ACADEMIA'S GOLDEN AGE

ACADEMIA'S GOLDEN AGE

Universities in Massachusetts
1945–1970

RICHARD M. FREELAND

New York   Oxford
OXFORD UNIVERSITY PRESS
1992

Oxford University Press

Oxford   New York   Toronto
Delhi   Bombay   Calcutta   Madras   Karachi
Petaling Jaya   Singapore   Hong Kong   Tokyo
Nairobi   Dar es Salaam   Cape Town
Melbourne   Auckland

and associated companies in
Berlin   Ibadan

Published by Oxford University Press, Inc.,
200 Madison Avenue, New York, New York 10016

Oxford is a registered trademark of Oxford University Press

Library of Congress Cataloging-in-Publication Data
Freeland, Richard M., 1941–
Academia's golden age : universities in Massachusetts, 1945–1970 /
Richard M. Freeland.
p. cm.   Includes bibliographical references (p.) and index.
ISBN 0-19-505464-4
1. Education, Higher—Massachusetts—Boston—History.
2. Universities and colleges—Massachusetts—Boston—History.
I. Title.
LA306.B7F74   1992
378.744′61—dc20   91-15670

1 3 5 7 9 8 6 4 2

Printed in the United States of America
on acid-free paper

For
Daisy M. Tagliacozzo
And
Francis L. Broderick

Institutions are more important than individuals. But only individual men and women, when they have the strength, can transform and enrich the things which institutions transmit to successor generations.

JEAN MONNET

Acknowledgments

For the entire period of work on this project, I have been associated with the University of Massachusetts at Boston, mostly in administrative positions. My campus community has assisted me in countless ways. I am grateful to Chancellors Claire Van Ummersen and Robert Corrigan for supporting two sabbaticals, and to Provost Robert Greene, who helped arrange a special summer's leave. I could take time away only because Edna Seaman and Howard Cohen were so willing to fill in for me and so able to do so. I also owe an enormous debt to numerous colleagues whose conversations, insights, and collegial assistance over the years have contributed to my understanding of higher education. Several have provided helpful comments on this manuscript, including Howard Cohen, Jim Fraser, Zee Gamson, Fran Malino, Joan Tonn, Robert Wegner and Robert Wood.

I have benefited from the assistance of people at other institutions as well. I am grateful to the Ford Foundation, and especially to Dorothy Marshall and Harold Howe, for approving the small grant that enabled me to begin this project, and to the National Endowment for the Humanities for research support, efficiently administered by Nadina Gardner. I profited immensely from three residencies: first at the Harvard Business School, where I was sponsored and generously tutored by Alfred D. Chandler; then at the Harvard Graduate School of Education, where David Kuechle, Nancy Hoffman, Arthur Levine, and Lee Bolman were especially helpful; and finally at the Rockefeller Foundation's scholarly residence in Bellagio, for which I wish to thank Nan Robinson, Susan Garfield, and Roberto and Gianna Celli.

My efforts to understand the various Massachusetts universities included in this book were advanced by a large number of colleagues at these institutions. I am especially appreciative of the men and women with direct experience of these campuses who were willing to be interviewed or to comment on portions of my drafts. These individuals are listed in the bibliography under the appropriate institution. I was also aided by documents collections at each of the universities I studied. I specifically want to thank archivists Helen Samuels and her associates at M.I.T., Paul Fitzgerald at Boston College, Russell Miller and Robert Johnson-Lally at Tufts, and Albert Donnelly and Andrew Calo at Northeastern.

Acknowledgments

All scholars build on the work of others. I owe a special intellectual debt to four individuals. Laurence Veysey's book on the early development of American universities has provided a model of academic history. David Riesman, who has produced the richest body of work on higher education of any living scholar, has provided generous assistance at several points in this project. Alfred D. Chander has written the best institutional analyses I have encountered. Hugh Hawkins, who possesses a vast knowledge of American educational history, was a constant source of assistance and encouragement.

Several friends and colleagues read portions of the manuscript and provided useful criticisms, including Fawzia Assaad, Maritza Barrios, Chester Finn, Roger Geiger, Mary Katzenstein, Margaret Marshall, Pauline Maier, Sandra Morgan, Diane Ravitch, William Rawn, Frederick Rudolph, Anne Sa'adah, Rennie Shepen, and Barbara Taylor. I want particularly to acknowledge eight friends who, at critical times in the course of this project, set aside their own work to help me past difficult moments: Thomas Brown, Edward Greene, Allen Guttmann, Bruce Kuklick, Joan Liem, Ernest Lynton, Diane Paul, and Kenneth Waltzer. Sheldon Meyer and his associates at Oxford University Press, David Bain, Scott Lenz, and Joellyn Ausanka, have been a steady source of professional help. Karen Michalec, Leslie Hannigan, and Angela Wren have been able research assistants. Danny Marcus was an expert proofreader. Much of the work on this book has been done during long, isolated hours in two places that I have come to love: the Isle of Springs on the coast of Maine and Waitsfield in the Green Mountains of Vermont. To the people who sustain those lovely communities and who tolerated, on numerous occasions, an incommunicative scholar in their midst, I am deeply grateful.

Above all, I want to thank the two individuals to whom this book is dedicated: Daisy M. Tagliacozzo and Francis L. Broderick, both colleagues at UMass/Boston and close friends. Daisy, a talented dean and gifted sociologist, has tried to teach me to think systematically about organizations. Frank, as campus chancellor, historian, and teacher, has been both model and mentor. The two together, more than any others, have inspired my work and helped me believe that my own, slowly unfolding scholarly efforts might yet yield something of value. For Daisy and Frank I feel gratitude and affection beyond the bounds of acknowledgments, or even words.

Boston Mass.   R. M. F.
June 1991

Contents

ACADEMIA'S GOLDEN AGE

Introduction

This book began as an exploration of a paradox in the history of American universities. In the twenty-five years following World War II, the student population served by these institutions became more diverse and the societal purposes they served became more varied. Yet, during the same period, universities themselves became more alike. The contradictions were easy to observe. It was obvious that the academic and social backgrounds of students—and consequently their needs, skills, and interests—became more heterogeneous in the postwar years, yet the undergraduate curricula of universities increasingly stressed highly academic subjects, especially the arts and sciences. Similarly, universities pursued a well-documented trend toward greater involvement in practical affairs and social problem solving in the 1950s and 1960s, while also adhering to a narrowing focus on doctoral programs and research in the basic disciplines. I wanted to understand the forces, both internal and external to campuses, that promoted this puzzling conjunction of converging characteristics and expanding functions. I also wanted to assess the academic and social consequences of this pattern.

The decline of institutional diversity was only the most startling of a number of apparently inconsistent developments associated with an era of historic growth among universities. Almost as curious was the fact that, while expansion occurred mostly to accommodate increased demand for college education, institutional attention to teaching diminished, as did concern about the undergraduate curriculum. Meanwhile, graduate programs, whose chief function was to train college teachers, tended to slight preparation for instructional work and to nurture research skills. Indeed, as growth intensified academia's role in socializing the nation's youth, universities dismantled the programs of general education that were the primary vehicles they had created for that purpose. More broadly, the active involvement of universities in the definition and resolution of social problems went hand in hand with the consolidation of an academic value system quite remote from most Americans.

Even the increasing heterogeneity of the student population was not free of contradiction. Academic leaders claimed credit for making their institutions more democratic during the postwar years by reducing traditional barriers to admission—including those of income and race. Yet, in terms of social class, universities in 1970 were more differentiated from one another than they had been in 1945, and the expansion of college attendance by minorities was not greatly different from enrollment increases by whites.

This volume explores the paradoxical nature of postwar change through a close analysis of eight Massachusetts universities from 1930 to 1980, with emphasis on the quarter-century after 1945.[1] At the start of the postwar era, these institutions—Harvard, the Massachusetts Institute of Technology, Tufts, Brandeis, Boston University, Boston College, Northeastern, and the University of Massachusetts—were remarkably varied, not just in their origins and stages of development but also in their functions, aims, and campus cultures. During the 1950s and 1960s, universities in Massachusetts illustrated the national pattern of declining diversity, becoming more alike in their programs, their faculties, their students, their financing, their organization, and their conceptions of institutional purpose. Upon close examination, however, declining diversity has not seemed the only—or even the most important— aspect of postwar change among these campuses. Equally impressive was their continuing distinctiveness. Indeed, no moderately astute observer, visiting them in 1970, would have confused one with another. During the 1970s, moreover, explicit and self-conscious trends toward re-differentiation were apparent.

The detailed histories of individual universities confront us, then, with a paradox inside a paradox. The challenge becomes not only to account for diminished diversity and the contradictory developments associated with that tendency, but to understand the simultaneous persistence of variation. Ultimately these phenomena force us beyond strictly historical concerns toward basic questions about our national system of universities. What features of that system reinforce its capacity to perform the multiple and often conflicting functions it has undertaken? What forces tend to undermine its social effectiveness? How, on balance, do we evaluate the contributions of these institutions during one of the most important periods of academic growth in the nation's history?

The primary advantage of Massachusetts as a setting for studying academic change is the variety of its universities.[2] In the years before World War II, when this analysis begins, Harvard was already well established as the country's leading campus, unique in many ways but representative also of the private, eastern schools that had constituted the nation's academic elite for generations. M.I.T., its center of gravity firmly fixed in its undergraduate programs in engineering, was the country's preeminent technical institute. Boston University and Tufts were two Protestant institutions that had followed different paths of development, the first as a sprawling, diversified "municipal university," the latter as a smaller campus modeled on the traditional New England college. Boston College had taken root as one of the nation's first Catholic and Jesuit universities, while Northeastern had grown out of the Y.M.C.A. as a technically oriented campus for working-class commuters.

In a setting densely populated with private institutions, public higher education had grown less vigorously than in other parts of the country. The state's primary public campus in 1940 was Massachusetts State College in Amherst, renamed the University of Massachusetts only in 1947. M.S.C. had evolved from shaky beginnings as an agricultural college to include undergraduate work in the arts and sciences and graduate programs in a small number of scientific fields. Brandeis, the eighth school in this study, was founded just after the war as the nation's first Jewish-sponsored secular university.

The book makes no claim that these institutions represent a scientific sample of American universities or that Massachusetts is a typical academic environment. On the contrary, Massachusetts is unique, harboring one of the greatest educational concentrations in the country, with an unusual emphasis on private schools. It is also true, however, that other states or regions that might provide a context for examining a group of disparate campuses have their own special characteristics. Despite such differences, most studies of the years following World War II have concluded that basic trends and the social forces that drove them were similar in different parts of the country.[3]

Given parallel tendencies across regions, much can be gained from considering institutions located in a single geographical area, and Massachusetts contains most types of universities to be found in the United States. The author hopes that focusing on these schools will help us understand the differing ways in which diverse campuses and their leaders responded to common patterns of change in the social, political, and economic environments of higher education.

≫

At the national level, the heightened postwar interest in graduate education and research represented a fundamental change of emphasis that first appeared among leading universities. Prior to World War II, the most socially important function of these schools, especially private ones, was undergraduate education. Universities served the nation chiefly by training a new generation of leaders in government, business, and the professions, and they achieved status by attracting the most talented students and producing the most influential alumni/ae. Even before the war, however, deep changes in the social significance of knowledge began to shift attention toward the advanced academic functions, and the war dramatically accelerated this tendency. Social progress in a range of areas—economic growth, national security, and public health—became linked in the minds of governmental and business leaders to intellectual and technical innovation. Institutions with highly developed research capabilities gained influence and prestige. The new academic world was sustained and symbolized in the 1950s and 1960s by rising federal investment in university-based research and graduate education, especially in scientific fields.

The postwar years also produced a rapid enlargement of the academic system. An expanded youth population—the postwar "baby boomers"—combined with increased rates of college attendance accounted for this phenomenon. The expansion was related to the nation's enhanced appreciation of knowledge and expertise, since the new interest in college stemmed from a heightened need for formal training for many jobs. But growth also reflected the democratization of higher education, as young people from modest backgrounds and those with average skills were encouraged to pursue college-level studies.

As established universities grew and new ones were created to accommodate more students, the new priorities emerging in the upper echelons of the academic hierarchy decisively influenced patterns of institutional change. Expanding campuses that had little or no tradition of scholarly distinction and enrolled moderately selective or nonselective student bodies based plans for development on the revised academic concerns of the postwar years. Institutions historically characterized by distinctive missions and constituencies—campuses that served particular geographic regions or religious groups; institutions supported by public funds or oriented toward local, commuting populations; and college-centered and special purpose universities that emphasized undergraduate, professional, or technical education—tended to converge on a common conception of purpose and academic organization modeled on the nation's most prestigious universities.

Change at universities in Massachusetts replicated the national pattern. Harvard and M.I.T. led the way, seizing the opportunities of the 1950s and 1960s to accomplish goals deferred during the Depression and the war: expansion of graduate programs, especially in the basic sciences, and recruitment of research-oriented faculty to build concentrations of scholarly expertise. The shift of focus at the top of the regional hierarchy was quickly registered at the secondary and tertiary levels. Prior to World War II, no university in Massachusetts outside of Cambridge placed major emphasis on research, and some academic leaders (for example, the presidents of Northeastern and Tufts) stressed their opposition to scholarship as a central function of their campuses. After 1945 every university in the study began to define research as a vital objective.

Graduate development was also stressed by every campus, including those, like Massachusetts State and Boston College, that had been highly circumscribed in their post-baccalaureate activities before the war. To support the new emphases on advanced academic functions, area schools sought scholars trained at leading research universities; many, indeed, came from Harvard and M.I.T. In contrast to earlier generations, faculties of the postwar era were oriented more toward the professional values of academia than the specific traditions and purposes of their campuses.

Undergraduate change followed a similar evolution toward elite models, as all universities in the area gave heightened attention to the liberal arts, the traditional focus of bachelor's-level education at leading institutions. Campuses that historically had served commuting students from the immediate vicinity, especially B.U. and B.C., sought to upgrade their student bodies by standard academic criteria and to create traditional residential settings, complete with dormitories to attract out-of-state students and facilities to support extracurricular functions. As they made these changes, the region's former urban universities enrolled students from more affluent backgrounds and de-emphasized or eliminated low-status programs, especially those with an occupational orientation or those serving evening and part-time students. By 1970 these Massachusetts institutions were far more alike in whom they served and what they offered than they had been thirty years earlier.

≫

The postwar accomplishments of higher education, evident both nationally and locally, were impressive. Expansion created the world's first system of mass higher education. Historic impediments to attendance—income, sex, geography, religion, and race—were reduced. While higher education became more democratic, the scholarly attainments of the nation's campuses also rose. Undergraduate and graduate programs at top-ranked universities became more intellectually demanding than they had been previously. American scholars, who traditionally had looked to Europe for leadership, emerged as dominant forces in many academic disciplines.

These specifically academic gains were paralleled by educators' increased contributions to the practical affairs of the nation through the creation of new knowledge to support technical progress and through direct participation as experts in solving social problems.

The overall pattern of growth and change from the mid-1940s to the late 1960s constituted a true golden age in academia. The prestige of higher education soared. Money flowed to the campus and public support rose to an all-time high. Both government agencies and business leaders courted professors for their specialized wisdom. State legislatures, like the national Congress, appropriated vast sums to finance expansion. In 1963 John Kennedy proclaimed an explicit national interest in higher education and became the first president to propose legislation intended specifically to promote its development.[4]

Beginning in the mid-1960s, however, colleges and universities entered a period of financial and political difficulty. The student protest movement, initially associated with public issues like the war in Vietnam and the civil rights movement, soon turned into an attack upon the academy itself. Before the "time of troubles" ended in the early 1970s, the social position of higher education was weakened severely, and academic leaders were more concerned with defending their institutions against criticisms than with shaping new demands for funding. Within higher education, moreover, there began a wrenching process of self-examination expressed in an outpouring of books, articles, and reports by prestigious commissions—not to mention endless debates on individual campuses. At the center of the ferment was one central question: did the disarray of the late 1960s represent historical bad luck, an unfortunate by-product of uncontrollable external events—as apologists tended to argue—or, as critics contended, did it reflect flaws in the pattern of postwar expansion that so recently had seemed so beneficent?

This author and most academics of the period felt distressed and confused as the professional world to which we had dedicated our lives began to unravel.

I was one of the many young scholars who entered the profession in the 1960s, buoyed by the excitement of those years and inspired by the importance of higher education as a positive social force. My early experiences stirred concern, however, about the obvious discrepancies between the propensities of our institutions and the requirements of our new social functions. I believed intuitively that the contradictions and paradoxes associated with our rapid growth were related in some fashion to the political turmoil in which we were enveloped. Like many other members of my profession, I was eager to comprehend the roots of our difficulties. This book represents my effort to do so.

Existing studies of higher education contain three primary traditions for understanding institutional change. The first and oldest of these, associated with figures like Thorstein Veblen, Abraham Flexner, and Robert Maynard Hutchins, stresses the impact of ideas, especially about academic purposes.[5] From this perspective, universities are—or ought to be—guided in their development by principles that define their proper functions. This tradition lives on in faculty debates and presidential addresses, but most recent scholarship discounts the significance of philosophic contention as a primary cause of change among universities. Indeed, the two most prominent schools of contemporary analysis emphasize institutional factors that have minimal intellectual or even academic content.

One such tradition, associated with sociologists like Joseph Ben-David, Martin Trow, and Burton Clark, focuses on competition among universities for students, faculty, status, and support. These analysts argue that universities change functions and policies largely in response to the pressures of the academic marketplace. There is disagreement, however, about the impact of competition on institutional diversity. Some, like Ben-David and Clark, argue that competition promotes diversity as campuses seek distinctive niches. Others, like Laurence Veysey and David Riesman, contend that competition causes universities to imitate each other.[6] Another body of literature stresses the interplay of forces within institutions as a source of change. In recent years, writers like Victor Baldridge and Karl Weick have characterized universities as collections of interest groups—faculty, students, staff, and trustees—and have depicted change as the result of power struggles among them.[7]

These alternative perspectives have produced varying accounts of academic developments following World War II. One debate has involved the extent to which universities were active agents of their own evolution or were passively shaped by external forces. A prominent treatment of this issue by Clark Kerr in 1963 argued that, in the early postwar years, universities were transformed by a series of outside pressures—especially government policies and demographic shifts—that campus leaders were helpless to control. A related issue has been the relative significance of nonacademic social forces and more specifically academic changes. On the latter side of this question, the influential assessment by Christopher Jencks and David Riesman in 1968 stressed the increased power of faculty as the principal force in directing change. Both Kerr's perspective and that of Jencks and Riesman downplayed the significance of executive leadership. In contrast to traditional notions of the college president as a cultural hero, recent studies, like that of Michael Cohen and James March in 1974, typically portray campus officials more as hapless mediators buffeted by contending forces than powerful leaders of academic communities.[8]

There are methodological difficulties with the entire literature on postwar academic change. This is hardly surprising, since the task of tracing developments among three thousand diverse colleges and universities scattered across the continent presents immense challenges. The most prominent studies, like the Jencks/Riesman volume, are broad surveys based on social scientific techniques. These analyses can have great value in identifying general trends but are less successful at explaining variations associated with specific campuses or providing detailed explanations of evolutionary processes. Another class of volumes includes impressionistic reviews by participants and commissions—Kerr's book is an example—but such studies, however perceptive, tend to express the concerns of a particular moment and to lack a systematic basis for their conclusions. There are, additionally, numerous treatments of specific kinds of institutions—from research universities to community colleges—or of special topics—like academic finance or undergraduate education. But these accounts are limited in their focus. Volumes that review individual institutions in depth are mostly celebratory exercises written partially for promotional purposes.

So far, this rich literature contains no general history of the postwar period that offers an integrated view of change at the campus level among universities generally by focusing on a small number of institutions of different types. Yet this is a vital form of analysis. Despite the growth of government influence and suprainstitutional regulating bodies, our system of universities remained throughout the postwar period (and remains today) preeminently an aggregation of institutions. It is, ultimately, the interplay of forces at the campus level that we most need to understand—hence, this book's emphasis on detailed histories of several diverse universities.

An examination of the postwar evolution of universities in Massachusetts makes it clear that declining diversity registered both the new social pressures from outside higher education and broad trends within academia itself. The federal government created new funding programs to support scholarly research and promote graduate education, and the region's universities obediently adopted the new priorities. As the aims of federal programs evolved in the postwar years, the concerns of scholars shifted with them. The academic professional associations became more organized and assertive, and the norms of these organizations began to determine the practices of individual campuses in areas ranging from personnel policy to curriculum to governance. Similar pressures for conformity, with similar consequences, flowed from the accrediting associations.

The evidence of externally driven change was not limited to tangible pressures from funding and regulating agencies. The new conception of academic excellence associated with leading universities exercised an overwhelming hold on the thinking of leaders at nonelite campuses. It seemed, indeed, that a hidden but irresistible power was directing change at universities in Massachusetts into similar channels and rejecting initiatives that deviated from the preordained pattern.

Yet, within the broad trends, continuing institutional variations were everywhere apparent. Boston College retained its Catholic identity, symbolized by a strong Jesuit presence, just as Brandeis readily communicated its relationship to the Jewish community. M.I.T. retained its central emphasis on scientific and technical work and honored its traditional commitments to undergraduate, professional education and to involvement in practical affairs. Tufts worked at perpetuating its historic focus on undergraduate teaching in the arts and sciences. Northeastern continued to stress practical programs for young people from working-class backgrounds. In all these instances, the outward appearances of the campuses and of the students (though less of the faculty) bespoke fundamental differences in populations served, sources of financial support, curricular emphases, and characteristics of campus cultures.

The distinctiveness of these universities at the end of the golden age reflected several factors. In the first place, the forces that influenced broad patterns of change most strongly, especially financial support for research and enlarged public demand for college education, had different impacts on individual campuses depending upon their histories, capabilities, and orientations. M.I.T. readily attracted federal support, while Northeastern struggled to obtain a modest share. Harvard was quickly deluged with applications for admission, while interest in Tufts grew gradually. Moreover, large systemic forces constituted only a portion of the external influences that affected these universities. Each was also susceptible to a set of local pressures that mirrored its sources of revenue and students, its form of organization, and its pattern of corporate control. B.C.'s embeddedness in the structure of the Jesuit order mattered greatly, as did the relationship of the University of Massachusetts to the state legislature. After 1970, moreover, worries that federal support was diminishing and student demand softening prompted renewed efforts among these institutions to define more precisely their special niches in the academic marketplace.

The entire constellation of external forces—both systemic and local—left considerable room for maneuver by campus leaders. Many factors influenced the exercise of that discretion. Ideas and values played a role. The Catholicism of the B.C. hierarchy influenced decisions about the curriculum. The educational commitments of Tufts's leaders shaped choices about personnel and graduate education. Progress in scientific understanding affected program development at M.I.T. Social concerns arising from the civil rights movement swayed admission policies at several campuses.

The distribution of internal power and the characteristics of campus organization also mattered. Leaders at Northeastern could institute dramatic changes quickly because of campus traditions of strong executive authority. The hierarchy at B.U. was constrained by a history of decentralization. In addition, the quality of campus leadership was important, despite end-of-the-period scholarly analyses minimizing the significance of executive authority. The most impressive patterns of change were invariably associated with skillful and effective presidencies.

The multiple forces producing change at the campus level can be aggregated into three broad categories. The first of these was institutional ambition, which was expressed in a continuous competition among universities for prestige and resources. The second driving force was ideas, including academic knowledge, cultural and professional values, and conceptions of institutional purpose. The third factor, organizational dynamics, involved the political characteristics and administrative capabilities of universities, especially struggles for power among key internal subpopulations. These three forces roughly correspond, of course, to the three strands of interpretation in the literature on postwar change. Their simultaneous significance underscores the need for an integrated view of evolutionary processes in higher education. For the sake of economy, I shall refer to this system of forces as the institutional complex.

While it is possible for purposes of analysis to speak of the components of the institutional complex, none of these forces operated in isolation. Each of them—institutional ambition, academic ideas, and organizational dynamics—connected individual campuses with specific external economic, social, political, and professional environments. Indeed, the distinction between "inside" and "outside" forces was often blurred. For example, federal science policy was clearly an external force, but for most of the postwar years the key government offices were controlled by individuals with campus affiliations (often with M.I.T. or Harvard) whose actions, within the external context, were affected by internal perspectives.

The elements of the institutional complex were also interconnected within universities. Ideas could only exert influence if they had well-positioned advocates, so we cannot disassociate the importance of ideas from the internal distribution of power. Similarly, power within campuses was directly related to the competitive pressures of the academic marketplace. Indeed, the capacity of an individual or group to enhance institutional prestige or to acquire resources was a primary source of standing within the influence system of universities.

Despite the complexities of the change process, this study has persuaded me that over extended periods of time the factor that has most influenced the evolution of universities in Massachusetts has been competition among campuses for prestige and resources—with each other and with universities around the country. Ultimately, the other elements of the institutional complex tend to follow patterns deriving from the position and strivings of each school in the academic marketplace. This interinstitutional competition, moreover, has deep roots in historical divisions and conflicts—of religion, class, and ethnic group—within the fragmented social structure of the state.

It is, then, the sources and character of competition among universities that we most need to understand if we are to comprehend the paradoxical nature of academic change during the golden age. It is the consequences and limitations of a system based on competition that we most need to assess in evaluating how well universities served the nation during their period of maximum prosperity and influence. In pursuing these concerns through the study of individual campuses over a fifty-year period, we also shall see how competition promoted institutional diversity in some circumstances and in others fostered its decline.

⇌

The first chapter of this volume introduces the universities in the study, emphasizing their traditional links to the various subcultures of Massachusetts, outlining their patterns of development prior to World War II, and describing the historic dynamics of competition among them. The second chapter establishes the resource environment and intellectual context of postwar change at the national level, illustrating general patterns with examples from universities in the study. This chapter compares the visions of academic purpose expressed by educators in the late 1940s with the actual character of institutional development.

The next four chapters—3 through 6—explore the evolution of the eight institutions between 1945 and 1970. Chapter 3 compares changes at Harvard and M.I.T., two institutions that placed primary emphasis on research and graduate education. Chapter 4 discusses Tufts and Brandeis, both of which focused on undergraduate education in the arts and sciences while trying also to build strong research and graduate programs. Chapter 5 reviews developments at three institutions—Boston University, Boston College, and Northeastern—that, before the war, chiefly served commuting students from the city and region. The last chapter in this part, Chapter 6, describes the growth of public higher education in the commonwealth, concentrating on the University of Massachusetts.

Drawing on the material in the four institutional chapters, Chapter 7 analyzes the workings of the institutional complex during the 1950s and 1960s. This chapter also reviews the adaptations of the eight universities to the new, less-expansive circumstances of the 1970s and considers their responses to various reform proposals that achieved widespread acceptance among academic leaders in the latter years of the golden age.

One final note. This is a long book, full of detail for the reader who wishes to understand change at particular universities. Those interested chiefly in broad patterns and ideas may wish to focus on Chapters 2 and 7, which summarize trends from the beginning of the postwar period through the 1970s. Such readers may refer to the intervening institutional chapters for elaboration of specific references that occur in the more general essays.

Readers who do review the detailed histories may sometimes feel, especially if they have had direct experience with one of these universities, that I have failed in places to adequately represent the texture and range of life on individual campuses. To this charge, I regretfully plead guilty, acknowledge the

limits of my scholarship, and extend apologies, though I do believe I have identified the most significant changes. Work on this volume has impressed me,
above all, with the complexity of universities as human constructions, capable
of engaging simultaneously in a multiplicity of activities, some in apparent
opposition to others, and of pursuing behavior that is at once self-interested
and idealistic, institutionally aggrandizing and socially helpful. Universities,
like the country itself, are hard to see. It is my hope that this book, despite its
limitations, will help us to see them more clearly.

PART ONE

Contexts

CHAPTER ONE

Academic Development and Social Change: Higher Education in Massachusetts before 1945

In October 1948, James B. Conant, president of Harvard, journeyed from Cambridge across the Charles River to address the fiftieth anniversary convocation of Northeastern University. Though the ceremonies on N.U.'s new Hungtington Avenue campus occurred only two miles from Conant's offices in Harvard Yard, in academic terms the two settings could not have been separated by a greater distance. Harvard was the nation's richest and most distinguished institution of higher education, the alma mater of generations of regional and national leaders in government, business, and academia. Northeastern, only recently cut loose from the Y.M.C.A., still struggling to obtain proper facilities, was an obscure, local school offering practical training to working-class students. Indeed, Conant's appearance at Northeastern eloquently symbolized the variations that existed among institutions that called themselves "universities" in the United States at the end of World War II, and Harvard's president made these differences the subject of his talk, which he titled "Diversity in American Education."

Conant's speech was a hymn to institutional variety as an academic characteristic particularly appropriate for a democracy. "There would be a contradiction in terms," Conant said, "if we had an American system," in the sense of an organization "logically constructed, well-integrated . . . and administered from the top down" like those of continental Europe. The opportunity of individuals from any background to better their positions in this country's "fluid and free society" would be inhibited by centralization. For Conant, the colleges and universities of Massachusetts illustrated democratic higher education at its best. "We have here in this section of New England," he observed,

a number of academic organizations designed to provide educational facilities for young men and women . . . These institutions are diverse in their history and their specific objectives and cover a wide spectrum of educational opportunity. Between us there are but few gaps in the type of advanced instruction we offer. We each have our own mission . . . Taken as a whole [we] represent as diversified a program of post–high school education as can be found in the United States.[1]

In celebrating the variability of the nation's universities, Conant found an ideal way to narrow the embarrassing difference in status between himself and his hosts. Indeed, the leaders of Northeastern were proud of their institution's distinctive qualities, its departures from the traditionalism of Harvard, and President Carl Ell's plans for the postwar years emphasized his university's special character.

Conant's talk also reflected a central theme of national debates in the late 1940s. This was a time when leaders in government and academia, made newly conscious of the social importance of higher education by the war, were feeling their ways toward educational policies appropriate for the conditions of a new era. In these discussions, no premise was more widely accepted than the importance of preserving functional diversity among institutions. That diversity, as represented by the local campuses of which Conant spoke, involved much more than alternative academic theories. Higher education in Massachusetts in 1948 was a contemporary embodiment of the conflict-laden social history of the commonwealth.

Prologue: Three Centuries of College Building, 1636–1929

Harvard and the Colonial College

Harvard became the first seat of higher education in British North America as part of a wave of institution building in the 1630s and 1640s by the Puritan elders of Massachusetts Bay.[2] The new college—like the common schools, the compulsory education laws, the grammar schools, and the Cambridge printing press—expressed the colonists' belief that general learning and respect for scholarship were essential ingredients of a Christian community. Created as an arm of both church and state, supported by government grants and private donations, Harvard's role was to train the clerical elite of the commonwealth's integrated Congregational theocracy. In its ties to a sponsoring religious group, Harvard provided a prototype for the colleges founded during the colonial period, and a majority of its graduates became ministers until well into the eighteenth century. But pre-Revolutionary Harvard was not a Congregational divinity school. Formal preparation for the ministry began only after completion of the undergraduate degree, and a secondary function from the beginning was to provide liberal education for young gentlemen of the colony.

The early patterns proved durable. Harvard's formal links to the church survived until 1843 through a reservation of seats on the Board of Overseers for Congregational ministers. The college was incorporated into the state constitution after the Revolutionary War, and elected officials were guaranteed a majority on the Overseers until 1851. They retained *ex officio* seats until 1865. The classical undergraduate curriculum, with its prescribed work in ancient languages, mathematics, and philosophy and its strict system of memorization and recitation, lasted into the 1860s.

Within Harvard's basic framework, however, change was continuous and at times dramatic. The most significant evolution was toward the secular, as the proportion of undergraduates preparing for the ministry diminished steadily after the 1640s. In the eighteenth century, as the grip of orthodox Calvinists on Massachusetts weakened, liberals within the church achieved a dominant position on the Harvard Corporation and turned the college into a center of advanced thought. The most important evidence of liberal modernizing was the increased emphasis on science, including the introduction of experimental work by the faculty. The Medical School was established in 1782, part of a quickening pattern of change following the Revolutionary War that culminated in the dramatic events of 1805–1806, when the Unitarians captured both the Hollis Professorship of Divinity and the presidency. New professional schools of Law and Divinity were founded in 1817 and 1819. The Lawrence Scientific School followed in 1847. Harvard hired its first European-trained scholars, who called for more freedom for students, a wider array of subjects, and greater attention to creative scholarship. Harvard's last minister-president, Thomas Hill, appointed in 1862, saw that additional changes were needed and tried to lead the transformation advocated by faculty reformers. But the obstacles were formidable, and Hill was not the man to overcome them. Harvard in the 1860s remained closer to the modest, prototypical colonial college for Massachusetts that it had been than to the standard-setting modern university it was to become.

The man who could lead Harvard into the modern academic era, Charles W. Eliot, was inaugurated in 1869, following a classic Harvard contretemps between the Corporation and the Board of Overseers.[3] As a less-than-distinguished chemist, Eliot was opposed by both the scientists, who disparaged his achievements, and the classicists, who feared his progressive views. But Eliot had a genius for administration and understood what was needed for Harvard to retain its social influence as breeder of a regional elite.

Eliot believed that the traditional college, with its rigid curriculum and preoccupation with "virtue and piety," had become irrelevant to producing successful leaders for the industrial, urban nation of the late nineteenth century. Influenced by his observations of German universities, Eliot saw that conditions favored academic institutions dedicated to the secular achievements of the intellect, places that would nurture contemporary thinking on socially significant subjects and enable ambitious, talented men to demonstrate their abilities. The former objective required a faculty composed less of faithful teachers than of productive scholars for whom the campus would provide the conditions for creative work. The latter implied a shift of focus from undergraduate, liberal education to graduate work in the most important professional fields.

During his remarkable forty-year presidency, Eliot pursued his priorities relentlessly. A separate Graduate Department was delineated within the Faculty of Arts and Sciences in 1872. The existing graduate shcools were modernized and expanded one by one. A Graduate School of Business Administration was founded in 1908. The instructional staff grew from less than sixty at the beginning of Eliot's tenure to about six hundred at the end and adopted modern academic norms. Departments were established along disciplinary lines, and the Ph.D. became the standard credential for faculty status in Arts and Sciences.

Eliot was aided by the fact that his presidency coincided with a period of local prosperity and a spirit of philanthropy among citizens that brought large donations to the university. Eliot's Harvard paid the best salaries in American higher education and acquired academia's most extensive library and largest endowment. These resources enabled the college in Cambridge to attract leading scholars from the United States and Europe, who, in turn, drew students from beyond New England.

Eliot's innovations were hardly unique, but his skill in implementing them was exceptional. When he retired in 1909, he was widely acknowledged as the most influential educator of his day, and his university, so recently a Puritan college for New England, was recognized as the leading center of scholarship and graduate training in the United States.

Despite his successes, Eliot stirred criticism, especially within the Harvard community. The harshest indictments came from those who believed his efforts to build the advanced academic functions had weakened the College. Indeed, Eliot fostered revolutionary changes at the undergraduate level, particularly the replacement of the classical curriculum with a system of electives. This reform left faculty members free to teach and students free to take whatever courses they deemed appropriate. As an inevitable result, courses proliferated, and standards became uneven. Moreover, partially to finance his innovations, Eliot began a program of expansion, and the College became sprawling and disorganized. The president's detractors were strengthened by a decline in applications at the beginning of the twentieth century that threatened Harvard's status as well as its solvency. The accumulating criticisms apparently affected the governing boards. In selecting a successor, they turned to one of Eliot's most persistent adversaries, a lawyer turned political scientist, A. Lawrence Lowell. Among other qualifications, Lowell possessed the connections to local wealth that would be needed for Harvard to regain financial strength.[4]

Lowell's presidency proved a striking counterpoint to Eliot's, lasting long enough—twenty-four years—to define a distinct era, while stressing, with comparable determination, different aspects of intellectual life.[5] Lowell led reform of the undergraduate program, giving it new structure through concentration and distribution requirements that became a pattern for colleges throughout the nation. To intensify and control the undergraduate experience and use it to strengthen character as well as intellect, Lowell built residence halls, hoping to foster skills in social interaction among individuals from varying backgrounds.

Fundamentally, Lowell was out of sympathy with the concepts of modern scholarship and academic organization that had been adapted from German precedents during the Eliot years. He rejected an exclusive focus on intellectual values and believed that undirected student exposure to a fragmented collection of courses and professorial specialities was unlikely to engender liberal learning. Lowell hoped to recast Harvard along the familiar lines of Oxford and Cambridge, with tutorials and general examinations replacing the course-credit system as a basis for graduation. Though he failed to install his program in every department, by the end of his term the policy was widely adopted, and the College employed enough tutors to support this form of instruction for every undergraduate.

While Eliot had been criticized by Harvardians concerned about the college, his successor was accused of neglecting research and graduate education. Worse, Lowell's detractors blamed him for granting faculty appointments to mediocre candidates, some of them personal associates, who shared his priorities. Harvard's reputation as the nation's leading scholarly community, firmly established under Eliot, seemed threatened. "One hears," wrote Bernard De Voto, "that the distinction of this department has lapsed, or that there is much dead wood in another, or that the best [graduate] students of a given field now go to Chicago or Columbia or Wisconsin." While such criticisms failed to acknowledge genuine progress under Lowell, during his years Harvard did move less vigorously than other leading universities in building the advanced functions. As Lowell's presidency wound down in the early 1930s, a chorus of faculty opinion advocated radical change. "Let the College rest awhile," pleaded De Voto; "it is time to give us back the university."[6]

Tufts, Boston College, and the College Movement

Harvard was one of only nine colleges founded before the Revolution, but independence and the forces it unleashed, especially population growth and the settlement of western lands, prompted a rash of institution building in the late eighteenth and early nineteenth centuries. By one estimate, nearly two hundred fifty colleges were founded between 1800 and 1860, often in remote places with minimum financial support. Though some failed, most survived, and by the Civil War, the young republic boasted over two hundred entities calling themselves colleges or universities—compared with four in the United Kingdom.

A number of factors contributed to "the college movement," including the creation of the first state universities. The most important work, however, was done by Protestant organizations animated by local boosterism, religious sentiment, sectarian competitiveness, and the need to educate their ministers and their young. The Universalists, a small sect centered in the Northeast, decided in the 1840s to create a "literary institution" embodying their special commitment to religious tolerance. After an extended effort to raise funds and obtain a site, the new college was established in 1853 in Medford, Massachusetts, just north of Cambridge, on a hilltop donated by Charles Tufts. Tufts College was to be one of two Massachusetts schools that would evolve into universities from foundations laid down between the Revolution and the Civil War.[7]

The second, Boston College, represented a different aspect of the college movement: the gradual emergence of Catholic higher education in a predominantly Protestant society. Though the nation's first Catholic college was founded at Georgetown in 1789, few others were added until the mid-nineteenth century. Initially, the limited scope of Catholic college building mirrored the modest size of that religious group in the nation's population. Even after the great migrations of the 1830s, however, Catholic higher education developed slowly. Most of the newcomers were peasants with little means to support or orientation to seek advanced learning.

Nonetheless, the creation of Catholic colleges became a minor theme of academic expansion in the decades prior to the Civil War. This was especially true in Massachusetts, a point of entry for Irish immigrants where the Society of Jesus was dedicated to educational work. The state's first Jesuit institution, Holy Cross in Worcester, opened in 1843 but was beyond the geographical and financial reach of the large Catholic population of Boston. Throughout the 1840s and 1850s, Jesuit and Catholic leaders sought support for a college in the capital city. A building was constructed on Harrison Avenue in the South End between 1858 and 1860—but the new institution, called Boston College, would not accept its first students until 1864.[8]

Tufts and B.C., like many of the colleges founded before the Civil War, struggled to survive with meager resources. Tufts opened in 1854 with "one building, four professors, and seven students," the entire result of three years' work following the gift of land from Charles Tufts.[9] Problems in attracting both students and money persisted for several reasons. The Universalist sect was neither large nor wealthy, and its ability to support Tufts was compromised from the beginning by efforts to launch a second college at St. Lawrence in western New York.

The existence of St. Lawrence also weakened Tufts's attractiveness to graduates of Universalist secondary schools, a problem deepened by the declining importance of these feeder institutions as the public schools grew. Pressed, Tufts's leaders sought supplementary sources of enrollments and financing, especially within the commonwealth. Programs were designed to attract local students unable to afford Harvard or interested in a more practical form of education than was available there. A "philosophical course" that omitted requirements in classical languages was initiated, and an engineering program was started.

Tufts's evolution into a school for local boys provided a basis for subsidies from the state, which greatly aided the college during the nineteenth century. The pattern of adding programs to reach new groups expanded during the long presidency of Elmer Capen from 1875 to 1905. A contemporary of Eliot, Capen, like his Harvard colleague, was impressed with the university form of organization. Under his leadership, Tufts built a graduate school that offered both master's and doctoral degrees, expanded the Divinity School, and acquired existing, free-standing, medical and dental colleges as well as a secondary school. By the early years of the twentieth century, Tufts College, while retaining its traditional name, was a "university *de facto*," enrolling almost a thousand students and employing one hundred seventy-five faculty members.

Tufts's pattern of development prior to 1905 enabled it to survive its early financial difficulties but produced festering internal tensions. Despite efforts to draw students and support from outside the Universalist organization, ties to the sect remained strong. The college continued to depend on the church for financial contributions, and Universalists controlled the trustees and the presidency. For the faithful, the heart of Tufts remained the liberal arts program, and the professional schools were appendages frequently used to subsidize the college. President Capen, a Universalist minister, viewed Tufts in these terms and did not install the values of a modern university with anything like Eliot's determination.

The professional programs, however, had become the largest part of Tufts, and the alumni of these units resented their secondary status. Thus, conflict between the Universalist-dominated hierarchy and a growing alumni/ae organization was inevitable and became chronic. The problem was symbolized by the mismatch between the name "Tufts College" and the school's university-like collection of programs. The Faculty of Arts and Sciences, Tufts's most important internal constituency, shared the trustees' focus on the college and resisted Capen's new priority on graduate work, but they also objected to the governing board's domination of institutional affairs. Between 1905 and 1919, these various divisions produced confusion and two brief unhappy presidencies.

As World War I came to an end, the trustees, now with alumni/ae representatives, sought a solution to Tufts's difficulties by turning to one of their own, a successful local businessman and alumnus, John A. Cousens. Cousens proved an intelligent, humane leader who gave the college stable guidance until his retirement in 1937. His task was eased in the 1920s by good times. As the nation prospered, demand for higher education grew, and financial support came more easily.

Buoyed by these conditions, Cousens conceived a plan for Tufts that he hoped could win support from the institution's several constituencies, resolve ambiguities about institutional purpose, and establish Tufts as "one of the outstanding centers of learning in America." Adopting an idea popular among academic leaders in the 1920s, the president proposed to divide Tufts in half. A large, two-year "college" would offer general education in the arts and sciences and be open to all graduates of Massachusetts high schools. A smaller, more selective "university" would enroll top students for upper-division and graduate work in a selection of professional fields. This design, Cousens felt, would allow Tufts, with its small endowment, to maintain the large enrollments needed for financial reasons while achieving a reputation for high academic standards.

Cousens devoted much of the 1920s to promoting his plan but failed to win adequate support, especially from the faculty. By the end of the decade, he was looking for a new scheme to lift Tufts, once conceived as a proud, Universalist alternative to Harvard and Yale, from the middling academic position into which, too comfortably in Cousens's view, the college had allowed itself to settle.[10]

B.C. was as limited as Tufts in its early years.[11] When the city's Catholic college finally opened in 1864, only twenty-two boys presented themselves to a faculty of three Jesuit priests. In truth, the new school could not properly be called a college at all in the American sense of the term. It was organized on the European plan of Jesuit education, incorporating both secondary and collegiate courses in a seven-year program of classical studies. All of the initial students required lower-level work. Boston College did not produce its first bachelor's degrees until 1877.

The college developed slowly but steadily during the nineteenth century. The city's Irish community was expanding and, despite much poverty, included many families who could afford educational opportunities for their sons. The Irish were beginning to produce successful businessmen and professionals capable of supporting the college, and B.C. consistently found the financing required to construct and maintain its facilities. The diocesan hierarchy was helpful, and the Society of Jesus, by contributing most of the faculty, ensured the necessary instructional capability. Enrollments in the high school and college reached two hundred fifty by 1880, climbed to three hundred by 1885, and topped four hundred by 1900, making B.C. the largest Jesuit college in the United Sates.

Early in the twentieth century, an ambitious new rector and president, Father Thomas I. Gasson, S.J., aspired to turn B.C. into the "greatest Catholic college in America." In Gasson's view, two steps were essential: separation of the high school and college to bring the latter into conformity with accepted American practice; and the establishment of a proper campus. With the assistance of Archbishop William O'Connell, an alumnus, Gasson secured a magnificent site on a promontory in Chestnut Hill, just outside the city.

Following a successful fund-raising program, Gasson moved B.C. to its suburban home in 1913, leaving the high school behind in the South End. So began the daily ritual, which would characterize the college for decades to come, in which hundreds of city boys rode the streetcar to the Lake Street terminus and hiked up the long hill to attend classes on the "Heights." The opening of the Chestnut Hill campus coincided with a spurt of growth. The first freshman class in the new location contained as many students—four hundred—as had the college and high school combined only thirteen years earlier.[12]

B.C.'s association with the Catholic church and Jesuit order, though tying it to a rich and enduring educational tradition, restricted academic development. All major decisions were made by nonacademic Jesuit authorities. The order's regional provincial, not the rector-president of B.C., controlled the finances and the assignments of teaching priests. The general in Rome appointed the rector-president and retained authority over the curriculum. These Jesuit officials typically were more concerned about B.C.'s role in strengthening the Catholic faith than its intellectual advancement. In appointing a campus head, for example, the general's main interest was the candidate's ability to provide spiritual leadership.

Change came slowly. The separation of high school and college, begun in the 1880s, was not completed until 1919. The traditional Jesuit curriculum, with its requirements in classical languages and Catholic theology, was retained with little modification throughout the nineteenth century. The faculty continued to be composed mainly of priests, whose academic training rarely exceeded the master's level. While many colleges and universities were being transformed by the wave of change represented by Eliot and Capen, B.C. and its sister Jesuit institutions were largely unaffected.[13]

By the early years of the twentieth century, Jesuit educators were becoming aware that the order's resistance to change posed serious problems. Regional accrediting associations were exerting pressures for standardization, and Jesuit refusal to conform threatened the order's educational legitimacy. By 1920 multiple concerns prompted a small group of academics, led by Father Edward Tivnan of Fordham, to nudge the order toward academic modernization. Officially constituted by the provincials and general as an Inter-Province Committee in 1921, Tivnan's group worked for a decade on a reform agenda: revising the curriculum, strengthening libraries, cultivating ties to lay alumni, and, above all, training Jesuit faculty at the doctoral level. In 1925, one year after the committee called for a new emphasis on graduate education, B.C. established its own graduate school of arts and sciences and began offering doctorates. Four years later, the college created its first graduate professional school in law.

In the end, however, the Inter-Province Committee failed to persuade the provincials or the general of the need for aggressive efforts to upgrade the order's academic institutions. Fearing conflict with the National Catholic Education Association as well as loss of regional autonomy, the provincials resisted the committee's call for a national organization of Jesuit schools and colleges. In 1931 the Inter-Province Committee was disbanded with its reforms largely unaddressed.[14]

M.I.T., Massachusetts Agricultural College, Boston University, and the Age of the University

During the second half of the nineteenth century, a new wave of academic institution building occurred, comparable in scale but different in character from the college movement of pre-Civil War years. By mid-century, in fact, reformers like Francis Wayland were asserting that the traditional colleges, with their focus on religion and classics, were out of step with the nation's expanding middle class, the chief potential constituency for higher education. These attacks were buttressed by alarming references to an enrollment crisis. In 1870 President Barnard of Columbia asserted that the proportion of young men attending college had declined steadily between 1838 and 1869.

The latter year, coinciding with Eliot's appointment, is often taken as the beginning of the "age of the university," during which many established colleges were transformed and a generation of institutions created. By 1909, when Eliot finally retired, complex universities—with their diverse curricula, their aggregations of graduate and professional schools, their large student bodies, and their professionalized faculties—had replaced traditional colleges as the nation's dominant form of academic organization. In association with these changes, enrollments increased sharply, rising fivefold in four decades.[15]

Academic change in the age of the university was a multifaceted phenomenon, but two developments stood out: the heightened attention to practical concerns and the expanded importance of graduate instruction and scientific research. The theme of "utility," so expressive of late nineteenth-century preoccupations with industrial growth and social mobility, had been present, of course, long before the Civil War in the technical institutes like Rensselaer, in some of the state universities, and even in traditional offerings in law, medicine, and theology. With the Morrill Act of 1862 and the wave of state universities and land-grant colleges that flowed from it, however, industrial and agricultural programs moved to center stage. In Massachusetts two schools were supported with federal revenues. The Massachusetts Institute of Technology, founded in Boston as a private institution in 1861, was adopted as the state's college for the "mechanic arts" in 1863, the same year that Massachusetts Agricultural College was created in Amherst, ninety miles to the west.

Private higher education also flourished anew, aided by the immense individual fortunes of the period. Stanford, Chicago, Cornell, Johns Hopkins, and Vanderbilt were all begun on the basis of single gifts, and philanthropy generated a cluster of local universities embodying the spirit of the age. Worcester Polytechnic Institute, devoted to mechanics, manufacturing, and agriculture, was established by a hometown donor in 1865. Twenty-two years later, another successful native of Worcester County created Clark University, committed exclusively to graduate education and research. The most ambitious initiative was Boston University—an effort by three Methodist laymen to combine British and German educational concepts. B.U. was founded in 1869 with a gift from Isaac Rich of $1,700,000, the largest educational contribution yet made by an American.[16]

M.I.T. was the brainchild of William Barton Rogers, a scientist and scientist's son, who believed that the industrial revolution called for a new type of education simultaneously more practical than the traditional classical training and broader than the offerings of the technical institutes. Clear about the dependence of technology on science, Rogers thought that instruction combining basic subjects with applied fields would produce the creative, pragmatic men needed to lead the country's emerging industrial economy. Although Rogers was not a Bostonian, he wanted his school located there, since he regarded the city as the nation's "most forward looking" in both education and industry.

During the 1840s and 1850s, he explored various possibilities. One option was creating a new unit of Harvard, but Rogers rejected this course because his ideas seemed unlikely to flourish in a place committed to "the old education." He preferred a limited-purpose institution dedicated to his specific goals. When the legislature, the Great and General Court of Massachusetts, decided in 1859 to reserve space in the Back Bay landfill for educational projects, Rogers proposed an institute of technology. In 1861 he was granted both land and charter. The assignment of Morrill Act funds two years later provided a reliable source of operating income.

During the 1860s and 1870s, Rogers assembled a faculty, built a facility, and designed a curriculum stressing scientific and technical subjects. Public response was strong, and within ten years of the founding, Rogers claimed that M.I.T. "has already taken the first place among the scientific schools of the U.S." The positive trends continued during the last two decades of the nineteenth century under Rogers's successor, Francis Amasa Walker. When Walker retired in 1897, the Institute was the nation's largest and most complete school of applied science and engineering, employing over fifty faculty and enrolling a thousand students, 40 percent of whom came from out of state, many from foreign countries. Throughout these early years, the Institute remained dependent on the commonwealth for financial support, since neither Rogers nor Walker was successful in building an endowment. M.I.T.'s local ties were conveyed by its nineteenth-century nickname—"Boston Tech."[17]

Despite the success of Rogers's ideas, the effort to balance science and its applications begat continuing tensions. This problem was especially severe in the late nineteenth and early twentieth centuries. In a period of weak and changing leadership, champions of the technical side achieved a dominant position and impeded the advancement of basic research. The appointment of Richard Maclaurin as president in 1909, however, gave power to a leader who understood the potential of Rogers's initial conception.

A physicist with a practical inclination, Maclaurin wanted M.I.T. to evolve from a technical institute into a "scientific university." This new type of institution would add two elements to Rogers's design: first, research and graduate work in fundamental disciplines like physics and chemistry; second, an intensified learning environment at the undergraduate level based on residential facilities and a strenthened program of liberal education. Both steps were intended to undergird a continuing focus on the practical applications of scientific progress. On the strength of his inspiring vision, Maclaurin rallied the Institute's supporters to build a badly needed campus in Cambridge.

The campaign for the Cambridge campus dramatized M.I.T.'s natural relationship with the nation's industrial executives, many of them alumni. These were years when leading businessmen were becoming as impressed as was Maclaurin with the economic importance of scientific research, and M.I.T.'s president parlayed that shared perception into large contributions, especially from Coleman du Pont and George Eastman. By the end of World War I, Maclaurin had defined M.I.T.'s chief constituency in terms of this new elite.

When financial pressures heightened after the war, he turned to industrial leaders once again, this time proposing formal links between the Institute and corporate sponsors. Under the "Technology Plan," Maclaurin intended to write contracts with specific companies that guaranteed, for an annual fee, access to the intellectual resources of M.I.T., assistance in solving technical problems, and a steady flow of trained men.[18]

Though Maclaurin suffered an early death in 1920, the Technology Plan sustained a new stream of activity during the postwar decade under his successors Ernest Nichols and Samuel Stratton. Ironically, given Maclaurin's goal of using corporate support to build a "scientific university," the plan had the effect of channeling energies away from academic problems toward practical work of immediate value to industry. The Stratton period, in particular, like the early years of the century, was a time when the balance between technical and scientific concerns shifted excessively toward the former. By the time Stratton retired at the end of the decade, key members of the Corporation, joined by a cadre of scientists on the faculty, were convinced of the need for renewed attention to basic science.[19]

The state's other Morrill Act institution, Massachusetts Agricultural College, achieved less impressive development in the nineteenth century and also lagged behind the land grant colleges of other states.[20] As late as 1896, the college enrolled only eighty-eight students, employed just two dozen faculty, and offered an undergraduate program that had changed very little since the 1860s. Within this modest framework, however, the college could boast some areas of distinction. Like other land grants, M.A.C. was concerned with agricultural research, and the faculty did important experimental work that brought a measure of national, even international, recognition. In the 1880s and 1890s, this aspect of M.A.C. was enhanced by a state appropriation for an experiment station and by federal research support under the Hatch Act.

By the end of the century, modest graduate programs in the basic sciences and mathematics as well as in agriculture, botany, entomology, and veterinary science expressed the college's strengths. Agricultural education for undergraduates remained, however, the heart of M.A.C. All students were required to complete a sequence of courses in farm-related subjects as well as in appropriate scientific fields. The social sciences and humanities were viewed as supplements to the basic curriculum and remained undeveloped, and no other occupational or professional programs were available.

A number of factors accounted for M.A.C.'s limited progress. The decision to separate agricultural and industrial education in Massachusetts—a pattern not widely adopted—cut the college off from the most dynamic aspect of the state's economy while linking it to a sector where Massachusetts was bound to be a minor force. The existence of a well-established group of academic institutions in the commonwealth limited M.A.C.'s potential to move into new fields. The school's relationship to state government on Boston's Beacon Hill also was problematic. While it enjoyed quasi-official status as a public college, it was independently organized and was expected to fend for itself once the campus was acquired and federal funds were provided. Only when M.A.C. faltered in the 1880s did the General Court commit itself to continuing support.

M.A.C. was held back also by a disinclination among the college's supporters and members to expand beyond original purposes. The state's farmers—the most important source of political influence—wanted the campus to concentrate on their concerns. M.A.C.'s president in the 1890s, Henry Goodell, was one of four founding faculty and was content with a restricted path. While private and public institutions in Massachusetts and around the nation experimented with new educational forms and a broader range of functions, Goodell and his colleagues devoted themselves to serious but circumscribed efforts to improve basic science related to agricultural education and research.

In the early years of the twentieth century, several forces pushed M.A.C. toward a wider view of its possibilities. By virtue of its low cost and respectable reputation, the college was attracting talented students eager for educational opportunities beyond agriculture. Some began an organized movement for a broad program in the arts and sciences and a change in the college's name to Massachusetts State College. The state chapter of the American Federation of Labor was even more ambitious, arguing that the commonwealth should enlarge M.A.C. into a full-blown university comparable to the public institutions of the Midwest. The college's new president, Kenyon Butterfield, shared the view that M.A.C. was not realizing its potential, and he mounted a successful effort to expand the institution and increase financial support. By 1916 the undergraduate student body had grown to six hundred and become more cosmopolitan than in earlier years; the faculty numbered seventy-two; new facilities had been added; and the college had enhanced its reputation for both education and scholarship.

Ultimately, however, growth was constrained by internal as well as external factors. Butterfield himself was basically committed to an agricultural vision. His reforms stopped short of introducing new fields. His most striking innovation was an extension program that carried M.A.C.'s services to outlying communities. The disinclination of Beacon Hill to foster development also remained a hindrance. Indeed, in the 1920s the college's position worsened in this respect. A constitutional amendment in 1918 resolved ambiguities in M.A.C.'s status and brought it clearly under government control. Shortly thereafter, the college was made a subunit of the Massachusetts education bureaucracy. This change so limited institutional initiative that Butterfield resigned, and the college sank into a period of stagnation.

Though the 1920s were discouraging years, the forces working to improve the college continued to be evident. Able students enrolled in increasing numbers—by 1930 half came from the Boston area—and M.A.C. sent a larger percentage of its graduates to advanced work in science than any other agricultural college. Student and alumni/ae groups as well as organized labor kept up pressure for a change in the college's name and for authorization to offer the arts degree. Their efforts finally succeeded in 1931 as M.A.C. was renamed M.S.C., stirring hopes for a surge of innovation in a curriculum that remained, according to the centennial historian, "basically . . . the scientific agricultural program which had been designed by the founders in 1867."[21]

While M.I.T. and M.A.C. were created as special-purpose institutions linked to particular sectors of the state's economy, B.U. was intended to be large and comprehensive, fully reflective of the university movement. The first president, William F. Warren, planned undergraduate colleges patterned on Oxford and Cambridge, but B.U.'s central concerns were to be at the advanced levels. Warren wanted graduate faculties similar to those at German universities—especially in law, medicine, and theology, as well as the arts and sciences.

B.U. was to be modern in other respects as well. The founders were committed to coeducation in all units, a pattern new to New England in the 1870s. Like Johns Hopkins, Chicago, and Clark, B.U. was to be urban. Its relationship to the Methodist church involved not the formal sponsorship typical of ante-bellum colleges but close informal connections. Warren was an ordained minister, and most of the trustees were Methodists, as were most of the liberal arts faculty. B.U. would be concerned with religion, but the interest was ecumenical rather than sectarian. Even the School of Theology, a former Methodist seminary absorbed into the new university, was nondenominational—it became a pioneer in training ministers for a range of faiths. The founders understood that they were creating an academic, not a religious, institution.

As planned, the most important achievements of the early years occurred in graduate education. Following the creation by incorporation of the School of Theology in 1871, the School of Law was founded in 1872, and the School of Medicine followed a year later, through merger with the New England Female Medical College. Warren insisted that all three schools adopt high standards and employ current ideas about professional training. Within a few years, B.U. enrolled more students in its graduate programs than either Harvard or Yale. The School of All Sciences, renamed the Graduate School of Arts and Sciences soon after it opened in 1874, was a comprehensive, separately organized enterprise at a time when Eliot was beginning graduate training as an appendage of Harvard College. B.U. awarded its first Ph.D. in 1877. Other units of Boston University founded in the early years included a small, relatively exclusive College of Liberal Arts that prided itself on high standards, even smaller Music and Oratory units (the latter suffered an early demise), and a College of Agriculture based on cooperative arrangements with M.A.C.

Despite the early successes, B.U.'s progress during the late nineteenth century was impeded by difficulties that threatened bankruptcy by the onset of World War I. In fact, financial concerns had been present from the beginning. Even before the university received it, the Rich estate had been depleted through economic reversals. Expansion to obtain tuition income became imperative, and the high standards of the College of Liberal Arts were sacrificed to growth in the 1880s. By 1900 this unit enrolled over five hundred students, and the university's leaders were eager to attract even more applicants. Concern focused on B.U.'s evolution as a female-oriented institution at the undergraduate level. In the 1870s men had constituted two thirds of the students in the College of Liberal Arts, but the proportions gradually reversed, and in the early years of the twentieth century, women accounted for 60 to 70 percent of this unit.

Financial pressures also limited B.U.'s ability to support a faculty of the first rank. Salaries remained low, and important fields were neglected. In the nineteenth century, B.U. depended on M.I.T. to supply its scientific courses and maintained its own staff chiefly in the humanities. In 1905 the resident faculty of arts and sciences numbered only twenty, of whom eight taught foreign languages.[22]

The combination of financial and enrollment pressures produced a set of difficult questions about the future of B.U. The university lacked the wealth and glamour to develop further as the elite institution envisioned by its founders. There was, for example, no proper campus, and the several schools were located in scattered facilities around the city. Enrollment potential was limited, however, by relatively high charges, a reputation as a school for women, and the absence of practical programs that could attract a broader clientele.

During a fifteen-year administration that began in 1911, President Lemuel Murlin, like his predecessors a Methodist minister, tried to resolve B.U.'s problems of identity and finance through two parallel efforts. First, he repositioned the institution as a "municipal university" offering an array of undergraduate degrees to local students. Schools were opened in Business, Education, Secretarial Science, Religious Education, and Fine Arts. These initiatives were not solely a response to B.U.'s difficulties. They expressed also the reformist impulses of the Progressive era, a sentiment felt with particular strength by the Methodists, who undertook a general reorienting of their universities toward urban residents.

Murlin's policies succeeded in their social as well as their institutional objectives. In the expansive years that followed World War I, enrollments grew rapidly, making B.U. one of the largest universities in the U.S. by the time Murlin retired in 1924.

The president was less successful in the second part of his program, a campaign for endowment that failed to achieve its goals. This disappointment hastened Murlin's departure and reinforced B.U.'s dependence on enrollments and tuition. These would need to be obtained, it was now clear, by serving large numbers of commuting students through the new collection of practical programs.[23]

Radcliffe, Jackson, Northeastern, and Social Reform—Feminism and Progressivism

As the university movement of the late nineteenth and early twentieth centuries was transforming higher education with new ideas about the functions of academic institutions, the movement itself was reshaped by the pressures of a turbulent period. Two social causes of these years—feminism and Progressivism—had far-reaching implications for academia. Each influenced established institutions, and each produced a cluster of schools committed to its particular goals.

The history of higher education for women followed different courses from region to region. Coeducation first appeared in the antebellum colleges of the West, both public and private. In Massachusetts and the rest of the Northeast, however, the tradition of masculine exclusivity was firmly rooted and tied to the dominance of private schools. Not surprisingly, in this context, the leaders in female education were single-sex and private. The seminary founded by Mary Lyon in the 1830s in South Hadley was an early attempt that encountered resistance when it sought to become a full college. It was not until the 1870s, when Smith and Wellesley were created on the model of Amherst and Williams, that advanced education for women became acceptable in the commonwealth. Shortly thereafter, Mary Lyon's seminary won a new charter as Mt. Holyoke College.[24]

With the exception of B.U., founded at the same time as Smith and Wellesley, the state's existing universities, private and public, resisted feminist claims. Harvard's Eliot, though a reformer and modernizer who supported the expansion of opportunities for women, was a determined foe of coeducation. In response to proposals from local advocates, however, he did consent, in 1878, to establish the "annex"—later incorporated as Radcliffe College with its own charter from the legislature—where female undergraduates could take Harvard courses from Harvard professors in a setting strictly separated from Harvard College.

For years, the Tufts trustees fended off pressures to admit women, despite the Universalists' commitment to coeducation in their other academic institutions. Only in 1892, by which time advanced learning for women was no longer controversial, did they relent. Even then, the policy of coeducation proved short-lived. In 1910, worried that Tufts was becoming female-dominated—a problem B.U. encountered in the same period—the trustees created a separate school for women, Jackson College, on the Radcliffe pattern.

Unlike their western counterparts, neither of the state's land grant campuses, M.I.T. and M.A.C., displayed much interest in coeducation—though females were eligible for admission to both, and a few actually attended. As late as 1916, the graduating class at M.A.C. included only two women. Not until male enrollments were depleted by World War I did the state's agricultural college think seriously about educating women. The Jesuits at Boston College thought about such matters even less. Women would not gain admission to B.C.'s programs until the late 1940s.[25]

The impact of Progressivism on higher education occurred later than that of feminism, appearing in the final two decades of the nineteenth century and peaking between the Spanish-American War and World War I. As both a social and a political phenomenon, Progressivism assumed many forms and focused public attention on a number of issues, including corruption in government, monopolistic practices in industry, and the impoverished circumstances of urban and immigrant communities.

Within academia, the Progressive impulse was expressed as a new readiness to engage social problems beyond the campus. The classic example was the University of Wisconsin under President Van Hise, who made public service a central concern. As part of the "Wisconsin idea," faculty members were encouraged to work with government agencies and social-welfare organizations on societal problems. At the same time, the university initiated "extension" courses for the general population. Academic leaders understood, of course, that the new, service-oriented activities brought political benefits.[26]

The advantages of Progressivism were especially evident to educators in Massachusetts with links to state government. Faculty at M.A.C. and M.I.T. were involved with applied research in agriculture and industry from an early time, and the patterns endured. The first agricultural experiment station was established by the state college in the 1880s, and Maclaurin's Technology Plan was a later version of the same idea. Extension courses were part of M.I.T.

from the beginning, especially through an association with the Lowell Institute, and M.A.C. developed its own version of extension during the Butterfield administration. But academic Progressivism in Massachusetts was not limited to publicly supported institutions. Murlin's policies at B.U. were greatly affected by Progressive ideas. Another example was the initiative of A. Lawrence Lowell in 1911 to link Harvard, Boston University, Boston College, Tufts, and Wellesley with the Lowell Institute to offer courses for the general public.[27]

Like feminism, Progressivism produced a set of academic institutions in Massachusetts expressing the movement's special values. Simmons College opened in the 1890s to offer practical programs for working-class women, and Suffolk Law School, which would evolve into Suffolk University, was founded in 1908 to make legal education more widely accessible. Similarly, the directors of the Boston Y.M.C.A. decided, in 1896, to organize their long-standing program of lectures and evening courses into an Evening Institute for the city's growing population of young men who lacked the means to attend a private college. This was the modest beginning of Northeastern University, destined to become one of the largest and most important academic institutions in the commonwealth.[28]

In creating the Evening Institute the directors of the Y.M.C.A. were acting within a broader movement among the nation's Ys that produced a number of schools and colleges in the early years of the twentieth century. But the directors were animated by more than Christian concern for the well-being of young men from rural and immigrant backgrounds. Through their ties to Boston's business community, they understood that the region faced a shortage of trained workers and that the unruly new arrivals were needed to maintain economic expansion. The dual impulse to provide opportunities for students with few resources while working with industry to produce competent manpower was built into the foundations of Northeastern and became a defining characteristic of the school.

From the beginning, in fact, the Evening Institute was operated as a business, with courses and programs offered or canceled depending on student willingness to register and pay. The first director, Frank Palmer Speare, though trained as a school teacher, proved a gifted entrepreneur with ambitions for his enterprise far beyond those of his board. After a period of experimenting with course sequences, Speare moved into full-scale, degree-granting programs. The first was the Evening School of Law, established in 1898. During the next fifteen years, the director launched an eclectic set of ventures with mixed results. Successes included an Automobile School with programs for owners as well as mechanics (1903), an Evening Polytechnic School offering technical subjects ranging from chemistry to clay modeling (1904), a School of Commerce and Finance (1907), a prep school (1909), and a Co-operative Engineering School (1909). The failures, quickly disbanded when they could not pay their way, were a School of Advertising, a School of Applied Electricity and Steam Engineering, and an Evening College of Liberal Arts.

In mounting programs, Speare was animated less by an educator's sense of mission than a promoter's readiness to see what worked in the marketplace. The new Institute became a vehicle for innovation. The Evening School of Commerce was the first program of its kind in the nation. The Engineering School adopted a pattern begun at the University of Cincinnati—called cooperative education—through which students paid their way by alternating periods of study and work. Flexibility fostered growth, and by the beginning of World War I, the Institute enrolled over thirty-six hundred students in 376 courses. Moreover, by trial and error, Speare evolved a rounded educational mission for his school. Stressing practical studies in fields of occupational opportunity, the Institute offered programs in two formats: evening, part-time studies for employed adults, and day courses for full-time students on the cooperative plan. In 1916, after two decades of operation, Speare persuaded the directors to seek legislative authority to organize his baccalaureate-level programs under the name of Northeastern College. With this initiative, the Institute took a clear, if partial, step toward independence.

As a new addition to the commonwealth's collection of colleges and universities, Northeastern was an anomaly. It lacked the support from a religious organization that had provided the initial impetus for Harvard, Tufts, B.C., and B.U. (Like the Y itself, of course, Northeastern retained a strong Protestant flavor with links, through its board, to the city's social and economic elites.) It enjoyed no sponsorship from state government as did M.I.T. and M.A.C. or, for many years, Harvard and Tufts. It had no facility, apart from the rooms it utilized at the Y. Its operating expenses came entirely from tuition and fees, and its minuscule endowment was built by husbanding what Speare called "profits." Its small full-time faculty had the status of industrial employees rather than professional scholars, and most courses relied on part-timers hired from industry. It maintained a strange array of programs ranging from the avocational to the technical to the preparatory to the collegiate.[29]

But Speare and his colleagues persisted and, in the years of academic growth following World War I, expanded their fledgling college. In 1920 they gained legislative approval to award degrees in engineering. In 1922 they changed their name to Northeastern University. In 1923 they won expanded degree-granting authority.

Speare's adventurousness continued to manifest itself. A wartime experiment with a branch campus in Worcester prompted additional ventures in Springfield, New Haven, Bridgeport, and Providence. The Automobile School, having outlived its usefulness, was closed. A day, co-op–based, College of Business Administration was opened. The Evening Polytechnic School evolved into the Lincoln Institute, which contined to offer technical courses at night. In 1929 Speare and his associates acquired a parcel of land close to the Y's new facility on Huntington Avenue with the intention of constructing a proper campus. It was on this site, nineteen years later, that James Conant of Harvard, *ex officio* captain of the nation's academic establishment, celebrated Northeastern as a welcome and respectable sister institution in the region's democratic educational system.[30]

Historical Dynamics of Academic Change

The Roots of Competition Among Universities:
The Problem of Resources

Each university in Massachusetts was created by a specific component of the state's population to advance goals of interest and benefit to itself. The early histories of these schools, however, demonstrated the importance of competition among them in determining patterns of institutional change. Initially, each was embedded in an organizational structure dominated by representatives of its founding constituency and oriented toward that group's religious, intellectual, social, or economic goals. So long as these campuses remained closed to outside influences, change derived mostly from the slow evolution of purpose among its sponsors. Isolation rarely lasted for long, however. The most fundamental force against insularity was the need for funds.

Money to support academic work came from three sources: private philanthropy, student payments, and government aid. Harvard, the state's first college, was established with a grant from the Great and General Court and regular subventions from the commonwealth were indispensable well into the nineteenth century. Private donations, including the famous bequest from John Harvard, were also important from the beginning, and accumulating grants strengthened the young college decade by decade. Students always bore part of the costs.[31]

During the two centuries that Harvard remained the lone college serving the commonwealth, its struggles to obtain funds were those of an academic outpost in a comparatively undeveloped society. With the founding in the mid-nineteenth century of other colleges, institutes, and universities, however, and the general growth of academia following the Civil War, the situation began to change. For several of the newer schools, support from sponsoring communities was insufficient to ensure existence even on a modest scale. The inevitably expanding ambitions of campus leaders increased financial appetites. The need or desire for supplementary help inspired efforts to broaden bases of support. Such initiatives, in turn, frequently modified—and sometimes compromised—the schools' initial purposes.

It was only a matter of time before campus drives for survival and development brought the area's schools into competition for resources with each other and with other colleges and universities outside the region. Over time, the terms of competitive engagement evolved along with social, economic, and academic conditions, but the competition itself—and the pressure for change that it exerted—remained constant.[32]

Efforts to attract students from the immediate vicinity provided an early context for interinstitutional competition. All area schools served mostly local students during the second half of the ninteenth and first half of the twentieth centuries. Moreover, the percentage of the state's high school graduates attending college remained small throughout these years, reaching only 20 percent by 1922. As late as 1929, half the undergraduates at both Harvard and M.I.T. came from Massachusetts, and most of the rest came from New

England. Student bodies at B.U. and Tufts in the 1920s were drawn largely from nearby towns, with a sprinkling from beyond the state. B.C., Northeastern, and M.A.C. were resolutely local in orientation. The parochial character of student bodies was symbolized by the fact that, into the 1930s, none of these schools, save Harvard and M.A.C., provided housing for a significant proportion of its enrollees. Even at Harvard, most students lived off campus, since the first of Lowell's houses for upper classmen opened only in 1930.[33]

The competition for students was especially intense among institutions characterized by modest academic reputations, heavy reliance on tuition payments, and weak claims on the loyalty of particular college-going constituencies. Schools that combined these circumstances with a limited array of undergraduate offerings were vulnerable to shifts of curricular fashion. At different points, Tufts, B.U., and Northeastern all needed to expand enrollments to earn more revenue, and all three did so by diversifying their programs to reach additional clienteles.

Tufts's Capen expressed his dismay over the unseemly spectacle of academic entrepreneurship as early as 1880. "The spirit of competition," he wrote, "which is fierce in every branch of business, extends even to our educational institutions."

> Neighboring colleges are straining every nerve to obtain students; established courses of instruction are extended and new ones are introduced . . . attractions unknown to our New England institutions a quarter century ago are presented to the young man who contemplates entering an institution of learning . . . Although it would be neither wise nor dignified for us to enter into this scramble, the fact remains that we must be progressive and aggressive if we expect Tufts College to maintain the rank it has among New England institutions.[34]

The "scramble" for enrollments deeply affected the character of institutions. Capen's policy of program diversification turned Tufts from a Universalist college into a comprehensive university, thus fostering internal tensions that would plague the campus for decades. B.U.'s Murlin eschewed the elite goals of the school's founders and stressed service to the local community. In doing so, he stretched his campus beyond its physical and organizational capacities, creating problems that would dominate the administrations of his successors. The impact of the academic marketplace on Northeastern was even more fundamental. From the beginning, the offerings of the Evening Institute were determined by Speare's eclectic, business-oriented approach to academic innovation. By contrast, the schools most likely to retain their programmatic emphases over time were those like B.C., Harvard, and M.I.T. that had the firmest hold on a steady stream of applicants as well as a reliable base of monetary support that limited their dependence on tuition.

The competition for students had a political as well as an entrepreneurial dimension. This fact stemmed from the power of the commonwealth to grant institutional charters designating the fields in which degrees could be offered. Academic leaders quickly learned the uses of politics in protecting their interests. Harvard, for example, achieved a privileged position in medicine by persuading state authorities to restrict entry to the field by other campuses. The charters issued to Tufts, Amherst, and Holy Cross all prohibited degrees in medicine. When Capen's Tufts sought relief in order to merge with the Boston College of Physicians and Surgeons, a representative from Harvard appeared before the legislature to oppose the change. Fortunately for Tufts, Harvard's political standing had declined since the seventeenth century, and the request was granted. Northeastern encountered similar opposition when it sought to expand beyond nondegree courses. The charter granted to Speare and his colleagues in 1923 excluded the B.A. and B.S. as well as degree programs in medicine and dentistry.[35]

Following Harvard's lead, other Massachusetts universities sought direct funding from the state. Politics therefore constituted a second arena in which they competed for support. In fact, state aid was a common feature of academic finance during the second half of the nineteenth century after the legislature dedicated revenues from the sale of Back Bay lands for educational purposes. Relationships between Beacon Hill and academia were rarely smooth, however. The financial history of Harvard was littered with complaints about the unreliability of politicians, and Tufts had to petition the legislature three times before it received an initial grant.

The most significant manifestation of academic contention for government dollars involved the resistance of private institutions as a group to the growth of public higher education. In this, they were largely successful, as could be seen in the sluggish progress of the state college. Nationally, the years following the Civil War were a time of rapid expansion among state-financed institutions. Massachusetts, however, participated only marginally in this movement. Educational historians have explained the phenomenon by noting the absence of a significant local constituency. This was true. Protestants were involved with the schools they had created; Catholics preferred their own institutions; and politicians remained indifferent. However, academic leaders from the independent sector also worked actively to keep support for public institutions from developing. Eliot, for example, was an outspoken critic of state funding, even though Harvard had depended for years on the commonwealth.[36]

The politics of public-private conflict were illustrated by the movement to expand state-supported higher education in the early years of the twentieth century. Initiative came from several quarters: students and alumni/ae of M.A.C., who wanted to upgrade their college; the labor movement, which was interested in low-cost education for its members; and the Massachusetts Board of Education, which proposed a state university in the Boston area. In 1922 the legislature formed a commission to review the commonwealth's needs. The commission found that Massachusetts ranked twenty-first nationally in the proportion of its young people attending college but recommended against a tax-supported university, citing additional capacity among private institutions.

This result reflected the views of commission chair Murlin of B.U., whose financially strapped campus was trying to expand in these years. As an alternative, the commission proposed a system of community colleges focused on technical programs. Even that proved unacceptable, however. Cousens exemplified the opposition. While favoring two-year institutions, Tufts's president campaigned against public sponsorship. Massachusetts would not create a state university until 1947 or a community college system until the 1950s.

The efforts of universities like B.U. and Tufts to fulfill needs met elsewhere by public institutions influenced their own character as much as that of M.A.C. Cousens's proposal to create a lower-division college open to all graduates of area secondary schools was clearly related to his concern about the proposed system of state-sponsored two-year colleges. Murlin transformed his campus into a kind of public institution under private sponsorship. In some instances, indeed, independent universities formally accepted functions at the request of government agencies, as when B.C and B.U. designed teacher-training program for the Boston School Department or when the state Department of Education offered extension courses through the independent sector.[37]

The search for philanthropic support constituted a third arena in which area universities competed for resources. Private donations played a central role in the establishment of every college in Massachusetts, including M.A.C. An inability to continue attracting gifts could push a campus toward particular developmental policies, as when Murlin's shortcomings as a fund-raiser forced reliance on tuition—and therefore expansion—or M.A.C.'s poverty led to dependence on the government.

Success in attracting revenue, on the other hand, introduced another kind of distortion into campus decision-making processes. If, for example, a large proportion of contributions came from a single source, a college could be cut off at the pleasure—or displeasure—of the donor. Tufts's relationship to the Universalists illustrated the point. Early in the twentieth century, the university's leaders wanted to end their sectarian ties, but financial dependence on the church rendered this goal impractical and led them, in fact, to maintain their failing Divinity School, renamed the Crane Theological School in 1905. Long-time trustee Austin Fletcher consistently used the influence gained from large donations to demand policies consistent with his personal conception of Tufts. Attempts to diversify sources of gifts presented a different difficulty. That strategy pushed academic leaders toward an ecumenical blandness and pluralism that conflicted with distinctive educational purposes.[38]

When philanthropic support could be transformed from budgetary sustenance into endowments, particularly unrestricted ones, its advantages were greatly increased. Indeed, well-endowed institutions were much less subject to external pressures for change than were those that relied on student payments or annual giving. Eliot understood this fact well, telling his inaugural audience that Harvard's greatness depended on freedom, and Harvard's freedom depended on wealth. Eliot's good fortune in turning income from investments into a primary source of operating revenue was one of his most important achievements. Though other universities in Massachusetts established endowments in the late nineteenth and early twentieth centuries, none was remotely as large as Harvard's or as important a contributor to annual expenditures. Despite its eminence, for example, M.I.T. did not amass substantial funds under Rogers and Walker, chiefly because Harvard so thoroughly monopolized local philanthropy.[39] This fact provided the background for a fascinating chapter in the history of interinstitutional combat in Massachusetts as well as a classic illustration of the impact of competition for private gifts on institutional character.

Eliot wanted to absorb M.I.T. He proposed merger four times between 1869 and 1909. These initiatives attracted support among Institute officials, including two presidents, partially because of their school's persistent financial problems. Many Institute loyalists, on the other hand, resented Harvard's overtures and actively resisted them. The 1904 chapter of this drama produced a student brawl on the streets of Boston.

One enthusiast of merger was Lawrence Lowell, who was a member of the M.I.T. Corporation before succeeding Eliot at Harvard. Indeed, soon after his elevation to the presidency, Lowell revived the old question for a fifth time. His initiative coincided, however, with the appointment of Maclaurin at M.I.T., who proved combative. The Institute's new president used his inaugural address to express firm opposition, winning a thunderous ovation from the partisans in Symphony Hall. Soon afterward, however, when Maclaurin sought money from local donors to build the Cambridge campus, he received such a chilly reception that the Institute considered moving to another city.

Ultimately, Maclaurin solved his problem by identifying a new constituency of corporate leaders and alumni/ae across the country who helped build the campus and, indeed, move the Institute to a higher level of academic work. His success turned M.I.T.'s traditional weakness in local fund-raising into a source of strength and played a major role in transforming the Institute into a national institution. Thus, M.I.T.'s evolution as a cosmopolitan campus had a deep root in the competition among local universities for philanthropic support.[40]

The atmosphere of interinstitutional competition for resources did not preclude collaborative efforts. For years, B.U. relied on M.I.T. for scientific instruction and offered agriculture through M.A.C. B.C. also cooperated with M.I.T. and forged a relationship with Tufts to help its graduates win admission to the Tufts Medical School. Northeastern's efforts to open the Evening School of Law were actively aided by law deans at Harvard and B.U. Even Harvard and M.I.T. designed joint programs once the Institute's independence was ensured. Interinstitutional cooperation was facilitated by the pattern of overlapping associations among individuals and universities—like Lowell's ties to M.I.T. and Harvard—that characterized Massachusetts higher education.

Despite such connections, competitive pressures tended to dominate interinstitutional discussions, as the Harvard–M.I.T. case illustrated. Negotiations always involved close calculations of mutual advantage, and proposals that made educational sense, such as the attempts of Tufts and B.U. to design joint programs in law, medicine, and dentistry, were often defeated. In the late nineteenth and early twentieth centuries, competition for students, government aid, and philanthropic support constituted a fundamental force in shaping area universities.[41]

The Roots of Competition among Universities:
Social Conflict and Institutional Prestige

Beyond surviving, the universities of Massachusetts sought to progress. The impulse to improve had multiple roots and meanings. It partly flowed, of course, from the desire of the cleric and scholar to find a deeper truth or a higher religious meaning and of educators to inspire students to greater achievement. Eliot summoned his inaugural listeners to a new age for the college in Cambridge in the name of academic excellence, a rhetorical tradition followed regularly by his successors at Harvard and elsewhere.[42]

From the outset, however, calls to campus communities to do better typically referred to a comparative as well as an intrinsic conception of achievement. It meant doing better than others—especially other schools. When De Voto expressed concern about Harvard at the end of the Lowell years, he spoke of losing ground to Chicago, Columbia, and Wisconsin. Harvardians constantly measured their position against Yale and Princeton in the East, and, later, Michigan and Berkeley among the major state schools.

Leaders of other institutions in Massachusetts demonstrated equal concern about their relative standing in their spheres. Tufts's early leaders worried about their position relative to St. Lawrence, and Cousens solicited support by proclaiming that his struggling campus should become "one of the outstanding centers of learning in America." Rogers's proudest claim was that M.I.T. had achieved "the first place" among scientific and technical schools in the United States. B.C. kept a wary eye on Holy Cross, Fordham, and Georgetown, as well as Notre Dame, and Gasson stirred local enthusiasm by urging his little Jesuit school to become "the outstanding Catholic college in America." The impulse to be good in comparative terms was closely related to the competition for resources, since it was always easier to attract donations, grants, and applications when one was offering association with high academic status.

In the localistic world of Massachusetts higher education in the late nineteenth and early twentieth centuries, the competition among institutions for prestige expressed not only academic strivings in relation to other schools but also social divisions among the state's religious, ethnic, economic, and regional communities. Relations among such groups were rarely easy. On the contrary, the history of the commonwealth was notable for a high degree of hostility and stratification along lines of social difference. Schools born of the hopes of distinctive communities carried also those communities' resentments. The explicit function of these institutions as vehicles for the development of individuals was complemented by a less-explicit role in the advancement of their constituencies: academic progress for the campus signified social achievement by its supporters. Beneath institutional ambition lay social conflict.[43]

Interclass tension in academia had its origins in the link between Harvard and the Puritan elite in the seventeenth century. Though the Puritans ultimately lost control of the college, though religion, indeed, waned as a social force, Harvard's affiliation with the region's wealthiest and most powerful citizens survived. As Samuel Eliot Morison put it in his tercentenary history: "Harvard in politics has always reflected the sentiments of the ruling class in Boston." During years when the college in Cambridge was the state's only institution of higher learning, opposing elites battled for its control.

Social conflicts also prompted the creation of competing schools. The founding of Williams and Amherst in the early nineteenth century expressed orthodox outrage over the Unitarian conquest of Harvard, regional animosity between eastern and western parts of the state, and class resentments between a rural yeomanry and the cosmopolitan, mercantile class of the coast. Similarly, among the forces contributing to the founding of Tufts, B.U., and M.A.C. in the mid-nineteenth century was middle-class anger over Harvard's preference for wealthy applicants. These institutions all stressed their intention to enroll young people whose financial backgrounds denied them access to the state's leading campus. Religious feeling added to the tension among schools sponsored by differing Protestant sects: Unitarian Harvard, Universalist Tufts, and Methodist B.U.[44]

The development of M.I.T. reflected another form of intergroup division, rooted in the relationship between occupation and social position. William Barton Rogers argued that education at M.I.T. would be democratic in its concreteness and practicality, in contrast to the more abstract, theoretical—and aristocratic—emphases of classical learning, as practiced by the self-satisfied scholars of Cambridge. In fact, as the Institute evolved into the nation's leading engineering school, a tie between its academic specialities and social class did develop. Engineering became a field—and M.I.T. a school—for ambitious, upwardly mobile, middle-class graduates of the public schools. Established families preferred a traditional immersion in the liberal arts for their offspring. Early partisans of M.A.C. were moved by feelings of resentment between the small-town and rural constituencies they served and the urban, metropolitan communities to which their private competitors were tied.[45]

The relationship between academic institutions and patterns of social stratification proved durable and was especially apparent among undergraduate students. In the 1920s, Harvard continued to educate mostly the sons of socially well-positioned Protestant familes, though it also enrolled small percentages of Jews and Catholics, some from modest Boston neighborhoods. Indeed, though Lowell initially liberalized Harvard's admission policies—a reaction to the declines in enrollment of the last Eliot years—in the 1920s, he presided over a social narrowing of the College. Two policies accounted for the change: first, the Corporation took the unprecedented step of limiting freshman admissions; second, Harvard raised tuition three times in rapid succession, doubling its charges in less than a decade—following a fifty-year period of marginal change. Both policies were defensible on practical grounds—enrollment limitation as a response to the expansion of applications after World War I; tuition increases as a reflection of prosperity and inflation—but such considerations do not explain adequately the shift of emphasis.

Lowell thought Harvard was too accessible. He was particularly worried about an influx of academically talented Jews from the large second generation that was completing high school in these years, especially in New York and Boston. Lowell earned himself a permanent reputation for bigotry by proposing a Jewish quota—and allowing racial segregation in the dorms. These policies expressed Lowell's conviction that Harvard College should nurture the Yankee, Brahmin values with which he had been raised, and that this mission required the student body to be drawn largely from the College's traditional constituency. He thought there should be room for the gifted sons of newer groups, but their number should be limited to ensure their integration into the mainstream. The new policies of restricting freshman admissions and raising tuition served Lowell's purposes by increasing Harvard's bias toward graduates of a few preparatory schools and major public high schools in Boston, New York, and Philadelphia.[46]

Student bodies at the state's other Protestant institutions in the 1920s further reflected the state's social divisions. Tufts and B.U. continued to attract students from their sponsoring religious communities and remained overwhelmingly Protestant despite the increasingly Catholic character of Boston. An exception to this rule was the Tufts Medical School, which enrolled a large proportion of Catholics, but this derived more from a wish to restrict the admission of Jews than from Universalist liberalism. Tufts and B.U. were places for middle-class students who lacked the abilities required at Harvard or M.I.T. The great majority of undergraduates at both institutions came from the public schools of the region, and many lived at home and worked their way through college. In 1929 half the students at B.U. were paying half or more of their own educational costs. Tufts's program in engineering and its link to a medical school made it especially attractive to scientifically oriented males. B.U. held a special appeal for females interested in education, office work, nursing, and social service.

Northeastern served students from families a step lower on the social hierarchy than Tufts and B.U. N.U.'s emphasis on business and engineering, its total inattention to the refinements of liberal education, and its educational formats—cooperative education for younger students and evening programs for adults—mirrored its historic orientation toward the area's working class. As guarantors of educational opportunity for the impecunious, the universities of the Boston area—especially Northeastern, B.U., and B.C.—played far more important roles than the state college in Amherst. M.A.C.'s remote location, which made it impossible for most students to live at home, drove the costs of going there above those of the commuting schools of the metropolitan area, and the lack of employment opportunities near the rural campus made it difficult for low-income students to combine work and study. M.A.C. in the 1920s was an institution for the children of comfortable middle-class familes from the small towns of western Massachusetts and, increasingly, the Boston area as well.[47]

Boundaries of class, faith, and region within the Protestant community were historically less sharply drawn than the divide between Protestants taken together and the region's more recently arrived Catholics. Much has been made of Protestant–Catholic, or Yankee–Irish, conflict in Massachusetts, and popular mythology has simplified social patterns that were actually nuanced and complex.

Yet the long-remembered conflicts were real enough. Zealous Calvinists banned Catholics from residence until 1780 and barred them from state office until 1822. The immigrants of the mid-nineteenth century entered a social context containing much intolerance. As evidence of anti-Irish and anti-Catholic feeling accumulated, Massachusetts seemed to many newcomers to pit a struggling Catholic community against a homogeneous religious establishment. Negative predispositions toward Protestants brought across the Atlantic by the new arrivals exacerbated the problem.

Education became one of many contexts in which Yankee–Irish resentments were enacted. In the 1840s and 1850s, the Protestant-dominated state government repeatedly rebuffed petitions from the Society of Jesus to charter Holy Cross and Boston College. Once established, these schools entered a separate educational universe and had minimum contact with Protestant academics. Their isolation was partly voluntary, partly enforced. Protestants often regarded Catholic education as dominated by religious concerns and therefore intellectually inferior as well as anti-American. Such attitudes received an explicit expression from Eliot when Harvard dropped B.C. and Holy Cross from a list of colleges whose undergraduate degrees would be fully recognized by the Law School. Catholics, on their side, frequently saw Protestants as biased and threatening. They were often uninterested in ideas beyond those sanctioned by their faith.[48]

Tensions between the Protestant and Catholic communities and their educational institutions persisted into the twentieth century. As the Catholic population grew, these feelings became important political forces. An especially charged topic was government support for schools and hospitals. Yankee comfort with public subsidies for Tufts and M.I.T. did not extend to Holy Cross and B.C., much less to parochial schools at the elementary and secondary levels. Yet, Catholics had grown strong enough in the legislature to demand equal treatment for their institutions. Resolution of this matter was achieved only by passing a constitutional amendment prohibiting state aid to all private schools, secular and religious. Boston College itself became an important symbol of the gathering strength of the Catholic community. The new campus on the Heights in Chestnut Hill was part of a pattern favored by Cardinal O'Connell, who loved to locate Catholic institutions on the hills around Boston to proclaim the progress of his countrymen and co-religionists.

In the early years of the twentieth century, Catholic universities and colleges were even more inclined than their Protestant counterparts to enrolling students from their sponsoring faith. Enrollment patterns among Catholic institutions also reflected class divisions, just as they did at Protestant campuses. For affluent Catholic families, the most popular choice was Holy Cross, or possibly one of the out-of-state institutions like Georgetown. Boston College in the 1920s enrolled local commuters from modest families.[49]

Because of the association between universities and specific subcultures, each school's academic prestige became emblematic of the social standing of its sponsoring group. From the early days of the commonwealth, Harvard's academic eminence was inseparable from the social dominance of its clients and patrons, and gradations of academic prestige among the state's other campuses mirrored differences in the social position of their constituencies. This linking of academic standing to social acceptance fueled the anger of leaders at B.C. when Eliot questioned their graduates' preparedness for Harvard's Law School. The same phenomenon gave intensity to the long-standing friction between Harvard and M.I.T. When the Institute's alumni roared approval of Maclaurin's defiance on the merger issue, they expressed class feeling as well as campus pride.

The hunger for social prestige provided part of the motivation for educational leaders to seek academic advancement for their schools: success promised not only the satisfactions of institutional progress but enhancement of social position for the nonacademic communities they represented—and from which they typically had come. Indeed, academic progress generally involved upward shifts in the social level of students. In advocating his reorganization plan in the 1920s, Tufts's Cousens urged his colleagues to stop thinking of their institution as "a poor man's college and an asylum for the children of the foreign-born." In Cousens's view, improving Tufts's academic reputation required it also to attract more students from the "best families."[50]

Another corollary of the link between social and academic prestige was that universities enrolling upwardly mobile students often felt pushed to adopt the educational patterns of high-status institutions. The movement among students at M.A.C. for a full program in the liberal arts exemplified this phenomenon, which in due course would affect Northeastern as well. Herein, however, lay a dilemma for campus leaders, since it was not easy to integrate the particularistic goals of traditional constituencies with the claims of upward academic mobility. To the extent that M.A.C. retained its historic orientation toward agriculture, its potential for academic progress was limited; to the extent that it sought higher status, it would be constrained to expand and blur its mission. Similar problems confronted the Jesuits of B.C., the Universalists at Tufts, and the engineers at M.I.T.

Even Harvard encountered conflicts between social commitments and academic goals. Lowell's efforts to make the College a more effective agency for promoting Brahmin values were perceived in some quarters, particularly among faculty members like De Voto, as jeopardizing Harvard's academic reputation. In the end, of course, these conflicting pressures could never be resolved fully, at Harvard or the state's other universities. They could only be balanced and accommodated in the context of each historical moment within each academic community. They constituted, however, a consistent element in the equation of pressures that shaped the evolution of universities in Massachusetts between the Civil War and the Depression.

Ideas, Power, and Competition

The discussion so far has emphasized the impact of competition among universities for resources and prestige on institutional character. In this context, the analysis has considered campuses as whole entities contending with the dual pressures of the academic marketplace. In fact, however, colleges and universities were rarely unified internally. From the beginning, they contained distinct subpopulations, and every group—faculty, students, board members, and administrators—wanted different things and had somewhat different conceptions of their institutions. Over time, as schools took on new functions, the roll of interest groups lengthened. Faculties and students in new fields, financial supporters with varying perspectives, and alumni/ae oriented toward the past all made their claims. The developmental trajectories traced out by universities in Massachusetts were inevitably influenced by jostling among these constituencies. Intramural contention, in turn, was shaped by the relative power of the participants within campus political systems and by the positions of the schools themselves in the larger arena of interinstitutional competition.

Debates about how local universities should develop took many forms and produced myriad, often unpredictable alliances and animosities. One prototypical conflict pitted the founders and their successors, typically members of a nonacademic, sponsoring community serving on a governing board, against the scholars who constituted the heart of an institutional community. In the seventeenth and eighteenth centuries, Harvard weathered numerous clashes between Puritan governors, with their commitment to theological orthodoxy, and the Cambridge academics, whose tendencies were liberal and innovative. Parallel tensions occurred at Tufts in the late nineteenth century as dedicated Universalists struggled to maintain collegiate values at a campus transforming itself into a modern, diversified university. At B.C., conflicts of priority between the nonacademic Jesuit hierarchy and the order's educators were apparent by the early 1900s.

Policy debates did not invariably cast trustees and nonacademics as conservatives and faculty members as progressives. It was the Harvard Corporation that appointed Eliot to the presidency in 1869, thus opening the way for dramatic change. It was M.I.T.'s board, in the late 1920s, that concluded the Institute must shift emphasis from industrial problem solving to basic science. Indeed, campus communities—especially administrators and faculties— sometimes resisted academic change. For years, leaders at M.A.C. were pushed by their students, alumni/ae, and external groups to take a more expansive view of the college's possibilities. In the early twentieth century, B.U.'s trustees reduced the faculty's role in academic appointments because the professors were reluctant to consider activities outside the liberal arts.

The situation within institutional communities, moreover, was often fragmented. Presidents and faculties, and subgroups within faculties, disagreed about priorities. Cousens wanted Tufts to be a center of innovation but found his faculty complacent. In the early twentieth century, the scientists and engineers at M.I.T. warred over the relative importance of their interests. Other constituencies also were hard to characterize in any consistent fashion. The alumni at Tufts, less involved with Universalist purposes than the trustees, supported Capen's policy of program diversification in the 1880s. But alumni could also exercise convervative influence, as was the case at Harvard on the issue of education for women.[51]

The difficulty of establishing a definitive pattern linking specific elements of academic communities to predictable tendencies of academic policy stemmed partly from the interplay between ideas and power. It is always problematic, of course, to distinguish the thoughts from the interests of an individual or group. When conservative Universalists at Tufts opposed Capen's efforts to diversify, were they acting from religious conviction or political concern or both? When the engineers battled the scientists at M.I.T., were they advancing an intellectual cause or defending institutional turf?

The answers to such questions are invariably contextual and specific. Indeed, the perspectives of participants in these debates sometimes shifted with changes in their institutional roles. As a young instructor promoting reform at Eliot's Harvard, Lowell was a tireless proponent of faculty prerogatives in curriculum planning; following his appointment to the presidency, however, he nurtured a newly formed student government as a means of combating faculty power. Perspectives also shifted with altered understandings of campus needs in competition with other colleges and universities. Eliot's priorities changed radically during his forty-year presidency with his deepening grasp of how best to ensure Harvard's eminence. Jesuit reformers of the early twentieth century were animated as much by awareness of the weak position of their institutions as by intellectual disagreements with their conservative opponents.[52]

However difficult it is to separate the contributions of conviction and interest in shaping the thoughts of participants in intramural policy debates, it is clear that what mattered most in determining the outcome of these controversies—at least in the short run—was the relative power of the contending advocates rather than the intrinsic merits of their ideas.

In traditional colleges, presidents were well positioned to exercise executive authority. These men, many of them ministers, were often highly regarded representatives of their institutions' sponsoring constituencies. This fact gave them legitimacy as educational leaders with governing boards as well as with faculty and students. The schools they governed were small, and the range of subjects taught was limited. Most presidents, moreover, possessed extensive formal powers in matters of faculty status and compensation, unencumbered by requirements of due process, the pressures of faculty committees, or even the constraints of explicit policy. Not surprisingly, therefore, educational historians typically have used presidential administrations to define periods of campus development, an emphasis justified by the stories of Massachusetts institutions. Powerful figures like Eliot at Harvard, Rogers and Walker at M.I.T., Capen at Tufts, or Gasson at B.C. held the keys to change. Periods of institutional drift—at M.I.T. at the end of the nineteenth century, at Tufts in the early twentieth—were typically associated with weak leadership. Discerning members of governing boards understood that their most important power was naming the president.

Even in the late ninteenth century, however, presidential success depended on conditions as well as personal qualities and formal powers. Eliot had the good fortune to serve during a period of great wealth and philanthropy among Boston's Yankees, and Gasson benefited from the growing prosperity of the Irish community. At the same time, the accomplishments of talented leaders, like Warren of B.U., were limited by adverse circumstances. We must, therefore, consider the relationship between power within institutions and competition among institutions for resources. A central source of Eliot's power and of Lowell's after him lay in each man's ability to attract Yankee wealth. Speare dominated Northeastern like a captain of industry because, entrepreneur that he was, he exercised detailed control over new financial initiatives and the internal distribution of funds. By contrast, campus heads at Tufts were weakened because they traditionally played marginal roles in monetary affairs. Cousens transformed the Tufts presidency when he insisted on a primary voice in budgetary decisions.[53]

Governing boards, like presidents, possessed extensive power in nineteenth-century institutions. As leading representatives of the nonacademic communities whose aspirations these schools expressed, board members had standing to influence educational decisions through both collective and personal authority. As conduits for contributions from sponsoring constituents and as individual donors, their influence acquired an even firmer basis, a fact illustrated by Fletcher's tenure on the Tufts board.[54]

As a general pattern, the professoriate in traditional colleges possessed minimal power outside the curriculum and student discipline. This situation derived from the weakness of the faculty in determining the relative position of the campus. With respect to the competition for resources, most professors had no direct function whatever. Many were, literally, dependents of their institutions and therefore of governing hierarchies. Faculties were more powerful when they controlled or benefited from restricted endowments—as at Harvard—or when they could command resources independently—as was the case with the engineers at M.I.T. Among universities in Massachusetts, however, the Cambridge campuses were atypical.

With respect to the competition for prestige, most faculty also played limited roles. During an era when few professors were publishing scholars and research itself was a minor theme in academic life, campus reputations derived largely from their nonacademic characteristics. Here again, the faculties of Harvard and M.I.T. contained exceptions to the general rule, but even in Cambridge, most scholars lacked visibility beyond their own schools' walls. The stature of the president, the social position of board members, the significance of education within the sponsoring community, the status of the constituency itself, and the aura of tradition played larger roles in determining the standing of most early colleges than the specific intellectual achievements of faculties.[55]

Other campus subpopulations were also weak in relation to presidents and governing boards. The power of students was akin to that of customers, though the involvement of student groups in promoting change at M.A.C. suggested the potential of an organized student movement in a political context. The influence of alumni/ae was limited by the fact that little emphasis was placed historically on annual giving programs of the kind that became common after World War II. Here, again, there were exceptions. At Harvard, the alumni acquired the power to elect overseers in 1865 and became an important source of donations in the early 1900s. B.C. also established an alumni fund at the end of the nineteenth century, and alumni/ae at Tufts were important participants in the struggles between 1905 and 1919.[56]

The Professional Challenge to Hierarchical Power

While conditions that reinforced the roles of presidents and governing boards lingered on in the late nineteenth and early twentieth centuries, the rise of the university form of organization contained forces that would ultimately transform the balance of academic power. It was one thing, in the relatively fixed curriculum of the traditional college, for minister-presidents to dominate their modest academic communities; it was quite another for them to exercise authority over the burgeoning faculties of turn-of-the-century universities with their multiplying scholarly specialities. During this same period, the growing role of higher education in producing useful knowledge and training professional practitioners was shifting the terms of interinstitutional competition from social and religious issues to academic and professional ones. This change, too, would impinge on the discretion of presidents and governing boards.

The development that most challenged the traditional academic order was the emerging professionalism of the faculty, especially their organization into discipline-based societies transcending the boundaries of particular universities. The first academic professional organization was actually formed in the 1840s, but the movement did not become significant until thirty years later. Sometimes, specialists split off from a preexisting general organization, as when, between the 1870s and 1890s, the American Association for the Advancement of Science spawned the American Mathematical Association, the American Chemical Society, and the Botanical Society of America. Sometimes, new groups, like the Modern Language Association, were created from scratch. While the specific history of this process varied from field to field, the underlying forces were similar. Scholars with common interests wanted to communicate with each other and promote the development of their specialty. Founding a society, creating a journal, and holding periodic meetings were natural expressions of these impulses. On occasion, mitosis was hastened by resistance to new fields within established groups, but the formation of new and splinter organizations accompanying the establishment of disciplines was bound to occur more or less as it did, rooted as it was in both an intellectual and social logic.[57]

The professionalization of academia proceeded in historical tandem with the transformation of colleges into universities. As academic leaders worked to build centers of graduate training and research, they needed the scholarly expertise the new associations could provide. Harvard's Eliot, noting the difficulty he had experienced in the early years of his presidency in finding outstanding scholars, welcomed professional groups as aids to his own efforts.

The complementary aspects of professionalism and institution building were particularly evident in the emergence of the academic department as the fundamental unit of universities. In traditional colleges, faculties were aggregations of individuals appointed by presidents. Before the Civil War, some institutions, Harvard among them, created schools (for medicine, law, and arts and sciences) and even departmental structures within these larger entities, but the pattern was not widespread, and the categories were broad. The practice of assembling scholars into departments defined by research specialities, and linking departments together into schools headed by deans, was not common until the late nineteenth century.[58]

The implications of these changes for the distribution of power gradually became manifest. As recognition within the professional associations and publication in the societies' journals came to be the touchstones of scholarly status, the new groups began to claim authority to evaluate the work of their colleagues with a minimum of interference from nonspecialists. Similarly, at the campus level, academic departments fought for control over their own affairs, especially in matters of personnel. Some leaders, like Eliot, welcomed this development and thought it advanced the interests of their institutions, even though it also curtailed administrative power. By the 1920s, the primary responsibility for recommending faculty appointments had devolved to departments at most of the nation's leading universities.

At less-prestigious institutions, however, traditional patterns often remained. Even M.I.T., while formed into academic departments, had not yet created schools, and department heads were appointed and closely supervised by the president. Academic appointments were made by the head and president with no required participation by other faculty. Presidents retained similar powers at Tufts and M.A.C. Northeastern and B.C. represented an even earlier stage. At neither place did faculty members possess any of the independence that came with professional status.[59]

The reallocation of power associated with professionalization involved more than mutual agreement by scholars and administrators. Presidents did not always yield their prerogatives readily, and professors were animated by motives more complex than intellectual progress. For many faculty members, in fact, professional values and departmental forms provided a political framework for resisting control by the increasingly hierarchical and bureaucratic organizations that universities were becoming in the late nineteenth century. These were years when private money was flowing into higher education and providing a basis for institutional growth as well as the further enhancement of administrative power. In this potentially oppressive context, the department could be a protected enclave within which scholars exercised a measure of authority and control.

The fullest expression of professionalism as an assertion of faculty power was the formation in 1915 of the American Association of University Professors. The founders of the A.A.U.P explicitly intended to create a faculty-based counterforce to administrative structures on matters of importance to all scholars, like academic freedom. For this reason, some presidents viewed the A.A.U.P. as a kind of labor union and objected to its initiatives. Leaders who resisted the claims of professionalism, both substantive and political, faced a dilemma, however, if they also wished to enhance the stature of their institutions.[60]

They faced a parallel dilemma from accrediting agencies, which were beginning to appear in the late nineteenth century, though their maturation trailed somewhat behind the learned societies. The rise of regional and professional accrediting organizations was driven by the problem of maintaining educational standards in the *laissez-faire* world of American higher education in the years following the Civil War. The significance and implications of accreditation were illustrated by its emergence as a force in Massachusetts, which occurred in the second decade of the twentieth century in medicine.

The initial impetus came from the American Medical Association, the professional organization of physicians, which in 1903 created the Council on Medical Education to establish standards for training doctors. Before the new council could proceed very far, however, Abraham Flexner's study of medical education for the Carnegie Foundation in 1910 drew widespread attention to the shortcomings of the nation's medical schools. As part of his study Flexner inspected the Tufts Medical School, pronounced it unsatisfactory, and recommended that it be closed. Tufts fared somewhat better with the A.M.A. itself, but faced increasing pressure after 1910 to provide better support and to maintain more rigorous standards. Ultimately, to avoid being forced from the field—as were a number of universities in similar circumstances—Tufts was compelled to stop diverting funds from medicine to other programs and to build an endowment specifically for the school, improve facilities, change policy in faculty hiring and compensation, and raise admission requirements. Tufts's problems in medicine were a hint of things to come for it and other struggling Massachusetts institutions in a number of fields, including dentistry, engineering, education, as well as, by mid-century, the basic arts and sciences.[61]

Like professionalization, accreditation affected the distribution of power within campus communities. Historically, the dean of Tufts Medical School had little recourse, save resignation, when the trustees drained revenues from his budget. Following the advent of accreditation, however, trustees and presidents needed to attend to complaints from deans or faculty who buttressed their arguments with references to recognized agencies—and could signal their concern to the certifiers if they were ignored.

Presidents and governing boards did not always welcome such intrusions on their authority—any more than those of the new professional societies. There was limited room for resistance, however, since the imprimatur of accreditation became an emblem of legitimacy in a growing number of fields. The pressure was especially pronounced for low-status institutions like Tufts in medicine and Northeastern in engineering. For them, accreditation became essential for protecting their positions in the competition for both students and dollars. Well-established campuses like Harvard and M.I.T. had less to fear. Indeed, representatives of elite campuses typically played leading roles in forming accrediting groups and drafting standards. For example, the first chair of the Committee on Engineering Schools of the Engineers' Council for Professional Development (E.C.P.D.), whose standards were to have a major impact on the evolution of Northeastern, was the president of M.I.T.

In diminishing the power of traditional campus hierarchies, both professionalism and accreditation tended to diminish institutional diversity. Indeed, the fostering of standards applicable at many colleges and universities was the essential purpose of these movements, and that purpose sometimes conflicted with the maintenance of distinctive institutional cultures. No school faced this dilemma more starkly than B.C., with its historical orientation toward sectarian values that conflicted at key points with acceptance by the new regulatory agencies. B.C. was only an extreme case of a general problem, however. Cousens of Tufts consistently railed against the accrediting agencies for demanding uniformity and inhibiting innovation at the campus level.[62]

By the 1920s, however, it was clear that academic status required accommodation with professional norms, even if these challenged particularistic campus traditions and the power of presidents, board members, and nonacademic sponsoring constituencies. Indeed, there was in these years a rough correlation between the degree of freedom from domination by external, nonacademic sponsors enjoyed by universities in Massachusetts and the academic standing of these institutions. Those schools least encumbered by outside control—especially Harvard and M.I.T., whose lay governing boards, though informally linked to nonacademic constituencies, had the power and orientation to act in the best educational interests of their campuses—were unchallenged as scholarly centers. Those that were controlled most directly by nonacademic organizations—B.C., M.A.C., and Northeastern—were least advanced. When N.U.'s leaders sought professional advice about fund-raising, they were informed that separation from the Y.M.C.A. was essential. Their consultants argued that no university could achieve respectability or attract financial support if it were governed by a group not committed primarily to academic goals.[63]

The Long Pause, 1929–1945: University Development in Depression and War

Harvard, M.I.T., and the Dream of the Research University

In the early 1930s, Harvard and M.I.T. needed presidents. The two campuses anticipated the pending changes with more than usual interest because, at both, the 1920s were years of growing concern about the priorities of incumbent leaders. Complaints about Lowell's focus on undergraduate education paralleled worries that M.I.T.'s Stratton was too oriented toward technical problem solving. These criticisms implied that both men emphasized the concerns of external constituencies at the expense of intellectual values.

In fact, Lowell and Stratton came to their presidencies from careers outside higher education—Lowell was a lawyer and amateur scholar, Stratton was a government official—and they thought of their schools as fundamentally dedicated to meeting manifest societal needs. While this orientation linked them with important institutional traditions, it impeded their understanding of academic change in the early twentieth century, especially the importance of research and graduate education and the professionalism that flowed from these functions. As the governing boards of Harvard and M.I.T. debated the selection of new leaders, they were implicitly deciding how best to reconcile their institutions' historic social roles with their commitments to national leadership in academic terms.

The M.I.T. Corporation acted first, offering the presidency in 1930 to Karl Taylor Compton, a physicist from Princeton with a reputation as a brilliant research scientist. Three years later, the Harvard Corporation chose James Bryant Conant, chair of the Chemistry Department, highly regarded scholar, and outspoken opponent of Lowell's policies. In some respects, the new leaders embodied traditional differences between the two campuses: Conant was a Bostonian who had earned his undergraduate and graduate degrees at Harvard and spent his entire career on the Harvard faculty; Compton had no prior connection with the Institute and no ties to New England. Yet the similarities between the two men were striking. Both were Ph.D.s and professional academics. Both were research-oriented scientists educated in American universities but steeped in German ideas about scholarship. Both, indeed, belonged to a new generation of intellectuals who believed the United States should achieve the primacy in science long held by Europe, and both believed the institutions whose presidencies they were assuming should lead the nation in this direction.

Conant and Compton represented new priorities for their institutions. Though a Bostonian, Conant was solidly middle class and had no ties to the Brahmin elite that for generations had controlled the Harvard presidency. A scientist's scientist, committed specifically to his discipline and broadly to academic excellence, he was uninterested in disseminating the values or securing the position of a particular community or class. Compton, though attentive to links between basic science and its applications, was, above all, an academic investigator. He was more concerned with promoting sound scholarship than with meeting the immediate needs of corporate sponsors. By selecting professional scholars, the two governing boards stressed intellectual strengthening. The two decisions marked critical divides in the evolution of Harvard and M.I.T. as modern universities.[64]

The most thoughtful members of the M.I.T. Corporation saw no conflict between academic science and industrial development. By the early 1930s, leading corporate executives realized that scientific research was the basis of technological progress. This fact had implications for corporations as well as universities. An economy not supported by science was likely to stagnate. An institute of technology concerned chiefly with engineering risked loss of academic prestige and obsolescence in practical terms.[65]

Compton believed M.I.T. had to change radically to maintain its position as "the nation's leading technological institution." He wanted to elevate basic science, traditionally viewed as support for engineering, to a quality and significance equal to engineering itself. Indeed, he thought scientific research should be a central objective of the Institute, a proposal he saw as truly revolutionary:

> No educational institution, to my knowledge, has ever . . . giv[en] attention to the efficiency of its research program comparable to that which it gives to teaching. No institution has such great possibilities in this direction as the Massachusetts Institute of Technology. I can imagine no investment for public welfare so likely to secure large returns as one which would permit the latent creative powers of this institution to become really active.

Compton restricted the industrial work of the M.I.T. faculty to projects possessing fundamental significance and educational potential. He made appointments in the basic disciplines, replaced the chair of the Physics Department with a young theoretician from Harvard, and initiated a campaign to finance research laboratories for chemistry and physics. At the same time he cut out long standing "deadwood in M.I.T.'s curriculum" in fields like mining engineering, and electrochemical and sanitary engineering.

The new president's plans included changes in M.I.T.'s educational program as well as its student body. He believed an expansion of graduate education, especially in science, was "absolutely necessary . . . for the sake of the Institute's prestige . . . because graduate students are the most highly selected." He also noted that graduate students would set an example for the undergraduates and help the school retain its most creative faculty. Higher admission standards for undergraduates were essential. Compton wanted the Institute to produce "leaders who will be able to handle the big and difficult problems of organization, production and new development" rather than the skilled technicians for whom the campus was traditionally known. In his first year, he limited freshman places—something M.I.T. had not previously done—and saw the resulting decline of in-state enrollments as an indication of higher stature. Simultaneously, he pressed for a reduction of technical and professional work in the undergraduate curriculum and an increase in nonscientific subjects. He even created a new Division of Humanities to ensure attention to the liberal arts. To make the Institute more attractive to broad-gauged applicants, Compton began planning dormitories as well as athletic and social facilities.[66]

Though the new president was popular, his policies were not universally embraced. Some faculty argued that undergraduate teaching would suffer from the focus on research. Others complained that more attention to basic science and the liberal arts would weaken professional education. More generally, traditionalists worried that Compton was abandoning the vision, first articulated by William Barton Rogers, that M.I.T. should offer a "new" education rooted in practical and "democratic" concerns, in contrast to the classical, abstract, and class-based preoccupations of conventional universities. Compton vigorously combated these doubts, insisting that his policies represented an updating, not a relinquishment, of Rogers's ideas.

The truth lay in the middle. Unquestionably, Compton's priorities were intended to make M.I.T. more like the well-established, Ivy League universities with which the president was most familiar. He would later observe that M.I.T. was comparable in orientation to Harvard and Chicago (a comment Rogers would not have made), and he was delighted in 1934 by the Institute's acceptance into the Association of American Universities (A.A.U.). But Compton also believed his reforms would enhance undergraduate professional education and improve M.I.T.'s ability to meet the practical needs of society. In fact, he had undertaken a complex balancing act with the dual goals of preserving what was strongest and most distinctive about the Institute and moving it closer to the mainstream defined by the nation's elite campuses. Here was a challenging venture, containing great potential for both institutional progress and organizational conflict.[67]

While M.I.T. was edging toward Harvard, the decision of the Harvard Corporation to appoint Conant recognized the need for the nation's oldest university to embrace the science-based notions of research and advanced education that Compton was bringing to the Institute. In contrast to Lowell, who worried about curriculum and student life, Conant believed his primary job was to appoint outstanding faculty members, support their work, and let the rest take care of itself. "A university [is] a collection of eminent scholars," he told a member of the Corporation during the search process. "If the permanent professors [are] the most distinguished in the world, then the university [will be] the best university."

Conant faulted his predecessor for insufficient attention to intellectual attainment in faculty appointments. He believed that Lowell had done harm by "filling up the young ranks with mediocre men whose merit consisted largely of their willingness to be tutors . . ." Conant also had strong views about Harvard's students, whom he expected to be serious about learning. He had no interest in assisting "young gentlemen born to the purple" to obtain an "appreciation of the 'good life.'" He was distressed that percentages of upperclass and private-school boys had increased during the 1920s. The new president believed in fierce competition for entry and wanted applicants judged on their academic abilities. For students as well as faculty, Conant sought to raise the intellectual level as high as possible. It was time, he argued, for Harvard to stress "intensification" rather than expansion.[68]

Conant quickly made plain the meaning of intensification in academic appointments. Junior faculty members in Arts and Sciences were instructed to limit tutorial work and do more research. Deans and chairs were informed that junior colleagues should not to be retained indefinitely but must be reviewed for permanent appointments after a fixed period. It was clear that such reviews would stress scholarly achievements. The potentially dire implications of these policies were obvious, and Conant tried to implement them gradually. Nonetheless, his first attempt to do so—by denying reappointment to two young economists—produced a storm of controversy. Faced with a challenge to his leadership, Conant was pressured into a review of personnel policy by a committee of professors.

The resulting report included recommendations that he could welcome, including the required tenure review after a fixed period. Other suggested policies, however, threatened his goals. In particular, the committee wanted clear statements that faculty possessed the primary power in personnel decisions and that teaching and research were equally important. Believing that committees of colleagues would not be tough enough on junior associates, Conant resisted faculty primacy, arguing that academic appointments were chiefly an administrative responsibility. This contention, though true to Harvard's traditions, was not widely understood, and Conant's position heightened the turmoil. In the end, in peril of being forced from office, the new president accepted the committee's recommendations.

Conant regarded his acquiescence as only a tactical setback. Over the next several years, he recaptured the ground he had lost by appointing *ad hoc* committees, containing eminent academics from outside Harvard, to advise him on permanent appointments. This innovation had two consequences. It provided the president with a new source of authority, since the outsiders were a professionally credible counter to faculty opinion. It also centered attention on published scholarship, since external experts could not judge the teaching abilities or general scholarly qualities of individuals with whom they did not work. Through the *ad hoc* committees, Conant won the biggest battle of his tenure. He institutionalized the presidential role in personnel decisions and focused such decisions on the activities he deemed most important to secure Harvard's position as the nation's leading university.[69]

Conant's pursuit of intensification in undergraduate admissions led to two closely related objectives. The first was to raise intellectual standards; the second, to make the undergraduates "more representative [of the nation] in terms of both geography and family income." The latter purpose expressed Conant's distaste for the notion that Harvard should be the preserve of a privileged caste and his corresponding openness to talent from all sectors of society. These views, in turn, were rooted in his intellectual interests, democratic values, and middle-class background, as well as his conviction that merit-based admissions would strengthen Harvard's educational leadership and ensure its connection, in a highly mobile society, to future leaders and shifting centers of power.

Conant incorporated his ideas in a program of National Scholarships, which offered financial support to residents of western and southern states. Implementing this policy was problematic, however, since it required Harvard to judge applicants from distant places and unknown schools. Conant's engagement with this issue made him a proponent of objective tests, particularly the recently developed Scholastic Aptitude Test, which was used to assess scholarship requests and proved encouragingly predictive of academic performance.

The National Scholarships had great symbolic importance, but their short-term impact on Harvard's student body was modest. The number of awards was limited by finances, and though most went to boys from public schools, the percentage of private-school graduates in the entering class was almost the same in 1940 as in 1930. Conant's intentions were more evident in a small but clear shift away from Massachusetts and the Northeast among freshmen. These results suggested that it would be easier for Harvard to alter the geographical composition than the social class of its students. Ties to the region remained strong, however, as Conant discovered in his conflict-laden efforts to promote non-Bostonians for seats on the Corporation. Change at Harvard was going to be incremental, but the academic values the new president asserted in personnel decisions and admission policies contained the potential to transform the nation's oldest college far more dramatically than was evident during the 1930s.[70]

Compton and Conant were visionary leaders, but the early years of their presidencies, coinciding with the Depression, proved a difficult time to accomplish changes that required new resources. The biggest successes of both men in the 1930s involved tightened standards—Conant's personnel policies; Compton's reductions in support for weak departments—but these steps were aided by financial pressures. By contrast, building capacity in research and graduate education was expensive. Fellowship funds were essential. Facilities and equipment were required. Teaching loads needed to be kept low. Despite the relative wealth of Harvard and M.I.T., neither had the flexibility to redirect large sums to support new priorities. Moreover, neither president had much success raising new funds, though both tried.

The Depression was especially difficult for M.I.T., which had further to go academically and financially than Harvard and lacked Harvard's ability to attract foundation support. Compton wanted to expand the faculty and increase salaries, which were well below those of top universities, but could do little on either front. Moreover, by making the Institute's relatively high tuition a more significant barrier to attendance, economic conditions impeded Compton's efforts to improve the quality of the students. Indeed, shortly after announcing higher admission standards, Compton faced a decline in applications and had to recruit vigorously simply to maintain enrollments.[71]

Both Compton and Conant repeatedly expressed frustration over the absence of means to translate their visions into reality. Under these circumstances, Compton began advocating federal funding for scientific research as the only means of achieving the requisite level of support. In a series of speeches, he pointed out that the United States lagged behind other countries, including the Soviet Union, in encouraging scientific work. In 1933 he was asked by President Roosevelt to chair the Science Advisory Board, which was charged with studying the scientific activities of the federal government. The board's report recommended federal assistance for university-based research, but the idea did not attract broad political support.

Multiple factors explained the failure. Academicians were divided on the question of federal aid, many preferring to rely on the established, though limited, capabilities of private foundations and universities rather than risk government involvement, and Compton had to overcome resistance even among his colleagues on the board. Conflicts between the natural and social sciences added to the difficulty. The most fundamental problem, however, was lack of conviction about the importance of science among political leaders and the general public. In fact, both Compton and Conant were concerned about an anti-intellectual mood in the country, and both used their presidential platforms to combat this sentiment. The need to make such arguments, however, only added to their discouragement. As the decade ended, neither was hopeful that the resources required to pursue scientific research at the levels they believed desirable could be obtained.[72]

The outbreak of war in Europe occasioned a new diversion of attention from academic goals. As early as 1939, Compton began organizing the Institute for a military emergency, and in 1940 Conant abandoned the nonpolitical stance of his early presidential years and became an active interventionist. Once the United States entered the war, many faculty and administrators took leaves to assume government posts. The two presidents also accepted assignments in Washington. Instructional activity increasingly focused on federally sponsored training programs. As Conant put it: "After Pearl Harbor and until V-J Day . . . Harvard was primarily a university at war." Compton described M.I.T. in similar terms.

Looking back on the fifteen years from 1930 to 1945 from the perspective of a later time, Conant would be impressed by the degree to which change at Harvard was retarded by external circumstances. Had these catastrophes not occurred, he though, much that happened in the 1950s and 1960s would have come sooner. He labeled the period "the long pause."[73]

Nonelite Private Universities in Depression and War

Though Conant and Compton were often discouraged between 1930 and 1945, their institutions were shielded from adversity by their endowments, their connections to private wealth, and their secure standing in student markets. For the area's other private universities—Tufts, Boston University, Boston College, and Northeastern—these were difficult years. Their most important sources of financial support—tuition and philanthropy—were imperiled; students were less able to pay and donors less ready to give. Competition for local support intensified as each sought enrollments and revenues from diminished regional reservoirs.

The specific impacts of Depression and war varied. Tufts suffered least. Its smallness and respectability enabled it to retain enrollments during the 1930s, and revenue from endowments and gifts helped with operating expenses.

When wartime conscription depleted student bodies at many colleges and universities, Tufts was protected by coeducation and the exempt status of medical and dental students. Finances were strained, but no faculty members were terminated or reduced in salary. Tufts even found a way to help its staff earn extra pay—and to acquire additional institutional income as well—by providing liberal arts courses for free-standing occupational schools.

The picture was quite different at Boston University, which had grown into one of the nation's largest universities during the 1920s on the strength of tuition income. B.U. lost enrollments and, lacking adequate endowments to maintain itself, cut salaries to avoid layoffs. B.C. and Northeastern, low-budget and low-tuition institutions that served specific clienteles and did not rely on gifts, came through the Depression with minimal damage. Both were aided by small payrolls (B.C. utilized unpaid priests in the classroom; N.U. used part-timers). The war was hard on both campuses, however, as their all-male student bodies were decimated. Both laid off faculty in the early 1940s.

In forcing private universities to struggle to sustain themselves, the Depression and war dramatized their vulnerability to uncontrollable economic and political events. The new significance of national politics as both threatening and benign was particularly striking for institutions that regarded themselves as independent. During the 1930s, the willingness of the Roosevelt administration to allow stipends from relief and employment programs to be used for tuition proved vital in helping private universities retain students. A few years later, a new national policy, the draft, reduced enrollments. Then new government programs, this time military training programs like Engineering, Science, and Management War Training and R.O.T.C., produced new sources of students and revenue. By the end of the war, educational leaders had learned to regard federal policies as major factors in their economic calculations.

Academics also had absorbed a new spirit of engagement with national issues, for their participation in military training programs was motivated by patriotism as well as practical need. Indeed, from the perspective of a later time, the enthusiastic manner in which universities in Massachusetts reoriented themselves to help the government prosecute the war was one of the most impressive aspects of the period. Their activities went far beyond enrollment-producing training contracts and included, through the Key Centers project, efforts to promote enthusiasm for the government's policies.[74]

Faculties, meanwhile, were learning about their own vulnerability to economic and political crises. When costs needed to be reduced, the professoriate was the most likely element of institutional communities to suffer, initially through worsened working conditions—higher teaching loads and less support—and then through salary cuts or layoffs. Though this was inevitable, given that instructional salaries represented high percentages of budgets, it was also a source of anxiety, frustration, and anger. As we have observed, none of the area's nonelite university faculties played a major role in academic personnel decisions. None of them had direct representation on policy-making bodies.

Professors encountering the Depression and war from positions of structural impotence drew appropriate conclusions about the need for effective organization. Faculties at both Tufts and B.U., encouraged by local chapters of the A.A.U.P., became more aggressive in pressing for enhanced security and compensation and for greater involvement in decision making. At Northeastern, businesslike administrators were able to cow hesitant initiatives toward forming an A.A.U.P. chapter, but even here, the Depression and war stirred faculty concerns that would soon lead to demands for greater power and protection.[75]

With academic leaders focused on institutional maintenance and national defense between 1930 and 1945, plans for development, spurred by conditions of the 1920s, were relegated to the background. Beneath the surface, however, the old competitive thrusts toward upgrading remained strong, and leaders did what they could to advance their positions while awaiting the return of better times. Tufts's John Cousens, for example, defeated in his first attempt to create "one of the nation's major centers of higher education," spent the 1930s pursuing a new vision. Abandoning the idea of a large, unselective lower-division college, Cousens now proposed to recast his two core units—the School of Liberal Arts (for men) and Jackson College (for women) as small, selective, residential units comparable to New England's elite colleges. He believed this change would attract the well-prepared and affluent students that were needed to improve the college's standing. Simultaneously, he hoped to build Tufts's small cluster of graduate and professional schools, especially in medicine and dentistry, into quality programs and centers of institutional prestige. The constellation of programs that Cousens now envisioned would be something unique in the region: a small-scale university (unlike Murlin's B.U.), focused on undergraduate, liberal education (unlike Conant's Harvard), but also offering opportunities for advanced education in a few, well-chosen areas (unlike Amherst or Wellesley).

Unfortunately, the 1930s were the worst of times for the changes Cousens projected. Far from being able to admit undergraduates more selectively, Tufts hustled to keep enrollment at established levels. Raising funds for new dormitories was out of the question, and financial pressures also precluded improvements in the professional schools, which actually lost ground. The problems were especially severe in the programs of engineering and medicine, which were criticized by their respective professional associations as underfunded and ill-equipped.

Amidst these various difficulties, Cousens did manage one great success: the Fletcher School of Law and Diplomacy. A restricted bequest from Austin Fletcher, Tufts's longtime trustee and benefactor, allowed the president to concentrate resources in this new graduate enterprise, pay higher than normal salaries, and even persuade Harvard to become a co-sponsor. Such steps enabled Cousens to recruit top faculty, launch the school with great fanfare, and attract able students from a national pool. Exhilarated, Cousens pronounced the opening of Fletcher "the most important event in the history of Tufts College." Indeed, the new unit quickly became a singular example of the enhanced academic standing that Cousens sought for the entire campus.[76]

Cousens died in 1937, ending Tufts's longest twentieth-century presidency and leaving behind a well-integrated institution broadly supportive of his developmental directions. As his successor, the trustees selected his personal favorite, the dean of Arts and Sciences at Rochester, Leonard Carmichael. An active alumnus and son of a former dean of the Theological School, Carmichael had close ties to the college and its Universalist traditions. He also represented something new in the Tufts presidency: he was not only a scholar but a research scientist—a behavioral psychologist. In appointing such a man to replace a nonacademic, businessman/churchman president, the trustees were bringing to Tufts the same orientation toward professional academic values and scientific scholarship that the appointments of Conant and Compton had brought to Harvard and M.I.T.

The new president quickly justified Cousens's confidence by affirming his predecessor's vision of Tufts as a small, selective university centered on undergraduate liberal education with a modest cluster of graduate, professional programs. He also made clear his intention to revise collegiate traditions by stressing research within the Faculty of Arts and Sciences. His hope was to combine this new emphasis with Tufts's tradition of undergraduate education, since he did not believe his school could build successful graduate programs in a regional context dominated by Harvard and M.I.T. His conception was unusual and would have been difficult to implement anywhere. It would be especially challenging at the college in Medford where, for two decades, the administration had done nothing to encourage faculty scholarship. Carmichael had little immediate opportunity to address such matters, however. Within a year of his appointment, Europe was at war, and the new president found himself attending to the manifold problems of the military emergency.[77]

Tufts's attempts to position itself as a small, elite university were paralleled by the efforts of Boston University to cope with bigness. Murlin's policy of expanding B.U. as a service-oriented "municipal university" following World War I alleviated long-standing concerns about enrollment and finance but produced problems of space and organization. At the time of Murlin's retirement in 1924, B.U.'s main facilities were located in Copley Square, to which the university had moved only twenty years earlier. Already, however, the new quarters were inadequate. Some units were renting space near the square. Others were scattered about the city. These physical arrangements compounded chronic problems of administrative coordination rooted in B.U.'s early history as an assemblage of previously free-standing schools and Murlin's recent addition of new programs. B.U. in the 1920s was less a unified institution than a collection of independent units, each with its own facility, admission policy, curriculum, and faculty.

Murlin's successor, Daniel Lash Marsh, believed B.U.'s problems could not be overcome without building a proper campus, as M.I.T. and B.C. recently had done. Murlin actually had initiated planning for such a facility on a site west of Kenmore Square in the early 1920s. Land acquisition was in full swing when Marsh was appointed, though some trustees believed the project beyond B.U.'s financial capabilities. Marsh persuaded his board to proceed, however, and threw himself into the project. He conceived an elegant row of limestone Gothic buildings along Commonwealth Avenue, backed by lawns that sloped downward to the Charles River.[78]

For Marsh, the creation of a campus and a unified organization were not only goals in themselves but prerequisites for academic upgrading. Marsh distanced himself from Murlin's view of B.U. as a service-oriented local institution and revived the founders' vision of a leading national university, albeit one with strong ties to Boston. Here was a theme to which Marsh would return repeatedly, never missing an opportunity to recall B.U.'s glorious early days, never failing to trumpet an indication of national recognition.

In truth, however, the new president could articulate B.U.'s academic potential only vaguely. Trained as a Methodist minister—the fourth in the line of B.U. presidents—and lacking scholarly experience, he represented a disappearing tradition of educational leadership. Unlike Conant, Compton, and Carmichael, Marsh had little grasp of the forces changing higher education. He showed scant understanding of the growing importance of science, graduate education, and research, or the role of disciplinary organizations, in establishing the standing of universities. At a time when Carmichael was skeptical about Tufts's Theological School, Marsh was stressing B.U.'s role in promoting religion.

Lacking specific educational ideas, Marsh expressed his conception of B.U. most clearly in his plans for the new campus. He understood, for example, that the kind of university he wanted had to be residential and to enroll students from a broad geographical area. Dormitory facilities were part of his plans from the beginning. His belief in the importance of religion determined his architectural centerpiece: a magnificent bell tower reproducing the most prominent feature of St. Botolph's church in Boston, England. Unfortunately, Marsh began his capital campaign as the nation's economy was collapsing, and he was promptly forced to defer his plans and cope with the challenge of maintaining his overbuilt institution. He made a new start in the late 1930s, actually erecting one building and acquiring others, but World War II brought new delays. Throughout the war, as Marsh worried about enrollments and military contracts, he was waiting for a time when he could focus on the construction program that he believed held the key to B.U.'s future.[79]

The contrast between developmental ambitions and immediate realities during the long pause was especially dramatic for Boston College—and for Jesuit higher education nationally. The period began badly for those within the Society of Jesus who, during the 1920s, had tried to improve the order's colleges and universities. Following the disbanding in 1931 of the Inter-Province Committee, the chief vehicle of the reform movement, the order entered a period of drift in matters of education.

In the mid-1930s, a series of events drew new attention to the problems that the reformers had stressed. In 1934 the American Council on Education, an umbrella organization for several national educational associations, issued a report on graduate studies that failed to list a single Jesuit university as equipped to award advanced degrees. Adding insult to injury, the A.C.E.

endorsed programs at two non-Jesuit Catholic institutions, Catholic University and Notre Dame. For the leaders of the New England province and of B.C., the painful message of the A.C.E. report was reinforced by the work of a visiting committee from the Association of American Universities that found B.C. too academically undeveloped to offer the doctorate and recommended closing the Ph.D. programs created in the 1920s.

The A.C.E. report moved the father general to order "a systematized attempt to secure for our educational activities their due recognition and rightful standing . . ." The general endorsed steps the reformers had been advocating for years, especially the need to meet lay accrediting standards and to provide teaching priests with advanced academic training. Demonstrating awareness of emerging sources of academic prestige in the United States, the general urged Jesuit universities to build high-quality programs of graduate education and research and to forge ties to academic professional societies. To implement his policies, the general mandated a national organization of Jesuit schools and colleges cutting across provincial boundaries and headed by a national secretary reporting directly to him. To this post, he named a leading member of the reform movement, Father Daniel M. O'Connell, giving him the rank of "commissarius" to ensure his authority over the provincials.[80]

O'Connell's appointment and the creation of the national organization— the Jesuit Educational Association (J.E.A.)—inaugurated a new era among Jesuit colleges and universities. O'Connell began an institution-by-institution reform program with a visit to B.C., where he endorsed the critical findings of the A.A.U. committee, ordered the discontinuation of all Ph.D. programs until A.A.U. approval could be secured, and emphasized the need for faculty and administrators with doctorates from A.A.U.-approved institutions.

O'Connell's directives must have been received with mixed feelings by the leadership of the New England province and especially by B.C.'s rector-president in the early 1930s, Dr. Eugene Gallagher. As a member of the Inter-Province Committee in the late 1920s, Gallagher was sympathetic to O'Connell's stance, but he and his superiors were aware of the province's limited resources and knew they would need time to meet the new requirements. The biggest problem, not just at B.C., was faculty training. The order's response was the "special studies" program through which intellectually talented young priests, having completed initial training in Jesuit institutions, were sent to leading graduate schools for advanced work.

Meanwhile, the Depression was on, followed by the war, and a succession of rector-presidents at B.C. concerned themselves with immediate problems. The most important programmatic initiatives of the 1930s were the founding of undergraduate schools in social work and business and revision of the curriculum in arts and sciences to include majors and a less restrictive core. It now became possible to graduate without Greek. These changes continued the broadening of B.C.'s reach that had begun in the 1920s but were not central to the longer-term effort to enhance the university's stature in secular terms. Those hopes, however, would need to await the end of the war, the return of better times, and the emergence of a new generation of Jesuit scholars who were, in the late 1930s and early 1940s, just beginning their graduate studies.

The new vision of academic respectability would also remain subject to complex crosscurrents within church and order, both of which still were concerned primarily with religious goals. Of particular importance would be the attitudes of the provincials, who traditionally controlled Jesuit activities in their areas. Father O'Connell's abrupt replacement in 1937 provided a sharp reminder of the strength with which the nonacademic regional hierarchy could resist change emanating from extraprovincial authority.[81]

Northeastern, like Boston College, continued in the 1930s to be subject to control by a nonacademic sponsor—the Y.M.C.A. Though the former Evening Institute had established a degree of independence, the legal name remained "Northeastern University of the Y.M.C.A." and the Board of Trustees was dominated by directors of the Y, who treated the university as a subunit of the parent organization. Like their counterparts within the Society of Jesus, however, Speare and his colleagues in the administration of Northeastern were becoming aware of the difficulties of building a university under nonacademic auspices. In Northeastern's case, the problem was brought to a head by the efforts to raise funds for the Huntington Avenue campus and to achieve accreditation from the Engineering Council for Professional Development. In both contexts, Northeastern's leaders learned that separation from the Y was essential.

In 1935 they won legislative approval to drop reference to the Y from their name and also obtained general degree-granting authority comparable to that held by other private universities. A year later, the board endorsed a reorganization plan creating an independent, self-perpetuating corporation empowered to choose the trustees. While ensuring that directors of the Y could no longer dominate the board, the new organization continued Northeastern's close ties to its Protestant business constituency. Support from this community would be essential to guarantee the financial and physical development of the university.

While pressing for independent status, Speare planned the new campus. The design included six buildings to be constructed in an austere, modernist style that expressed the university's pragmatic educational philosophy. Obtaining capital funds, however, proved no less difficult for Northeastern during the Depression than for B.U. Prodded by the E.C.D.P., Northeastern did erect a first building in 1937–1938, and a second, much smaller, structure in 1941. Once the U.S. entered the war, however, further progress was impossible.

At this point, Speare, now seventy, retired from the position he had held for over forty years. Able, under Northeastern's centralized organization, to select his successor, he chose Carl Stevens Ell, longtime dean of Engineering, director of the Day Colleges, and, for a number of years, *de facto* manager of the university's internal operations. More an administrator than an entrepreneur, but one committed to his predecessor's concept of Northeastern's purposes, Ell was determined to put the university on a stable footing by finishing the campus and creating an endowment.

Ell intended also to attain academic respectability by concentrating on the day programs in Engineering and Business and cutting back Speare's marginal, academically suspect ventures, including the branch campuses. His concern with academic respectablity had led him in the mid-1930s to support a movement within the faculty to establish a College of Arts and Sciences, though he viewed the new unit chiefly as support for professional programs. In general, however, the new president was less interested in program development than in consolidation, an orientation rooted in his basic conservatism and his view, common among educators of the 1930s, that demand for higher education had peaked in the 1920s and was not likely to exapnd in the foreseeable future.[82]

Ell's wish to enhance the academic standing of his university paralleled the goals of Carmichael at Tufts, Marsh at B.U., and the academic reformers within the Society of Jesus. The common impulse of these institutional communities between 1930 and 1945 to move their institutions upward in the academic hierarchy represented a continuation of the historic competition among them for prestige, just as their common efforts to survive the Depression and war extended their rivalry for resources. Under the conditions of the long pause, the competition for resources was necessarily paramount. The competition for prestige was bound to reassert itself, however, as soon as external conditions gave scope for schemes of campus development.

Within institutional communities, as among them, Depression and war promoted some forms of tension while masking others. We have seen, for example, how the financial pressures of these years heightened conflicts between administrators and faculties. At the same time, by suppressing plans for upward repositioning, conditions of the 1930s concealed latent tensions between external constituencies, who stressed social, economic, or religious goals, and educators eager to improve their universities in academic terms.

Among the Jesuits, for example, there was great potential for conflict between reformers who wanted Boston College to meet secular standards as a modern university and traditional priests and officers interested in religious goals. Between 1930 and 1945, however—as the reform movement began the slow process of training future faculty while administrators wrestled with immediate economic pressures—the two groups could coexist with minimal friction. Similarly, at B.U. it was not easy to see how Marsh could reconcile his emphases on religion and local service with his plans to remake his university as a national leader. With development of the Charles River campus deferred and enrollments falling, however, Marsh and his colleagues did not need to choose among competing long-term goals. At Tufts, the hidden issues were academic: how could Carmichael's focus on scientific research be meshed with the tradition of undergraduate, general education that expressed the college's roots in Universalist liberalism?

Perhaps the sharpest conflict between developmental goals and traditional purposes could be found at Northeastern. No university in Massachusetts attached more importance to maintaining its distinctive character than the newly independent spinoff from the Y.M.C.A. Speare, Ell, and their colleagues frequently quoted Henry Wriston on the topic of institutional diversity in higher education: "Instead of being all things to all students, let each college choose its function, state it with clarity, and pursue it with integrity." What this meant for Northeastern was detailed in a campus brochure:

> Northeastern . . . was built to meet the needs of men. It was not started with a theoretical purpose, based upon an abstract educational philosophy . . . It has refused to duplicate . . . other institutions. It has kept uppermost the question: "What are the needs of society?" It has not been swayed by the question: "What are other educational institutions doing?"

Ell and his colleagues, however, *were* being swayed by what other institutions were doing and *were* attempting to duplicate conventional educational patterns. In part, this impulse toward orthodoxy was being forced upon them by the requirements of accreditation, but Ell's commitment to making Northeastern respectable was prompted by ambition as well as pressure. Fundamentally, this goal expressed a belief that Ell shared with many academic leaders: by enhancing the prestige of his institution he would increase the value of its degree and thereby better serve the students for whom it had been established—in Northeastern's case, working-class boys from the local community.

This logic, though powerful, avoided the central dilemma of academic mobility: how to increase prestige by becoming more like the best-established universities and yet retain the particular commitments—to a student group, a set of programs, and a system of values—that embodied an institution's distinctive purposes. The dilemma was implicit in the following passage of Northeastern's brochure:

> An institution which confines its purposes to basic courses . . . can eliminate the high cost of expensive laboratories, research apparatus, and research courses, and can operate much more economically and . . . better educationally when viewed from the standpoint of student development and growth. Such an institution can appropriately place its emphasis upon teaching as the major function of its faculty [and thereby avoid] that half-hearted type of service which often characterizes the research expert, who looks upon teaching entirely as a necessary evil . . .[83]

This statement accurately described Northeastern in the 1930s. But when judged against Ell's goal of furthering N.U.'s reputation, it becomes problematic. These were years, after all, when the presidents of the area's leading universities, Conant and Compton, were asserting the supremacy of research and graduate education, the very activities Ell was minimizing. If Conant and Compton represented the forces of the future, it was hard to understand how Northeastern could concentrate on undergraduate teaching, shun research, and still achieve academic respectability. The dilemma would be further complicated by Northeastern's practice—common among universities in Massachusetts—of recruiting faculty trained in Cambridge. If, on the other hand, Northeastern's quest for prestige led it toward the new orthodoxy that Conant and Compton were defining, it was hard to imagine how it could sustain the distinctive commitments that were the heart of its reason for being.

Public Higher Education in Depression and War

The circumstances of the long pause had different implications for the newly renamed state college in Amherst than for nonelite private universities. As applications declined at Tufts and B.U. in the 1930s, they increased at Massachusetts State. Between 1929 and 1940, the college grew by 53 percent. Staff and facilities were stretched to their limits and still failed to keep pace with demand. As rising numbers of students were turned away during years when many could not afford private tuition, public attention focused on the limited opportunities for low-cost higher education in the commonwealth in comparison with other states. This atmosphere revitalized long-standing interest in making the former agricultural college a full university. In 1935 the Massachusetts Federation of Labor proposed that the curriculum be expanded to include engineering. At the end of the decade, the alumni/ae association endorsed the university movement and began a campaign for legislative approval.

Simultaneous with revived local interest in M.S.C. came the benefits of the New Deal. The impact of federal programs on public institutions during the 1930s was much greater than on their private counterparts. Public colleges and universities were aided not only by the availability of relief payments to cover tuition charges but also by special programs applicable only to them. For example, the Bankhead–Jones Act of 1935, which provided support for research related to agriculture, doubled federal funding at M.S.C. in one year and allowed an immediate addition of fifteen faculty members. Federal dollars also supported building programs on public campuses, enabling the college to add a library and a dormitory. Thus, while nonelite private universities struggled to maintain themselves and worried that the era of expansion in higher education might be over, the state college experienced progressively more-encouraging conditions.

This environment persuaded M.S.C.'s new president, Hugh Potter Baker, as well as the trustees, to join the campaign to create a University of Massachusetts. On the eve of World War II, the old agricultural college in Amherst seemed close to being transformed into the kind of comprehensive public institution that earlier had developed out of the land grant movement in the western states.[84]

It was not to be, however. The timing was poor. When the bill designating M.S.C. as the state university was submitted to the legislature, Europe was already at war and Pearl Harbor only a year away. The attention of lawmakers inevitably turned toward the international crisis. At the same time, conscription eased the pressure on admissions, and the college became involved with the same issues of national defense and military training that preoccupied private universities. The war did not produce a sense of crisis about resources at M.S.C., as it did at the state's nonelite private institutions. Coeducation, combined with the high demand for admission, kept enrollments satisfactory, and wartime training programs helped retain the faculty and staff essentially intact.

Quite apart from the immediate emergency, moreover, the declining birth-rates of the 1930s had prompted the legislature to consider cutting back collegiate programs—an unpromising context for expansionist proposals. Interest in M.S.C.'s future lapsed.

The political forces that traditionally had restricted public higher education in Massachusetts also contributed to the defeat of the university movement. Broad support for a system of state-sponsored institutions was absent, and the advocacy of labor and alumni/ae was offset by opposition from other quarters. Elements within the agricultural community continued to oppose a broadening of the college's program beyond their interests. The town of Amherst was against growth. Key private-sector leaders, apprehensive about their own plans for development, worked against the movement with varying degrees of intensity. In 1938 Daniel Marsh, who was launching a capital campaign for B.U.'s Charles River campus, used an invitation to M.S.C.'s seventy-fifth anniversary to speak against expanding public higher education and to urge the use of tax dollars for private institutions.

The college itself was divided. Some of the faculty wanted to maintain an emphasis on agriculture. Others focused on enhancing the liberal arts. The hottest campus issue of the 1930s was whether the college should offer a program leading to the B.A. degree. President Baker and the trustees were ambivalent about university status, as their late-in-the-day endorsement of the alumni/ae effort implied. Indeed, despite the pressure on admissions, for most of the 1930s Baker, whose background was in forestry, stressed his lack of interest in expansion and focused on incremental improvements in agricultural and technical fields. He initially opposed labor on engineering, then endorsed a minimal program. He did not support the movement for a B.A., which prevailed through the efforts of students, faculty, and alumni/ae.[85]

In this fragmented environment, the General Court showed little inclination to act. The position of the state college on Beacon Hill continued to be weak in the 1930s. With its "western" orientation, its ties to the Republican Party, and its reputation for anti-Catholic bias, M.S.C. was poorly positioned to benefit from the shift of legislative power toward urban, ethnic Democrats. Political response to the new pressures on admissions had been limited throughout the 1930s. No review of the state's educational needs comparable to the study of the early 1920s was initiated. The administrative restrictions that had led Butterfield to resign remained in place. Modest increases in appropriations for staff were balanced by decreases in funds for facilities. The college's leaders and supporters became so impatient with the legislature's refusal to add dormitories while insisting upon higher enrollments that the alumni/ae association created an independent building authority.

Given this record, it was not surprising that the bill to create a state university did not get far on Beacon Hill, notwithstanding the optimism that fueled the university movement at the end of the 1930s. Despite a positive report from the Committee on Agriculture, the legislative leadership allowed the proposal to languish without debate until the end of the last prewar session.

After that, little public emotion was stirred by the fact that Massachusetts State College remained, after three-quarters of a century, among the least developed land grant institutions in the United States.[86]

Jews and Higher Education

There was another academic dream, rooted in one more subculture, that had to be deferred during the years of the long pause. This dream belonged to the Jewish community and was a modern-day echo of the tradition of denominational college building that had flourished prior to the Civil War. It was a puzzling fact that American Jews, despite their orientation toward scholarship and education, historically had been far less active than either Protestants or Catholics in creating academic institutions. Indeed, prior to World War II, few Jewish colleges were established, and these were sectarian and concerned chiefly with religious training. Among them, the leaders were Hebrew Union in Cincinnati and Yeshiva in New York. The Boston version was a small teacher-training college, Hebrew Teachers College, established in Brookline in 1921.

A number of factors limited Jewish sponsorship of colleges and universities. Prior to the immigration of the late nineteenth century, the American Jewish community was small in comparison with the Protestant and Catholic groups. Moreover, before World War I, despite the ethnocentrism of nominally nonsectarian institutions, the modest numbers of Jews seeking admission were reasonably successful, even at leading schools like Harvard, Yale, and Princeton. Harvard had built strong ties of loyalty and philanthropic support with the upper strata of Jewish society in Boston and New York.

As this history of affiliation with essentially Protestant universities implies, there was among American Jews an assimilationist impulse that impeded the creation of identifiably Jewish colleges. Other factors reinforced the pattern, including the high cost of building academic institutions by the time the Jewish population was large enough to support them, the relative poverty of many recent arrivals, and preoccupation with the well-being of relatives and co-religionists in Europe.[87]

The paucity of colleges and universities oriented toward their faith and culture began to be an important issue within the Jewish community in the 1920s. By this time, the number of young Jews was increasing markedly, as the children of turn-of-the-century immigrants reached college age. The recent arrivals, mostly of eastern European origin, were less inclined toward assimilation than their earlier, western European predecessors. Moreover, this was a time of rising restrictions on Jewish admission to established colleges, a result of the convergence of increases in Jewish applicants and the nativism that followed World War I. In this context, leading Jews began urging their community to build its own academic institutions.

The most prominent exponent of college building was New York rabbi Louis Newman, who was inspired by the concept of a nonsectarian Jewish university. As Newman imagined it, the new institution, like many leading colleges and universities, would be created and supported by a particular faith but open to students from all backgrounds. Ultimately, he believed, the school would be absorbed by American culture and would be no more Jewish than "Brown is Baptist, Princeton is Presbyterian, and Harvard is Congregationalist." Such an institution, Newman argued, would help ensure educational opportunities for Jewish youth while serving as a monument to Jewish achievements. To its faculty would be drawn the most eminent Jewish scholars. In its program, despite its nonsectarian character, special attention would be paid to Judaic studies.

Throughout the 1920s and 1930s, Newman promoted his idea, but it proved controversial. Some expressed ancient hesitations about a specifically Jewish institution. Others regarded the proposal as a compromise with bigotry. Still others pointed out that a single university could do little to ensure opportunities for large numbers of young people. Though some leading Jews were excited by Newman's advocacy, he enlisted no broad support. Moreover, the blatant anti-Semitism of the postwar years that had provided a context for Newman's efforts proved short-lived. Though discrimination against Jews in higher education remained an issue, the prosperity and institutional expansion of the late 1920s softened its edges. The onset of the Depression in 1929 focused the attention of American Jews on other pressing issues: economic disaster at home and abroad, increasingly troubling reports of events in Europe, and ultimately, the war and the Holocaust.

In time, despite Newman's efforts, interest in a Jewish university faded. An effort by the B'nai B'rith to implement Newman's vision in the early 1940s attracted a number of Jewish leaders but again failed to arouse general interest. The idea of a Jewish-sponsored university thus receded into the background, to join the dreams of other upwardly mobile subcultures—the Catholics at B.C., the middle-class Protestants at Tufts and B.U., the working-class students at Northeastern, the engineers at M.I.T., and the champions of M.S.C.—in waiting for conditions that would permit their schools to flourish in a manner commensurate with their own dignity and accomplishments.[88]

CHAPTER TWO

The World Transformed:
A Golden Age for
American Universities, 1945–1970

In the years following World War II, academic leaders in Massachusetts participated in a national debate about the social role of higher education in the era that lay ahead. They also experienced the beginnings of a period of expansion for universities that would continue, more or less uninterrupted, for twenty-five years. Change in this postwar golden age involved an ongoing interaction between ideas and opportunities: the first concerning the public purposes of higher education; the second promising glory for institutions and advancement for academic interest groups. For most of the period, the dominant view—inside and outside of higher education—was that expansion was improving the academy as well as the country, but the turmoil of the late 1960s raised fundamental doubts about the character of postwar change.

Academic Ideas and Developmental
Opportunities in the Postwar Years

Impact of World War II

Although World War II entailed difficulties for universities, their extensive involvement in the military effort stirred a new awareness of the social importance of academic work. This habit of thought extended into the postwar period, as educators, exhilarated by wartime patriotism, looked for new ways to contribute to social problem solving. As they did so, they exhibited a further effect of their recent experience: a tendency to focus on national concerns—as distinct from regional or local ones—far more intensively than they had done before 1940.

The country's agenda was long. The human costs of the war, and the even more-frightening possibility of atomic conflict, made the importance of maintaining peace evident. Europe had precipitated two wars in a generation and now lay in ruins. The United States, suddenly the preeminent power of the globe, would have to pioneer in shaping a stable world order. In some, the nation's new international prominence aroused a sense of urgency about discrimination and inequality at home. More broadly, world leadership implied a need to maintain military and economic power and the technological vitality on which they depended. Many educators believed they had important roles to play in all these contexts—through training leaders, forming attitudes, and advancing knowledge. As one college president put it: "Events . . . have shaken the complacency of many university communities and compelled educators to . . . make [their] maximum contribution to a decent, well-ordered, free and peaceful society."[1]

Belief in the importance of addressing social issues was paralleled among academics by conviction that their wartime activities would have a positive effect on attitudes toward higher education. Indeed, even as they struggled with war-related problems, many educators saw the crisis as a chance to prove the value of intellectual work to a skeptical society. Mindful of the financial pressures of the long pause, they anticipated stronger public support in the postwar period—and new opportunities to pursue developmental plans delayed by adverse circumstances.

The comment of M.S.C.'s Baker was typical: "Out of the bitter struggle of war will come future demands for . . . greater opportunities for all people . . . The promise for state supported growth of colleges and universities . . . is great." The heightened expectations included hopes that the federal government, whose assistance had been vital during the Depression, would continue channeling resources toward academia. Carmichael of Tufts expressed this idea frequently. "It is possible," he wrote, that "patterns of connection between the government and the colleges now evolving as war expedients will allow the endowed educational institutions of the country to serve the nation's welfare in peacetime as well."

As the references to their particular types of universities in the comments of Baker and Carmichael implied, the prospect of new government aid raised important questions about what kinds of support might go to various campuses. The war created a new context for competition among universities even as it revealed new opportunities for public service.[2]

Two war-related federal programs were particularly important for higher education: during the conflict itself, the organization of scientists to develop military technology; in the latter years of the war and the early postwar period, the inclusion of educational entitlements among the benefits for veterans in the G.I. Bill. Both programs offered opportunities for individuals and campuses to contribute to the military effort. Both dramatized the significance of higher education for governmental officials, political and business leaders, and even the general public. Both revealed an awareness among educators of the advantages that could derive from participation in national programs.

The story of academic science during World War II began with the conviction among leading scientists and engineers, as the crisis developed in Europe, that their expertise was essential to the government's preparations for American involvement. One of these men, Vannevar Bush, president of the Carnegie Institution in Washington, persuaded President Roosevelt to charge a small group to plan for the mobilization of the nation's scientific capabilities. Roosevelt gave the job to Bush, who created the National Defense Research Committee. The N.D.R.C. quickly became the key link between the military hierarchy and academic science. As the nation's participation in the war intensified, the committee evolved into a new federal agency, the Office of Scientific Research and Development (O.S.R.D.). This organization was based on an important innovation in the relationship between the federal government and the scientific community. Rather than creating free-standing, government-managed research-and-development facilities, as had been done during World War I, Bush's group subcontracted specific projects to campus-based scientists, who continued to work in university laboratories. Using this system, Bush and his colleagues produced a series of technical achievements, the most spectacular of which was the atomic bomb, widely assigned a crucial role in the Allied military effort.[3]

So impressive was the record of O.S.R.D. that, as the war ended, Roosevelt asked Bush for an analysis of science's potential to contribute to national development in peacetime. Bush's 1945 report was a passionate statement of the role of scientific research in industry, defense, and medicine and of the importance of federal funds in guaranteeing the strength of science. The following year, President Truman appointed a cabinet-level committee, the President's Scientific Research Board, chaired by his close advisor John R. Steelman and including Bush himself, to consider the federal interest in scientific work. The board's report, published in 1947, affirmed Bush's views and recommended that "by 1957 we should be devoting at least one percent of our national income to research and development." The report also proposed a National Science Foundation to administer federal grants for basic research and urged the government to adopt O.S.R.D.'s practice of channeling support directly to university-based investigators.

In arguing that the nation had an interest in basic research, Bush was voicing ideas about science that academics like Compton and Conant had been advancing for years. In particular, the idea that the federal government should finance scientific work had been a prewar cause of Compton's, and he had used his platform as chair of the Science Advisory Board in the 1930s to promote ideas similar to those of the Scientific Research Board. In fact, Bush had been Compton's vice president before going to the Carnegie Institution, and the two shared an awareness of M.I.T.'s difficulties in obtaining financial support for research. Not surprisingly, therefore, both Bush and Compton were quick to see the possibilities of the war for demonstrating the importance of science and establishing a precedent for federal funding. As early as 1941, Compton wrote that "the military emergency is serving to bring educational staffs into closer contact with industry and . . . government" in a way that "presage[s] a new prosperity for science and engineering after the war."

Bush drew heavily on his former associates in the Cambridge scientific community, especially at M.I.T., to staff his wartime agency. Compton himself was one of the first men to join the Central Committee of the O.S.R.D. The group also included Frank Jewett, president of the National Academy of Sciences and of Bell Labs, member of the M.I.T. Corporation, and a close friend of Compton's who had actively supported the effort to strengthen science at M.I.T. during the 1930s. The fourth member of the Central Committee was Conant, and the fifth was Richard Tolman, an M.I.T. alumnus on the faculty of Cal Tech. The men brought in to staff the O.S.R.D. at the second and third levels further tightened the connection between Washington and Cambridge.[4]

The experience of the O.S.R.D's leaders in working for increased support for science during the prewar years and their perception of the potential significance of the war in advancing their cause inevitably affected their thinking about the operations of the wartime agency, including the all-important decision to award federal funds directly to campus-based scientists. In this context, the report of President Truman's Scientific Research Board should be seen not only as a general indication of the war's impact on science but also as a specific and aggressively pursued victory for Bush, Compton, and their colleagues. As the postwar era dawned, they had reason to hope that the federal government would become the adequate source for financing scientific work—and the development of academic institutions devoted to science—that for so long had eluded them.

The veterans' education program, like the O.S.R.D., was created by government officials to serve purposes related to the war, but like the scientific agency, it became a vehicle through which segments of the academic community advanced their own agenda—in this case, the expansion of educational opportunities. The fundamental purpose of the G.I. Bill was to help integrate returning soldiers into civilian life. Those planning for demobilization worried that problems would arise if large numbers of veterans sought jobs in an economy no longer stimulated by the war. Realizing that a program to encourage former soldiers to enter college would be helpful, they asked for assistance from the American Council on Education, headed by Dr. George Zook.

The A.C.E. recognized that any program of educational entitlements for servicemen would affect colleges even as it served the nonacademic purposes of the government. Most important, a veterans' program would boost enrollments decimated by the war. The idea raised, however, a number of long-term issues that proved divisive within the A.C.E. For example, the program had the potential to bring higher education within reach of many who could not previously afford college. For some, this was a welcome chance to open the academic gates. Included in this group was Zook himself, a New Deal liberal and former president of the University of Akron, who for years had advocated the use of public funds to expand access to higher education. Others, including Conant, believed that higher education should remain elite and favored a limited program for veterans.

The prospect of federal support for tuition also uncovered tensions between private and public institutions. The latter worried that reimbursing students for full costs would favor the former. In the end, the A.C.E. suggested compromises on all these issues, while presenting a united front on the question that concerned educators most: that the program preserve the independence of all academic institutions from federal control.

Although questions about the impact of the proposed veterans' program on academia were important to educators, who saw the entitlements as a precedent, such considerations were marginal for governmental planners as well as legislators. In testimony before Congress, the primary force behind the G.I. Bill was the American Legion, which wanted the broadest possible program for its constituents. It won benefits more generous than the compromise put forward by Zook's organization: support for one year of college for nearly all veterans with a year's service or less and a further year for each additional year served.

Throughout the deliberations, academics cast themselves as willing participants rather than lobbyists for an education bill. This stance, as well as the relative ease with which factions within the A.C.E. reconciled their differences, reflected the fact that few regarded educational entitlements as a central element of the demobilization effort. Estimates of potential college attendance under the veteran's legislation ranged from one hundred fifty thousand to several hundred thousand per year, with total participation over the life of the program not likely to exceed seven hundred thousand. An activity on this scale, while helpful to universities and interesting as an experiment, was not likely to produce major change in higher education.[5]

The veterans surprised everyone and grasped the chance to attend college in totally unexpected numbers. For most of 1946, M.I.T. received four thousand applications per month—an extreme example of a common pattern. Between 1945 and 1949, about 2,200,000 former servicemen enrolled in college through the G.I. Bill, more than three times the maximum figure projected during the war. Sixty thousand former soldiers applied to Harvard alone. Educators responded with the spirit of patriotism—and gratitude—characteristic of the early postwar years. Conant told his Overseers: "The society of free men on this continent has another chance to realize its aspirations; the world has another chance to organize for peace. The youth of our country made this possible."

Although caught by surprise, educational leaders took every possible step to accommodate the demand. Enrollments at many institutions rose far beyond normal capacity. Special administrative and counseling mechanisms were created. Curricula were streamlined to help veterans complete their work rapidly. Year-round schedules were adopted, and graduation requirements were relaxed. Credit was awarded for work done in military service. Refresher courses and noncredit programs for poorly prepared veterans were implemented. It was an inspiring and generous time, providing a challenge that elicited from academics a maximum desire to adapt themselves and their institutions to the unusual needs of a special group.[6]

For educators like Zook, the enthusiasm of the veterans and the response of academics constituted a political bonanza. The popularity of higher education had been strengthened by the war; now it soared. A federally assisted effort to enlarge the educational system suddenly seemed possible. President Truman was, after all, seeking ways to extend the New Deal into new areas of domestic life. Eager to seize the moment, Zook persuaded the president to appoint a commission on the national interest in higher education—the first review of this subject ever ordered by a chief executive. Zook himself won appointment as chair, and most of the members shared his prospective.

The President's Commission on Higher Education was dominated by individuals from teaching and service-oriented public institutions and experimental private colleges with disciplinary backgrounds in education and in occupational and technical fields. The influence of the progressive education movement of the prewar years, with its emphasis on socially responsive schools, was clearly in evidence. Representatives of the academic establishment—people, like Conant, who were skeptical about Zook's democratizing agenda and who had resisted the idea of turning the veterans' program into a pilot project for it—were scarcely visible at the table. There were few commissioners with backgrounds in the arts and sciences or the elite professions, and none were from the nation's most distinguished universities, private or public, or the most prestigious colleges. The commision's report, issued in several volumes in late 1947 and early 1948, expressed the hopes of its constituency for a vastly expanded, socially engaged system of higher education, supported by an infusion of federal dollars. Specific recommendations included scholarships and direct aid to public institutions.[7]

The reports of the two presidential commissions of the early postwar years contained recommendations for national policy on issues that had preoccupied the academic community in the years before World War II. The President's Scientific Research Board was concerned with supporting research in science and technology as well as with graduate and professional education in scientifically oriented fields, matters of concern to men like Compton and Conant. The Zook commission focused on questions of interest to those—like Ell of Northeastern or Murlin of B.U.—who had fought to make higher education less oriented toward social elites, less dominated by tradition, and more concerned with the practical affairs of life. In proposing new federal programs to address these issues, the two commissions advocated sweeping changes, with highly unpredictable consequences, in the nation's institutions of higher education.

Both reports were bound to be controversial. They were issued, moreover, at a time when academics, inspired by the war and hopeful about new developmental opportunities, were already considering academia's postwar role. Many colleges and universities formed planning committees. States and educational associations established special commissions. The aggregate result was an intense and wide-ranging public debate. As the president of the Carnegie Foundation exclaimed in 1950: "At no time in the history of this country has there been so much ferment and stir about the ends and means of education." Competing opinions appeared in the pages of newspapers and popular journals. The recommendations of the presidential commissions provided a focus for much of this discussion.[8]

Among the many reactions to these two reports, none contained a more thoughtful or comprehensive alternative perspective than the work of the Commission on Financing Higher Education, jointly sponsored by the Rockefeller Foundation and the Association of American Universities. Officers of the foundation shared the view of many educators that the financial problems produced by the Depression—especially among endowed institutions—remained unaddressed. After a series of preliminary conferences with institutional leaders revealed not only continuing economic worries but also widespread discomfort with the recommendations of the two presidential commissions, the foundation decided to sponsor a broad examination of higher education, with particular reference to financial problems.

In contrast to the two governmental commissions, the Rockefeller group was dominated by representatives of leading private universities. Its chair was Paul Buck, dean of Arts and Sciences at Harvard, and its membership included senior officers of Johns Hopkins, Cal Tech, Stanford, and Brown. In essence, the Rockefeller group was a vehicle through which academia's traditional elite responded to the reforming propositions of the two public bodies on the central issues facing higher education: who should go to college and for what? and how should graduate education and research be developed? In offering different answers to these questions, the three reports summarized much of the postwar debate. Moreover, they each addressed the most fundamental questions of all: what system of higher education would best serve the nation? and how should that system be organized and financed?[9]

Who Should Go to College and for What?

The most controversial recommendation of the Zook commission was that facilities for higher education should be enlarged so that, by 1960, 49 percent of the country's eighteen- to twenty-one-year-olds would receive at least two years of college, and 32 percent would attend for a full four years. Increased public expenditures, including the new program of federal scholarships, would subsidize the expansion. While arguing that these proposals were consistent with recent trends and responded to needs made clear by the veteran's program, the commission recognized that its ideas would appear revolutionary to many Americans. Less than 16 percent of the college-age population was receiving advanced education in 1940.

The commission justified its recommendations on two grounds. First, it pointed out that current enrollments were artificially depressed by nonacademic barriers, including finances, regional variations in opportunity, and discrimination against religious and racial groups, especially Negroes and Jews. These inequities, the commission argued, denied the nation the full talents of many citizens, were inconsistent with American ideals, and were intolerable at a time when democratic and totalitarian values battled for popular allegiance. The commission also criticized universities for focusing excessively on "verbal skills and intellectual interests" and for ignoring "many other aptitudes—such as social sensitivity and versatility, artistic ability, motor skills and dexterity, and mechanical aptitude and ingenuity." The commission's estimates of the numbers that could benefit from higher education assumed that programs would be developed for the wider range of talents that, in its view, should be cultivated. It recognized that "if these proportions of American youth are to be admitted to institutions of higher education, we shall have to provide a much greater variety of institutions than we now have to meet the needs."[10]

The Rockefeller report agreed that admission policies should be free of bias, and it joined the Zook commission in urging admission policies based on merit. It also acknowledged the "startling fact" that less than 50 percent of the most gifted young Americans attended any form of college, and it advocated an expansion of financial aid programs. Unlike the Zook commission, however, the Rockefeller group did not emphasize educational inequality as a major problem for academic institutions. It stressed that "colleges and universities are among the least discriminatory institutions in American society" and argued that the main difficulties lay in individual motivation, secondary schooling, and family finances. The Rockefeller group had little inclination to expand the interests and talents with which colleges were concerned. "The primary purpose of higher education," it observed, "is the development of . . . intellectual promise and . . . [the capacity to] deal with abstract ideas . . . and to reason . . . upon the basis of broad conceptual schemes." The Rockefeller report estimated that 25 percent of the population—half the figure suggested by the Zook commission—could profit from college and argued against educating a significantly enlarged proportion of young people. It opposed any federal scholarships beyond the veterans' program.[11]

At the heart of the differences between the two reports were divergent views about the implications of "democratic" values for higher education. For the Rockefeller group, there was no conflict between democracy and elitism. Admission procedures must be fair and accessible, but they could also be highly selective. The Zook commission was less ready to accept a system that limited its advantages to the few. In its view, democracy implied not only fairness of treatment but also equality of status for a wide range of abilities and fields.

The comments of academic leaders in Massachusetts typified the spectrum of campus-level responses to the Zook–Rockefeller debate. Conant, true to his prewar ideals, insisted with the Rockefeller group that the national interest required recognizing differences in individual ability. He wanted to make Harvard more, not less, exclusive in terms of academic standards, and he doubted the wisdom of conferring social status on an expanding set of "semiprofessional" occupations by requiring four or more years of postsecondary education not demanded by the fields themselves. In contrast, Marsh of B.U. and Ell of Northeastern, siding with Zook, argued that democratic admission policies implied opening their doors as widely as possible. Both thought their universities should embrace the changing requirements of employment markets by continuously developing new occupational programs.[12]

Liberal Education, General Education,
and the Quest for Democratic Community

During the twenty years preceding World War II, one of the liveliest topics of academic discussion involved the educational consequences of the increased emphasis on science and the corresponding decline of the traditional curriculum. This change, some argued, had weakened attention to the development of character by making undergraduate work too intellectual and also had shattered the ability of college to transmit a common culture. Sectarian institutions, especially Catholic ones that had chosen to retain requirements in philosophy, theology, and ancient languages, had avoided curricular disintegration, but most American institutions could not rely on religious imperatives to achieve coherence or maintain values.

In the prewar years, these concerns gave rise to two broad movements to reform the curriculum. The first stressed exposure to the arts and sciences through required courses. Although it took many forms, this pattern was associated particularly with Columbia in the 1920s and the University of Chicago in the 1930s. The second movement emphasized the nonintellectual elements of undergraduate education: emotional capacity, physical health, and social skills. Initially conceived—for example, in the General College at the University of Minnesota—as an alternative to the liberal arts for students in two-year colleges, this movement influenced four-year institutions as well. It was especially evident in the development of guidance programs, residential facilities, and extracurricular activities. Both of the movements were referred to as "general education" at one time or another, though they were rooted in markedly different conceptions of the boundaries of academic work.[13]

Concern about the social contributions of higher education at the end of World War II introduced new intensity into the debate about general and liberal education. The Zook commission asserted that "liberal education has been splintered by overspecialization" and argued that "the failure to provide any core of unity in . . . higher education is a cause for grave concern." It concluded that "the crucial task of higher education today . . . is to provide a unified general education" that will transmit a "common cultural heritage towards a common citizenship." Zook and his associates recommended a series of goals for all college programs—including several concerned with family life, physical health, emotional adjustment, and ethical behavior—that aimed at both intellectual breadth and personal and social development.

The Rockefeller report also stressed the importance of shared goals for undergraduate learning, but it set much narrower limits on college curricula. Liberal education, the Rockefeller group argued, should seek "a quality of mind" by "liberat[ing] the spirit of man from superstition and ignorance while cultivating . . . enduring values and the capacity of discriminating judgment." The two committees agreed on the goals of undergraduate education but differed on the means. The Zook commission argued that socially constructive behavior should be taught directly by "redefining liberal education in terms of life's problems as men face them," while the Rockefeller report asserted that desirable personal qualities could best be nurtured indirectly, through studying the academic disciplines of the arts and sciences.[14]

Among many institution-based efforts to address the issues of common learning in the postwar years, the most conspicuous was the report of the Harvard Committee on General Education in a Free Society—frequently called the "Redbook" because of its crimson cover. The committee included humanists and social scientists and was charged by Conant and Buck to produce "a concept of general education that would have validity" not only at Harvard but also at colleges and schools throughout the country. Published in 1945, the Redbook argued that general education should "look first of all to [the student's] life as a responsible human being and citizen." Education must be concerned not only with imparting knowledge and skills but also with producing the "good man" and the "good citizen" by developing values, wisdom, a sense of cultural tradition, and the capacity for emotional and gregarious life. The committee translated its formulations into concrete terms by proposing that Harvard create three required, interdisciplinary courses for undergraduates—one from each of the disciplinary divisions—to provide a shared body of knowledge and also design a series of upper-class electives infused with the spirit of general education. Conant hailed the document as "the dawn of a welcome day" in which colleges and universities could organize themselves to "both shape the future and secure the foundations of our free society."[15]

The Harvard Redbook found a wide readership and had a major impact on discussions of undergraduate curriculum reform. Its inspired defense of general education expressed the social idealism of the period. It applied the imprimatur of the nation's leading university to a cause hitherto considered marginal by most academics. In suggesting, moreover, that the ambitious goals of general education could be achieved by restructuring traditional materials in a limited portion of the curriculum, the Harvard committee offered a middle course between broadening undergraduate studies to include nonacademic concerns—as the Zook commission would suggest—and standing pat with the traditional liberal arts—as the Rockefeller group would prefer.

Despite the eloquence and apparent practicality of the Redbook, events quickly demonstrated that the academic community would not agree on a single conception of general education. As many approaches to this issue were offered as there were faculties to debate it, and agreement proved elusive even within institutions. Sometimes, as in the famous programs at Harvard and Amherst College, general education courses were specifically designed as broad introductions to areas of knowledge. In other instances, general education more closely resembled a distribution requirement, and students simply chose from more or less standard disciplinary courses. Even at Harvard, the Faculty of Arts and Sciences was unable to overcome disciplinary boundaries and rejected the notion of a single basic course in the three areas of knowledge, voting instead to offer several options in each category. Tufts's Carmichael represented an extreme position. Intensely conscious, as a psychologist, of differences among students, he was fundamentally opposed to common requirements and preferred his institution's prewar emphasis on individually tailored programs.[16]

Beyond basic requirements, the general education movement provoked a wide variety of programmatic innovations in the late 1940s and early 1950s. Several institutions, including Harvard and Boston University, strengthened international coursework, as had been recommended by the Zook commission, to support the nation's new position of world leadership. A more controversial topic was religious studies. The Zook commission had not made reference to religious belief, and the Redbook explicitly rejected religion as a basis for infusing values or unity into undergraduate education. The advice naturally went unheeded in schools like B.C. and B.U. with strong religious traditions or church sponsorship, but even M.I.T. made new efforts to support the religious lives of students from different faiths. The strengthening of campus life offered another important context for general education. Marsh proposed a new student-faculty assembly to help train students in the workings of democracy. M.S.C. created programs in health and guidance to aid the maturation of the whole student.[17]

In the end, postwar debates on general education more clearly reflected diversity of perspective and cultural tradition than the new unity that Conant had welcomed so hopefully. Indeed, despite the tendency among academic leaders to explain their initiatives in terms of newly perceived national needs, the programs actually instituted, as well as the concerns that lay behind them, were remarkably continuous with patterns of development during the 1930s. With few exceptions, the atmosphere of the late 1940s impelled institutions and their leaders to redouble efforts along lines charted before World War II and the Cold War infused them with a new sense of democratic urgency.

Research and Graduate Education
for a Technological Age

The recommendation of the President's Scientific Research Board that the national government support research and graduate education presented the Rockefeller group with a dilemma. The panel's members agreed that universities could foster progress in defense, health, agriculture, and industry, and as officers of leading universities, they appreciated the benefits for higher education of federal funding. They were particularly enthusiastic about grants for basic research through a National Science Foundation, as distinct from the applied and development-oriented projects typically sponsored by the armed services.

The Rockefeller group believed, however, that the Scientific Research Board, composed largely of nonacademics, had failed to consider troubling questions. Some concerns involved matters of balance within and among academic institutions. What would be the impact on instruction of a sudden outpouring of money for research? Would support for natural science weaken general education, social science, and the humanities? On the other hand, if federal support were extended into the social sciencies, would it not lead educators into controversial policy issues for which academic research could not produce definitive answers? There was also concern that the proposals would benefit some institutions more than others. What, for example, would the Scientific Research Board's program do for liberal arts colleges that did little research in natural science? Alternatively, was there not a danger that political pressures would force the government to distribute funds too widely, thus dooming the entire effort to mediocrity? Administrative issues lurked as well. By what criteria would government officials make awards? Would bureaucrats enforce an unwelcome uniformity or place unacceptable controls on the work they supported?[18]

As the Rockefeller group deliberated in the late 1940s, the burgeoning Cold War resulted in a continuing flow of federal funds for defense-related work, though in amounts much reduced from wartime levels. The Office of Naval Research played a particularly important role in this phenomenon. The need to write contracts gave academic leaders and government officials opportunities to resolve some of the administrative issues associated with the Scientific Research Board's recommendations. Design work on the National Science Foundation also proceeded during these years, and the enabling legislation, adopted in 1950, contained important protections for academic institutions, including peer review of requests for funding.

These developments relieved some of the anxieties of the Rockefeller group, but questions about the implications of federal aid remained. In its report, the panel took a middle position, endorsing the programs already in existence, including the National Science Foundation, but opposing any expansion. "Higher education . . . needs time," the group asserted, "to digest what it has already undertaken and to evaluate the full impact of what it is already doing under federal government assistance." It urged academic institutions to seek alternative sources of funding for postwar development.

As the ambivalent conclusions of the Rockefeller group implied, the lines of postwar debate were less starkly drawn on questions related to academic research than on enrollment policies and general education. This was not surprising, since most universities regarded teaching as their primary responsibility. The Zook commission and the Rockefeller group actually agreed on most issues in this area. In an atmosphere dominated by uncertainty about the impact of new federal action, individual institutions worked out policies according to the logic of their positions and their goals.[19]

The differing perspectives on government investment in science among academic leaders whose universities focused on research were illustrated by the views of Compton and Conant. Not surprisingly, given his history of advocacy, Compton embraced the opportunity to undertake federally assisted work. While he was eager to strengthen basic research, he stressed the country's need for help in defense and announced that M.I.T. would continue to manage large-scale military projects similar to those undertaken during the war. Conant was more wary. A fiscal conservative, he worried that acceptance of contract work would expose Harvard to financial risk. Governments were political bodies and policies could shift suddenly. Moreover, while Conant's wartime experience had increased his appreciation of applied work, he thought fundamental knowledge was the country's most pressing need. For these reasons, Conant barred Harvard from involvement in the large technical projects that Compton was ready to accept.

The two leaders also disagreed about classified work. Compton regarded secret research as undesirable in a university setting but unavoidable under conditions of the postwar years. Harvard adopted a general rule against research contracts under which results could not be published freely.

The contrasting attitudes of Conant and Compton expressed divergent institutional interests as well as alternative philosophies. Harvard was not oriented toward applied research, having reduced such activities during the Lowell years, and its scientists had little interest in projects that did not involve basic questions and the possibility of publication. M.I.T. retained a central focus on engineering, despite Compton's new emphasis on science. Harvard was, moreover, much richer than M.I.T., and its leaders could hope, in a way their Institute counterparts could not do, to accomplish their developmental goals through funding sources other than the national government. Finally, since science and technology had always been the Institute's central interests, leaders at M.I.T. were not worried about programmatic imbalances that might result from increased funding for those fields. Thus, the two leading universities in Massachusetts became prominent exponents of opposing positions on federal support: Conant's Harvard sought to limit reliance on government funds and to strengthen itself through other means; Compton's M.I.T. welcomed federal contracts as both duty and opportunity.[20]

Research was always linked to graduate and professional education. Interest in advanced training had been moderated during the decades prior to World War II by the same forces that had produced the general education movement, but the postwar atmosphere put graduate studies high on the academic agenda. Bush pointed out in his 1945 report, for example, that the development of science required not only support for current work but also the training of future scholars. Conant suggested limiting federal financial aid to graduate students in a handful of scientific and medical fields. There was even talk at M.I.T. of abandoning undergraduate education to concentrate on graduate training. The issue was broader than science, however, since the war had demonstrated the importance of specialists in a variety of academic, technical, and managerial fields. Both the Zook commission and the Rockefeller group wanted to increase the supply of professionals.[21]

Two major questions were raised about graduate education in the early postwar years. One was advanced by the Zook commission, which criticized universities for past tendencies to stress specialized academic studies rather than fields of national need. Pointing out that most holders of Ph.D.s spent their lives doing something other than scholarly research, the commission advocated programs for teaching and nonacademic careers. A second concern involved the potential for graduate education to reduce attention to undergraduate teaching. This issue was repeatedly introduced in faculty discussions at M.I.T. in response to Compton's proposals to strengthen graduate education and research. Compton's response provided a model for advocates of advanced work at all institutions: graduate and undergraduate education, like teaching and research, were mutually reinforcing, not conflicting, priorities. A heightened effort in graduate work, he claimed, would inevitably enrich the educational environment for undergraduates.[22]

University and Society: Academic Values, Institutional Diversity, and Interinstitutional Competition

Debates of the late 1940s on questions ranging from enrollment policy to curriculum change to research often turned on underlying disagreements about the social functions of universities. At the same time, the thoughts of academics on social issues were affected by the possibility that the federal government might channel large sums toward their institutions precisely because they could assist in solving national problems. The contrasting perspectives of the two presidential committees—the Zook commission and the President's Scientific Research Board—and the Rockefeller group illustrated the complex interplay within the institutional complex of academic ideas and interinstitutional competition for support.

The presidential commissions began with a common charge: to identify ways in which colleges and universities could meet national needs. The members of the President's Scientific Research Board, all government officials, were asked to consider how scholarly expertise could foster technological progress. The task given Zook and his colleagues was broader: to examine the "objectives, methods, and facilities [of higher education] . . . in light of the social role it has to play." The commission responded with a statement of fundamental assumptions:

> The social role of education in a democratic society, is at once to ensure equal liberty and equal opportunity . . . and to enable the citizens to understand, appraise and redirect forces, men and events as these tend to strengthen or to weaken their liberties. In performing this role education will . . . [be most successful] if its programs and policies grow out of and are relevant to the characteristics and needs of contemporary society. Effective democratic education will deal directly with current problems.

Did the society need more trained people in occupational fields? Higher education should add the necessary programs. Did the country face social problems ranging from racial prejudice to poverty to troubled families? Academic institutions should alter their curricula to address such questions. Did technical problems need to be solved? Academia should put its shoulder to the wheel. The country needed scholars with "a passionate concern for human betterment, for the improvement of social conditions and of relations among men" who could "apply at the point of social action what the social scientists had discovered regarding the laws of human behavior."[23]

In viewing universities as social agencies that should assume whatever functions they could usefully undertake, the Zook commission was drawing on educational ideas with deep roots. Academic institutions typically grew out of the religious, economic, or social purposes of particular communities, and continuing ties to external groups perpetuated their concern with nonacademic issues. Other patterns reinforced the social involvement of universities. One was the rise of public service during the second half of the nineteenth century.

A second was the spread, during the same period, of career-oriented programs. The clearest expression of the social theme was the development of state universities and land grant colleges with their central commitment to promoting economic progress.

Other strands of academic tradition, however, pulled educators in a different direction. American universities inherited from their European antecedents an impulse toward self-regulation and separation from the outside world rooted in the medieval church. In modern times, the desire for autonomy was strengthened by Germanic ideas about academic freedom. From these perspectives, universities were best understood not as creatures of society but as independent entities dedicated to transcendent goals like "truth" and "knowledge." So conceived, they should not constantly adapt to social needs. Indeed, the evolution of universities in the United States fostered an association between academic autonomy and scholarly achievement, since the most prestigious institutions were those with a high degree of independence from external, nonacademic control.

Contending perceptions of the proper relationship between universities and external communities had turned the nation's academic history into an ongoing saga of battles between "insiders" and "outsiders." The rise of professionalism in the late nineteenth century was only one example of a phenomenon that began with disputes between Puritan governors and Harvard scholars in seventeenth-century Cambridge. The academic debates of the late 1940s made it clear that the postwar period would be an important new chapter in this ancient story.

Many educators were appalled by the views of the Zook commission. The members of the Rockefeller group, for example, stressed limits on the social involvements of academic institutions. Their report began not with an analysis of contemporary concerns but with an explication of academic traditions. It identified four functions of universities and colleges: liberal education, professional education, graduate education and research, and public service. Of these, public service, direct efforts to address social problems, was accorded least emphasis. Higher education's primary response to societal needs, in the view of the Rockefeller group, should be to "contribute the trained experts, the scholars, and the leaders" who could work on these issues. The Rockefeller report affirmed many characteristics of higher education that the Zook commission attacked: its relative exclusivity, its emphasis on the development of individuals, and its focus on specialized knowledge. The report resisted the notion that major change was needed. "What higher education has been doing," the group argued," must still be done."[24]

It would be a mistake, however, to draw the lines between the Zook commission and the Rockefeller group too sharply. Zook and his associates respected academic freedom, pure scholarship, and liberal learning. The Rockefeller report praised public service and urged colleges to help individuals become citizens. Both acknowledged that historical conditions had produced many kinds of academic institutions in the United States. Indeed, both reports saw this diversity as the special genius of American higher education, a clear difference from the centralized national systems of Europe. Both linked diversity with democracy and stressed that federal policy must protect this aspect of academia. The Zook commission advocated federal support to promote diversity, but the Rockefeller group felt that government involvement would threaten diversity by concentrating influence in Washington.[25]

The philosophical disagreements between the Zook commission and the Rockefeller group could not be separated from the financial interests of their respective constituencies. The institutions represented on Zook's panel were likely to benefit from extensive federal involvement in higher education. For example, the funding of scholarships for large numbers of Americans not previously equipped, financially or academically, to attend college was bound to strengthen enrollments at the nonelite, practically oriented institutions that dominated this commission. On the other hand, the Rockefeller group's conservative estimates of the numbers of Americans who could profit from college were a logically essential element of their effort to demonstrate the viability of a system heavily dependent on private support.

The Zook commission's recommendation that institutional aid be granted only to public institutions would produce a windfall for a sector of the academic community with which it was strongly aligned. This possibility was bound to frighten the establishment figures on the Rockefeller group, since it would shift the balance of academic power against private schools. Even proposals that would allow everyone to benefit, such as the call for research aid by the President's Scientific Research Board, were worrisome to the authors of the Rockefeller report, since the long-term pressures of politics on any governmental program would diffuse funds widely among regions and campuses, inevitably weakening the positions of well-established universities. At the same time, such institutions were likely to prosper if nongovernmental sources of funding continued to be dominant, as the Rockefeller panel urged, since they possessed the strongest ties to philanthropists, foundations, alumni/ae groups, and private industry.

The impact of the Zook commission's recommendations and the Rockefeller report, as well as of the numerous other studies and statements produced during the postwar years, is hard to measure. These documents clearly affected academic debates at the campus level, but government response was thin. The National Science Foundation was one specific outcome, and some federal funding for research and technology-based development continued to flow. No legislation, however, was proposed or enacted based on the recommendations of the Zook commission. At a minimum, these debates on the functions and values of higher education documented the concerns of a generation of educators on the eve of the greatest period of academic development in the nation's history. In terms of the institutional complex, they provided benchmark statements of academic ideas against which observers of a later time could assess postwar change.[26]

The Three Revolutions: Enrollments, Finances, and Faculty

During the 1950s and 1960s, the traditional scramble for resources as well as the balance of academic power underwent striking transformations. Both students and dollars, which had been in short supply between 1930 and 1945, became much easier to acquire as young people applied to college in greatly increased numbers and financial support from a variety of sources became available at levels unimaginable before World War II. As institutions grew in response to the new conditions, demand for faculty—the third key resource for universities—intensified. This phenomenon greatly improved the historically weak organizational position of the professoriate. Other factors, especially the rise of government-funded research, further empowered professional scholars. Thus, as educational leaders considered the debates of the late 1940s in relation to their own institutions, they confronted changes in the context of interinstitutional competition for resources and shifts in the relative power of subgroups within campus communities.

The Revolution in Patterns of College Attendance

The question of who should go to college, so intensely discussed in the postwar years, was only partially susceptible to the determinations of educational leaders. They could urge governments to encourage or limit attendance. They could make admission policies receptive or restrictive. But the disposition of potential students to apply or not to apply, the capacities of families to support their children's educations, and the reactions of politicians to public pressures to expand educational opportunities were important and uncontrollable factors in the equation. The response of the veterans to the G.I. Bill demonstrated how widely actual conditions could diverge from prior expectations. The educators of the postwar years knew all this, and, even as they argued about who *should* go to college, they wondered who *would* do so.

Uncertainty about enrollments after the servicemen completed their studies dominated the late 1940s and early 1950s. Some, like Conant and Baker, argued that the veterans' program had introduced higher education to a new group of Americans who could not have afforded college before the war and that demand from younger siblings and friends of the former soldiers would generate continuing growth. Others, like Ell, remembered the falling birthrates of the 1930s and regarded the postwar expansion as a temporary aberration. In 1947 the United States Office of Education issued a report leaning toward Ell's side of the argument: national enrollments would peak at about 3.3 million in the late 1940s, the U.S.O.E. projected, and then would decline toward about 3 million, at which level they would remain for a decade.[27]

Difficulties in predicting enrollment trends were compounded by uncertainty about federal policies. The Zook commission's recommendations for federal scholarships and institutional aid resulted in several years of fruitless debate and anticipation. During these same years, the nation's continuing need for military manpower posed new threats to enrollments. Discussions of peacetime conscription, like wartime planning for veterans' benefits, did not focus on education, but academic leaders had to consider the impact of legislation in this area on their institutions.

The crucial question was whether students would be allowed to defer military service to complete their studies. Some, like Conant and the A.A.U., opposed deferments as fundamentally unfair; this position was strongest, however, among academics whose institutions were not worried about enrollments. Most educational leaders favored deferments, and the A.C.E. lobbied vigorously to obtain them. Their success led Conant to comment derisively on a draft policy "designed to keep the colleges full of students." The new selective-service law was a victory of sorts for academia, but the outbreak of the Korean war in 1950, followed by federal legislation extending the G.I. Bill to veterans of the new conflict, created additional uncertainties about enrollments.[28]

While various federal proposals were alternately promising prosperity or disaster, academics were learning firsthand about educational demand in the wake of the veterans' program. Enrollments of ex-servicemen rose to 1.1 million in the fall of 1947, then dropped to less than 400,000 by 1951. Despite this reduction, total enrollments increased in 1948 and 1949, lending support to the view that postwar trends would not follow the patterns anticipated in the late 1930s. When enrollments did fall in 1950 and again in 1951, many observers thought the long-anticipated decline associated with the end of the veterans' subsidy was arriving. But in 1952, the numbers turned upward, confounding the expectations of planners yet again. Additional confusion arose from the differential impact on institutions of postwar shifts in student demand. The bulk of the post-veterans' growth occurred in the public sector, while many private universities experienced a decline in applications.[29]

The atmosphere of uncertainly about long-term demand for higher education began to change in the early 1950s. Ralph Van Meter, Baker's successor as president of M.S.C., renamed the University of Massachusetts in 1947, was among the first to identify the new situation. "It appears certain," he wrote in the fall of 1951, "that pressure for admission will increase sharply in the last part of the decade." Tying together the increased birthrates that began in the early 1940s and the higher rates of attendance of the late 1940s, Van Meter argued that applications would overwhelm academic facilities by the 1960s. After 1952 national enrollment statistics lent support to Van Meter's contention that a basic change had occurred in the percentage of young Americans wishing to attend college. The upturn in enrollments of that year initiated a new pattern of steady expansion at a time when the impact of high birthrates during the 1940s was still years away. Between 1952 and 1960, the number of young Americans enrolling in college increased from 2.1 million to 3.6 million, while the proportion attending rose from 14 percent to 22 percent.

By the mid-1950s, there was a consensus among academics that higher education faced fundamentally new conditions. In 1955 the American Association of Collegiate Registrars and Admissions Officers issued a report called "The Impending Tidal Wave of Students." A year later, President Eisenhower's

Committee on Education Beyond the High School gave even more visible attention to the issue. The expansion was going to be rapid and sustained. Both the Association of Registrars and the president's committee estimated that by 1970 colleges and universities would be enrolling triple their current numbers. The new projections radically altered the focus of academic planning. Leaders stopped worrying about maintaining their institutions in uncertain times and concentrated on ensuring adequate places—and appropriately trained faculty—to accommodate the expanded applicant population that would appear after 1960.[30]

Several analyses were offered to explain the increased interest in college. To a substantial degree, the pattern continued a trend dating from the nineteenth century, but World War II seemed to have changed the country in basic ways. The Zook commission, though much criticized, appeared to have anticipated accurately a new impatience with restrictions on social mobility and with privileges based on class and race. Men from all social groups had died in battle, and Nazi Germany had made clear where racial prejudice could lead. The accomplishments of expatriate Jews were dramatizing the blindness of bigotry, not least within higher education.

Institutions, also affected by the democratic emotions of the war, actively encouraged applicants from all segments of society. The veterans' program not only stirred an appetite for higher education among new groups but also engendered an appreciation among academics of admission policies based on merit rather than family history. Moreover, the increasingly technical and bureaucratic character of industry, combined with the interest of employers in applicants with formal training and credentials, was convincing young Americans that college was an economic necessity. At the same time, an unprecedented prosperity, which began almost immediately after the war, brought college within reach of many more Americans than had been the case in the 1930s.[31]

The long-anticipated "tidal wave" of applications for college admission arrived as predicted in 1960, and the nation's system of higher education expanded to accommodate it. During the following decade, college and university enrollments grew from 3.6 million to 7.9 million, and the proportion of the nation's youth attending college—32 percent in 1970—came to approximate the figure that the Zook commission, to the distress of many academics, had advocated. The number of colleges and universities jumped by a third during the 1960s, while average institutional size tripled. The expansion occurred in every region and among all types of institutions, though the shift in enrollments from private to public institutions that began right after the war continued. In 1950, about 50 percent of the college population was attending a publicly supported campus; by 1960 the figure had grown to 59 percent; and by 1970, to 73 percent.[32]

Not everyone was enthusiastic about the growth in numbers of those seeking higher education, as would be expected from the debates on enrollment policy of the early postwar years. John Gardner, president of the Carnegie Corporation, expressed the doubts of many as the momentum of expansion was building in the 1950s:

> We send great numbers of our youth on to college without any clear notion of what they will get out of it, but simply in pursuance of a vague notion that "college is an opportunity that should not be denied them." This makes no sense at all.[33]

Such reservations, however, counted for little in the rush of postwar development. During the 1950s and 1960s, with only passing attention given to the issues raised by Gardner and others, educators and political leaders, responding to overwhelming public pressures, concentrated on building the world's first system of mass higher education. The task of evaluating this phenomenon would be the work of another time.

The Revolution in Financial Support

Postwar change in the financial circumstances of higher education was even more dramatic and less expected than the new patterns of college attendance. In the late 1940s, as educators considered the enlarged social role they hoped to play, the most worrisome obstacles were economic. Inflation was making it difficult to maintain the activities established before 1940. Faculty salaries, which had made little progress during the Depression and war, were losing ground in comparison to those of doctors, dentists, and lawyers. Higher costs compounded long-neglected problems of maintenance and rendered new construction especially difficult. The authors of the Rockefeller report summarized the situation in 1952: "The educational administrators of our day are so preoccupied with the effort to protect the educational achievements of the past . . . that they can give little attention to educational advancement." One question haunted all discussions of new academic possibilities in the early postwar years: who would pay the bill?[34]

The economic position of higher education was illustrated by the nation's wealthiest institutions: endowed, private universities. These schools historically had depended on private philanthropy, but this income source was becoming less reliable. Endowment income, which provided 30 percent of the revenues of private universities in 1930, contributed only 16 percent in 1950. Several factors explained the change, including reduced returns on investment since 1929, lower rates of giving resulting from the progressive income tax as well as the Depression and war, and postwar enrollment expansion that outstripped investment growth.

Institutional leaders hoped to offset some of the loss through annual fund drives, especially campaigns oriented toward alumni/ae, a technique that few universities had exploited systematically before the war. There was little reason to believe, however, that annual giving, which historically had contributed less than 10 percent of current income, could make up for a continued erosion of endowments. A 1947 report sponsored by the Rockefeller Foundation noted that academics felt "bewilderment and doubt about the appropriate solution" to the loss of support from investments.

The severity of the situation varied among institutions. At Harvard, with the largest endowment in the country, the importance of fund income declined only moderately between 1930 and 1950. Still, Conant told the Corporation that additional funds would be needed to make any new ventures possible. At Tufts, with its modest financial base, the change was more severe, and Carmichael identified the weakness of endowments as his institution's most urgent problem. Compton observed that M.I.T. needed new capital comparable in significance to the gift from George Eastman in 1912 that had financed the Cambridge campus. All these presidents were convinced, moreover, that no conceivable program of private giving would be adequate to sustain research programs at needed levels, especially in the physical sciences. In this area, a federal program of the type proposed by Bush and the President's Scientific Research Board seemed essential. Even Conant moved toward this position, albeit reluctantly.[35]

As endowments declined in significance, payments from students became more important. Private university income from tuition and fees increased as a proportion of total income from 56 percent in 1940 to 65 percent in 1950. Some of this change was merely the mirror image of reduced contributions from investments. The major explanation, however, was the expansion of enrollments, coupled with increases in tuition. The enlarged role of tuition and fees was problematic for several reasons. Since it resulted partly from higher prices, it represented a trend that could restrict access to college and also limit the student market. If inflation in the general economy continued, moreover, it was doubtful that prices could be pushed higher, even though costs would climb. Finally, the association of higher revenues from students and enrollment growth linked budgets to a source that most educators considered highly uncertain. These concerns were particularly pertinent at institutions where traditions of philanthropic support were strong and where revenues from expanded enrollments held the key to institutional development.[36]

While both philanthropy and student payments seemed unreliable in the late 1940s, government support appeared likely to increase in scale and importance. Publicly supported institutions were less vulnerable to economic pressures between 1930 and 1945 than their private counterparts. Indeed, during years when most private universities were neglecting facilities and postponing new construction, state universities experienced a building boom. The value of the physical plant at public institutions doubled during the 1930s and doubled again in the 1940s, a result of New Deal public works programs and postwar financial surpluses of state governments. Moreover, state appropriations for academic institutions grew slightly during the 1930s and rapidly during the 1940s. In the early postwar years, state universities experienced growth in total appropriations and in support per student, while private universities faced declining per-student income. There were differences from state to state, but even in Massachusetts, with its tradition of low support for public higher education, the late 1940s were years of enlarged government funding.

The strength of state appropriations at a time of financial uncertainty for their own campuses aroused fears among leaders of independent institutions that the balance of power between the two sectors was shifting permanently. Compton noted that the financial situation "threatens the continued leadership and even the continued relative effectiveness of privately supported institutions," and he emphasized the need to position M.I.T. securely in an educational world dominated by state schools. Public educators were, indeed, optimistic about the future in the early postwar years, though they had worries of their own. They were particularly concerned that, over time, political pressures would push up enrollments more rapidly than appropriations, a pattern illustrated by the experience of Massachusetts State in the 1930s. They also shared their private counterparts' apprehensions about inflation, increased dependence on student payments, and even endowments, which were important at a number of public campuses.[37]

The first and most important indication that the postwar economic position of higher education was going to be radically different from what most educators of the late 1940s anticipated came from innovations in federal policy. As so often had been the case, the change stemmed not from increased appreciation of the inherent value of academic work but from the perception that colleges and universities could serve a nonacademic purpose.

In the early 1950s, the decisive developments were the Cold War and the Korean conflict, which generated support for applied, defense-related research-and-development projects. For several years in the 1950s, federal funding for university-based research, both basic and applied, grew incrementally to a total of $169 million in 1955. Then, in 1957, the Soviet launching of *Sputnik I* created the shocked impression that America was falling behind Russia in science. Government support for academic work jumped quickly to $356 million in 1959. For the next decade, federal aid grew steadily, reaching close to $2 billion by 1968. In the mid-1960s, the federal government accounted for more than 70 percent of all separately budgeted, university-based research support.

Throughout the period, defense-related work was a mainstay of government spending. Within this context, however, aid for basic work grew more prominent, effectively realizing Bush's vision of universities as the nation's primary resource for scientific progress. During the mid-1960s, federal support also broadened into new areas. As domestic policy issues moved to the top of the political agenda, research allocations from the domestic departments of government—especially Health, Education and Welfare—became more important. The government also created two new funds, paralleling the N.S.F., to support the arts and humanities. The direct impact of all this spending on academia was, however, highly concentrated. During the 1960s, ten institutions—Harvard and M.I.T. among them—received approximately 30 percent of all research support, and twenty institutions received between 45 and 50 percent. There was little movement in and out of this select group.[38]

Research was not the only area where federal policies had a major effect on academia. In the immediate postwar years, in fact, educators were as concerned with student aid and direct institutional support as with research, though the Zook commission's proposals in these areas were not enacted. Discussions of federal action to expand the nation's academic system were kept alive, however, by the prospect of the tidal wave of students projected for the 1960s, and in 1957 President Eisenhower's Committee on Education Beyond the High School recommended a comprehensive program, including support for facilities construction, student aid, and institutional grants.

The *Sputnik I* crisis finally created a political environment in which an enlarged federal role was viable. The first significant legislation was the National Defense Education Act of 1958, establishing scholarships and fellowships, together with aid for new programs in specified fields. Additional training programs were created in the National Institutes of Health, the Atomic Energy Commission, and the National Science Foundation. After 1960, as higher education became a concern of social policy as well as national security, federal programs came rapidly. Bills were enacted to support campus building, expand educational opportunities in the health professions, strengthen the study of other countries and foreign languages, and increase aid to students from low-income backgrounds. Support for educational programs through the three endowments was expanded. A new G.I. Bill for veterans plus amendments to the Social Security Act provided additional sources of financial aid.[39]

By the late 1960s, Congress had created an array of programs that channeled money toward academia, although no overall national policy with respect to higher education had been formulated. There were, however, some general trends. The most important was that nonresearch support was directed largely to student aid, some granted directly to individuals and some administered by institutions. By 1968 student aid programs equaled sponsored research in total dollar support, and these two areas accounted for two-thirds of the federal budget for higher education. The largest part of the remaining third paid for facilities and equipment, while only 10 percent supported educational programs. During the 1960s, moreover, student aid was increasingly concerned with ensuring access to college, and financial need became a dominant consideration in determining eligibility for federal support.

Overshadowing particular programs and legislative patterns was the aggregate effect of federal funding during the 1950s and 1960s. Prior to World War II, revenue from federal sources was a negligible part of the current income of the country's private institutions of higher education—less than 1 percent in 1940; by 1970 the national government was providing nearly 23 percent of the operating funds of these schools. The change for public campuses was less pronounced but still substantial: from 10 percent of current funds in 1940 to 17 percent in 1970.[40]

Federal support was not the whole story of the postwar revolution in the economics of higher education. As public systems expanded to absorb increased enrollments, state allocations also grew markedly, rising from $492 million in 1950 to $5.8 billion in 1970, a gain of over 1,000 percent. At the same time, a strong economy and sustained public support enabled institutions to mount fund-raising campaigns for amounts that could not have been imagined before 1940. Much of the money came from traditional sources—alumni/ae, private individuals, and foundations, but new tax incentives prompted corporations to greatly expand their donations to academia. Between 1950 and 1970 voluntary annual giving from all these sources increased by 675 percent, from $240 million to $1.86 billion. In addition, with demand for college places intense and family income growing, colleges and universities increased tuition charges rapidly, vastly expanding revenue from this historic source. Annual receipts from students rose by over 1,000 percent in twenty years, from $395 million in 1950 to $4.4 billion in 1970.[41]

Educators had difficulty grasping the significance and scale of the new financial environment, but the basic story was evident in the summary numbers. Aggregate spending by all institutions of higher education rose from $2.2 billion in 1950 to $21 billion by 1970. This golden age of financial support, when funding could be found for almost any worthwhile educational proposal, stood in stark contrast to the gloomy expectations of educators in the early postwar years and to the difficult realities of the long pause. A single comparison highlighted the change. Between 1930 and 1950 institutional expenditures per student had risen somewhat more slowly than per capita G.N.P. During the next two decades the relationship was reversed with a vengeance as academia's outlays increased at more than double the rate of national productivity.[42]

The Triumph of the Professoriate

The perception of the mid-1950s that academia was approaching a period of expansion generated widespread concern about faculty shortages. Estimates of new Ph.D.s that would be needed varied with enrollment projections, but no one disputed the basic problem. An influential report in 1955 by the Ford-sponsored Committee of Fifteen summarized the situation as follows:

> . . . between now and 1970 about 135,000 doctorates will be awarded . . . Even if all these new Ph.D.s were to become teachers, we would, by 1970, need approximately 350,000 more college teachers than we shall probably train in our doctoral programs . . . To expect that by 1970 the proportion of college teachers holding the Ph.D. degree will have declined from the present 40 percent to 20 percent is not statistical hysteria but grassroots arithmetic.

President Eisenhower's Committee on Education Beyond the High School incorporated a similarly alarming appraisal in its 1957 report.

As higher education grew in the late 1950s, the Ph.D. shortage seemed to materialize. Biennial surveys by the National Education Association reported that the proportion of doctorates joining faculties of four-year colleges and universities was well below the 40 percent baseline identified by the Committee of Fifteen. These reports encouraged a conventional wisdom that the mismatch between supply and demand was producing a deterioration of faculty quality. This perception, in turn, moved educators to focus on raising salaries to attract talent. The president's 1957 committee noted that the economic circumstances of faculty had eroded in recent decades and urged a doubling of salaries over a five- to ten-year period. Fearful of competition for professors and aided by an improved financial environment, institutional leaders made salary enhancement a priority.

Nathan Pusey, Conant's successor at Harvard, exemplified the attitudes of the time. Pusey was conscious that Harvard traditionally had set national standards for faculty pay, and he recognized a threat from rapidly growing and well-financed universities in other regions. Improving salaries became the central goal of his presidency. Nationally, faculties achieved their prewar purchasing power by 1958. For the next ten years, real income grew steadily as pay rose at rates well above inflation. Working conditions got better in other ways as well: fringe benefits were expanded, support staff and facilities were improved, and teaching loads were reduced.[43]

The actual expansion of college faculties between 1955 and 1970 approximated the predictions of the Committee of Fifteen, increasing from two hundred thousand in 1952–1953 to five hundred thousand by 1970. The Ph.D. shortage, however, turned out to have been a false alarm—at least in terms of formal credentials and aggregate numbers. Existing graduate programs expanded, and additional institutions moved into doctoral-level education. Between 1948 and 1969, annual production of Ph.D.s increased from about four thousand to over twenty-six thousand. As a result, the proportion of terminally trained faculty at four-year colleges and universities actually increased somewhat across the period. A number of factors explained the new attractiveness of professorial careers, including improved material rewards, the high status of academia during the 1950s and 1960s, and the social idealism of college graduates. The true situation became clear only in retrospect, however, and the perceived shortage of teachers dominated discussions of graduate education into the late 1960s. Such perceptions were encouraged by the limited availability of highly talented scholars and the increased number of campuses trying to attract them. Competition in the top layer of academia bid up compensation levels for the entire professoriate.[44]

The position of college faculties was further strengthened, both economically and politically, by the growth of support for scholarly work from noninstitutional sources, especially the federal government. The new dollars were, of course, part of the general prosperity that supported better pay and conditions. Equally significant was the fact that faculty were able to obtain funds as direct grants to themselves. As Carl Kaysen put it, this development "had the effect of supporting the community of professionals—the professor and his peers—as against the power of the educational institution and its administrators." Indeed, a faculty member able to win outside funding not only achieved a measure of independence but also became a source of institutional income. With academic jobs plentiful, scholars gained a major advantage in negotiating terms of employment—and in asserting other interests.[45]

The position of faculties was enhanced also by the increased emphasis on research that flowed from federal policies. In the 1950s and 1960s, American scholars, especially scientists, achieved the international eminence Conant and Compton had envisioned twenty years earlier. The graduate school replaced the college as the most important component of many universities, and research productivity became a vital measure of institutional standing. In this context, well-known scholars became increasingly valuable contributors to campus reputations, and judgments about research carried greater weight in decisions on hiring and promotion. Moreover, the trend toward ever more sophisticated and specialized research, already a source of professional power in the late nineteenth century, continued to erode the capacity of administrators to evaluate specific research achievements. In combination, these facts shifted power in matters of academic personnel toward the faculty.

The circumstances of the postwar decades spawned an era of professional ascendency that involved much more than improved working conditions. The discipline-oriented professional associations that were formed in the late nineteenth and early twentieth centuries flourished as never before. Their memberships increased along with their influence. Part of their new strength resulted directly from academia's growth. As large numbers of Ph.D.s joined new or expanding institutions, often in remote locations, the disciplinary societies provided them with crucial links to others in their fields. The new emphasis on research reinforced this phenomenon.

As faculty members became more specialized, they were more likely to find colleagues with common interests in professional groups than on their own campuses. Institutions also came to rely on scholarly associations in new ways. For example, universities planning Ph.D. programs turned to them for guidance and sometimes for formal accreditation, just as administrators used them to assess faculty scholarship. As learned societies achieved greater authority, activity within them—service on committees and election to key offices—became important measures of scholarly standing.

The associations also influenced national policy. This was especially true outside the hard sciences, which were well established in Washington by the end of World War II. Social science organizations lobbied for research support for their fields and for protecting funded projects from political control. The American Council of Learned Societies was influential in promoting the National Endowment for the Humanities.[46]

The expanded role of the professional societies on matters of interest to specific disciplines proceeded in tandem with a more assertive stance by the American Association of University Professors on matters of general policy. The A.A.U.P. was especially concerned with issues of compensation and scholarly autonomy. Its decision in the 1950s to publish information on salaries at individual campuses promoted interinstitutional competition in faculty pay.

Even more important were the A.A.U.P.'s guidelines on the standing and treatment of faculties. The most fundamental of these was the 1940 Statement of Principles on Academic Freedom and Tenure. This document not only asserted the central importance of academic freedom but also argued that tenure was its indispensable adjunct and that clearly stated norms and procedures were vital in matters of academic personnel. In subsequent years, these guidelines were supplemented by others, including the 1958 Statement on Procedural Standards in Faculty Dismissal Proceedings, the 1961 Statement on

Recruitment and Resignation of Faculty Members, and the 1964 Statement on Standards for Notice of Nonreappointment. In combination, these A.A.U.P. policies provided the basis for investigations by the association of complaints by aggrieved faculty members against their institutions, actions that occasionally led to formal censure. The guidelines also emboldened faculties on individual campuses to advocate change in local policies.[47]

The new power of faculties, both substantive and political, transformed the manner in which academic decisions were made at the campus level. Bolstered by A.A.U.P. guidelines, faculties at universities in Massachusetts worked to replace the administrative discretion common in the prewar decades by formal statements of faculty rights, including rules, procedures, and criteria. At Boston University, the first published statement of academic personnel policy was issued in 1946. Revisions of this document during the 1950s and 1960s steadily expanded faculty prerogatives and protections. At less-developed institutions, the process progressed more slowly. The Northeastern faculty did not establish an A.A.U.P. chapter until Ell retired in 1959. The first formal statement of personnel policy came shortly thereafter, as did a conventional tenure system. By 1970, however, with some local variation, especially at Harvard, codified rules governing personnel decisions were the norm at universities in Massachusetts.[48]

As in the late nineteenth century, the expanded role of professional societies developed simultaneously with enhanced power for academic departments. Here, again, the most dramatic shifts involved academic personnel decisions, where departments and faculties gained much greater power than they had possessed before World War II.

The evolution of M.I.T. illustrated the change. The Institute traditionally had maintained a high degree of central administrative control over academic matters. In the postwar decades, however, as federal money flowed and Compton's vision of a campus focused on research and graduate education became a reality, administrators learned that advanced, specialized work in basic fields could not be supervised with organizational tools appropriate for undergraduate programs in engineering. They were forced to grant more autonomy to subunits as well as individuals, not only in judging faculty qualifications but also in setting research priorities and building graduate programs.

The same process was replicated at campus after campus around the country. By the end of the period, academic personnel decisions at low-status institutions like Northeastern were being made, as they were at elite campuses like Harvard, on the basis of recommendations from departments and faculty committees with which administrators differed at their peril.[49]

Perhaps the most impressive indication of the faculty's altered position was the broadening of its formal involvement in institutional policy-making. A crucial early step was typically the formation of an elected senate (or its equivalent) to represent faculty interests to campus administrators. The B.U. faculty, with memories of reduced salaries and longer hours during the Depression and war still fresh, organized a Senate in the late 1940s. Their colleagues at the University of Massachusetts did so in 1957, and Northeastern came along in the

1960s. While senates often focused initially on issues of compensation and personnel policy, in time they expanded their concerns to include priorities in program development, resource allocation, and even administrative organization.

An additional arena for the assertion of faculty power was the selection of administrative leaders, from department chairs to presidents. In the 1930s, presidents were typically appointed by trustees with no formal—and little informal—consultation with the faculty. Deans and chairs were chosen by presidents. With some notable exceptions, especially the selection of presidents and deans at Harvard, formal mechanisms for involving faculty in choosing administrators became normal in the postwar years. The A.A.U.P.'s Statement on Government of Colleges and Universities in 1966, issued jointly with the A.C.E. and the Association of Governing Boards of Colleges and Universities, expressed the expanded expectations of the professoriate and acceptance of the new rules by administrative leaders.[50]

Disarray and Reassessment: A Second Debate on Academic Values

The End of the Golden Age

The circumstances that supported generalized development for higher education after the mid-1950s—rising demand for college education, increasing revenues from several sources, and solid public and political support—ended with remarkable speed and drama. The change began in the late 1960s as educators considered an unexpected problem: despite expanding resources, the financial position of academia was deteriorating. The most visible statement of the new situation was Earl Cheit's study, alarmingly entitled *The New Depression in Higher Education*, published in 1971. Cheit reviewed financial data from forty-one campuses and found, at most of them, that costs were rising more rapidly than income.

Universities in particular, especially private ones, were experiencing problems. Cheit's sample included Harvard, which he thought was "headed for financial trouble," and Boston College, which was already "in financial difficulty." Cheit's study confirmed what institutional leaders already knew. A national projection based on Cheit's data concluded that over 60 percent of the country's colleges and universities were in a financially precarious position.

The sudden concern about money produced a chorus of appeals from educators for increased support, especially from the federal government. The debate of the early postwar years about direct grants to institutions was revived. This idea, which had been controversial when the Zook commission first proposed it in 1947, was now widely accepted in academia. By 1968 every major institutional association—from the American Association of Junior Colleges to the A.A.U.—favored institutional aid. Parallel appeals were made by groups of private campuses to state legislatures in Massachusetts, New York,

California, Texas, and Oregon. For most public officials, however, the pleas for new assistance at a time when higher education seemed more affluent than ever was shocking and paradoxical.[51]

The financial crisis was only the first of a series of problematic developments in the late 1960s and early 1970s. The second attracted even greater attention. Beginning in 1964, the nation's campuses encountered, for the first time in recent memory, sustained protest activity by students. At first, these incidents were not seen as a serious problem for higher education. Early demonstrations were peaceful, and many occurred off campus. They were regarded as expressions of frustration over traditional student issues, like parietal rules, or as understandable responses to disturbing public events, especially the civil rights movement and American intervention in Vietnam.

With the widely publicized episode at Columbia in 1968, however, student protests acquired an altered and, for academic leaders, a more threatening aspect. Incidents became more frequent and more violent. Grievances increasingly focused not on the misdeeds of governments and businesses but on those of universities themselves. Beseiged campuses were characterized as corporate bodies that ignored and exploited their impoverished urban neighbors, as willing participants in American foreign policy, and as oppressive agents of a social "establishment." In Massachusetts alone, major strikes occurred at Brandeis in 1967 and 1969, at Northeastern in 1968 and 1970, at M.I.T. in 1969 and 1970, and at Boston College in 1970.

The crowning event was the police "bust" of a group of students who had taken over the administration building at Harvard in April 1969. Few images captured more poignantly the contradictions of the period than televised clips of local police advancing among the trees of Harvard Yard to subdue unresisting undergraduates. One year later, the drama reached a grim climax when National Guard troops, summoned to control demonstrations at Kent State in Ohio and at Jackson State in Mississippi, fired on and killed several students.

The Harvard, Kent State, and Jackson State confrontations illuminated the incapacity of educators to contain these crises—and even to understand them. Where had all this anger come from? Why did responses based on traditionally accepted values—reason, individual responsibility, and the rule of law—produce new outbursts? Why was so much violent emotion being directed against the university, which academics considered the most liberal social institution in the nation?

The termination of "student unrest" was as puzzling as its onset. The summer of 1970 marked the high point of disruptive activities. Although American involvement in Vietnam continued for another three years, although issues of civil rights and racial tension remained unaddressed, and although problems in the relationships of universities to government agencies and neighboring communities persisted, during 1970–1971 the student protest movement inexplicably, even "eerily" (to use the word of a *New York Times* reporter), dissipated. Subsequent episodes tended to be isolated and short-lived. For educational leaders, the new peacefulness offered a chance to assess the impact of recent events.[52]

Throughout the "time of troubles," academic leaders worried about damage to their political position, especially their hopes for increased federal aid. By the early 1970s, it was apparent that the credibility of higher education was seriously compromised. Many politicians were more inclined to ask what was wrong on the nation's campuses than to entertain requests for aid. In the new atmosphere, long-simmering doubts among policymakers, particularly about the utility of federal investments in scholarly research, were reinforced.

In part, the new skepticism toward academia betokened a rightward shift in the country's political attitudes—a change to which the student protest movement seemed to have contributed. In 1968 and 1970, conservative candidates for office denounced equally the behavior of students and the vacillations of educators. The election in 1968 of Republican Richard Nixon signaled the altered political mood, which was quickly expressed in financial terms. Beginning that year, the pattern of generous annual increases in federal support for research that had begun in 1953 was replaced by one of constant dollar reductions. Other areas of federal funding also contracted, as did assistance from nonfederal sources, including alumni/ae. Despite these setbacks, the hope persisted as the new decade began that higher education could recapture its developmental momentum.[53]

At this point, new problems disrupted the calculations of academics. For years their claims for support had been linked to expanding enrollments. In the early 1970s, however, the demand for higher education appeared to be leveling off, and there were even indications that the number of students might diminish in the foreseeable future. Several factors were involved. Rates of college attendance, which had risen steadily since the 1940s, were becoming stable. Some thought, on the basis of studies showing that college was losing its economic value and that the supply of trained graduates was outstripping employment opportunities, that they would actually decline. New demographic projections revealed that the bulge of young people produced by high postwar birthrates was passing out of the educational system: annual increases in the eighteen-year-old population would diminish during the 1970s and be replaced by absolute reductions during the 1980s.

In combination, these facts implied that the expansion of the nation's educational system was finally catching up with applicant pressure. Suddenly academics found themselves worrying less about providing sufficient spaces than about keeping their facilities full. By 1973 public education authorities in Massachusetts had concluded that existing projections overstated the need for places in the state's colleges and universities in 1980 by as much as two hundred thousand.[54]

The successive crises of the late 1960s and early 1970s changed academia's mood abruptly. As recently as 1966 and 1967, as the first evidence of financial problems appeared, educators had manifested confidence in their work and their public position. Five years later, self-critical and defensive, many were preoccupied with understanding what had gone wrong with their institutions. A flood of books and articles appeared to explain and lament the change, including works by Jacques Barzun, Robert Nisbet, Adam Ulam, and Paul

Dressel. A gathering of scholars agreed that higher education's era of "triumphalism" was over.[55]

Study commissions were assembled. The first and most important of these was the Carnegie Commission on Higher Education, funded by the Carnegie Foundation and headed by Clark Kerr, former president of the University of California and an early casualty of student unrest. Created in 1966 to consider higher education's economic condition, the Carnegie commission expanded its activities over the next several years, evolved into the Carnegie Council on Policy Studies, and ultimately produced, in dozens of reports and monographs, the most comprehensive review of American higher education ever undertaken. Other groups evaluated finances, including committees of the A.A.U., the A.C.E., and the National Science Board.

Campus unrest produced its own crop of commissions, the most important of which were the A.C.E.'s Special Committee on Campus Tensions, led by Sol Linowitz, and President Nixon's Commission on Campus Tensions, chaired by former Pennsylvania governor William Scranton. As concern broadened, several groups undertook comprehensive reviews. President Nixon appointed a Task Force on Higher Education, under New York University president James Hester. Nixon's Secretary of Health, Education and Welfare appointed a commission of his own, chaired by Frank Newman of Stanford. From within higher education, the Assembly on University Goals and Governance, associated with the American Academy of Arts and Sciences, formed a study group. In the 1960s as in the 1940s, the impulse toward assessment at the national level was paralleled by efforts among the states and institutions.[56]

The reviews of the late 1960s and early 1970s represented the first systematic appraisal of higher education by academics since the early postwar years. In the intervening period, educational leaders had been preoccupied with expansion and development and mostly had assumed that more of the same meant institutional and social progress. The second great postwar debate thus paralleled the first, and the two together framed the years of growth.

Many old issues were reconsidered: who should go to college and for what? what kind of education should be common to all undergraduates? how well were graduate education and research meeting national needs? was the academic "system" properly constituted? how should financial responsibility be distributed? how should educators think about their social functions? In essence, the period of reappraisal was a time for academia to evaluate its collective accomplishments—and review again its basic values—during higher education's postwar golden age.

The Ambiguous Triumph of Democratic Higher Education

Among the changes that educators of the late 1960s regarded most proudly was the reduction of obstacles to attending college. The most egregious forms of discrimination in admission—explicit limitations against blacks and Jews; more subtle barriers for other religious and ethnic groups—had been largely eliminated. The use of merit-based criteria, especially scores on aptitude and achievement tests, had shifted the focus of admissions judgments from social background to academic accomplishment. The expansion of public institutions combined with greatly increased scholarship programs at private schools had brought college within reach of talented students from any income level or geographical background. Educational opportunities for women had grown increasingly similar to those for men. Even in Massachusetts, with its history of sexually segregated campuses, coeducation had become the norm. Harvard, Boston College, and Northeastern were all admitting women by the 1950s. Sheer numerical expansion encompassed all these changes and embodied a clear victory for the policy preferences of the Zook commission.

The reassessments of the 1960s made it clear that Zook and his colleagues had not only predicted the future but had won the philosophical debate. No major study committee argued for limiting access to higher education as the Rockefeller group had done in the early postwar years. The new consensus mirrored a shift in the political and social climate of the nation. By the 1960s, Americans were far more egalitarian than they had been before the war.

Broad support for mass higher education also expressed the widespread conclusion among academics that growth had been good for all kinds of institutions, a perception not present in 1945. After the war, educators at elite campuses had worried that increased access would dilute higher education intellectually and diffuse resources too widely. The intervening years were to show that revenue could be obtained to support both an enlarged academic industry and increased budgets at major institutions. It also became evident that mass access had brought many talented youngsters into the system without a general lowering of standards. Indeed, studies of the 1960s revealed that the average mental ability of college students had remained approximately constant. Moreover, elite universities had been able to raise their requirements for admission despite the general emphasis on access. Typical freshmen at Harvard or M.I.T. were much stronger academically in the 1960s than their counterparts in the 1930s.[57]

Despite the successes of democratic admission policies, the reassessments of the late 1960s were not complacent. Indeed, the nearly universal emphasis, in reports from commissions representing all types of institutions, was on further liberalization. The Carnegie commission proposed that the nation move toward "universal higher education" by removing all remaining barriers to college. For most educators, greater access meant opportunities for all social groups at all kinds of institutions. The nation's leading universities no less than its community colleges were urged to do better in enrolling members of disadvantaged groups.

This concern, surprising among representatives of the world's most democratic educational system, derived from a number of factors, the most important of which was the position of African Americans. The Newman report noted that while college-going rates among blacks had increased, so had rates for whites and that the relative change was not dramatic. It also pointed out that blacks were much better represented in the student bodies of second- and third-tier institutions than at leading ones. In a social and intellectual atmosphere deeply affected by the civil rights movement, few academics would defend the racial implications of the elitist values that James Conant had advanced so passionately twenty-five years earlier. As the Newman report put it: "Minority enrollment across all the spectrum of colleges and universities is important, not only because of high persistence rates at four-year colleges, but because of the need for improved access to graduate schools and to further participation in American life generally."[58]

The ambiguous record of higher education in enrolling minority students was part of a broader pattern that troubled educators of the late 1960s. Despite twenty-five years of democratic admission policies, college enrollments still reflected a high degree of class isolation and stratification. Indeed, Jencks and Riesman concluded that college enrollments across the nation were more stratified by class in the 1960s than they had been in the 1930s and 1940s. Part of the problem, ironically, flowed from the widespread use of objective tests, which in practice favored economically advantaged students and resulted in a slight increase in the importance of social class as a factor in admissions decisions.[59]

The records of universities in Massachusetts, while broadly consistent with national trends, also illustrated variations of pattern among institutional types. The most obvious changes occurred at nonelite private institutions bent on improving their academic standing. In the 1930s, B.U., B.C., and Tufts had enrolled significant numbers of students from middle- and lower-middle-class local families. By the late 1960s, all three were focusing on affluent students from broader geographical pools. The pattern at the University of Massachusetts was somewhat different. In prewar days, the state college in Amherst had been less oriented toward the financially underprivileged than the private urban universities of Boston. Still, M.S.C. had enrolled many young people from modest-income families in the western part of the state as well as the metropolitan area. During the 1950s and 1960s, however, the percentage of students from the commonwealth's lowest-income groups declined at Amherst. By the 1960s, only Northeastern in the private sector and the new Boston campus of UMass continued to emphasize programs for residents from low-income families.[60]

Harvard presented a more complex pattern. Conant harbored a transparent distaste for the College's reputation as a haven for privileged graduates of northeastern prep schools, and he sought, before and after the war, to enroll students from more diverse backgrounds. His goals were maintained after he retired in the early 1950s and were buttressed with expanded scholarships and greater efforts to recruit students from public high schools. In principle, then, the Harvard student body became more open to students from lower economic strata after the war. It is difficult, however, to document significant change in the economic backgrounds of Harvard students. Available evidence suggests, in fact, that during the 1950s and much of the 1960s, Harvard was growing more rather than less restrictive in class terms, though the trend appears to have changed at the end of the period. Harvard's admission policies during the golden age suggest the illusory nature of geographical scatter as an indicator of socioeconomic diversity. Students of the 1950s from widely separated suburban schools probably had more in common than boys from different neighborhoods of Boston in the 1930s.[61]

The discovery that important segments of higher education had become more economically exclusive while the entire system was expanding and becoming more democratic surprised educators of the 1960s. These were years when leaders at many institutions, affected by national concerns about poverty and urban decline, were making special efforts to enroll disadvantaged students, particularly minorities. Such programs could be misleading, however. For the most part, they constituted a thin countercurrent in the upward economic drift of student bodies that, in earlier years, actually had included larger numbers from modest-income families.

Research and Graduate Education in the Postwar Years

Along with creating the world's first system of mass higher education, the greatest postwar accomplishment of American academics was the strengthening of research and graduate training. Prior to World War II, the underdevelopment of these activities, especially in scientific fields, was a source of concern, and educators of the late 1940s who had differed on other matters had agreed that the advanced academic functions needed to be improved. Better-trained, better-supported scholars would be required for the United States to achieve leadership in technology-dependent areas of defense, medicine, and industry. If undergraduate enrollments were going to expand, the nation's graduate schools would have to produce more teachers.

The reassessments of the late 1960s celebrated academia's accomplishments in response to these challenges. Spurred by the revolution in financial support, especially federal funding, higher education had greatly increased the quality and volume of both research and advanced training. The change was particularly evident at a limited number of elite universities that reoriented their priorities in the postwar years and became "research universities," institutions that regarded their central purpose as the production of new knowledge.

Harvard and M.I.T. became leading examples of the new institutional pattern, which had implications for many areas of academic life. Decisions about hiring and promotion were increasingly dominated by judgments about scholarly work as distinct from teaching effectiveness. Indeed, keeping time-consuming instructional commitments to a minimum was essential in research universities, and lower-level instructional work was often delegated to graduate students at campuses that adopted the new model. Other forms of support for faculty scholarship—expanded clerical and technical assistance and improved facilities and equipment—were also essential. These changes greatly increased instructional expenditures per student, which is why federal dollars were so important.

In association with higher education's new emphasis on research and graduate education, the military, economic, and social advances foretold by Bush and President Truman's Scientific Research Board had materialized, as conditions in Massachusetts made plain. The state's depressed prewar industrial economy had been revived by thriving, technology-oriented industries, many of them linked to national defense programs and university-based research. The teaching hospitals of the Boston area had become international centers for research and advanced medical care. Most local observers agreed that changes at M.I.T. and Harvard had been instrumental in producing these developments. The A.A.U.'s 1968 report, "Federal Financing of Higher Education," articulated the academic consensus: "Looking forward, almost the only certainty about higher education . . . is that the demands placed upon it will continue to grow . . . Even more than at present, business and government will turn to higher education for new knowledge and technologies . . ." The report urged an expanded federal investment in graduate training and research.[62]

Despite its importance, the growth of federally financed research was a source of continuing discomfort within the academic community. In the late 1940s, there had been division about federal funding, illustrated by the contrasting positions of the Zook commission and the Rockefeller report. Here, as in the area of enrollments, Zook and his colleagues had seen the future more clearly. Some of the worries of the Rockefeller panel also proved prophetic, however. Federal policies *did* disturb prior balances among the disciplines, divert attention from undergraduate education, produce differential financial benefits among institutions, and subject academia's research agenda to determination by government officials. Harvard's Pusey spoke for many educators when he wrote that "it is difficult to exaggerate the impact on colleges and universities of the increased attention paid to science in the postwar years." Academia clearly concluded, however, that the benefits of federal assistance outweighed such difficulties, and government restraint in controlling actual research programs relieved the most serious worries of the early postwar years.

Patterns of change at Harvard and M.I.T. demonstrated the irresistible role that federal funding played in the development of university-based research. The Institute had embraced federal funding promptly and enthusiastically in the 1940s. By doing so, it had been able to achieve Compton's dream: the engineering school of prewar days transformed itself into a research university, and its departments and graduate programs achieved top national ratings, not only in science but also in the social sciences and humanities.

Observing such changes at institutions that had accepted federal funding unhesitatingly, Harvard's leaders realized that their efforts to limit dependence on government support could jeopardize their competitive position. The costs of maintaining leading departments and providing scholars with the freedom and support needed to perform at peak levels was beyond the means of even the nation's richest institution. After 1960, Harvard set aside the reservations expressed by both Conant and Pusey and allowed federal funding to grow rapidly as a proportion of the campus budget. As a consequence, the policies governing contract research at the two universities in Cambridge moved closer together. If Harvard could not resist, who could?[63]

The shift of emphasis toward research involved more than federal funding and extended beyond elite campuses. After 1945, every university in Massachusetts came to define research as a vital function. At the most fundamental level, the change expressed the imperatives of intellectual modernization. As the base of knowledge expanded in the postwar years, the challenge of keeping educational programs current was increasingly daunting to campus leaders, especially at institutions like UMass/Amherst and Northeastern, which historically had stressed scientific and technical fields. In this context, the idea took hold that teaching faculty, even those working exclusively with undergraduates, must be directly involved in the advancement of their fields. For most of these institutions, the availability of federal support was essential, but external funding was not the sole basis for modifying priorities. Even when noninstitutional resources were unavailable, universities were moved by the altered academic values of the 1950s and 1960s to increase their attention to scholarly research.

The atmosphere of reappraisal precipitated after 1968 by student unrest produced a wave of doubts abut the new priorities of the postwar years. The A.C.E.'s Special Committee on Campus Tensions found agreement among students, faculty, trustees, and administrators that "the professorial role—particularly in major universities—has become so distorted in the direction of research and scholarly achievement that many faculty seriously neglect their teaching function." No group expressed this view more eloquently than the Assembly on University Goals and Governance, which was dominated by leaders of the nation's foremost research universities. Higher education, the assembly declared, had been overtaken by a "production ethic" that "gauges scholarly performance by the crudest of measures: [the accumulation of] bibliographical citations. It is time," the assembly argued, "to upgrade the art of teaching."[64]

Concern about indifference toward teaching focused attention on graduate training. Here the educators of the late 1960s confronted another paradox of the golden age. In their 1947 report, the Zook commission had coupled its call for expanded graduate programs with recommendations for reform. If colleges were to expand through the adoption of more democratic admission policies, the commission had argued, the next generation of faculty would need more preparation for their teaching responsibilities and greater understanding of the breadth of knowledge and its applications than was common in Ph.D. programs in the prewar years.

Graduate education indeed had expanded, not only on elite campuses but also at places that had no significant graduate activities before the war. In this rush of growth, however, the exhortations of Zook and his colleagues were largely ignored. Ph.D. training changed very little during the postwar years, as sociologist Logan Wilson discovered when he repeated in the 1970s his 1942 study of the academic profession. Some institutions, Tufts among them, tried to create new kinds of graduate programs that stressed teaching skills, but few of these efforts produced concrete results. Indeed, during the 1950s and 1960s, graduate school faculties and the programs they administered became more intensely preoccupied with research in restricted academic specialties than ever before.

The assembly was a harsh judge. It found that graduate programs "are frequently pedantic, emphasizing a narrowness of focus that has little importance for the individual's intellectual and personal development" and "tend to neglect the development of skills in teaching." Here was an analysis emanating from the upper echelons of the academic profession that paralleled the criticisms made over two decades earlier by Zook and his service-oriented reformers. A similar analysis led the Carnegie commission to urge the "growth and acceptance of the Doctor of Arts degree for students primarily interested in a teaching career."[65]

The calls for greater attention to pedagogical skills seemed sensible in light of the fact that most universities explained their efforts to build graduate programs by reference to the need for more teachers. But such exhortations tended to have a hollow, even pious, ring. They were rarely linked to any plausible description of how change might occur without damaging other desirable goals, or even to a persuasive analysis of the underlying causes of the problem.

Academics had debated the relationship between research and teaching for years. Some argued that good teaching was inherently inseparable from research and that the best scholars were also the best instructors; others claimed that research, especially of the scientific type that became dominant in the postwar years, required skills of little use in teaching undergraduates. During the 1950s and 1960s, as institution after institution devoted more attention to research and graduate education, the trend of opinion was toward the former position. The shift was largely a matter of fashion, however, unsupported by systematic research. Nor was careful examination of this question undertaken by the major study commissions of the late 1960s. Indeed, some of these groups adopted contradictory positions. The assembly, despites its criticism of excessive attention to research and narrow forms of graduate training, observed that "the most stimulating university teaching generally occurs when the individual is actively engaged in significant scholarly research."[66]

In this intellectually confused universe, individual institutions struggled with the relationship between research and teaching according to the perspectives of their leaders. There was considerable variation. Most campuses continued to assert commitments to both teaching and research. For those, like Harvard, that had moved furthest toward research, such statements came to have little bearing on the ways faculty were actually evaluated. Other campuses made impressive efforts to stress teaching effectiveness in reviewing faculty work. In Massachusetts, Tufts and UMass/Boston were notable in this respect.

Even at institutions that adopted the research ethic quite fully, there remained groups within administrations and faculties that pressed for attention to teaching. Such efforts proceeded, however, against formidable pressures. The dominant situation was summed up in 1963 by the dean of faculty at Brandeis, Leonard Levy, in response to a complaint from his president about declining faculty interest in teaching. "Like it or not," Levy wrote, teaching and related activities . . . are almost impediments toward advancement in the profession. The road to preferment, position and profit only passes through, and sometimes passes by, the classroom . . . The scholar who crystallizes DNA or wins a Bancroft prize receives all the publicity, advancement and take-home pay, regardless of how much or how well he teaches.[67]

The expectation that emerged after 1970 that academia's period of expansion was ending produced additional dilemmas in the area of graduate education. Suddenly the calls for continued expansion that had dominated commission reports in the late 1960s were discredited. The shifting perspective of the Carnegie commission registered the change. In a series of reports between 1970 and 1972, the commission first revised downward its initial recommendation for graduate school growth, then urged a halt to further development, and finally argued for cutting back programs already in place.

By the early 1970s, the worries about excessive graduate expansion merged with concerns about diminished attention to teaching to produce a consensus among the study commissions. From every side came calls to concentrate high-cost, high-quality programs of graduate education and research at a limited number of well-established institutions while reemphasizing teaching at most campuses. How this shift would be accomplished, however, given the general reorientation of universities toward the advanced academic functions, was difficult to see.[68]

The Nature of Undergraduate Education

The anger that many students displayed toward their campuses during protest activities was a puzzle. While most study commissions viewed unrest as a response to social and political problems outside the university, they tended also to believe that student dissatisfaction evidenced shortcomings within academia. The Newman panel observed that postwar expansion had been accompanied by "a large and growing number of students who voluntarily drop out," and it concluded that "college is failing to capture the attention and engage the enthusiasm of many students."[69] Indeed, events of the late 1960s led educators to be far less self-congratulatory than they had been only a few years earlier. No major commission argued, as the Rockefeller report had done twenty years before, that, on the whole, colleges and universities were doing what they should be doing and doing it well. The emphasis was on reform.

Most observers felt that reduced attention to undergraduate teaching contributed to student dissatisfaction, but deeper forces also seemed to be at work. Particularly impressive to educators was the realization that postwar expansion had fostered a generation of "involuntary students." Perhaps the pressure to attend college arose from recognition that a degree had become a prerequisite for upward mobility. Perhaps it stemmed from the expectations of parents or peers or from an intensified sense of status requirements. Or perhaps it represented the absence of other options, a situation exacerbated by the exposure of nonstudent males to conscription.

Whatever the reason, educators were surprised their students did not feel, as earlier generations had done, that higher education involved a choice and was a privilege. This perception undermined the moral position of academics—for how could they maintain standards and expel those who did not measure up when the costs of failure had risen so high? Several of the study commissions concluded that the problem of involuntary students or "reluctant attenders" could be addressed only by severing the link between higher education and certification for employment. According to the Assembly on University Goals and Governance, the nation's youth needed "alternative paths to intellectual and professional development."[70]

While noncollegiate alternatives seemed useful, they could not be expected to address important parts of academia's problems. The most severe student unrest occurred at leading universities, which enrolled the nation's most intellectually talented youngsters, poor candidates for designation as involuntary students. Was the undergraduate experience, therefore, problematic in some way, even for the academically oriented? This question led to a second line of analysis. In expanding to accommodate more students, it was widely observed, institutions had reproduced too readily traditional forms and practices—particularly full-time attendance for four years, preferably on a residential campus, right after high school—that were not suitable for some members of increasingly diverse student bodies.

Postwar expansion, indeed, had gone hand in hand with an intensified emphasis on the traditional liberal arts. The Newman report noted that public colleges and universities, historically the strongholds of occupational education, had become progressively more focused on arts and sciences. The Hester commission found the same pattern in two-year colleges. Baccalaureate-level programs also had become more intellectual, abstract, and conceptual, while concern for the personal development and socialization of students had waned. As the Newman report put it: "The present trend is for colleges to become a single type of institution which offers one mode of acquiring skills and knowledge." The Carnegic commission concluded that academic institutions had converged toward a common model of undergraduate education, both in content and form. There was wide agreement that more diversity in the organization and character of undergraduate learning was needed.[71]

Patterns of development in Massachusetts confirmed these generalizations. At every major university, with the exception of Northeastern, the greatest growth in the undergraduate curriculum occurred in the arts and sciences. To some extent, of course, the stress on traditional subjects was a logical extension of enrollment policies. As universities admitted more affluent, well-prepared applicants, student bodies sought out programs modeled on those of leading campuses. But clearly, too, institutions preferred the arts and sciences. Even at Northeastern, occupational programs were modified to include more attention to liberal learning. The two new universities of the postwar years, Brandeis in Waltham and the Boston campus of the University of Massachusetts, both concentrated on these subjects. The former institution attracted academically gifted, financially comfortable, well-educated students who were likely to attend graduate school; the latter drew low- and moderate-income commuting students for most of whom the baccalaureate would be the final degree. Yet the undergraduate programs of the two campuses differed only marginally; both offered variants on a traditional liberal arts program.[72]

The preferential treatment accorded the arts and sciences in postwar growth patterns would have astonished the educators of the 1940s. Despite their disagreements, the Zook and Rockefeller groups had concurred that diversification of academic programs to accommodate more interests and abilities would be essential if higher education were going to enroll a larger proportion of the nation's youth. Instead, academia adopted the Rockefeller position that college should be concerned with abstract, academic subjects while also embracing the Zook emphasis on expanding the college-going population. By the late 1960s, this paradoxical development seemed problematic to many observers.

The Demise of General Education

Along with the question of who should go to college, the most hotly debated issue of the early postwar period had involved "general education": what core of learning should be common in the experience of every undergraduate? In the atmosphere of the mid-1940s, with its high idealism and national unity, the notion that general education could help students become citizens had captured the imagination of academics, and many institutions had created programs. Interest in this subject, however, proved ephemeral. In retrospect, publication of the Harvard Redbook marked more the end than the beginning of intense concern with general education, and the reassessments of the late 1960s lamented the lapse. The comment of the Carnegie commission was typical: "General education is now in trouble. What was once our greatest success is now becoming our greatest failure."[73]

The demise of general education was essentially a decline in requirements. The evolution of Harvard's program exemplified the pattern. Under the policy adopted in 1949, Harvard's freshmen and sophomores were offered twelve basic courses from which they had to select one in each of three broad areas of knowledge. By 1955 the faculty had increased slightly the selection of introductory courses from 12 to 17, but in the early 1960s the number passing muster as elementary general education courses mushroomed. By 1963, 55 had been approved; by 1969, 101. Reviewing this history in the early 1970s, Harvard's Dean Henry Rosovsky observed that the College had "reached an uneasy compromise between extremes, allowing enough freedom to make the constraints seem arbitrary, while constraining choices just enough to require justification of the limits . . . The drift toward a (qualified) free elective system . . . has gradually eroded the legitimacy of General Education . . ."

Some institutions were more persistent than Harvard. Both Boston College and M.I.T., which had long traditions of curricular prescription, maintained reasonably structured undergraduate programs throughout the period. A few institutions, such as the University of Chicago and St. John's, even continued to place particular emphasis on general education. Despite such variations, the thrust of change across the period, especially in the 1960s, involved a steady reduction of nonmajor requirements. The Carnegie commission concurred with Dean Rosovsky that many institutions had been gradually re-creating versions of the free-elective system that Charles Eliot had introduced in the late nineteenth century. Dismay at the educational consequences of Eliot's system, of course, had provided the initial impetus for the general education movement in the 1920s.[74]

As the references to Eliot suggested, the postwar decline of general education represented to some extent a normal, periodic swing in academic fashion. Such shifts often mirrored social and political trends, and these forces were at work in the 1950s and 1960s. The hopeful, positive postwar spirit of democratic community that had inspired general education was quickly overtaken by a more negative, nationalistic emphasis on opposing communism. McCarthy-era attacks on intellectuals weakened higher education's connection with the broader community. Under seige, the scholarly community's innate impulse toward autonomy and separation from society reasserted itself.

These tendencies were further encouraged by a social conformity during the 1950s that inspired educators, as a counterthrust, to promote individualism rather than reinforce group consciousness. The atmosphere of the 1960s, as opposition to the war in Vietnam gained momentum, pushed this evolution to a logical extreme. By the end of the decade, the 1940s' celebration of constructive social involvement was replaced by emphases on opposition to social constraints and the virtues of dissent. No major academic commission of the late 1960s argued that preparation for active citizenship should be a goal of higher education. Things had changed, the Carnegie commission observed, and academics were now more concerned with preparing students to evaluate than to participate in society.[75]

For many educators, the student protest movement provided an explicit link between the nation's social problems and the erosion of curricular structure. Aroused students of the 1960s frequently objected to institutional restrictions on their educational freedom, and faculties often responded by removing requirements. The most thoughtful reassessments of the late 1960s, however, traced the erosion of general education to more important phenomena than academic spinelessness in the face of hostile undergraduates.

The truth, the Carnegie commission argued, was that scholars of the 1960s, in contrast to their postwar counterparts, doubted their ability to say, with any precision or hope of agreement, what the purposes of undergraduate education actually were. The advancement of knowledge, especially in science, and an expanded interest in non-Western cultures had made the essential core of learning elusive. Academic training had become more specialized and rarely encouraged future faculty to contemplate the outlines of literate culture or the relationship between intellectual development and social values. As higher education grew in sophistication, moreover, interest in extracurricular activities, viewed in the 1940s as an important part of the undergraduate experience, had largely evaporated.

In essence, the reassessments of the 1960s asserted that academia's concern with general education had been swept aside by graduate education and research and that university-based colleges were now dominated by the priorities of graduate schools. A 1964 report on undergraduate education at M.I.T. illustrated the new spirit: "We faculty members are doing our own professional work. We find it open-ended, exciting and rewarding, both intellectually and emotionally. Our aim is to introduce students to the same kind of experience and reward as quickly and efficiently as we can." From this perspective, debates about the basic purposes of undergraduate education held little interest. The M.I.T. report did not discuss the preparation of students to be citizens in American society; rather it expressed the faculty's interest in educating members of the "technological community."[76]

In their reviews of general education, the study commissions of the late 1960s tended toward the same conclusion they had reached in broader assessments of undergraduate programs: institutions of higher education had moved toward a single model of learning dominated by the disciplines of the arts and sciences and committed to academic values associated with these disciplines. In confronting the consequences of this pattern for general education, the study commissions conveyed deep confusion. Most expressed distress and called for renewed efforts. But the plight of general education seemed closely tied to developments that the commissions themselves lauded, especially the strengthening of graduate education and research. None of the study groups, moreover, made any serious effort to discuss the content of general education or to explain how these programs might be revived. Something in the process by which a wide variety of institutions had evolved in the postwar years had led them to stress other goals. But exactly what forces were responsible for the unfortunate pattern, and how, if at all, they might be counteracted, remained obscure.[77]

Academy and Society: The Intensified Postwar Relationship

Debates of the 1940s had revealed deep divisions among educators about the relationship between universities and the broader society. The Zook commission had argued that academic institutions were social agencies that should adapt to changing public needs; the Rockefeller group had stressed academic traditions that transcended nations, periods, and practical problems. The Zook commission had urged greater engagement of academia in social problem solving, while the Rockefeller report warned of dangers from federal grants to support such activities. Here, as in so many other areas, the vision of Zook and his colleagues proved the better guide to future developments. Educators of the 1960s agreed that the postwar years had brought an enormous increase in the social involvements of universities.

Some aspects of the change were implicit in the growth of enrollments and the strengthening of research. The enthronement of the college degree as a credential for individual mobility greatly enhanced the social function of academia, as did the nation's heightened dependence on scholarly expertise. Moreover, growth had turned higher education into an economically significant industry in its own right. A study commissioned by a consortium of Boston-area universities found that expenditures by academic institutions and their employees were vital elements of the regional economy. Campus growth also involved universities in complex, often tense, relationships with immediate neighbors.

Most striking to the study commissions of the 1960s was the progressive deepening of academia's involvement in social problem solving, from managing military development projects, as at M.I.T., to working with municipal anti-poverty agencies, as at Brandeis and Northeastern. These were precisely the kinds of activities about which the members of the Rockefeller panel had been apprehensive, fearing that academics would lose their political neutrality and become mired in social controversy. The student protest movement revealed this concern to have been well-founded, especially in connection with defense-related work. When angry demonstrators at M.I.T. and elsewhere indicted their institutions as accomplices of unpopular government policies, they were enacting a consequence of academic reliance on federal dollars that the Rockefeller report had predicted two decades earlier.[78]

By 1970 many leaders were convinced that higher education's social involvements had gone too far. Some activities, especially classified work for government or industry, seemed inconsistent with academic values. Others, like managing military or industrial-development projects, brought little educational or scientific benefit. The President's Commission on Campus Tensions saw the burgeoning of academia's "service" function as a primary cause of its troubles. The commission argued that universities had given so much attention to applied research and social problem solving—and diverted so much attention from teaching and scholarship while becoming powerful and rich—that they had lost the moral respect traditionally accorded them.

The view that higher education's difficulties in the late 1960s and early 1970s flowed from excessive and unselective engagement with nonacademic matters was part of a broader analysis of postwar change that was widely repeated in the commission reports of the period. The essence of this perspective was that higher education had lost control of its affairs in the face of overwhelming external pressures that had been primary determinants of postwar change.

Phenomena ranging from accepting large numbers of veterans in the early postwar years, to increasing enrollments during the 1950s and 1960s, to becoming involved in contract research and social problem solving for the federal government were cited consistently as instances in which academia took on additional functions as a result of new social demands. If higher education seemed confused in its purposes, dislodged from its traditional scholarly centers, and torn by internal conflicts, the cause was often located in its vulnerability and responsiveness to demands from outside its walls.[79]

The emphasis on nonacademic forces as a cause of change was new. The historic image of colleges and universities as "ivory towers" tended, of course, to stress their insulation from the concerns of the practical world and their freedom to pursue autonomous, scholarly purposes. This classic characterization of universities as "closed systems" was prominent in the literature on academic organizations well into the 1950s.

It proved impossible to sustain, however. By 1963 Kerr had published his landmark essay arguing that academic institutions of the postwar years were being driven and shaped by social, economic, and political pressures. Increasingly, universities were depicted as "open systems" whose evolutionary trajectories were determined by their dependence upon the external environment for support and approval. A comprehensive statement of the altered assessment was provided by Daniel Katz and Robert Kahn in 1966. Parallel analyses appeared in the writings of Burton Clark, Francis Rourke and Glenn Brooks, and J. B. Lon Hefferlin. As Kerr put it at the end of the period:

> Dependent on demography, dependent on the judgment of public authority, dependent on the comparative performance of competitors, dependent on the mercies of the mass media, open to the surrounding community, vulnerable to attacks against its inadequacies, higher education . . . is becoming more conscious that it is a subsystem within the total society and that it does not lead a life entirely of its own design.[80]

It was inevitable, of course, that as universities became more-important agencies of social development they would be subjected to increased external pressures of various kinds, including government regulation. Nonetheless, the perception among educators that academia had responded too indiscriminately to external demands produced a consensus in the commission reports for a general pulling back. The Carnegie commission offered a statement of principle to guide the process. "The campus is an academic institution," the commissioners stated:

> We consider it a contradiction when the campus takes on functions which are at odds with the inherent nature of academic life. We also consider it inefficient when an academic institution takes on non-academic operations which can be performed as well or better by other institutions . . . Higher education should serve society by serving the cause of knowledge; it should serve the cause of knowledge by protecting the freedom of its members and the essential independence of its institutions; and it should protect freedom and independence by responding with consideration to the needs of society and by safeguarding its own universal values of thought and expression . . .

Prodded by such exhortations and by angry, questioning students, many campuses, M.I.T. among them, adopted new policies and administrative structures to restrict their relationships with nonacademic agencies.[81]

Professional Power and the Decline of Institutional Diversity

Not all observers shared the view that academia's connection with outside society had intensified in the postwar years. The Newman panel drew attention to opposing tendencies. Noting that faculty members had become more specialized and abstract in their knowledge, more limited in their experience to academic life, and more divergent in their values from the mainstream of society, Newman and his associates argued that most professors were no longer able to "provide students a perspective that extended beyond the limits of the campus."

One expression of this shift, Newman and his colleagues pointed out, was the academization of the undergraduate curriculum. Indeed, nothing symbolized the movement away from society more clearly than the altered focus of debates on general education from preparing citizens to nurturing social critics. When educators of the 1940s considered their role in strengthening a "common culture," they meant the culture of the surrounding society, the nonacademic culture of which they were a part; when their counterparts in the 1960s complained that coherence had gone out of the curriculum, they were worrying about the lack of a structured introduction to the academic disciplines.[82]

The paradox to which Newman and his colleagues drew attention—that academics had become more removed from society while their social responsibilities had expanded—was rooted in a deeper contradiction of the postwar period: that power in higher education flowed simultaneously in opposite directions. Even as influence over academia's affairs moved toward external forces and agencies, the power of faculty insiders also was growing. The primary chroniclers of the latter change were Jencks and Riesman, who argued that the postwar shift of institutional power from administrative hierarchies to faculties led colleges and universities to converge toward common values and ideas—what Riesman called a national "academic culture"—associated with the professional academic disciplines.

The Jencks/Riesman assessment was echoed repeatedly by the study groups of the late 1960s. The Carnegie commission claimed that the American tradition of institutional diversity recently "began to be reversed by a trend toward homogenization. The major direction of this homogenization has been toward science, research, and graduate study and, for the individual faculty member, toward identification with a single discipline." The Newman panel offered a similar analysis: "As we have examined the growth of higher education in the postwar period, we have seen disturbing trends toward uniformity in our institutions, growing bureaucracy, overemphasis on academic credentials, isolation of students and faculty from the world—a growing rigidity and uniformity of structure that makes higher education reflect less and less the interests of society." The assembly put it this way: "Women's colleges seek men; religiously based schools are turning non-sectarian, technical schools add humanities, liberal arts colleges aspire to become graduate universities, and public state systems find political protection in copying each other. Residual differences have not vanished; the tendency, however, has been unmistakable: toward greater uniformity."[83]

Amid the multiple ironies of postwar academic change, none was more striking than the decline of institutional diversity. On the central value of such diversity, the educators of the late 1940s, so divided on other issues, had found ready agreement. Both the Zook commission and the Rockefeller group had advanced their proposals in the name of preserving diversity. Centralized, European-style systems of higher education had been universally scorned as undemocratic and inconsistent with the country's pluralistic traditions. Catholic institutions (like Boston College), engineering schools (like M.I.T.), urban universities (like Northeastern and B.U.), teaching-oriented, college-centered institutions (like Tufts), and public institutions (like UMass) had all made the maintenance of their unique characteristics a central goal of postwar development.

Conant's speech at Northeastern's fiftieth anniversary observance in 1948 had celebrated and perfectly symbolized this common perspective. But in the 1950s and 1960s, as the nation's educational leaders responded to the pressures and opportunities of the golden age, the goal of preserving institutional diversity seemed frequently to have been set aside. When, at the end of the period, academics took time to review twenty-five years of change, they were surprised, and more than a little chagrined, by what they found. Most of the study commissions issued calls for renewed attention to the value of diversity.[84]

The Roots of Paradox

Concern that colleges and universities had become too much alike to serve the nation's diverse educational needs was part of a critical consensus about postwar change that emerged from the reassessments of the late 1960s. Though there were differences of emphasis among the major commission reports of these years, an impressive feature of them—and a point of difference between the educational debates of the late 1940s and the reappraisals that took place twenty years later—was the extent of agreement on several important questions.

All the major reviews endorsed the pattern of mass higher education that had emerged in the postwar period and called for an extension of access to groups not fully integrated into the academic mainstream, especially African Americans. There was an equally unanimous dismay at the degree of class stratification that remained in a system whose members believed it had become progressively more democratic. Regret about the neglect of general education was also widespread, as was belief that higher education was rewarding research at the expense of undergraduate teaching. Other common themes were evident: that undergraduate programs had become too standardized, too academic, and too rigid to provide adequate alternatives for the variety of students who now attended college; that graduate education was giving too much emphasis to research skills and neglecting areas, especially teaching, where most faculty would spend most of their efforts; that academic institutions had become too closely associated with government policies and practical problem solving; that colleges and universities, while assuming a steadily more important role in socializing young Americans, had become more remote from the dominant culture in terms of their values as well as their interests.[85]

The critical consensus of the late 1960s was compelling and even inspiring. Yet it was strange to find academic leaders, reviewing a period in which higher education had grown more rapidly than ever before, had acquired an enhanced role in the life of the nation, and had achieved international leadership in many scholarly disciplines, adopting so negative a posture.

To some extent, of course, the questioning atmosphere expressed the defensiveness of educators after the period of student unrest, a mood markedly different from the middle 1960s. But the critical themes of many reassessments reflected more than a transient disorientation, since several of these ideas, like the importance of general education or the need for reform in graduate training, had been widespread in the 1940s.

Too often, however, the reports of study groups and commissions offered their critical appraisals one idea at a time, without presenting an integrated picture of postwar change that portrayed academia's successes and failures as part of a single, interconnected pattern. Too often, moreover, these reports had a scolding, moralistic, and hortatory quality that avoided analysis of the underlying causes of academia's problems. Too often, in fact, these reports begged the obvious question: if so many leading educators agreed on the need for certain kinds of reforms, and had so agreed for some period of time, why had higher education so stubbornly and consistently gone astray?

Why indeed? The answer required an analysis of the processes by which change occurred in the nation's academic system. To the extent that the commission reports addressed this issue, they stressed the two streams of influence that we have observed: the pressure of new social demands and the strength of academic professionalism. In the face of these powerful forces, the reports repeatedly asserted, academic institutions had been essentially reactive. Their passivity derived not only from the irresistibility of nonacademic and extrainstitutional forces but also from the diffusion of power among internal constituencies and the erosion of administrative authority that were secondary effects of external change.

This analysis led to the one theme of the reappraisals of the late 1960s that had not been debated in the 1940s: the problem of governance. In the early postwar years, educators had not worried about the capacity of their institutions to formulate policies and act in an orderly way; debate was about the actions they should take. By 1970 this was no longer true. Commission after commission argued that academic government had broken down at the institutional level and that universities had devolved into collections of warring interest groups. Similar assessments appeared in the scholarly literature on academic organizations. Most of the study commissions thought this situation problematic. For academia to regain its balance as well as its respectability, it was widely asserted, the restoration of authority on campus was an essential prerequisite.[86]

Macro-level explanations of postwar change were clearly important, and it is also easy to understand why educators were preoccupied, during years when social and professional pressures on academia were increasing exponentially, with the impact of external forces on their institutions. It is also easy, in the context of the student protest movement, to see why universities would be perceived as lacking the power to control their own affairs.

Still, the emphasis on broad forces; reactive, undirected change; and administrative helplessness obscured important realities. In particular, such analyses understated the extent to which universities could be initiating agents capable of setting goals and manipulating external forces for their own ends, even as they were responding to them. This was particularly the case at the institutional level, where leaders retained considerable authority and discretion in shaping responses to environmental forces. Even at the systemic level, however, academics could not accurately be characterized as merely acquiescent in the face of outside forces. Some of the major public policies of the postwar period—including the veterans' program, the expansion of public higher education at the state level, the rise of federal research funding, the character of selective-service legislation—reflected the concerted efforts of educators to influence government action.

In minimizing the potential for controlled institutional initiative in the change process, the common focus on macro-level forces and reactive policies also depreciated the significance of variations in response patterns among universities that were affected by common forces and pushed (or pulled) in similar directions.

To understand postwar developments more fully, it is necessary to move beyond generalizations to an examination of change at the campus level. In particular, it is necessary to consider the interactions of forces within the institutional complex as these were manifested in specific settings. Such an analysis provides the focus for the next four chapters of this book. Before turning to that review, however, it is important to consider the implications of the discussion so far for the workings of the institutional complex in the postwar period and to add one additional element to the general context of change.

We have noted shifts in each of the three elements of the institutional complex. The comparison of the academic debates of the 1940s and the 1960s revealed major changes in academic ideas and values, and these were linked to substantive intellectual developments as well as to modified perspectives, both inside and outside academia, about higher education's social role. We also have observed widespread modifications in organizational dynamics, especially with respect to the enhanced power of the faculty and the reduced role of administrators and external, nonacademic sponsors. Our assessment of individual universities will tell us more about the impact of both these trends.

A central proposition within the idea of the institutional complex is that one of the three elements—institutional ambition expressed in an ongoing competition for resources and prestige—is the most powerful. Resources, of course, were always essential, and our earlier review of the pre-World War II histories of universities in Massachusetts stressed the impact of efforts to obtain them on both academic ideas and organizational characteristics. A crucial fact about academia's postwar golden age was that the twin revolutions in college attendance and financial support made resources readily available. From the mid-1950s to the late 1960s, few universities were forced to alter programs or priorities to obtain money or students. The primary arena for interinstitutional competition, then, shifted to prestige. Here, as the reviews of the late 1960s made clear, the golden age brought fundamental change.

The rise of the research university established a new model of institutional excellence—and therefore of legitimacy and prestige—in the upper echelons of academia. The central tenet of this model was that the university whose faculty was most productive in research, as measured by publications in important scholarly outlets and, increasingly as the period advanced, by success in attracting outside funding, was the best university. The model incorporated a clear hierarchy of values: it celebrated modern, scientifically oriented research above traditional forms of interpretive or synthetic scholarship; investigation of basic problems above applied work—and therefore the arts and sciences above professional fields; research over teaching; and graduate-level training above undergraduate education. It also retained more traditional indicators of academic prestige: selective admission policies, residential facilities, and strength in the liberal arts and the elite professions. By the early 1970s, the various elements of the new model were sufficiently well established to be equated by a leading educational sociologist with the idea of academic quality, without any sense that they represented only one kind of quality, or quality viewed from a particular perspective.[87]

By becoming research universities, leading institutions altered the terms in which other campuses, occupying positions of lesser prestige, understood the requirements of upward academic mobility. Increasingly, to establish legitimacy in the eyes of crucial constituencies—students they hoped to attract, donors they hoped to impress, or faculty they hoped to recruit—campus leaders felt they needed to point to the contributions of *their* scholars or the excellence of *their* doctoral programs. Efforts by universities in Massachusetts to develop at the graduate level revealed the extent to which such policies were driven by the impulse to raise status at least as much as by intellectual values or social needs.

The most striking examples occurred at places that began the postwar period in the lowest positions on the prestige hierarchy. The case of Brandeis is particularly illuminating. The primary goal of President Abram Sachar was to move his fledgling institution up in the nation's academic ratings as quickly as possible. Although Sachar and his colleagues, inspired by the general education movement of the early postwar years, initially stressed undergraduate work, they quickly realized that a young campus could not readily gain recognition by that path, however fine their programs might be. To achieve status, they needed to attract leading, research-oriented scholars, develop Ph.D. programs, and provide the necessary conditions for scholarly productivity, including limited teaching responsibilities at the undergraduate level. These things could be bought for cash by leaders with the shrewdness and wherewithal to do so, and Brandeis possessed ample amounts of both. In the mid-1950s, the new campus shifted its priorities toward research and graduate education. Within a few years, it achieved high ratings nationally in several disciplines. In the process, the initial focus on undergraduate education weakened. A faculty committee declared the general education program dead in 1965. The Brandeis pattern was repeated, with variations, at every upwardly mobile university in Massachusetts.[88]

The compelling nature of the new model of institutional prestige goes a long way toward explaining the central paradoxes of the postwar period. Why was general education neglected despite repeated expressions of its importance? As the Brandeis story makes clear, upwardly mobile institutions could gain little prestige by stressing this goal. Indeed, by diverting the time of faculty, general education conflicted with the development of research and graduate education. Why did so many institutions shift their admission policies toward the most academically accomplished and most affluent, even though this change was at odds with professed commitments to egalitarian social goals? Because attracting better students was an important step toward raising institutional status and an important means of keeping research-oriented faculty. Why did most institutions ignore repeated calls to reform graduate education by giving greater emphasis to teaching? Because research-oriented doctorates were the most highly prized in the new model of academic excellence. Why, finally, was there a decline of institutional diversity despite innumerable statements of its importance and despite the increased range of functions performed by universities? Because, in the golden age, resources permitted it and student markets supported it.

Notwithstanding its overwhelming influence on patterns of institutional development, the new model of academic prestige was always adapted and mediated, at the campus level, by the interplay of academic ideas, organizational dynamics, and competitive pressures specific to that setting. This fact brings us back to the central paradox of our story: Massachusetts universities moved closer together in fundamental ways during the postwar years while simultaneously retaining their traditional distinctiveness. Their special qualities posed a vital question: were they simply the "residual differences" the Assembly on University Goals and Governance dismissed so disparagingly, or did they represent a genuine differentiation of function in response to multiple social needs? Implicit in this problem is another: on balance, did competition among institutions promote or diminish institutional diversity under the conditions of the golden age? On the answers to these questions must turn our judgment about the effectiveness of our system of universities in carrying out the broadened social role that academia assumed in the years following World War II. We shall be in a better position to undertake such an evaluation after examining patterns of change at individual campuses.

PART TWO

Institutions

CHAPTER THREE

Emergence of the Modern Research University: Harvard and M.I.T., 1945–1970

Harvard and M.I.T. were ideally positioned to exploit the advantageous possibilities for development that arose after World War II. Both did so, pursuing routes that reflected their different histories, stages of development, organizational characteristics, and current priorities. Both became, in the process, contrasting versions of a modern research university, together helping to define a new institutional model for the nation's academic community.

From Depression to Prosperity: The Early Postwar Years

Assessing Peacetime Possibilities During World War II

For most universities, World War II continued the difficult circumstances of the Depression, but the wartime role of academics also fostered hopes for recognition and growth in the postwar years. This optimism prompted organized planning for institutional development well before the end of the war. As Conant put it in 1943: "The period immediately following the cessation of hostilities . . . will be a time when [Harvard's] educational house can be put in order, when changes perhaps long overdue can be made most readily." The leaders of M.I.T. anticipated even more dramatic gains. Referring in 1944 to the Institute's contributions to the war effort, Compton observed that "the value, effectiveness and prestige of the Massachusetts Institute of Technology have never been at so high a level; this is certainly a strategic vantage point from which to initiate the next advance."[1]

The prewar years at Harvard had left little doubt about the "changes . . . long overdue" on which Conant would focus. From the beginning of his presidency, he had insisted that Harvard's goal should not be expansion but "intensification": the raising of intellectual standards within established programs and the reducing of concern with the social, localistic values associated with Harvard's Brahmin traditions. The two major expressions of these policies prior to 1940 had been the efforts to tighten scholarly standards for promotion in the Faculty of Arts and Sciences and to attract more able undergraduates by recruiting in public and non-northeastern secondary schools.

As Conant anticipated the postwar years, especially in the context of the veterans' program, he was aware that the new popularity of higher education might support a level of growth that had not been possible during the Depression, but he continued to oppose expansion. If demand for admission increased, Conant argued in the mid-1940s, Harvard should raise standards, not increase in size. Meanwhile, his university should take advantage of the fluid transitional period after the war to strengthen academic values in as many faculties and programs as possible.[2]

Conant's interests were concentrated in two closely related areas of activity: graduate education and research, especially in Arts and Sciences. He was convinced that basic research would play an expanding role in American life and would become, therefore, an increasingly vital function of universities. "It seems to me clear," he wrote in 1948, "that in the next few years it is the advancement of knowledge which will need the greatest encouragement and support." With high scholarly standards now required for permanent appointments, the keys to increasing Harvard's research productivity lay in providing adequate financial support for the faculty and attracting the most gifted young scholars to the Graduate School.

The Depression and war had left Conant pessimistic about endowments as a source of increased support for faculty scholarship. His financial worries undoubtedly helped persuade him to set aside his concerns about federal intervention and to advocate government subsidies for research. In the absence of such assistance, he feared, the most gifted scholars would gravitate toward industry and research institutes, and universities, especially private ones, would not be able to play the national role he thought possible for them.

In determining the quality of faculty research, the availability of talented graduate assistants seemed to Conant as important a factor as financial support. He also believed that training the next generation of scholars, no less than producing new knowledge, was "the first duty of the modern American university." Prewar patterns of graduate admission had not been encouraging, however. In Conant's view, arts and sciences had not done as well historically as medicine and law in attracting "the best brains and well-developed, forceful personalities," and he thought this problem would become more severe after the war because the veterans, having lost crucial years, were likely to favor the quick route to success offered by the professional schools. Attracting outstanding graduate students would be further complicated by competition from the best public universities of the West, which offered excellent opportunities at costs well below Harvard's. Harvard would have to recruit actively and offer more financial aid. Here, as in the area of research, Conant's advocacy of federal funding was rooted in his concern that private institutions, even one as wealthy as Harvard, could not maintain their positions without such help.[3]

In his public statements, Conant described universities as a balance of activities encompassing research, professional education, general education, and student life. His sponsorship of general education through the Redbook committee testified to his seriousness about the full range of university functions. It also was evident, however, that Conant hoped the trumpeted role of academic science in winning the war had stirred public support for universities expressly identifying research and graduate education as their central functions. If that proved true, Harvard's president was ready to spend the remainder of his term reshaping the nation's first college as a research-oriented university. How, under these hoped-for circumstances, the balance ultimately would be struck between the new priorities and the traditionalist claims of general education remained uncertain as Conant and his colleagues turned their attention from the wartime emergency to peacetime possibilities.

To the leaders of M.I.T., enlarged support for research and advanced education seemed an even more important basis for institutional progress than was the case at Harvard. When the war began, the Institute had achieved only modest gains in the directions advocated by Compton: greater emphasis on basic science, research, and graduate education and a broadening of the undergraduate curriculum combined with efforts to attract a more intellectual, less narrowly talented student body. Accepted into the Association of American Universities only in the mid-1930s, M.I.T. remained more the technical institute it traditionally had been than the focused research university its leaders wanted it to become.

The war, however, produced a remarkable effect. Suddenly the Institute was at the center of national affairs. Its leaders became the directors of the nation's effort in military science. Especially important was the experience of managing well-supported, interdisciplinary, war-research laboratories, most notably the Radiation Lab. Compton was so impressed with the work of these labs that he proclaimed a vision of a new "super-institute of technology" that would maintain under peacetime conditions the scale and technical capacity that M.I.T. created during the war. The military labs also brought to M.I.T. a group of accomplished American and European scientists who fostered a more cultured and cosmopolitan tone than had prevailed among the engineers of prewar years. In effect, World War II provided a taste of the academic environment Compton sought to establish, and he made it clear, in his readiness to continue defense-related work and his advocacy of federal support, that he intended to preserve M.I.T.'s enhanced function, status, and ambiance as much as possible.

In 1943 and 1944, Compton reported plans for postwar development based on a major expansion of educational programs, research activities, and staff. He noted a range of fields—"electronics, instrumentation, methods of propulsion, mechanisms for control of machinery, calculating devices, energy sources, plastics, organic chemistry, food technology, mechanics of materials, hydraulics, applied mathematics"—in which there had been "extraordinary developments" in recent years. He predicted that all these innovations would play "important roles in the scientific and industrial activities of the near future." He reported that the Corporation's Executive Committee already had set aside resources to support initiatives in these areas, including funds to expand interdisciplinary research facilities. Especially significant was a $250,000 appropriation to create the Research Laboratory of Electronics to carry on the work of the Radiation Lab. Compton also listed plans to build a residential campus that would attract students and to raise faculty salaries in order to lure academic talent. These developments would be associated with an upgrading rather than an enlargement of M.I.T.'s undergraduate student body. For Compton, as for Conant, the possibility of expanded demand for education after the war was more interesting as a means of raising standards than as an opportunity for growth.

The costs of change on the scale envisioned by Compton would be high, but the leaders of M.I.T.—buoyed by the recognition and support of the war years—were hopeful that the necessary support, probably including federal funds, would be forthcoming. After the frustrations of the long pause, the moment for rapid institutional progress seemed finally to have arrived.[4]

M.I.T. always had evolved in contrast to its elder sister institution in Cambridge. Its leaders had taken pride in their scientific, practical, and democratic commitments as distinct from Harvard's aristocratic and humanistic traditions. In many ways, Conant and Compton perpetuated this history of contrasts in their approaches to the postwar period. Conant's focus on returning to Harvard's prewar scale and configuration of programs was balanced by Compton's enthusiasm for change. Conant's doubts about the prospects for expansion contrasted with Compton's ambition and optimism. Above all, Conant's refusal to house large-scale, defense-related, applied-research programs differed sharply from M.I.T.'s willingness to continue such activities.

To some extent, the points of divergence between Harvard and M.I.T. expressed different stages of development as well as contrasting commitments. The Institute community had good reason, financially and academically, to welcome new opportunities more eagerly than Harvard. In fundamental ways, however, the institutional visions of Conant and Compton rested on common values. Both were representatives of the generation of American academics who believed their country and its universities should assume international leadership in scientific research, and both were determined to strengthen science, research, and graduate education. Consistent with these emphases, both also sought to place greater stress on intellectual values in undergraduate education by increasing selectivity in admissions and basing judgments of applications on measurable tests of academic ability. Thus, some of the traditional contrasts between Harvard and M.I.T. existed, within each campus, in tension with shared aspirations and commitments. The ultimate impact of these tensions on both schools was another question for the future as the postwar period began.

Postwar Restoration at Harvard

Conant remained in the presidency for seven years following World War II, resigning in late 1952 to become U.S. high commissioner to Germany. Though his postwar presidency exactly equaled his prewar term, he never refocused his attention fully on Cambridge after 1945, and his major initiatives remained those of the 1930s.

In truth, Conant's interests were transformed by his experience in Washington, and in the late 1940s he abandoned his prewar rule of noninvolvement in public affairs outside education and played a continuing, active role in national politics. He attended the Moscow conference in 1945 as an advisor to Secretary of State Byrnes, served during 1946 on the committee that drafted the Acheson–Lilienthal plan for controlling atomic energy, and helped organize the Committee on the Present Danger in 1950.

These activities required Conant to distance himself somewhat from the pressures of the Harvard presidency. That role, in any case, had become less congenial, as prewar battles between himself and the faculty and less-than-comfortable working relationships within the Corporation had taken a toll. Important duties, especially leadership of Arts and Sciences, were delegated to a provost—his choice was historian Paul Buck—and, during the last years of his term, Conant exercised only a general supervision over the affairs of Harvard.[5]

Conant's disinclination to press for major changes after the war reflected not only his personal interests but also his assessment of the circumstances of his institution and of higher education generally. His postwar presidency coincided with the years of uncertainty during which many educational leaders anticipated a contraction of their industry following the veterans' program and also worried about future financial support. Throughout these years, Conant insisted that Harvard should return to its prewar scale of operations as soon as the emergency expansion to accommodate veterans became unnecessary. Although enrollments ballooned above fourteen thousand in 1947 (representing big increases in every unit except the Medical School), by 1952 Conant had reduced Harvard's size to approximately ten thousand (only two thousand above the 1939 level), and he hoped an additional reduction of a thousand could be achieved.

Conant was also conservative about expanding programs and faculty. He did not share Compton's enthusiasm for maintaining the interdisciplinary research labs that had been created during the war and endorsed only reluctantly Buck's efforts to establish the Russian Research Center. He regularly stated that major initiatives would require new funding, and he doubted the availability of such resources. He undertook no large-scale fund-raising efforts in the postwar years (although he did preside over an expanded effort to obtain annual contributions from alumni), and he resisted reliance on newly emerging sources of support, especially by keeping Harvard's use of federal research dollars at a modest level. In his final report, Conant warned against the "deficit financing" associated with "temporary grants from foundations or government contracts." The deteriorating political environment of higher education that came with the advent of McCarthyism after 1950 added to Conant's pessimism. In combination, the demographic, financial, and political circumstances of the early postwar years sustained Conant in the view that Harvard should not undertake significant new commitments.[6]

Given the nature of Conant's leadership, the changes that occurred at Harvard between 1945 and 1952 were ones that flowed naturally from the policy initiatives of the prewar years and the externalities of the postwar situation. As things developed, these changes were not insignificant, although they did not represent the clear pattern of administrative initiative that might have derived in more expansive times from Conant's vision of a research university.

An example was the altered character of the undergraduate student body. From the beginning of his presidency, Conant had wanted to attract students who were "more representative in terms of both geography and family income" than those who traditionally had come to Harvard. These objectives expressed not only his distaste for artificial barriers to talent but also his belief that the College should incorporate more fully the values of the Graduate School and his conviction that Harvard should build links to new centers of wealth and power beyond the Northeast. Conant's prewar efforts to modify admission policies, especially the program of National Scholarships, had been a disappointment, but postwar circumstances proved conducive to success.

The first indications of a new atmosphere in the College came from Harvard's encounters with women and veterans. Both the Radcliffe students who joined undergraduate classes during the war and the older men who arrived after 1945 brought a greater academic seriousness than had been present before 1940. Their presence built support for Conant's emphasis on merit-oriented admissions and standardized tests to evaluate applicants. A decision to retain coeducation was made in 1947 without controversy (though with cautious attention to alumni response). At the same time, Harvard initiated a national effort to recruit talented undergraduates through its regional alumni associations.

Throughout the postwar years, Conant stressed the importance of keeping Harvard within reach of students of limited means. A program of financial aid was established with the goal of supporting at least 25 percent of the undergraduates. Tuition was kept low. Conant authorized increases totaling only two hundred dollars—from four hundred to six hundred dollars—between 1945 and 1952, despite severe inflation and a national trend toward higher student charges. At the end of his tenure, Conant took a final step to institutionalize his democratic philosophy by creating a new deanship empowered to coordinate admissions and financial aid, thus ensuring a maximum chance to enroll able students without regard to their financial circumstances. To this new post, he appointed Wilbur J. Bender, an architect of the National Scholarships in the 1930s and a man passionately committed to opening Harvard's gates more widely. In the context of the national trend toward greater interest in college, Harvard's efforts produced a steady rise in applications from nonveterans.

With demand growing while Conant was scaling back enrollments, admissions became much more selective. Between 1945 and 1952, the rejection rate doubled in comparison with the 1930s—from the 20 percent range to the 40 percent range—marking a basic divide between the comfortable, parochial, class-oriented, prewar atmosphere of admissions and the competitive intensity of the postwar years. From Conant's perspective, the change brought a welcome enhancement of academic standards, but the gains were far less clear in terms of his wish to make Harvard's students more representative of American society. In 1952, for example, the percentage of freshmen from outside the Northeast was only 1 percent higher than in 1940, although the emphasis within the northeastern states continued to shift from Massachusetts and New England to New York and the Middle Atlantic region. Shifts in the social origins of Harvard students are harder to measure, but, to the extent that the distribution between public and private school backgrounds was indicative, postwar change also was modest. In 1930, about 44 percent of Harvard's freshmen came from public schools, compared with 48 percent in 1952.[7]

While policies on admission and enrollment were "intensifying" Harvard College in ways Conant felt appropriate for a research university, a parallel evolution was occurring in the professional schools. It had become clear before the war that Conant was comfortable with only two approaches to graduate education. The first, pursued in the 1930s in Arts and Sciences, Dental Medicine, and the Medical School, emphasized faculty research and the training of future researchers. The second involved the preparation of elite practitioners in such intellectually demanding fields as law and business. In the postwar years, these emphases were heightened and extended to additional units.

Conant encouraged all graduate schools to return to prewar enrollment levels as demand for admission expanded in the late 1940s. Here, as in the College, the intensified competition for places was increasingly mediated by meritocratic standards. Conant was particularly proud of the Law School. As late as 1937, Law had accepted "virtually any graduate," but after the war it pursued selective admissions with great success. The stronger emphasis on research was especially evident in the Medical School, where the number of post-doctoral investigators in medical science expanded rapidly while that of future M.D.s remained at prewar levels. Similar priorities were evident in Public Health, which was reorganized in 1946 to broaden its scope and increase research productivity. In both the Medical School and Public Health, federal research dollars provided vital support for change. In the same years, the Graduate School of Engineering was dissolved, and its faculty was re-created as the Division of Engineering and Applied Physics within Arts and Sciences.[8]

The boundaries of Conant's vision of graduate education were illustrated most clearly by his continuing efforts to reform the Graduate School of Education. In the 1930s, he had endorsed a scheme for this unit based on the Law/Business elite-practitioner model. The heart of the plan was a new master's degree for teachers, the M.A.T., to be supervised jointly by the faculties of Education and Arts and Sciences, with the latter group ensuring academic rigor. During the war, however, cooperation between the two schools had broken down, and by 1945 no organizational basis for the joint degree remained.

It occurred to Conant at this point that education might not belong at Harvard, but he believed too deeply in the social importance of this field to abandon it altogether. A new conception of the "Ed" School was developed, this one based on the research model. A small faculty rooted in the social sciences would conduct policy research and train an elite corps of administrators and analysts. Conant believed in the new plan but failed to raise adequate funds to support it or to recruit a distinguished social scientist to the deanship. The dean he finally appointed, Francis Keppel, quickly abandoned the new plan and returned to practitioner training by resurrecting the M.A.T. In the end, neither of Conant's models of academic quality worked in a professional field in which the primary challenge, always, was the training of school teachers (who probably could never be quite brilliant enough for Harvard's president) and in which scholarly research lacked a clear focus and disciplinary basis.[9]

Conant's failure to bring the Graduate School of Education within his idea of a research university was an exception to the general pattern of his presidency. Indeed, despite the undramatic, incremental nature of change in the postwar years, the cumulative impact of Conant's leadership was decisive for the future of his institution. At the time of his appointment in 1933, Harvard still was dominated by the Brahmin, Yankee, "collegiate" traditions that Conant's predecessor, Lowell, had epitomized. By 1952 Conant's emphases were well entrenched. New standards for hiring, promotion, and tenure placed primary value on scholarly distinction and research productivity. Graduate and professional education were now seen as the heart of Harvard's educational mission. Admission to most units had become competitive with acceptance increasingly based on academic criteria.

The culture of Harvard had been altered also, in part due to external events. The Depression and war had reinforced Conant's impulse to replace local and regional perspectives with national and international concerns. The Holocaust had exposed the implications of comfortable prewar parochialisms, while the appointment of several expatriate Jews strengthened the shift toward cosmopolitan and scholarly values. Harvard's leaders were now aware that private donations from the region's elites no longer constituted a viable financial basis for institutional development. In 1947 Conant undertook the ultimate—and long-delayed—effort to transform Harvard by replacing Bostonians on the ruling Corporation with representatives of other regions. He fought a long battle to fill a vacancy with a prominent Baltimore attorney instead of a young Boston banker favored by some of the fellows. Conant won, but the costs were high, and the episode added to the somewhat sour atmosphere that characterized Conant's final years.

Conant regarded the changes he promoted as no more than shifts in the balance among Harvard's traditional concerns. The success of the general education program in the early postwar years supported this view. Though the modest requirements adopted in 1949 fell short of the Redbook proposals, the new courses attracted some of Harvard's most celebrated professors—Conant himself taught one—and students often remembered these courses as highlights of their collegiate experiences.

Despite its strengths, general education represented a weak countercurrent in the stream of change that Conant championed. The prominence of this program in the early postwar years expressed not only the idealistic mood of the nation and of higher education but also the absence of an environment in which Harvard could make dramatic advances on the central points of Conant's agenda. The continuing balance between undergraduate and graduate education, between teaching and research, between the old collegiate concerns and the new university values owed as much to Harvard's constrained resources—as husbanded by a fiscally conservative president—as to educational commitments.[10]

The Transformation of M.I.T.

Compton's vision of possibilities for institutional advance were quickly evident after the war. The atmosphere of M.I.T.'s "rapid mobilization for peace" was described by Compton's vice president, James Killian:

> Those who served on the Institute's governing boards . . . will long remember the excitement and urgency of reconversion. They will remember how a housing program for married veterans . . . was planned and started before federal funds became available. They will remember how we improvised to handle the tidal wave of applicants . . . They will remember the search for new talent in the war research laboratories, which . . . quickly brought to the Institute a remarkable group of "cream of the crop" graduate students and a number of major and outstanding faculty appointments . . . New programs were adopted, as in Food Technology, in Economics, in the Humanities, in Electronics, and Nuclear Science; departments were rebuilt and given new directions, as in the School of Architecture and Planning; new facilities blueprinted and financing started, as exemplified by the Gas Turbine Laboratory, the great Charles Hayden Memorial Library, and the Senior House.

The dramatic efforts to expand and develop M.I.T. reflected the belief of Compton and his colleagues that the war had so heightened public appreciation of science and technology that it would be possible to sustain initiatives aimed at international leadership in specific fields. As national figures, both Compton and Bush advocated more support for research and education in science and technology. As officers of M.I.T., they positioned their institution to catch a wave of cultural change that could carry it to the forefront of scientific advance.[11]

While the veterans provided a crucial part of M.I.T.'s postwar atmosphere, long-term developments in programs, faculty, and facilities were more important. Priorities were continuous with Compton's policies of the 1930s: the strengthening of science, both as an independent area of study and as a foundation for engineering; and the broadening of the curriculum, especially in the social sciences and humanities.

Of seventeen appointments to the rank of full professor between 1945 and 1947, six were in the basic sciences and mathematics, including new heads for the Chemistry and Mathematics departments. Two were in the social sciences. The largest number came in the Physics Department. New heads also were recruited for four of six engineering departments to achieve closer links with basic science. The new appointments relied heavily on contacts made through war research work. For example, in 1945 Compton sent a young physicist, Jerrold Zacharias, to Los Alamos to recruit as many top people as possible. The success of this and similar ventures produced a new standard for Institute faculty. "In every major appointment," wrote Killian, "we sought to answer affirmatively the question: is the candidate the best available man in the country, or even the world, to fill the post?" To reinforce the senior ranks, an additional fifty-one new faculty members were added at lower levels between 1945 and 1947.

Expansion of research capacity was even more striking than growth of instructional staff. Compton worked hard to maintain the research facilities built up during the war and continued to rely heavily on military contracts. In the first two postwar years, 442 research and support staff were hired, and in 1947 the total budget for contract research stood at ten million dollars, a reduction from the wartime peak but twenty times larger than the highest prewar level.

The impact of new activities was striking. In 1947 the full-time staff included 5,700 persons, compared with 1,500 before World War II. The budget quadrupled to fourteen million dollars. To accommodate growth, Compton and his colleagues undertook the most ambitious building program since the move to Cambridge. Facilities erected during the war with government support were taken over and converted. New construction was undertaken, including the residential complex across Massachusetts Avenue called "west campus." These investments symbolized the belief of M.I.T.'s leadership that World War II had been a turning point for their institution. The emergence of the old "Technology" as an international center for scientific research was symbolized and conspicuously celebrated at the Mid-Century Convocation in 1949, where international leaders from academia and government gathered to discuss the future of science and to hear Winston Churchill affirm the indispensable role of scientists (and of the Institute) in the war against Nazism.[12]

Despite the heady atmosphere, the advances of the early postwar years raised troubling questions about the Institute's basic character, its role among other institutions of higher education, and the internal distribution of power. Would the increased emphasis on science ultimately reduce engineering to secondary importance? Would advanced research and graduate work undermine historic commitments to undergraduate teaching? Finally, would the proliferation of new activities destroy traditions of small size, limited objectives, and a unified community? Would high levels of sponsored research place the Institute at the mercy of external forces?

By 1947 the pace of change had created sufficient concern on these points for Killian to suggest a faculty committee—called the Committee on Educational Survey—to "reexamine the principles of education that had served as a guide to academic policy at M.I.T. for almost ninety years and to determine whether they are applicable to the conditions of a new era emerging from social upheaval and the disasters of war." The chair was assigned to Warren Lewis, professor of chemical engineering, who had served with Compton at the N.D.R.C. and O.S.R.D. during the war.

The Lewis committee worked for two years, 1947 to 1949, while Compton and the Executive Committee proceeded to add faculty, programs, and facilities. With the broad directions of these initiatives, the committee was sympathetic, and at no point was it inclined to oppose the evolution that Compton was leading. The issues, rather, were how far the changes should go and how much they could be reconciled with M.I.T.'s traditional functions. The committee's report provided balanced answers to both questions.

Reviewing the Institute's history, Lewis and his associates argued that close links between science and engineering had been fundamental from the outset, despite some deviation from this path, mostly during the 1920s. They also noted that changes in the nature of technology were making such ties more important than ever. Thus, the Institute could embrace Compton's policies while remaining true to its traditions. The committee reported, for example, that it had considered abandoning undergraduate education—especially in professional fields—in favor of graduate work and research but had rejected this idea. In particular, it reaffirmed the baccalaureate degree as appropriate for engineering and opposed a shift to advanced training, as had occurred in law and medicine in the 1920s.

The committee also stressed that M.I.T. should limit expansion and maintain a clear focus on science and technology. It proposed a "four school" concept of organization based on separate units for Engineering, Science, Architecture, and Humanities and Social Studies (later changed to Humanities and Social Science). The latter unit was especially innovative and was associated with the committee's recommendation for a general education program even more extensive than that adopted by Harvard.

In some respects, the Lewis report argued that M.I.T. could have its future both ways on several major issues. Science, research, and graduate instruction could be advanced, while traditions in engineering, teaching, and undergraduate education continued to be honored. A limited focus on science and technology could be kept, while the curriculum was broadened and a School of Humanities and Social Studies equal to the other schools was developed. M.I.T. could remain small and unified while playing a dominant role nationally in its fields of emphasis. Reliance on contract research for financial support could continue while independence as an academic institution was maintained. There were reasons to doubt at least some of these comforting messages, but the Lewis committee reassured the Institute's traditionalists on the most worrisome points and constructed a conceptual bridge between a respectable past and a dazzling future.

Compton endorsed a document that entailed no major modifications of his plans. He especially welcomed the committee's emphasis on the undergraduate curriculum, though privately he expressed concern that the new School of Humanities and Social Studies could lead to an unwise expansion and loss of focus. The report was well received by both scientists and engineers. Even technically oriented faculty inclined to regret the changes anticipated by the report could not quarrel with the argument that their fields had moved closer to basic science. As historian Elting Morison has observed, it was the rise of electrical engineering, with its requirements in math and physics, and the decline of mechanical and civil, "that imperceptibly moved everybody towards Compton . . ." In rationalizing continued development that would accord with the new priorities of the 1930s, the Lewis committee opened the way to major organizational change with a minimum of conflict.[13]

The ebullience of M.I.T.'s leaders was tempered by nagging concerns about finances. The Institute's resources were vast, of course, in comparison with most universities. In 1940 its endowment ranked fifth nationally, and it had the ability to attract ongoing support in large amounts from private sources. Federal contracts provided additional funds. Still, the ambitious plans launched by Compton and his colleagues strained finances in the short run and implied a substantial increase in income over time. Compton continued to express confidence that federal support would grow, but in the late 1940s the future of government science policy remained unclear. Indeed, the Zook commission was proposing an aid program that specifically excluded private institutions. Moreover, even if government support continued, the Institute's leadership worried about losing their independence by relying on such assistance.

Expanding income from traditional, private sources also seemed problematic. The prospect of a capital campaign was uncertain in the early postwar years, as Conant's pessimism about new resources was illustrating at Harvard. Private foundations were no longer willing to use their funds to build endowments or basic facilities. M.I.T.'s last capital campaign, in the 1930s, had not been successful, and it was not clear that universities could attract any longer the large contributions that had been forthcoming in the late nineteenth and early twentieth centuries, such as Eastman's crucial gift during the Maclaurin years. At the same time, return on the existing endowment was declining as a result of lower rates of return and inflation. Between 1940 and 1948, the Institute's endowment income per student (after removing the temporary bulge of veterans from the calculation) diminished from $500 to $350. In this uncertain financial environment, M.I.T.'s leadership took a series of steps to secure their financial position while continuing to campaign for federal support of academic science.

The most ambitious initiative was a twenty-million-dollar capital campaign announced in 1948 and kicked off by the Mid-Century Convocation in 1949. Noting that this would be the second largest fund drive ever undertaken by a private institution, Compton characterized M.I.T.'s effort as a test to "determine whether privately supported institutions . . . in the free enterprise system will continue their effectiveness and leadership." The theme of ensuring the continued excellence and supremacy of private universities in the face of an expanding role for public institutions—and in the cultural context of the Cold War, with its anti-collectivist implications—was a continuing element of this campaign. While launching the fund drive, Compton also installed a variant of the old Technology Plan established by Maclaurin after World War I. Corporations would be asked to contribute large sums over a period of years in return for special privileges. A new Industrial Liaison Office was established to coordinate the effort.[14]

Having initiated an ambitious financial program, Compton resigned the presidency to become chairman of the Corporation, a position created for his predecessor, Samuel Stratton, but vacant since Stratton's death in 1931. The decision combined personal and institutional considerations. His health was poor, and he had been subject to heart disease in middle age, suffering his first stroke in 1936 and a succession of minor ones in subsequent years. At age sixty-one, he needed to husband his energies, and the chairmanship permitted him to maintain an important local role while responding to regular calls for participation in national affairs. Compton was also concerned that his vice president, James Killian, might accept an offer to move elsewhere unless he were promoted to the presidency, and he was prepared to step aside in favor of his longtime aide, who was promptly installed by the Corporation.

For the next six years, until his death in 1954, Compton devoted himself to representing his institution and its needs to the public. He traveled widely to address alumni/ae groups and lobbied corporate leaders in support of the financial campaign and the Industrial Liaison Program. He also served briefly as chairman of the Research and Development Board of the Department of Defense, a position that afforded him close contact with developing national priorities in applied science.[15]

While the capital campaign was addressed to M.I.T.'s long-term financial health, the Institute had an immediate need for cash to support its expanded operations. The Industrial Liaison Program helped by providing "rather large sums for . . . research and advanced education," but the task of serving business also resulted, as Compton put it, in "the warping of desirable programs." In this financial context, enlarged tuition revenues became an essential component of the Institute's short-term strategy, and the veterans' program became the vehicle by which this strategy was carried out. Like Harvard, M.I.T. allowed its enrollments to expand far beyond normal levels to accommodate the needs of veterans. By 1947 total enrollments neared fifty-seven hundred, over two thousand above the "stable" level Compton had projected in 1944 for the postwar years. This expansion was coupled with tuition hikes in 1947 and 1948, the years of maximum veterans' enrollment, to increase revenues to levels sufficient not only to support the new scale of operations but also to finance development projects.

The importance of increased tuition revenues became especially apparent after the peak of veterans' enrollments had passed. Like Conant, Compton had indicated in his plans for the postwar period that M.I.T.'s interest in growth was limited and that, if applications increased, the Institute would use the situation chiefly to raise standards. The expansion to accommodate veterans had been undertaken as a temporary measure to meet a national need. In the late 1940s, however, the Institute sought to maintain enrollments close to the 1947 peak, and when the numbers dipped by modest amounts in 1950 and 1951— to forty-nine hundred in the latter year—Killian expressed alarm and mounted a recruitment campaign. To some extent, the maintenance of expanded enrollments supported the Institute's educational objectives, since most of the growth occurred in science and in graduate programs. It also became clear, however, that, despite their goal of raising academic standards, the Institute's leaders were ready to pay a price in quality in order to maintain size. In the four years between 1948 and 1951, freshman applications declined from thirty-four hundred to twenty-five hundred, while the number admitted increased from eleven hundred to twelve hundred.[16]

M.I.T.'s policies in the areas of enrollment, financial development, and federally sponsored research illustrated the risks that Compton and his colleagues were prepared to accept in order to mount their program of change. In all these areas, M.I.T.'s leaders, eager to reshape their technical institute as a research university, made compromises that their more conservative, better-established colleagues at Harvard found unacceptable. The potential problems were apparent and were carefully debated but seemed modest in relation to the possibilities of the time. Moreover, looking ahead, Compton and his associates anticipated that evolving government policies, expanded private support, and increased public interest in science and in technological education would establish reliable bases for sustaining their reconstructed institution at its enhanced level of activity and eminence.

New Conditions, New Leaders, New Perspectives

The departures of Conant and Compton from active leadership at Harvard and M.I.T. ended an era of academic change in Cambridge. Both had redirected priorities toward those activities, especially research and advanced education, that, in their shared view, defined the mainstream of academic advance, but both had served during two decades in which the potential for development was limited by exceptional difficulties. As they exited, however, more hopeful circumstances were emerging. The erratic student markets of the 1930s and 1940s were being replaced by an extended period of strong demand for undergraduate programs. The expansion of academic institutions that was becoming a national phenomenon ensured jobs for the products of leading graduate schools. New possibilities for financial assistance—including government aid and increased parental income—made it clear that the long period of uncertainty about resources was coming to an end. In the early 1950s, having been repositioned by the transforming presence of two forceful leaders, both Harvard and M.I.T. faced circumstances conducive to major advances along well-defined lines.

The new conditions were quickly registered at the Institute. In 1951 the capital campaign was brought to a successful conclusion, with $25.4 million raised. This success convinced M.I.T.'s leaders of their ability to raise funds from private sources at a level unimaginable before the war. Simultaneously, following the outbreak of war in Korea, federal expenditures for defense research increased sharply, initiating a period of national rearmament that would continue for two decades. No one at M.I.T. doubted that the military build-up would bring large-scale support to the campus. At the same time, the worrisome situation in admissions reversed itself. In 1952 applications turned upward after declining for two years, beginning a period of growing demand for the Institute's programs.[17]

M.I.T.'s new president, James R. Killian, Jr., had been associated with the

Institute since his undergraduate days in the 1920s. In 1939, after a period with the *Technology Review,* ultimately as editor, he had become Compton's executive assistant and during the war had assumed major administrative responsibilities while Compton concentrated on national affairs. Appointed vice president in 1945 and president in 1948, Killian was the first alumnus to achieve the Institute's highest administrative office.

So compatible were Killian's ideas with those of his predecessor that the change in leadership was scarcely noticeable, especially with Compton continuing as chairman of the Corporation. By the early 1950s, however, Killian was convinced that the primary goals of the Compton years—national leadership in scientific research and in graduate instruction in science and engineering—had been achieved and that the times offered an opportunity for a new stage of evolution. Emphasis now could be given to diversifying M.I.T.'s sphere of activity while preserving and strengthening its position in its traditional fields.[18]

Killian's conception of a broader Institute included two basic components. First, he wanted to redesign the undergraduate program to attract more versatile, less technically oriented graduates who could become leaders in industry and government, not just staff scientists. Compton had hoped for such a shift since the 1930s, but in the early 1950s, with the program of general education in place, with the School of Humanities and Social Studies on the way, and with prospects for a steadily increasing demand for admission, the transition seemed within reach. The second aspect of Killian's vision complemented the first: to extend the range of the faculty and program by recruiting outstanding persons outside the sciences and promoting interactions among scholars from different fields like those that had proved so productive during World War II.

The prospect of changing the character of M.I.T. produced an exciting intellectual environment within the campus community. The Institute was to become a full university, but not a classical one like Harvard. Killian believed strongly in maintaining his school's distinctive character. "A great university," he later wrote, "must possess [an] institutional personality . . . that is an amalgam of tradition, past accomplishments, standards, and values . . ." M.I.T.'s new president, however, was less a visionary who could enunciate an enriched conception of M.I.T. than a gifted organizer who could elicit ideas from the community he led. He evoked a new model for M.I.T. through widespread, informal discussions within the faculty and administration.

The unique strength, manifestly, lay in science and its applications, and the formula that evolved was a diversified institution in which not just explicitly scientific topics but also science-related social and philosophical issues and scientific modes of thought would be emphasized. M.I.T. was at last to blossom into the "scientific university" of which Richard Maclaurin had dreamed before World War I. The School of Humanities and Social Studies would stress quantitative approaches to the social sciences and the social implications of technology. A separate School of Industrial Management also would be established, based on an existing program in the School of Engineering. This unit, too, would focus on points of contact between management disciplines and scientific techniques. To house the new M.I.T. and symbolize its transition toward educational goals and patterns associated with more conventional universities, residential facilities would be enlarged. Killian summarized the new ideal in a phrase that expressed his wish to synthesize M.I.T.'s tradition of limited purposes and practical studies with the characteristics of a modern, research-oriented university: M.I.T. was no longer to be an institute of technology, he announced, but a "university polarized around science, engineering, and the arts."[19]

The new president of Harvard, Nathan Marsh Pusey, felt no comparable need to reinvent his institution. Harvard, after all, was the model against which other universities measured themselves and from which others—especially M.I.T.—attempted to differentiate themselves. The challenge at Harvard, Pusey felt, was to reverse the cautious policies of the final Conant years and open the campus to a more contemporary and expansive spirit. What this general view might mean would have to be determined, Pusey thought, in the context of particular schools and programs. He had no specific views about academic directions in which Harvard should evolve comparable to those with which Conant or Lowell had entered their presidencies earlier in the century.

Pusey was an alumnus, like every Harvard president in anyone's memory. He had taken both his undergraduate and graduate degrees in classics and had embarked on a teaching career at Wesleyan shortly before World War II. His first major administrative responsibility had come in 1944 when he was chosen president of Lawrence College in Appleton, Wisconsin, a position he held at the time the Corporation called him back to Cambridge. As both teacher and president, Pusey had won an enviable reputation, yet his selection was a surprise, not least to Pusey himself. He had not cultivated ties to Harvard since his student days. Having been born and raised in Iowa, he was hardly in the Boston tradition that had produced Eliot, Lowell, and, with a modern twist, Conant.

He had not campaigned for the job. Speculation about the Corporation's reasons for selecting him centered on his ties to the humanities and to undergraduate education, possibly useful correctives after twenty years of Conant. There was also talk of his potential capacities as a fund-raiser, since he had been successful in this respect at Lawrence. He possessed impeccable credentials as a conservative, midwestern Christian at a time when universities were coming under attack—especially from a senator from the new president's state—as havens for suspect and alien ideas. Since the Corporation retained their tradition of conducting presidential searches in absolute secrecy, such explanations remained little more than educated guesses. In subsequent interviews, members of the Corporation made one thing clear: the group had wearied of Conant's propensity to involve himself in external affairs and wanted a leader who would devote himself to Harvard.[20]

Pusey's understanding of the conditions affecting higher education diverged sharply from those of his predecessor. He rejected (what he understood to be) Conant's belief that the era of American growth had ended, and he was impressed by indications of increased demand for education and expanded support for academic research. He thought the 1950s and 1960s would be years of opportunity, and he wanted Harvard to assert national leadership, not only educationally but also financially. Pusey felt that Harvard's policies set national standards, and he had observed, as a college president in the 1940s, how Conant's restrictive attitudes made it difficult for other institutions to respond to the opportunities of the postwar years. Pusey envisioned a new period of development for Harvard, though the directions of change remained undefined.[21]

Consolidating the New Focus:
Research and Graduate Education

Pusey's Early Years: Uncertain Academic Directions

In 1960 Pusey reflected on his first eight years as Harvard's president. "If there has been a single, dramatic change within our universities within the past two decades," he wrote, "it is the enormous amount of research now done within them . . ." Pusey placed his own institution at the center of this trend and believed the change had altered Harvard's educational priorities. "Simply stated," he later wrote, "Harvard's purpose is to conduct research and to produce a continuing flow of highly trained people for a wide variety of careers . . ." The new focus on research and graduate education represented, Pusey believed, the triumph in Cambridge and America of German academic values over the British tradition of liberal undergraduate education that had dominated top universities before World War II.

The new priorities were, of course, those of Conant, whose intellectual roots were in German science. Indeed, in a memoir written in the 1970s following his retirement from Harvard, Pusey argued that the enhanced role of science had been the driving force of change during his presidency. "It is difficult," he wrote, "to exaggerate the impact made on colleges and universities by the increased attention paid to science during these years . . . [it] flourished . . . as never before, and in the process universities were transformed. They became fully committed research, as well as teaching institutions . . . The graduate school . . . finally and unquestionably supplanted the college as the major institution of higher education in the United States." It was also clear to Pusey that "what encouraged and sustained this great development—indeed what made it possible—were the very large sums" made available by the federal government to support both scientific work and the training of scientists.[22]

Pusey's readiness to celebrate the values of the research university emerged gradually during the early years of his presidency. Indeed, in the middle 1950s, as he worked toward understanding the complex institution he now led, Pusey directed administrative energy toward other concerns. An early priority, for example, was undergraduate expansion. Assuming his duties at a time when educational leaders were beginning to grasp the enrollment pressures that would appear after 1960, Pusey believed that Conant's policy of scaling back undergraduate numbers—a policy still being applied in 1953 and 1954— would have to be reversed. He began planning for new houses and asked the

Committee on Educational Policy of the Faculty of Arts and Sciences to provide guidance. The committee reported that expansion would enjoy little faculty support and, indeed, would arouse much opposition, an attitude that was reaffirmed in a second committee review in 1960.

Faced with resistance, Pusey did not press the matter of growth. In fact, Harvard College expanded only marginally (9 percent) during an eighteen-year presidency that coincided with the most intense increase in demand for undergraduate education in the nation's history. The little growth that did occur resulted from reduced attrition rather than increased admissions, since Harvard accepted progressively fewer applicants during the 1950s and 1960s. By the middle 1950s, noting strong faculty support for enlarging graduate enrollments in Arts and Sciences, Pusey was arguing that Harvard's response to public pressures for enhanced undergraduate opportunities should be the training of Ph.D.s.[23]

Pusey's appreciation of the significance of postwar interest in scientific research and of enlarged federal support also evolved slowly. His early reports did not draw attention to these matters. In fact, in addition to the College, the programs that Pusey identified as requiring special attention at the beginning of his presidency were Divinity and Education. His efforts to restore the Divinity School marked with special clarity the change from Conant, who had no interest in religion and wanted to shut down Harvard's school, which he regarded as moribund. Pusey launched a campaign for Divinity within days of his appointment, devoted much personal attention to the effort, and told faculty members that the "queen of theology" would again receive her proper due.

Pusey agreed with Conant, however, on the need to be conservative about federal financial support. He reaffirmed his predecessor's policies that Harvard should not depend for the salary of permanent appointees on external funds, should not conduct classified research in peacetime, and should not manage large-scale, applications-oriented research and development facilities. Pusey's dean of Arts and Sciences, McGeorge Bundy, summarized the Harvard view that outside funds should be accepted only to support activities that the faculty was independently inclined to pursue: "Our business with the government," Bundy wrote, "was a product of choices by our faculty, not the other way around."

Within this policy context, the importance of federal research support during Pusey's first years remained at the level allowed by Conant, about 10 percent of income for departmental instruction and research and 17 percent of total income. In his fund-raising appeals, Pusey stressed the importance of maintaining established balances among the disciplines against the press of federal support toward science. He was proud that his exertions kept support for the humanities growing as rapidly as for the sciences during the 1950s. When the Soviet launching of *Sputnik I* evoked calls from many academic leaders for greater efforts in scientific research and education, Pusey downplayed the event. The Soviet triumph, he told readers of his 1958 report, carried no mandate for change at Harvard.[24]

M.I.T. Seizes the Moment

The leadership of M.I.T. displayed much greater clarity than their Harvard counterparts about the proper relationship of their institution to the new circumstances of higher education. On the subject of sponsored research, for example, especially research supported by the federal government, President Killian outlined the Institute's policies in the following terms in 1953:

> . . . The Institute prefers not to limit itself to any narrow or doctrinaire definition of what is appropriate research for an educational institution . . . We know from extensive experience that sponsored research can enrich our educational program, and we do not share the extreme view sometimes expressed that sponsored research ipso facto is bad for education . . . In addition, we have recognized an inescapable responsibility in this time of crisis to undertake research in support of our national security which under normal circumstances we would choose not to undertake . . .

Indeed, as defense-related federal subsidies for academic science turned upward following the outbreak of war in Korea, M.I.T. quickly established itself—by a wide margin—as the nation's leading recipient. A special Division of Defense Laboratories was established to manage this work, much of which occurred in two large units, the Lincoln and Instrumentation labs. By 1952 the Division of Defense Labs was conducting federal projects costing over fourteen million dollars annually. In this same year, M.I.T.'s total receipts for current expenses from the national government, chiefly for sponsored research, exceeded thirty-one million dollars (71 percent of operating income) compared with six and a half million dollars (18 percent of operating income) at Harvard.[25]

Although Killian initially attributed some of the Institute's participation in federally sponsored research to the national-security crisis of the early 1950s, the close relationship between M.I.T. and the government was maintained and even intensified in subsequent years. By 1957, just before *Sputnik I,* government contracts for sponsored research had nearly doubled from the 1952 level to fifty-nine million dollars. Institute faculty and staff met regularly with high-ranking military and national security officers in a series of "summer studies" intended to identify emerging policy problems, especially in national defense. From these collaborative retreats came a steady flow of new research contracts for M.I.T. The Institute's ties to the federal scientific and defense bureaucracies were further strengthened by Killian's appointment to the newly created post of White House science advisor in November 1957, a month after the Soviet space triumph. Repeating the pattern established by Karl Compton seventeen years earlier, Killian went to Washington, where he played a central role in shaping the nation's response to the Soviet technological challenge, including the massive expansion of federal support for academic science.[26]

Killian's presidency established a pattern of development that was maintained throughout the 1960s under his two sucessors, Julius Stratton (1957–1966) and Howard Johnson (1966–1971). Both were insiders chosen through a closed process within the Corporation. Stratton was a physicist who had spent his entire professional life at M.I.T., had headed the Research Laboratory of Electronics, had supported actively the new directions of the Compton and Killian years, and had served under Killian as provost and vice president. Johnson, a former professor of management, was completing a term as dean of the Sloan School (as the School of Industrial Management was renamed) at the time of his election. Both choices emphasized continuity, as did Killian's return as chairman of the Corporation in 1959, a position he would retain until 1971.

During both presidencies, with government support flowing liberally, federal and defense-related research expanded steadily. By 1968 the annual federal subsidy for M.I.T.'s research program reached $150 million, compared to a total Institute budget of $3.7 million in 1940. On the strength of this support, interdisciplinary research labs multiplied from five in 1949 to nineteen in 1969, broadening out from engineering and science into fields of social policy, as in the C.I.A.-sponsored Center for International Studies.[27]

Despite their strong, continued endorsement of sponsored research, M.I.T.'s leaders were not unworried about their reliance on the government. The problems were numerous. A basic fear was that federal support would bring federal control. Many projects, moreover, had a short-term character, and shifts of policy direction could create problems for a university. There also tended to be an emphasis on design and development of new technology in this work rather than on the basic research of primary interest to academics. There was, finally, the troubling need for secrecy on some contracts, as well as the danger of excessive association in the public mind between M.I.T. and the military authorities.

In response to their worries, the Institute's leaders attempted during the 1950s and 1960s to raise private support as financial counterweights to federal dollars. These efforts resulted in a marked expansion of corporate assistance, especially after 1960. The scale of government funding became so great, however, that private contributions could make only a marginal difference. For much of the 1950s, federal revenue accounted for 93 percent to 95 percent of M.I.T.'s sponsored research. Fund-raising successes in the 1960s lowered the percentage to the 83 to 86 percent range. Efforts to reduce the orientation toward military work were aided by the extension of federal programs into nondefense areas, particularly the basic sciences and the social sciences, in which M.I.T. was building strength throughout the postwar years. Nonetheless, military funding continued to dominate federal subsidies. In 1968, for example, the special defense labs accounted for two-thirds of the Institute's sponsored projects, and military funding of department-based research accounted for another significant portion.[28]

M.I.T.'s willingness to continue expanding federally supported and defense-related research was based on its leaders' conviction that, despite zones of discomfort, the arrangements were good for M.I.T. and good for the country. After all, a long list of scientific and technical achievements emanated from the interdisciplinary labs, and numerous educational innovations were inspired by the new discoveries. Government officials, moreover, were proving themselves sensitive to issues of academic freedom and institutional autonomy and responsive to scholarly interests in basic research. Beginning in the late 1950s, in fact, the military agencies began devoting a percentage of their budgets to basic work.

As an added protection for academic values, the special defense labs enabled M.I.T. to maintain a degree of administrative separation between the large-scale, highly applied, and often classified projects for which bureaucratic controls were strongest and the Institute's central organization. Many of the researchers employed by the labs did not receive academic appointments and could not directly influence Institute policies on questions of education and scholarship.

In addition to all this, there was the inescapable fact that M.I.T.'s goal of maintaining national leadership in scientific and engineering research left it with little alternative to federal and military dollars. By 1968, 32 percent of faculty salaries during the academic year were being paid through sponsored projects, and 82 percent of summer salaries was financed in this way. Indirect support through overhead payments also became vital. By the late 1960s, overhead charges on sponsored contracts exceeded 30 percent of current expenses. For most of the 1950s and 1960s, in fact, total income to M.I.T. from federal projects never constituted less than 70 percent of operating revenues, and these resources regularly exceeded by a factor of three the revenue available for departmental instruction and research from endowment, tuition, and annual giving combined. Additional federal subsidies were also available in large amounts to construct research facilities. No alternative source of funds existed that was remotely capable of sustaining scientific and technical work on the scale undertaken by M.I.T. during these years.[29]

Graduate Education at M.I.T.

M.I.T.'s leaders were as clear in the middle 1950s about the need to emphasize graduate instruction as they were about the importance of expanding research. Killian expressed none of Pusey's ambivalence on this matter and never argued that M.I.T.'s response to increasing national demand for college admission should be enlarging the undergraduate program. Indeed, once Killian focused on external pressures to expand undergraduate admissions—in 1953, following his brief season of concern about falling enrollments—he stressed the importance of limiting the entering class. He froze freshman enrollments at nine hundred, approximately the class size reached during the peak years of the veterans' program. Once established, the freeze became fixed policy. It was reaffirmed by Stratton at the beginning of his presidency, which coincided with the arrival of the national tidal wave of high school graduates, and maintained under Johnson.

The policy of limiting enrollments had its roots, Killian explained, in the need to create an academic environment that would attract—in the continuing competition with industry and other universities—the top-flight scientists and engineers upon whom the Institute's research program depended. As he put it in 1955: "The urgent need now . . . is for more research and graduate study in order to create the environment for attracting first-rate imaginative teachers. The engineering profession can no longer depend upon a system of undergraduate professional education," and M.I.T. could not maintain its leading position unless it abandoned that traditional emphasis.

While undergraduate admissions were frozen, no comparable controls were established for graduate enrollments, the only restraint being "the availability of space and staff in the respective departments." During Killian's ten-year presidency, graduate students increased by 65 percent (from fifteen hundred to twenty-five hundred) with the most rapid advance coming in scientific fields at the doctoral level. The expansion continued under Stratton and Johnson, reaching thirty-nine hundred by 1969. New doctoral programs were mounted in deliberately chosen fields: economics, political science, psychology, sociology, philosophy, and linguistics. By the late 1960s, total graduate enrollments surpassed undergraduate, a fact that expressed the change in M.I.T. since 1940, when undergraduates had outnumbered graduates (who were then largely master's degree students in engineering) by four to one.[30]

Graduate expansion, no less than research, depended on federal assistance. Here, once again, sponsored projects were crucial, since they typically included funds for staff positions that became research assistantships. By 1968, 80 percent of graduate-student salaries paid by the Institute were charged to research contracts. Indeed, the financial dependence of both faculty and graduate students on external support became so great that the capacity of an individual department or field to expand or mount a graduate program came to depend on that unit's ability to attract outside—chiefly federal—funds. Government dollars also were vital in providing fellowships and traineeships. By the late 1960s, 25 percent of all graduate students receiving financial aid—which included almost the entire graduate student body—was supported by federal stipends in addition to the 50 percent of aid-receiving graduate students who were supported by research contracts.[31]

With developmental policies clearly focused on research and graduate education and with lavish support from the federal government, M.I.T. flourished in the 1950s and 1960s and became one of the nation's leading research universities. The strength and breadth of the Institute's programs were reported in the national survey of faculties and graduate programs conducted by the American Council on Education in the late 1960s. This survey, based on the reputation achieved by sixteen hundred graduate departments among their disciplinary colleagues nationally, ranked each faculty on a six-point scale from "not sufficient for doctoral training" to "distinguished" and each program on a four-point scale ranging from "not attractive" to "extremely attractive."

In its traditional area of emphasis—engineering—all of M.I.T.'s faculties were ranked "distinguished"; and all its programs, "extremely attractive." The Departments of Electrical Engineering and Mechanical Engineering ranked first in terms of faculty as well as program, while Civil and Chemical achieved slightly lower ratings that clearly placed them among the leading departments in the nation. In ten scientific fields offered by the Institute, every faculty was rated in the top category, as was every program but two. The average rank of M.I.T.'s faculty in the ten fields was 5.5; the average program rank was 6.1.

As impressive as the Institute's achievements in engineering and science was its record in the social sciences and humanities, in which graduate programs had not existed prior to 1950. Among the four social science departments where M.I.T. offered doctoral programs, two, Economics and Political Science, achieved top ratings for faculty and program, and both were also ranked among the handful of leading national departments. The Psychology Department fared only slightly less well, being ranked twelfth and thirteenth in terms of faculty and program. Only in sociology did M.I.T. fail to achieve national recognition. In the humanities, the Institute had made a more modest effort, but two departments, Linguistics and Philosophy, were rated among the national leaders, with Linguistics ranking first in both faculty and program. A separate ranking of professional schools affirmed that M.I.T. had maintained its traditionally high position in architecture while building a School of Management that also was considered one of the best in the nation.

These surveys made it clear that M.I.T.'s leaders had achieved the central institutional goals shared by Compton and Killian in the early postwar years: to retain a leading position in engineering, science, and architecture while broadening the Institute's programs and achieving national prominence in a limited number of new fields where the special character of the Institute could be exploited. By the time Julius Stratton retired from the presidency in 1967, the old technical institute demonstrably had become, as the remembered version of Killian's formula had it, a "university polarized around science."[32]

M.I.T.'s remarkable development in the 1950s and 1960s provided one of the clearest examples nationally of the new focus on research and graduate education and the role of federal funds in fostering this development. Indeed, when Clark Kerr attempted, in the early 1960s, to describe the postwar evolution of higher education, he identified the "federal grant university" as a major new phenomenon of the period. By this time, in fact, federal research funds constituted more than 50 percent of the budgets of Stanford, Princeton, and Cal Tech; and government dollars provided the essential ingredient at most universities that became research centers in these years. Throughout the period, however, M.I.T. consistently led the nation in the amount of federal dollars received.

The Institute's early commitment to sponsored research made it a national laboratory for crafting administrative and financial policies to govern the management of external funds. The prewar Division of Industrial Cooperation became the model of a separate administrative structure for external projects that nonetheless had close financial ties to academic departments. The wartime Radiation Laboratory, and later the Lincoln and Instrumentation labs, became prototypes for administering large-scale, federally sponsored projects such as the Lawrence Laboratory at Berkeley and the Jet Propulsion Lab at Cal Tech. The procedures for writing research contracts between the federal government and academic institutions were first worked out at M.I.T. When tensions developed between government and academy, M.I.T. was likely to be prominent in finding solutions. The M.I.T. faculty also played a leading role in reviewing the impact on academic and educational work of externally supported activities and drafting institutional policies designed to protect academic norms and values.[33]

Harvard Accepts the Postwar World

While M.I.T. was becoming the prototypical federal-grant university, Harvard was seeking to maintain its position atop the academic hierarchy while also keeping its distance from the government. Throughout the 1950s, Harvard's reliance on federal dollars remained unusually low among major universities. From the beginning, however, there were exceptions in fields where government support proved vital for maintaining research programs. The clearest cases were the Medical School, Dental Medicine, and Public Health, where, in each instance, government funds quickly grew beyond 50 percent of total income.

Following *Sputnik I,* as federal largess flowed with increasing generosity, Harvard found it difficult to maintain limits. Other institutions were demonstrating with unanswerable force the academic and institutional benefits of government subsidies. In 1960 Pusey initiated a review of Harvard's policies. This analysis concluded that the early fears of government control had proved unwarranted and that the overall effect of federal support was not only benign but, in specific fields, essential. During the 1960s, the proportion of Harvard's income represented by federal funds jumped sharply. By 1967 government dollars accounted for more than 40 percent of Harvard's budget for departmental instruction and research, compared with 10 percent ten years earlier.

Programmatic changes accompanied the liberalization. Interdisciplinary research centers on the M.I.T. model, which Conant had resisted in the early postwar years, flourished under Pusey. In 1963 he identified eleven such units as indicative of Harvard's intellectual vitality. Among them, and symbolic of Harvard's changed perspective, was the Joint Center for Urban Studies, a policy-oriented collaborative enterprise with M.I.T. Indeed, Pusey's Harvard became deeply engaged in social problem solving in the 1960s, a fact to which the president drew attention in his 1967 report. A new Institute of Politics was concerned with "urgent present social and political problems." The School of Education was actively working for civil rights. The faculty and students of the Law School were "increasingly involved in public activities and practical affairs." The "evidences of a changed spirit at work" at Harvard multiplied across seven pages.[34]

The financial and programmatic changes of the 1960s did not mean that Pusey and his colleagues had set aside their reservations about government support. On the contrary, Pusey felt that the nation would never "outgrow a need for Ivory Towers," and, even in reporting Harvard's social contributions, he wrote regretfully of the "trumpeting outside . . . for action" that was making "cloistered learning . . . almost something to be deprecated." Caught by a cultural tide for which he had little sympathy, Pusey struggled to differentiate what he saw as Harvard's controlled relationship with the government from that of institutions—like M.I.T.—that had accepted federal funds more indiscriminately. Over time, however, the differences became progressively blurred. In the end, for example, Pusey was unable to maintain the balance of support among disciplines to which he initially had aspired. In 1969 a faculty committee summarized the inevitable: the sciences were rich, the social sciences less so, and the humanities least affluent of all.[35]

The clearest lines that Harvard drew involved the refusal to participate in classified research or to undertake management responsibilities for large-scale development projects. These two policies were closely related, since classified research tended to occur within the framework of development-oriented activities. Both policies reflected principled academic positions and had real consequences. For example, Harvard declined to participate in the C.I.A.-sponsored Center for International Studies, which provided a major boost to Political Science at M.I.T.

Harvard's restraint, however, did not conflict in any serious way with its institutional interests. Harvard scientists were eager to publish their findings, were generally successful in obtaining funding of the type they wanted from the National Science Foundation and the Office of Naval Research, and exerted no pressure on Pusey to accept classified activity. Moreover, individuals inclined to do classified work were not prevented from doing so as private consultants under Harvard's rules. In general, however, large-scale applied projects had little inherent attraction for an institution that had decided in the 1920s to concentrate its scientific work in the basic disciplines. With respect to the third of Harvard's three "self-denying ordinances" about federal funds— the refusal to make permanent appointments based on this form of support— Harvard ultimately relented and awarded tenure in the Medical School, Dental Medicine, and Public Health on the basis of external funds.

Perhaps the most important measure of Harvard's ability to maintain its independence from the government stemmed from Dean Bundy's claim that, during the 1950s, his university undertook only those federally supported projects that were defined internally by the interests of the faculty. Given the independent way in which faculty members and research teams identified their interests, any judgment about the durability of this standard is problematic. It is clear from his 1967 report that Pusey himself doubted Harvard's adherence to this posture. One study concluded that the School of Education was shaped and reshaped by changing federal policies.

By the late 1960s—despite Pusey's concerns and despite his institution's unparalleled independent wealth—the similarities between Harvard's relationship to the government and those of other research-oriented universities had become far more important than the differences. Thus, while M.I.T. was dramatizing the enormous institutional benefits that flowed from welcoming federal aid, Harvard was demonstrating the irresistible importance of these funds to an institution disposed to keep its distance. Pusey's successor summarized the logic of Harvard's evolution succinctly: "There was no turning back . . . Distinguished medical schools and science departments simply could not exist without government support. Although universities lost some of their independence in the process, few educators were troubled so long as appropriations rose year after year with few tangible ill effects."[36]

At Harvard, as at M.I.T., the expansion of government-supported research activities was associated with a shift in the character of the student body toward more advanced levels. In the Graduate School of Arts and Sciences, enrollments doubled between 1957 and 1967—while the size of the College grew only slightly. In the Medical School, the number of research associates and post-doctoral fellows expanded rapidly while that of future M.D.s remained stable. Federal funds were also vital in financing this aspect of Harvard's growth, as high percentages of the advanced students were supported by government fellowships and traineeships.

As always at Harvard, the overall pattern of change was complex, reflecting both programmatic diversity and administrative decentralization. The graduate professional schools less directly affected by federal support than Arts and Sciences or the Medical School—for example, Law, Business, Divinity, and Design—pursued policies that reflected the internal logic of their fields and situations. Unquestionably, however, as Pusey acknowledged, the moving edge of change was in fields where government policies financed a shift of institutional emphasis toward research, graduate education, and science. In all these fields, Harvard's readiness, in the end, to accept dependence on federal support allowed its departments to retain their competitive position in relation to other research universities. The rankings of graduate faculties and programs of the late 1960s in the sciences, social sciences, and health professions placed Harvard's departments among the handful of national leaders in every field.[37]

The Economics of Academic Progress

The Revolution in Costs

The priority assigned to research and graduate education, combined with increased competition for outstanding faculty and students, raised operating costs dramatically. In 1952–1953, Conant's last year, Harvard's academic departments spent about $2,100 per student for educational and research activities. By 1967–1968, the figure had risen more than fourfold—to $9,300. The comparable figures at M.I.T. were $4,400 (1953) and $11,500 (1968). A significant portion of increased per-student expenditures—$3,400 in the case of Harvard, $4,300 at M.I.T.—were directly attributable to and supported by external contracts. Even after sponsored projects were subtracted from the institutions' budgets, however, their per-student cost increases were formidable: from $1,900 to $5,700 (200 percent) at Harvard, and from $1,600 to $4,400 (175 percent) at M.I.T.

These additional dollars had to be supplied from traditional sources of revenue—tuition, gifts, and endowment income—in daunting amounts. In 1953 Harvard's expenditures for departmental instruction and research, a figure that excluded government contracts, totaled $21.8 million, an increase of about $10 million during Conant's twenty-year presidency. By 1968 the comparable figure was $86.6 million, a sixteen-year expansion under Pusey of $64.8 million, or 297 percent, triple the rate of growth under Conant.

A portion of these increases, of course, resulted from inflation and expanded enrollments. A rough calculation of the impact of these two factors after 1953, however, produces a 1968 expenditure budget for Harvard's academic departments of only $34.2 million. The remaining $52.4 million in increased costs must be explained by basic changes in the economics of education and research at Harvard. A similar expansion of aggregate costs occurred at M.I.T.[38]

On both campuses, the shift of emphasis from undergraduate to graduate and post-doctoral education played a major role in financial change. Advanced programs were inherently more expensive than collegiate instruction in terms of faculty time per student, as well as costs of laboratory, library, and office facilities. Budgets were further increased by the need to provide financial aid to attract talented graduate students in the national competition among research universities. Pusey reported that the "costs of educating graduate students are from three to ten times as great as those of educating undergraduates; the cost of post–post-graduate programs are still higher . . ."

Undergraduate education also became more expensive during the 1950s and 1960s. Several factors contributed to the change. There was a need to modernize courses, especially in scientific and technical fields. It also was essential to provide more financial support for undergraduates, partially to offset the tuition raises that were instituted to meet expanded revenue requirements, partially to keep these increasingly pricey institutions accessible to students from modest backgrounds, and partially to compete with other universities for able students.

The largest factor in pushing up undergraduate costs, however, was the greater number of courses taught, often to small audiences. To some extent, this phenomenon reflected the expansion of knowledge, but at least as important, probably more so, was the fact that faculty members, under pressure to maximize research productivity, inevitably sought to teach their scholarly interests, not only in graduate seminars but in undergraduate courses. Even Conant, who had done more than anyone else to promote research at Harvard, came to lament the "absurd" proliferation of specialized offerings, a process that was to accelerate under his successor.[39]

The costs of attracting and sustaining faculty advanced markedly during the golden age, with salaries playing a major role. Since Eliot's years, the Harvard faculty had been the best paid in the nation, but Conant's conservative financial policies had resulted, by the late 1940s, in a deterioration of Harvard's position. Pusey was determined to reassert primacy in this area, and he also had strong feelings about the general need to increase academic compensation in parallel with advances in other professions. He granted three across-the-board raises in his first four years and continued to press for increases thereafter. His success was recorded in two 1967 studies ranking Harvard first nationally in average salary, first in starting salaries for full professors, and second in starting salaries for associate professors.

Staying ahead of the competition was to prove more difficult during the golden age than it once had been. As institutions vied for recognition, many were willing to pay extraordinary amounts for academic stars—a practice Harvard consistently rejected. By 1967 the mean salary of full professors at Harvard had risen by 66 percent from the 1952 level. The competition for outstanding junior faculty produced even greater increases—81 percent—at this rank.

Higher salaries counted for only a portion of the increased costs of supporting the Harvard faculty. Institutions also competed over fringe benefits, research facilities and support, teaching loads, teaching assistants and graders, and opportunities to offer specialized fields. Since Harvard was eager to strengthen research, many of these pressures were reinforced by institutional policy, and related trends further added to operating costs. Harvard increasingly supported faculty and staff who worked only on research. The administrative apparatus was expanded to relieve faculty of nonacademic duties. Additional space was required for all these activities. Taken together, these changes meant that between 1953 and 1968, while the university's enrollment grew by only 32 percent, total salaries, wages, and fringe benefits, including positions funded on grants and contracts, nearly quadrupled, and more square footage was added to Harvard's facilities than during any previous administration.

These increased costs represented progress of two important kinds: for academics as professionals entitled to respectable compensation for extraordinarily demanding work; and for Harvard as a center of scholarship of expanding national and international importance. Of these gains, Pusey was immensely proud. "There can be no thought of 'clamping down on expenses' in the ordinary sense," he wrote in 1967. The issue was how to expand revenue.[40]

As an upwardly mobile institution, M.I.T. placed a high priority on maintaining the pace of faculty compensation and support that Harvard was setting. Compton's emphasis on raising the Institute's historically modest salaries had produced some gains by the late 1940s, but a 1948 review pointed out that parity with leading universities had not been achieved. At the beginning of his presidency, Killian identified further progress on salaries as his first financial objective, and by 1958, the year he left office, M.I.T.'s average compensation was comparable to major private universities. Advances continued under Stratton and Johnson, and by 1968 M.I.T.'s salaries ranked sixth nationally, surpassed only by Harvard, the University of Chicago, Cal Tech, Stanford, and Claremont. Other compensation and benefits at M.I.T. also followed the general pattern of Harvard. Teaching loads were reduced as research was given greater emphasis. Full-time researchers were added to the staff in large numbers. Support staff and facilities expanded rapidly.[41]

The Search for Nonfederal Revenues

At both Harvard and M.I.T., it was necessary to expand income from nongovernment sources, partially to meet costs not covered by sponsored projects and partially to retain independence. Pusey's wish to limit federal aid resulted in intense pressures to strengthen support from endowment, gifts, and tuition. Harvard's president believed, in fact, that his campus should set the pace nationally in meeting the costs of the new academic priorities. In this context, he was critical of Conant, whose conservative financial policies, Pusey believed, had retarded the postwar development of American higher education while leaving the "so-called 'richest university in the world' desperately in need of increased revenue." Raising Harvard's financial horizons became a central goal of Pusey's presidency. While he did not succeed in containing Harvard's reliance on federal dollars, his efforts to increase revenue from other sources constituted one of the major accomplishments of his presidency.[42]

Pusey especially wanted to maintain the vitality of Harvard's endowment. In 1948, hoping to increase fund income, the Corporation had transferred much of the responsibility for the endowment to an independent investment firm. This innovation proved highly effective: between 1948 and 1962, the market value of the general investment account, the central pool containing most of Harvard's funds, increased by about 150 percent—from two hundred million to five hundred million dollars—entirely on the basis of appreciation and turnover within the portfolio.

For Pusey, however, the central challenge was attracting new capital. In 1958, after several years of planning, he announced the Campaign for Harvard College, with the goal of obtaining over eighty million dollars. Although this was "by far the largest amount ever sought by an educational institution," Harvard raised over a hundred million dollars in less than two years. Emboldened, Pusey launched additional drives, the largest of which—with a goal of $160 million—was announced in 1966. Through a series of campaigns between 1953 and 1968, Pusey brought in nearly $350 million in capital resources for Harvard, an annual average of nearly $22 million. These successes, combined with the effective management of existing funds, increased the market value of Harvard's investments by 275 percent to $1.2 billion in 1968.

Pusey was particularly proud that the proportionate contribution of investment income to expenditures for departmental instruction and research remained steady—at about one-third—despite rising costs. Even more impressive was the less-publicized fact that Harvard under Pusey actually lowered—to about 60 percent—the proportion of investment income used for current expenses. The president himself was only the chief contributor to these results. Under Conant, fund-raising had been decentralized, and initiatives among Harvard's various schools, encouraged by Pusey, were incorporated in the totals.

Pusey presided over revolutionary increases in the scale of gifts and grants received to support current operations. Before World War II, like other private universities, Harvard conducted only a modest alumni giving program, and contributions from this source had not played a major role in the university's financial structure. Increased postwar financial pressures, however, led Harvard to intensify its efforts. This practice had begun under Conant, but in Pusey's first year, total contributions to the four largest funds (College, Law, Business, and the Medical School) totaled less than a million dollars. By 1963 these four funds were bringing in nearly three million dollars, and in 1970 total contributions to all alumni/ae funds rose to six million dollars.

Pusey's Harvard also took a leading role in exploiting the increased availability of philanthropic outlays by corporations and foundations. From these sources, Harvard received just under two hundred million dollars in gifts and grants for current use between 1953 and 1968, an annual average of more than twelve million dollars. Along the way, annual gifts were transformed into a major element of Harvard's financial support, accounting for approximately 25 percent of current expenditures for departmental instruction and research during the Pusey years. When these totals are added to capital gifts, the overall fund-raising of Pusey's first sixteen years was approximately $550 million. The annual average in new contributed funds of over $35 million very nearly exceeded the institution's total budget from all sources in Conant's last year, even after adjusting for inflation. During the 1960s, Pusey's annual fund-raising comfortably exceeded Conant's largest total budget.[43]

With respect to Harvard's third major source of nongovernment income—tuition—Pusey felt an obligation to obtain the maximum amount that fairly could be asked. He had criticized Conant for resisting tuition increases, feeling that "Harvard's policy was in fact undermining the whole teaching profession: for most colleges and universities relied heavily on tuition . . . How could less prestigious institutions . . . justify setting tuitions at higher rates when Harvard refus[ed] to move?" He was aware, moreover, that the student markets of the 1950s and 1960s, backed by general prosperity, would support higher charges.

Pusey reversed Conant's emphasis on tuition restraint soon after his appointment. Undergraduate tuition, which stood at $600 in 1952, was raised by $200 in 1953, by another $200 in 1956, and by $250—to $1,250—in 1958, for an overall doubling in five years. The president repeatedly explained the increases in terms of the need to raise salaries, a goal that also was emphasized in the Campaign for Harvard College. Contributions for faculty salaries were the least-successful part of the fund drive, however, and the pattern of tuition hikes continued. Charges were raised in two-hundred-dollar increments in 1962, 1964, and 1966; and in 1968 stood at two thousand dollars, for a total increase since 1953 of 233 percent. As a result of these changes—and similar policies in the professional schools—the contribution from student payments to Harvard's expenditures for departmental instruction and research held steady throughout the Pusey years, between 34 and 38 percent, despite sharply escalating budgets.[44]

Pusey did not escape criticism for his emphasis on student charges. At the time and later, however, he defended his policies vigorously. His most important assertion was that the increases were only making up for an extended period during which the academic profession was kept in scandalously impoverished conditions. He also stressed Harvard's success in expanding scholarship, loan, and work-study support at the same rate as it heightened tuition (although not at the same rate as total increased costs to students).

These were forceful arguments, but they did not alter the fact that Pusey's emphasis on tuition income meant that Harvard's undergraduates and their families were subsidizing the university's new emphasis on graduate education and research, an emphasis that was a primary cause of increased costs. Throughout the period, undergraduates paid the same tuition as advanced students in Arts and Sciences, even though the cost of their education to Harvard was much lower. In important ways, of course, the undergraduate program was enhanced by the university's intensified intellectual environment and greater prestige, but questions about the relationship of student charges to institutional priorities remained. The dean of Arts and Sciences put it this way in the early 1970s: "Today we are undoubtedly a far bigger enterprise: in numbers, in range of skills, in functions" than in the early 1950s; "but, in my opinion, our undergraduates have benefitted relatively little from these improvements . . . [and] have not received [their] fair share of the recent additions to our resources."[45]

Although M.I.T.'s leaders were much more comfortable with their reliance on government support than were their Harvard counterparts, the Institute consistently sought ways to limit dependence on federal subsidies by increasing income from traditional sources. The successful capital campaign of the late 1940s was only the first of a series of progressively more-ambitious efforts. Indeed, in relation to its resources in the early 1950s, the Institute was even more successful than Harvard between 1953 and 1968 in attracting revenues from private contributions. M.I.T.'s income from private gifts and grants grew by 450 percent during these years, compared with 260 percent at Harvard. Endowment earnings also increased by 450 percent, in contrast to 270 percent at Harvard. During the 1950s, new development at M.I.T. made it necessary to use relatively high percentages of contributed funds for current expenses, but, during the 1960s, Stratton shifted the emphasis to endowment building in order to provide a secure, continuing balance to external funds.

M.I.T.'s sustained effort to raise private money achieved a measurable reduction in its reliance on the government, though the overall role of external funds remained immense. Indeed, Stratton's policies had the effect of moving M.I.T. closer to Harvard by placing greater stress on traditional sources of income, even as Harvard was moving closer to M.I.T. by accepting reliance on federal support. Thus, the financial strategies of the two institutions, radically different in the early postwar years, tended to converge during the 1950s and 1960s. Tuition charges at the two institutions also moved upward in tandem, though the Institute was more restrained in this respect than Harvard, a pattern that probably reflected M.I.T.'s stronger orientation toward middle-class families, as well as its greater readiness to fund increased costs through federal subsidies.[46]

Undergraduate Education in the Research University

Changing Students, Changing Faculty,
Changing Priorities

At both Harvard and M.I.T., there occurred during the 1950s and 1960s a progressive abandonment of the structures, as well as the spirit, of general education. At the same time, the Institute's work in undergraduate professional education became less compatible with its other commitments. These changes stemmed from shifts in the intellectual ability and precollege preparation of undergraduates and from the altered priorities of the two institutions and their faculties.

The limits on new admissions established by both campuses in the early 1950s remained in place while demand steadily increased. At Harvard, for example, freshman applications grew from 3,100 in 1952 to 5,200 in 1960 and to 7,200 in 1967; while the number accepted decreased from 1,900 to 1,500 to 1,400. These numbers, in the context of admission policies stressing academic talent and of the strengthened secondary programs of the post-*Sputnik I* era, produced entering classes of unprecedented ability and preparation. As early as 1960, admission dean Wilbur Bender observed that increased selectivity since 1952 had produced "the greatest change in the Harvard student body in a short time—two college generations—in our recorded history," and standards continued to rise for the remainder of the decade. M.I.T., with its specialized clientele, experienced a more modest expansion of applications—from three thousand in 1952 to thirty-nine hundred in 1967—but the Institute, too, accepted fewer students in the latter year than in the former. At both universities, heightened selectivity eliminated the previously sizable proportion of academically undistinguished students from the bottom of the freshman class and raised the average level of ability. At Harvard, the median freshman of 1960 would have stood at about the 90th percentile in 1952. At M.I.T., the lower half of the class entering in 1962 had College Board scores equivalent to the upper half of the entering classes a decade earlier.[47]

The curricula designed in the early postwar years had to be reevaluated in light of the more intellectually advanced entering freshmen. One goal of general education was to introduce untrained minds to basic fields of inquiry, but this purpose seemed less relevant as freshmen became more sophisticated. In 1955 Harvard established an advanced-standing program that enabled many new students to bypass some or all of the first year and thereby miss the introductory courses that were the heart of general education. A similar program was installed at M.I.T.

At the Institute, the admission of better-prepared students posed even more fundamental problems. Increasingly, M.I.T. students, like their Harvard counterparts, viewed their baccalaureate education as a preparation for graduate school. This fact raised questions about the Institute's historic commitment to undergraduate professional education. By the mid-1950s, the M.I.T. faculty was divided between those who advocated a radical reduction in the technical (professional) aspects of undergraduate work and an expansion of emphasis on basic science, and those who held fast to the tradition of combining practical and theoretical concerns.[48]

While student change exerted pressure on the curriculum from one direction, faculty change pressed from another. Indeed, the intensified focus of both Harvard and M.I.T. on graduate education and research rendered general education—with its requirement that professors involve themselves with broad intellectual issues—an increasingly burdensome distraction. At Harvard, senior faculty became less willing to participate in general education courses and readier to accept a variety of offerings as meeting the College's slender requirements. Junior faculty members, on the other hand, were under great pressure to publish in their specialties in order to maximize chances for promotion or ensure their marketability at other institutions. Introductory instruction became the province of graduate students hired as teaching assistants.

Both Killian and Stratton lamented reduced attention to undergraduate teaching at M.I.T. The solution, Stratton argued, was to bring the curriculum into alignment with faculty research interests. Since the talented students of the 1950s and 1960s were well equipped to undertake advanced work in the disciplines, the direction of change was predictable. Harvard's freshman seminars, introduced in 1959, let undergraduates work with senior professors on topics closely linked to scholarly specialities. Even these courses proved too burdensome for most full-time faculty, however. In the end, most freshman seminars were taught by part-time instructors. M.I.T.'s Undergraduate Research Opportunities Program (U.R.O.P.), initiated in 1969, was a more successful response to the same basic insight.[49]

Curriculum Reform in the 1960s

By the early 1960s, discrepancies between the assumptions of the educational programs established after the war and current institutional conditions had become too obvious to ignore. In 1962 Stratton established the Committee on Curriculum Content Planning, chaired by Jerrold Zacharias, to review the Institute's undergraduate offerings. The following year, Franklin Ford, Bundy's successor as dean of Arts and Sciences, charged a faculty committee led by Paul Doty to assess Harvard's general education program. The reports of these groups, together with the intramural debates they fostered, bore witness to the altered view of collegiate education that had emerged in Cambridge during the preceding decade.

The members of the Zacharias committee, released from their teaching duties, devoted two years to a course-by-course analysis of the M.I.T. curriculum. When the report appeared in the spring of 1964, Stratton called it "the most extensive review of our undergraduate program since the basic philosophy of the Institute was set forth by William Barton Rogers."

The post-*Sputnik I* emphasis on achieving the maximum possible level of scientific achievement was clearly in evidence. The central passages of the Zacharias report recommended a focus on advanced work for gifted undergraduates rather than on a broadly conceived concept of general education. The main goal of the undergraduate program, the committee wrote, must be "to prepare those of our students who can do so to reach the frontiers of knowledge early in their most creative years" while also attempting "to strengthen those students who feel the need of a sequential, complete and formal schooling." The relationship of this new emphasis to faculty research interests was explicit. "We faculty members are doing our own professional work. We find it open-ended, exciting and rewarding, both intellectually and emotionally. Our aim is to introduce students to the same kind of experience and reward as quickly and efficiently as we can."

The Zacharias report was a victory for those who believed the Institute should stress academic rather than professional goals at the baccalaureate level. The committee urged additional requirements in basic science and fewer in applications. They also proposed to make the curriculum less prescriptive by allowing students to choose among alternatives and to pursue special interests intensively. With respect to the humanities and social sciences, the Zacharias committee had little to say, in contrast to their predecessors on the Lewis committee, for whom the strengthening of humanistic and social values had been a priority. Without extensive discussion, the Zacharias committee endorsed a recommendation of the faculty of humanities and social science that Institute requirements in these fields be made more flexible.[50]

The work of the Doty committee at Harvard was far less detailed than that of its counterpart at M.I.T. The committee noted that recent modifications of general education had shifted emphasis in a number of ways: undergraduate requirements were now less concerned with historical understanding, allowed more room for non-Western subjects and for science, and were less prescriptive about how the goals of general education should be met. Even more important had been changes like advanced placement and the freshman seminars, which forced the committee to wonder "to what degree are the important educational innovations in the College now going on outside rather than within the framework of general education."

Concluding that general education as originally conceived had become progressively less central to the undergraduate curriculum but wishing to affirm the broad principles of the program, the committee redefined general education in terms more consistent with recent changes. The Doty report recommended "the introduction of new subjects, advanced work and course sequences that would permit students to develop a particular interest in greater depth. Specialized departmental courses were welcomed as an alternative way of meeting General Education requirements." The emphasis of the Redbook on a common core of basic courses was to be replaced with a loosely conceived distribution requirement. The recommendations were adopted after an inconclusive faculty debate that bore no resemblance in intensity to the discussions of general education that took place directly after the war.[51]

The reforms of the early 1960s acknowledged problems with general education that had begun to appear almost as soon as these programs were established. In important ways, the limitations were intellectual and cultural. The ideas of the elder statesmen of the 1940s represented less a common, American culture than the classical educational values of the nation's academic and social elite. By the 1960s, Conant himself acknowledged the "painful necessity" of "throwing overboard my assumption that a unified, coherent culture was possible in a democratic country" and of recognizing that "a pluralistic ideology must be the basis of a democracy." Cambridge was, in any case, further removed from the mainstream of society than ever. While the Lewis committee debated the roles of M.I.T. graduates as American citizens, the Zacharias report spoke of educating members of the "technological community." Where the Redbook committee was concerned about the common values of a national culture, the Doty committee focused on the importance of sampling a range of academic fields.

The reforms of the 1940s—even at M.I.T.—also underestimated the extent to which both the perspective of science and the progress of knowledge generated by scientific discovery would make it difficult for scholars to agree on a core of essential knowledge and values. By the 1960s, the faculties of Harvard and M.I.T. possessed neither the consensus needed to sustain the old formulations nor the will to construct new ones. It was hardly surprising, therefore, that curricular change in these years expressed an impulse to let undergraduates choose among subjects, confront a diversity of perspectives, pursue individual interests, and, in the end—not unlike graduate students—assume responsibility for their own intellectual progress.[52]

In the wake of the Doty report, the number of courses acceptable for general education credit at Harvard escalated quickly, rising from 55 to 101 between 1963 and 1969, with increasing emphasis on topical courses of current interest. The movement toward flexibility was reinforced during the latter half of the decade by pressures from undergraduates who were readier than earlier student generations to insist upon courses of their own choosing. Such pressures led to the introduction of programs like Afro-American and Visual and Environmental Studies that the faculty, on its own, probably would not have established. The ultimate expression of student-sponsored education was a two-semester sequence titled "Social Change in America" and "The Radical Perspective" taught to 760 undergraduates in 1968–1969 by a collection of graduate students and friends under the loose supervision of two junior members of the Social Relations Department.

Curriculum change at M.I.T. was more restrained during the late 1960s than at Harvard, a fact that reflected the Institute's stronger tradition—rooted in the special character of scientific and technical subjects—of deliberation and control in matters of undergraduate education. In 1967, for example, the Institute's faculty rejected recommendations calling for further reductions of requirements. The direction of change, however, was similar on both campuses, and President Johnson regarded the trend toward greater flexibility as both inexorable and beneficial. "The opportunity to participate in the choice of one's own program," he wrote, "produce[s] a greater sense of responsibility and most likely some gain in standards of performance." A faculty committee took a more skeptical view in a 1970 analysis. "We have enlarged the scope of freedom of the first two years," the committee observed, ". . . without developing the unifying principles which that freedom requires if it is to lead to something more than eclecticism . . ."

In later years, there was a tendency at both Harvard and M.I.T. to attribute the disintegration of undergraduate programs to the unique pressures of the late 1960s. Such analyses forgot that the basic decision to deemphasize structured programs occurred earlier in the decade, without pressure from students, and reflected chiefly the revised priorities of institutions and faculties.[53]

Admission Policies in the 1960s

The subordination of undergraduate programs to graduate education and research generated questions about admission policies as well as curriculum. Excess demand made it possible to enroll undergraduates with sufficient talent to function as apprentice scholars, slightly younger (but often brighter) versions of graduate students. Such policies would have ensured maximum coherence among undergraduate, graduate, and research activities; and at both Harvard and M.I.T., strong voices, chiefly within the faculty, urged that intellectual capacity be the only consideration in judging applicants. This standard, however, if rigorously applied, would have clashed with entrenched traditions at both campuses, particularly the conviction that baccalaureate-level programs should prepare students for more than academic careers and the belief that learning was fostered by student diversity. The conditions of the 1960s made it necessary for campus leaders to review established balances between academic ability and other considerations in admitting undergraduates.

At Harvard, the tension between academic and nonacademic criteria focused on the policies of Wilbur Bender, the man Conant appointed in 1952 to build a more aggressive admission function for the College. Bender was committed to student diversity in terms of academic talent and regional and class background. During Bender's tenure Harvard finally enrolled a genuinely national student body, as the proportion of freshmen from non-northeastern schools rose from 28 percent in 1952 to 56 percent in 1960. At the same time, Bender resisted pressures to sacrifice diversity to brilliance. "The top high school student is often, frankly, a pretty dull, or bloodless, or peculiar fellow," he observed, and his policies were responsible for the fact that the number of students with exceptional minds increased very little during the 1950s despite the rise in admission standards. Bender's orientation brought him into conflict with a number of faculty members, especially several scientists, who believed he discouraged gifted students from coming to Harvard.[54]

By 1960 continuing conflict over admission policy for the College led Bundy to appoint a special committee under Franklin Ford, then a professor of history, to review the entire matter. The committee's recommendations were carefully balanced. Bowing first to academic values, the report agreed that, since Harvard's unique qualities "lie, above all, in the realm of the intellect," the College must "in making final admission decisions . . . opt for intellectual promise." The committee also noted, however, that the number of applicants with exceptional gifts was limited, possibly no more than 1 percent of the pool, and that, in selecting from the remaining large group of highly intelligent applicants, the College must look at other qualities that "make men outstanding in government or business, in the liberal professions and the arts, even though they would never achieve distinction in the library or the laboratory." Thus, there was little choice, in the committee's view, but to continue current efforts to balance the claims of intellectual and other abilities while offering "a broad hospitality to talent."

In truth, Harvard's institutional requirements permitted no basic alteration of admission policy, even if the pool of applicants had allowed one: it was vital that the College continue to forge close ties with future leaders in industry and government and to maintain a strong and supportive alumni/ae network, and these necessities limited the extent to which purely academic values could dominate policy.

Ford's committee also addressed the sensitive issue of Harvard's concern with enrolling students from moderate-income and disadvantaged backgrounds. Bender's final report in 1960, written while the committee deliberated, included an unrestrained attack on Harvard's inattention to this matter, as manifested in the "steady stream of tuition increases" that Pusey had instituted to improve faculty salaries and finance increased costs. Noting that the median family income of scholarship holders had risen from the 58th percentile nationally to the 75th and that nonscholarship holders undoubtedly represented an even higher-income group, Bender reported that "Harvard is rapidly becoming a college serving only upper-middle-income families" and would soon "cut itself off from most of America." Bender was bitter that scholarship aid had not kept up with the total cost of attending Harvard, and he was especially angered by a 1959 decision of the Faculty of Arts and Sciences to eliminate contributions to scholarships from funds it controlled in order to enhance faculty salaries.

Bender was criticized by his superiors for inaccurately characterizing Harvard's student profile, but subsequent analyses have substantiated his contention that Harvard was becoming less accessible to moderate income students during the 1950s. A study by the treasurer's office concluded, for example, that Harvard's tuition rose from 40 percent of national per capita income in 1952 to 70 percent in the early 1960s. Even with the large increases in scholarships of which Pusey was so proud, such a change was bound to be forbidding to many potential applicants of limited means. Ford's committee acknowledged that, notwithstanding the post-Conant emphasis on democratizing Harvard's admission policies, the economic base from which the College drew was narrowing. The committee did not express great concern on this point, however, and concluded that "the faculty should not, under present conditions, expect too much socio-economic variety in the College." Ford himself felt it was important to use limited scholarship resources to attract minority students.

As the 1960s wore on and national attention focused on problems of social and racial equity, the bland disinterest of Ford's committee in Harvard's accessibility became unacceptable. The most striking result of the changed perspective was an increase in minority enrollments from 1 to 10 percent of the undergraduates between 1960 and 1970, with most of the shift coming at the end of the decade. This was a major achievement.

The broader issues that Bender had brought so forcefully to the institution's attention did not go away, however. In 1963 students from families with nonprofessional and moderate-income breadwinners accounted for 28 percent of the freshman class, and over the next five years the figure never climbed higher than 34 percent. The slight increase was aided by the growth of Harvard's scholarship program, which made it possible, after the mid-1960s, to divorce admissions decisions from considerations of financial capacity. A 1970 review concluded, however, that Harvard students continued to come, overwhelmingly, from professional and managerial families with incomes far above the average. The accomplishment of Harvard admissions during the 1960s with respect to socioeconomic diversity involved less a reversal of the patterns Bender had criticized than resistance to a further narrowing of the financial backgrounds of Harvard students that might have occurred in the context of steadily increasing competition for admission.[55]

The problem of balancing academic and nonacademic concerns in admitting freshmen took a different form at M.I.T. Questions of regional and class background, for example, were not central for the Institute, since it had enrolled a national—and international—student body earlier than Harvard and continued to be attractive chiefly to upwardly mobile, middle-class students. During the 1960s, like most other academic institutions, the Institute gave greater attention to minorities and women, but its specialized character made progress in this respect difficult to achieve while also shielding it from the pressures experienced by Harvard and other comprehensive institutions. Indeed, it was exactly the Institute's specialized character—and how much that character should be altered as M.I.T. evolved from a technical college into a research university—that generated the most important questions about admission policies in the 1950s and 1960s.

M.I.T.'s leaders since Compton had associated institutional progress with enrolling larger numbers of broadly talented, versatile students who were headed for top positions in industry and government—in short, students of the kind found at Harvard and other Ivy League schools. This goal prompted Killian and Stratton to broaden the undergraduate curriculum and create the residential campus, and probably influenced their decision to freeze the size of the undergraduate program.

The conditions of the golden age, however, made it possible for the Institute to attract progressively more-talented students capable of mastering steadily more-demanding courses in math and science. The tension between achieving greater variety and enrolling math-science whizzes proved difficult to resolve, and by the late 1960s the M.I.T. community was divided over the issue. A 1969 review by the Committee on Undergraduate Admissions reflected the dilemma. Committee members readily agreed that greater breadth and diversity were desirable. They were unready, however, to recommend changes in established admission criteria that gave greater emphasis to abilities in math and science than was the case at comprehensive universities or to propose that the Institute recruit students likely to major in nonscientific subjects. Though some members of the faculty would support such changes, others would strongly oppose them. The committee concluded that there was too much uncertainty within the faculty about the essential character of the Institute to provide a firm basis for policy change.[56]

The ambiguous outcome of debates about admission policies at Harvard and M.I.T. reflected real problems arising from broad patterns of postwar change. Harvard's evolution as a research university was not, in the end, entirely harmonious with collegiate traditions that stressed the preparation of economic and political elites. M.I.T.'s thrust toward leadership in scientific research tended to reinforce a history of specialization even as the Institute's leaders sought more-broadly talented students. At both universities, the claims to access of disadvantaged groups conflicted with the escalation of academic standards. These intersecting forces produced policy resolutions at the two institutions that reflected the traditional differences between them. Within this complex pattern, however, the dominant direction of admission policies from the mid-1950s to the late 1960s involved a steady raising of intellectual standards. Reviewing these years from the disappointed perspective of a later time, David Riesman would characterize them as "meritocracy triumphant."[57]

Organizational Dimensions of Academic Change

A Tale of Two Cultures

In the years preceding World War II, Harvard and M.I.T. displayed markedly different organizational characteristics. In terms of formal structure, Harvard was a federation of functionally distinct subunits, loosely coordinated through arrangements based more on historical understandings than written rules. M.I.T. emphasized limited purposes and maintained an authority structure that was centralized, pyramidal, and, for an academic institution, relatively formal. The ramifications of these dissimilarities were manifold.

At Harvard, the dominant units traditionally were the several faculties, each of which exercised considerable control over its own affairs in areas ranging from admission and curriculum (where authority was formally delegated) to personnel (where the faculty had acquired the power to initiate recommendations) to finances (where each faculty had jurisdiction over its own endowments and was largely responsible for its own solvency). Though patterns varied, most faculties evolved internal governance structures through which the professoriate exercised authority directly. Such structures tended to include, as in Arts and Sciences, an entrenched system of mainly self-regulating departments. By accepted custom, little effort was made to foster university-wide discussion of major issues. The ruling statutes provided for a University Council containing members from each faculty, but the body was never convened.

Within Harvard's diffused organization, the president possessed a few areas of direct authority, such as the ability to appoint deans, raise and allocate new funds, and control communications between the faculties and the governing boards. Explicit executive powers, however, were largely negative, staff support traditionally minimal, control of free dollars circumscribed, and capacity to discipline individual faculty members limited by Harvard's early commitment to academic freedom and tenure. A Harvard president's ability to move his institution depended more on achieved influence and success in attracting resources than on formal authority. The exercise of leadership in such a system was inherently problematic, and Harvardians enjoyed quoting the observation of former president Holyoke: "If any man wishes to be humbled and mortified, let him become president of Harvard College."[58]

At M.I.T., the central administration was empowered historically to manage campus activities quite directly. Working with the Executive Committee of the Corporation, the president controlled revenues and allocated budgets, appointed department heads and supervised their work with no intervening structure of faculties or deans, and charted directions of institutional development that were reinforced by decisions about budget and personnel. In contrast to Harvard, the Institute emphasized organizational unity and achieved this through structures dominated by administrators. The central body for policy discussions was the Faculty Council, which included the president as chair and the heads of all departments and professional courses. The standing committees of the Council also were dominated by members of the administration. Major policy matters were brought before the entire faculty for discussion, but this was hardly a body that could take initiatives independently, especially when the committees through which policies were drafted were tied closely to the administrative hierarchy.[59]

The organizational differences between Harvard and M.I.T. reflected far more than alternative administrative theories. The major influence centers at Harvard were the Faculty of Arts and Sciences, with its largest component in the humanities, and, to a lesser extent, the old and established professional faculties, especially those of Law, Business, and the Medical School. The Corporation was dominated by lawyers drawn from Boston's leading firms. The Harvard community thus reflected the professionalized values and self-regulating habits of the occupations favored by Boston's social elite. Harvard was also a large, old institution in which innumerable pockets of power had been carved out through three centuries of restricted endowments, organizational in-fighting, and bureaucratic deals.

M.I.T. was younger and less entrenched in every sense. Its centers of gravity were engineering and business, relatively new professions that were more comfortable with hierarchy than those that dominated Harvard. The members of the Corporation tended to be corporate executives. The Institute's close ties to industry and its focus on technological change required more administrative coordination than was needed in a university dedicated to humanistic learning.

The historic differences between Harvard and M.I.T., though important, should not be sketched too sharply. Despite the limitations of the Harvard presidency, the administrations of Eliot and Lowell demonstrated the enormous power inherent in the position. Despite the centralization of formal authority at M.I.T., the Institute's leaders traditionally placed a high value on achieving wide support before proceeding with new initiatives.

Compton's efforts to make M.I.T. less a technical institute and more a university generated pressures for a greater sharing of power. The strengthening of the scientific departments in the years before World War II, for example— including the importation of major figures from Harvard—led to a more active role for the faculty in the areas of curriculum and personnel. Faculty pressures also produced a clearer formulation of policies governing academic appointments. In the early postwar years, the Lewis committee reported widespread concern about the lack of faculty participation in governance. The committee concluded that the Institute had become too large and complex to retain its traditional organization, and the proposal to establish four schools, each headed by a dean, represented an impulse to decentralize.

Compton also saw the need for a more complex structure. He understood that continuing the interdisciplinary research centers developed during the war would create new administrative issues. He may also have believed that the establishment of separate schools for engineering and science would allow the sciences to grow with less inhibition. The changes of the Compton years, however, did not reduce administrative authority markedly. The manner in which the president and Executive Committee formulated, funded, and implemented plans for postwar development involved a high level of initiative and discretion. The Lewis committee was important in rationalizing M.I.T.'s future, but it mainly ratified policies already launched by Compton and his associates.[60]

Although Conant was a forceful leader who created a major tool of administrative authority in the *ad hoc* committees, the dominant impact of his term was to extend Harvard's traditional decentralization. In part, this result flowed, as did the parallel tendency at M.I.T. under Compton, from presidential efforts to strengthen the status and professionalism of the faculty. Though Conant simultaneously sought interdisciplinary cooperation through the extradepartmental University Professorships, he rightly concluded that this device had little impact on interactive patterns among professors. He honored the twentieth-century practice by which Harvard presidents left the professional schools largely to themselves, except when they encountered difficulty—as did Education. Indeed, he reinforced the customary financial independence of the various faculties—a tradition locally referred to as letting "each tub stand on its own bottom"—by making each responsible for its own fund-raising.

Conant had little interest in increasing the administrative capacity of the president's office as Harvard's operations became more complex in the postwar years. Prodded by the pressures of the veterans' program, however, he did create an administrative vice presidency to relieve himself of worries about budgets, physical plant, and other nonacademic matters. Perhaps his most significant structural innovation was the position of provost, which relieved him of direct responsibility for Arts and Sciences. (His initial intention had been to have this office supervise the deans of the professional schools also, but he retreated in the face of opposition.)

Conant's administrative changes left him relatively free, in the postwar years, to involve himself in national affairs, but it also left the Harvard presidency less well-defined than previously. The role no longer involved direct leadership of Arts and Sciences, but it had not been repositioned to provide overall coordination to Harvard's other faculties. At the end of Conant's years, Harvard was more a federation of semiautonomous units than ever before.[61]

Contrasting Administrative Approaches;
Common Academic Pressures

History presented Killian and Pusey with different organizational mechanisms through which to respond to the conditions of the golden age, and the styles of the two men heightened the contrast. Killian, who had graduated from M.I.T.'s course in administration and was steeped in the Institute's centralized traditions, saw organizational change as a necessary adjunct to academic development. Pusey, a classicist who had learned administration on the job at a liberal arts college, possessed some of the academic's disinterest in (and disrespect for) formal administration and was not inclined to ponder the links between organization and scholarly work.

These differences in orientation went hand in hand with developmental agendas that shared common impulses and contained similar organizational implications. Both institutions grew rapidly, adding faculty, staff, and facilities. The number of administrative units multiplied on both campuses as budgets increased geometrically. Both stressed research and graduate education, especially in the sciences, with concomitant shifts in the focus of faculty interests, the character of student bodies, and sources of funding. Both, as they grew, were inevitably drawn into more complex relationships with external agencies ranging from the federal government to private foundations to the City of Cambridge.[62]

Early in his term, Killian decentralized authority to a new layer of middle-level administrators. The four-school concept was implemented, and deans were given broad authority over their units. The position of provost was created to supervise educational work that fell outside the schools and oversee the interdepartmental research centers. This role was subsequently upgraded to a vice presidency for academic affairs, with general responsibility for education and research. Two additional vice presidencies, one in finance, the other in industrial and governmental relations, were established. Moreover, at the top of the organizational pyramid, a division of labor evolved through which the chairperson of the Corporation, beginning with Compton, assumed active responsibilities in the areas of fund-raising and policy development.

Paralleling the new administrative hierarchy, Killian put in place a series of coordinating mechanisms to balance the dispersion of administrative power. He was especially proud of the Academic Council through which he integrated the work of his deans and vice presidents. The Academic Council met regularly to consider policy matters of Institute-wide significance and major questions in the areas of personnel and resource allocation. Intensive summer sessions were used to define strategic priorities for the succeeding year, which then provided the basis for presidential supervision of each dean and school. An elaborate budget development and review process was created, coupled with long-range financial and personnel planning that included projections of needs and revenues and demographic profiles of Institute faculty. Killian's successors, Stratton and Johnson, continued the emphasis on organizational development. During the 1960s, M.I.T. became a pioneer in the use of computers to support administrative decision making, and in 1968 the Institute established an Office of Organizational Systems to provide ongoing, computer-based support for managerial decisions.[63]

Though Harvard was both larger and more complex than M.I.T., Pusey established no system of coordination comparable to that developed at the Institute. Moreover, despite the growth during his years—the number of departments in Arts and Sciences alone rose from forty-one at the end of World War II to fifty-four in the early 1970s—Pusey vigorously sought to maintain the tradition of limited central administration that he inherited from his predecessors. Indeed, he eliminated the position of provost that had been Conant's chief organizational change. There was little increase in staff support directly available to the president and equally little strengthening of staff capacity for the single vice president. "If there was a criticism of my administration," Pusey would later note with more pride than regret, "it would be that I was still trying to run Harvard as though it was small."

Pusey's spare administrative style was characterized after his retirement by Kenneth Andrews, a professor of management from the Harvard Business School in the following terms:

> The President, depending principally on his Deans to run their own affairs, has elected to use his staff principally as advisors, with each assistant reporting separately to him on problems in his area. He has preferred not to have staff meetings and has apparently depended in lieu of staff discussion upon what in President Eliot's case was called an "imperial grasp of fact" and a personal ability to appraise the soundness of advice offered to him without the cross check of other staff members' opinions. He has resisted suggestions that he share responsibility for educational leadership with a deputy or provost and he has maintained a primary interest in the life of the College, with which at least until recent years he attempted to remain in close contact. He has retained the statutory authority of presiding, when possible, at the meetings of all the principal Faculties throughout the University. He has convened a Council of Deans [which has functioned as a] mutually informative and informal advisory luncheon group.

No formal budget process on a university-wide basis was established, and patterns of financial management varied from faculty to faculty. There was no university-wide long-range planning mechanism. Pusey tended to concentrate his own attention on the manifold problems of day-to-day administration as they arose and to use the Corporation to help him attend to ongoing administrative matters while allowing "major questions demanding top-level attention to come to the Corporation too late and without the kind and quality of staff work that would permit definitive consideration and prompt decision." To the extent that significant new administrative capacity was developed at Harvard between 1953 and 1968, it occurred in the various faculties at the initiative of deans, a phenomenon that Pusey endorsed and which further strengthened Harvard's already strong pattern of decentralized administration.[64]

Given the radically divergent organizational traditions of Harvard and M.I.T. and the opposing administrative inclinations of their leaders, it is hardly surprising that the two institutions took different approaches to managing the most significant trends of the golden age—the growth of externally funded research and the expansion of graduate education. M.I.T. began immediately after the war to write formal policies and procedures concerning the receipt of government funds, and by the early 1950s an elaborate system of controls was in place, including the provision that any major research proposal required the approval not only of the appropriate department head and dean but also of a new Committee on Sponsored Research, composed of senior administrative officials. The Division of Industrial Cooperation, later renamed the Division of Sponsored Research, directly managed all the financial affairs of sponsored projects. Harvard, despite its much greater initial reluctance to accept external funds, established no comparable system of controls, and patterns of activity developed in an *ad hoc* fashion reflecting the inclinations of individuals and the disposition of particular faculties.

M.I.T.'s efforts to control funded research proved problematic as federal funds flowed with abundance and as the Institute, on the strength of these dollars, evolved into a research university. A 1963 study by a faculty committee argued, in fact, that efforts to "exercise control and surveillance in the ways traditional among certain other types of formal organizations will in the end destroy the very characteristics that make academic institutions generally, and M.I.T. in particular, uniquely attractive to competent, creative faculty members."

The committee urged "a high degree of individual autonomy, accompanied by a high degree of personal responsibility among all members of the faculty" on matters of sponsored research. The Committee on Sponsored Research was abolished and replaced by a faculty Committee on Outside Professional Activities, charged to provide general guidance on policy matters and informal advice to individuals upon request. The new group, however, proved insignificant as a mechanism of control and found its chief role in matters of grant administration. In the end, the pattern of externally funded projects at both Harvard and M.I.T. was largely guided by the individual decisions of specific researchers and research units in response to externally determined targets of opportunity and with minimal central coordination.[65]

A similar phenomenon of converging organizational patterns occurred in the area of graduate education. For the first part of the postwar period, responsibility for the administration of advanced programs at M.I.T. was lodged in the dean of the Graduate School, working with a committee of the Faculty Council, which he chaired, called the Graduate Policy Committee. The dean and his committee were responsible for admissions, the awarding of graduate fellowships and assistantships, and the enforcement of academic standards.

In early 1958, after a period of growing dissatisfaction, an *ad hoc* review committee recommended that central administrative control of graduate education be ended. "Only the departments can select the most promising applicants for their specialized fields and attract them to M.I.T. by appropriate assistantships and fellowship appointments," the committee insisted. "Only the departments can determine the depth and scope of knowledge of their fields which students must attain." The committee proposed the decentralization of administrative authority to the various departments with the dean and a renamed committee assuming responsibility for more general tasks of coordination and long-range thinking.

The impact of the new system, which was quickly implemented, was soon apparent in the area of admissions. As academic vice president, Stratton was concerned about the rate of graduate growth, and, when he became president, he attempted to limit expansion. His policies were markedly unsuccessful, however, as graduate enrollments regularly outstripped the guidelines he set. In his final report, Stratton expressed frustration, observing that these programs had "grown like Topsy" and that advanced education at the Institute was "singularly lacking in clarity and coherence of educational philosophy."

Thus did efforts to exercise central control of graduate program development give way to decentralized, uncoordinated growth. The pattern toward which the Institute evolved was the one with which Harvard began, at least in Arts and Sciences: direct departmental control of graduate enrollments, fellowships and programs with minimal central effort to coordinate development or set general goals across departmental lines.[66]

The Triumph of Research Culture

The erosion of the authority of M.I.T.'s central administration and the further decentralization of Harvard's organization represented basic consequences of their academic priorities. In their common evolution as leading research universities, power flowed inevitably toward professors. The trend toward faculty self-regulation was inherent in the increasingly complex and specialized nature of scholarly work. As research and graduate training came to be the dominant goals of both universities, the ability of administrative leaders to make judgments about curriculum and scholarly activities decreased. This change was especially clear at M.I.T. as a prewar faculty with large numbers of engineers holding master's degrees was replaced by scientists with Ph.D.s. The shift toward faculty autonomy was also influenced by the manner in which major academic developments were financed. With money flowing directly from external agencies to individuals and organizational subunits, and with both institutions dependent on such funds to subsidize their ambitions, those who could attract support took on a high degree of individual authority.

Recruitment standards further augmented faculty power. Both universities were committed to attracting the "best men available" in their fields for senior appointments in an intensely competitive market, and neither pressed potential appointees for commitments to specific institutional goals. Under these circumstances, scholars the institutions sought acquired enormous bargaining power in establishing conditions of employment. At both universities, indeed, the kind of activity most valued was less and less the work of the institution and more and more the work of individual researchers. Not surprisingly, the M.I.T. faculty acquired the dominant position in academic appointments long held by its counterpart at Harvard, and departmental collectivities supplanted deans and department heads as the major force in academic personnel decisions. Both faculties, in the end, became more loosely linked aggregations of professionals and less communities integrated through shared commitments or programmatic goals.[67]

The diffusion of administrative authority was one of a set of centrifugal forces introduced into the organizations of Harvard and M.I.T. by the academic priorities of the golden age. The multiplication of subunits and ancillary activities at both universities brought into the institutional communities many individuals connected only marginally with the central and continuing academic life of each campus. Nonfaculty research associates, graduate assistants on teaching fellowships, and technical personnel—most of whom had no long-term prospect of faculty appointments—grew in number. Junior faculty, on whom both universities relied for large amounts of instructional work, acquired a tenuous connection to their schools as the chances for advancement to the senior ranks decreased.

As the peripheries of both institutional communities became larger and more diffuse, the capacities of the governing boards to maintain effective contact with and oversight of their sprawling activities decreased. To some degree, at Harvard, the weakening connection between the Corporation and the internal organization flowed from the limited supervisory capacities of the president's office. The comparison with M.I.T. makes it clear, however, that even in a superbly organized and staffed administrative structure, the ability of the governing boards to provide a strong, coordinated organizational center diminished during the 1950s and 1960s.

Fundamental shifts in the underlying character and culture of both universities were part of the pattern of change. With respect to the faculty, for example, it became decreasingly likely that senior appointments would go to persons with some prior connection to the institution, either by having received a degree there or having taught there as a junior faculty member. Indeed, as the Harvard faculty expanded during the golden age, the process of cultural change that Conant had initiated through new standards for hiring and promotion led to the progressive replacement of representatives of the New England culture to which Harvard historically was linked by a cosmopolitan collection of scholars bound not by ties of school or region or ethnicity but by a common commitment to scholarship at the highest levels. When Pusey tried to assert one aspect of Harvard's traditional culture by identifying it as a Christian institution, he stirred one of the major uproars of his presidency and quickly learned how far his alma mater had moved. The ancient connections between the Harvard student body and New England also weakened and ties to greater Boston virtually disappeared as the undergraduate population became fully national. The financial base of the university moved to Washington and to a national constituency of alumni/ae and friends. Both Corporation and Overseers were nationalized, and the presidency ceased to be reserved for a Bostonian.

An analogous evolution occurred at M.I.T. In the prewar years, the Institute's ties to industry dominated the structure of its educational programs and the activities of its faculty and fostered an institutional value system rooted in an instrumental, technocratic view of knowledge and learning. M.I.T.'s evolution as a "university polarized around science" and supported by new sources of income led to a progressive weakening, though by no means the disappearance, of corporate influence.[68]

As the Yankee culture of prewar Harvard and the corporate culture of prewar M.I.T. receded in the postwar years, they were gradually replaced at both universities by a homogenized research culture that had academic as well as instrumental dimensions. The academic side of this value system, expressed in the policies and attitudes of Conant, sought scholarly excellence in all aspects of institutional life. This academic culture recognized intellectual achievement, measured by the most objective standards available, as the only fully acceptable criterion for the admission of students and the selection of faculty, and deviations from this norm required elaborate explanation—as was apparent, to take one example, in discussions of undergraduate admission policy at Harvard in the 1950s. The central constituencies of the academic culture were the scholarly disciplines and the learned societies they sponsored, for it was these groups, and only these, that could confer a reputation for excellence. As the academic culture, with its emphasis on professional ties, gained strength, the bonds of institutional community weakened.

Academic culture was, in essence, the culture of the faculty, especially that of arts and sciences—just as prewar institutional cultures had expressed the values of dominant external constituencies—and its ascendancy registered the growth of professorial power at both institutions in the postwar years. While the academic culture partook of democratic ideals in its emphasis on individual merit, its deepest roots were not in any social, ethical, or religious value but in the culture of science, what Talcott Parsons has called the "cognitive complex"; the highest expression of this culture was the advancement of knowledge. Thus, the academic side of the research culture of the postwar years admired above all else a particular kind of intellectual achievement quite different from that associated with the humanist scholars who were the academic stars of Harvard before the war and whose achievement lay in the mastery of a sociocultural tradition that they helped preserve, synthesize, define, and transmit.

The instrumental dimension of the research culture, drawn more from the traditions of M.I.T. than of Harvard, valued activities that utilized basic knowledge to solve technical and social problems. This value was particularly encouraged by federal funding, which tended to draw Harvard toward M.I.T. (as Pusey reluctantly acknowledged) even as M.I.T. was drawn toward Harvard by the changes begun by Compton. The convergence of the two universities in Cambridge upon the common standards and commitments of the research culture was symbolized by a growth of combined activities in the postwar years, including the Joint Center for Urban Studies, the Cambridge Electron Accelerator, a joint program for training math and science teachers, a new School of Health Sciences and Technology, and numerous arrangements for cross-registration of students and shared faculty activities. Indeed, as M.I.T. developed in new areas of the social sciences and the humanities, it frequently sought to complement disciplinary strengths already established at Harvard and appointed numerous former Harvardians to staff its expanding departments.[69]

The Resilience of Institutional Culture

The common impact on the organization and character of Harvard and M.I.T. of the academic priorities of the postwar years did not eliminate the organizational differences between them. Despite administrative change, M.I.T. was a more coordinated and structured institution than Harvard at the end of the period, as it had been at the beginning. The Institute's budget process, for example, continued to be centralized and hierarchical with no provision for collective faculty involvement. Indeed, the machinery for faculty participation in governance at M.I.T.—apart from such areas of specific concern as research, academic personnel, and curriculum—remained underdeveloped even as the administrative apparatus became well staffed and highly sophisticated—an organizational situation precisely the opposite of Harvard's.

Both universities remained, moreover, complex, multidimensional organizations with long histories, restricted endowments, and highly tenured faculties, and neither was capable of revolutionary change, even if that had been a goal, which it was not at either place. Harvard, for example, continued to have flourishing professional schools like Law and Business that did not adopt the research ideal but continued to train elite practitioners and to promote faculty who were outstanding teachers in these terms. The engineering faculty at M.I.T. continued to be largest, and the Institute's continuing readiness to take on major technical development projects had no counterpart at Harvard. Equally distinct was M.I.T.'s special relationship to the national security apparatus. Both also harbored faculties and subunits that did not fit comfortably into their institutional cultures: Education at Harvard, for example, and Humanities at M.I.T. Even within the activities that were common to both universities, significant differences remained, as was evident in the divergent emphases of admission policies and undergraduate curricula that remained throughout the period.

Harvard, moreover, continued to be a sprawling, decentralized, pluralistic campus while the leadership of M.I.T. still sought—albeit with increasing difficulty—to preserve the notion of institutional unity. This difference had both administrative and substantive implications. Programmatic decisions at Harvard were made on an *ad hoc* basis in the context of specific schools and departments with little reference to a broader conception of the university. At M.I.T., choices were made through a coordinated process and informed by an impulse to stress the substance, methods, and implications of science. In fact, the new fields that flourished most readily—economics, political science, linguistics, and management—were frequently those where the association with mathematics and science was an asset.

The emphasis on unity at M.I.T. is best symbolized by the remarkable continuity of its postwar leadership: Compton, Killian, Stratton, and Johnson. Killian and Stratton were lifelong members of the M.I.T. community who had been active in the change process that Compton began in the 1930s. All three of Compton's successors served extended administrative apprenticeships before ascending to the presidency. Three of the four chaired the Corporation upon leaving the executive office.

Most fundamentally, despite their common adoption of the values of the research culture, Harvard and M.I.T. retained different centers of gravity defined by the academic and instrumental dimensions of this value system. Harvard, with its core of arts and sciences and its history of resistance to applied work, admired basic research above all else and honored the individual scholar working alone in the laboratory or library. This resilient pattern was compatible with the values of Harvard's constituency of cultivated, affluent professionals who typically cherished the ideal of humanistic learning and believed in the beneficent effect of that ideal on society. Pusey summarized Harvard's emphasis succinctly:

> Though universities have a concern and responsibility toward the everyday world, their primary, their fundamental responsibility lies totally elsewhere. This is for basic investigation, for the pursuit of learning almost for its own sake . . . It is possible for a university to slip into a servile relationship with the culture in which it finds itself and so betray its real reason for being.

M.I.T., despite the rise of basic science and the introduction of the humanities, still viewed knowledge mainly in terms of utility—an orientation that fit well with the Institute's military and corporate patrons. Morison has distinguished the special character of M.I.T. from that of Harvard and other conventional universities in the following terms:

> Historically the object of . . . scholarship in traditional universities has been to obtain a more accurate description and fuller understanding of the given conditions—of the nature of things and of human experience. At M.I.T. the aim, for much of its history, has been to learn what you needed to know to improve the machinery and so, presumably, to make things work better. As a result the Institute tended to become more directly engaged in the world around it than its older counterparts did. And then [between 1945 and 1960] when the expanding machinery increasingly altered the given conditions of this world and brought pressure to bear on the conduct of its affairs, it was natural for those in the Institute both by the work they did and their cast of thought, to take a larger part in what was happening.[70]

The convergence of these two universities on the values, forms, and activities honored by the research culture represented not an abandonment of their historic commitments but an adaptation to the most important conditions of higher education in the years following World War II. In the process, both lost some distinctiveness and some autonomy but simultaneously achieved their own goals—both academic and competitive—and preserved their central characteristics not only intact but strengthened. Indeed, one of the most important observations that must emerge from a comparison of Harvard and M.I.T. in the golden age is that their different approaches to matters of organization appeared to work equally well. Both the centralized, coordinated, and rationalized style of M.I.T. and the decentralized, *ad hoc* manner of Harvard proved effective instruments of organizational progress—at least under the congenial circumstances for development that existed from the mid-1950s to the late 1960s.

The Old Order Changes

Two Clouds, One Storm

Pusey's report for 1966–1967 contained a note of concern that contrasted distinctly with the triumphant accounts of previous years. Two issues worried Harvard's president: student unrest and finances. The next year, Johnson of M.I.T. drew attention to the same two problems, which, as both men understood, were interrelated. Student disruptions, in Cambridge and around the country, were typically directed against policies of the federal government, whose threats to reduce aid to higher education were the chief source of fiscal uncertainty. In terms of long-range institutional health, finances seemed particularly important. In the short run, however, the student movement occupied center stage. In 1970 both presidents, in the wake of draining protest actions, announced their resignations, symbolically ending the golden age in Cambridge.[71]

Encountering New Financial Realities

Apprehensions about money became a constant theme of Pusey's reports during the late 1960s. In 1968 he noted that federal support to Harvard actually declined for the first time in many years, that Arts and Sciences closed the year with a deficit, and that a number of Harvard's professional schools were at risk from the further reductions in governmental aid that he anticipated. "It is hard to see," he wrote, "how a measure of retrenchment can be avoided." The following year, the university announced an operating deficit of $760,000—its first in recent memory—and the shortfall grew to $1.3 million in 1971. Such figures were misleading, since the Corporation continued to add a portion of endowment income to principal, but the situation was serious enough to prompt a thorough review of Harvard's financial position.

A preliminary study was provided in 1970 by two Kennedy School faculty members with extensive backgrounds in public affairs, economist Francis Bator and policy analyst Graham Allison. Stressing the rise in operating costs during the 1960s, their report expressed doubt that revenues from Harvard's traditional sources could offset the loss of federal support. "The outlook for the next year is bleak," they concluded, and "the long-run portent, though less certain, is also bleak." Bator and Allison questioned whether Harvard was organized adequately to cope with the economic universe that lay ahead.

Bator and Allison were particularly skeptical about the wisdom of maintaining the system of "each tub on its own bottom," at least in the form that had been employed in recent years. This structure, they argued, expressed the absence of any "coherent model of the university that could compel agreement on priorities and choices" in a constrained fiscal atmosphere:

> There is something peculiar about the notion that it is somehow right for a great
> university to be shaped more or less by happenstance, by the largely uncoordi-
> nated entrepreneurial activities of deans, professors, and administrators, and
> the proclivities of donors.

"Over the long run," the two economists asserted, "both structural change and new kinds of finance may be necessary if Harvard is not to deteriorate in scope, range and intellectual quality."[72]

M.I.T. was even more vulnerable than Harvard to reductions in governmental support. While federal research funds to the Institute grew at a rate of 6.3 percent per year in constant dollars between 1961 and 1965, the increases stopped and then turned into slight declines after 1967. Beginning in 1969, the Institute experienced a steady erosion in the number of federal fellowships and traineeships available for its graduate students. By 1970 M.I.T. was projecting deficits even larger than Harvard's: three million dollars for 1971 and a total of ten million dollars over the next three years.

It was a measure of the Institute's inherent strength that, in 1971, Johnson could initiate a program of privately funded fellowships that replaced much, but not all, of the loss in graduate support from Washington. Despite such indications of resilience, however, Johnson repeatedly expressed concern about the implications of changed government policies and felt that the areas of greatest importance to M.I.T.—science and engineering—were in particular danger. "The financial problems ahead for higher education are horrendous," he told readers of his 1971 report. "New forms of [federal] support must be devised if the long-term interests of our society are to be protected. It is almost that simple."[73]

Encountering Student Protest: Harvard

Nothing was simple, however, for academic leaders in the late 1960s, least of all maintaining an atmosphere conducive to federal aid to higher education. The first major protest incident at Harvard was triggered by a visit from Defense Secretary MacNamara in 1966, the second by a recruitment session with a representative of the Dow Chemical Corporation in 1967. A third episode occurred in December 1968 in connection with faculty discussion of Harvard's affiliation with the Reserve Officers' Training Corps (R.O.T.C.).

Throughout this period, Pusey and his associates were doubtful that local unrest would take the extreme forms that had appeared at Berkeley and Columbia. Harvard, the accepted analysis held, would be spared major difficulty because there was "no widespread 'alienation' of the student body, no breakdown in communications between students, teachers and administrators in an academic community with decentralized power and remarkable integration of all its parts." Pusey was pleased when Mario Savio, leader of Berkeley's Free Speech Movement, visited Cambridge and was largely ignored by students. In the fall of 1967, he felt confident enough to fling at student radicals his famous taunt, publicly labeling them "Walter Mittys of the left . . . who play at being revolutionaries . . ."

In truth, however, undercurrents of disaffection were building throughout the Harvard community during the 1960s, not all of them tied to external political events. A study of the Graduate School of Arts and Sciences discovered problems of morale among the students and raised questions about the effectiveness of Harvard's programs. Blacks pressed for greater recognition of their concerns, especially the need for a program in Afro-American studies, and students generally demanded involvement in decision-making procedures. A survey of the faculty revealed weak institutional commitment within the junior ranks. An increasingly politicized faculty harbored organized liberal and conservative caucuses.

How much these various divisions and discontents contributed to the explosive events of April 1969—when the optimism of Harvard's leaders was rudely shattered—remains an open question. Contemporary accounts tended to cite student dissatisfaction with their Harvard experience as part of a volatile mix of national and local concerns. One systematic survey cast doubt on that thesis, however, noting that polled students expressed positive feelings about Harvard both before and after the "bust." In this view, external social and political issues were the source of student rage.[74]

Whatever the truth about causes, the events themselves were clear enough. On April 9, a group of students led by the campus chapter of Students for a Democratic Society seized an administration building in Harvard Yard, expelled the deans, and demanded the abolition of R.O.T.C. and a student voice in selecting faculty for Afro-American studies. Believing that a prompt show of resolve would contain the incident, Pusey called in local police the next morning to clear the building.

Though he had hoped to set a national example for effective response to protest actions, Pusey's decision proved a serious miscalculation. Following the bust, student and faculty support rallied to the occupiers. A strike was called which lasted for two weeks while negotiators sought to restore order. The crisis was resolved only by a faculty vote to accept student demands with respect to R.O.T.C. and Afro-American studies. The latter decision prompted Henry Rosovsky, subsequently dean of Arts and Sciences, to resign from the program planning committee. He called the vote "an academic Munich."

Student unrest at Harvard did not end with the strike. The subsequent two years produced a series of episodes, but no issue or event (including the Kent State–Cambodia moratorium in the spring of 1970) matched the scale or intensity achieved following the bust. In the early 1970s, organized protest actions fragmented and dissolved, their ultimate meaning and value exceedingly uncertain.[75]

The events of April 1969 produced an orgy of institutional analysis. Even before the bust, the Faculty of Arts and Sciences established a committee to consider the implications of the initial R.O.T.C. protest. Then, in the midst of the crisis, an *ad hoc* Committee of Fifteen was assembled to identify reasons for the students' actions and to adjudicate disciplinary questions. In the fall of 1969, at the request of the Overseers, Pusey established a university-wide committee on governance under economist John Dunlop to undertake its own wide-ranging assessment. These exercises were unable to shed much light on the causes of protest activities. Indeed, the focus of discussion quickly shifted from the substantive issues that prompted student actions to the manner in which the university responded to the crisis. A consensus emerged that the building takeover had exposed profound difficulties with Harvard as an academic community and organization.

The Committee of Fifteen offered an analysis that was repeated in slightly different versions by other groups and individuals. Harvard's troubles, the committee asserted, were symptomatic of the "crisis of the modern university."

> The traditional university was a certain kind of community, quite hierarchical, yet, in the case of Harvard, integrated. The vast expansion of Harvard's teaching and research, greater diversity in the student body and in the faculty have shaken the old kind of community and led to increasing stratification and strains.

With the old institutional bonds weakened, the committee continued, the formal structures that sufficed in an era of shared norms became inadequate to maintain communication and resolve conflict. The students of the late 1960s were demanding and disillusioned and turned their frustrations upon the university. The Faculty of Arts and Sciences, with its committees and town-meeting form of government, was unable to manage the manifold issues of substance and process that were suddenly presented. The other faculties functioned in their own separate spheres. The governing boards, pressed by external concerns, grew remote from the internal life of the campus. No mechanisms existed to bridge the gaps between Harvard's components. The president, overburdened by responsibilities, inclined to address issues on an *ad hoc* basis, and fundamentally out of sympathy with important themes of contemporary culture, was not able through personal authority to provide a center. Thus, when the crisis came, the committee concluded, Harvard did not possess the reservoir of loyalty that could prevent escalation or the structural means to communicate among its parts to find solutions or the imaginative leadership to overcome the other deficits.

In the vacuum that existed after the bust, Harvard depended upon the *ad hoc* efforts of respected individuals—members of the Corporation, faculty, and senior administrators—to restore order. Archibald Cox was designated by the Corporation as official crisis manager. Dunlop, who replaced Ford as dean of Arts and Sciences, became a pivotal figure in reassembling Harvard's broken pieces. The organizational disarray implied by these arrangements profoundly shocked the university's leadership. Harvard was discovering how much it had changed since the days when President Lowell could make a major decision on his own authority. The university's chaplain summarized the dominant assessment with a combination of arrogance and dismay that was characteristic of post-bust Harvard. "There is a certain terrible sense," he told his audience one Sunday that spring, "in which excellence destroys community."[76]

Encountering Student Protest: M.I.T.

Indications of organizational strain were apparent at M.I.T. in the late 1960s just as they were at Harvard. An early instance was Stratton's final report in 1966. Drawing attention to the Institute's rapid development in the years since World War II, the outgoing president worried that growth might have exceeded the university's capacity to absorb change and that the tradition of institutional unity was being lost. He was especially concerned about the uncontrolled development of graduate education, the failure to integrate the humanities, and the quality of undergraduate education. In Stratton's view, M.I.T. had reached a "critical juncture in its history." He doubted the wisdom of further initiatives and argued that "we have now rather staked out the principal boundaries of our academic territory, and . . . have come to a time for consolidation and deepening." One of his final acts was to constitute a committee to review the Institute's graduate programs.

Intraorganizational tension became much more evident during Johnson's presidency in the late 1960s. M.I.T. was, of course, a highly vulnerable target of protest because of its association with the national security apparatus, particularly the armed forces. It was hardly surprising, for example, that the work of the Instrumentation Lab on guidance systems for ballistic missiles became a focus of student—and faculty—criticism.

As had been true of the R.O.T.C. and Afro-American studies issues at Harvard, however, questions about M.I.T.'s military ties were embedded in a network of questions that divided the campus community. Stratton's committee on the Graduate School had proved unable to make recommendations because of unbridgeable disagreements among its members about future growth. A similar split about the character of the student body was exposed by the work of the admissions committee. A survey of faculty revealed problems of morale and institutional loyalty among the scientists, the group on which the Institute has based its progress in the postwar years. Student activists pressed for a greater voice in campus affairs.[77]

By 1969 Johnson was convinced that two steps were needed to keep the Institute on a steady course. The first was a review of the work of the special defense labs—Instrumentation and Lincoln—to assess the appropriateness of continuing M.I.T. sponsorship. A committee of faculty, students, alumni, laboratory staff, Corporation members, and administrators was charged with the task under the chairmanship of Dean William Pounds of the Sloan School. In May, following weeks of testimony, the committee issued a preliminary report recommending major changes, including a balanced program of contract work that included more attention to social and domestic problems. The committee specifically concluded that the Instrumentation Lab's work on missile systems should be halted. The recommendations were reissued with little change as a final report in October 1969 and adopted on a trial basis by the Corporation.

Johnson's second initiative in the spring of 1969, as Harvard struggled to recover from the bust and strike, was to propose a broad review of the Institute's goals and directions comparable to the work of the Lewis committee in the late 1940s. In June, Johnson charged a planning group to make recommendations about the new study and emphasized the need "for participation . . . of as many members of our community as possible." The committee got the hint. In its August report, it suggested a commission composed exclusively of faculty and students that would stimulate "the broadest possible active participation of the many diverse components which make up the M.I.T. community." In September, Johnson appointed the new commission from a list of nominees supplied by various student and faculty entities under the leadership of Kenneth Hoffman of the Mathematics Department.[78]

In November 1969, the wave of student protest that had broken over Harvard the preceding April reached M.I.T. A group of students, joined by associates from around the city, announced a "November action" week consisting of rallies, parades, and mock trials, including a march on the Instrumentation Lab. Anticipating the possibility of a major confrontation, Johnson and his colleagues formed advisory groups of faculty and students whose members were asked to keep in touch with events and meet regularly with senior administrators.

Members of the advisory groups were present for the week's major event at the Instrumentation Lab on November 5. While they failed to prevent a tense encounter, which included a police action to keep the lab open, they provided a vehicle for discussion among various constituencies of immediate events as well as underlying attitudes. With the changes in Institute policy on the lab already in place, with the Commission on M.I.T. Education at work on a broad review of campus activities, and with intensive efforts to maintain communications among administrators, faculty, and students, neither the November action nor a subsequent episode in January escalated into a general strike or crippling protest.[79]

By 1970 it was clear that M.I.T., no less than Harvard, faced major issues about its program as well as its organization. The effort to put the work of the Instrumentation Lab on a more viable basis proved unsuccessful, partially because external funding for the more-balanced program recommended by the Pounds committee was not available, partially because of continuing controversy about the nature of the lab's work. In May 1970, Johnson announced his conclusion that M.I.T. should formally divest the lab—now renamed for its founder, Stark Draper—though he believed that Lincoln could continue as part of M.I.T. Johnson's recommendation was costly, given the lab's role in contributing overhead funds to Institute budgets, and it was especially difficult in the context of federal cutbacks in contract research. The decision, nonetheless, was critical not only to the continued work of Draper but to the reestablishment of consensus within M.I.T.

Indeed, Johnson's entire approach to determining the labs' futures, like the thinking that led to the Commission on M.I.T. education, was characteristic of the Institute's habit of planned change. Through carefully structured processes, M.I.T. consistently institutionalized developmental impulses and channeled into constructive interactions energy that would otherwise have gone into confrontation or produced frustration and disillusionment. It must be acknowledged, of course, that, in the context of the late 1960s, M.I.T.'s central focus on engineering, a traditionally conservative field, provided ballast against the forces that led to protest movements on many campuses. Still, it is striking that the Institute, despite much greater exposure than Harvard on the substantive issues raised by student demonstrators, avoided the kind of generalized crisis that occurred at its elder sister institution.[80]

Two Presidential Resignations

Pusey's decision to leave office following the 1970–1971 academic year ended an extended presidency during which Harvard had changed dramatically. Johnson's parallel announcement a few months later completed a much shorter term that had continued an evolution dating back to the early postwar years. Pusey's decision surprised nobody. He no longer possessed the authority to lead, and he also had lost the desire to do so. His departure occasioned little regret, but those with balance acknowledged an honorable educator who had the misfortune to lead Harvard in times with which he was out of step and whose rigidity of perspective made him effective in combating external attacks from Senator McCarthy but denied him the flexibility to maneuver in the face of internal conflict.

Johnson's announcement was more unexpected, but he, like Pusey, was worn down by recent events and welcomed the chance to succeed Killian as chair of the Corporation, where he would be shielded from the day-to-day pressures of the presidency. Both men understood, moreover, that their institutions faced fundamentally changed conditions—a different financial context, an altered political environment, and new educational issues. Such circumstances, as Johnson put it, called for "new ideas" and "new responses" that could not come easily from leaders who had survived periods of turmoil but wearied of their offices.[81]

CHAPTER FOUR

Evolution of the College-centered University: Tufts and Brandeis, 1945–1970

Tufts College, traditionally focused on undergraduate education in the arts and sciences, responded to the opportunities of the postwar years with new emphases on research and doctoral-level programs. A new name, "Tufts University," signified the change. The leaders of Tufts intended, however, to retain a primary emphasis on undergraduate work. During these same years, a new university, Brandeis, sponsored by a group of American Jews, joined the state's academic community. Brandeis's founders also conceived their institution as centrally concerned with undergraduate education, although they too intended to build a modest array of graduate programs, especially in the arts and sciences. In projecting their development during the 1950s and 1960s, Tufts and Brandeis set out to become different versions of a distinctive institutional idea: the college-centered university.

The Postwar Years at Tufts

Looking Ahead During World War II

By the early 1940s, President Leonard Carmichael of Tufts, like his counterparts at Harvard and M.I.T., had come to regard World War II as a time of opportunity, despite immediate, war-related problems of enrollment and finance. Carmichael's wartime reports referred repeatedly to new possibilities arising from the military emergency. He welcomed a Navy R.O.T.C. unit to Medford as a chance for greater visibility as well as for public service. He speculated that increased awareness of international issues would benefit the Fletcher School.

Most important of all, given Tufts's history of straightened finances, was the possibility of new federal support. "It is . . . not too early," Carmichael told his trustees in the middle of the war, "for all of us to do what we can to see to it that the men who administer our postwar education [at the federal level] . . . have an appreciation of the importance to this nation of colleges and univer-

sities with varied objectives and varied bases of administration and support."
If federal funds were to become available, Carmichael wanted to be sure that
private institutions got their share, and he assured his board that "every effort
is being made to maintain our relationships with the armed services . . . so that
Tufts's peculiar qualities—a university-college in which teaching and research
go forward together—may be maintained . . ."[1]

Carmichael's reference to the "peculiar qualities" of his institution
expressed his commitment to the idea of Tufts espoused by his predecessor,
John A. Cousens: a small, elite, liberal-arts program for undergraduates
capped by high quality graduate schools in selected professional fields. This
conception had developed slowly during the 1920s and 1930s as Tufts's leaders sought a way to reconcile the institution's historic yearning for Ivy League
status—a Universalist Harvard or Yale—with its actual circumstances.

The reality of Tufts, as Carmichael encountered it upon his election in
1939, remained far from Cousens's vision. The campus included two academically unexceptional undergraduate colleges of liberal arts (one male, one
female), both enrolling chiefly middle-class, commuting students; an undergraduate engineering program rated one of the weakest in New England; two
once-independent and still quite separate professional schools in Boston, for
dentistry and medicine, the second of which had been placed on probation by
the American Medical Association in 1935; and the new Fletcher School of
Law and Diplomacy, Cousens's hope for the future. All these units were beset
by financial problems.

Soon after his arrival, Carmichael announced that his goal was not radical
change but a general strengthening within the existing configuration of programs. Like Conant of Harvard, he believed the times called for upgrading
rather than expansion. He also shared with Conant, and with M.I.T.'s Compton, the view that academic improvement should be pursued by raising intellectual standards for both faculty and students, especially in the basic disciplines. Carmichael's academic values, like those of his two counterparts in
Cambridge, were rooted in his training as a research scientist. Tufts's new president was a physiological psychologist and was only the second academic professional to hold a position historically reserved for a Universalist clergyman
or an elder of the church. Indeed, though Carmichael was an alumnus and the
grandson of a Theological School dean, his view of Tufts had no more to do
with the Universalist church than Conant's ideas about Harvard derived from
Congregationalism. When Carmichael spoke of Tufts's "peculiar qualities," he
was referring not to religious traditions or social ideas but to academic characteristics.

Tufts in 1940 was in a middle stage of evolution between its Universalist
past and its future as a modern university. Important strains of the campus's
religious heritage remained. Church members still comprised nearly half the
trustees and a large proportion of the nonlocal students. The campus continued to receive financial support from the sect. The Divinity School, however,
was moribund, and Universalist culture at Tufts had devolved into a generalized secular liberalism and humanism. This atmosphere was only moderately

receptive to Carmichael's emphasis on the hard-edged values of science and research.

Any plans for Tufts's academic development, Carmichael felt, would have to take into account the dominating local presence of Harvard and M.I.T. Though he shared the intellectual aspirations of Conant and Compton, Carmichael doubted that Tufts could become a large university and graduate center, and, soon after assuming office, he downgraded Tufts's mediocre, teaching-oriented master's programs in the arts and sciences. What was possible, he believed, was to improve the research productivity of his faculty while also stressing undergraduate education of high quality. In this conception, the existing professional schools, properly strengthened, were important both because they gave Tufts the aura of a university and because they reinforced the arts and sciences. The Medical School, for example, attracted undergraduates who hoped to continue their studies in medicine and also offered opportunities for faculty involvement in advanced education and research. The Fletcher School offered similar advantages in the social sciences.

Carmichael's central emphasis, however, was on improving students and faculty in the arts and sciences. These hopes provided the context within which he responded to the wartime N.R.O.T.C. program that brought to Medford trainees from southern and western states where Tufts planned to recruit after the return of peace. Carmichael's ambitions also were stirred by Tufts's involvement in war-related scientific projects. These allowed the campus—as they had allowed M.I.T.—to expand its research capacities much more rapidly than would otherwise have been possible.[2]

Balancing Enrollments, Dollars, and Admission Standards

During the middle 1940s, Carmichael consistently emphasized his goal of maintaining Tufts at its established size while increasing student quality. He was aware of speculation that demand for higher education might increase after the war, and his response echoed Conant and Compton: Tufts should use any expansion of applications as a chance to become more selective. As he put it in 1946: "May the postwar period . . . see each year not a larger but an ever finer Tufts."

The disposition against growth extended to all of Tufts's degree programs, but special attention was given to recruitment for the two colleges of liberal arts. Early in his presidency, Carmichael had hired a new dean of admissions, a former graduate student of his from Rochester named Nils Wessell. As soon as the war ended, Wessell began a campaign to attract students from beyond the local area. As an expression of their intent to upgrade the student body, Carmichael and Wessell decided in 1946 to require College Board tests of all applicants, a practice associated with the selective private institutions they sought to emulate. During these same years, planning was initiated for dormitories, recreational buildings, and other amenities typically found on elite, residential campuses.

Given Carmichael's goal of limiting expansion, the veterans' program presented Tufts with an opportunity as well as a dilemma. Like other local colleges, Tufts was flooded with applicants in 1946 and 1947, many from able and motivated students. This sudden chance to increase selectivity was balanced, however, by pressure to grow beyond desirable limits, and Carmichael's solution, again paralleling Conant and Compton, was to permit temporary increases followed by a reversion to smaller numbers. By 1947 Tufts was enrolling thirty-six hundred students, 70 percent more than in 1939, and the admissions office was turning away eighteen applicants for every acceptance. In 1948, noting that demand from veterans would soon decline, Carmichael reiterated his intention to scale back. The next few years, however, were a disappointment. Between 1947 and 1952, the year Carmichael announced his resignation, Tufts's enrollments declined by only two hundred. The outgoing president noted this figure with regret, writing that it was "not a source of satisfaction" to him and expressing again his perennial hope that Tufts would become "better not bigger."[3]

The discrepancy between actual enrollments and Carmichael's goals was explained by Tufts's familiar financial problems. The criticisms of Engineering and Medicine in the late 1930s translated into claims for increased expenditures. New facilities of every sort were needed. The plant suffered from long-deferred maintenance. Faculty salaries remained embarrassingly low. Tufts's capacity to meet these needs through new fund-raising was limited, and continuing discussions of a financial drive bore no fruit until after 1950, when the "Second-Century Campaign" was launched with a goal of $4.2 million. Help from this source thus came too late to meet immediate postwar requirements. At the same time, Carmichael's hopes for federal aid beyond subsidies for scientific research were frustrated when the proposals of the Zook commission failed to win support. (Carmichael would not have welcomed approval of Zook's recommendations in any case. He was outraged by the suggestion that institutional aid should be limited to public institutions.)

In the absence of assistance from private or public sources, Carmichael, like his predecessors in the Tufts presidency, turned to tuition. In this context, the increased enrollments of the veterans' program were a blessing, and the fact that these students came with federal backing enhanced the benefit, since prices could be raised without jeopardizing applications. In the first two postwar years, Tufts raised tuition by 50 percent over the 1939 level, the largest increase among universities in Boston. Between 1947 and 1952, Carmichael instituted five tuition hikes in the School of Liberal Arts.

The arithmetic of higher enrollments and higher prices was inexorable. At the height of the veterans' program in 1947, tuition income was 137 percent above the 1939 level. By 1952 it was up another 22 percent despite a moderate decline in enrollments. The new money was used for facilities for Engineering and the Medical and Dental schools and also for construction and maintenance projects on the "hill." Observing his resources-starved institution absorb a steadily growing budget, Carmichael's hopes of reducing enrollments faded. He noted in 1948 that the question of "how to reduce student numbers in the present period of increasing costs is . . . the basic problem of Tufts today." In fact, when enrollments in Liberal Arts and Engineering began to fall after the veterans completed their studies, Carmichael expressed concern and took steps to maintain the student body at the 1947 level, in part by increasing the sizes of Jackson College, Fletcher, and the Medical and Dental schools.[4]

In the process of maintaining high enrollments, expanding tuition revenue, and improving Tufts's facilities, Carmichael was forced to abandon the goal of raising student quality. Indeed, once the inflated application pressures from veterans abated, the degree of selectivity in the School of Liberal Arts settled back into approximately the prewar pattern. In Carmichael's final year, Tufts had slightly under 2.4 applicants for every Liberal Arts seat, compared to slightly over 2.4 in 1939. The continuing Navy R.O.T.C. program brought Tufts a somewhat more cosmopolitan student body in the late 1940s than had been present earlier, but the overall change in student quality or character appears to have been insignificant.

Actually, Carmichael did more than sacrifice quality to numbers in the postwar years. He also was moved by financial pressures to expand Tufts's least selective and most academically marginal enterprise, the affiliated-schools program of the extension division. This activity, initiated as a source of revenue during the Depression, involved contracts with independent, special-purpose schools to provide general education for students in technical and vocational curricula. In 1948 Carmichael added the Forsyth School for Dental Hygienists to the list of affiliated schools, followed by the Nursery Training School of Boston in 1951. Recognizing the importance of the affiliated-schools program, Carmichael folded the extension division into a new Division of Special Studies headed by a dean, an ironic counterpoint—given the president's academic values—to the earlier decision to downgrade the graduate school and eliminate the dean of graduate studies. In the early postwar years, the affiliated-schools program and the two colleges of liberal arts earned surpluses that covered deficits and financed improvements in Tufts's struggling professional schools.[5]

Upgrading the Faculty

Carmichael's goal of strengthening his faculty also proved difficult to realize under the conditions of the late 1940s and early 1950s. There were some gains. As federal research support expanded, Tufts obtained an impressive share. By 1952 the combined faculties were attracting nearly three million dollars in government contracts, and Carmichael—whose personal standing and connections to federal authorities played a major role in this development—asserted in his final report that these funds had "made over our institution from a college into a small teaching and research university." The expanded research program helped Carmichael expand his faculty from 570 full- and part-time persons in 1938 to 990 by 1952. Moreover, Tufts's total research income in Carmichael's final year was only slightly lower than Harvard's, and—with an operating budget of less than six million dollars compared to thirty-four million dollars at Harvard—government dollars represented a significantly higher proportion of revenues.

The aggregate numbers were misleading, however, since sponsored research was concentrated in a few large projects and left most departments untouched. Moreover, Carmichael himself was not prepared to demand scholarly productivity as a general requirement of the faculty, even for those newly hired in the postwar years. The officer responsible for coordinating sponsored projects reported in 1953 that research was viewed as beneficial but not mandatory, since teaching remained Tufts's central responsibility. This was clearly a shift of emphasis from the Cousens years, when research had been regarded officially with grudging skepticism, but it hardly sustained Carmichael's hopeful parting claim that Tufts had been transformed into a center of scholarly productivity.

Indeed, despite his ambitions, Carmichael was able to do very little to support scholarly work. In 1946 he identified the steps necessary to attract a faculty of high standing: salaries would need to be improved, teaching loads reduced, and time made available for study and research—including a program of sabbaticals. During the remaining years of his presidency, Carmichael made only scant progress in all of these areas. Minimal salary increases were granted, for example, but, compared with the steps being taken at Harvard and M.I.T., Tufts's efforts were modest and did nothing to enhance the institution's relative position.[6]

Carmichael also continued to oppose new graduate programs in the arts and sciences, even on a selective basis, although his faculty voted in 1947 to reestablish the Ph.D. degree. The president's skepticism reflected not only his doubt that Tufts could compete with more established universities but also his view that Tufts lacked the financial base adequately to support advanced work. It was also the case, however, that between 1945 and 1952 Carmichael used surplus revenues earned by the colleges of liberal arts to meet pressing facilities requirements. Thus, the patterns of the postwar years were as much a matter of priorities as of resources, and Carmichael had concluded that improving the campus and underwriting the acceptability of the professional schools were primary objectives. To meet these goals, under the constrained circumstances of the times, he neglected matters that were essential to raising Tufts's scholarly sights.[7]

Carmichael's Departure

As Carmichael left the presidency in 1952, he expressed mixed emotions about the changes of his years. His policies, building on those of his predecessor, had ensured that Tufts would evolve as a diversified and reputable university of at least modest proportions. He had overcome the most pressing deficiencies of Engineering and Medicine and could report full accreditation for the former. He expressed special pride in the Dental School, which had consolidated its dominant position for clinical training in New England during the postwar years, and in Fletcher, which was attracting national attention. He had fostered emphases—not yet realized in practice—on enrolling a national, residential, undergraduate student body and strengthening the research orientation of the faculty. In recognition of these priorities and of a commitment to maintaining them, Carmichael urged his trustees to rename "Tufts College" as "Tufts University."

The overall tone of Carmichael's final report, however, was more apprehensive than celebratory. He was disappointed that he had been forced to enlarge the student body and that he had made so little progress on faculty salaries. These failures, he reported, reflected the central fact that Tufts still lacked the resources to finance its ambitions. The Second-Century Campaign, moreover, represented only a modest step toward improving the situation. The endowment, which stood at eleven million dollars, was far smaller than those of the institutions to which Tufts liked to compare itself. Tuition income thus remained vital, but the erratic student markets of the early 1950s rendered this income source problematic as well. In closing his valedictory, Carmichael stressed the uncertainty of Tufts's prospects. "The future usefulness of Tufts," he told his trustees, "will in large measure depend upon a constructive working out of its continuing financial problems."[8]

The Founding of Brandeis

Reviving the Idea of a Jewish-sponsored University

As Carmichael and his associates struggled to find a successful formula for Tufts, in the nearby suburb of Waltham a university was being established whose evolution would provide a provocative comparison to the century-old college in Medford. The new institution, named Brandeis after the leading American Jew of his generation, represented a dream that had been nurtured for decades within the nation's Jewish community: to create a secular and non-sectarian campus as emblematic of Jewish achievements as the nation's leading Protestant schools were of the accomplishments of that faith.

In undertaking their venture at a time of academic expansion, the builders of Brandeis would prove especially fortunate, although it would be several years before this fact would become apparent. In attempting to fashion a university that was closely linked to Jewish culture and also representative of high scholarly values, the founders faced a dilemma that had troubled many colleges and universities since the late nineteenth century. It was here that the first of the parallels between Tufts and Brandeis suggested itself.

The leaders of Tufts had been working for decades to reduce their dependence on the Universalist church and find an alternative basis for their development as a modern academic institution, while also retaining important aspects of their traditional collegiate culture. The early history of Brandeis would compress this long-playing educational drama—the confrontation of the universal values of academia with the specific commitments of a particular subculture—within a brief but intense period. The main actors in the first chapter of this story were a rabbi, an academic, and a group of successful businessmen.

The rabbi was Israel Goldstein, a New Yorker, a Zionist, and a prominent activist in Jewish causes. In the years prior to World War II, Goldstein had become interested in the efforts of fellow New Yorker Louis I. Newman to establish a Jewish-sponsored, nonsectarian university. Newman's idea, however, had proved controversial, and interest in the topic waned during the 1930s. With the return of peace, Goldstein directed his attention to Newman's proposal once again.

He did so in a period of great importance in Jewish history. As the awful consequences of the Holocaust came to light, the United States was emerging as the leading center of Jewish life and culture. At the same time, Israel was being born. In Goldstein's mind, a new university could serve an "essentially Zionist purpose." He wanted to strengthen Jewry as a distinct community within the American population and foster links between the United States and Israel.[9]

In early 1946, one of Goldstein's associates learned that a medical college in Waltham, Massachusetts, Middlesex University, was near bankruptcy and was seeking new sponsorship. Middlesex had been known for refusing to adopt a Jewish quota—its leaders blamed their financial difficulties on vindictiveness by the A.M.A. for the school's liberal policies—and the Jewish community was a group to which the college was prepared to turn. Prompted by Goldstein's friend, Middlesex contacted the New York rabbi, who made an exploratory visit.

Goldstein discovered an institution with remarkable possessions: a hundred-acre campus, largely undeveloped, among rolling hills; a small group of solid but ill-maintained buildings; a closed medical school; a struggling veterinary school and pre-veterinary program; and a charter authorizing degrees in the arts and sciences, medicine, and veterinary medicine. It was obvious to Goldstein that Middlesex was in desperate straits but that the facility had immense potential. "What a glorious place this campus could become," he wrote. "Most impressive of all were the site, the setting, the elevation, the view," which included, from a quiet hilltop, the Charles River, a reminder that the pastoral campus was only ten miles from Boston and its famous universities.

The visit convinced Goldstein that Middlesex "was intrinsically worthy of becoming . . . a great Jewish-sponsored university." He assembled a committee from the New York Jewish community, but also included a Boston lawyer named George Alpert. He reached agreement with Middlesex to take over the campus in exchange for assurances that the New Yorkers would try to maintain the existing operation and revitalize the medical and veterinary programs. Simultaneously, aware of the need for a well-known educator, Goldstein enlisted Albert Einstein, then at Princeton, who lent his name to the fund-raising effort in the hope that the new university would shelter refugee scholars. By February 1946, Goldstein and his group had acquired the assets and charter of Middlesex, established the Albert Einstein Educational Foundation, and set the fall of 1947 as the date for opening their new university.[10]

Goldstein and his New York associates, none of them educators, underestimated the challenge of establishing an academic institution, especially one intended as a symbol of the American Jewish community. The new university—the name Brandeis was adopted in the summer of 1946—would open a year behind schedule in 1948, and the thirty months between the acquisition of Middlesex and the arrival of the first students were marked by a series of crises and changes of leadership. Along the way, the new project was forced to overcome an effort in the legislature to revoke the charter and a parallel attempt to deny the veterinary school eligibility for funds under the G.I. Bill. Goldstein was able to face down both challenges, which never represented broad opposition, by emphasizing the need for additional facilities to meet the applicant pressures of the early postwar years. Indeed, Goldstein won endorsement of Brandeis from an impressive list of individuals, including Governor Tobin and Cardinal Cushing, as well as Compton of M.I.T. and Marsh of B.U.

The central problems of the initial period occurred within the Brandeis organization and were particularly focused on Einstein's role. The first eruption came in the fall of 1946 when the physicist, apparently angered by Goldstein's aggressive efforts to organize the new university and raise funds, threatened to withdraw. When it proved impossible to resolve the conflict, Goldstein removed himself, fearing that loss of Einstein would jeopardize the project.

Goldstein's departure left Brandeis leaderless, as Einstein was not prepared to give the enterprise more than peripheral attention. The initiative fell to Alpert, who tried to press ahead. He recruited six other Boston businessmen, all, like himself, highly accomplished but several of whom lacked formal education or broad connections in the Jewish community. Alpert, however, also had trouble with Einstein, and in 1947 the physicist carried out his earlier threat to resign. Subsequent negotiations between Alpert and Goldstein about the rabbi's return also failed, precipitating a walkout by the New Yorkers who remained from Goldstein's initial group. Brandeis was left in the hands of Alpert and his associates.[11]

The conflicts among Einstein, Goldstein, and Alpert have never been fully explained. While they clearly involved three strong and difficult personalities, they also expressed broad tensions within the American Jewish community in the early postwar years. For example, Einstein's political sympathies were internationalist and socialist, and these commitments made him ambivalent about the Zionist movement. One dimension of the conflict between Goldstein and Einstein appears to have involved the latter's repugnance at Goldstein's efforts to use Brandeis to promote nationalist sentiment of any kind. George Alpert, the successful offspring of a modest family, was animated by the intense feeling for the United States characteristic of many Jews of his generation and background. Alpert's patriotism was not incompatible with Goldstein's Zionism, but he had little understanding of Einstein's left-wing internationalism. Einstein's efforts to obtain the Brandeis presidency for British socialist Harold Laski enraged Alpert and deepened the tension between the two men.

By the fall of 1947 (the originally projected opening date for the new university), battles involving the relationship of Brandeis to one or another strain of contemporary Jewish culture threatened the entire enterprise. After eighteen months, the Brandeis project had lost its most important sponsor, raised little money, abandoned the idea of reopening the medical and veterinary schools, was in the hands of a group of obscure Boston businessmen, and possessed no leader capable of organizing a new academic institution.[12]

At this low point, Alpert and his colleagues offered the presidency to Abram Sachar, a well-known Jewish historian and leader, a faculty member at the University of Illinois, and the recently resigned president of the B'nai B'rith Hillel Foundation. Sachar was familiar with the troubled history of efforts to establish a nonsectarian, Jewish-sponsored university and was deeply attracted to the idea. He had participated in an unsuccessful effort along these lines in the early 1940s and had been on the original list of Brandeis supporters recruited by Goldstein. Sachar had no illusions at the time Alpert approached him, but he also saw the possibilities: the Middlesex campus; the availability of a state charter with broad degree authority; the readiness of the Brandeis family to lend their name; and the existence of a group of sponsors who, despite obvious limitations, possessed strong commitment and ample cash.

Sachar pressed hard about financial support, asking Alpert's group to cover any deficits he might incur in the first four years. He also insisted upon complete control over academic affairs and voiced his belief that the sponsorship needed to be broadened. When Alpert and his associates agreed to all his terms, Sachar accepted. This was March 1948, only half a year before the scheduled opening, but the Sachar appointment marked a turning point in the short history of the new university. Brandeis now had a leader who, as time would show, was perfectly suited to the challenge ahead. He would preside, during the next twenty years, over one of the most remarkable success stories in the history of American higher education.[13]

Imagining Brandeis

Abram Sachar was the first professional academic to lead the Brandeis project, and he harbored a different perception of the possibilities than had Israel Goldstein. The two men did share a starting point: Brandeis should symbolize Jewish achievement and therefore must pursue high academic quality. As Sachar put it: "If they [the Jews] are going to create a symbol, it better be a symbol of excellence . . . We had to have a Harvard/Yale/Princeton/Columbia/Dartmouth kind of a school . . ." What this meant to the new president in concrete terms was left unspecified in the early going. Sachar was more an entrepreneur than a planner, and the programmatic character of his new university would become clear only as the school evolved. His emphasis on academic and social prestige did have implications, however, that separated him from Goldstein.

A premise of Sachar's thinking was that Jewish culture could not provide the institutional center. That place had to be occupied by the established academic disciplines, and the major effort must be to build these into first-class offerings, attractive to students from all faiths and staffed by scholars from any background. Within this framework, there would be some room for Jewish themes. Sachar would prove receptive, for example, to the life sciences and music as fields in which Jews had achieved distinction. He also saw a role for Judaic studies and for international programs, especially ones that linked Brandeis to Israel. Extracurricular life would provide additional opportunities for the expression of Jewish traditions. But the "Jewish component," as Sachar called it, would be kept at the margins. For the new president, the emphasis had to be on academic excellence as defined by the nation's most prestigious campuses.

Sachar's educational ideas flowed from his aggressively conventional vision. The new university would start as a college of arts and sciences and later add graduate work because that had been the evolutionary sequence of Ivy League schools. Brandeis would not focus on advanced professional schools at the beginning and would never develop undergraduate professional programs because this was not the pattern at the nation's elite universities. Brandeis would not emphasize innovative or experimental approaches to undergraduate education because this was inconsistent with the symbolic need to represent excellence. Sachar had no interest in the reforming exhortations contained in the 1947 report of the Zook commission. The basic text for designing the undergraduate program would be the Harvard Redbook. Obtaining accreditation would be given top priority.

The Brandeis student body would be national, relatively small, and exclusive because in the American academic tradition these characteristics were associated with quality. While Sachar rejected any notions of racial and ethnic quotas for Brandeis, with their hateful associations for Jews, the new university also would not become a haven for Jews discriminated against elsewhere, important as this idea had been in the movement to create a Jewish-sponsored university. Sachar did not think such an institution ever could represent quality. From the beginning, Sachar recruited key personnel from the most established institutions. His first two aides, David Berkowitz and Clarence Berger, had been at Harvard. Emphasis was placed on attracting faculty from the Ivy League.[14]

With the appointment of Sachar, the underlying purpose of Brandeis shifted subtly but crucially: from directly promoting Jewish objectives to indirectly strengthening the position of Jews by establishing an institution of quality. For Sachar, Brandeis was to be a corporate gift from the Jews to American society, a fulfillment of a Jewish obligation to higher education. He looked forward to a time when the Jewish origins of the university actually would be obscured—as had happened with the sectarian roots of leading Protestant institutions. Here was an aspiration that made little sense to a man like Israel Goldstein, who, for the remainder of his life, would be critical of Sachar for giving insufficient stress to Jewish culture in the development of the new university.

What Sachar's vision captured, with an unerring eye for gradations of social and academic prestige, were the educational ideas and institutional forms most closely associated with elite higher education in the late 1940s.

When Brandeis's first president was inaugurated in Boston's old Symphony Hall, the scene of so many academic ceremonies for the state's universities, it was the Harvard Glee Club, on loan for the occasion, that sang in celebration.[15]

Launching the New University

In the fall of 1948, six months after Sachar's appointment, Brandeis opened its doors with an arts and sciences faculty of 13 and 107 freshmen. For the next six years, Sachar and his colleagues built incrementally on this base. A new entering class was added each year until a full, four-year program was in place. This early period demonstrated that the new university could attract good students, despite the slackening of demand for college admission affecting many academic institutions in the late 1940s and early 1950s. By 1950, in fact, the Brandeis student body boasted scores on standardized tests well above national means in all areas and represented twenty-four states, though half came from Massachusetts and another quarter from New York.

Simultaneously, Sachar mounted a vigorous effort to recruit faculty by seeking out veteran instructors who were prepared to spend their final years in a new venture and young persons from major universities to whom Brandeis could offer rapid advancement. Making full use of the trustees' commitment to cover early deficits, Sachar offered high salaries, gave instant tenure, and landed a number of distinguished scholars. Among the pioneers were Ludwig Lewishon in literature, Everett Hughes in sociology, Max Lerner in American civilization, Irving Fine in music, Saul Cohen in chemistry, Leonard Levy in history, Albert Guerard in comparative literature, Herbert Marcuse in political science, and Abraham Maslow in psychology. In 1953, setting a regional speed record, Brandeis received full accreditation as an undergraduate college of arts and sciences from the New England Association of Colleges and Secondary Schools.[16]

Sachar displayed a particular genius in public relations and fund-raising. He was aware, when he assumed the presidency, that past efforts to create a nonsectarian, secular, Jewish university had experienced trouble attracting money. As recently as 1945, Newman had published an article drawing attention to this fact. Goldstein's efforts to promote Brandeis had confirmed Newman's analysis: the New Yorker had failed to win support among either Orthodox or Reform Jews, and the project's early supporters—including Goldstein, Alpert, and Sachar—belonged mostly to the Conservative branch of Judaism. In this pattern, however, Sachar sensed not difficulty but promise. As he later put it, reflecting on his first encounter with Alpert and his Boston associates:

> As I listened to them they reinforced the conviction that there was enormous power in the constituency they represented, a power that had been completely misunderstood and overlooked by those who glamorized letter-head names. These remarkable men all had the traditional Jewish awe of education . . . Most of them had no university of their own. Here they found an ideal identification, and they were determined to fashion it into the proudest of symbols, regardless of what it required in energy and resources.

Thus did Sachar define a natural constituency for his enterprise: first and second generation Jews, chiefly of eastern European origin, mainly uneducated beyond high school, and oriented toward assimilation within American culture but retaining a strong Jewish identification. Such men, Sachar knew, could be moved by his stirring, ambiguous conception of a first-class university established by their community and symbolic of their success from which the Jewish identity gradually would disappear.[17]

Sachar also knew the money was there, not just in Boston but in major Jewish communities across the nation. Indeed, creating a national constituency for Brandeis was an early priority for Sachar, and to accomplish this he needed to add highly visible Jewish and academic leaders to Alpert's gritty band of local enthusiasts. His success in this regard was a crucial step in positioning his institution. Soon after his appointment, the Brandeis board was expanded to include prominent philanthropists (Joseph Proskauer, Mrs. Adele Rosenwald Levy), businessmen (Israel Rogosin and Jacob Shapiro), academics (Paul Klapper and Isador Lubin), and public figures (Eleanor Roosevelt).

By Brandeis's second year of operations, development offices were functioning in Boston, New York, Atlanta, Los Angeles, and Chicago, and a collection of fund-raising organizations—Brandeis Women; Friends of Brandeis Music—were created. At this early stage, expenditures for development and public relations exceeded the budget of the faculty. A stunning array of fund-raising devices was employed. The "Brandeis Associates" provided recognition for individuals who contributed a hundred dollars or more annually. Testimonial dinners at which wealthy friends and colleagues of an individual were invited to pay tribute—with the proceeds going to Brandeis—were organized at a rate of forty per year. Endowed chairs were proposed to honor recently deceased celebrities, and friends and admirers were asked to provide the funding. "Air safaris" to the Brandeis campus brought potential donors to Waltham.

Most important, Sachar traveled the country speaking to individuals and groups. He made an annual visit to the Palm Beach Country Club in Florida, regularly netting a quarter of the university's operating budget. Before such audiences, Sachar eloquently related Jewish history and culture to the promise of Brandeis. It was time, he always argued, for "the people of the book," now prospering in their adopted home, to establish a great American university. Those who witnessed these occasions were moved, sometimes awed, by the grandeur of Sachar's vision. Neatly structured giving programs added tax advantages to emotional rewards for donors.

The money poured in. Annual gifts and grants rose from one million dollars in 1950 to two million in 1953 and to four million in 1956. These successes were complemented by proportionately large revenues from student charges, as the Brandeis constituency proved ready and able to pay high tuition rates to gain access to the unique new university for their children. Brandeis even made profits from its dormitory and dining-hall operations.

Sachar's financial virtuosity allowed the new campus to sustain high instructional costs while also making rapid progress on the physical plant. By the spring of 1951, the former Middlesex facilities were completely refurbished, a master plan for campus development was completed by Eero Saarinen, and construction was begun on one million dollars' worth of residential and social buildings. Observing this astounding record, while their own better-established institution was struggling to raise five million dollars during a multiyear capital campaign, the leaders of Tufts must have experienced large measures of both respect and frustration.[18]

The money Sachar raised was, inevitably, Jewish money, a fact that was consistent with the president's concept of Brandeis as a gift from the Jews to their countrymen. Financial progress also symbolized, however, the extent to which, despite Sachar's goal of creating a nonsectarian university, the specifically Jewish character of the enterprise was the key to its early success. The faculty and staff were almost exclusively Jewish. So, too, were the students.

Brandeis's attractiveness to talented Jews fearful of discrimination elsewhere contributed greatly to its ability to enroll able undergraduates in an environment of intense interinstitutional competition for enrollments. From the beginning, however, the new university made special efforts to attract students from other religious groups. Non-Jews were placed in prominent positions in the admissions office. A sports program was intended to appeal to Catholics and Protestants. Sachar also emphasized the recruitment of non-Jewish foreign students whom he thought would be less likely than their American counterparts to stay away. The admissions office even proved ready—despite official denials—occasionally to admit non-Jews with lower qualifications than some Jews who were rejected. None of these efforts had much impact, however, and Brandeis quickly became an overwhelmingly Jewish institution in every significant way outside the formal curriculum.

From Sachar's perspective, Brandeis's Jewish character was not surprising and was, in fact, precisely the pattern associated with the early years of the Protestant institutions he so much admired. He continued to express confidence that Brandeis would evolve into a nonsectarian, general university, just as Harvard, Yale, and Princeton had done. In affirmation of this goal, he dedicated, in the mid-1950s, an "interfaith area" in which separate chapels would be built for students from each of the nation's three major religious traditions.[19]

Institutional Mobility in the Early Golden Age

The Importance of University Status

By 1953 leaders at both Tufts and Brandeis believed the time had come to ally themselves more explicitly with postwar academic values by strengthening their images as universities rather than colleges. The two institutions arrived at this point, however, by strikingly different routes.

Tufts had taken on the form of a university in the late nineteenth century, but the name "Tufts College" had been retained, partially because the heart of the institution—for trustees, presidents, faculty, and alumni/ae—continued to be the undergraduate colleges and partially because, for most of the twentieth century, no great advantage would have flowed from altering Tufts's identity. By the early 1950s, however, universities had begun to emerge as the leading force in higher education. It was to universities, now, that associations of high academic standards were most readily attached. Tufts's recently retired president, Leonard Carmichael, had taken a number of steps to change Tufts into a proper university, especially by stressing the need for more research.

In choosing Carmichael's successor, the trustees effectively endorsed his views by appointing one of his closest associates, the former dean of men and director of admissions for Liberal Arts and current vice president, Nils Y. Wessell. Wessell's inaugural speech proclaimed his commitment to Carmichael's goal of lifting Tufts's academic sights within the established configuration of programs, and he reiterated his predecessor's proposal to rename the campus "Tufts University."

Wessell's belief that the period ahead would offer opportunities for upward mobility was based on his awareness of the new conditions of the early 1950s, especially the prospects of increased demand for admission and enhanced federal assistance. Wessell also possessed a good sense of public relations. He knew he would have an easier time attracting students, faculty, and money if he could make his pitch in the name of a university. In 1954 the trustees agreed to the proposed name change.[20]

While Tufts had been for decades a university with the name of a college, Brandeis, during its first years, was a college with the name of a university. Indeed, some members of the board and faculty wanted to remain a four-year institution, which had been Goldstein's original conception. For Sachar, however, there was never any doubt that Brandeis should develop the advanced functions, though he had few specific ideas about how to do so. By the early 1950s, however, much of the initiative for academic planning had shifted to the faculty, and from this quarter came advocacy for instituting an emphasis on graduate programs and research.

An important champion of this perspective was chemist Saul Cohen, who joined Brandeis from industry in 1950 and quickly became chair of the School of Science and a faculty leader as well as confidant to the president. It was Cohen, more than anyone else, who brought to Brandeis the values of modern science, which had been given little attention in the early years when Sachar's recruitment emphasized humanists oriented toward general education. Cohen was not impressed by the scholarly achievements of the initial faculty in the sciences. He doubted, moreover, that Brandeis could attain academic prestige by stressing undergraduate education. Quality in that arena was too amorphous, he thought, too difficult to document, for a new campus to compete with established places. The keys to rapid upward movement for Brandeis, in Cohen's view, lay in scholarly distinction and doctoral training, where excellence could be achieved and demonstrated quickly if sufficient resources were available.

From Sachar's perspective, Cohen's reasoning was on target. Though not personally research-oriented in modern, professional terms, Sachar understood that success in creating a Jewish version of an Ivy League school depended upon attracting recognized scholars. Cohen was persuasive that Brandeis would be more successful recruiting for a university—with all that the label implied about support for research and opportunities to work with gifted students on an advanced level—than for a college. An official planning document expressed the new strategy:

> Its origins and timing gave Brandeis little choice but to become a university . . . To a school committed to excellence, the small, liberal arts college concept offered limited foundations upon which to build. Contemporary conditions . . . require a complex of facilities, a faculty staffed by sophisticated researchers and scholars, and students who view the B.A. as a passport to advanced learning. The average, traditional liberal arts colleges . . . were ill-equipped to meet the new needs. The in-depth resources of such great schools as Swarthmore, Carleton and Amherst might stand their ground; it was another matter for a fledgling institution such as Brandeis. Academic talent was flowing increasingly toward the "university colleges" . . .

In 1953, the year that Brandeis's baccalaureate degree programs gained accreditation, Sachar established the Graduate School of Arts and Sciences. Like Wessell, Sachar was convinced that the 1950s would be a time of opportunity for institution builders. Two years later, in 1955, he created the new position of dean of faculty and gave the job to Cohen.[21]

At both Tufts and Brandeis, the impulse to achieve university status was combined with a wish to retain collegiate virtues and avoid the negative characteristics of large universities, especially the neglect of undergraduate education and of individual students. In his inaugural address, Wessell qualified his emphasis on making Tufts a true university by stressing the importance of limiting expansion and fostering good teaching. Tufts should strive, he asserted, to become a "small university of high quality," and he underlined the distinctive value of this aspiration by pointing out that few institutions could be characterized by those four words.

Sachar, seeking a principle that would reconcile the emphasis on graduate education and research represented by Cohen and sentiment among some board and faculty members favoring a collegiate institution, also adopted the "small university" concept, which was in any case philosophically appealing to him. On both campuses, therefore, plans to exploit the favorable conditions of the 1950s included efforts to define and institutionalize the special qualities that could be achieved by restricting growth.[22]

Defining the College-centered University

The leaders of Brandeis, unencumbered by the rigidities of established institutions, were particularly free to chart a new course. At his inauguration, Sachar had defined Brandeis's focus as "the development of the whole man, who grounds his thinking in fact, who is intellectually and spiritually alert to the needs of a growing society and to the role he should play in it." For those planning Brandeis's development, Sachar's emphasis meant that progress toward university status must be combined with a continued stress on liberal learning at the undergraduate level. The graduate school would not be allowed to grow beyond a third of the size of the college, and while scholarship would be encouraged, its potential relationship to teaching would be exploited.

Indeed, Brandeis would require all faculty members, even those recruited mainly for their scholarly standing or potential, to teach undergraduates regularly, and Sachar and his colleagues would seek out professors who "would not come reluctantly" to this balance of emphases. A limited number of fields would be developed. In science, for example, Cohen restricted Brandeis to four disciplines—chemistry, physics, biology, and mathematics—and he emphasized a limited range of specialties within these, focusing especially on areas of intellectual change.

While avoiding the tendency toward excessive specialization in education associated with modern scholarship, Brandeis's leaders also planned to avoid the vocational training and social problem solving associated with service-oriented universities. The only undergraduate program with any practical flavor would be a limited teacher-certification sequence within the arts and sciences. The Graduate School would build doctoral programs in the basic disciplines. Only a few advanced professional programs, carefully selected, would be established, and Brandeis would avoid duplicating programs in place elsewhere while stressing the most advanced and theoretical aspects of the fields chosen. Applied research would be limited.[23]

The transition to university status was more complex at Tufts than at Brandeis. The first step was a symposium in the fall of 1955 on "The Role of the Small University in American Higher Education." Delegates from over two hundred campuses came to Medford to discuss scholarship, religion, teaching, and engineering education in institutions of limited size. Simultaneously, Wessell obtained funds from the Carnegie Corporation for an extensive self-study through which a dozen committees and nearly seventy members of the faculty and staff would develop a master plan for future development. The self-study, though cumbersome and attenuated, proved a successful exercise in collective decision making, and when the final report was issued in 1958, project director Leonard Mead was able to claim unanimous endorsement of a series of major policies.

The dominant theme of the self-study report was that Tufts should restrict expansion while raising quality in every aspect of its operations. Only the Graduate School of Arts and Sciences should grow, to about three hundred students, and Ph.D. programs should be developed in every department. The Medical and Dental schools should shift from training practitioners to producing researchers and specialists and should seek to recruit national student bodies.

While the size of the Graduate School should be allowed to double, Tufts's emphasis should continue to be on the liberal arts colleges, since undergraduates in these two units still would outnumber graduate students by seven to one. In the same vein, the report recommended a general strengthening of faculty research while retaining a primary emphasis on teaching and on pursuing efforts to integrate teaching and scholarly activities. Also in the name of quality, Tufts should reduce its commitments to the College of Special Studies (renamed, along with the other undergraduate units, after the campus put the word "university" in its title) and should either raise standards in the affiliated-schools programs until they were comparable to the other colleges or eliminate them altogether.

The recommendations were compatible with Wessell's own thinking. As he put it in 1959, following trustee endorsement of the self-study, Tufts should not "cater to all or even a majority" of educational needs but should limit itself "to those pursuits of man which demand breadth as well as special competence." Since "breadth comes from a proper emphasis on the liberal arts and sciences," Tufts should retain its historical commitment to these fields, insisting that they form part of the education of all students, including dentists, foreign service officers, and engineers, as well as undergraduates. Wessell's advocacy of these limited goals expressed philosophical commitment and also recognized reality. He doubted that Tufts could marshal the resources to support more extensive development of the advanced academic functions.[24]

A central emphasis on the arts and sciences at both the baccalaureate and advanced levels; a particular focus on general and liberal education for undergraduates; an aversion to intellectual specialization; an insistence that graduate program development and faculty research be organized to enhance undergraduate learning; a distaste for vocationalism, especially in undergraduate programs; a reluctance to encourage service-oriented activities by the faculty: these values—in conjunction with a general disinclination to expand and diversify—were the major elements of the small university concept as defined at Tufts and Brandeis in the 1950s.

Beyond these shared dispositions were important differences between the two institutions. Tufts had to take account of historical commitments that were marginal to Wessell's vision in areas like dentistry and the affiliated-schools programs. The founders of Brandeis were in a position to conceive a pure embodiment of their current values.

The central themes of projected development had much in common, however, and Sachar and Wessell asserted similarly distinctive roles for their institutions. Neither would follow the path being taken by research universities like Harvard and M.I.T., in which graduate training and faculty scholarship seemed likely to dominate and weaken undergraduate education. Both rejected the model of urban and service-oriented institutions like B.U. and Northeastern, with their heavy emphasis on practical subjects and their tendency to become massive bureaucracies. Sachar and Wessell each acknowledged, in fact, an affiliation of purpose with the nation's leading liberal arts colleges, though both also insisted that their status as universities would enable them to achieve higher intellectual standards and offer a greater range of subjects than was possible at most four-year schools.

While Tufts and Brandeis hoped to remain explicitly collegiate in spirit, they rejected the traditional notion that colleges should embody the particularistic values of their sponsoring ethnic and religious groups. The authors of Tufts's self-study asserted that the historic Universalist commitments to "virtue and piety" were no longer relevant to a discussion of institutional aims. Wessell shared this view. Indeed, he regarded Tufts's tie to Universalism as an impediment to academic progress since, unlike the Unitarians, the Universalists were small-town people with limited vision, resources, and ambitions. Replacing Universalist and alumni/ae board members with accomplished, successful, cosmopolitan trustees was a major goal of the Wessell years. In a similarly ecumenical spirit, planning documents at Brandeis gave no emphasis to the special Jewish possibilities of the new university.

For leaders of both institutions, collegiate values had become synonymous with the liberal arts and sciences, conceived as a rounded body of learning representing the vital intellectual inheritance of modern civilization. Sachar, Wessell, and their colleagues were also clear about the association of the liberal arts with institutional prestige. Their central emphasis on these fields, as well as their adherence to other aspects of the small university concept, had everything to do with their common ambition of making their institutions as much like Ivy League universities as possible.[25]

Building the College-centered University

In the hopeful environment of the middle 1950s, encouraged by the expanding need for college teachers and ready support for educational institutions, Wessell and Sachar moved toward their interpretations of the college-centered university. Between 1957 and 1960, even before the self-study was completed, Wessell and his colleagues expanded the Graduate School by establishing new Ph.D.s in chemistry, physics, psychology, humanistic studies, and sociology. At the end of the decade, graduate enrollments began to rise and, equally important, to shift from the traditional cadre of part-time teachers pursuing master's degrees to full-time, apprentice scholars working on doctorates. By 1960 Wessell was claiming major progress toward the goals of the self-study. He characterized Tufts as a "threshold university" that was "on the edge of greatness" and possessed a "potential for unusual distinction."[26]

Progress at Brandeis was even more dramatic. In the six years after the founding of the Graduate School, under Cohen's skillful leadership the campus launched thirteen Ph.D. programs and created the first graduate professional school, the Heller School of Social Welfare. By 1960 Brandeis's Graduate School of Arts and Sciences was as large as its counterpart at Tufts—with just under two hundred students, virtually all full-time doctoral candidates.

As impressive as the pace of development was the rapid attainment of eminence in several fields. Biochemistry illustrated the opportunistic approach that Sachar and Cohen employed. A potential donor wanted to support research on Hodgkin's disease, a difficult project for a campus without a medical school. Cohen suggested research in biochemistry, an emerging area where a new campus could make a mark, as an alternative. Sachar and Cohen then recruited two prominent scientists and built a graduate department around them, quickly gaining national visibility. Similarly, rapid movement was accomplished by parallel means in literature, mathematics, history, and music.

Cohen understood that Brandeis had a limited window of opportunity, during its early years, to install a critical mass of faculty with the highest scholarly standards, and he used his position to make sure the moment was not lost. He established a tenure system both to create an appropriate setting for the accomplished scholars around whom he hoped to build and to ease out some of the early faculty who could not survive a rigorous review. Mathematics, for example, was completely restaffed under Cohen's guidance. In 1961, only thirteen years after its opening, Brandeis was granted a charter for a Phi Beta Kappa chapter. Once again, the new university in Waltham established a speed record in achieving a significant academic recognition.[27]

Both Sachar and Wessell understood that an essential ingredient of the college-centered university was the presence of intellectually talented undergraduates. To some extent, the impulse to enroll selective, national student bodies was rooted, at both Tufts and Brandeis, in the knowledge that prestige was linked to undergraduate admission standards. Sachar and Wessell also understood the logic that had driven enrollment stabilization at M.I.T. in the 1930s: an institution wishing to develop faculty research and graduate education needed to enroll undergraduates who could thrive in a demanding atmosphere and attract the interest of a scholarly faculty. For both these reasons, the strengthening of collegiate student bodies was a major part of building the small university in the 1950s.

From the time of his appointment, Wessell argued that Tufts should limit undergraduate expansion, emphasize recruitment on regional and national bases, build more dormitories and recreational facilities, and rely on the anticipated tidal wave of high school graduates to bring an elite group of undergraduates. The admissions subcommittee of the Carnegie self-study endorsed this emphasis, asserting that the baby boom was about to present Tufts with a chance to become truly competitive with the Ivy League. For most of the 1950s, however, this goal remained only a hope. Wessell was able to avoid major expansion of the two undergraduate colleges and did make progress in enriching the residential atmosphere, but selectivity did not increase. Unlike better-established institutions like Harvard and M.I.T., Tufts experienced only modest growth in freshman applications during the 1950s. Educational demographics made Wessell and his colleagues confident that the demand would come, however, and the 1950s was a time of anticipation and preparation.

At Brandeis, with its appeal to Jewish students and its instant national network of contacts and supporters, the 1950s were years of rapidly increasing selectivity. By 1959, when Brandeis first achieved the undergraduate student body of twelve hundred envisioned as its stable enrollment, the admissions office received 2,325 applications and accepted only 688, making the new university somewhat more competitive than Harvard in terms of numbers, although not in terms of the S.A.T. scores of entering freshmen. New York now replaced Massachusetts as the largest source of students, and there were substantial matriculants also from New Jersey, Pennsylvania, Illinois, Ohio, and Connecticut, with twenty-two states represented.

The impressive statistics hid lingering problems, however. In the mid-1950s, the admissions office expressed concern about the quality of Brandeis's students and drew attention to difficulties in attracting talented males and non-Jews. (Females outnumbered males by two to one.) The admissions staff also worried about their inability to attract children of cultivated, professional families, graduates of private schools, and individuals residing outside major metropolitan areas.[28]

Growing Pains and Upward Mobility

Along with the progress evident in the middle and late 1950s, both Tufts and Brandeis manifested tensions that were inherent in their separate versions of the small-university concept. At Tufts, the problems were rooted in the difficulty of transforming an old, entrenched organization with limited resources. Wessell, like Carmichael before him, could talk about scholarship, but altering the reality of a teaching-oriented faculty was another matter, especially given the policy of nonexpansion. In 1959 an accrediting team noted that less than half the Faculty of Arts and Sciences possessed a doctorate and more than a quarter had only a bachelor's degree. Both numbers compared poorly with the universities Wessell hoped to emulate.

The accrediting team also noted that "the volume of research activities at Tufts is at present so limited" that the issue of excessive dependence on outside funds, which was beginning to worry leaders at research-oriented institutions, was hardly a concern. Indeed, the dollar value of sponsored research at Tufts actually had declined since the Carmichael years. The scholarly weakness of the faculty raised questions about the university's ability to mount credible doctoral programs, and the accreditation team, while endorsing Tufts's plans for advanced work, noted that new faculty would be required in all areas.[29]

The doubts expressed by the 1959 accreditation team drew attention to the financial implications of Tufts's plans. The expansion of the faculty would require additional revenues, of course; so would the other changes needed to increase scholarly activity: lower teaching loads, higher salaries, improved library and laboratory facilities, and fellowship support for graduate students.

Wessell understood the costs of his ambitions and spent much of his time during the 1950s trying to improve his financial base. He created a new alumni/ae organization and worked hard to activate local affiliates around the country. He appointed a vice president for development to seek out gifts from individuals, foundations, and corporations. Both efforts proved effective by Tufts's standards. During Wessell's first five years, annual giving by alumni/ae increased from $78,000 to $432,000, and annual gifts grew from $75,000 to $534,000. These gains, combined with some expansion of revenue from students, enabled Wessell to enlarge the budget by 57 percent between 1953 and 1958, with emphasis on raising faculty salaries and improving facilities.

Wessell's ability to strengthen Tufts's finances without expanding enrollments in the regular programs was a major achievement and accounted for much of the optimism on campus during the 1950s. At the same time, there was evidence of financial strain. Tufts's salaries still ranked far below those of top private colleges and universities. Wessell still was forced to depend on revenues from the College of Special Studies—indeed, he expanded these programs substantially during the 1950s—even though both he and the self-study committee wished to curtail this type of activity. Tufts still relied on current income for capital improvements.

The report of the accrediting team and the recommendations of the self-study committee at the end of the decade confronted Wessell, yet again, with Tufts's historic gap between resources and ambitions. The self-study committee estimated that an immediate expansion of the operating budget by three million dollars (33 percent) was required, plus twenty-two million dollars in nonrecurring expenditures. In fact, in fiscal year 1958, Tufts was spending only nineteen hundred dollars per student from all sources (excluding auxiliary services), compared with thirty-five hundred dollars at Harvard. For Wessell, the task of building Tufts's finances was only beginning.[30]

The tensions that developed at Brandeis during the 1950s were quite different from those at Tufts. In particular, Sachar's continuing success as a fundraiser and entrepreneur removed most of the financial pressures that haunted Wessell and his colleagues. Brandeis was able to recruit faculty and plan new facilities with little sense of constraint. The Brandeis faculty quickly surpassed their counterparts at Tufts in academic credentials and compensation. Of the 214 faculty recruited by the end of the decade, 49 (23 percent) had Ph.D.s from Harvard, and another 59 (28 percent) held doctorates from Columbia, the University of Chicago, Princeton, or Yale.

The problems derived from the achievement. Committed to building a reputation for academic excellence, Sachar's faculty, under Cohen's leadership, tended inevitably (even eagerly) to replicate the patterns of the established institutions from which they had come. As Ph.D. programs were developed, the emphasis on undergraduate education was correspondingly reduced, while teaching loads were lightened to foster scholarly work. Cohen believed in hiring outstanding scholars and turning them loose, without worrying too much about what or how much they were teaching. The catalogue soon mushroomed, with a large number of specialized courses taught to small groups of students. Such policies helped the campus move rapidly toward Sachar's goals but, if carried too far, posed problems for Brandeis's self-proclaimed commitments as a college-centered university focused on undergraduate general education.

The general education program, indeed, was one of the first places to show the strain between collegiate and university impulses. As institutional attention focused on building the disciplines as a basis for graduate work, the earlier emphasis on an interdisciplinary core curriculum proved difficult to sustain. "The first major break with the core curriculum," according to a review by a faculty committee, came in 1955–1956 and was brought on by "the introduction of graduate education and departmentalization." In that year, the faculty eliminated the second-year general education requirement in a student's area of concentration, thus opening the way for more attention to disciplinary work. Subsequent years brought a further loosening of core requirements, and by the late 1950s, numerous members of the faculty—which was no longer dominated by the small group of committed founders—were expressing doubts about the basic idea of general education. The Redbook's emphasis on broad, general learning had begun to seem intellectually thin. A need was being felt to pay greater attention to the early cultivation of gifted student intellects.

The new educational concerns of the Brandeis faculty were, of course, exactly parallel to those being expressed at Harvard during the late 1950s. Brandeis also seemed inclined toward solutions similar to those favored by their colleagues in Cambridge: greater flexibility for students in selecting courses; more room for advanced work in the disciplines; and greater emphasis on individualized work through seminars, tutorials, and honors programs. By the end of the decade, the Brandeis faculty was debating the creation of freshman seminars modeled on those recently instituted at Harvard. But at Brandeis, support for general education remained strong enough to produce, in 1958–1959, a limited counterrevolution in the form of a series of policies reducing options for meeting general education requirements and thus reasserting, if only modestly, the value of a common intellectual experience for undergraduates.

In the area of research, too, the pattern of development at Brandeis was beginning to mirror events at leading graduate institutions. While Sachar's initial commitment to broad learning and general education had fostered a balanced research program, patterns of federal research support began to pull Brandeis—like Harvard—increasingly toward the sciences. Of four million dollars in sponsored research contracts at Brandeis at the end of the 1950s, more than three million dollars were supporting scientific work.

In a range of areas—faculty training and interests, teaching loads, undergraduate curriculum reform, and research activities—the directions of development at Brandeis were following patterns being traced out by the nation's leading research universities. Yet the idea of retaining a distinctive role for Brandeis as a college-centered university remained. As one official document put it: "Brandeis has achieved university status without sacrificing the values of intimate directness and teaching excellence commonly associated with the unattached liberal arts college." How to give continuing meaning to this commitment while also competing for academic acclaim was a central dilemma for Sachar and his colleagues as they completed the first phase of their transition from college to university.[31]

The 1960s at Tufts

The Golden Age Reaches Medford

"The year 1960," Wessell observed in a report to his trustees, "must mark the beginning of a noteworthy era of decisive action and high purpose . . . if the decade we are entered upon is to see Tufts meeting the full obligations thrust upon it by world events and by the resulting demands of national security and survival . . ."[32] The new decade did seem, in fact, to justify high hopes for the traditional New England college now reaching for university status. The long-anticipated tidal wave of high school graduates was finally arriving, and federal funds for research and training were beginning to flow freely.

For the next six years, until he resigned in the spring of 1966, Wessell led his campus along paths of development that he and the self-study committees had defined during the 1950s: raising standards in the two undergraduate liberal arts colleges; building the Graduate School of Arts and Sciences; strengthening the scholarly productivity of the faculty; and bringing the College of Special Studies into conformity with university-level standards and practices.

A Changing Student Body

Tufts welcomed the inevitable rise in freshman applications after 1960 more determined than ever to limit undergraduate expansion and increase selectivity. As the new decade unfolded, admissions statistics seemed to justify the school's long-held hopes. Applications to the College of Liberal Arts rose from fifteen hundred for the fall of 1959 to thirty-five hundred for the fall of 1967. The figures for Jackson College were only slightly less impressive: from twelve hundred to twenty-five hundred. At the end of Wessell's presidency, the dean of admissions reported proudly that Tufts had the "largest applicant-matriculant ratio in the country." The increased demand enabled Tufts to recruit, finally, the nonlocal, residential student body toward which its plans had been directed since the 1920s. During the 1960s, the percentage of undergraduate students from Massachusetts fell from 61 percent to 31 percent, while numbers from other regions, particularly the mid-Atlantic states, rose steadily.

The increase in Tufts's geographic range and selectivity did not produce all the changes that had been anticipated. Mean S.A.T. scores for male students in Liberal Arts increased only slightly, and the high school class rank of entering freshmen actually declined—markedly. At the beginning of the decade, 70 percent of male freshmen came from the top quintile of their secondary school classes; by 1968 the figure had fallen by almost half to 37 percent. Although the Admissions Subcommittee of the Carnegie self-study had hoped that Tufts's freshmen would become more like Harvard's, little progress was made in this respect. College Board scores of Harvard's entering freshmen were rising somewhat during these years also, so that by 1967 Tufts's students stood in about the same relation academically to their Harvard counterparts as in 1960.[33]

Tufts's admission policies during the 1960s had a greater impact on the social background of the undergraduates than on their average intellectual ability. The decline in high school rank of entering freshmen undoubtedly reflected the fact that Tufts was recruiting from more competitive high schools than previously, not that the students were less bright. What the new students clearly were was more cosmopolitan, better prepared, and wealthier than earlier Tufts classes. In this sense, the undergraduates did become more like those at Ivy League institutions. By the end of the decade, the distribution of family income at Tufts was similar to Princeton and Brown, and the percentage of Tufts's students drawn from nonprofessional and working-class families actually fell below the figure for Harvard. The number from private secondary schools rose steadily and by the end of the decade was hovering just below 40 percent, while Harvard's percentage had declined to just above that proportion.

As the egalitarian concerns of the 1960s took hold in academia, Tufts, like other elite campuses, became concerned with its accessibility to disadvantaged applicants. The most important expression of the new mood involved efforts to enroll blacks. Wessell first drew attention to this issue in 1965, and by 1968 the dean of admissions was able to report fifty new black students on campus, double the number of the recent past. At the end of the decade, Tufts's undergraduate minority enrollments reached 10 percent, a record comparable to Harvard's during these years. This was an important achievement, though it did not alter the fact that Tufts' students were becoming progressively more advantaged as the college's traditional, local, middle- and working-class constituency was replaced by residential students drawn from regional and national pools.

Tufts's movement away from its traditional role as provider of educational services for local residents was registered also in the College of Special Studies. The largest shift came in the affiliated-schools program, which was no longer financially necessary and was not congruent with Tufts's plans for higher academic status. The Admissions Subcommittee of the Carnegie self-study had expressed the wish to end these programs, and the self-study Executive Committee, more measured in its approach, had recommended that no new affiliations be undertaken and that standards be raised to those of the other undergraduate colleges. Wessell pursued the course proposed by the Executive Committee. The affiliated schools were given the option of complete merger with Tufts or departure. Merger threatened these schools with loss of control over their curricula and admission policies, and two left to form affiliations with Northeastern. Three others elected to merge. While these changes were occurring, the College's evening program was being slowly eliminated. By the end of Wessell's presidency, the College of Special Studies, established as a community service program for part-time students seeking specialized degrees, had been transformed into a home for conventional undergraduate professional programs.[34]

Graduate Education and Research

While Liberal Arts, Jackson, and Special Studies were being upgraded in the 1960s, the Graduate School of Arts and Sciences grew. The establishment of doctoral programs, begun in the late 1950s, continued after 1960 with new offerings in biology, English, government, history, classics, drama, economics, and French. In addition, new programs were created in several engineering and health-science fields. By the end of the decade, Tufts had twenty-two doctorates and thirty master's programs, almost all created between 1957 and 1966.

With this explosive development, pressure to expand the Graduate School beyond the three hundred students recommended by the Carnegie self-study developed quickly and won Wessell's support. By the fall of 1968, the Graduate School enrolled a total of 804 students and was, by a wide margin, the fastest growing unit on campus. Graduate students in Arts and Sciences now constituted 15 percent of Tufts's total enrollments, compared with 4 percent in 1958. The change was even greater than suggested by these percentages, since most 1958 enrollees were teachers taking courses on a part-time basis, while many of Tufts's graduate students in the late 1960s were attending full time.

Parallel efforts focused on strengthening the faculty in scholarly terms. Between 1958 and 1968, the number of full-time appointments in Arts and Sciences increased by over 60 percent (from 133 to 208), with emphasis on hiring Ph.D.s likely to be productive scholars. Average teaching loads were reduced from ten to twelve hours per semester to fifteen hours per year. Sponsored research, which had declined during the first years of Wessell's presidency, expanded again after the crisis brought on by *Sputnik I*. Between 1958 and 1967, financial support for sponsored projects increased by more than 100 percent (from $2.1 million to $5.5 million), with the health sciences contributing the major share.[35]

Other units of Tufts also enhanced their roles during the 1960s in directions anticipated by the self-study. The Medical School, which Wessell valued as a major contributor to Tufts's image, retained a fixed size while student interest and federal support expanded. By the end of the decade, it was attracting a national constituency. In an atmosphere of increasing attention to international issues, the Fletcher School also grew stronger, although competition from other universities made it difficult for Tufts to retain its early lead in international affairs. The Dental School received less support from Wessell, who regarded the field as a low-level activity that did not really fit at an elite private university. The central casualty of the 1960s, however, was the Crane Theological School. Once the spiritual center of Tufts but now a financial as well as—in Wessell's view—an academic drag, Crane finally was closed, symbolically ending Tufts's long affiliation with the Universalist church.

When Wessell left office in 1966, he rightfully could claim success in achieving many of the goals toward which Tufts had been moving since Cousens defined a modern conception of the institution in the 1930s. The undergraduates now were drawn broadly from the northeastern and middle Atlantic states, and 75 percent lived in university housing. The faculty was better trained and paid than ever before. The professional schools had consolidated their positions on the foundations of accreditation and professionalization achieved under Carmichael. Wessell also had amended the Cousens/Carmichael formula by emphasizing the growth of the Graduate School of Arts and Sciences, which was now a substantial enterprise, offering a wide range of master's and doctoral programs. The entire record was impressive indeed and confirmed Tufts's right to be called a university rather than a college, as Wessell had insisted be done in his inaugural address in 1953.[36]

The Costs of Upward Mobility

Wessell had devoted much of his energy during the 1950s to strengthening Tufts's fund-raising organization, and the changes of the 1960s put these initiatives through a severe test. The decade began with the announcement of a capital campaign to raise $7.5 million for faculty salaries, financial aid, and facilities. Though Wessell initially hoped to set the target at $11 million—he and the trustees were dissuaded by a consultant's report on Tufts's fund-raising potential—the new campaign was the largest in the university's history. It concluded in 1963 with approximately $5 million actually raised, though a promised bequest of $2.5 million allowed Tufts to claim that the campus's goal had been met.

The new funds did not shield Tufts from financial stress, however, as costs rose more rapidly than anticipated. The Carnegie self-study had estimated that its recommendations would lead to a 33 percent increase in annual operating expenses. Between 1958 and 1967, the budget actually tripled. The trustees adopted endowment management policies stressing income over appreciation to ease the pressure, but this provided only partial relief, since Tufts's investment funds remained small for a campus of its size and scope. Increased income from sponsored research also produced limited help, since Tufts's gains in this area, while encouraging after the poor record of the 1950s, were modest in comparison with competing schools. Tufts actually lost ground in the national rankings of institutions receiving federal support.

Confronted by a mismatch between resources and costs, Tufts was forced, as so often in the past, to turn to its students for the difference. In the decade following the self-study, Tufts raised tuition from $850 per year to $1,900, which kept its prices similar to Harvard's. These increases were decisive in producing the shift toward a more affluent student body, since Tufts's ability to offset the increments with financial aid was restricted. In 1960 Harvard budgeted $434 in scholarship funds for every undergraduate. The comparable figure for M.I.T. was $308; for Tufts, $194. Harvard gave 32 percent of its students grants averaging 77 percent of tuition. M.I.T. gave 27 percent grants averaging 67 percent of tuition. Tufts gave 24 percent grants averaging 48 percent of tuition. Wessell was sensitive to the impact of rising charges on Tufts's ability to stress academic talent rather than financial background in admissions decisions. In 1964 he told his trustees that "no other factor over which we have direct control exerts a greater influence in determining the caliber of our entering classes."

In the end, however, there was a limit on Tufts's ability to increase prices, and the university was forced to abandon the no-growth policy for undergraduates recommended by the self-study Executive Committee in 1958. In fact, between 1958 and 1968 undergraduate enrollments grew by 20 percent, with almost all of the expansion coming in Jackson College. A faculty-administration planning committee explained:

> Since, during the late 1950s and the 1960s, the University was striving to increase faculty salaries and to attract strong new faculty members, no paring could be undertaken there. Tuition rates were raised each year, but the University felt the need to keep such raises in line with those of other colleges. So, with reluctance, in recognition of both the increasing demand for places and inevitable fiscal pressure, enrollments were allowed to rise annually.

The cycle of increasing costs, rising prices, and expanding enrollments perpetuated Tufts's tradition of greater dependence on student payments than was typical of leading private institutions. In 1967 more than half of Tufts's expenditures for departmental instruction and research were provided by charges to students, compared with approximately a third at Harvard and M.I.T.[37]

Tufts's unanswered financial problems contributed a note of concern to the admiring atmosphere surrounding Wessell's departure. Wessell himself focused attention on this matter. Pointing out that the financial pressures of the years ahead "will make [those of] the last decade seem modest," the outgoing president observed that Tufts was in a "critical situation" and was confronted with a "giant task." Like other private university presidents of the late 1960s, Wessell hoped that increased public support, especially from the federal government, would come to the rescue. The trustees appointed an acting president—the choice was Vice President Leonard Mead, former director of the Carnegie self-study—while taking stock of the rapid, not fully assimilated changes of the recent past.

The largest factors in increasing Tufts's operating costs during the Wessell years had been the president's efforts to expand the faculty, increase salaries, and build the Graduate School. In 1958 the Faculty of Arts and Sciences included 133 persons, and their total compensation costs were $860,000, which produced a compensation-per-student figure of $340. By 1967 this faculty had expanded to 218—more than triple the rate of enrollment growth—while salaries had increased and teaching loads had been reduced. Total faculty compensation in 1967 stood at $2.9 million, and compensation per student had risen to $873.

In the year following Wessell's departure, Mead and the trustees commissioned a salary study to assess Tufts's relative position in the wake of the impressive improvements in faculty pay. The results were disappointing. In comparison with ten local and national institutions, Tufts ranked only ninth, lower than all but Boston University and far below Harvard and M.I.T. Tufts's salary scale merited only a *B* rating from the A.A.U.P., and, as Mead pointed out, per-student expenditures for faculty compensation were no better than 50 percent of those at Amherst and Williams, which did not support graduate programs.

Additional reviews of Tufts's expenditures for administrative compensation and libraries were undertaken, and these, too, revealed Tufts to be well behind its competitors. Perhaps most discouraging of all, given the exertions and hopes of the Wessell years, Tufts was actually losing ground in terms of total per-student expenditures for instruction and research compared with leading private universities. By the middle 1960s, Tufts's position in relation to Harvard was worse in this respect than it had been in 1940.

The results of Wessell's efforts to build the Graduate School also came into question following his departure. A national study—the Cartter report—gave poor ratings to Tufts's programs in 1966, and a year later, a team of consultants from the Council of Graduate Schools emphasized the risk for Tufts of further development at this level. The consultants questioned Tufts's ability to meet the costs in faculty salaries, financial aid, and library and research facilities that would be necessary to establish high quality. With a view to both the costs and the results of Tufts's efforts to build new doctoral programs, Mead urged the trustees to "deliberate long and hard" before committing themselves to the continued development of the Graduate School.[38]

The 1960s at Brandeis

Maintaining the Financial Pace

Throughout the 1950s, in contrast with Tufts, Sachar's fund-raising virtuosity had enabled Brandeis to achieve quickly a remarkable degree of academic success. "It is unwise to try to get over a chasm in two leaps," was his way of expressing the boldness of Brandeis's progress. In 1962 another financial coup provided the basis for a new surge of development that heightened differences with Tufts still further. In that year, the Ford Foundation made capital grants to a small number of promising private universities with the goal of helping recipients move into the first rank of academic institutions.

Ford's effort to increase the number of outstanding schools as the baby-boom generation reached college age—a project made especially important by the restrictive responses to increased demand by established institutions like Harvard and M.I.T.—ultimately played a major role in the development of eight universities, including Notre Dame, Stanford, Brown, and Vanderbilt, along with the fledgling, Jewish-sponsored university in Waltham. Sachar's successful campaign for a place on the list was testimony to his skills as a salesperson and to the academic stature that Brandeis already had acquired.

From Ford, Brandeis received a total of twelve million dollars in direct grants between 1963 and 1967, and because the award carried a three-to-one matching requirement, the Ford dollars helped Sachar expand geometrically his already successful fund-raising activities. In fiscal year 1963, the year before the impact of the Ford money was felt fully, the annual fund drive raised seven million dollars. The following year, the figure jumped to fifteen million dollars. For the next several years, as Ford funds came in, annual giving stabilized in the ten- to eleven-million-dollar range. In total, the capital grant was directly responsible for increasing Brandeis's resources by forty-five million dollars during the middle 1960s, allowing the new university to establish twenty-five endowed chairs and add a million dollars per year to the operating budget. The momentum, capacity, and prestige that came with these new funds helped Brandeis compete for additional financial support, including plant funds and sponsored research. Between 1963 and 1968, total annual expenditures for instruction and research increased by 100 percent (from ten million to twenty million dollars) while enrollment grew by only 57 percent (from 1,750 to 2,750).[39]

With money abundant, Sachar and his colleagues were able to maintain the pace of rising expenditures being set by leading private universities. Faculty salaries, having been set at a high level in the early years, remained competitive. In 1968 Brandeis's average salary ranked twenty-ninth nationally and was two thousand dollars higher than any other university in Massachusetts except Harvard and M.I.T. Annual expenditures for departmental instruction and research climbed close to fifty-two hundred dollars per student by 1967, slightly lower than Harvard, slightly higher than M.I.T., and well above other area institutions. A special fund was established to pay higher than normal salaries to outstanding faculty. Sponsored-research income was limited by Brandeis's relatively narrow range of programs, but these funds were sufficient to bring total expenditures per student in 1967 to seventy-four hundred dollars, compared with forty-four hundred at Tufts.

While the emphasis at Brandeis, necessarily, was on maintaining a high level of current expenditures, the new university's record of building its capital base was also impressive. By the time Sachar retired in 1968, he was able to boast that "the entire physical plant of eighty buildings—supplied and furnished with the most sophisticated equipment" and "representing a fully paid or pledged investment of $70 million" had been constructed on the hillside in Waltham that Israel Goldstein had viewed as an unkempt meadow only twenty years earlier.

The weakest element of the financial picture was the endowment, which in 1968 had a book value of twenty-nine million dollars, a figure dwarfed by the invested resources of major private universities and considerably smaller than those of leading colleges like Amherst and Williams. Even here, however, Brandeis outstripped Tufts, surpassing by more than 30 percent in two decades the endowment Tufts had accumulated since its founding in 1830.[40]

Achieving National Prominence in
Graduate Education and Research

Expanded revenues accelerated Brandeis's transition from college to university. While undergraduate enrollments increased by a third during the 1960s, advanced students doubled to 735 and accounted for 25 percent of the student body by the end of the decade. Teaching loads, set at twelve hours in the 1950s, were reduced to nine or less by the early 1960s to facilitate research and graduate instruction.

Consistent with Sachar's initial policies, the emphasis remained on the arts and sciences. New doctorates were added in history, political science, philosophy, and linguistics. A graduate program in theater was established. Research centers concerned with communications, Judaic studies, and violence were founded. Previously established graduate programs were strengthened through the addition of new faculty, with emphasis on recruiting individuals oriented toward the advanced functions. The Heller School was expanded. Special efforts were made to exploit the early success in biochemistry by building in molecular biology and microbiology and moving into related fields in the medical sciences. At the end of the decade, Sachar won a new grant of nineteen million dollars to support biomedical research from the same donor, Lewis Rosenstiel, who had underwritten the initial effort in biochemistry.

The extent of change in the years of the Ford grant is suggested by the fact that the 163 full-time faculty hired between 1962 and 1966 almost equaled the 170 recruited prior to 1962. Moreover, many of the new appointments were at the senior level, so that, despite the new hiring, the Brandeis faculty had a considerably higher percentage of senior faculty in 1970 than in 1960.[41]

When the results of Brandeis's rush toward university status were evaluated in the A.C.E.'s ranking of graduate faculties and doctoral programs at the end of the 1960s, the record was astonishing. Of fifteen graduate departments reviewed, eleven were placed in the top category ("distinguished" or "strong"), and the remaining four were given the second rating of "good." With respect to its programs, Brandeis received somewhat less-striking scores, with only two in the top category, eight in the second, and six in the third, undoubtedly reflecting the newness of Brandeis's efforts.

The A.C.E. evaluations made it clear that Brandeis had acquired the talent in field after field to compete for recognition with the nation's leading universities. In the life sciences, all four of Brandeis's faculties were ranked in the top twenty nationally; three were in the top fifteen, and biochemistry was ranked eighth. Other departments placed in the top twenty were math, music, philosophy, anthropology, history, sociology, and linguistics. By comparison, none of Tufts's graduate programs made it into the top thirty, and none of its graduate faculties or programs was ranked in the highest category. Even in health-related fields, where Tufts was aided by a well-established medical school, the new university in Waltham far outdistanced its sister institution in Medford.[42]

Becoming a University College

During the 1960s, the undergraduate college became, ever more clearly, a "university college." It now was embedded in a full university and was dominated by students preparing for graduate school. To a degree, of course, these qualities had been present from the beginning. Even in its initial years, Brandeis had attracted unusually talented students, and 56 percent of those admitted between 1948 and 1958 went on to advanced programs. In the middle 1960s, however, the number continuing their education rose to 70 percent, with large groups accepted at the nation's leading universities.

Such results reflected the elevated academic profile of Brandeis undergraduates in the 1960s. Median combined S.A.T. scores for the classes admitted between 1961 and 1967 ranged between 1298 and 1334, somewhat below Harvard (which maintained average combined scores between 1375 and 1400) but well above Tufts (where the comparable figures were 1225 and 1256). Two-thirds of Brandeis's undergraduates in the 1960s were in the top 10 percent of their high school classes, generally in academically competitive secondary schools, and over 80 percent were in the top quintile.

Within the pattern of rising undergraduate standards, Brandeis—like Tufts, Harvard, and M.I.T.—undertook special efforts to increase minority enrollments. The Transitional Year Program, established in 1968, brought underprepared black students to Brandeis for a year of financially supported precollege work. Those who completed the program were eligible to apply for regular admission, though policy required them to compete on equal footing with other applicants. Sachar once described the T.Y.P. as "one of the proudest things I ever did" because it enabled Brandeis to expand educational opportunities for blacks without adopting quotas or other discriminatory devices, approaches that were, for evident historical reasons, anathema to Sachar and to many Jewish educators. As at other selective colleges, however, the T.Y.P. represented a secondary theme within the overall movement of admission policy toward higher academic standards. By the middle 1960s, Sachar was able to report that a widely used national guide to American colleges listed Brandeis as one of the most selective colleges in the nation.[43]

The Hazards of Early Success

Despite Brandeis's progress, the new university's position contained troubling elements. Two problems, in particular, gave cause for concern—both, ironically, involving areas were Brandeis was unusually successful: financial development and undergraduate admissions. Sachar's prodigious skills as a fundraiser enabled Brandeis to advance at an extraordinary rate, but the movement was based on his ability, year after year, to obtain large amounts of current contributions. With the advent of the Ford grant and its generous matching provisions, both the budget and the effort needed to support it jumped sharply.

Throughout these years, annual giving accounted for about a third of the operating budget, but the amount required for this purpose rose from $3.6 million to $6.9 million. Additional financial pressure came from the constant expansion of facilities, which resulted in heavy indebtedness and rising plant operating costs. While Sachar raised the funds, or obtained pledges, to finance the construction of his projects, the enlarged operating expenses were an additional claim on annual budgets. By 1968, with the Ford funds coming to an end and Sachar nearing retirement, the challenge of maintaining the new university's financial operation loomed large.

The issue in admission policy involved the size and character of the applicant pool. This was a matter that bore directly on Brandeis's financial position, since expanding enrollments always represented—as the history of Tufts demonstrated—a potential response to budgetary problems. During the 1960s, Brandeis began to encounter the limits of its attractiveness to undergraduates. Between 1961 and 1967, years when the tidal wave of young Americans was flooding into academia and producing increases in applications of 70 percent at Harvard and 40 percent at Tufts, applications to Brandeis grew by 20 percent. Although the numbers accepted rose only modestly each year, Brandeis was less selective in 1967 than in 1961 and enrolled a higher percentage of students from a few metropolitan centers in the Northeast in the latter year than in the former.

The admissions statistics reflected two realities, one involving Brandeis's appeal for Jewish applicants and the second its lack of attractiveness to non-Jews. The university's early success in enrolling substantial numbers of highly qualified Jewish students derived, in part, from the widespread belief in the Jewish community, well-founded in prewar history, that leading private universities would discriminate against Jewish applicants. By the 1960s, radical changes in admission practices since the war had reduced this concern. Talented Jewish students now were far more confident of their ability to gain entrance to elite private institutions than had been the case twenty years earlier, and many preferred that alternative.

The 1960s also demonstrated the difficulty of attracting non-Jews. Though gaining admission to a highly regarded undergraduate college became more difficult for all applicants in these years and though Brandeis won an enviable academic reputation, the new university made little headway in reaching beyond its original constituency. Brandeis, like M.I.T., was learning the difference between recruiting talented students within a well-defined market niche and appealing to a broad range of potential applicants.[44]

Brandeis's problems in expanding its applicant pool dramatized the gap between Sachar's original vision of a Jewish-sponsored, nonsectarian, Ivy League university and the actual character of Brandeis as a specifically Jewish enterprise. Sachar always had known, of course, that the evolution he envisioned would take time. Harvard, Yale, and Princeton needed generations to outgrow their sectarian roots. Sachar clearly hoped, however, to limit as much as possible the perception of Brandeis as a university for Jews. In this, he largely failed, and his nonsectarian vision became, over time, more a dominant myth than a description of institutional reality or even a guide to policy.

It was also true, however, that the consequences for Brandeis of retaining a Jewish identity were far less negative than Sachar anticipated. In 1948 the newly appointed president doubted that a university perceived as Jewish could be regarded as first class. Brandeis's record in the intervening years demonstrated that a Jewish identity and a reputation for academic excellence were compatible in postwar America. Indeed, these years revealed that Brandeis's meteoric ascent owed much to an awareness of its Jewish character—by donors, potential faculty, potential students, and charitable foundations. Sachar's genius involved less his ability to obscure this fact than his success in turning it to advantage. There was in all this an encouraging measure of social change. At the end of his presidency, nonetheless, Sachar continued to proclaim the hope that Brandeis would lose its Jewish identity. By the late 1960s, it was becoming evident that this long-held goal was more important for ensuring a broad base of student interest and financial support for Brandeis than in helping it gain acceptance as an outstanding academic institution.

Organization, Leadership, and Institutional Change

The Colleague as Leader; the Autocrat as Entrepreneur: Two Approaches to Academic Progress

Wessell and Sachar were as different in their styles of leadership as were the institutional settings within which they pursued their similar academic goals. Wessell thought of himself as a member of the Tufts community. He came there as a young man, grew up there professionally, knew everybody on campus, and spent much of his social life with Tufts people. He was well-liked, and he returned the affections of his institutional family. Wessell's ambitions for Tufts were those of a fond colleague and a consensus-oriented politician. He sought broad support for the changes he advocated and had little taste for organizational conflict—or perception of conflict as a potential contributor to constructive change.

Sachar was cut from a different cloth. An archetypical entrepreneur, he was determined to move Brandeis ahead through the direct exercise of his own will. Unlike Wessell, he did not come to an established institution from the outside. He, quite literally, had created Brandeis. He tended to minimize the accomplishments of early leaders like Goldstein, and he thought the role of the founding trustees was to cover costs while keeping out of his way. He was, by inclination, a one-man band—or orchestra (with full chorus)—and he harbored a personal vision of what Brandeis should represent, for both Jews and non-Jews. Consensus was not his goal, and he had no aversion to conflict. Indeed, he quoted with pride the assessment of Abraham Maslow, one of the distinguished scholars who joined Brandeis in the early years. "When we're all dead," Maslow told a reporter, "when the personalities are forgotten, nobody will know whether Sachar was loveable or unloveable. All they'll see are the consequences, what happened here. All they'll see is a great university."[45]

It was no accident that Tufts and Brandeis were led during the golden age by such different personalities. Wessell was chosen as the favorite son of an outgoing president by an institutional community that was comfortable with him and possessed no sense of urgency about change. Sachar was brought in to rescue a foundering operation whose survival was in doubt. The divergences of style and philosophy that separated the two men were reflected not only in their mandates but also in the character of their accomplishments and, ultimately, in the manner of their resignations, which occurred within two years of each other.

Tufts as an Organization

The organization that Wessell inherited from Carmichael in 1952 was in a transition that mirrored Carmichael's role as bridge between the traditional college and the modern university. In many respects, Tufts continued in the 1950s to follow norms and patterns established during the early years of the century. The academic organization was spelled out in the "new plan" of 1903 that divided Tufts into several "schools": Liberal Arts, Engineering, Divinity, Graduate Arts and Sciences, as well as the Medical and Dental schools. The first four of these were grouped together as "the Department of Arts and Sciences." This organization required that policies involving any of the schools in the Department be considered first by the appropriate "constituent" faculty and then by the parent body. The Medical and Dental schools, always a distinct universe both geographically and organizationally, remained outside the overlapping relationships of Medford and were constituted along conventional lines as separate units, each with its own dean and faculty.

As Tufts developed, new units were incorporated into the pattern. Jackson College became officially a school within the Department of Arts and Sciences, while Fletcher was set up with its own dean and faculty. Tufts's complex and inevitably sluggish structure was not without critics, but it worked well enough, partially because the constituent faculties left each other alone and partially because, under trustee bylaws, the role of the faculty in governance was highly circumscribed.

Throughout the first half of the twentieth century, formal power remained almost exclusively with the administrative hierarchy. Deans were appointed by the trustees upon the recommendation of the president, and chairs were appointed by the president in consultation with deans. All appointments to the faculty were made by the trustees upon the recommendation of the president, who normally conferred with the appropriate dean and chair. There was no role for the faculty in personnel decisions, nor any formal procedure or criteria to govern the actions of the trustees in this area. Appointments without limit of time, promotions, and salary adjustments were granted or not as the president and trustees saw fit in individual instances. Committees of the faculty were appointed by the president.[46]

During Tufts's early history, financial affairs were controlled entirely by the board, the president being excluded from participation under the bylaws. This arrangement inevitably produced tension between executive and board, especially in the hands of aggressive trustees, like Austin Fletcher, who believed their contributions to Tufts entitled them to exercise detailed supervision over internal affairs. During the long presidency of John Cousens (1919 to 1937), however, the locus of power shifted to the chief executive. At the beginning of his term, Cousens won a formal role in financial administration, and in succeeding years, his competence and durability kept the board from intruding unduly into matters of campus administration.

Cousens's attention to detail, fairness, and decency were such that few complaints arose during his years, despite depression conditions that prompted faculties elsewhere to organize to protect themselves. He worked hard, in fact, to preserve the informality of Tufts. He resisted proposals for explicit rules and procedures in the area of personnel. He opposed a pension system and policies on academic freedom and tenure. He declined to hire professional administrators, preferring to rely on his own efforts, a minimal staff, and the assistance of the faculty. As it was defined during Cousens's long tenure, the Tufts system of organization had the form, though not the spirit, of highly centralized administrative power. Members of the college often referred to "the Tufts family," and Cousens ruled not as a commanding executive but as a benign paterfamilias, paying close attention to the ideas and sensitivities of his community while retaining all discretion for himself.[47]

Representing a different generation than Cousens's and coming from an academic background, Carmichael recognized the necessity of organizational change. In 1940, when the Tufts chapter of the A.A.U.P. proposed an elected committee to advise administrators on grievances brought by individual faculty, Carmichael was ready to cooperate. He also supported trustee endorsement of the national A.A.U.P.'s statement on academic freedom and tenure and urged board approval of a modest pension system. In the area of administration, too, Carmichael realized that Tufts was behind the times. He created the positions of vice president, dean of men, and director of admissions and later added a provost, research coordinator, and dean of administration, as well as several lesser posts.

The cumulative organizational changes of the Carmichael years left in place all the major patterns consolidated under Cousens. Faculty appointments and promotions remained largely matters for informal consultation between president, dean, and department chair. There was no written personnel policy. Financial decisions and major policy issues were worked out between the president and appropriate trustee committees. Vital administrative responsibilities, such as directing the all-important Second-Century Fund, continued to be handled by faculty members on part-time assignment.

To some degree, the limited character of change during the Carmichael years can be ascribed to the conditions of the Depression, war, and early postwar years, which left little time for organizational niceties. But Carmichael's wish to change Tufts's paternalistic system of decision making also was circumscribed. He had scant inclination, for example, to refer questions of institutional policy to faculty committees. Indeed, after a disappointing experience with one such exercise early in his term, he never again sought the advice of such a group on major questions.[48]

Wessell and Participatory Governance

Although Wessell was a Carmichael protégé, he signaled early his intention to create a new atmosphere. He committed himself to increasing faculty salaries, a need that Carmichael had recognized but not fulfilled, and he delivered on this pledge. He also adopted a consultative approach to policy development. As Vice President Tilton put it in 1954: "Tufts College is rapidly becoming a truly cooperative effort. Participation by faculty, by alumni, and by students in planning and developing effective operating conditions is a reality . . ."

The most obvious example of Wessell's style was the Carnegie self-study, with its numerous subcommittees scrutinizing every aspect of Tufts and its final report representing a laboriously constructed consensus. Wessell believed that the academic changes he sought could be accomplished most readily by stimulating his habitually passive and self-doubting faculty into new levels of activity. He also believed that the institutional environment he was creating would play an important role in attracting new faculty. Prodded by Wessell, departments that, as the self-study revealed, "had not held a meeting for many years," were moved into action. One concrete expression of this atmosphere was the large number of new graduate programs rapidly developed in the various arts and sciences disciplines.

Faculty involvement in decision making became a hallmark of the Wessell years. A self-study subcommittee provided Tufts's first written statement of academic personnel policies, and much of this work was incorporated in Tufts's first faculty handbook, issued in 1958. The 1962 version of the handbook guaranteed tenured faculty a role in senior appointments in their own departments and in the selection of chairs.

In comparison, however, with the prerogatives exercised by a highly professionalized faculty of arts and sciences, such as Harvard's, the gains achieved at Tufts in the 1950s and 1960s were modest. It was not until the late 1960s, for example, following Wessell's retirement, that faculty committees routinely considered major personnel decisions prior to administrative review. No written statement of criteria for the award of tenure and promotion was developed until 1970, although the desirability of such a policy was identified by the Carnegie self-study. A faculty/administration committee, reviewing Tufts's governance arrangements in the late 1960s, concluded that the faculty role was far more limited than at numerous other institutions or than recommended by A.A.U.P. guidelines.[49]

While diverging from Carmichael in the area of governance, Wessell followed his predecessor's policy of strengthening Tufts's administrative organization. During his first five years, he established a new development office headed by a vice president, reorganized the alumni/ae relations function, appointed a director of publications, and added capacity to the business management, record keeping, facilities planning, and student-affairs offices. Despite these initiatives, Wessell did not feel he could devote primary attention to internal administration, since Tufts was in such urgent need of advocacy with external groups. The 1959 accreditation team observed, in fact, that greater attention to administrative organization was needed. As time went on, Wessell found himself attracted to the idea developed at M.I.T. of dividing responsibilities for external relations and internal administration between a chancellor and a president.[50]

Sachar and One-Man Rule

Determined to control every aspect of Brandeis, Sachar was reluctant to create any formal organization for his new university. At first, of course, a high degree of informality was to be expected. The "university" was the president, a couple of assistants, and a dozen faculty seated around a dining-room table. But Sachar's approach to administration remained unchanged through the mid-1950s, by which time Brandeis employed over a hundred professors and enrolled nearly a thousand students. Still, there was no chief academic officer and no dean of students.

Sachar worked through a series of young, inexperienced aides who assumed large responsibilities with no delegated authority and kept the president involved in all aspects of campus life. He personally reviewed the file of every applicant whom his admissions committee was inclined to reject, and if the case involved an important constituent, he either overruled the committee or sent an individual letter of explanation. He was not eager to establish academic departments, which he saw as enclaves of faculty prerogative, and he organized the teaching staff into four interdisciplinary "schools"—Humanities, Science, Social Science, and Arts—delegating no authority to these units or to their chairpersons, whom he appointed without consultation.

There was no defined faculty role in academic personnel decisions and, indeed, no academic personnel policy. Sachar regarded the hiring and development of the Brandeis faculty as his personal responsibility. He was slow to acknowledge a role for the faculty in these decisions even after disciplinary groups were well established. In selecting professors, moreover, Sachar employed idiosyncratic standards linked to his symbolic goals for Brandeis, which led him, on occasion, to insist upon appointing a luminary whom his faculty did not regard as substantial or to reject an important scholar whose personal qualities might tarnish the image of the new institution.

Sachar created no structures for faculty or student governance, preferring to rely on what he called "informed consensus." In 1950 he did establish a Faculty Advisory Committee on Educational Policy that had no defined powers but served as a consultative body on important matters. All other faculty committees—the administrative board, admissions, scholarships—were chaired by Sachar himself or by one of his assistants and were dominated by members of the administrative staff.[51]

In the middle 1950s, a number of pressures converged on Sachar to relinquish personal control and form a more conventional organization. The burgeoning scale of the operation, the demands of fund-raising, and the rapid progress of campus construction were all generating needs for administrative attention that were outrunning even Sachar's prodigious capacities. The shift of emphasis to graduate education, moreover, implied a more complex organizational structure and a higher degree of autonomy for disciplinary subunits. In addition, both faculty and staff, as well as some trustees, were growing impatient with the president's autocratic style. This was hardly surprising. The faculty in particular, having been recruited from major research universities, and including a number of accomplished, senior members, was bound before long to insist upon the prerogatives of established faculties in areas like academic appointments.

In 1954 Sachar was persuaded to commission a thorough analysis of Brandeis by a management consulting firm. Their report expressed admiration for the new university's educational progress, but amazement at the primitive character of its administration. Calling Brandeis's staffing pattern "the least adequate the consultants have ever observed," the report catalogued a host of problems: the absence of plans in crucial areas like enrollment and program diversification; the nonexistence of written policies for any major area of operations; excessive reliance on the individual efforts of the president compounded by his use of inexperienced, poorly paid assistants and by the lack of a professional bureaucracy; utilization of poor financial controls that rendered the educational program among the most costly in the country; plus a host of managerial failings in areas like the library, residential facilities, business affairs, and the physical plant. The report proposed a series of deans and administrative officers with clear patterns of authority, proper academic departments, a more active role for the trustees in planning institutional development, and a series of technical and procedural reforms.

Even before the consultant's report was completed, Sachar responded to the criticisms of his leadership. His decision in 1955 to appoint Cohen as dean of faculty was paralleled by a second appointment in the area of student affairs. Over the next several years, additional offices were created, including a dean of administration with wide-ranging responsibilities for business and plant activities. Academic departments were established—a step Cohen felt was essential for Brandeis to develop graduate work—along with a formal governance structure based on an elected faculty Senate with written charter, a plenary faculty meeting empowered to make recommendations on a range of subjects, and a system of faculty committees and school councils. A student counterpart to the Faculty Advisory Committee on Educational Policy also was created. Written personnel policies were produced with a high degree of faculty involvement. Another of Cohen's projects was the first faculty handbook, which provided written statements on conditions of employment for individuals and described the faculty role in decision making.[52]

By the early 1960s, Brandeis had moved a long way toward organizational structures similar to those of other American universities. It was obvious to everyone, however, that Sachar's acceptance of these changes was limited and grudging. He negotiated the handbook with Cohen line by line. Indeed, he allowed his dean of faculty little actual authority and went through a series of individuals in this role in rapid succession. The governance system granted minimal power to the professoriate, since the elected Senate was allowed only to discuss issues while the much larger and more amorphous faculty meeting could make formal recommendations, and then only on the basis of reports from committees that continued to be appointed and controlled by Sachar. Sachar retained the right to designate department chairs without any formal advice from the faculty, and school councils were made up entirely of these appointed officers. The president also continued to insist upon an initiating role in faculty recruitment.

Sachar was not shy about explaining his conception of his role, which was based on his belief that Brandeis must maintain a strong presidency in order to become a major academic institution. Addressing the local chapter of the A.A.U.P. in 1963, Sachar made it clear that he could give at least as well as he was getting on the issue of governance. He observed that most faculty regarded the trustees as unlettered merchants with no right to be taken seriously on educational matters and saw the administration "as a combination of aggressive public relations and spectacular mendacity." At the same time, he believed that faculty attributed to themselves only the most high-minded motives and based their claims to institutional power on their greater commitment to educational values. Sachar attacked both the negative and positive sides of these images. He defended his trustees as diverse and socially engaged, drew attention to his own role in bringing superior faculty to Brandeis, and wondered aloud if "the unlovely yearning for the fast buck" was "known among academicians."

Sachar possessed a particular view of both administrative and faculty commitments. He argued that administrators were concerned with the well-being of the entire institution, while faculty tended to care chiefly about their disciplines. This analysis was the basis of his conception of governance: "Faculty should be given every leeway where the welfare of their own discipline is involved," but should only be "called upon for counsel in the planning and the development of the totality of the university." University government should involve the "advice and consent" of the faculty, but the zone of consent should be narrow and the zone of advice wide.

Sachar spoke from both conviction and experience. He believed that excessive faculty power in the universities of Europe and Israel had led to institutional paralysis. He felt his faculty frequently opposed important initiatives, often for self-interested motives. He was convinced that the interests of Brandeis were served when the new institution was guided to the maximum extent possible by his own vision and will. He hardly could be expected, after all, to cede to the professional academics he had hired or to the trustees he had rescued anything like a decisive role in determining the future of the symbol of Jewish achievement that he was nurturing so carefully.[53]

Wessell vs. Sachar: Institutional Mobility

The contrast in leadership style between Wessell and Sachar is instructive, since their accomplishments differed markedly. Both men set out, in the mid-1950s, to transform their collegiate institutions into proper universities. By the late 1960s, Brandeis had established a clear, though limited, identity at the graduate level, with high national rankings in several fields. In the same years, the expanded Graduate School at Tufts was foundering, and even its strongest departments had achieved no better than modest national standing.

A number of factors worked in Sachar's favor in this comparison, including the more generous financial resources available to him and the more flexible organizational context in which he was building. Between 1959 and 1970, the Brandeis faculty of arts and sciences expanded from 133 to 285, an increase of 152 persons, or 114 percent. During the slightly shorter period from 1958 to 1968, the Tufts faculty grew from 133 to 208, an aggregate expansion of only 75 persons, or 56 percent. Thus Sachar, whose hiring pattern before the mid-1950s had also established a generally stronger base for graduate development than existed at Tufts, was able to recruit twice as many new faculty as Wessell and to offer higher salaries.

Brandeis's advantages should not be overstated, however. The pace of growth at Tufts and the resources available there provided ample potential for developing at least some areas of unquestioned excellence. Tufts, moreover, was well established in particular fields, most notably health sciences, where it possessed a strong medical school and where opportunities existed to obtain federal support for graduate education and research. Yet in every health-related scientific field—biology, biochemistry, molecular biology, and psychology—where both universities were offering doctorates in the late 1960s, the Brandeis programs and faculties were rated well above their counterparts at Tufts. Some of the difference must be attributed to the contrasting approaches to organizational change employed by the two presidents.[54]

Wessell sought to strengthen Tufts by building support for his goals within the existing faculty and drawing his colleagues into developmental activities. He took no steps that angered his community, or parts of it, in substantial ways. He left largely in place an entrenched group of chairs who represented the Tufts tradition of modest scholarly attainment and served extended, open-ended terms. The review of academic personnel policy by one of the Carnegie self-study subcommittees, completed five years after Wessell assumed office, noted no major changes in requirements for promotion and tenure.

Standards, however, were rising, if only incrementally. The Ph.D., for example, was becoming essential for advancement in most cases, and publication was increasingly emphasized, but these changes were being instituted in modest steps that did not disrupt the peaceful evolution of the Tufts community. Wessell's most controversial tenure decision involved rejecting a candidate who had done no scholarship and was not an outstanding teacher. Faculty complained not because excessively high standards were employed but because tenure was denied to a candidate recommended by the department.

The self-study report emphasized the need to increase salaries and reduce teaching loads, and both objectives became priorities for Wessell. In raising compensation, however, Wessell gave greater emphasis to improving the position of the faculty in place than to bringing in new people at a higher level. By the late 1960s, Tufts was most competitive with other institutions at the rank of full professor and least competitive in the categories of assistant professor and instructor, for which new faculty were being hired. Wessell was aware that his policies might be costing Tufts the chance to attract talent, but his feeling for his colleagues denied him the ruthlessness to channel resources toward new people. He felt the existing faculty had remained with Tufts through difficult times and deserved to benefit from prosperity.

The atmosphere at Tufts was expressed in a discussion of turnover in the Carnegie self-study. The committee noted that the average faculty member stayed for ten years, a low departure rate that indicated a high level of contentment. The report commented that "some individuals would interpret this finding as meaning that the environment is too stable . . . and perhaps we are living in 'happy mediocrity.'" It suggested a study of the careers of individuals who had left Tufts to determine "whether we tend to lose some of our top-flight staff members." Such a report could not have been written by representatives of a faculty whose attention had been focused on the need for higher standards of performance.

The comfortable, step-by-step approach to organizational change adopted by Wessell was registered in the modesty of measurable progress in increasing Tufts's academic standing. Wessell believed, however, that his approach was the only one that could work at Tufts given its collegial traditions and its large cadre of tenured professors. A bolder, more-divisive style risked alienating many faculty whom Wessell hoped to stimulate to greater contributions.[55]

Sachar's approach to raising the scholarly reputation of his institution created a distinctly different climate. He believed his faculty tended to resist the appointment of scholars more accomplished and promising than themselves or the investment of resources in new fields. He did not hesitate to assert his will against these attitudes when he felt the interests of Brandeis required such action. He proceeded with several projects—the Heller School, the Lemburg Center for the Study of Violence, and the Wein Scholarships—over faculty objections, while also insisting upon individual appointments, frequently at high salaries, that were not popular with the relevant department. He also supported Cohen when his first dean of faculty moved strongly, sometimes—as in the case of mathematics—brutally, to raise Brandeis's sights in the area of research. In the end, however, he was not ready to allow even an effective ally like Cohen to exercise too much power. The rapid turnover of deans and presidential assistants was a measure of the extent to which he continued to regard Brandeis as his personal creation and fief.

Sachar elaborated his attitude in an account of his presidential years published after he retired. Acknowledging that he sometimes exercised power with a minimum of support, he argued that a leader must behave differently in the process of building an institution than would be appropriate in a more-established setting. This position was probably part thoughtful explanation and part *post hoc* rationale. What remained clear was his focus on institutional outcomes as opposed to collegial feelings. In these terms, by any measure, Sachar's achievements were extraordinary. The rise of Brandeis between 1948 and 1968, with its rich meaning for the Jewish community, was far more important, Sachar clearly felt, than some ephemeral distress.[56]

Wessell vs. Sachar: Organizational Climate

The organizational costs of Sachar's ambitions for Brandeis became increasingly evident during the middle 1960s. His modest concessions to participatory governance failed to satisfy the faculty. Between 1962 and 1968, pressures grew on him to accept greater constraints on presidential power, and he found it necessary to make a series of structural and procedural adjustments, each linked to an area of tension between him and his community.

Rules governing academic appointments and promotions were revised to ensure faculty initiative and to subject hiring proposals by the president to faculty review. Guidelines to guarantee due process in cases involving academic freedom were established after Sachar angrily admonished a professor for criticizing American policy during the Cuban missile crisis. Procedures governing the appointment of department chairs were rewritten to require initial recommendations from senior faculty and to limit terms of office. New patterns for appointing academic deans mandated prior consultation between the president and the Senate. Sachar encountered the most open challenge to his authority in the appointment of deans. In 1968 he attempted to name as graduate dean an individual not supported by the tenured faculty. The matter quickly became acrimonious and resulted in protracted negotiations. Ultimately, a compromise was adopted in which Sachar's choice was installed on an acting basis subject to review and reconsideration after one year.

While the tug-of-war between Sachar and his faculty continued, the president was faced with an increasingly rebellious student body. Brandeis undergraduates were notable for contentiousness from the early days—tuition increases and parietal rules produced organized protests in 1957 and 1961—and this pattern intensified in the middle 1960s, as students nationally became more aggressive in expressing their views. Efforts to exercise greater control over social life produced a series of incidents, the resignation of a dean of students, a drug bust, and another mass demonstration against parietal rules. These events also resulted in repeated encounters between Sachar and student leaders, complete with inflamed coverage in the campus newspaper. In 1965 it became necessary for the president to establish a special committee of faculty and administrators to meet with students to negotiate terms of peaceful coexistence.[57]

Tensions between the Brandeis administration and the student body amplified the struggles between the faculty and Sachar and produced an increasingly tense atmosphere on campus. As this situation continued, showing no signs of resolution, responsible faculty leaders and trustees became concerned that the climate was hurting the university's standing as well as its fund-raising ctivities. Such people began to feel that Sachar had done what he could do and that Brandeis needed new leadership. These views were conveyed to the president.

Under growing criticism and pressure, Sachar finally concluded, in 1967, that he should leave the presidency. Though brought to this decision against his will, he was allowed to resign in an honorable fashion, at the conclusion of twenty years of leadership, with full ceremonial recognition of his accomplishments. But the manner of his departure was painful and constituted part of the price that he and the Brandeis community paid for his and its remarkable academic success.[58]

No such bill came due at Tufts. Both outsiders and insiders noted high morale during the late 1950s as a result of the president's consultative style. A team of outside consultants, reviewing Tufts's position in 1960, discovered that, after eight years as chief executive, Wessell remained immensely popular while also being regarded as a strong leader. The consultants heard no negative comments about the president. Wessell's ability to project a more impressive image of Tufts to the general public than his predecessors had done further enhanced an internal sense of Tufts as a collective enterprise.

The congenial atmosphere was maintained throughout Wessell's term, and his departure was genuinely regretted and experienced as a loss within the Tufts community. Wessell himself, though ready by 1966 to leave the presidency, was reluctant to end his association with the campus and was attracted to the idea of becoming chancellor on the M.I.T. model partly for this reason. Thus, the sense of Tufts as a collegial association, even as a "family"—an increasingly archaic term that the authors of the Carnegie self-study still found applicable—was maintained, even reinforced, during years when the nation's educational leaders, especially at schools that had evolved into large, research universities, were becoming concerned about the fragmentation of their campus communities. Reviews of conditions at Tufts in 1968 by two faculty/administration planning committees, one focused on undergraduate education and the other on graduate programs, did not feel it necessary to comment, as did counterpart groups at Harvard and M.I.T., on discontents in various components of Tufts or latent conflict over institutional purposes.[59]

There were limits, however, to Wessell's success in fostering an atmosphere of common enterprise. The 1968 undergraduate long-range planning committee complained that Tufts lacked a sense of community, and it proposed a series of changes—including a unified structure for the Faculty of Arts and Sciences, new forums for faculty participation in decision making, and new campus facilities—intended to reinforce a feeling of shared purpose. The parallel committee reviewing graduate programs argued that strong administrative leadership was necessary because few faculty members or departments were able to think in terms larger than their individual and disciplinary self-interest. Moreover, the atmosphere of self-doubt, of inferiority in an academic context dominated by Harvard and M.I.T., continued to manifest itself at Tufts and to reduce the readiness of individuals to identify with the university in Medford.[60]

Such signs of community weakness in these years should not be interpreted as presidential failures. Indeed, it is hard to imagine a chief executive more skillful than Wessell at moving his organization gradually ahead while also nurturing its sense of collectivity. The fractures in that structure are best understood as indications of the limits of collegiality in academic institutions. The dream of an association of scholars was only partially compatible with Wessell's efforts to transform Tufts into a modern university. The question that Wessell's leadership posed was this: given Tufts's limited progress in the advanced functions, how much benefit to undergraduate education derived from his patient efforts to nurture morale? This is a matter to which we shall want to return.

Dilemmas of the College-centered University

Maintaining the Collegiate Focus

From the mid-1950s through the late 1960s, Tufts and Brandeis remained faithful in important ways to the small-university concept. Both Wessell and Sachar continued publicly to emphasize this idea. While other universities expanded to fifteen thousand or twenty thousand students and beyond, these two institutions, despite strong applicant pools, pursued modest growth while seeking to increase their selectivity. In 1968 Tufts enrolled less than five thousand students in all its programs; Brandeis, less than three thousand. Both were among the smallest universities in the nation, and both ranked high in the intellectual calibre of their collegiate programs.

Both universities also remained focused on the arts and sciences and avoided the temptation to diversify into professional fields. Wessell concentrated on new graduate programs in the basic disciplines, developed no new professional fields, and pressed for a liberal emphasis in the applied curricula already in existence. Brandeis continued to offer exclusively the liberal arts at the undergraduate level and created only one graduate professional school, which adopted a highly academic character and awarded only the Ph.D. Indeed, in what he identified as the most difficult decision of his presidency, Sachar rejected an opportunity to build a medical school in New York linked to Mount Sinai Hospital—and thus to build ties to the nation's wealthiest and most important Jewish community—on the ground that such an enterprise would divert too much attention from Brandeis's essential activities in the arts and sciences.

As enunciated by their leaders, the aspect of Tufts and Brandeis that most distinguished them from other universities was their central concern with undergraduate liberal education. Both Wessell and Sachar claimed that their schools would avoid the tendency, which they perceived at research-oriented institutions, to neglect collegiate work as they developed the advanced functions. Both asserted, in fact, that controlled growth, judicious planning, and careful monitoring would produce graduate and research activities that would complement undergraduate programs.[61]

Throughout the 1960s, in fact, the scale of graduate development at Tufts and Brandeis did remain relatively restricted. By the end of the decade, graduate students in arts and sciences on both campuses numbered approximately seven hundred, in each case about 25 percent of total enrollments in these disciplines. At Harvard and M.I.T., graduate enrollments accounted for 35 percent and 54 percent respectively of all arts and sciences students.

The similarity in scale of graduate work at Tufts and Brandeis hid important differences, however. At Tufts, only a modest percentage of graduate students (about two hundred of seven hundred) were enrolled in Ph.D. programs—the rest were master's students, including many school teachers, who had no thought of advanced work or research. At Brandeis, most graduate students were full-time doctoral candidates preparing for academic careers. This difference reflected the comparative success of the two institutions in building advanced programs. That contrast, in turn, must be attributed in part to the divergent attitudes of their leaders toward the idea of the college-centered university.[62]

Undergraduate Education at Brandeis:
The Costs of Academic Success

Sachar's priorities for Brandeis were clear from the outset. He sought the highest possible standing in the shortest possible time. This objective, rooted in his symbolic view of his university, helped make Sachar an eloquent advocate of undergraduate education in the late 1940s and early 1950s, when the collegiate ideal represented the mainstream of elite academic thinking. Sachar was essentially an institutional opportunist, however, and as attention shifted toward graduate education and research, he was ready to make adjustments. In this process, research capabilities became the primary consideration in assessing faculty performance.

This change, though critical to Brandeis's ascent in the academic hierarchy, was not entirely comfortable for Sachar, who retained old-fashioned views about scholarship and teaching. In 1963 he complained angrily that his campus was becoming "less and less teacher oriented. Reputation, prestige, advancement, depend more and more on outstanding scholarship and research." This was true enough, but the emphasis, as Dean of Faculty Leonard Levy patiently informed his president, was a correct reflection of his own priorities:

> Like it or not, teaching and related activities . . . are almost impediments toward advancement in the profession. The road to preferment, position and profit only passes through, and sometimes passes by, the classroom; publication, not teaching, pays off. . . . The administration itself endorses the 'publish or perish' criterion, for . . . the scholar who crystallizes DNA or wins a Bancroft prize receives all the publicity, advancement and take-home pay, regardless of how much or how well he teaches . . .

By the late 1960s, Brandeis was ready to reject truly gifted teachers if there was not also an impressive record of publication.

The emphasis on research produced insistent pressures from the faculty to reduce teaching assignments, and accommodations, worked out in *ad hoc* arrangements between deans, chairs, and individual scholars, were an inevitable implication of Brandeis's rapid progress. Official policies continued to state that all faculty taught three courses each term and that each was actively involved in undergraduate instruction. In fact, however, no system of monitoring this policy was established. In 1964 the dean of undergraduate studies, Milton Sacks, wrote a long memo to Sachar pointing out that many faculty members were teaching much less than called for by official policy, possibly as little as one course per term—and this not infrequently an advanced, specialized course for a relatively small group of students.

Sacks's memo upset Sachar and precipitated a debate about teaching that lasted for several years. In this discussion, it became clear to Sachar that Brandeis's practices were not unlike those of leading, research-oriented institutions with which he was competing for faculty and reputation. In the end, little modification in teaching loads was attempted. On the contrary, the major policy change arising from this debate was reduction of the required course load for undergraduate students from five courses per term to four. Although the formal rationale for this shift was that it permitted young minds to concentrate more intensively, the underlying goal was to diminish the instructional responsibilities of the faculty.[63]

The thinness of commitment at Brandeis to the ideal of the college-centered university was further reflected in the evolution of the undergraduate curriculum. After 1960 the old general education program—established in the early years and retained, despite some erosion, throughout the 1950s—came completely apart. Alternative courses to meet distribution requirements proliferated rapidly. Growing numbers of advanced placement students skipped introductory work altogether. A review of the situation by a faculty committee in 1965 produced the following conclusion:

> You may turn with some wry amusement to the statement [in the] current undergraduate catalogue to find an essential reiteration of the rationale of general education given in 1950–51. The substance has passed beyond knowing. Vestigial remains of "core curriculum" may still be found in individual courses, but the faculty has voiced little support for universal requirements. . . . The original conception of general education at Brandeis may have been unattainable. For a brief period and for a variety of reasons, Brandeis came closer to realizing the intentions of the Harvard Redbook than Harvard College ever did. The tremendous growth and diversity of Brandeis have relegated "general education" to second rank. . . . Your committee saw no way nor any necessity to attempt to reconstruct the Brandeis of 1950 in 1965.

The review committee seemed to lament the passage of general education, with its high hopes for producing "moral, decision-making" individuals and providing a "universally shared experience." It recognized, however, that general education courses had sometimes been superficial, that there could be no intellectual agreement on the pattern of courses most likely to produce the "whole man" that general education idealized, and that education in disciplinary specialities had become the primary, often the only, interest and capability of the faculty.

Under these circumstances, the most that Brandeis could do was provide "abundant offerings in rich and available forms" in the various fields of knowledge, establish a reasonable distribution requirement, and shore up the advising system to ensure that each student was given help in assembling a program of liberal education. These sensible recommendations recognized the realities of Brandeis in the middle 1960s and represented a surrender of collegiate to university values as the inevitable implication of the young school's extraordinary success. In 1969 the general education program was formally abolished and replaced by a distribution requirement.[64]

Keeping the Faith at Tufts

The history of the collegiate ideal at Tufts was quite different from that at Brandeis. Wessell wanted his campus to develop research and doctoral programs, but he also expressed a continuing seriousness about undergraduate education that qualified his pursuit of upward mobility as a university. He persistently held up the ideal of the committed teacher who was also an accomplished scholar as the appropriate faculty member for Tufts. Criteria for promotion and tenure continued to reflect a balance of these concerns. Wessell repeatedly urged his faculty to commit energy and imagination to undergraduate education.

The Experimental College was a case in point. In 1962, persuaded that Tufts needed more innovation and flexibility in its undergraduate programs, Wessell charged a faculty committee to consider a new unit that could provide a protected home for curricular initiatives. The committee's endorsement led to the most significant change in Tufts's collegiate program during Wessell's presidency. The emphasis on innovation also led to the Tufts Seminar on Undergraduate Education, which brought together educators from all over the country. In 1968 the Tufts faculty endorsed an unusual program allowing students to create individual "Plans of Study" as an alternative to a conventional disciplinary major.

In sum, Wessell, much more than Sachar, took the concept of the college-centered university literally and sought formulae through which Tufts could stress undergraduate teaching and learning while also establishing itself as a proper university. Wessell's attitude forms part of the reason that Tufts moved less successfully and dramatically than Brandeis in developing its graduate and research functions.[65]

How much difference did Wessell's and Tufts's attitude toward education, like the president's concern with faculty morale, actually make in the experience of students? This is a difficult question for the historian to answer. There is an obvious difference between documenting presidential actions or policies and forming conclusions about what actually happened in the classroom. What can be discussed with confidence, however, is the atmosphere on campus with respect to the collegiate ideal and the extent to which the local culture, and the president as chief spokesperson for that culture, directed energy to this aspect of the institution's work. On this level, there was a clear difference between Tufts and Brandeis.

In the late 1960s, two faculty committees assessed Tufts's programs in the arts and sciences. Both expressed a continuing commitment to the idea of college-centeredness that was absent from the reviews conducted in the same years at Brandeis. The Undergraduate Long-Range Planning Committee opened its report with the triumphant declaration that Tufts "is not a multiversity where the undergraduate college is almost an extracurricular operation, nor is it a rural college where research and scholarship are peripheral. Tufts has available the best of the 'small university' and the best of the 'college.'" The Graduate Long-Range Planning Committee stated "emphatically" that "we see no evidence at Tufts to support the view that the graduate program has attracted" faculty that neglect undergraduate education.

The graduate committee was concerned, in fact, that the Tufts faculty remained excessively wary of doctoral programs. It also pointed out that Tufts had not succeeded in designing doctorates that complemented the undergraduate curriculum. In the committee's view, Tufts's efforts were largely copies— and not very good ones—of conventional, research-oriented programs at major universities. Noting that few graduates of Tufts's programs were likely to pursue careers in research and that most would be teachers or workers in industry and government, the committee urged their colleagues to create new Ph.D. programs more compatible with the real needs of their students.

The undergraduate committee also identified problems. Its report repeatedly emphasized that the curriculum had become a preprofessional experience centered on the disciplinary majors and viewed by the faculty as preparatory to graduate work in an academic field. The committee urged more attention to the nonprofessional side of undergraduate education, advocating new general studies programs, revised distribution requirements, and a new program of freshman seminars.[66]

The Continuing Tension Between College and University

The stories of Tufts and Brandeis in the golden age are tales of two universities confronting a dominant tension of the period—that between the traditional priorities of the college and the new concerns of the university. That there were conflicts and trade-offs between these two value systems and that the two campuses resolved the choices they faced differently expressed not only the contrasts between Tufts and Brandeis but also the underlying difficulty on any campus of achieving a satisfactory balance between the claims of undergraduate education on one side and advanced training and research on the other. By the time he left the presidency, even Wessell was sounding discouraged on this point. In his final report, he wondered aloud if Tufts had been pursuing a "shibboleth" and if it were time to structure institutions in which "teachers teach and scholars undertake scholarship." A few years after his departure a faculty planning committee endorsed a far more critical assessment of the impact of graduate work on undergraduate programs than offered by the undergraduate and graduate committees in the late 1960s.[67]

An important element of the dilemma that faced Wessell and Sachar in shaping college-centered universities was the pervasive influence of the nation's leading research universities, represented locally by Harvard and

M.I.T., on institutions with other missions. The fact of such influence, how-ever, was hardly surprising. These institutions defined the pinnacle of the aca-demic prestige system, and to improve one's position—a central goal for both presidents—was, inevitably, to become more like them. The faculties of Tufts and Brandeis, moreover, were drawn heavily from the graduate schools of these universities, and the Harvard contingent, in particular, was strong at both. Discussions about faculty roles and responsibilities, including teaching loads, or about the importance of research or about the organization of grad-uate programs frequently referred back to Harvard as model and standard.[68]

Even in the area of undergraduate curriculum, where Tufts and Brandeis most would be expected to seek their own formulations, there was a tendency to follow Harvard. At Brandeis, for example, the evolution of the collegiate program from general education in the late 1940s to freshman seminars and advanced placement in the 1950s and to electives within a loosely structured distribution requirement in the 1960s reproduced the fashions of Cambridge. Tufts showed somewhat more independence, although the freshman seminars adopted in 1968 were a variant of the program introduced at Harvard nearly a decade earlier.

Given the pressure on Tufts and Brandeis to conform to the dominant edu-cational ideas of the golden age, it is important to remember that undergrad-uates could find at these institutions advantages that were less readily available at large, diversified research universities dominated by their graduate schools or at massive service universities with their dazzling arrays of professional and academic programs. Faculty members at Tufts and Brandeis were more readily available to undergraduates than at Harvard. Less of the undergraduate pro-gram was conducted in large classes or turned over to teaching assistants, and at Tufts, in particular, greater efforts were made to encourage undergraduate teaching. The small scale of both places, the relative isolation, and the tradi-tional collegiate environment made a difference. As even the critics of the new emphases on research and graduate education acknowledged, moreover, the strengthening of these functions had clear benefits for undergraduates in terms of an intensified intellectual environment as well as a greater variety of course offerings.

It is important to remember, too, that the period from the mid-1950s to the late 1960s was a time of multidimensional progress at both universities. Wessell and Sachar could make their quite different exits confident that their faculties were academically stronger and better paid than fifteen years earlier, their students more selectively admitted, their facilities improved, and their revenues enlarged. The histories of Tufts and Brandeis in these years are chronicles of advancement, combined with some success in fostering a special environment for undergraduate education in a university context. That their qualities as colleges proved, in the end, to be less distinctive and more com-promised than had been anticipated accounts for the tone of disappointment that tended to seep through justly prideful reviews of change at both institu-tions.

The 1960s End Early and Gently at Tufts

During the year of Mead's acting presidency, 1966–1967, the sense deepened among the trustees that Tufts had become overextended under Wessell. It was obvious that additional investments on a large scale would be needed to bring the new doctorates to a respectable standard, and there was no confidence that such resources could be obtained. There remained, moreover, ambivalence within the Tufts community about Wessell's efforts to build the advanced functions. The trustees signaled their own views by electing as president Burton C. Hallowell, executive vice president of Wesleyan University in Connecticut, a campus noted chiefly for excellence in undergraduate education. Hallowell's reputation as a cautious administrator was a further indication of the official mood.

In a series of statements, the new president articulated his perception that Tufts had allowed the specialized values of the modern university to dominate the campus. Ironically, given Wessell's policies and the views of the Undergraduate Long-Range Planning Committee, Hallowell characterized Tufts as a "multiversity" and announced his intention to restore coherence, collegiality, and broad participation in governance. He was particularly concerned about the impact of recent changes on undergraduate education, which, he asserted,

> has both lost and gained in the last twenty years. It has gained from the upgrad-
> ing . . . in virtually all the specialized fields since World War II. . . . At the same
> time undergraduate teaching has suffered compared with earlier years. . . .
> There is what one astute observer has called the loss of a "sense of any indepen-
> dent mission" on the part of undergraduate colleges. They seem to be becoming
> an adjunct to the graduate schools.

Hallowell called for "reconsideration" of the direction and rapid growth of Tufts's Graduate School of Arts and Sciences, stressing the need for greater emphasis on "breadth, vision, versatility, and wisdom"—the traditional virtues of general education—in the undergraduate program.[69]

Financial conditions, including reduced federal support for graduate work, reinforced Hallowell's conservative instincts. During his first year, fiscal year 1968, Tufts incurred its first deficit after a period of balanced budgets, though some of the change reflected more rigorous accounting than had previously been employed. The pattern continued for the next two years, despite tuition increases. By fiscal year 1970, the accumulated deficit exceeded two million dollars, an amount larger than total annual gifts for noncapital purposes in that year. Tufts's salaries, which gained in comparison with other institutions between 1960 and 1966, began to slip again. Cheit's study identified the Medical School, historically a drain on Tufts's finances, as "in serious financial trouble."

Hallowell himself commented repeatedly on budgetary problems. He noted in 1968, for example, that "we need more faculty in several areas, but our finances made these additions difficult to effect." He saw Tufts's worries as embedded in the broader fiscal dilemmas of higher education in the late 1960s. "The needs of students educationally," he observed, "and the willingness of society to support those needs seem to be moving in opposite directions." He was not optimistic about solutions. "The central economic question in higher education," in his view, "concern[ed] its ability to design techniques which combine quality in the educational function with higher productivity by the faculties. Nowhere . . . has this difficulty been satisfactorily faced and solved."[70]

Tufts had its own version of the late 1960s. There was a wrenching and divisive debate about the status of the R.O.T.C. on campus. There were student protests related to university policies on minority hiring and federal actions in Vietnam. There was a drug bust. An Afro-American cultural center was established. New structures to involve students in governance were created. Efforts were made to engage the university more actively in social problems, including a widely acclaimed project that brought medical services to inner-city Boston and rural Mississippi.

None of the protests produced a major crisis in Medford, however, where campus culture traditionally contained an element of passivity and where Wessell had worked hard to preserve a spirit of community; nor did any of the innovations lead to a fundamental rethinking of the university's mission. As the decade ended, Tufts was embarked on a period of consolidation, and Hallowell was calling for a comprehensive assessment of current programs before recommending new initiatives.[71]

The 1960s Blow up at Brandeis

In February 1968, six months after Sachar announced his readiness to step aside, the Brandeis trustees offered the presidency to Morris B. Abram, a partner in a prestigious New York law firm and national president of the American Jewish Committee. For Abram, the Brandeis position was a long-held dream, and he was, as he himself thought, a natural choice to succeed Sachar. Although not a professional academic, his law degree and his Rhodes Scholarship gave him respectability as an intellectual. His work for the American Jewish Committee and his presidency of the Field Foundation had won him prominence in Jewish philanthropic circles. His record as a crusading southern lawyer in the early years of the civil rights movement, subsequent assignments as American representative to important U.N. commissions on human rights, and his political activism during the Kennedy–Johnson years had earned him national visibility in liberal circles.

Despite his lack of academic experience, Abram held strong views about higher education. He was a champion of general education and was eager to reassert the importance of undergraduate teaching. He wanted, at the same time, to "prune the luxuriant growth of graduate programs, resist proposals for new ones, and rationalize teaching loads." His skepticism about academia's orientation toward disciplinary specialization led him to propose university professorships cutting across departmental lines, an idea that Conant had tried with little success at Harvard. He was aware that Brandeis had allowed the catalogue to thicken with specialized courses, and he hoped to cut these back. He wanted to move his university in new directions and grew particularly excited about building a law school geared toward public policy.[72]

Abram's ideas, with their almost quaint reference to his student days at Oxford, would have aroused faculty resistance at the most congenial of universities in the late 1960s. At Brandeis, they guaranteed conflict. Faculty-administration contention was already a way of life, and the president's priorities challenged central features of the school's meteoric rise. Tension between Abram and his faculty built quickly. An early discussion with a department about resources produced an antagonistic exchange about the tenure prospects of a young instructor who was a talented teacher with little publication. An initial meeting with the faculty Senate turned into a chilly standoff: the faculty wanted to discuss its role in governance; Abram grew righteous and said he wanted to discuss education. Soon the professors were calling for the appointment of a provost. Abram's ideas about university professorships and a new law school stirred more antipathy than excitement and went nowhere.

The new president fared no better with the students. One early meeting turned into an angry exchange about investment policy. Another became a tense discussion of "relevance" in undergraduate education, during which Abram lectured his visitors about a high British economic official who had studied only the classics at Oxford. Soon Abram found students averting their eyes as he passed them.[73]

The biggest problem was the blacks. Abram arrived in Waltham to find an aroused group of African-American students pressing for action on a series of measures, including a black studies program and minority scholarships, to which Sachar had agreed in the waning months of his presidency. To Abram, a classic liberal, policies rooted in special treatment for black subjects and black individuals were patronizing and discriminatory, the opposite of what he had championed during years in the civil rights movement. He was ready, reluctantly, to honor most of Sachar's commitments, but he let the students know what he thought of their views.

He reaped a whirlwind. In January 1969, African-American students seized Ford Hall and began an eleven-day siege that proved to be the stormiest moment of a generally turbulent period of campus history. By skillfully mobilizing moderate opinion and avoiding violence, Abram waited out the strikers and brought the incident to a quiet end. The success did not resolve basic tensions, however, or rally the campus to its new leader. On the contrary, the episode seemed to drain constructive energy from Abram's young presidency.

The administrative apparatus was also a problem. The biggest headache, from Abram's perspective, was Sachar, who continued to play an active role in campus affairs from his new perch as university chancellor. The builder of Brandeis was not ready to release his dream child into the care of another, and he and Abram became openly antagonistic even before the new president's inaugural. Abram became convinced that Sachar was working to undermine him with former colleagues, especially within the administration. The staff, moreover, in Abram's perspective, was made up of "layers of administrators who reveled in their practiced skills of bureaucratic infighting, a very useful craft which I abhorred and have never mastered." The one senior appointment that he made was greeted with hostility and produced what Abram saw as a "cabal . . . in the senior administration" to "expel [the appointee] as a foreign object."[74]

All in all, Abram's initial period in the Brandeis presidency was a disaster, and by the middle of his second year he had had enough. When an opportunity arose to run for the U.S. Senate from New York, he found himself eager for the change. Discussions with trustees about the terms of his remaining were perfunctory. By the spring of 1970, he was back in New York for a campaign that never got off the ground.

Abram's subsequent account of his time at Brandeis was a bitter indictment of academic politics in the late 1960s. The students appeared to him as ill-mannered, mindlessly radical, and thin on conviction, ready to drop their opposition to the war as soon as their personal interests were protected. The administration was a vipers' nest of intrigue. The faculty was self-interested and weak. Against such corruption, his own high-mindedness had proved ineffective. "I could cope with greed, hypocrisy, and slander when I encountered them in the caucus room or in the marketplace; I cannot, however, bear the defilement of my abiding illusion, not to say ideal, that a place of higher learning is sacred and that Brandeis was symbolic of the Jewish devotion to that ideal . . ." He had imagined himself in the presidency as a "Renaissance prince." He found he needed to be a "keeper of the peace, not through reason or persuasion, but by buying off troublemakers."

Abram saw with accuracy places where Brandeis needed attention, but he was too much an outsider to academia and too unready to learn its ways to find constructive means to address them. He saw the excesses of the period astutely but conveyed little sense of deeper, more positive, redemptive impulses in his community, or in the scholarly profession more broadly, that could provide a basis for progress. The campus was not ready to accept a leader who fancied himself a Renaissance prince, but it needed something more than a keeper of the peace—and it was unfortunate for both university and president that these were the only alternatives Abram could see.[75]

As the new university entered the post-Sachar era, major issues awaited answers: how to maintain financial health with the Ford money coming to an end and a fund-raising genius headed for retirement; how to ensure a continued flow of top undergraduates; how to build on the limited academic base that was now in place; and how to define the university's ambiguous relationship with the Jewish community. Brandeis had ended a brilliant, if contentious, first act, but conditions would not allow a mere continuation of Sachar's formula.

In turning to Charles Schottland, the respected dean of the Heller School, for the acting presidency, the trustees won themselves time to think carefully about the next move. Schottland led Brandeis for two years, during which the volatile issues on which Abram's presidency had shipwrecked still needed to be faced: black studies, the antiwar movement, and localized student discontents, including complaints about overcrowding in introductory classes. These were not calm times—they included a bank robbery and murder involving radical Brandeis students—but Schottland kept the university functioning and relatively stable. While there was little forward motion on any basic issue, Schottland's record won him the title of president in January 1971. His term remained, however, a holding action while the trustees sought a leader who could give the campus the second act it so badly needed.[76]

Transformation of the Urban University: Boston University, Boston College, and Northeastern, 1945–1972

Boston's three local, private, teaching and service-oriented, commuter universities—Boston University, Boston College, and Northeastern, classic urban universities in the years before World War II—undertook to change themselves in fundamental ways during the golden age. B.U., reaching back to its nineteenth-century origins, sought to re-create itself as a comprehensive regional and national university. Boston College, drawing on the ancient academic traditions of the Society of Jesus, worked to become the nation's top Jesuit university and a leading force in Catholic intellectual and professional life. Northeastern, with its philosophical roots in service to the low-income population and business community of Boston, tried to balance its historic concerns with a new impulse toward national prominence in cooperative education.

All three invested heavily in graduate education and research, and B.U. and B.C., in upgrading their undergraduate student bodies, shed their identities as local, service-oriented campuses. At the end of the period, only N.U. remained centrally committed to the functions of an urban university, though it, too, had taken steps to reduce its emphasis on local service.

Postwar Boom: Veterans, Growth, and Capital Accumulation

Getting Ready for Good Times

Boston's three nonelite, private universities were hit hard by World War II, but campus leaders were conscious of predictions that the return of peace would bring a new period of expansion. By the middle of the war, Presidents Marsh of B.U. and Ell of Northeastern and the provincial Jesuit hierarchy that governed B.C., frustrated by fifteen difficult years, were turning their attention to postwar opportunities. Throughout the war, Marsh later wrote, "we kept getting ready" to "jump quickly" after the fighting stopped. Ell was equally eager. "When the war is over," he wrote in 1943, "Northeastern will be prepared."[1]

Boston University and the Charles River Campus

The senior president among the universities of Massachusetts, B.U.'s Marsh was in his middle sixties during World War II and was determined to make concrete progress toward his institutional goals in the short period in office remaining to him. Since his appointment in 1926, he had emphasized three aspects of B.U.: its religious heritage as a nonsectarian, Methodist university with a strong School of Theology; its public-service role as a diversified educational resource for the Boston area; and its academic possibilities as one of the nation's largest universities with a full range of graduate and professional programs. In 1943 he appointed a Committee on the University in the Postwar World to consider how B.U. could enhance itself in all these areas. The group's report became the basis for postwar planning.

Both the committee and Marsh affirmed B.U.'s traditional concern with religion. For Marsh, a Methodist minister, the classical Protestant values of virtue and piety remained essential components of B.U.'s mission. Repeatedly stressing these concerns in postwar discussions of general education and student life, he argued that B.U. must give ecumenical encouragement to formal religious practice. The Committee on the University in the Postwar World, largely faculty members, placed much less emphasis on religion and proposed only to establish an undergraduate department of religion and expand the Graduate School of Theology. Although these recommendations constituted a minor element in the committee's program—some members saw them as a sop to Marsh—they appeared to satisfy the president, who seemed, in fact, to attend to religion more in his speeches than in his plans. For both president and committee, the central ambition was to improve the position of Boston University as a secular, academic enterprise.

When Marsh spoke of "jumping quickly" after the war, he was referring to his ambitious plan to construct a campus on the Charles River site near Kenmore Square. For decades, B.U. had operated in buildings scattered throughout the city, and Marsh regarded the creation of a proper home as an essential basis for raising academic stature. The impulse to build B.U. into a national university was a consistent theme of his presidency. He frequently observed that B.U. was the first proper university in the United States because it first combined British and German traditions. He began early to build dormitories for students from beyond the Boston area, never missed an opportunity to associate B.U. with Harvard and M.I.T., and drew attention to every hint of national or international recognition. In depicting B.U. in such terms, however, Marsh was aware of being more hopeful than descriptive. He knew that his institution functioned principally as an unselective, urban, commuter university.

The expansion of Boston University in the years following World War I had been based on local, service-oriented programs, chiefly practical, in fields like education, business, health, social service, and even secretarial and office work. The Graduate School of Arts and Sciences was small, undistinguished, and concerned mainly with training teachers at the master's level. Both Marsh and his planning committee celebrated community service. Noting that "an institution of Boston University's character must always be attuned to the educational needs of the area it serves" and stressing the "democratic" character of its admission policies, the committee emphasized the creation of programs, mostly undergraduate, in career-oriented fields. It also called for one- and two-year nondegree and junior college courses, flexible program packages for non-traditional students, and a significant expansion of adult education programs, summer school, and extension work. At the same time, both committee and president recommended steps to lift B.U.'s academic sights, including "widen[ing] B.U.'s geographical sphere of influence" by recruiting from beyond Boston, emphasizing scholarly research, and raising compensation for the faculty.[2]

There was no contradiction for Marsh and his associates in simultaneously strengthening their service-oriented functions and raising their stature in academic terms. Boston University was large and complex and had room for multiple purposes. Indeed, some programs, particularly the School of Medicine, the School of Theology, and the College of Music, had achieved a measure of recognition before the war. There was no reason why some units could not advance academically while others served the practical needs of the region.

The two visions of B.U. were also linked financially. Since the university lacked both a substantial endowment and major fund-raising capabilities, most resources for development would have to come from student payments. Mounting large programs and earning surplus revenues thus held the key to upgrading. While Marsh and his committee had different priorities—Marsh wanted dollars to build his campus while the committee hoped to improve salaries—everyone understood that progress required expansion. As the committee put it: "Boston University cannot afford long periods of research and investigation" before starting new programs. "We need to be more pragmatic, more resourceful, more expeditious than some other institutions." Deans and faculty should be "zealous in consideration of new opportunities."[3]

Securing the Future of Northeastern

Like Marsh, Ell of Northeastern possessed a settled conception of his campus born of long association. Though different in both temperament and style from his predecessor and mentor, Frank Palmer Speare, Ell was devoted to Speare's idea of Northeastern as a "community service" institution with limited and distinctive purposes. Both men stressed practical training on the co-op model for local, working-class, male students who lacked other educational opportunities. Both defined "service" as meeting the manpower needs of area businesses. Ell eschewed the ambitions for academic status expressed by Marsh, but he did seek to increase Northeastern's respectability. He attached great importance, for example, to achieving acceptance from accrediting and institutional associations in N.U.'s fields of emphasis, and he encouraged faculty members to be active in relevant professional organizations. His particular objective was to put Speare's shoestring operation on a secure basis by building an endowment and a facility. The outbreak of war, coinciding with the start of his presidency, slowed progress on the Huntington Avenue campus, but Ell used the time, aided by seven faculty committees, to draft an extensive "plan of operation" for the postwar period.

Ell believed that the key to making N.U. a proper university lay in the three "day colleges": Engineering, Business, and Liberal Arts, with the latter serving chiefly to support the other two. He stressed the need to build carefully within these areas and advocated a return to the prewar pattern of four-year, cooperative education for most students. He did not project substantial expansion for the three central units. The only major change would be retention of coeducation, introduced during the war as an emergency measure to bolster enrollments.

Ell explained his conservative plans, so different from those of B.U., in terms of institutional commitments. "We believe," he wrote, "that the long-established programs of the University, its method of operation, and its policies on admissions, should continue." He sought to maintain Northeastern's "distinctive mission" and not to become "just another institution." He noted that increased demand for higher education might permit the school to alter its character, but he rejected this possibility, insisting that "Northeastern has a definite mission and that this mission shall be accomplished."[4]

Ell's restrained plans did not imply fundamental disagreement with the free-wheeling, market-oriented conception of community service articulated by Marsh and his colleagues. On the contrary, Ell described Northeastern in terms remarkably similar to those used by B.U.'s wartime planning committee. To meet the needs of the community, he wrote, N.U. must be a "dynamic," "developing," and "flexible" institution, ready to create new programs in response to changing conditions. The emphasis in admission policy should be on access rather than selectivity. In contrast to the ebullient Marsh, however, Ell was a cautious man, and he was skeptical about postwar growth. His plans for the day colleges assumed that future demand was not likely to exceed the level of the 1930s.

Ell's uncertainty did not prevent him from wanting to exploit any opportunities for expansion that might occur after the war. He believed he could accomplish this through evening and part-time programs. Utilizing part-time faculty, often from industry, and facilities designed for the day colleges, these activities entailed no long-term financial commitments. Through them, Northeastern could expand and contract readily in response to fluctuating markets. If the unpredictable postwar years offered opportunities for rapid growth and new initiatives, Ell planned to respond with entrepreneurial development in these arenas.

For Ell, as for Marsh, the expansion of service-oriented programs was closely linked to financial concerns. Northeastern, like B.U., had little experience with fund-raising. A program of annual giving by alumni was only organized in 1943 and could not be expected to yield large amounts in the immediate future. Resources to build both campus and endowment would have to come from student payments. In essence, the plan was to use surplus revenues—what Speare had called "profits"—from low-cost evening and part-time programs to secure the position of the day colleges, whose affairs would be managed in a much more conservative manner.[5]

Boston College and the Society of Jesus:
Sustaining the Reform Movement
During World War II

Early in the war, the Jesuit Education Association, now headed by Father Edward B. Rooney, decided that it was vital, despite the crisis, to continue the upgrading of the order's colleges and universities that had been launched in the 1930s. In particular, it was essential to maintain the Special Studies Program, through which intellectually gifted young priests were receiving advanced academic training. Special Studies was the order's main vehicle for producing faculty members capable of staffing a modern university, and the war threatened to divert these future scholars to other activities. It would be "fatal," the Executive Committee and Board of Governors agreed, "to let this program lapse even for a few years" lest the order not be in a position to "take our place in the ranks of the leaders" of the "inevitable postwar education resurgence." The Executive Committee urged provincials to "continue and, where possible, increase" assignments to Special Studies.

Other elements of the reform movement also continued during the war. The J.E.A. pressed its effort to win acceptance for a Jesuit university into the A.A.U., and debated the advantages of asking the Vatican to grant "pontifical university" status to one of its institutions. In late 1943, the J.E.A. created a Committee on Postwar Jesuit Education "to make a blueprint . . . [that] will aim at making our schools more effective in the postwar world." The committee's 1945 report stressed the pursuit of distinctive Jesuit goals combined with the modernization of curricula in the arts and sciences, especially the latter. The report also urged expansion in professional fields and greater selectivity in admissions in order to produce more influential alumni. A 1947 communication from the father general reaffirmed the mandate to Jesuit universities in the United States to stress scholarly work at the highest academic level.[6]

The impulse to use the period of the war to build strength for the postwar years was fully shared by the New England hierarchy. During the two years after Pearl Harbor, the New England province led the nation in assigning young Jesuits to graduate studies. At the same time, the provincial leadership reiterated its intention to build Boston College into a center for graduate education. As one participant in these efforts later wrote, "the administration of the New England province . . . had determined during the depths of the

Depression and World War II that Boston College was, indeed, going to become a university."

The products of the Special Studies Program began arriving in Chestnut Hill in 1941. Over the next seven years, fourteen freshly minted Jesuit Ph.D.s were placed on the Heights campus, an extraordinary infusion of talent for an institution whose religious teachers traditionally possessed only master's degrees. The appointment in 1945 of a new rector-president, Father William Lane Keleher, more oriented toward his pastoral than his academic functions, had little impact on this development, since institutional power rested chiefly with the provincial, Father John J. McEleney, who was determined to strengthen B.C. academically. As the war came to an end, the long-delayed effort to transform the traditional Jesuit college into a regional university was well under way.[7]

Traditional Missions and Institutional Mobility

The postwar plans of B.U., B.C., and Northeastern were, in their details, as diverse as the universities themselves, and in each case, campus leaders stressed the importance of preserving their particular characteristics and commitments. At the same time, their plans conveyed a common impulse to improve academic status by adopting some of the functions, values, and organizational forms of the nation's leading universities. Prospective conflicts were implicit in all these visions: B.U.'s hopes to be both local and national; N.U.'s to be both unique and respectable; and B.C.'s to be both Catholic and academic.

To the educators involved in postwar planning, these tensions seemed manageable and even constructive. None of these universities was in any immediate danger of losing its special qualities or abandoning its traditional constituency by becoming too much like the most established institutions. While places like Harvard and M.I.T. provided a kind of magnetic pole for schools eager to improve their positions, the towers of Cambridge remained as remote from Boston's three local universities as was the geographical pole from the ships' compasses it activated. Leaders at B.U., B.C., and Northeastern had no reason to doubt that they would serve their upwardly mobile students well by reaching for some of the characteristics, and therefore the prestige, that elite campuses conferred upon their more privileged clients.

Another point of similarity among Boston's three local, commuting universities was their dependence on student payments to finance new development. None of them possessed a substantial endowment or connections to major sources of private wealth. There were some differences in their positions. The war was particularly hard on the two all-male universities, Northeastern and B.C., whose leaders learned an important lesson about the advantages of coeducation. B.C., which relied on unpaid Jesuits for a large part of its faculty, had access to a "living endowment" that made it less dependent on enrollments for faculty salaries than B.U. or Northeastern. At bottom, however, these variations were of marginal importance for planning purposes. The major source of revenue for all of them was tuition. Unlike elite institutions, which subsidized students, these universities kept costs low and could expect to make money by adding enrollments. None of them was inclined—as were Harvard, M.I.T., and even Tufts—to restrict growth. If their dreams were to be realized, expansion was not only desirable but also necessary.

The Veterans' Program: Public Service and Institutional Windfall

Given the orientations of B.U., B.C., and Northeastern toward public service, program development, and growth, the flood of applications from returning veterans provided an ideal beginning for the postwar period. For leaders of these universities, the pressure to adapt and expand programs to serve G.I.s was a chance for a fast start on long-frustrated plans. Marsh captured the spirit of the moment when he observed that "the upheavals wrought by the war and the reconversion to a peace-time program have given this university an opportunity—and we have seized the opportunity by the forelock."

In 1945 B.U. opened an evening law school oriented toward working veterans and also began an undergraduate business program through the Evening College of Commerce. A year later, a two-year unit, the General College, was created, followed the next year by a new School of Public Relations based on the Journalism Department of the College of Business Administration. Enrollments in previously established colleges and schools were expanded to the limit of capacity. In 1947–1948, the peak year for the veterans, B.U. enrolled over fourteen thousand students in its degree programs, more than triple the number registered in the last prewar year, and Marsh reported proudly that his university was serving over thirty thousand students in all its activities.

At Northeastern, where the cautious Ell was not ready to build new units in response to a short-term surge of applications, growth in daytime degree programs was confined to the three established colleges—Engineering, Business, and Liberal Arts—but day enrollments still jumped by 74 percent over the 1939 level, reaching 4,225 in 1948. Meanwhile, Ell encouraged both explosive growth and entrepreneurial development in evening programs, which were placed in the hands of an energetic new dean. In 1948 Northeastern enrolled over eleven thousand students across all its degree and nondegree activities, more than double prewar registration levels.

At Boston College, the veterans helped make possible the rapid development of professional programs called for by the J.E.A.'s Committee on Postwar Jesuit Education. The College of Business Administration, a marginal operation enrolling seventy-three students in 1939, grew to nearly fourteen hundred by 1948. The Law and Social Work schools were also expanded, and new units were established for Dramatic and Expressional Arts and for Adult Education. With admissions to Liberal Arts also swollen, B.C.'s overall enrollments reached seventy-two hundred in 1948, nearly triple the number served before the war.[8]

At all three universities, tuition increases added to the revenue generated by sudden growth. By 1948 B.U.'s tuition was 38 percent above the 1939 level; B.C.'s was up by 40 percent; and Northeastern's by 50 percent. While such raises derived from a number of factors, including high postwar inflation and the suppression of tuition during the Depression, there can be no doubt that the guarantee of federal reimbursement for the full tuition costs of veterans allowed these schools to raise fees rapidly, with little fear of losing applicants.

B.U. illustrated the effect of revenue-oriented enrollment and tuition policies. In fiscal year 1948, total receipts from tuition and fees, which constituted 78 percent of current income, reached $6.2 million, a 266 percent increase over 1940. These dollars, in turn, enabled Marsh to expand the faculty, increase salaries, provide scholarships and fellowships, and support the professional activities of the faculty. Between 1945 and 1949, the instructional budget quadrupled while enrollments only doubled. For B.U.'s aging president, however, the central priority was the Charles River campus, and he restrained operating expenses to earn surpluses for the building program. In fiscal year 1948, 35 percent of current revenues, amounting to more than two million dollars, was used to finance new construction. On this basis, supplemented by conventional fund-raising, Marsh put up six buildings, including homes for Liberal Arts, Theology, the Graduate School, facilities for science and administration, and the chapel that was to bear his name.

Boston College and Northeastern employed variations of the B.U. formula. Both used surplus earnings simultaneously to increase endowment and support construction. Building programs on Huntington Avenue and the Heights proceeded less rapidly than along the Charles River—a new facility for Business and a classroom and office building at B.C.; a student center, a library, and a program of property acquisition at Northeastern—but the emphasis on using operating profits for capital accumulation was common to all three. Thus did the federal government, through the G.I. Bill, provide the basis for Boston's struggling private universities to launch programs of institutional development in the early postwar years.[9]

The common emphasis on growth and diversification reinforced these institutions' traditional roles as urban universities serving local residents. All three stressed undergraduate programs in practical fields where demand was strong. All three pursued unselective admission policies, enrolled mainly commuting students, and allowed registrations in various programs to fluctuate in response to applicant pressures. All three created part-time and nondegree programs for older students.

In pursuing such policies, these campuses aligned themselves with the democratic, egalitarian impulses urged by George Zook's Commission on Higher Education. Campus leaders, indeed, explained their policies in terms that echoed Zook and his colleagues. Marsh, responding to charges that expansion was diluting academic quality and adversely affecting student life, argued that growth expressed B.U.'s democratic commitments. "Boston University wants students," he wrote, and in large numbers, because

> in a democracy, leadership always emerges from the common crowd . . . Our students are a cross-section of the country, representing every stratum of soci-

ety. Seeing our educational opportunities and responsibilities in [this] light . . . sanctifies our work and lends it an unspeakable solemnity and beauty.

Ell issued a major restatement of his view of Northeastern as a "community-service university," placing his emphasis on growth in the context of his dedication to "meet[ing] the changing needs of the students and the community."[10]

Shifting Emphasis in the 1950s

Maintaining Enrollments and Capital Programs after the Veterans

After 1948, as applications from returning G.I.s began to decline, leaders of B.U., B.C., and N.U. sought ways to maintain the high enrollments that were supporting their development programs. In an atmosphere of uncertainty about student demand, each added programs and sought new clienteles to offset the losses of veterans.

B.U. opened a School of Nursing in 1946 and, shortly thereafter, added a School of Industrial Technology and an Evening Division. Altogether, in the five-year period between the end of the war and Marsh's retirement in 1950, five new schools were established, while existing programs were modified to expand their enrollment potential. The emphasis on expansion and program development continued after Harold Case replaced Marsh in 1951. The General College was expanded into a degree-granting Junior College and the old College of Music was transformed into a School of Fine and Applied Arts during the new president's first two years. As enrollments in some fields declined, the new units were expanded to take up the slack. The Junior College and Fine Arts quickly became two of the largest parts of B.U.

Similar policies were evident at Boston College and Northeastern. Ell, who was especially worried about declining enrollments, retained his reversible approach to growth. While Marsh and Case were creating one school after another and hiring full-time faculty to staff them, Ell added no units to his day program and worked to maintain enrollments in the existing colleges, particularly by continuing coeducation. In 1953 he closed the School of Law because he did not think it could continue to compete profitably for students. At the same time, he pursued maximum expansion through the Evening Division, doing a lively business in part-time and nondegree programs. When the Korean war presented a new threat to enrollments, Ell responded with the largest R.O.T.C. unit in the nation.

The leaders of Boston College emphasized the further development of professional education while also moving into programs for women and adults. In 1947 B.C. took a hesitant step toward coeducation by establishing a School of Nursing on Newbury Street. Other new units, like the Institute of Adult Education and the College of Business Administration continued to grow. As at B.U., a change in leadership had no discernible impact on the policy of expansion and diversification. By 1950 the Jesuits had a new provincial, Father William Fitzgerald, and a year later Father Joseph Maxwell replaced Keleher as rector-president, but the emphasis on maintaining B.C.'s size continued. In 1952 female students were brought to the Heights for the first time, with the opening of a coeducational School of Education.

The efforts of Boston's three urban universities, all dependent on local students, to continue expanding as demand diminished, fostered intense competition for applicants. The combative spirit was illustrated by B.C.'s decision to open a School of Education in the midst of a dip in enrollments produced by the Korean war. During the late 1940s, it was observed on the Heights that large numbers of aspiring school teachers from Irish and Italian families were graduating with good records from Boston University. There was no doubt that the Jesuits could take this Catholic clientele away from the Methodists, provided they were willing to accept women. Education was, in any case, a field in which the provincial hierarchy was interested, since the need for teachers was about to increase as the baby-boom generation approached elementary school. Thus did a calculation about competitive advantage reinforce the order's educational judgment about appropriate directions for new development.[11]

The continuing emphasis of B.U., B.C., and Northeastern on growth at a time of uncertain public need for expanded educational facilities highlighted the financial dependence of these institutions on student payments. Having finally gained momentum—after fifteen years of Depression and war—in developing capital resources, all three campuses were eager to continue earning operating surpluses. Though all three undertook some fund-raising in these years, none could attract sufficient amounts to sustain its development program. Instructional costs, therefore, especially faculty salaries, were kept low, and tuition was pushed up in order to maximize the availability of working capital.

The atmosphere fostered ingenious financial strategies. B.C. adopted accounting procedures that treated the educational services provided by Jesuits as if the institution actually paid for them at the going rate for lay faculty. This meant that apparent costs, on which the official budget was based, tuition set, and expenditures publicly reported, far exceeded real outlays. The discrepancy between true and reported costs was accumulated in a special fund, called the Loyola Fund, from which Maxwell obtained revenues for his building program. At Northeastern, Ell instituted a student activities fee and deposited payments in a special account controlled entirely by him and not reported on annual financial statements. Continuing to support student activities from general revenues as enrollments remained high, Ell gradually accumulated large sums that provided seed money for capital projects.

At B.U., Marsh not only captured operating surpluses but also utilized earnings from the modest endowment as well as large amounts of principal to obtain funds for the construction program. By 1948 about 39 percent of B.U.'s endowment was invested in new buildings rather than in income-producing securities. Marsh, in particular, was severely criticized for his financial machinations, which were much more visible than those of his fellow presidents. Faculty members at B.U. charged their president with jeopardizing the academic program by expanding excessively and diverting revenues from the instructional budget. Marsh, however, was undeterred. He was convinced that the Charles River campus held the key to B.U.'s future, and he was determined to have the facility in place before he retired. The proudest passage of his final report proclaimed "a quarter mile of solid Gothic façade extending along Commonwealth Avenue, magnificent buildings of Indiana limestone, rising six stories high."[12]

The new conditions of the middle 1950s had important implications for B.U., B.C., and Northeastern. As it became clear that expanded demand for college was not a passing phenomenon, the leaders of these three institutions became confident, for the first time since the war, that they could sustain their enlarged operations for an indefinite period. In 1953 Case called for a doubling of B.U.'s enrollments by the end of the decade, further increases after 1960, and continued emphasis on new facilities. In fact, B.U. ballooned to twenty thousand degree-seeking students by 1958–1959, while Case continued to restrain costs to earn surpluses and steadily added buildings to the new campus.

A similar pattern occurred at Boston College, which expanded to a historic high of seventy-five hundred by the fall of 1958 while maintaining low salaries and low operating costs, and making rapid progress on the construction program. With dollars flowing into the Loyola Fund—in 1958 the contributed services of teaching Jesuits, who constituted 21 percent of the faculty, were valued at $835,000—Maxwell became B.C.'s greatest builder, adding nine structures to the campus, including homes for Law and Education as well as an athletic complex. Maxwell also used surpluses to increase B.C.'s tiny endowment from $2.6 million to $4.1 million.

The altered environment of the middle 1950s even affected the most cautious of the three presidents. Ell now focused on expanding the day colleges rather than preparing for shrinkage. Between 1953 and 1959, these units grew by more than 50 percent, and total enrollments approached twenty thousand. Northeastern even jumped into the competition to train future teachers by opening a College of Education, the only college established during Ell's twenty-year presidency. Throughout these years, like Maxwell and Case, Ell used surplus revenues to enlarge N.U.'s capital assets. When he retired in 1959, the Huntington Avenue campus contained eight buildings and the endowment stood at $12 million, compared with $400,000 at the beginning of his presidency.[13]

Changing Priorities at Boston College

The new confidence in demand for admission allowed the leaders of Boston's urban universities to shift attention from the entrepreneurial strategies of the early postwar years toward activities that would strengthen institutional prestige. Graduate development and research began to be priorities. The early postwar emphasis on diversification into practical fields gave way to the liberal arts and sciences, and a new interest emerged in recruiting students from beyond the metropolitan area and building residential facilities. While the new focus on quality and status did not become dominant at any of these universities in the 1950s—the pressure to earn income to support capital development was too great—these themes moved into higher relief as academic leaders felt their ways toward new combinations of long-standing local, democratic, service-oriented missions and the tantalizing possibilities of the golden age.

The six-year term of Maxwell at B.C. (from 1952 to 1958) illustrated the shifting priorities. A veteran administrator, Maxwell had served as dean of Arts and Sciences at B.C. in the 1930s and as rector and president of Holy Cross during World War II. For two decades, he had championed the cause of academic reform and had earned a reputation as hard-driving and demanding. The general's decision, undoubtedly influenced by Fitzgerald, to install the province's strongest educational leader at B.C. reflected the order's ambitions for the Chestnut Hill campus, and a heightened academic spirit was apparent from the beginning of Maxwell's presidency.

While pressing the effort begun in the early 1940s to bring academically well-trained Jesuits to B.C., Maxwell also emphasized the recruitment of lay Ph.D.s. The growing core of academic professionals became the president's agents of reform. One committee wrote B.C.'s first standards for hiring and promotion. A second became the first faculty committee on "rank and tenure" and began demanding evidence of scholarship for advancement. A third undertook a self-study of the College of Arts and Sciences. The self-study committee represented Maxwell's focus on the liberal arts as central to intellectual strengthening. In fact, after opening the School of Education, Maxwell added no new undergraduate programs in practical fields. Instead, he stressed the reinstitution of Ph.D.s, which had been suspended after the devastating critique by the A.A.U. in the 1930s. He succeeded in three fields: economics, history, and education.

The self-study committee provided Maxwell with a broad agenda for change. It insisted that B.C. judge itself not only by the values of church and order but also by the standards of secular accrediting agencies. It complained that the college was attracting "ordinary *B*" students who generally spent "little more than ten hours per week" on academic work. It advocated tighter requirements, a wider range of offerings, tougher disciplinary majors, and honors courses for superior students.

Maxwell did not need prodding to upgrade the student body. In 1952 he abolished the archaic practice of administering a unique admissions test and began requiring all applicants to take the College Boards or obtain appropriate certification from their high school principal. A year later, he ended the traditional practice that allowed each dean to control admissions to his own school and created a new office directly responsible to the president. Instituting a program of active recruitment, something B.C. had not previously done, Maxwell created presidential scholarships and sought applicants from beyond the Boston area. To house the new, more qualified students he hoped to attract, he built the first permanent dormitories on the Heights campus.[14]

Maxwell's ability to raise the intellectual level of Boston College was limited by a number of factors. The relatively weak faculty base with which he began was only beginning to be changed through new appointments. One indication of B.C.'s situation was that the new dean of graduate studies, brought in to preside over the development of Ph.D.s, came to his position fresh from his own doctoral work at Georgetown. Maxwell's primary emphasis on expansion and construction further restricted academic upgrading. It was difficult to change the student body as long as enrollments were being increased without much growth in applications. In fact, at the end of Maxwell's term, as at the beginning, B.C. was primarily a school for "day hops" from the Boston area, and there was little increase in the proportion of nonlocal students or in the level of preparation. In 1958 less than 10 percent of the students were living in dormitories, and many of these were athletes recruited for the college's traditionally strong intercollegiate teams. Similarly, Maxwell's insistence on low salaries and high teaching loads compromised his ability to attract lay faculty. More than half the faculty of Arts and Sciences held undergraduate degrees from B.C.

Academic progress was also complicated by debates within the Jesuit order about how to respond to the expanded demand for access to college. The guidelines for admission to Catholic institutions published by the National Catholic Education Association placed only modest emphasis on intellectual ability: baccalaureate programs were to be accessible to at least the top third but not more than the top half of high school graduates, and as much weight was to be given to social and personal qualities as to intellectual talent. In 1954 J.E.A.'s Director Rooney initiated a review of admission practices at Jesuit institutions. The resulting document reflected divisions within the order about the role of its colleges. General statements of policy stressed the need to accommodate increased numbers of Catholic high school graduates through expansion, but the section on procedures emphasized raising academic standards and increasing selectivity. In the end, provincials were left relatively free to set policies for their regions.[15]

Though academic change under Maxwell was circumscribed, his presidency marked a basic divide for Boston College. He was chosen more for his academic strengths than his pastoral qualities, and his goal of gaining acceptability in secular terms implied a new impulse to associate B.C. with mainstream academic values. The concern about admission standards expressed a new emphasis on educating talented Catholics headed for influence in the professions rather than protecting the faith of the local population. B.C.'s emerging aspiration to exert social influence was symbolized by the Citizen Seminars, instituted in the middle 1950s, which brought together Boston's Yankee business establishment and its Irish political leadership, two historically antagonistic groups, to discuss the city's economic future.

The order's efforts to change the character of B.C. shared a common impulse with the activities of Abram Sachar and his colleagues at Brandeis. Both groups saw their institutions as vehicles for elevating the social status of their sponsoring communities through affiliation with elite values. There were, however, fundamental differences between the two campuses. The Society of Jesus, both locally and nationally, remained committed to a sectarian curriculum and was much less interested than Brandeis in serving students from other religious groups. Indeed, while Sachar sought to minimize the "Jewish component" of his university in the 1950s, B.C. reaffirmed its undergraduate requirements in theology and philosophy with minimal change and continued to staff these crucial, values-shaping courses with Jesuit priests. Thus, B.C.'s leadership hoped to remain explicitly Catholic while also achieving high academic standing in secular terms. The viability of this strategy, over an extended period, was the deepest question raised by the changes initiated during the Maxwell years.[16]

Drifting Toward the Golden Age at B.U.

Boston University's new president, Harold Case, was far less oriented toward changing the character of his institution than was Maxwell. Indeed, the most striking fact about Case's leadership was his tendency to affirm all the institutional objectives of the Marsh years. Like Marsh, Case was a Methodist minister, and his public statements stressed religion and values as central concerns of Boston University. Similar to his predecessor, however, Case found little opportunity to translate his religious interests into concrete policies and programs. The modest chapel, erected at the focal point of the campus where Marsh had hoped to build an imposing cathedral tower, stood as a permanent symbol of the diminished role of religion at Boston University.

With respect to B.U.'s academic purposes, Case, like Marsh, stressed different and potentially contradictory policies on alternate occasions. He consistently affirmed B.U.'s role as an urban, service-oriented university, with democratic admission policies and strong ties to Boston and its working-class students. No less enthusiastically, he welcomed every evidence that his campus was making progress toward recognition as a major research university. The unfocused, even amorphous, image of B.U. projected by Case reflected important realities of a decentralized institution that had been pieced together from previously independent units, that still operated in scattered sites, and that aspired to higher status as a regional or national university while remaining linked, in numerous practical ways, to its local community. Two years of work by a long-range planning committee in the early 1950s produced a shapeless report giving equal emphasis to every conceivable institutional goal and concluding, with admirable candor, that a modern university must be "all things to all people." Physicist Robert Cohen described the atmosphere at B.U. in the 1950s this way:

> There was no objection to any professor or department being first rate, and there was no encouragement either. The administration was benevolently neutral. It was a mediocre place, but it was like a fruitcake, and it was studded with wonderful bits and pieces.

Case's central emphasis was growth and construction. In this, he had little choice, given the desperate inadequacy of B.U.'s facilities and the trustees' determination to proceed with the new campus. The logic that had dominated Marsh's thinking still held: for B.U. to have an academic future, especially one involving intellectual progress and institutional mobility, the building program was a prerequisite. Presidential attention to the academic character of the university that would reside within the new halls would have to be the work of a later time.[17]

Despite his focus on administrative matters, Case's adherence to Marsh's vision of a transformed and upgraded university was evident in his continuing emphasis on widening B.U.'s geographic reach. In 1952 about 80 percent of B.U.'s students came from Massachusetts, most of them commuters from the Boston area. By 1959, with applications rising, only 57 percent of new freshmen came from within the state, and many of these were residential students from outlying suburbs and towns. B.U. was changing its constituency, and Case worked hard to provide dormitory space for the more affluent, less local applicants the campus was now able to attract. He also played a key role in guaranteeing the future of the School of Medicine, a historic source of institutional pride that the trustees had neglected in recent times. In 1957 Case persuaded his board to accept a federal construction grant that implied a long-term commitment to creating a modern facility and adequate funding base for the school.

Curricular change in the late 1950s, carried out by B.U.'s component parts with little central direction, reinforced the drift away from service to the local community. As it became clear that the campus could easily maintain its enlarged enrollments, the entrepreneurial pattern of program development that had been followed in the early postwar years ceased. After 1954 no new undergraduate units were established, and the thrust of development shifted to the graduate level. At the same time, B.U. scaled back its work in technical and occupational education. The College of Practical Arts and Letters was closed. The Junior College was reorganized as a College of Basic Studies to feed students into four-year programs. The College of Industrial Technology was recast as a College of Engineering. Within several occupational programs, the emphasis on technical work was reduced and replaced by greater attention to the liberal arts and sciences.[18]

All of these shifts of emphasis—from undergraduate to graduate programs, from technical to liberal education, from entrepreneurial development to strengthening established units—moved the university closer to the configurations and priorities of higher-status institutions. If the advantageous conditions for academic development continued, B.U. seemed headed toward fundamental change in its character and mission.

New Possibilities at Northeastern

The new conditions of the middle 1950s induced even the conservative Ell of Northeastern to adopt a more expansive view of his institution's possibilities.

Throughout his long tenure, Ell had stressed that Northeastern should remain a limited-purpose university, focused on the practical needs of working-class and adult students from Boston and uninterested in replicating the academic forms of elite campuses. This perspective was reiterated in 1953 in a major restatement of mission, formally adopted by the trustees, characterizing Northeastern as

> a community service institution . . . primarily concerned with teaching at the undergraduate and graduate levels . . . in programs for which there is genuine demand and which are not adequately provided by other colleges and universities in the Boston area.

Northeastern's interest in research, the statement concluded, was limited to those activities "which will be stimulating and helpful to the faculty as a means toward the enhancement of instruction."

These emphases continued to describe Northeastern during Ell's final years, but as the opportunities of the times became clear, new and more academically ambitious themes began to surface. Impressed by government and industry support for research and graduate education, Ell began focusing on these areas, speaking of the need to establish endowed chairs to attract the "best scholars" and emphasizing the importance of "original thinking in the sciences and humanities." Among his last initiatives as president were the first graduate program for full-time, day students (a master's in engineering), the creation of the Graduate School, and a start on construction of a graduate center.

Ell was equally impressed by new possibilities in admissions. Noting the likelihood of a massive increase in applications after 1960, he observed that "seldom, if ever, will a greater opportunity come to any university to meet with increased excellence and widened scope of academic programs . . ." The references to "excellence" and "widened scope of academic programs" represented distinctly new notes for Ell, who launched an effort to recruit students on a regional and national basis and began a program of dormitory construction to accommodate a residential student body.[19]

The Mixed Motives behind Institutional Change

To distinguish between those aspects of development at B.U., B.C., and Northeastern in the 1950s that represented remnants of the "democratic," growth-oriented policies of the early postwar years and those that conveyed new impulses toward elite academic values is to separate analytically themes that were actually blurred and overlapping. The intertwining of motives was evident in the common effort to recruit students from beyond Boston and Massachusetts and to build dormitories for the new clienteles. This trend clearly involved opportunistic impulses to enhance institutional status, but there were also defensive reasons to seek a broader geographic base. All three universities depended financially on maintaining their already enlarged operations. However, the urban population that they traditionally served was changing in ways that rendered it a dubious long-term source of students for large universities. Indeed, these were years when Boston, like other American cities, was experiencing a loss of middle-class families to the suburbs, and urban schools and neighborhoods were beginning their tragic postwar spiral of decline.

In 1959 Harold Case expressed concern about Boston's decreasing high school population and the difficulty B.U. was having attracting applicants from suburban towns. He argued that B.U. must shift toward a more residential student body to protect its enrollments. Conscious of the same phenomenon, Ell established an off-campus center on Route 128 outside Boston—the major area of new industrial development in the region—to keep his evening programs within reach of Northeastern's traditional adult, working customers. Ell, too, believed that his institution must shift toward a residential student body in order to protect its scale.

Other factors reinforced the logic of forging ties to new areas. The economies of Massachusetts and New England had been weak for years, and other regions of the country seemed likely to experience more dynamic development. Ell, in particular, believed that his university, with its orientation toward industry, had to seek contacts with regions of industrial growth. There was also the possibility that Massachusetts might follow the lead of other states, including nearby New York, and expand its historically small system of public higher education as demand for access to college increased. Though the legislature took no concrete steps in the 1950s that foretold such a development, there were rumblings of the possibility, and an expanded public sector would be a formidable competitor for local students from low- and moderate-income backgrounds. Thus prudence reinforced and justified ambition for the leaders of the three universities upon which residents of metropolitan Boston historically had relied for educational opportunity.[20]

By the late 1950s, as they readied themselves for the much heralded tidal wave of applicants, Boston's urban universities were poised for progress in academic terms. The foundations of change had been laid, and leaders at all three were acutely conscious of the opportunities that the 1960s would bring. Turnover in the presidency at two of these schools added to the sense of new potential. In 1957, with Maxwell's term drawing to an end at B.C., the general and provincial turned to one of the president's young lieutenants, Father Michael Walsh, chair of the Biology Department, a product of the Special Studies Program, and a member of the famous "class of 1948." A year later, at Northeastern, the aging Ell personally selected a successor, former Business dean Asa Knowles, who had been president of the University of Toledo since 1951. Only B.U. would not experience a change of presidents. As American higher education entered the most promising period for institutional development of the twentieth century, Harold Case seemed likely to remain in office for the foreseeable future.

The "Bonanza Years" at Boston College

The Special Studies Program
Produces a President

The new president of Boston College, Father Michael P. Walsh, S.J., assumed his duties in February 1958, as Congress signaled a new enthusiasm for higher education in hearings on the National Defense Education Act. Forty-six years old, a Jesuit since graduating from Boston College High School in 1929, Walsh exemplified the new breed of academicians nurtured by the order during the 1930s and 1940s. Trained as both priest and scientist, with a Ph.D. from Fordham, Walsh was a devoted son of the church who believed that Jesuits must embrace modern academic values to achieve the position to which they aspired: intellectual leadership among Catholics and broad influence in American society. Walsh's hero was Father Robert I. Gannon, president of Fordham in the 1930s and an early leader of the reform movement. During the 1950s, like many thoughtful Catholics, Walsh had been moved by the writings of John Tracy Ellis lamenting the poverty of Catholic intellectual life and the low quality of Catholic colleges. "My basic message," Walsh stated,

> is that never in history has there been an educational institution so involved in the life of its time and so powerful to shape its time as the modern American university. Unless there is significant and first-class Catholic participation in top-level university activity, then the Mystical Body of Christ will be deprived of a voice in this most critical area of leadership. American and therefore . . . world society is going to be influenced more by American universities in the decades ahead than by any other social institution. The purpose of the American Jesuit university therefore is to become an ever stronger factor in this shaping of society *ad majorem Dei gloriam.*

Walsh's deepest concerns transcended the order as well as the church. As the son of Irish immigrants in Boston, he was painfully aware of the Catholic history of second-class citizenship and of past discrimination—as he saw it—against Catholics by Protestant universities like B.U. and N.U. He believed the low status of Jesuit schools both reflected and perpetuated the restricted social position of Catholics. Despite such feelings, he admired what he viewed as the Protestant virtues of flexibility, tolerance, and honesty, and he saw the traditional inwardness of Catholic colleges, their emphasis on protecting faith by shutting out secular influences, as self-defeating.

Animated by ambition—a word he would have rejected—for both his religious and ethnic communities, Walsh worked tirelessly as a young faculty member of B.C. to enhance the intellectual level and academic prestige of his campus. He built up the premed program, urged his superiors to challenge B.U. in education, and was active on committees established by Maxwell to enforce professional standards in personnel decisions and heighten academic demands on students. He was often frustrated by Maxwell's emphasis on expansion and construction and was eager to improve B.C. as a scholarly enterprise.[21]

As he contemplated the presidency during the winter of 1958, Walsh had no doubt about his priorities: academic standards had to be raised much further; better students recruited; superior, chiefly lay, faculty hired; and conditions created that would satisfy a talented student body and a productive, professional faculty. His vision, ultimately, was to transform B.C. into the leading Jesuit university in the nation and challenge Notre Dame's supremacy among all Catholic schools. Walsh knew his plans would be expensive and that fundraising, traditionally an amateurish enterprise at B.C., would need to be emphasized.

Walsh also knew the politics of his task would be challenging, given the power of traditionalist forces within the order. He had watched closely as two dedicated academics, Fordham's Gannon and his own predecessor, Maxwell, had fallen from official favor for pushing their causes too aggressively. He knew that academic leadership within the complex political environment of the Society of Jesus required subtlety. For the tactical requirements of his position, Walsh was ideally equipped. An Irishman to the bone, the new president was a lifelong student of Boston politics and had absorbed its lessons and arts. His comfortable charm and disarming manner reminded one observer of "Spencer Tracy playing Frank Skeffington in *The Last Hurrah*," an apt description that captured Walsh's complexity and drive as well as his gentle humor. Over the next ten years, as the cresting wave of high school graduates and public support flooded into the nation's colleges, Walsh evolved into one of the most effective academic politicians in the modern history of Boston. His presidency would be remembered on the Heights as "the bonanza years."[22]

Upgrading the College of Arts and Sciences

Walsh's central goal was to increase radically the intellectual level of the undergraduate students—all male—in the College of Arts and Sciences. He believed that C.A.S. held the key to B.C.'s status and influence, and he had no interest in admitting women to this unit or using it to meet the educational needs of disadvantaged local students. He especially wanted to recruit future Ph.D.s—in addition to potential doctors, lawyers, and businessmen, the traditional professions of B.C.'s brightest graduates—who could form Ellis's intellectual elite while ensuring the academic prestige of Boston College.

Walsh sensed opportunity in admissions. He knew that Catholic secondary schools, particularly those run by the order, were improving during the postwar years as part of the same movement that was raising standards at B.C. and were largely overlooked by recruiters from leading universities. He understood that Catholic parents preferred to send their children to Catholic universities and that Catholic school principals would try to prevent students from attending Ivy League colleges. He was aware also of the administrative sluggishness of other Jesuit campuses that were not organized to compete with a well-conceived admissions campaign.

Having identified an "untapped" source of good students, Walsh moved aggressively into this market on a national basis, ignoring hitherto sacrosanct regional boundaries of the Jesuit provinces. Retaining personal control over admissions, he appointed a new director, expanded scholarships by diverting dollars from the Loyola Fund, and directed that financial support be channeled toward the most promising young minds without regard to financial need. Over the ten years of Walsh's presidency, student aid rose from $360,000 annually to $2.7 million, and the number of students assisted increased sixfold. Emphasizing excellence rather than expansion in Arts and Sciences, Walsh established and enforced enrollment limits for that college for the first time in B.C.'s history.

The results of Walsh's initiatives were quickly evident. In 1960 a faculty committee noted "with great pleasure the conspicuous progress made in raising . . . admission standards and the part played in this by . . . vigorous recruiting." Between 1959 and 1968, the College Board scores of freshmen rose steadily, and the proportion of in-state students dropped from 80 percent to 50 percent. The numbers from the immediate Boston area fell even more precipitously. Walsh also stressed dormitory construction, turning a minor theme of the Maxwell years into a centerpiece of his administration. By 1968 nearly a quarter of B.C.'s full-time undergraduates were living in university housing.

As he moved toward increasingly selective, intellectually oriented admissions, Walsh was conscious of the latent conflict within the order over admissions policy that had surfaced in the middle 1950s. When the J.E.A.'s Rooney attempted to reopen this issue in 1958, Walsh supported a policy of quiet resistance among the provincials, who argued successfully that the matter had been settled by the earlier discussion.[23]

In tandem with his campaign to attract better students, Walsh strengthened the program and faculty to appeal to his talented and cosmopolitan recruits. He wanted research-oriented, lay scholars, who could carry B.C.'s colors in the competition for academic recognition. He was particularly eager for faculty who had received degrees or taught at leading research universities— above all, at Harvard—because they brought instant status and could use their ties to the journals, funding sources, and other agencies of the scholarly establishment to help their less well-connected colleagues.

One key to the hiring effort was salaries, which were traditionally low at B.C. Walsh was especially critical of Maxwell's stinginess in this area and pushed hard to be competitive with nonsectarian universities. Here, as in other matters, Walsh was influenced by Gannon, whose success at Fordham was based on his readiness to outbid non-Catholic rivals for top lay faculty. By the end of Walsh's term, B.C.'s minimum and average salaries achieved *A* ratings from the A.A.U.P. at all ranks but full professor. The new pattern of compensation made B.C. a salary leader among Catholic schools—the average salary was almost identical with Notre Dame's—and placed it in the top 5 percent of all academic institutions in the U.S. Among universities in Boston, B.C.'s salaries in the late 1960s were comparable with those of Tufts, ranking below Harvard, M.I.T., and Brandeis, but above B.U. and Northeastern. Walsh also lowered teaching loads, expanded laboratory and library facilities, and offered faculty fellowships, summer grants, and travel awards. Incentives were reinforced by a promotions policy that stressed publication—a departure from earlier emphases on teaching that had been maintained through the Maxwell years.

By the end of Walsh's term, more than 60 percent of the faculty of Arts and Sciences had been hired under the new rules, as the full-time staff of the College grew from (approximately) 210 to 330. The percentage with doctorates rose steadily, to 75 percent by the end of the period, mostly from secular universities. A survey of all B.C. faculty completed shortly after Walsh retired showed that 40 percent of those with doctorates came from ten research universities, with the Harvard contingent of forty-eight by far the largest, more than double the group from any other school. Only 14 percent—approximately the size of the Harvard group—had doctorates from any Catholic university. As the lay professoriate grew, the Jesuit faculty contracted, both absolutely and proportionately. In 1959 the 120 teaching Jesuits at B.C. constituted a third of the total full-time faculty and close to half those in Arts and Sciences. By the end of Walsh's term, there were only fifty-seven teaching Jesuits at B.C., 10 percent of the total faculty and 15 percent of Arts and Sciences.[24]

Walsh's major programmatic goal—strengthening the Graduate School of Arts and Sciences—flowed directly from his desire to attract research-oriented scholars. He believed he could not recruit and retain such a faculty without providing graduate programs for status and graduate students to justify advanced courses and serve as research assistants. The Graduate School became one of B.C.'s fastest growing units, doubling in size between 1958 and 1966, while Walsh also tripled—to nine—the number of Ph.D.'s offered.

Walsh retained a clear-eyed view of graduate work at B.C. He regarded the program he had encouraged as undistinguished and intended chiefly to gratify the faculty, an assessment that was confirmed in the late 1960s when the A.C.E.'s rankings failed even to mention B.C.'s programs. Walsh hoped his top undergraduates would be too ambitious to settle for B.C.'s Graduate School and would seek admission to Harvard and other top schools. He felt that the intellectual elite he hoped to produce needed to sharpen their talents in competition with the best and would not blossom fully if their education were restricted to Catholic settings. By that stage of development, Walsh reasoned, their faith would not be threatened by exposure to secular influences. Walsh also believed that B.C.'s status would be greatly enhanced if its students could gain entry into leading graduate programs, and he worked hard to build relationships with Pusey and Bundy to smooth the way for B.C.'s graduates in Cambridge. One of Walsh's favorite statistics involved the percentage of alumni pursuing advanced degrees. Seventy percent of those who entered the College of Arts and Sciences in 1960 continued their education—a dramatic shift from earlier times—and the percentage rose in subsequent years.[25]

Walsh's interest in the arts and sciences led him to neglect the professional programs that had been a focus of B.C.'s development in the early postwar years. The major exception at the beginning of his administration was law, which he viewed as a potential source of prestige and influence. He upgraded the Law School, closing its traditional evening program to enhance its academic image and make it eligible for membership in Coif, an honorary scholastic society. Other faculties and schools, however, felt the benefits of the Walsh years passing them by. Early in Walsh's term, an administration-faculty committee, commenting on the campaign to recruit better students, complained that "progress has not been uniform among the schools" and noted "an increasingly serious disparity" between students in C.A.S. and those in Business and Education.

Such complaints had little impact. Walsh continued to channel financial aid toward future scholars and kept the undergraduate professional programs on the Maxwell pattern of unselective expansion to earn surplus revenues for his developmental priorities. The professional programs, indeed, remained local in orientation while Arts and Sciences "went national." Walsh's enrollment policies produced an ironic outcome. Despite his putative emphasis on excellence rather than growth, B.C. expanded more rapidly during his term than Maxwell's—from seventy-five hundred to ninety-five hundred in ten years. Moreover, university-wide admissions selectivity changed very little, partially because B.C.—like M.I.T. and Brandeis—recruited in a limited market and did not experience the same growth of applicants during the golden age that occurred at other universities in Boston. In addition, Walsh's disinterest in coeducation in Arts and Sciences and Business Administration cut the campus off from a large pool of talented students.[26]

Financing Upward Mobility

Walsh's use of income from students to support scholarships reflected the underlying financial weakness of his institution and the vast difference between B.C. and leading universities. Maxwell had subsidized development by keeping costs down and generating operating surpluses, but Walsh believed the price of that financial strategy was mediocrity. From the beginning of his presidency, he knew he could not increase scholarships, support a lay faculty on competitive salaries, reduce teaching loads, expand the Graduate School, and construct new facilities without also finding new sources of revenue in large amounts.

Impressed by the success of Father Hesburgh at Notre Dame in using fundraising techniques developed by secular universities, Walsh decided to imitate his archrival from the little Holy Cross order. Believing that the key to philanthropy in Boston was a business community still dominated by Yankees, Walsh formed an advisory board—he called it his Board of Regents—composed chiefly of non-Catholic businessmen and financiers, and he cultivated this group by seeking its advice on policy issues. Simultaneously, he hired a director of development and quietly planned a major campaign. In 1961 Walsh announced a fifteen-million-dollar drive, intended as the first phase of a decade-long effort, that expressed his determination to move B.C. into the modern world of academic finance in a single step. His ambition is indicated by comparison with Tufts—a richer and better-established institution—where Wessell was mounting a scaled-down program for seven and a half million dollars. The Board of Regents provided the contacts needed for success by 1965, and two years later, B.C. mounted an even more aggressive effort with a goal of twenty-five million dollars.

To complement the fund drives, Walsh developed glossy public relations materials, which were striking for their lack of reference to the Catholic character of B.C., intensified the annual giving program, and introduced investment techniques to earn maximum interest on funds. These efforts not only supported increases in faculty pay but also enabled Walsh to build fourteen new buildings, a larger expansion of facilities than had been accomplished under the construction-oriented Maxwell.[27]

Despite Walsh's successes as fund-raiser and money manager, his policies strained the resources of his underfinanced university. B.C.'s historically low instructional expenditures rose more rapidly than those of other universities for a combination of reasons. Faculty growth outstripped student expansion, partially to offset reduced teaching loads, and the student-faculty ratio dropped from 18.4:1 in 1961 to 13.7:1 in 1970. The shift to a lay faculty denied B.C. its greatest traditional economy and compounded the impact of salary increases. In 1958 B.C.'s direct costs of instruction were less than six hundred dollars per student, about 50 percent of the twelve hundred dollars spent by B.U. Over the next ten years, B.C.'s expenditures nearly tripled, while B.U.'s did not even double, and in 1968 B.C.'s per-student costs of roughly sixteen hundred dollars were 80 percent of those at B.U. Financial pressures limited the progress Walsh could make in building the endowment. He actually added less to B.C.'s funds in current dollars than did Maxwell, and investment income decreased as a percentage of the budget during his term. Sponsored research did not help much either, as B.C.'s faculty was only beginning to attract external support.

With rising costs only partly offset by new sources of revenue, B.C. remained basically dependent on tuition. At the end of Walsh's term, 86 percent of current costs was borne by student payments, down from 99 percent in 1958 but far above the 33 percent associated with well-endowed private institutions, or even the 54 percent of a moderately well-supported institution like Tufts. This translated into a doubling of tuition from eight hundred to sixteen hundred dollars during Walsh's ten-year term, a rate of price increases less steep than the rise in B.C.'s costs but still tops among private universities in the Boston area. Historically, B.C. had been the lowest-charging local university, but by 1967 its tuition exceeded those of B.U. and Northeastern.

Higher prices spotlighted the dependence of Walsh's efforts to raise the status of his campus upon attracting a more affluent student body—as well as a more talented one. The upward pressure of tuition on student-income level was only slightly lessened by Walsh's use of Loyola Fund revenues for scholarships, partially because the amounts were modest and partially because Walsh used them to attract gifted undergraduates rather than needy ones.

As Walsh's term drew to a close, the financial signals were ominous. B.C. incurred a small deficit in fiscal year 1968 (Walsh's final year) that was covered by transfers from the Loyola Fund, and the prospects for succeeding years were problematic owing to the rate at which his policies were pushing up expenses. In particular, the pressure on instructional costs was going to grow as new lay faculty moved toward the senior ranks, where salaries had not risen as much as at the junior levels. It was clear, indeed, that the structure of B.C.'s costs had become quite similar to those of good-quality, secular, private universities, while the revenue program was only beginning a comparable transition. To pay Walsh's accumulating bills, his successors would have to more than match his achievements as a fund-raiser.[28]

The Limits of Upward Mobility

Walsh's six-year period as president and rector ended in 1964, but the general asked him to continue, and Walsh stayed until 1968, becoming B.C.'s first modern leader to serve beyond the traditional term. The general's decision reflected the scarcity of qualified Jesuit successors but also endorsed the achievements of Walsh's presidency. These were confirmed in 1966 when B.C. was selected by the National Opinion Research Center as one of the most rapidly improving Catholic universities in the country, while Walsh was rated among the church's most effective academic administrators. Walsh himself, though aware that B.C. had accomplished only part of the evolution he was promoting, was not modest about the changes of his years. He believed he had led B.C. past Notre Dame as the nation's premier Catholic institution, and in a final report, he declared that Boston College "has taken its place among major American universities."

Such comments were understandable, but they exaggerated B.C.'s relative progress. While none of B.C.'s graduate programs or faculties achieved sufficient stature even to be rated by the A.C.E.'s survey in the late 1960s, other Catholic institutions, notably Notre Dame, Georgetown, and Fordham were mentioned frequently. The roughly two million dollars in sponsored research that the faculty was attracting placed B.C. at about the same level as Northeastern and well below Tufts. Even in the area of Walsh's greatest focus, the undergraduate program in Arts and Sciences, B.C.'s standing remained modest. A respected national survey in 1967 awarded B.C.'s departments only middling scores and gave the overall undergraduate program a rating at the low end of the middle range, below three other Jesuit universities—Georgetown, Fordham, and St. Louis—and far below Notre Dame. Mean verbal board scores for entering freshmen in the fall of 1967 were under 550, more than 50 points below the entering class at Tufts.[29]

These comparisons put Walsh's achievements in perspective; other Jesuit universities were progressing rapidly during these same years. Still, under his leadership, building on the base established by Maxwell, reflecting the spirit of the Johannine era and of Vatican II, B.C. moved out of the restricted, inward-looking world of traditional Catholic higher education and transformed itself into a respectable, modern university in secular, academic terms. A crucial plateau was achieved.

B.C.'s Dilemma: How to Be Faithful to the Church and Acceptable to the Profession

B.C.'s movement "into the academic mainstream," to use Andrew Greeley's celebratory phrase, posed difficult questions for the Jesuit community that had maintained B.C. for a hundred years: how modern, how research-oriented, how secular could their university become and still be an effective agency of the faith? Among the teaching Jesuits were men who feared Walsh was abandoning the central purposes of their university, though the president himself believed his policies were strengthening both church and order. This local debate mirrored a wider discussion within the Jesuit order in which Walsh emerged as a spokesman for the modernizing, university-oriented forces against those who favored a more Catholic and traditional perspective.

Competing attitudes toward change at B.C. were expressed with particular clarity in the mid-1960s, as Walsh focused on what he considered the ultimate arena of academic reform, the undergraduate curriculum in Arts and Sciences. No significant modernization had occurred during the Keleher and Maxwell years, and the program still derived largely from the *Ratio Studiorum,* the classic Jesuit educational prescription, and still was subject to approval by Jesuit authorities in Rome. Early in Walsh's term, the Latin requirement for the B.A. finally was dropped (with full presidential blessing), but in 1963 undergraduates still were required to take forty-three credits—fully 32 percent of their coursework—in the traditional core subjects of philosophy and theology. These courses were taught largely by Jesuits—the two departments accounted for a quarter of the Arts and Sciences faculty when Walsh assumed office— and included a heavy emphasis on Catholic doctrine.

Walsh viewed these requirements as archaic and was especially disturbed by the low intellectual level of the faculty, fearing they were more likely to discourage than fortify Catholic conviction in the brightest students while also alienating the best lay faculty. Walsh explained his eagerness to ease traditional requirements at a J.E.A. conference in 1962. Stressing the importance of promoting commitment, tolerance, and flexibility in undergraduates, he wondered aloud about the effectiveness of courses based on the particularities of Catholic dogma. He cited studies showing that a student's values were more affected by the total environment of a college, especially other students, than by classroom instruction. The best way to produce the graduates needed by the church, he argued, was to create a context that implicitly expressed basic values, not to hammer away on doctrine.

In actually redesigning B.C.'s curriculum, Walsh moved cautiously, hoping to minimize opposition from the Jesuit community and hierarchy. In a carefully structured process, a committee appointed by Walsh and dominated by his allies felt its way toward a formula acceptable to both lay faculty and teaching Jesuits. Requirements in philosophy and theology were reduced to nine courses, and the content of these subjects was made less "scholastic" and more academic. At the same time, a distribution requirement in the basic disciplines was established, ensuring roles for all the major departments and leaving B.C. with a well-defined core curriculum at a time when leading universities were dismantling their general education programs. An honors program was stressed, as were department-based majors. These incremental changes satisfied Walsh for the moment, since he believed the dynamic of change that he had initiated with such determination ultimately would overwhelm traditionalist forces. His perception was confirmed by subsequent reforms that, a few years after his departure, reduced requirements in philosophy and theology to four courses.[30]

Changes in the curriculum, together with the other policies of the Walsh years, turned B.C. more nearly into a Catholic Brandeis: a university broadly reflective of Catholic and Jesuit culture where teaching and scholarship mainly expressed secular academic concerns. How effective such an institution would be, ultimately, in advancing the specific goals of church and order that Walsh affirmed was an open question.

There were indications that B.C. was becoming markedly like its secular counterparts. The president of Wesleyan University, asked to review the curriculum reforms of the mid-1960s, cautioned that B.C. was aping too slavishly the patterns of leading research universities—becoming too departmental and disciplinary, too focused on graduate education and research—and ran the risk of neglecting its basic mission in undergraduate education. Walsh's academic vice president also worried about the "implicit derogation of teaching" associated with the emphasis on graduate education and research. Such concerns linked B.C. not only to Brandeis but also to Tufts and even Harvard and moved educational debate at B.C. into the center of contemporary academic culture. Indeed, while praising B.C.'s academic achievements, Greeley observed that the campus "had yet to devise anything in student life that was distinctively Catholic, or even distinctively religious."

By the mid-1960s, Walsh himself was feeling the need to reassert Catholic values. Noting a growing concern among Jesuit educators that the "religious functions of our colleges" have "been eclipsed in our dramatic drive toward intellectual excellence," he called for a new attention to "basic purposes . . . religious, moral and spiritual as well as intellectual." Unlike the order's conservatives, however, Walsh had no interest in re-creating the Jesuit campus of the past, dominated by large numbers of poorly trained priests. "It seems to me," he wrote,

> that . . . if the total faculty is a hundred, then fifteen Jesuit *scholar*-teachers [his emphasis] . . . will be more successful in impregnating the total faculty and student body with a Catholic view of life than will fifty or sixty Jesuits who are teachers but cannot be called scholars in the university sense.

Thus did Walsh reconcile his laicization of B.C.'s faculty with his implicit religious commitment. He could therefore celebrate the secularization of B.C., without ambivalence or irony.

He did so publicly in 1963 at a lavish centennial festival featuring a scholarly colloquium on the knowledge explosion. During that occasion, in a richly symbolic act acknowledging the conception of progress that pervaded the entire event and also recording the social ascent of the local Irish community, Walsh awarded an honorary degree to Nathan Pusey of Harvard. Half a century earlier, Pusey's university, traditionally viewed by Jesuits as a bastion of error, had refused to recognize B.C.'s degree. Now it was the citadel toward which Walsh pushed his brightest graduates, from which he sought his leading faculty, and through which he understood the imperatives of institutional change.[31]

The "Blooming" at Northeastern

*Asa Knowles Brings a Broadened
Vision to the Presidency*

In choosing Knowles as his successor, Ell believed he was turning over his campus to someone who shared his dedication to the principles that had guided Northeastern since the days of Frank Palmer Speare. Such confidence was well founded. Knowles was an Ell protegé, having begun his career at N.U. in the 1930s as Ell was assuming control of the university's internal affairs. Ell promoted Knowles into a series of positions, including the first deanship of the College of Business Administration.

Though he had been away for twenty years, Knowles fully understood Northeastern's twofold orientation: cooperative programs in professional fields for traditional students and part-time, evening programs for adults. His experience had involved him deeply in both areas. Further, Knowles realized that these educational ideas constituted not only a tradition of local service but also a strategy of survival in Boston's highly competitive academic environment. Northeastern specialized in jobs other universities considered marginal: educating nonelite students who needed to earn their way through college and cooperating with area businesses to provide technically competent middle-level employees.

Ell and his trustees knew the 1960s would be years in which to build Northeastern, not merely preserve its current form. While the challenge for Ell in the 1940s and 1950s had been to establish the campus as a free-standing institution, the job for Knowles was to put it on the map as a proper university.

Knowles was ready. He had earned a reputation as an entrepreneur in his previous administrative posts. In 1957, moreover, he had published an article that read like a manifesto for the development of Northeastern. He argued that demand for college admission would be even greater than generally anticipated and that the pressure would be especially strong at urban universities because of their proximity to centers of population and jobs. While public institutions would account for much of the inevitable expansion, some private universities would prosper by offering distinctive programs. He foresaw especially bright futures for co-op colleges that could help moderate-income students prepare for careers while aiding local industry solve manpower short-ages.[32]

Building Northeastern through Expansion
and Diversification

The first theme of Knowles's administration was expansion of programs already in place. Prior to his inauguration, the new president established a planning committee to formulate responses to the new conditions of higher education. This group recommended a slowing of growth at the undergraduate level, development of graduate work, and aggressive expansion of programs for adult, part-time students. Knowles moved immediately on the third of these proposals, noting that such an emphasis would serve the local community and strengthen Northeastern's finances.

A first step was the creation of a degree-granting unit, University College, to administer most part-time programs. This structure allowed the campus to organize curricula specifically tailored to adults—which meant courses that were less demanding and time consuming than those for full-time, day students—without jeopardizing the standing of its regular programs with accrediting agencies. Free to respond to market opportunities and set its own standards, University College quickly became a center of developmental activity. Relying on part-time faculty, following the principle that "convenience is more important than tradition," the new unit designed programs in business, technology, and liberal arts, established a policy of open admissions, and grew from four thousand students in 1960 to fifteen thousand by 1967.

A second vehicle emphasizing technical fields was created with the redesign of Lincoln Institute as a degree-granting entity called Lincoln College. This change allowed N.U. to expand its offerings in ways inappropriate for the College of Engineering, including two-year programs in applied science and four-year curricula in fields like commercial aviation. A third initiative was an Office of Adult and Continuing Education that sponsored nondegree programs, many of them oriented toward the training needs of new industries springing up along Route 128. By 1968 the new unit enrolled over forty-two hundred students.

While Knowles was aggressive in expanding part-time and nondegree programs, he also embraced rapid growth in the basic colleges, notwithstanding the recommendation of his planning committee to slow undergraduate development. Between 1962 and 1967, with applications mounting, the two largest colleges, Engineering and Business, added more students than during Ell's high-growth period in the 1950s, and Liberal Arts and Education grew even more rapidly. Total enrollments in the four units rose from just over six thousand in the fall of 1959 to thirteen thousand five hundred by the fall of 1967, thus adding more students in Knowles's first nine years than in the entire preceding history of the institution.

Expansion derived not only from the arrival of the postwar tidal wave of young people but also from energetic recruitment and public relations.

Knowles reached for additional students by following Boston's population out of the city. University College generated satellite facilities at several outlying locations. A mansion in Weston was acquired for Continuing Education. The boldest step came in 1964 when Northeastern opened an entire campus on a former military installation in Burlington—the heart of suburban growth outside Boston. By the late 1960s, the Burlington campus was serving over five thousand students in the programs of University College and the basic colleges.[33]

Rapid growth was reinforced by the second major theme of Knowles's administration: diversification. The new president was clear from the outset that he wanted to build both horizontally, by adding professional colleges, and vertically, through creating graduate programs. He was especially determined to promote horizontal growth and established a planning office to identify fields that could fit into Northeastern's co-op system and pay their own way. He was impressed with possibilities in the expanding service sector of the regional economy, notably health-related fields, where student interest was high, especially among women—whom Ell's Northeastern had not reached effectively—and where federal support was available. In the end, however, Knowles's initiatives had more to do with accident than planning.

During Knowles's first five years, Northeastern was approached by three external groups seeking university affiliations. The first was the Massachusetts College of Pharmacy in 1962. In 1964 the Harvard hospitals proposed a college of nursing and Boston-Bouvé, a school of physical education, seeking a new home following its break with Tufts, asked to come under N.U.'s umbrella. Knowles bought, and suddenly Northeastern had three new colleges.

A fourth, Criminal Justice, came somewhat later by a different route. Since the late 1950s, Northeastern had conducted continuing-education courses for the Boston Police Department, and after 1960 this activity became a department of University College. By 1964 the police wanted a comprehensive facility, and federal funds existed to underwrite such an enterprise. With Knowles's blessing, the entrepreneurs at Northeastern assembled these pieces into a plan for a new college, which opened in 1967 with federal, local, and foundation support. Thus, within eight years, Knowles doubled Northeastern's portfolio of basic colleges. In 1967 the new units enrolled nearly fourteen hundred students.

Knowles was more cautious with respect to graduate programs, reflecting his own uncertainty about Northeastern's role at this level and his awareness of reservations among the trustees. Even more than his predecessor, however, the new president was convinced that Northeastern must expand the advanced functions to achieve respectability, protect its position in technical and scientific fields, maintain ties to industry, and take advantage of federal largess. His analysis was affirmed by a faculty-administration committee.

In 1960 Knowles won trustee approval for doctoral work in chemistry, electrical engineering, and physics. The professional master's degrees established by Ell to serve part-time, evening students were converted into full-time, day programs. The graduate efforts in Education and Liberal Arts were upgraded and enlarged. Within a few years there were nine doctoral programs in the social and natural sciences. The new colleges also were urged to build graduate components. With support from the alumni, the School of Law, which Ell had closed in the early 1950s, was reopened, and two graduate professional schools, Actuarial Science and Professional Accounting, were established. All of these initiatives led to a doubling of Northeastern's graduate enrollments between 1960 and 1967.

The combined effect of Knowles's program of expansion and diversification brought total enrollments above forty-five thousand by 1967, compared with twenty thousand at the time he assumed office. Northeastern was now, the ebullient president proudly announced, the largest private university in the United States.[34]

Balancing Distinctiveness, Growth, and Upward Mobility

Knowles's emphasis on growth diverged from the policies of other upwardly mobile private universities in Massachusetts during the 1960s. Leaders of Tufts, Brandeis, and Boston College all saw these years as offering the chance to become more like their admired Ivy League counterparts by limiting undergraduate enrollments, becoming more selective, stressing the arts and sciences, scaling back commitments to practical fields and nontraditional students, and expanding at the graduate level.

Knowles, it must be emphasized, was far from indifferent to status. Indeed, he stressed the importance of winning a place for Northeastern at "the head table of academic respectability" through a "quest for higher academic stature." N.U.'s president was unusual among academic leaders in Massachusetts, however, in believing that his university could best enhance its position not by adopting the patterns of elite institutions but by stressing its distinctive qualities. Indeed, he believed the tendency of other institutions to pursue similar priorities represented opportunity for a campus willing to be different. His new colleges reflected the utility of this insight. Boston-Bouvé approached Northeastern because Tufts was forcing it to conform to the standards of a liberal arts college. The Harvard hospitals placed their nursing school at Northeastern partly because Boston University was not interested. Northeastern prospered in part-time and continuing education because other institutions were less interested in serving this market.

Knowles's appreciation of Northeastern's special possibilities was particularly evident in his attitude toward cooperative education. Convinced that the ties between industry and academy fostered by co-op guaranteed this system a continuing educational role, Knowles believed his campus could achieve national prominence as a leader in this field. The new colleges and graduate programs thus became vehicles for demonstrating the effectiveness of co-op outside the traditional domains of business and engineering, and Knowles was uncompromising in making new programs conform to this pattern.

Knowles projected himself and Northeastern into the front ranks of a new organization of co-op colleges—a movement that Ell, with his focus on Northeastern's local mission, had ignored—and from this platform, the new president became a national spokesperson and lobbyist for cooperative education. In 1964 he established a consulting service to advise institutions interested in adopting this format. By decade's end, the Center for Cooperative Education was carrying Northeastern's flag not only nationally but internationally.

Knowles's readiness to pursue an atypical version of academic status reflected his attention to audiences different from those addressed by other presidents. Sachar, Wessell, and Walsh, despite their differences, were all seeking status in academic and social contexts, reaching for recognition within the traditional disciplinary professions and among social elites and private contributors eager for association with a classy educational enterprise. Knowles, by contrast, focused on the business community, largely but not exclusively in Massachusetts, and on practice-oriented professional organizations and their counterpart accrediting agencies in nonelite fields where Northeastern was training middle-level workers.

Knowles's perspective was evident in his view of the liberal arts not as the core of Northeastern but as necessary support for professional programs, an attitude that led him to minimize commitments in these fields. It was equally apparent in his approach to the established professional colleges, where acceptance by accrediting authorities was the animating goal of academic change, and in adding new colleges, where support from external constituencies was a prerequisite for action. Knowles's unusual orientation was also manifest in his emphasis on graduate programs in fields like accounting and actuarial science, which grew out of carefully cultivated relationships with business organizations. Knowles's stress on nonacademic values and constituencies perpetuated his institution's long-standing affinity for M.I.T., rather than Harvard, as a model of educational excellence, and his selection of James Killian as his inaugural speaker was no less symbolic than Father Walsh's encomium to Nathan Pusey at B.C.'s centennial.[35]

Knowles was also aware, however, that educational institutions could succeed only up to a point by being distinctive—that students and families in selecting an institution, business executives in providing support, and prospective faculty members in considering appointments, had conceptions of a proper university that could not be ignored. He published an article regretting that conventions tended to force all institutions toward a single model of quality, but he was also a man prepared to deal with the world as he found it. Thus Knowles's strategy for Northeastern—like Killian's for M.I.T.—included plans to bring the campus more into conformity with mainstream academic forms than had been the case under Ell.

This aspect of his program was apparent in his approach to graduate education and research, which he knew had become hallmarks of the modern university, although neither was central to his personal interests or his vision of Northeastern. He placed a moderate emphasis on graduate programs throughout the university, but he also sought—with only partial success—to limit development at this level to fields, like science and engineering, where Northeastern had strength and where external support was available. He was even more cautious about research. He kept average teaching loads sufficiently high (twelve hours per term) to constrain scholarly work for most faculty, and he placed strict limits—5 to 9 percent of the operating budget—on the use of institutional funds to support this activity. He made exceptions to the policy of limited support for graduate education and research only in selected areas, like physics, where he offered large salaries, limited teaching loads, and significant support funds to recruit two faculty from M.I.T.

In his public relations during the 1960s, Knowles claimed major strides in graduate education and research. He published lists of sponsored projects, appointed a dean of research administration, and devoted large parts of his annual reports to these areas. Actual achievements, however, reflected his limited commitment. The total dollar value of sponsored research in fiscal year 1967 was $3.4 million, only slightly more than B.C., despite Northeastern's orientation toward science and engineering where grants from government and industry were readily available. The graduate programs in arts and sciences were too undeveloped even to warrant mention in the 1970 ratings published by the A.C.E. Only one program—in law—was included in a national evaluation of graduate professional schools published three years later.

Knowles also sought to make Northeastern into a more conventional university in terms of its undergraduate programs, including the quality and character of the student body and of the academic and extracurricular environment. He encouraged fraternities and sororities as well as student organizations and activities, including athletics, where the biggest thrills were provided by unexpected success in the traditional upper-class sport of rowing. He greatly expanded Ell's modest program of dormitory construction and stressed out-of-state recruitment. By 1968 a third of the thirty-five hundred entering freshmen came from other states, and by 1969 about a third of the undergraduate student body was housed in N.U.'s residential facilities.

From the beginning of his term, Knowles's speeches and reports argued that Northeastern's undergraduate program should increase in quality while also growing, and he moved early to establish uniform admission standards for the basic colleges. His focus on expansion, however, limited academic upgrading. A comparison with Boston College, where Walsh was much more single-minded about quality and status, is instructive. In the fall of 1966, freshmen entering B.C.'s College of Arts and Sciences had average S.A.T. scores 80 points higher than their Northeastern counterparts on the verbal test, and 60 points higher on the math. Only 40 percent of all Northeastern freshmen were in the top quarter of their high school classes. A respected national evaluation of undergraduate programs in the late 1960s gave Northeastern's programs, including the well-established offerings in engineering and business, no better than "fair" ratings on a four-point scale including "superior," "good," "fair," and "poor." The same survey gave Northeastern an overall rating of "fair" for its commitment to excellence, while rating B.C. and Tufts "good" and Brandeis "excellent."[36]

Maintaining N.U.'s Financial Traditions
in a Bull Market

Northeastern's relatively modest qualitative gains during the 1960s reflected not only different priorities from B.C., Tufts, and Brandeis but also Knowles's commitment to evaluating proposals as much in financial as academic terms. Northeastern, more than any other university in Massachusetts, traditionally viewed education as a business, and Knowles, working comfortably within this framework, was attentive to the capacity of new activities to cover costs and earn surplus revenues. By far the most successful initiatives in these terms were the highly profitable offerings of University and Lincoln colleges, which relied on part-time faculty and provided students with minimal support services. In 1968 these programs accounted for approximately a third of all student payments, far higher than their share of operating costs.

Northeastern's businesslike orientation was rooted in its historic lack of both endowments and wealthy patrons and had been expressed most clearly in Ell's dictum that current costs should always be covered by current revenues while donations should be sought solely for capital purposes. Neither Knowles nor his trustees was indifferent, however, to the fund-raising possibilities of the 1960s. On the contrary, financial development was a major goal from the beginning, and in 1961 N.U. launched a highly successful campaign, the Diamond Anniversary Development Program, through which Knowles sought aid from both government and foundations. Nonetheless, Knowles basically tried to maintain the financial traditions of Northeastern even as he expanded and upgraded his institution, focusing the D.A.D.P. on new facilities while meeting operating costs with operating revenues.

Since Knowles, like Ell, published virtually no financial information, it is difficult to say with precision how well Northeastern's programs fared in financial terms. Clearly it was a period of impressive expansion, as current income grew from $7.5 million in Knowles's first year to nearly $31 million in 1968. The increased revenue resulted in equal portions from larger enrollments and higher tuition, which was raised by 9 percent per year during the 1960s. Costs also rose steadily, of course, especially as a result of efforts to meet accreditation standards and build graduate and research activities, but overall income appears to have compensated for these higher expenses.

Knowles himself has stated that N.U. was "rolling in money" during these years to the point that he was afraid that fund-raising efforts would be hurt if N.U.'s true financial situation were made public. In fiscal year 1968, for example, revenue from student payments and program grants more than covered operating costs, providing nearly a million dollars to support plant development. Thus Knowles, unlike Walsh or Sachar, did not allow operating budgets to become dependent on gifts. This record is especially striking in light of the fact that, in comparison with other universities, Knowles was restrained about raising tuition, given his strategy of expansion among students from modest-income backgrounds. In the 1960s, Northeastern replaced B.C. as the least expensive private university in Massachusetts.[37]

The financial differences between Northeastern and B.C. or Brandeis were a direct reflection of contrasting academic priorities—and vice versa. Knowles's caution about research and graduate education was undoubtedly linked to his awareness that these activities could never pay their own way. Despite the university's affluence, he kept his faculty-to-student ratio high: the number of full-time students grew more rapidly than that of full-time faculty. His salaries remained low: Northeastern was clearly the lowest paying university in the area, earning only a *C* rating from the A.A.U.P. He used almost no institutional funds for scholarships: Northeastern relied on new federal programs in this area.

The Diamond Anniversary Development Program was intended to raise forty million dollars by 1973, when Northeastern would celebrate its seventy-fifth anniversary. Curiously, the forty-million-dollar figure was identical with the target established by Walsh for B.C., and both presidents were successful during the first half of the 1960s, though there were interesting differences. Nearly half of the fifteen million dollars raised by Boston College during this period, approximately seven million, came from alumni, while Knowles obtained only about a million of the twenty million dollars he reported from graduates. Knowles's success in obtaining support from industry was also circumscribed, amounting to only one and a half million dollars during the first phase of the D.A.D.P. The key to Knowles's fund-raising in the early 1960s was federal funds, chiefly for dormitory construction. Nearly fifteen million of the twenty million dollars he reported came from Washington, and federal matching requirements provided leverage in obtaining much of the private help.

During the second phase of D.A.D.P., between 1965 and 1969, Northeastern was able to expand support from private sources, so that fifteen million of the twenty-six million dollars raised during this period came from nongovernment contributions. By the late 1960s, Knowles and his colleagues were so optimistic that they upped the twelve-year target for the D.A.D.P. to sixty-five million dollars. During the first two phases of the campaign, Knowles increased Northeastern's buildings from ten to thirty-three, created the suburban campus in Burlington, acquired a Center for Continuing Education in Weston, a physical education center in Ashland, a marine sciences facility in Nahant, and established continuing education programs in Lynn, Weymouth, and Framingham. Of the $47 million raised, only $3.6 million were used to build endowment holdings.[38]

The Achievement and Vulnerability
of Northeastern

By the mid-1960s, Knowles had woven the various themes of his development strategy into a "triple service" model of Northeastern that he used in presentations to business and professional audiences, as well as to students and their families. Northeastern, he liked to say, had an urban mission in metropolitan Boston expressed through community service and adult education, a national mission manifested in the student body and co-op placements, and an international mission for leadership in cooperative education. These were, of course, marketing slogans, but they also represented real achievements and were testimony to Knowles's distinctive leadership. Long-time faculty members like Rudolph Morris, who subsequently published a memoir of his years at Northeastern, watched with amazement the process of institutional change that Morris called "the blooming."

In many ways, the new Northeastern played the role served by public urban universities in other metropolitan areas, and if there was a flaw in Knowles's formula, it was the potential difficulty of competing with tax-supported institutions for the modest-income, local students on which N.U.'s vastly enlarged operations depended. Knowles was attuned to this danger and kept a wary eye on Beacon Hill, hoping the state would continue its tradition of minimal interest in public higher education.

In 1962 Knowles was appointed to a special state commission to investigate the need to expand public colleges and universities. One policy question involved the possibility of a state university in the Boston area to serve the region's ballooning youth population. Along with several other commission members, Knowles opposed this idea and thought he had assurances that no such step would be taken until at least the late 1970s. He was amazed and angered, therefore, when the chairman of the commission, a state senator, announced one day in 1964 that the General Court was about to pass a bill establishing a Boston campus of the University of Massachusetts. Here, unexpectedly, was a potentially serious danger to Northeastern, but Knowles's protests and threatened resignation had no impact on a legislature suddenly committed to action. Thus, as Northeastern expanded in the late 1960s, Knowles and his colleagues cast concerned glances toward the new public campus beginning to take shape in temporary quarters only a few blocks away. UMass/ Boston was, for the moment, however, only a worry, given the success of Northeastern's programs. Knowles's ten-year report, published in 1969, recorded in triumphant tones the decade's record of growth and progress.[39]

The 1960s at Boston University

Completing the Charles River Campus

While Boston College and Northeastern were changing rapidly in the 1960s under ambitious new presidents, Boston University continued the broad pattern of development initiated by Daniel Marsh before World War II and maintained by Harold Case during the 1950s with only modest adjustments. The central goal was consolidation of B.U. in its new campus, and Case continued until his resignation in 1967 to focus attention on land and building acquisition, capital financing, and construction. In the 1960s alone, he produced six new instructional buildings, residence halls for over thirty-two hundred students, a library, a student union, an administrative center, and several ancillary structures. Plans for a sports complex, to bear Case's name, were also well advanced by the mid-1960s.

The only major unit not located along Commonwealth Avenue at the end of Case's term was the School of Medicine, which was to remain at its historic location near University Hospital in the South End. But here, too, physical progress was evident. In 1965 Case announced a ten-year, fifty-five million dollar capital program for a modern medical center, to house the medical school and the School of Nursing as well as health-related research activities. In the same year, while dedicating a building for the College of Basic Studies, Case announced that the master plan for the Charles River campus was at long last a reality. Getting to this point had required the primary attention of two presidents over a period of nearly forty years. It was an impressive achievement.

Case's continued emphasis on physical growth in the 1960s was not accompanied by fund-raising efforts even moderately commensurate with B.U.'s needs for capital financing. No program on the scale of those mounted by Walsh at B.C. or Knowles at N.U. was attempted. Indeed, throughout the decade, total private giving to the university—an institution now larger than Harvard—averaged approximately two million dollars annually and alumni/ae giving did not rise above four hundred thousand dollars in any year.

In the absence of donated funds, Case continued to rely on the operating policies that had subsidized campus development since the postwar days of Daniel Marsh: an emphasis on enrollment growth and tuition income to earn maximum current revenues, strict limits on expenditures for salaries and support services to achieve operating surpluses, and use of surplus revenues to obtain capital financing. Between 1959 and 1966, total enrollments grew from 15,000 to 22,500, through the addition of 4,800 full-time students and another 2,700 part-timers, while full-time undergraduate tuition rose from $950 per year to $1,550. During these years, total operating revenues (composed mainly of student payments) increased from $19.3 million to $54.8 million, generating annual and increasing surpluses that contributed over $28 million to plant development. Revenues generated through operating surpluses accounted for nearly 50 percent of total new plant funds obtained by B.U. between 1959 and 1967, while less than 25 percent of such funds were obtained through fund-raising activities.[40]

Academic Change Amid Physical Development

The evolution of B.U. as an educational institution in the 1960s proceeded in the highly decentralized manner that had been present from the start of the Case administration. The broad direction of change, moreover, continued to express the dream of transforming B.U. from a local, service-oriented campus into a more prestigious, national university. For both Marsh and Case, that vision provided the basic reason for the building program.

The extent of academic change at B.U. was highlighted during a comprehensive program review that Case initiated in 1965, the same year he announced completion of the Charles River campus. Convinced that a major period of development was now at an end, and mindful that B.U. had undertaken no university-wide planning since the early 1950s, Case was eager both to record the achievements of his years and to establish an academic agenda for the new facility. The elaborate process that he set in motion—including planning committees in every unit of the university, a central coordinating staff, and outside consulting assistance—did more to highlight the sprawling, undirected character of recent growth than to provide a blueprint for the future. A major reason for the inconclusive outcome was Case's decision to resign in the spring of 1966, just as the review was getting started. The final report did provide, however, a useful overview of the Case years. It also made clear the degree to which the new campus not only offered a setting for future academic improvements but also made such improvements a matter of strategic, particularly financial, necessity.

The most obvious change recorded in the review was in the nature of B.U.'s undergraduate population. The shift toward a more residential, less local student body that was begun by Marsh and continued by Case accelerated in the 1960s. By 1967 seven thousand students, more than half the undergraduates, were living on campus, compared with fifteen hundred at the beginning of Case's term sixteen years earlier. During this same period, the percentage of students from New England dropped from 93 percent to 52 percent and that from Massachusetts from 80 percent to 35 percent, with nonurban residents continuing to supplant local commuters even among in-state students. The bulk of the non-New Englanders was now drawn from the mid-Atlantic states, especially New York, New Jersey, and Pennsylvania.

In addition to coming from further afield, B.U.'s students in the 1960s were younger, more affluent, and better prepared academically than the commuters who had come by streetcar in the 1930s and 1940s. The changing student body reflected the extent to which conditions of the 1960s allowed B.U. to become more selective in admissions. Despite steady expansion, the number of applications per freshman seat grew from 1.7 in 1952 to 4.5 in 1967. Changes in student interests registered their altered social and academic backgrounds. The College of Liberal Arts, which enrolled 13 percent of the undergraduates in the 1930s and in the early postwar years—when almost all B.U.'s students sought technical and occupational programs—accounted for 32 percent by the mid-1960s.

The shift toward elite functions and subjects was further manifest in the emphasis on graduate education, the arena for most programmatic initiatives during the central years of the golden age. Between 1959 and 1966, thirteen advanced programs were created, chiefly master's degrees in professional subjects. In terms of enrollments, however, the change of emphasis from applied fields to the liberal arts that was occurring among undergraduates was also apparent at the graduate level. The Graduate School of Arts and Sciences was by far the fastest growing unit of the university in the 1960s, and by 1967 it accounted for the largest number of B.U.'s advanced students. Despite graduate growth, the ratio of undergraduates to graduates did not change markedly, due to the continued expansion of baccalaureate programs.[41]

Changes in B.U.'s students were mirrored by the faculty, which grew from 373 full-time members in 1948 to 969 in 1966, with a much higher percentage concentrated in arts and sciences at the end of the period. This shift was driven not only by growth in the basic disciplines but also by the consolidation of programs at one location. The new campus allowed all undergraduate instruction in the arts and sciences, traditionally offered to students in the professional colleges by separate faculties employed by those units, to become the exclusive province of the College of Liberal Arts. In his final report—noting that the percentage of faculty with Ph.D.s, had increased in recent years—Case spoke of the "growing prestige" at B.U. expressed in greater scholarly productivity and visibility.

Like Tufts, the area's other Protestant, nonsectarian university, B.U. weakened its ties to its roots in the Methodist church as it became academically more ambitious. In contrast to the postwar years under Marsh, and even the early years of the Case administration, the theme of B.U.'s role in fostering religious practice was almost invisible in the documents and public statements produced during the institutional review of the mid-1960s. For instance, a long essay on B.U.'s educational mission included in the summary report stressed commitments to teaching, research, and service and commented at length on the academic values associated with undergraduate liberal education. It made conspicuously little reference to religion, however, suggesting only that a committee look into this aspect of B.U. The outside consultants, Frederick Bolman and Miguel de Capriles, took a harsher view, recommending that the Methodist church be asked to assume financial responsibility for the School of Theology. The university, they argued, should not be putting scarce resources into an activity that was losing money and was unlikely to contribute significantly to future progress.

Summarizing the changes of the Case years, Bolman and de Capriles concluded that B.U.'s leaders had "already done much" to make their institution into "an outstanding, modern, private urban university, worthy of the historic city whose name it bears." The comment was accurate in describing the direction of recent development, but gentle in assessing the results. By the late 1960s, academic quality had become a central and problematic issue for Boston University.[42]

B.U.'s Dilemma: How to Make
the Transition from Quantitative Growth
to Qualitative Improvement

While celebrating B.U.'s growth, Case's parting review drew attention to the qualitative limitations of recent change. In a number of areas, the reports observed, B.U. was spending much less to support its programs than were other universities with which the campus hoped to be associated. Faculty compensation illustrated the point. Although B.U.'s salaries increased markedly over prewar levels under Case, they did not keep pace with major universities, and by 1967 the pay scale at every rank was below the average for all universities surveyed by the A.A.U.P. Salaries for full professors earned only a *C* rating, while salaries in all other ranks were in the *B* range. Among schools in the

Boston area, B.U.'s average salary ranked second from the bottom, only five hundred dollars above Northeastern and far below the highest paying institutions—Harvard, M.I.T., and Brandeis.

Other financial comparisons added to the sense of modest academic improvement. B.U. did not have a single endowed professorship in 1967. Its library budget ranked fifty-sixth among Association of Research Libraries, and its collection ranked third from last within the group. B.U. provided scholarship support to a smaller percentage of its undergraduates than any other private university in the Boston area except Northeastern, and its average grant was smaller than all but Northeastern and Tufts. Looking at the total budget for departmental instruction and research, B.U.'s expenditures per student in 1967 were only two-thirds those of Tufts, less than half those of Harvard or M.I.T. The emphasis on the building program also led to neglect of investments. During Case's sixteen-year presidency, B.U.'s endowment exhibited only modest growth (from thirteen million to twenty million dollars) and was now the same size as Northeastern's.

Reports of B.U.'s reputation in the late 1960s confirmed what the financial figures implied. A survey sponsored by the university itself found that B.U.'s image among opinion leaders in Boston had not been much enhanced as a result of growth and construction. While B.U. was seen as an improving institution, its faculty, students, and leadership were all regarded as mediocre, and it lacked a strong reputation for both academic quality and public service. A national evaluation of undergraduate programs gave B.U. a quality rating at the bottom of the middle range, slightly higher than B.C. and much higher than Northeastern, but well below Tufts and Brandeis. The A.C.E.'s evaluation of doctoral programs gave B.U. uniformly mediocre scores, with all faculties rated "adequate" (the second-lowest rating on a four-point scale) and all programs rated "acceptable" (also the second lowest of four possible scores).[43]

B.U.'s middling standing in the late 1960s expressed the paradoxical character of Case's approach to campus development: he attempted to change Boston University into a respected national university while following operating policies associated with low-status, mass-market institutions. Comparisons with B.C. and Northeastern reveal the problem. In its efforts to attract a younger, more affluent, better prepared, residential student body and to develop the arts and sciences and graduate programs, B.U.'s academic goals were similar to those of B.C. under Walsh. But Case, unlike Walsh, did not undertake a program of fund-raising and salary enhancement commensurate with his ambitions. Rather, he continued the financial pattern inherited from Marsh and relied on operating surpluses to support the construction program.

Case's financial strategy required a continued emphasis on growth, so that B.U.'s rate of expansion in the 1960s was more like Northeastern's than B.C.'s. Moreover, undoubtedly to protect the university's size, Case was restrained in raising tuition, so that student charges, which were closer to those of Harvard than of B.C. at the beginning of the postwar period, were by the late 1960s lower than B.C.'s and only slightly higher than Northeastern's. Finally, like Knowles, Case kept operating expenses low, which limited progress in hiring full-time faculty, increasing salaries, and providing financial aid. In essence, B.U. sacrificed academic quality to physical expansion in the short run. As Bolman and de Capriles put it: "In a sense, the recent capital improvements of Boston University have been subsidized by the faculty."[44]

Case's awareness that there had been costs as well as gains associated with his policies was implicit in his assertion that B.U. had completed an important stage of evolution and now could concentrate on academic progress. Indeed, the need to focus on substantive strengthening was a central theme of the self-study, which observed that B.U.'s uncontrolled growth during the 1950s and 1960s had aggravated the institutional shapelessness that had troubled the campus since before World War II. There was wide agreement among B.U.'s leaders that the university must now take steps actually to become the high-quality institution toward which both Marsh and Case had been vaguely pointing. The matter was put most succinctly by Bolman and de Capriles, who argued that B.U. must raise admission standards and place more emphasis on upper-division, graduate and professional programs and on research. To accomplish these goals, funds would be needed for salaries, scholarships, fellowships, and program support. The poor quality of campus life, reflected in low student morale, would need to be improved. The endowment would need to be built.

The consultants pointed out that intellectual upgrading, with financial policies to match, represented the only competitive strategy now available to B.U. With the University of Massachusetts building a major campus in the Boston area, Boston University could no longer hope to compete for local students based on modest tuition charges, as Northeastern was still trying to do. Having come so far in the transition from a low-cost, service-oriented urban institution to a more traditional and expensive residential university, B.U. had no option but to move further and faster along this path, betting that a better reputation could attract affluent students who could afford not to attend a public campus but lacked the credentials for admission to a leading private university.[45]

The question of financing much-needed academic improvements brought B.U.'s leaders face to face with the contradictions inherent in the development policies they had employed for two decades. Expanding enrollments further might make B.U. even less selective and weaken the university's already pallid academic image. Raising tuition dramatically would risk real income losses, since B.U. was already charging a high price in relation to its reputation. Continued suppression of operating costs would defeat hopes of raising quality. The situation was made more problematic by the fact that, even without a significant rise in per-student expenditures, costs were climbing more rapidly than income, and the university faced deficits within five years.

A search for alternative sources of income provided little solace. State aid was unlikely on both political and legal grounds. Increased federal support was possible but highly speculative. No organizational base for a major fund-raising effort existed. The budget director drew the necessary conclusion: "The only way, in the short run at least, is tuition." Thus, despite the need for upgrading, the self-study's projections for the period from 1967 to 1975 called essentially for a continuation of past practices: more enrollments and higher charges as the path to expanded revenue.[46]

The financial difficulties that came to light during the self-study were a source of concern but not alarm for the members of B.U.'s hierarchy. The good times that had supported the university's growth for two decades—based on strong student demand and generous federal funding—were expected to continue. The consensus was that, with the construction program now completed, B.U. could make the necessary shifts of emphasis, especially by restraining the use of operating income for capital improvements, and could begin employing surpluses to build endowment, raise salaries, and provide the other academic supports needed by a university of the first rank. The confidence of B.U.'s leaders was implicit in their decision, in 1967, to begin negotiations for air rights over Storrow Drive, the highway that separated the campus from the Charles River, in order to provide space for a new program of expansion.

The trustees did feel, however, that B.U. needed new leadership for the transitional period that lay ahead. It was time, some felt, to end the tradition of minister-presidents and install a proper academic, and the board pressed Case to leave before he was ready to go. As his successor, they chose Dr. Arland Christ-Janer, president of Cornell College, a small Methodist institution in Iowa. Likable, relaxed, devoted to humanistic and religious values, Christ-Janer seemed certain to keep the administration on good terms with its students during years in which campus unrest was becoming a national issue. The easygoing new president also embodied the trustees' view that the necessary academic progress could be made with only modest adjustments in the kind of leadership that had been employed at B.U. with obvious success for the previous twenty-five years.[47]

Institutional Mobility and Organizational Form

Traditions of Academic Organization at Boston's Urban Universities

Although by 1945 American universities had developed in a bewildering number of sizes and forms, certain features of organization had become common among those that had evolved furthest as intellectual communities. Three characteristics, in particular, had proved vital for fostering scholarly achievement. Of these the most fundamental was independence from external, nonacademic control. A second and more modern quality of leading universities was decentralization of administrative authority. Decentralization, in turn, implied an additional characteristic: the presence of an organizational culture that enforced high academic standards within relatively self-governing subunits.

As Boston University, Northeastern, and Boston College moved toward greater academic respectability in the postwar years, each struggled with organizational traditions that departed in one way or another from these three fundamental attributes. Since all three campuses changed significantly in academic terms during the golden age, their histories provide an opportunity to observe the relationship between organizational characteristics and substantive development.

Among Boston's urban universities, only B.U. was well-established as an autonomous academic institution in 1945. B.U. was governed by a large, self-perpetuating Board of Trustees (often called "the Corporation") that met only occasionally, rarely played a role in policy formation, and served mainly to link the university to the broader community. The powers of the board were exercised by a fifteen-member Executive Committee that, like its namesake at M.I.T. or the Corporation at Harvard, worked closely with the president in the ongoing administration of the campus. Other committees of the board worked with the individual schools in relationships similar to those of the visiting committees of the Overseers at Harvard. Northeastern, too, was an independent corporation, but its separation from the Y.M.C.A. occurred only in 1937. As the postwar period began, N.U. was just beginning to achieve a sense of itself as a free-standing university.[48]

Boston College was still controlled and operated by the Society of Jesus. Its academic activities were subject to religious authority, and the most important officer for B.C.'s community of Jesuit teachers was not the rector-president on the Heights, but the provincial in the order's regional headquarters, who was unlikely to have academic training or experience. Intersecting the provincial's authority was a second structure of external control, the Jesuit Educational Association. This was the national organization of Jesuit educators, and its executive director was appointed by the general in Rome. The authority of the J.E.A. and provincial came together in the province prefect of studies, a provincial official appointed by the J.E.A.'s executive director and charged to exercise oversight, in concert with the provincial, over all educational activities of his region. The order's control over its academic institutions was not reduced by the existence of "boards of trustees" that gave Jesuit universities an apparent structural similarity to their secular counterparts. These boards were appointed by the provincial and were constituted entirely of Jesuits subject to his authority.

B.C.'s subordination to external, nonacademic authority perfectly illustrated the relationship of campus autonomy to academic development. As one student of Catholic higher education has put it, the structure within which B.C. was embedded encouraged "obedience, discipline, loyalty, order, and respect for familiar, diffuse, particularistic, and ascriptive values" while directing suspicion toward "initiative, imagination, creativity and specific achievement and universal values"—essential qualities of an academic community. The system of Jesuit training did not produce strong academic leaders, and the tendency to attach greater importance to the role of rector than president made it unlikely that men with such capabilities would be appointed to head a college or university.

If a strong and academically oriented leader did achieve a presidency, the tradition of six-year terms undermined his capacity to produce change. He was likely, moreover, sooner or later, to find himself at odds with the order. Walsh's hero, Gannon of Fordham, ultimately had come into conflict with his superiors and had lost power. As an older man, he confided his discouragement to Walsh, telling the hopeful new president that the authority of the hierarchy would make it impossible for B.C. to achieve academic excellence.[49]

While two of Boston's urban universities began the postwar period as independent institutions, only B.U. possessed the second criterion of a modern academic organization—a decentralized system of internal authority. Within B.U.'s structure, as within Harvard's, the president's powers were circumscribed in a number of ways. His formal roles included chair of all faculties and of the University Senate, to which every faculty member belonged; of all committees of the Senate; and of the University Council, which was the Senate's operating arm. The University Council, his chief consultative body, was composed entirely of deans appointed by him and responsible to him. The president also had exclusive authority to recommend appointments and promotions—powers unconstrained by codified criteria or formal requirements of faculty involvement.

Limits on presidential power at B.U. began with an organizational culture that stressed consultation and consensus, qualities rooted in the university's traditional ties to Methodism. Indeed, Marsh liked to refer to B.U.'s organization not as a pyramid but as a circle with everyone on the same level and the president in the center, a kind of model Christian community. The president maintained a minimal staff—there was not even a provost—and attempted directly to supervise the work of nearly forty deans and directors. Well-established patterns of delegation and entitlement further limited central administrative control. The trustees had assigned to the various faculties legislative powers in matters directly related to their separate academic interests, including curriculum, and the system of school-specific committees of the board reinforced the independence of the units. B.U. also had entrenched policies on academic freedom and tenure that predated the formulation of statements on these subjects by the national A.A.U.P. in 1940.

Administrative control of academic affairs at Northeastern and B.C. was nearly total in 1945. N.U.'s leaders, indeed, habitually attributed their successes to their tradition of centralized authority, a pattern in which Ell received his training and to which he completely subscribed. Ell was convinced that only business-style management could preserve N.U.'s distinctive, circumscribed, market-sensitive mission while also achieving efficiency and economy. Autocratic and paternalistic, Ell regarded faculty members more as employees than professional colleagues and was opposed on principle to tenure, formalized criteria for personnel decisions, faculty participation in governance, and the A.A.U.P. The administrative apparatus he inherited from Speare was already highly centralized, and Ell spent the first years of his presidency further consolidating his control, especially with respect to finances.

At B.C., administrative authority was even more firmly rooted than at Northeastern, resting as it did on the vow of obedience that Jesuits owed their superiors. On the Heights, as at other Jesuit institutions in the prewar years, faculty participation in decision making was not even a topic, let alone a practice. Deans of colleges and chairs of departments, themselves typically priests, were appointed administratively. Notions of academic freedom and professional autonomy had no place in this system. The provincial moved his priests from campus to campus for teaching and administrative duties as he saw fit, often determined individual course assignments, and even selected texts.[50]

None of Boston's urban universities possessed an entrenched academic culture in 1945. At Northeastern and B.C., such a notion was entirely alien, and B.U.'s more conventional form of academic organization was not buttressed by shared commitments to high academic standards within the faculty. B.U.'s pattern of decentralization, indeed, was a reflection not of the professional stature of individual units, as it was at Harvard, but of the fact that the university had been assembled from previously free-standing entities. Though finances were tightly controlled on a university-wide level, the various schools, scattered about the city, continued in most respects to operate as independent entities. Each possessed its own admissions office, maintained its alumni/ae organization, designed its curriculum, established its personnel systems, and maintained its plant. Academic standards varied greatly from unit to unit.

From the perspective of Marsh and his trustees, as well as B.U.'s wartime planning committee, B.U.'s decentralization stood for weakness rather than strength, and a major reason for building the Charles River campus was to bring some unity to—and control over—an excessively fragmented operation. The impulse toward centralization was paralleled, however, by a movement within the faculty—intensely conscious of its inability to defend its interests during the Depression and war—to assert itself in administrative affairs. In 1944 the University Senate adopted a resolution sponsored by B.U.'s A.A.U.P. chapter calling for a Senate Council composed of elected faculty representatives.[51]

Organizational Change and Upward Mobility at Boston University

The two administrative trends evident at B.U. by the mid-1940s—increased bureaucratization of the central administration and greater faculty involvement in decision making—continued to dominate organizational change in the 1950s and 1960s. Latent conflicts between these movements did not become manifest during the golden age because Marsh and Case exercised their powers chiefly to control finances and pursue the construction program, leaving the subunits and their faculties relatively free to go their own ways on academic matters. Marsh, indeed, welcomed the new Senate Council, seeing it as complementary to his efforts to build a stronger university-wide organization.

Initially, the Senate Council focused on working conditions and the role of the faculty in personnel decisions. In its first year, it recommended procedures and criteria for all appointments and promotions. While reserving final authority in these matters to the president and allowing senior academic administrators to originate appointments, the Senate Council proposed that the faculty be empowered to initiate most personnel actions. It also suggested normal teaching loads, higher salaries, and a modified tenure policy along lines endorsed by the A.A.U.P. Marsh professed to welcome these initiatives and implemented most of them at once, while recommending trustee approval of the new tenure policy.

The pattern of formalization in the area of academic personnel continued under Case. Personnel procedures were reworked in 1956 and made more detailed. By 1962 the personnel policy was augmented by an "academic workload policy" defining reasonable expectations of the professoriate and making it clear that faculty owed allegiance to the profession as well as the university. The 1967 manual added a section stressing the responsibility of the institution to support, protect, and stimulate its instructional staff, while also recognizing the responsibility of the faculty to the university. By this time, the president's role in personnel actions was reduced to a veto power, which could be exercised only when accompanied by written explanations and could be appealed to the Corporation, and the right of senior administrators to initiate appointments was removed altogether. The 1967 manual also included a new section acknowledging the university's support for academic research.

While winning a dominant role in academic personnel decisions in the first two decades after the war, the B.U. faculty also sought to increase its influence over the selection of top administrators. When Marsh announced his decision to retire in 1951, faculty members asked for assurances from trustees that they would be formally involved in the search process; they were invited to form a separate, second-tier committee to interview candidates and advise the trustees. In 1954 the B.U. faculty requested participation in the appointment of deans, and this, too, was granted. By the late 1960s, the faculty manual also guaranteed that faculty members would be consulted in the appointment of chairpersons, though the ultimate right of the president and trustees to appoint chairs was retained.[52]

The expanded faculty role was the most striking organizational development of the two decades following the war, but B.U.'s administration was also evolving away from the minimal staff with which Marsh worked during the 1930s. The Committee on the University in the Postwar World argued in the early 1940s that B.U. was already too complex for the president personally to manage its affairs, and it recommended a university dean to coordinate academic activities in a manner paralleling the treasurer's role in finances. Marsh created the position immediately after the war as a staff function within his office.

The rapid growth of the university in the early postwar years quickly overwhelmed the modest changes undertaken by Marsh, however. In 1953 Case sponsored a review of B.U.'s organization by a team of consultants who recommended two vice presidencies, one for academic affairs and one for administration, to enable the president to concentrate on fund-raising. These changes were made, but they, too, proved inadequate to bring effective coordination to the sprawling, expanding campus. In 1959 another study resulted in a further expansion of the administration. Five vice presidencies were established—for academic affairs, student affairs, development, administration, and university affairs—making B.U. the first university in the Boston area to adopt an organizational form that was becoming common among the mushrooming multiversities of postwar America.

Despite the growth of B.U.'s administrative apparatus in the 1950s and 1960s, the university-wide review initiated by Case in 1965 drew attention to the fact that serious organizational problems remained. The president was still found to spend too much time on internal affairs and was again exhorted to devote more attention to fund-raising. Yet lack of central coordination was also a concern. B.U. still had no campus-wide registration and records system, making cross-registration between schools difficult. The School of Medicine continued to operate under a separate committee of the trustees rather than the president. The budgeting system assumed that each unit would retain its previous expense base and that change would be in the form of increments of varying sizes.

Most important of all, B.U. lacked any system to coordinate the general development of the university. There was no planning office or provision for university-wide governance review of proposed new units. By the late 1960s, B.U. was as much in need of improved administrative control as of intellectual upgrading. Indeed, given the absence of a pervasive academic culture within the faculty, the former was almost certainly a prerequisite for the latter.[53]

Northeastern Acquires a Conventional Form of Organization

While the members of the B.U. faculty were organizing an elected Senate Council and drafting rules to control academic personnel decisions in the late 1940s, their counterparts at Northeastern were just beginning to think of themselves as members of a profession rather than employees of an institution. In his memoir of these years, Morris recalls the shock generated by a move (easily defeated by a vote of the faculty) to exclude administrators from the faculty club. Despite N.U.'s tradition of administrative control, however, Ell sensed a need to bring working conditions into closer conformity with those of more developed institutions, partially to accommodate the mild restlessness within his own faculty, partially to create an environment into which he could recruit properly credentialed professors in a seller's market.

Ell instituted a retirement program, adopted a higher salary scale, and created what he called the "permanent faculty," an alternative to tenure that allowed him to promote individuals of proven worth without actually assuring them continuing appointments on an individual basis. He also took a tentative step toward faculty involvement in policy-making by creating an advisory committee containing some members of the teaching staff. In Northeastern's conservative context, dominated by engineering and business disciplines that tended to accept hierarchy and characterized by a generally undistinguished and not highly mobile faculty, these steps, though modest, were enough to prevent significant pressure for change.

In fact, Ell maintained his intense personal control of campus affairs to the end of his presidency. He continued after the war to enhance the central administration, consolidating support functions into single offices, adding new positions (such as alumni affairs), and eliminating activities (like the college prep program and the non-Boston divisions) that tended to divert attention from the main operation on Huntington Avenue. Ell's conservative style was expressed in the fact that he employed throughout his presidency the basic structures he had established in 1940, and he drew into key roles a remarkably small number of men, most of whom had long associations with Northeastern. A single vice president continued to coordinate internal affairs, and only two persons held this position during Ell's eighteen years. The six-member Executive Council of senior officers continued to be the primary center of administrative control, and only nine men, all directly responsible to Ell or the vice president, sat with this group between 1944 and 1954. Moreover, only one man, Robert Gray Dodge, served as chair of Northeastern's board during Ell's entire presidency, and sixteen others were trustees throughout this period.

Ell was aware that his situation was unusual in the exploding world of American higher education in the 1950s. "I doubt," he wrote in one of his final reports, "if any other college president in the United States has had such wholehearted support and at the same time such entire freedom to visualize, plan and direct the work of a college or university as I have enjoyed for the last twenty years."[54]

Knowles also enjoyed the exercise of power, but he was aware that the organization he had inherited was an anachronism emblematic of Northeastern's limited stature as a university, Ell's restricted vision of institutional possibilities, and the low professional standing of the faculty. Knowles's career included a period of Cornell, where he had learned the administrative culture of elite, mainstream universities, and he understood that his ambitions for N.U. implied a less autocratic form of organization and a more professional faculty. He also realized that Northeastern's staff was hungry for change after years of Ell's benign but domineering paternalism.

Reorganization became a central theme of Knowles's first years. His appointment, even before his inauguration, of several advisory committees signaled his receptivity to change, and he could not have been surprised when the Committee on Faculty Policy recommended an elected Senate and a complete restructuring of Northeastern's practices in hiring, promoting, and supporting its faculty. The Senate was established in 1961, with broad powers to advise the president on policy questions. At the same time, Ell's "permanent faculty" was replaced with a conventional tenure system along lines recommended by the A.A.U.P.

In its early years, the Northeastern Senate, like its counterpart at B.U. fifteen years earlier, concentrated on faculty standing, compensation, and benefits. By 1965 Northeastern had formally adopted (and published in a faculty handbook) procedures and criteria in the area of academic personnel that were similar in all significant respects to those in place at leading, mainstream universities, including guarantees of a dominant role for the faculty.

While involving the professoriate in institutional affairs, Knowles delegated more control over academic programs to the deans and directors, believing that the university could no longer be run effectively out of the president's office and that the addition of new units in Pharmacy, Nursing, Bouvé, and Criminal Justice required a less centralized pattern of control. An Academic Council of deans and directors was created to ensure coordination. A third theme of reorganization was the enlargement of Northeastern's central bureaucracy—a development also required, in Knowles's view, by his program of expansion. He created offices for planning, development, publications, alumni funds, and public relations and added personnel to a number of existing offices. During his first five years, the support staff, excluding secretaries and maintenance people, grew from about 140 to about 250.

By the late 1960s, Knowles's ballooning institution had adopted conventional patterns of organization and decision making in most areas of institutional life. It was also clear by this time that Northeastern had outgrown the pattern of second-level authority that Knowles had inherited from Ell—a single vice president and a small Executive Council. When longtime vice president William White retired in 1966, Knowles created seven vice presidencies, with jurisdiction over major sectors of campus life, a pattern adopted at B.U. seven years earlier. Symbolic of the organizational distance that Northeastern had traveled since Ell's retirement was the appearance of the first faculty-based search committee in the university's history as a means of filling one of the new deanships created during the restructuring of the mid-1960s.[55]

In promoting organizational modernization, Knowles amended Ell's principle that centralized power was necessary to preserve Northeastern's distinctive character. In essence, Knowles looked for the same kind of middle position on organizational matters that he sought on institutional character. Just as he was eager, up to a point, to make his school less distinctive than it had been by hiring conventionally trained Ph.D.'s and placing modest emphases on research and graduate programs, he was ready to bring his university into the administrative mainstream by surrendering some presidential authority. But Knowles was fundamentally a determined leader intent on controlling key decisions, and he retained critical powers, including the right to appoint deans and department chairs without consultation.

Knowles's lot was eased by an organizational culture that was acquiescent in the face of presidential initiative, even after the faculty had been formally empowered to exert more influence. In its early years, the Senate readily supported Knowles on major questions of institutional development, such as the creation of new basic colleges. As the 1960s continued, however, the faculty became more comfortable with the exercise of influence, the numbers hired since Ell's departure increased, and Knowles began to encounter resistance. In 1967 the proposed College of Criminal Justice stirred severe criticism in the Senate, and Knowles prevailed only by accepting changes that made the curriculum more academic. The following year, the Senate rejected a Knowles-sponsored Ph.D. in pharmacy, and then turned down a black studies proposal that the president endorsed. Indeed, though Knowles's term continued into the middle 1970s, the pattern of program diversification ended with the debate on Criminal Justice. When his idea for a School of Transportation Studies encountered opposition, Knowles dropped it.

Another sign of N.U's changing organization was that Knowles increasingly found himself pressured by the faculty to support measures he considered questionable, particularly the establishment of graduate programs in the humanities and social sciences. In these debates, he discovered the difficulty of controlling the changes he had initiated, and his pride in Northeastern's progress became tempered by frustration over his decreasing ability to dictate the course of development.

Still, business boomed during the 1960s. The organizational changes of the Knowles years were manifestly consistent with the university's need for adaptability in a time of growth, just as Ell's administrative philosophy had ensured control during years of fiscal constraint. The central question posed by Knowles's reforms was whether or not Northeastern retained the capacity to respond effectively if the prosperous conditions of the golden age suddenly ended.[56]

Boston College and the Limits of Progress
Within a Nonacademic Structure

The development of Boston College in the 1950s was aided by the provincial's eagerness to build a regional Jesuit university. In this context, the order's authoritarian structures were an asset. Maxwell, who was selected as rector-president because of his abilities as an academic leader, was allowed administrative latitude and was able to use his extensive powers to move quickly on key priorities—expansion, campus construction, revival of doctoral programs, and tightening of admission standards.

At the same time, however, the increasing numbers of lay faculty were altering the organizational environment. The secretive, hierarchical patterns of decision making that were acceptable to Jesuit faculty were problematic for their nonclerical colleagues. The 1953 self-study reported a quite un-Jesuit "dissatisfaction" because the faculty "was not always sufficiently informed of decisions and plans" and because "enquiries and suggestions . . . were not easily brought to the President's attention." The self-study recommended "greater participation" of the faculty in administrative affairs.

From Maxwell's perspective, the pressures emanating from the lay faculty contained benefits as well as difficulties. He saw that the presence of secular professionals could be used to justify policies associated with mainstream institutions, and he carefully balanced clerical and lay appointments to key committees, while also including Jesuits who shared his goals. The value of this approach was evident in the emphasis of the 1953 self-study on judging B.C. by the standards of secular accrediting associations as well as those of the order. Accommodation to lay expectations was also apparent in the adoption of conventional procedures for academic personnel decisions.[57]

Walsh, impatient with the slow pace of intellectual progress under Maxwell, was even more aggressive than his predecessor in promoting the laicization of the B.C. faculty. He was convinced that this was the only way to upgrade his campus, partially because he could control lay appointments but faced interference from the order when it came to Jesuits. Walsh understood that in recruiting a research-oriented, professionally trained, lay faculty, as well as in seeking academically ambitious students on a national basis, he was building powerful forces for change into his community.

Walsh's attitude was evident during discussions of undergraduate curriculum revision in the arts and sciences in the middle 1960s. Despite his Jesuit and Catholic loyalties, he quietly welcomed the initiatives taken by both lay faculty and students to reform B.C.'s long-standing requirements in philosophy and theology—including scandalously irreverent attacks on these courses in the student newspaper. Walsh also realized that the changes he was promoting required modification of the university's governance processes, and he took steps to provide a greater role for faculty in institutional affairs, while retaining the key powers of the presidency. Early in his term, for example, he created a Faculty Council composed of elected representatives from each school that was authorized to meet with the president four times a year to discuss a broad array of issues. He also created a University Planning Committee composed of deans and faculty members to write a ten-year plan for B.C.

Walsh was not eager to give away real power, however, and his steps toward participatory governance were minimal. The new Council had no specified role, and faculty committees continued to be appointed by Walsh independent of the Council and responsible only to him. He was careful, in fact, to appoint to the University Planning Committee individuals not likely to impede his own activities greatly. The committee operated for three years, issued long, diffuse, and inconclusive reports, and had no discernible impact. Walsh also retained the right to appoint deans and department chairs without consultation.[58]

Such broad presidential powers helped Walsh move efficiently on his own agenda, just as they had aided his predecessor, but he also realized that they could not be sustained. Internally, the faculty was not going to be satisfied over time with the half measures he had provided for their involvement. In fact, the 1964 self-study report in Arts and Sciences called for a more formalized faculty role in policy-making as well as elective procedures for choosing chairs and faculty committees. Externally, the university's relationship to the order was increasingly problematic. Walsh was impressed, for example, by the difficulties of managing the debate on undergraduate curriculum reform in an organizational context that ultimately required him to obtain approval of major changes from the general in Rome, though this entire review process was hidden from and unknown to his lay faculty.

By the mid-1960s, Walsh had come to agree with Gannon's observation that a Jesuit university could not achieve excellence within the confines of the order. He was not alone among Jesuit academics in this judgment. Indeed, in 1964 a group of Jesuit college presidents, many of them sharing Walsh's perspective, met at the Woodstock Theologate in Maryland, under the auspices of the J.E.A., to discuss organizational changes that could enhance the intellectual possibilities of their campuses. By this time, Father Paul C. Reinert, rector-president of the University of St. Louis and a prime mover in the effort to upgrade Jesuit universities, had succeeded Rooney as executive director of the association.

One approach that won wide support at the conference was the transfer of formal control of Jesuit schools from the order to lay boards of trustees. Such a change, it was felt, could be reconciled with retention of dominant influence by Jesuits—though not by the nonacademic Jesuit hierarchy—if strategically located positions could be reserved for members of the order, including presidencies, provostships, and chairs of philosophy departments. The times seemed ripe for this kind of change. The election of John XXIII to the papacy and the revolutionary recommendations of the second Vatican Council between 1962 and 1965 were inspiring broad movement to modernize the church, and a similar spirit led to the election of Father Pedro Arrupe as general of the Society of Jesus in 1965.

The moment of opportunity for Reinert, Walsh, and their colleagues came in 1966 when the general summoned the order's leaders to Rome for a General Congregation. The agenda called for a wide-ranging review of Jesuit activities, including higher education in the United States. Within the American delegation were a number of college presidents, and this group, led by Reinert, engineered approval of the new model of university organization developed at Woodstock. Jesuit universities could now be turned over to lay boards of trustees and the Jesuit communities that traditionally had owned and operated them would then be "separately incorporated"—constituted as independent entities, related to but distinct from the universities where they taught.[59]

The recommendations of the General Congregation triggered intense discussion and controversy within the New England Jesuit community. Holy Cross moved at once to adopt the new organizational form, and a regional task force recommended that Boston College and Fairfield follow suit. Walsh was delighted, and in 1968 he drafted new bylaws for B.C. creating a self-perpetuating Board of Trustees dominated by lay members but including some Jesuits to be appointed not from B.C. but from the national Jesuit community. Implementation of the new bylaws would constitute a crucial final step in the arduous process of freeing B.C. from structural constraints that, in Walsh's view, had long impeded its progress.

By 1968, however, Walsh was tired, in poor health, and eager to leave the presidency. He hesitated to press for separate incorporation unless he was ready to see it through. He was aware of strong resistance to change within the Jesuit community at B.C., and he was probably concerned also about the potential impact of a disruptive transition on the university's relations with its alumni/ae, whose support had been crucial to his fund-raising efforts. He elected to leave the task of establishing a new organization to his successor.

In characteristic style, however, Walsh took a step intended to guarantee eventual movement in his preferred direction. In his last year, he endorsed the creation of a new Academic Senate with full powers to involve itself in all university affairs. Faced with a governance body that inevitably would contain large numbers of the lay professional faculty that Walsh had been recruiting, the new rector-president would be hard-pressed to reconcile the requirements of the Jesuit hierarchy with those of his academic constituents. In fact, four years after Walsh's retirement, B.C. granted formal control of the university to a lay Board of Trustees.[60]

The Relationship of Organizational Structure to Academic Change

The histories of B.U., Northeastern, and B.C. during the golden age suggest two broad conclusions about the relationship between organizational form and academic progress. The first is that the characteristics commonly associated with elite universities—institutional autonomy, decentralization of internal authority, and the presence of a strong academic culture—do constitute a compelling model of university organization at the highest levels of scholarly achievement. B.U.'s independence was an evident asset in allowing quick responses to the shifting conditions of the postwar years, just as B.C.'s ties to the Jesuit order ultimately limited its progress. The broad direction of change at these institutions, as they sought to improve their academic positions, was toward greater autonomy supported by financial independence. Similarly, in other aspects of their organizations, these universities evolved toward structures and forms generally associated with leading universities. By the late 1960s, these three urban universities, having begun the postwar period with markedly different structures and cultures, had developed similar practices in most important areas of administration.

A second conclusion from these institutional accounts is that the relationships between organizational form and academic progress is complex and contextual. No easy formula for connecting the two emerges from these histories. The link between decentralized forms of decision making and academic development was especially variable. At Boston University, decentralization proved effective in promoting entrepreneurial growth, particularly in the early postwar years, but became a barrier to academic upgrading in the 1960s. At Northeastern, Knowles introduced some decentralization at an early stage to aid recruitment and induce his faculty to behave in a professional manner. Here, as at B.U., decentralization was more successful in promoting growth and programmatic initiatives than in raising quality. At B.C., by contrast, Walsh and Maxwell used the central powers inherent in their position to accelerate the change process in qualitative terms, and decentralization emerged toward the end of the period as a strengthened faculty pressed Walsh for more power.

The key variable in determining the role of centralized or decentralized forms of decision making involved the goals and culture of a particular campus. Decentralization proved capable of either promoting growth or quality depending on the nature of the faculty. Thus, while a decentralized system represented the ultimate organizational tendency of upwardly mobile universities, the steps by which an individual campus reached that point could involve an extended period of centralized control or, more likely, successive periods of centralization and decentralization depending on the school's stage of development as well as its strategy of change.

The Irony of the Urban University

Rethinking Withdrawal from the City
in the 1960s: B.U. and B.C.

Development policies at Boston University and Boston College during the golden age entailed a progressive deemphasis of historical ties to the city of Boston. This was inevitable given the focus of both campuses on raising institutional standing, since local service and academic status were antithetical values. Thus, as tuitions increased and out-of-state and suburban students replaced urban commuters, as curricular emphases shifted from occupational subjects to the arts and sciences and from the undergraduate to the graduate level, and as faculties became more cosmopolitan and professional, the bonds that historically had connected these universities to the city grew fewer and weaker.

In the mid-1960s, the movement away from Boston intersected with the sudden revival of interest, nationally and locally, in urban issues, especially conditions in minority communities. The pull toward involvement in social problem solving that was apparent at Tufts and Brandeis and even Pusey's Harvard was felt with particular poignancy at B.U. and B.C. where, for decades, campus leaders had prided themselves on service to the local population—and where local support remained critical for continued development. In this context, both Case and Walsh took steps to revitalize the ties to Boston that recent changes had diminished.

In 1965 Case created a new administrative entity, called "Metrocenter," to coordinate all of B.U.'s educational, research, and service functions "that directly related to the community." Though many of these activities brought B.U. into direct interaction with the city and its neighborhoods, Case emphasized that these involvements did not make Boston University a local institution. "It should be emphasized," he wrote,

> that our concern with the community is not restricted to Boston alone; rather, as an urban university, we are interested in urban life in general, in the phenomenon of the city as the life-sphere of Americans. Through our experience and research, wherever undertaken, we will make discoveries that would be applicable . . . across the country.

In this passage, Case found a formula for reconciling B.U.'s progressive disengagement from Boston itself with the impulse to affirm a role as an urban university: B.U. would use its location in Boston as an educational resource to help students gain insight into contemporary life, while also taking advantage of local surroundings to conduct policy-oriented research. This conception, which turned Boston into a laboratory to be used by the university rather than a sponsoring community to be served by it, was repeated again and again in the self-study that Case initiated during his last two years. The Bolman–de Capriles consulting report, for example, while urging B.U. to move even more aggressively toward an identity as a national, research, and graduate-oriented institution, suggested that the university think of Boston as "a vast variety of laboratory resources for intensive study and research and also for creative experimentation."

The final self-study report sounded the same theme. Pointing out that, despite the changes of the postwar years, B.U. remained linked to Boston much more closely than most other universities in the area, the report recommended that B.U. think of itself as "of the city, in the city, but not limited by or subservient to the city." In the view of the report's authors, B.U. should

> capitalize upon the opportunities that Greater Boston presents educationally for students not only from New England but across the country, for faculty as a cooperative education center and research laboratory, for the community of the University as a field of service, study and change . . . In responding to its urban context the first purpose of Boston University, then, is not to serve the practical and vocational needs of the local area but to serve the larger society and to explore the realms of basic research.[61]

While Case and his colleagues at B.U. were articulating a new conception of the urban university in the mid-1960s, Walsh was struggling with the realization that his policies were decreasing B.C.'s role in assisting the city's Catholic community that had nurtured the campus for a century and from which he himself had come. Concern about this trend was not new at Boston College. Indeed, throughout his term, Walsh was criticized by members of the Jesuit community on the Heights for abandoning the university's traditional mission in Boston. The University Planning Committee, for example, urged him to keep the evening law program open as "a valuable community service" and also advocated a limit on dormitory construction in recognition of B.C.'s "primary obligation to local students." In the early days of his presidency, Walsh was intent on academic upgrading and brushed such recommendations aside.

By the mid-1960s, however, his reawakened concern for B.C.'s "apostolic" functions combined with the mood of the times to reorder his priorities. In his final years, Walsh tried to direct institutional attention back to the city. He moved the School of Social Work to the Heights and added faculty to the school's budget. He sponsored an Institute for Human Sciences in which scholars would conduct research on urban problems. By this time, however, Walsh's presidency was drawing to an end, and the pattern of change that he had encouraged had moved beyond his control. He had no interest, moreover, in returning B.C. to anything like its earlier, locally oriented function. Unlike Knowles at Northeastern, Walsh actively supported the opening of a Boston campus for the University of Massachusetts since he knew it would serve students of the type that once had relied on B.C.

In the years following Walsh's departure, B.C.'s retreat from Boston, especially in terms of the student body, accelerated beyond anything he had imagined. The Institute for Human Sciences never established itself as a viable entity and was dropped by his successor. In the mid-1970s, Walsh accompanied B.C.'s president to the Mellon Foundation, then headed by Nathan Pusey, to appeal for funds under a program for urban universities. Pusey told Walsh that B.C. was not a credible applicant and that Northeastern had replaced Boston College as the university in Boston most actively involved in the life of the city. The incident was painful to Walsh, but he did not dispute Pusey's characterization.[62]

Staying on Course at Northeastern

Nathan Pusey was not alone in seeing Northeastern as the university in Boston that had done most to maintain its tradition of local service. In 1969, when the Carnegie commission sponsored a study of urban universities, its consultants selected N.U. as one of four private institutions nationally that were models of community involvement. The choice was clearly appropriate and was based less on specific responses to the political and social atmosphere of the mid-1960s than on the essential character of the campus. Far more than B.U. and B.C., N.U. continued to enroll local, commuting students from modest backgrounds. Far more than they, it continued to key its programs to the interests of area students and the character of the metropolitan economy rather than to academic conceptions of what would be most interesting or prestigious. Cooperative education continued to provide a means by which students could work their way through college while also gaining practical experience and entrance into the occupational world.

Northeastern was also active, however, in sponsoring Boston-oriented projects during years when public service became a priority on many campuses. Among these were a special school for high school dropouts, a community school in the South End, special courses for community groups and workers through the Center for Continuing Education, and a training program for inner-city teachers. Knowles was credited by faculty, students, and city residents for his responsiveness to local concerns. The praise extended to the growing population of black students, whom N.U. began to recruit actively in 1964 through scholarships funded by the Ford Foundation. Between 1966 and 1971 black enrollments at N.U. increased from 2.7 percent to 10.6 percent. Knowles endorsed the students' demands for an Afro-American Institute and a black studies program, and won trustee support for the institute even though the program was defeated in the Senate because of student insistence on controlling the curriculum.[63]

In stressing the importance of local involvement, Knowles was not to be understood simply as an idealist dedicated to Northeastern's traditional values. Doubtless, that was part of it. He believed in helping young people of modest means to obtain a useful education. He also understood, however, the strategic importance of Boston as well as the campus's immediate neighborhoods to his university—his dependence on the city for enrollments, money, and political support on issues like physical expansion. His worries about the threat to his local position posed by UMass/Boston undoubtedly contributed to his sense of urgency on these issues. Finally, Knowles understood how to exploit Northeastern's special qualities during years when foundations and government agencies were eager to fund projects addressed to urban problems. His remark to the interviewers from the Carnegie commission perfectly suggested his combination of dedication and managerial shrewdness:

> I have always felt that Northeastern should take the leadership in providing whatever services we could to the local community. Now the rest of the universities in Boston—Harvard, Boston University and Boston College—are getting on the bandwagon because they know that is where the money is.

The question that hovered around Northeastern's policies in the 1960s involved their durability. Other universities, starting with Harvard, had begun as local institutions and followed a path of increasing national influence and decreasing focus on the region as time went on and their prestige increased. B.U. and B.C. were only the latest universities to pursue this well-trodden path. Now Northeastern, the youngest private university in the city, had begun, under Knowles's guidance, to seek regional and national status in select areas and to recruit residential students from beyond the immediate area. Whether Northeastern in the 1960s was simply at an early point on a curve of mobility that would ultimately lead it, as it had led others, away from the local community, or whether, by contrast, it would remain dedicated to serving Boston as a continuing aspect of its culture, only future events would reveal. The precedents clearly suggested the former scenario. For the moment, however, Knowles and his campus deserved the praise they received for their contributions to the city. They were, as the authors of the Carnegie study put it, "a private university serving the urban proletariat."[64]

The Good Times End

Patterns of Change and Patterns of Disruption

If the end of the golden age on each campus can be defined as that moment when the atmosphere of relatively untroubled development and institutional self-confidence that was widespread in the 1950s and 1960s was superceded by new and problematic realities, then the final scenes of the period were quite different for Boston's three private urban universities. Boston College, in the years following Walsh's retirement, erupted in turmoil that drove his successor, Father W. Seavey Joyce, from office. The search for Joyce's replacement was informed by an urgent sense that B.C. was in trouble. Boston University encountered less turbulence, but the stresses of the period were sufficient to persuade Christ-Janer to leave after only two and a half years. B.U.'s confrontation with the precariousness of its position occurred most dramatically, however, not in the events surrounding Christ-Janer's resignation but in the process of choosing his successor. In that search, and especially in seeing themselves through the eyes of their ultimate selection, John Silber, the leadership of B.U. faced up to the need for significant change. At Northeastern, the durable Knowles rode out the tensions of the late 1960s and early 1970s with only moderate disruption of campus life.

To some extent, the severity of difficulties experienced by a particular campus during the time of troubles was a matter of chance: the presence of specific individuals in key positions—among students, faculty, or administration—could make a crucial difference in the nature of a protest incident. As we have seen in the cases of Harvard, M.I.T., Tufts, and Brandeis, however, the manner in which the tumultuous potentials of the period became manifest expressed much about the character of a school and about the manner in which it had evolved during the golden age.

Such a pattern was present among Boston's urban universities also. The institution that had taken the greatest risks in development and had pushed most forcefully to change itself—Boston College—hit bottom hardest. The university that stayed closest to its traditions—Northeastern—found its way through the period most smoothly. The campus that was least self-conscious about its position—Boston University—needed an outsider to articulate its circumstances clearly. To note these facts is not to offer an encomium to conservative leadership, since present dislocation can be the price of future progress; it is only to observe an order in events that often seemed, at the time of their occurrence, quite random.

Crash Landing at Boston College

The general and provincial had difficulty replacing Walsh. The possibilities were limited, since the successor had to be a Jesuit and preferably a member of the New England province. Walsh himself saw no obvious candidates and made no recommendation when asked. The selection of Joyce, Walsh's vice president for community relations and a former dean of the College of Business Administration, suggested an impulse toward continuity on the part of the hierarchy.

Like his predecessor, Joyce was a Boston boy who grew up in the order as the reform movement gathered momentum during the 1940s. He was also a product of the Special Studies Program, having completed a doctorate at Harvard, and joined the B.C. faculty shortly after World War II. He first achieved public notice in the 1950s as founder of the Citizen Seminars, then added to his reputation during his years in the vice presidency, though Walsh himself did not think Joyce was effective. The new president's goal was to build B.C. into "the outstanding Catholic university in the United States," an objective that Walsh would have endorsed readily, and the chief programmatic change of Joyce's years was also continuous with the recent past—the addition of six doctorates.

There were some differences of emphasis between the two men. Joyce was more eager than Walsh to foster a sense of B.C. as religion-centered, and he made the campus fully coeducational, something Walsh had opposed strongly. Joyce was more cautious than Walsh about lay control. He was ready for change but not for separate incorporation. When asked about his hopes for

B.C. following his resignation, he stressed that he had wanted to give the campus "a sense of class, of style," that he felt was lacking.[65]

Joyce's presidency never took root. Assuming office in the summer of 1968, the most difficult of times for academic administrators, he found himself embroiled in controversy and mired in administrative problems from the beginning. Much of the trouble stemmed from the same mix of national and local grievances that fueled student disruptions on many campuses. These elements were compounded at B.C. by conflict within the church and order arising from the reforms of Pope John XXIII, by the fact that B.C. had little experience of rambunctiousness in campus politics, and by Joyce's lack of agility in managing crises. B.C.'s alumni/ae were not accustomed to reading headlines in the local press reporting radical and disruptive student behavior at their alma mater or to seeing the student newspaper engaged in continuing, vitriolic attacks on campus leaders. Yet stories of both kinds became routine during Joyce's presidency, beginning with a series of incidents triggered by the tenure review of feminist author Mary Daly in the spring of 1969.

Joyce's task was made more difficult by the existence of untested or inadequate governance structures at every level. The administrative apparatus he inherited from Walsh was weak and unprofessional, heavily dependent on untrained Jesuits. This system worked well enough during the good times of the golden age under a skillful leader but proved inadequate, under the more stressful circumstances of the Joyce years, to compensate for the president's administrative limitations. For instance, the Senate that Walsh had created at the end of his term presented an opportunity for faculty, long denied a means to participate in policy-making, to air complaints. An expansion of the number of student senators at the beginning of Joyce's term enhanced the potential of this body for contentiousness.

While he was learning to live with a new source of advice and pressure from below, Joyce was also coping with a revised, and inherently problematic, supervisory structure. As an alternative to the full transfer of control to a lay board, Joyce established a two-tier system which granted broad powers of campus oversight to a Board of Directors, composed of both Jesuits and lay appointees, but reserved for the Jesuit members, as a separate Board of Trustees, certain crucial powers, including the selection of the president and the appointment of trustees and directors.[66]

The main substantive problem for Joyce—and one that aggravated his other difficulties—was financial. B.C. had prospered under Walsh, but the former president made little provision for a rainy day. On the contrary, his policies, especially in the area of faculty recruitment, workload, and compensation, stored up difficulties for the future, and Joyce was not the kind of skilled fiscal manager who could husband an overextended campus toward a secure financial future. The small deficit of fiscal year 1968 turned into large shortfalls in fiscal years 1969 and 1970 and Joyce had few places to turn for help. Despite his ties to the business community, he was not adept at fund-raising. The alumni/ae, on whom Walsh relied for the largest share of his gift income, grew less enthusiastic about contributing as campus tensions continued. The lay directors were not yet a strong enough group to provide major assistance, and Joyce's appeals to them produced limited results. Annual giving actually declined between Walsh's last year and Joyce's first, declined again between fiscal years 1969 and 1970, and then rebounded somewhat in fiscal years 1971 and 1972.

With no ready alternative and severely pressured for money, Joyce fell back on charges to students. In the fall of 1968, his first semester in office, he announced a 25 percent tuition increase, and this was followed by additional raises in each of the next two years. Enrollments were expanded to gain further income, especially in the fall of 1970, when the Joyce administration's aggressiveness in adding numbers produced an embarrassing housing crisis, forcing B.C. to erect modular dormitories on short notice. The effort to increase income was complemented with new economies, including a hiring freeze in fiscal years 1971 and 1972 and a salary freeze in the latter year. The 1960s were over at B.C.[67]

By Joyce's second year, a combination of factors—the difficulties of the times, new and untested governance structures, student and faculty dissatisfaction over sudden financial pressures, and Joyce's lack of political skill— proved a recipe for explosion. It came in the spring of 1970 in the form of a student strike to protest Joyce's second tuition hike. In temporarily bringing campus operations to a halt, this event focused the attention of both Joyce himself and his superiors on his shortcomings as a campus leader. Joyce's own doubts were manifest in his comment that he experienced "genuine terror" one night as a "mob" of shouting students approached his residence. In December, the provincial relieved him of the duties of rector, thus denying him a vital source of respect—and authority—within the Jesuit community.

In the succeeding months, Joyce tried to regain momentum through the appointment of a Priorities Committee of faculty, students, and administrators charged to draft a plan of development for the 1970s. Though the work of the committee generated much interest on campus, by this time Joyce's presidency was probably beyond saving. Another protest incident in December 1971 forced him to use police to clear a building, an action that contradicted everything he believed he was working for. The next month, under pressure from his board that he had no will to resist, Joyce submitted his resignation, which was promptly accepted.[68]

Boston University Confronts Its Position

The perception that B.U. was fundamentally sound but needful of incremental improvements, common among campus leaders at the time of Christ-Janer's appointment, was sustained during his brief presidency. His initial reports conveyed his own adherence to this view. He called for greater efforts in various directions—more research productivity and more direct involvement with the city—without predicting problems or ringing alarms. He initiated yet another university-wide planning exercise but gave it no clear direction. As anticipated, he proved adept at handling disruptive student behavior, and he guided his university through a series of incidents that, in less skillful hands, might have become much more problematic.

By his third year, he was generally thought to be doing a good job. As much as was possible in the 1960s, the students and faculty liked him, and while some alumni/ae and trustees complained about his conciliatory tendencies with students, the trustees as a group were satisfied. He even seemed to be enjoying himself. His sudden announcement in January 1970 that he wished to leave caught everyone by surprise. Subsequent accounts have not fully explained his motives, though the stresses of his job clearly had taken a toll. The conventional wisdom was that he simply burned out.[69]

B.U.'s trustees now found themselves looking for an executive under less auspicious circumstances than had existed three years earlier. Across the nation, student protests had turned the college presidency into a high-risk office. The structural problems identified by Case's self-study in the mid-1960s had become even more apparent. High on the list was money. In September 1970, Treasurer Perkins would put the matter bluntly:

> We are on a collision course . . . Last year our educational income went up 5%; our educational expenses went up 18%. It appears . . . that we must have $5 million of new current money each year just to stay even. The overriding question, of course, is how long we can obtain this needed amount by increasing tuition rates . . . One thing is certain—what worked in the 60s won't work in the 70s . . . If we don't come up with the answers, the 70s are going to be a rough ten years financially.

To make matters worse, the Boston campus of the University of Massachusetts was now a competitive reality, so the importance of academic progress was apparent. Indeed, members of the search committee—which included faculty and students for the first time in B.U's history—readily agreed that their campus "had reached a crossroads" and that "their task went well beyond filling a vacancy. It was to find someone who could lead Boston University to levels of strength and excellence the school had never known before." The committee also concluded that the university's leaders had established no clear definition of the changes that were needed or how they might be achieved. A *Life* reporter who followed the search closely summarized the committee's view: B.U. "appeared ready to take off, but it was uncertain where it should go . . . . It lacked even purposes to examine or goals to redefine." The committee accepted as its own task, and that of the president they were about to select, the imagining of Boston University's future.[70]

The early stages of the search proceeded routinely, and by the late spring of 1970, the committee agreed upon a candidate, only to be turned down after a month of negotiations. At this point, Christ-Janer left and was replaced on a temporary basis by one of the committee's own members, Dr. Calvin B. T. Lee, the young dean of Liberal Arts who had been one of the most effective participants in the search. During the summer and fall, Lee quickly established himself as an energetic leader and a plausible candidate for the permanent position.

Meanwhile, however, the committee was in contact with Silber, the controversial former dean at the University of Texas, who had achieved national visibility during a protracted battle with the Texas Board of Regents. To some members, Silber seemed a compelling possibility. He was a brilliant academic—a philosopher—who dazzled even his faculty interviewers with his intellect. His leadership qualities were obvious, and he had achieved a reputation as an effective administrator. After an astonishingly brief period of acquaintance with B.U., he offered persuasive, imaginative ideas about how the campus should develop. He was, however, aggressive and blunt to the point of rudeness, even brutality. He flaunted his congenital disability—a withered arm—in a way that seemed calculated to make others uncomfortable. He made no attempt to reinforce perceptions that B.U. was academically solid. On the contrary, he challenged faculty members on the committee about the quality of their departments.

Initially Silber's manner alienated most of the committee, especially the students. As the talks continued, however, his abrasiveness came to represent intellectual excellence—something all members felt was essential in the next president.[71]

By late fall, the committee had reduced its options to Silber and Lee. Both men seemed capable of doing the job. The choice was effectively between two views of the university, and for most members Silber fit the situation best. One of the students summarized the alternatives precisely: "Dr. Lee will take us slowly and carefully wherever we have to go. Dr. Silber will pick us up and throw us—and I'm afraid we need to be picked up and thrown." This assessment of Lee seemed fair. He told a student reporter that the next president would face two major issues—proposed changes in the university's governance system and the state of the current tenure process. These were not the priorities of a man inclined toward radical change.

Silber clearly was. Indeed, before the search ended the Texan provided his future colleagues with an unvarnished preview of his intentions. The committee's leading candidate was invited to meet the full board the evening before their final vote. The *Life* reporter provided the following account:

> Silber's speech was lucid and so blunt that it seemed calculated to offend every sensibility in the room. Boston University, he said, is an ugly place. He didn't like the looks of it and he meant to change it. Turning to a giant scratchpad . . . he described his vision of [the] future—a multilevel, multi-million dollar complex, with buildings rising from decks over streets and avenues.
>
> Switching to finances, Silber noted that BU's budget was in balance . . . but that this had been accomplished at the expense of educational excellence. BU might be in the black financially, but it was in the red educationally. And it wouldn't be able to get by much longer, even the way it was going. BU, he said, was a patient near to death, and he, Silber, was the surgeon who had been called in to see whether the patient could be saved . . .
>
> . . . the only way was to make BU competitive, which meant raising standards, hiring more faculty and making it a great teaching institution. It would have to happen almost overnight. He planned, he said to go out right away and

hire 30 of the finest teaching professors he could find, and hire more the next year, and the year after that, until he had about 200 . . .

Silber paused. He had arrived at his two conditions for coming. First, he said, he wanted a free hand to speculate with BU's unrestricted endowment . . . They might, of course, lose every penny of it, but this was a necessary gamble . . . secondly, he wanted the trustees to approve an immediate deficit of $1.5 million to pay the professors he was going to hire, and be prepared for bigger deficits in the future. He expected the trustees to get busy and start raising money . . . to dip into their own private fortunes if need be . . .

He wanted it clearly understood, Silber said in closing, that they didn't owe him the presidency at this stage and he didn't owe them an acceptance . . . If they weren't prepared to make a commitment, it would be a mistake for him to come. But if they were, he would be honored to be their president.

The trustees and search committee members, hearing this, could have reconsidered their preference for Silber if they had disputed the self-styled "surgeon's" diagnosis or prescription. In deciding, the following morning, to offer him the presidency, the leaders of B.U. faced up to the fact that they had been living on borrowed time academically and financially for too long.[72]

The Steadiness of Northeastern

Unlike B.C. and B.U., Northeastern encountered the political turmoil of the late 1960s unburdened by urgent questions of institutional strategy. The financial pressures of these years inevitably affected N.U., as they did most universities, but they were far less worrisome to Knowles, who had kept costs low during the years of growth, than to Joyce, whose campus had become accustomed to sharp rises in expenditures, or Silber, who believed B.U.'s future required major budgetary growth. Northeastern experienced even fewer problems in the areas of applications and enrollments, despite the opening of the University of Massachusetts at Boston. In fact, Knowles's apprehensions about UMass/Boston diminished in the late 1960s as the new public campus focused on fields—especially the arts and sciences—of secondary interest to N.U.' and chose a location on the southern edge of the city, less convenient to commuters than Huntington Avenue.

The key to Northeastern's stability was Knowles's dedication to maintaining the distinctive, circumscribed functions of his campus while also upgrading it. His rigid adherence to the co-op format in new programs kept N.U. competitive with the expanding public sector, though increased state scholarships—for which Knowles lobbied actively—also helped. His emphasis on occupational fields built on his campus's substantive strengths as well as its credibility in a specialized segment of the educational market. His insistence on examining new initiatives as much in fiscal as academic terms maintained N.U.'s pay-as-you-go tradition. Far from burdening Northeastern's budget as financial conditions worsened, the programs begun by Knowles in the 1960s allowed the campus to maintain its expanded scale of operations. In 1972 a third of N.U.'s entering freshmen chose majors that did not exist ten years earlier. Knowles's policies were less academically ambitious than those of Walsh or even Case, but they proved more durable in practical terms when the environment shifted.[73]

Strategic resilience could not guarantee political calm, however, and Northeastern experienced its share of student protests and faculty politics in the late 1960s. Student activism revolved around three issues—campus life, minorities, and the war in Vietnam. Between 1967 and 1972, there were a series of major incidents, including two large demonstrations linked to the war that involved the use of police, the issuance of a restraining order against the campus chapter of Students for a Democratic Society, and, during the Kent State–Cambodia demonstrations in the spring of 1970, a voluntary moratorium on classes.

The politics of these years often brought faculty members, including Senate majorities, into the field on the side of protesting students and revealed how much Northeastern had changed during its years of growth. Activist leaders, both students and faculty, frequently came from liberal arts departments traditionally considered marginal at N.U., a fact that stirred resentment among campus veterans. At the same time, the balance of numbers in favor of engineering and business served to constrain disruptive activities. A student poll in 1967–1968 showed a narrow majority in favor of government policies in Vietnam and overwhelming numbers supporting open recruitment by employers. When campus radicals mounted an attack on the R.O.T.C., nearly two thousand students petitioned the administration to retain it. Knowles himself, temperamentally and philosophically aligned with the conservative side of these divisions, privately fumed at much of the behavior he encountered in these years.

Despite such feelings, Knowles and his trustees honored Northeastern's traditions of pragmatism and flexibility and found ways through the crises with minimum disruption to campus operations. N.U.'s archaic rules governing campus life—no parietals in the dorms and a strict dress code—were modified with little fuss as soon as students organized against them. In repeated encounters with African-American students, Knowles offered positive and substantive responses—increased admissions, more financial aid, and new programs—with the net effect of strengthening Northeastern's links to the black community.

Demands for expanded roles by students and faculty in university affairs presented more complex problems. Although Knowles had advocated increased faculty participation in governance at the beginning of his term, he also believed, as he put it, that "when faculty and students become involved excessively in administrative matters, the institution tends to become stagnant." His approach to pressures for governance reform was to craft mechanisms that permitted participation while protecting the formal powers of the hierarchy. He opposed seats for students and faculty on the Board of Trustees. He persuaded his board, however, to create committees on student affairs and academic affairs as vehicles for communication with key constituencies. A new

President's Advisory Council dominated by students and faculty served a similar function within the administration.[74]

The atmosphere of N.U. was altered at least as much by the new fiscal and demographic concerns of the early 1970s as by the social turmoil of the late 1960s. While Northeastern avoided a crisis, it was clear by 1970 that the years of rapid growth were over. In his report for that year, Knowles stressed the need for economies in the face of new financial pressures and warned against increasing the burdens on students. Enrollments also stopped growing. In this context, the Senate, having grown more active during the late 1960s, sought new ways to protect faculty interests, especially by broadening their role in tenure decisions. Knowles and his trustees, equally apprehensive, pressed in the opposite direction. In 1972 the board established a limit of 60 percent on the proportion of faculty who could be tenured in any college. Additional conflicts arose over fringe benefits and salary increases.

The problematic dynamic continued: the administration trying to control costs, the Senate pressing for more information and power sharing. "By the fall of 1972," Knowles's biographer notes, "faculty-administration relationships had reached a point, it not of crisis, then of ever increasing tension." The tensions would continue in succeeding years, defining a new era at Northeastern and fostering a movement to unionize the faculty. In these stresses, as in those of the late 1960s, Knowles would demonstrate his flexibility and staying power, but he also wearied of the battles. As early as March 1973, he told his trustees that he was ready to leave. They prevailed upon him to remain until 1975, however, to complete the Diamond Anniversary Development Program and allow time for an orderly transfer of power to a successor.[75]

✴ CHAPTER SIX ✴

From State College to University System: The University of Massachusetts, 1945–1973

The conditions of the golden age liberated Massachusetts State College from the forces that had restricted its development since the nineteenth century. In spurts of growth linked to demographic and political cycles, M.S.C. mushroomed from a limited-purpose college into a comprehensive university and from a single campus in Amherst into a multicampus system, with units in Worcester and Boston and a statewide president's office. By the end of the period, UMass seemed finally to have joined its counterparts in western states as a full-fledged public university in the land grant tradition, with strong programs of graduate education and research built on a large undergraduate base and linked to public service activities of applied research and nondegree instruction.

The evolutionary process remained incomplete, however, and Massachusetts was still Massachusetts. The state's nonelite private institutions watched the public expansion nervously and organized to protect their interests. Other components of the public system, including the state colleges and a new network of community colleges, vied for support from an intensely politicized government still unsure of its role in higher education.

The Early Postwar Years

Wartime Planning for Postwar Development

Though the effort during the 1930s to transform Massachusetts State College into a full public university had ended in failure when the General Court shelved the enabling legislation, the university movement had gained important ground. In particular, by the end of the prewar decade, the loose coalition of students, alumni/ae, and organized labor that had kept the movement alive had stirred public interest and won support from the college's trustees as well as its president, Hugh Potter Baker.

Baker himself, with his roots in the scientific-technical traditions of land grant education, had been slow to endorse a broadened conception of his institution but once converted had become an eloquent and persistent advocate. Believing, despite his disappointment over the legislature's inaction, that World War II would foster increased interest in higher education and create new opportunities for M.S.C., Baker used his annual reports during the war to reiterate the central arguments of the university movement: that, in comparison with other states, Massachusetts was not providing adequate support for public higher education; that demand for places at the college far exceeded enrollment capacity; that the region's private institutions were not prepared to respond to the need; and that large numbers of Massachusetts residents were being forced to attend public universities in other states. In 1943, as progress of the Allied military effort foretold the return of peace, Baker wrote:

> If there ever has been a time in the history of the College when all having responsibility for its present activities and its future work should plan and work for an increase in both staff and physical facilities to the end that the College may meet its obligations to the public and the Commonwealth . . . it is now.

Early in the war, Baker began preparing for the opportunities he envisioned in the postwar period. By 1941 a faculty committee on postwar planning was formed. A survey of students and alumni in the armed forces was conducted to determine future areas of educational need. Baker himself devoted attention to the task of imagining the institution that might take shape in the postwar period. Not surprisingly, the plans that emerged from these activities called for the transformation of the old agricultural college into a proper state university. The divisional system of organization, under which the liberal arts and the sciences were housed in two separate schools—a relic of M.S.C.'s past as an agricultural college—was to be abandoned, and the campus was to be reorganized on the university pattern: a college of liberal arts surrounded by professional schools.

The range of professional offerings, moreover, was to be expanded, chiefly by building on established areas of strength. The program in rural engineering would provide the basis for a new school of engineering, a field of interest to the students surveyed during the war; traditional work in agricultural education would evolve into a broadened program of teacher preparation; animal husbandry would lead to a new school of veterinary medicine; and the School of Home Economics would be expanded to include nursing. At the same time, the social sciences would be upgraded to parallel the college's traditional strength in physical science, and an entirely new school of business administration would be organized. Baker and his colleagues even envisioned more extensive work in graduate education and research, though these functions, still closely tied to the college's traditional focus on science and agriculture, did not receive central attention. In connection with the planned changes, Baker and his associates considered it essential to increase the size of the instructional staff, raise faculty salaries to competitive levels, and expand facilities.[1]

The veterans' education program provided the first confirmation that Baker was right in anticipating new interest in public higher education after the war. Indeed, by 1943, well before the national government passed the G.I. Bill, Baker understood that the need to educate returning soldiers would create important leverage for the movement to upgrade the stage college. "It will be tragic," he told readers of his annual report, "if the thousands of Massachusetts men and women who are now in the armed services shall be forced to secure their educational experiences in state colleges and universities in other states because . . . the facilities of this college are not expanded." In 1944 a special planning committee on veterans' programs completed its work, and Baker requested a budget enlarged to accommodate demand from both veterans and civilians after the war. The following year, the college mounted an "unusually aggressive" effort to increase state support, mobilizing political help from the agricultural community, alumni/ae, parents, trustees, and other interested groups. "The College will be faced," wrote Baker during this campaign, "with the absolute necessity of securing additional teachers or turning away veterans."[2]

By early 1946, it was evident that the state's existing institutions—public and private—could not absorb the enrollments generated by the veterans, and Baker wrote Governor Maurice Tobin urging rapid expansion of publicly supported higher education, using one of the state's army bases as a temporary facility. Tobin created a special committee of college presidents to plan the state's response. In classic Massachusetts tradition, this group was dominated by representatives of private institutions: Conant of Harvard served as chair, and the membership included, along with Baker, Marsh of B.U., Keleher of B.C., Compton of M.I.T., Ell of Northeastern, and Carmichael of Tufts—plus the presidents of Williams College and Worcester Polytechnic Institute.

The plan drafted by Conant's committee followed the pattern Baker had recommended. Fort Devens, an army base forty miles west of Boston, would be turned into a campus and would be staffed and administered by M.S.C. The program would be limited to the first two years of college, after which students wishing to continue would transfer to Amherst. Fort Devens would be only a temporary facility, to be disbanded as soon as the bulge of veterans had been served. This plan proved highly effective; between 1946 and 1949, "Devens College" enrolled twenty-seven hundred students for whom educational facilities would not otherwise have been available.

Though hastily conceived under emergency conditions, the Fort Devens plan represented a fascinating mixture of educational ideas and institutional interests, and it perfectly reflected the forces that dominated state policy on higher education. The decision to offer only lower-division courses exemplified the intertwining themes. This scheme made academic sense in relation to the need for specialized facilities, available only at Amherst, for some upper-division programs, but it also expressed Baker's institutional ambitions, since it kept pressure on the legislature to build capacity at M.S.C. where additional enrollments could be expected within two years. At the same time, the plan was congenial to the Boston-area presidents who had no wish to accustom the state's taxpayers to having low-cost, four-year programs available in the eastern part of the commonwealth. Governor Tobin, a former mayor of Boston, had hoped to establish a full collegiate curriculum at Fort Devens, but he endorsed the presidents' proposals, and legislative appropriations to enlarge facilities at M.S.C. were immediately forthcoming. Baker's hope that the veterans would provide him with the means to stir public support for the state college appeared to be on the way to fulfillment.[3]

Despite the new possibilities, Baker himself had exhausted his administrative energies by the end of the war. Aging and ill, he lacked the strength to manage the veterans' program or lead the anticipated battle for expansion, which he knew would be difficult. In the spring of 1946, he resigned his position and issued a final report that acknowledged the frustrations of his presidential years. He complained of the commonwealth's indifference toward the potentialities of M.S.C., and he expressed his disappointment that "so little of a constructive nature" had been accomplished. Though he repeated his belief that the college had "fine promise for the future," he feared the patterns that traditionally had prevented public higher education in Massachusetts from flourishing could not be changed.[4]

An Altered Political Environment Emerges

As Baker was retiring in discouragement, there seemed reason to think that the political changes he had hoped for might actually be taking place. The surge of support for higher education being registered nationally among state governments in the late 1940s was also evident in Massachusetts. In 1945 the legislature sponsored, for the first time since the 1920s, a comprehensive review of state activities in this area. A special commission was appointed under the chairmanship of Senator Ralph Mahar, and Baker was named a member. Unlike most previous official commissions to study the problems of higher education in the commonwealth—the governor's committee on the needs of veterans' being the most recent example—the special commission was not dominated by independent schools. Indeed, the private sector had no representation at all. The new focus on higher education also revived interest in redesignating M.S.C. as the "University of Massachusetts." Five bills pointing in this direction were introduced in the General Court during the 1945 session.

Senator Mahar's commission proved friendly to public higher education. It established a subcommittee on the "university question" and made Baker the chair. In due course, the subcommittee recommended the long-awaited name change, and this proposal was enacted in 1947 without significant opposition. The final report of the special commission, issued in the spring of 1948, forecast a vast increase in demand for higher education, noted the seriousness of economic barriers to college for many talented young people, and dismissed the idea that private institutions could meet the situation. The commission recommended funding a new system of community colleges, expanding the state teachers' colleges to offer a wider range of programs, and enlarging and upgrading the newly designated University of Massachusetts to full "university status." The only dissents were three minority reports, each urging even more rapid growth of the state's educational efforts.[5]

The work of Senator Mahar's commission inaugurated a new period of political support for the Amherst campus. In 1946 and 1947, funds were appropriated to build four new educational buildings—including homes for engineering, physics, and home economics—and five new dormitories. The Alumni Building Corporation planned three additional dormitories. At the same time, the trustees decided to increase enrollments from twenty-seven hundred to thirty-five hundred by 1949, after which it was expected that the numbers would decline to about thirty-two hundred. Forty additional teaching positions were approved, supplemented by new research and extension staff, and a general salary increase was authorized. The pattern continued into the early 1950s. By 1952 the university's budget had grown to five and a half million dollars, a 400 percent increase since 1939. Physical facilities continued to expand beyond those required to accommodate the veterans.

The postwar progress of UMass was impressive, but it is important to keep the changes in perspective. Increased funding for public higher education was widespread in these years, and budgetary growth at Amherst between 1939 and 1952 was proportionately only slightly greater than aggregate increases in outlays for higher education by all state governments. Even in comparison with other New England states, the commonwealth's record remained relatively weak. Throughout the period, Massachusetts ranked last in the region by a substantial margin in dollars per capita spent for its university and in the ratio of seats at the university to the total population.

The expanded support for UMass clearly mirrored the general excitement about higher education stirred by the veterans' program (as well as effective lobbying efforts of the veterans themselves) and the national debate on higher education of the early postwar years. But deeper forces were also at work. The latent demand for access to low-cost, public higher education in Massachusetts was dramatized by the fact that applications to the university did not diminish as the veterans completed their studies. In 1949 the entering class at Amherst was 33 percent larger than its predecessor. In 1950, freshman enrollments again were up by 25 percent. The following year, the numbers increased by 47 percent. This pattern opposed national trends at both public and private four-year institutions, which registered declining enrollments in these same years.[6]

The special conditions of Massachusetts caused the university to experience early the heightened interest in higher education that was soon to be evident nationally and would be a continuing phenomenon of the golden age. A central question for the leadership of UMass involved the readiness of the state's political system to respond to these pressures. Did the political support of the late 1940s represent a short-term reaction to the excitement of the early postwar years? Or was Beacon Hill now ready to provide strong, continuing sustenance for the commonwealth's most important tax-supported academic institution?

Shaping the State's Public University

Baker's successor in the presidency, a specialist in pomology and horticulture named Ralph A. Van Meter, was the fortunate beneficiary of the new educational and political atmosphere. A seasoned administrator who had been dean of military programs during World War II and acting president after Baker resigned, the new president demonstrated a clear sense of the forces operating on his institution. In his first report, he cited the Zook commission on the importance of increasing educational opportunities and pointed to demand for admission to UMass to support his claim that this need was especially urgent in Massachusetts. He believed that the university was at last in a position to determine its destiny.

Van Meter outlined his views on institutional change at his inauguration, drawing heavily on plans for the Amherst campus conceived during the war. The emphasis, he announced, should be on establishing a strong College of Arts and Sciences surrounded by professional schools and supplemented by a full-blown Graduate School. In essence, the University of Massachusetts, finally free from the restrictive environment that had constrained it for so long, should move into the mainstream of state-supported higher education by becoming a comprehensive public university.[7]

During a seven-year presidency that lasted into the spring of 1953, when illness forced him from office, Van Meter systematically implemented his plans. An impressive number of professional ventures were launched: a combined School of Agriculture/Horticulture; new schools of Business Administration, Engineering, and Home Economics; new programs in Education, Physical Education, and Nursing. The Graduate School was reorganized and a set of M.A. programs was added to supplement the traditional M.S. and Ph.D. programs in the sciences. By 1951 the University of Massachusetts was offering thirty graduate degrees.

In numerical terms, the greatest expansion of the Van Meter years occurred in undergraduate programs in arts and sciences, where enrollments grew by more than 40 percent to about sixteen hundred. More students meant more faculty, and here also, the largest numbers were added in arts and sciences. Several academic departments were created. Sociology split off from History. Psychology was divided from Education. Languages and literature were reorganized into five units—English, German, Romance Languages, Fine Arts, and Speech. In 1951 Van Meter highlighted the changes by reporting that there were now more majors in liberal arts subjects, excluding the sciences, than in any other area of the curriculum, a shift that also reflected the burgeoning presence of women in the student body. Growth brought the need for more administration, and Van Meter created the positions of treasurer and provost to coordinate financial and academic affairs. The appearance of the latter office and the appointment to it of a man with graduate training in economics at Princeton rather than agriculture at a state university were indications of Amherst's evolution toward university status.

The changes *were* dramatic, but the deprivations of ninety years could not be offset by a brief flurry of activity. Indeed, when Van Meter left office in 1953, the University of Massachusetts was still far less developed than most public universities in the industrialized states outside the Northeast. Its total enrollment of thirty-five hundred in no way compared with the ten thousand at a typical state university. Its ratio of applications to admissions made it much more selective than its counterpart institutions. It lacked professional schools in high prestige fields like law and medicine, and its Graduate School of Arts and Sciences was small and limited at the doctoral level. Agriculture still received the largest share of the budget. Arriving in 1951, the new treasurer found the university "starved to death" with a totally inadequate library, salaries that were low by both regional and national standards, and no state support for research or extracurricular activities. For want of the necessary approvals, moreover, Van Meter had not been able to create the integrated, undergraduate College of Arts and Sciences that had been a primary campus goal since the middle of the war.[8]

The relatively limited pattern of postwar change at UMass was attributable not only to the school's history of underdevelopment but also to the continuing potency of forces that traditionally had constrained public higher education in the commonwealth. Van Meter himself, for example, shared the conservative view of his campus that was dominant among the faculty and staff. He advocated a selective approach to growth based on careful planning in well-established areas. He showed no interest in turning Amherst into a sprawling, eclectic enterprise along the lines of the giant public universities of the West. Nor did he display any of the freewheeling, market-oriented, entrepreneurship characteristic of Marsh at B.U. or Ell at Northeastern. More than either of these leaders, he stressed undergraduate education in the arts and sciences and graduate studies and scholarly work in these same fields. He even resisted proposals to establish professional schools in law, medicine, dentistry, pharmacy, and veterinary medicine on the ground that his school's resources were not adequate to do well the things it already had undertaken.

In admissions, Van Meter endorsed the Zook commission's concern about removing the income barrier to higher education, but, again in contrast to Marsh and Ell, he gave more emphasis to standards and selectivity than to access and growth. This orientation, too, was very much in the Amherst tradition. For years the campus had prided itself on high standards, and it continued in the postwar years to reject larger percentages of its applicants than B.U. and Northeastern and to enroll students from more affluent backgrounds than the private, urban universities of the Boston area. Basically, in expanding the Amherst campus, Van Meter hoped to enroll well-prepared, highly motivated, full-time students of traditional college-going age. He expressed no interest in adult education, which Baker had identified as a major field of postwar activity. Van Meter celebrated his campus as a "small university . . . [with] the potentiality for becoming . . . great in the quality of its work."[9]

Other factors reinforced Van Meter's restrained approach to change. The president was skeptical about the staying power of gubernatorial and legislative interest in higher education, and these doubts deepened his resistance to new enterprises. In fact, the Democratic governor from 1948 to 1952 showed little concern for the state's tax-supported academic institutions, and both governor and legislature largely ignored the recommendations of the Mahar commission. Moreover, Amherst's rural, residential character made it much more difficult to initiate educational ventures than was the case at urban, commuting schools. Latent tensions between the university and the state's private institutions could easily flare into direct conflict, as when Harvard, B.U., and Tufts joined forces in the early 1950s to oppose the funding of a public medical school. The politically weak, programmatically limited campus in Amherst was hardly in a position to challenge the educational giants of the state too boldly.

The university's financial structure introduced additional conservative tendencies into plans for growth. Unlike private universities or, indeed, public institutions in a number of states, the university's budget was unrelated to tuition payments, since receipts from students were deposited directly into the commonwealth's accounts while current revenues came chiefly from legislative appropriations. In this financial universe, UMass could not directly increase its resources by packing in additional students, as was occurring at B.U. and Northeastern. Indeed, experience had taught Amherst's leaders that high enrollments would not necessarily be followed by commensurate increases in annual budgets. The key to institutional development for the University of Massachusetts lay not in earning revenues to expand operating resources, build endowment, or construct facilities but in persuading the legislature that there existed a large unmet demand for higher education. As statistics on applications and admissions annually made clear, this condition was easy to demonstrate.

In the long run, the ability of the university simultaneously to remain a medium-scale, selective institution focused on academic quality and to portray itself as the guarantor of educational opportunity for the young people of the state was questionable. Already, there were pressures to enlarge public higher education more dramatically than plans for the Amherst campus envisioned. Senator Mahar's commission had expressed this impulse in recommending the enhancement of the state teachers' colleges and the creation of a community-college system, initiatives that could divert financial support from the university. Particularly worrisome to Van Meter was a proposal from the state C.I.O. to establish a campus of UMass in the Boston area. The president vigorously opposed this idea for the same reason that Baker had opposed it a few years earlier.[10]

Sooner or later, if pressures for admission persisted, the leadership at Amherst would be forced to confront the choice between expanding and diversifying more extensively than was their inclination or standing by while the state created additional, more accessible, educational agencies. This, however, was a political problem that Van Meter and his associates did not need to face in the late 1940s and early 1950s.

UMass in the 1950s

A New Leader Seeks to Break with the Past

Van Meter's heart attack in the spring of 1953 catapulted into the presidency the energetic young provost who had arrived on campus only a few weeks earlier, Jean Paul Mather. Mather was stamped from an entirely different mold than his predecessor. Having had no previous contact with the university, he did not share Van Meter's traditional perspective on the campus. Indeed, Mather tended to disparage those who wanted Amherst to retain a "small, comfy, homey atmosphere 'down by the pond.'" Prior to his appointment, he had worked at the A.C.E. with John Hannah, the legendary builder of Michigan State and "Midwest aggressive," who had told him that UMass needed attention and energy more than any public university in the country.

Mather's first months on the scene had convinced him that Hannah was right. The Amherst campus, he quickly concluded, had "just rocked along" in a comfortable pattern for much too long. Mather possessed a temperament that inclined him to see this situation as a delicious challenge. His motto came from the marines: "Go for broke." In his first months in office, a year before the trustees decided to make him Van Meter's permanent replacement, the 38-year-old acting president decided it was time to turn his sleepy school around.[11]

Mather's decision to push for major changes was not simply a projection of his personal inclinations. The new president was keenly aware of national estimates of increased demand for higher education associated with the approaching tidal wave of high school graduates. Indeed, during the last two years of his presidency, Van Meter had set the stage for his successor by drawing public attention to the imminent need for enlarged educational facilities.

Both presidents knew that the impending demographic changes were going to raise special problems for Massachusetts, where the neglected system of tax-supported colleges was too small to absorb significantly more students, and the dominant private colleges were unlikely to focus on regional needs. This state of affairs, in turn, had important implications for the University of Massachusetts, since the Amherst campus was all there was of public higher education in the commonwealth, apart from the teachers' colleges and technical institutes.

Mather, who had done graduate work in demography, calculated that if UMass merely continued to serve a constant percentage of the state's college-going high school graduates it would need to grow to approximately ten thousand students—nearly triple the fall 1952 enrollment—by 1965. A proposed change of this magnitude was bound to shock large segments of campus, public, and political opinion. But ten thousand was a modest target in relation to the foreseeable expansion of applicants. It was also a good, round number that had the political advantage, in relation to the private sector, of implying no increase in the state's proportional role in providing education for Massachusetts residents. Convinced that he was the man to make UMass into a major public university and to awaken the commonwealth to the importance of doing so, Mather made the goal of ten thousand students by 1965 the basis of his program.

With the support of the trustees, Mather announced his plans to a skeptical campus audience in the fall of 1953. Then he went public. An articulate, eloquent, engaging man with a sarcastic wit, he sought speaking engagements wherever he could arrange them. "I decided," he later recalled,

> I will become a bond salesman. I'll talk to any PTA group where they are trying to sell, in Goshen or anywhere else, a bond issue for an elementary school, and use that as a springboard for pointing out that these dear little children are going to need to go to college . . . Where are they going? You can't afford Harvard, Williams, Amherst, if you could get in.

Mather reinforced his public efforts by cultivating support from the press. He appealed directly and privately to the political leadership of the state, including the recently inaugurated Republican governor, Christian Herter. To policymakers he supplemented his concern about ensuring opportunities for young people with arguments about the interests of the state. He drew attention to the loss of talent that the commonwealth fostered by sending its youth to public as well as private colleges in other states. It was time, he told readers of his first annual report, for "the people of Massachusetts and their duly elected representatives" to "care for their own" by "recognizing the University of Massachusetts as the potential site for a revolutionary expansion and growth of public higher education."[12]

The Need for Institutional Independence

In Mather's mind, there was, beyond expansion, a second essential condition for the full development of UMass: relief from a paralyzing array of controls exercised by state officials over the administrative affairs of the university. These controls had grown up gradually in the years since 1919 when the Massachusetts Agricultural College had lost its independent status and had become a division of the State Department of Education. Though subsequent years had brought major changes at Amherst, the institution was even less autonomous in the 1950s than in the 1920s. Campus officials were required to obtain approval of many routine actions from one or another governmental agency. For example, expenditures of appropriated funds required the prior endorsement of the comptroller, as did transfers among accounts. Purchases of any consequence and all campus publications had to be channeled through the state purchasing agent. Even out-of-state travel by university employees required approval.

Most problematic of all, the personnel operations of the university, academic and nonacademic, were totally under the control of political and administrative agencies. All new positions, faculty or staff, had to be specifically authorized by the legislature and had to conform to criteria of the Division of Personnel and Standardization that applied equally to all governmental departments. Vacant positions could be filled only at the minimum salary for the designated grade, and salary increases occurred only through automatic step raises. Appointments to authorized positions had to be approved by the Division of Personnel. When vacancies occurred, the Division could downgrade the position before approving replacement—for example, from a full to an assistant professorship—or eliminate the position altogether.

State control of the university's affairs was a perpetual source of frustration for campus leaders. President Butterfield resigned in disgust shortly after the reorganization of 1919. Baker and Van Meter repeatedly drew attention to the problem in their annual reports, and some of Van Meter's colleagues attributed his physical collapse to tensions arising from his dealings with the state bureaucracy.

It is important to understand, in reviewing this situation, that substantial control of the activities of a public university by state agencies was in no way unique to Massachusetts. Indeed, the movement toward efficiency in government that had produced the reorganization of 1919 had been a national phenomenon, and many state governments had extended controls over their academic institutions during the interwar period. Within this pattern, however, Massachusetts was notorious. A national Committee on Government and Higher Education, chaired by Milton Eisenhower, characterized UMass in the 1950s as one of the most administratively constrained state universities in the country. The committee's report expressed particular concern about the role of the Division of Personnel and Standardization.[13]

For leaders of the Amherst campus, the complexity of existing administrative arrangements was only part of the problem. Equally important was the potential for politically motivated intervention by state officials, elected or appointed, in institutional decisions, especially in relation to hiring and admissions. The university's treasurer, Kenneth Johnson, described the system in the following terms:

> The idea was that if you had a vacant position, before anybody was offered a job, you went down and asked them who you put in the job. You didn't fill the job until they gave you the name . . . Sometimes the selection . . . would be made by somebody in the State House. It might be passed around the state to various other public officials, or elected officials, or even friends, of the people who happened to be in power at the time.

Johnson's account is almost certainly exaggerated, reflecting the distaste that he and many campus officials felt for Beacon Hill politics as much as actual experience. But the political and bureaucratic controls on hiring did foster abuses, especially in nonacademic hiring, and Van Meter had expended considerable energy resisting patronage pressures. It did not take long for Mather to conclude that the powers exercised by the Division of Personnel and Standardization posed a major obstacle to his hopes for the university. How could UMass attract and retain outstanding scholars under existing circumstances? It would be a battle to obtain approval from agency officials for the kind of people Mather hoped to bring in. Even if the required authorization could be obtained, who would accept an offer when salaries were so low in comparison with other universities and when raises could occur only through fixed annual increments unrelated to ability or performance? Mather was not one to mince words. "Anyone who read the name [of that agency]," he later recalled, "would know that this is a guarantee of mediocrity."

> These were men uneducated, controlling the destinies of an institution. Telling us, when we requested within the budget appropriation, the authority from these three "hacks" who literally and figuratively looked and acted as though they'd crawled out from under a rock, and had that much intelligence. And . . . the two top men in that division held their positions under a World War I dispensation of the Legislature which gave them . . . life tenure, short of discharge for moral turpitude; and I maintained that the act would have had to be performed in front of a district judge. I mean, there's no way to get away from these people.

This was a situation, the young president concluded, that had to end.[14]

The Political Economy of Academic Change

The political context within which Mather waged his twofold campaign for growth and freedom contained some helpful new elements. He had strong support from the Board of Trustees, which, in the years before World War II, had been reluctant to endorse efforts to build up the university. He had more potential allies in the legislature than his predecessors, as the postwar years had brought new individuals into state politics, including a number of veterans who had benefited directly from the G.I. Bill and possessed a clearer sense of the importance of higher education than earlier generations of lawmakers.

Public attitudes also were shifting in ways that were helpful to Mather. The broader interest in higher education that flowed from the veterans' education program was creating a more receptive audience for the president's arguments, and he won support from influential citizens' groups like the League of Women Voters. Even the agricultural community, which in the past had resisted a broadened vision of the university, proved ready to be helpful. Especially important was Mather's good fortune at the gubernatorial level. Christian Herter, a moderate Republican, a classic Yankee, and a cosmopolitan man, was just beginning a four-year period in office when Mather was appointed. Herter was responsive to the president's urgings about the importance of expanding UMass, and indeed, he made Mather's plans a priority in his first "state of the state" address. Herter's support remained steady throughout his two terms.

In the early going, the victories came quickly. During Mather's first three years, with Herter's endorsement, the legislature appropriated twelve million dollars in funds for construction at Amherst, a sum that exceeded by over two million dollars the total of all previous capital budgets for the school. Operating support also jumped rapidly. Mather was delighted. In a lyrical report written in the fall of 1954, the president expressed his appreciation and proclaimed that the state's political leaders finally had recognized "the need for greater public higher educational facilities." Mather was sufficiently confident to challenge the legislature's historic preference for expansion rather than academic improvement. He persuaded the trustees to halt dormitory construction until new facilities for teaching and research were provided. The money kept coming.[15]

Encouraged by success, Mather decided, in the summer of 1955, to open the second front of his campaign—the attempt to get out from under the Division of Personnel and Standardization. He drafted and submitted to the legislature a new law giving the university control over the hiring, promotion, and compensation of all of its employees. Delegating responsibility for the internal affairs of the campus to his provost, Mather went on the road to promote the "Freedom Bill." Between September 1955 and July 1956, he made over three hundred speeches on behalf of "the most significant single objective of the University looking toward improved quality." He won the endorsement of Governor Herter after agreeing to exclude classified and technical personnel from the plan. He met with editors of the major papers in the state to elicit helpful editorials.[16]

Mather's barnstorming turned into a bumpy ride, however. In essence, the Freedom Bill aimed to reduce the power of both the legislature and the bureaucracy, an outcome that numerous members of those bodies were unlikely to welcome. Moreover, Mather was still learning the state's political landscape and did not fully appreciate the depth of feeling that animated various sectors of opinion or the relationship of those sentiments to the university. He was surprised, for example, to discover that many Boston politicians were convinced that UMass, with its traditional ties to the Republican, Yankee, yeomanry of the "west," discriminated against Catholics in both admissions and hiring.

As an outsider and a Protestant, Mather had barriers to overcome with the legislature, and his witty, acerbic personality tended to enflame rather than soothe the latent hostility. In one speech, for example, he expressed his frustrations with the top officials of the Division of Personnel by commenting that their "knowledge of higher education would crowd a cufflink." As reported in the newspapers, the jibe was made to refer to the collective brains of the legislature, and Mather was summoned by the chairman of the House Ways and Means Committee to explain himself. He did not get very far, and, indeed, the withering published version of his remark took and became part of the state's political folklore.

After the cufflink episode, the battle for the Freedom Bill became truly nasty, as Mather found himself in a crossfire of ancient religious and ethnic hostilities. In the end, Mather got his bill—voted at a late night session during which he was called upon to prove his credentials as a Democrat—but the cost was high. When, shortly thereafter, the university attempted to exercise its hard-won freedom, it found itself challenged by the comptroller and required to obtain an opinion from the attorney general on the meaning of the new law.[17]

As time went on, the energy and enthusiasm associated with the first stages

of Mather's campaign for expansion gradually waned. The university continued to receive good support for physical development, but annual increments
in the operating budget did not sustain the enrollments that Mather and the
trustees had projected. Between 1953 and 1958, student numbers rose from
forty-one hundred to fifty-two hundred, a five-year increase that brought the
university only 18 percent of the way toward Mather's 1965 goal of ten thousand. There was little progress on the abysmally poor salary scale.

In the end, the university's expansion during the Mather years lagged
behind national figures for all public, four-year institutions in terms of both
budgets and enrollments. In 1958 the trustees were forced to refuse additional
growth until appropriations provided more money for programs. The loss of
momentum was reflected in Mather's annual reports. In 1957 he referred to
public apathy toward higher education and noted that progress on his plans
for the university was gradual. The following year, he complained that important forces within the state, notably leaders of private colleges, were resisting
the development of public higher education.

Many observers of the university's affairs, on campus and in the broader
political community of the state, attributed the slowing of Mather's campaign
to personal animosity against the president himself, especially among legislators. There was ample basis for this view. The tensions that surfaced during the
campaign for the Freedom Bill took firm root. As one legislative leader, a
staunch supporter of UMass and of public higher education, later recalled,
Mather was "dead right" on the issues but "lacked any sense of diplomacy." A
decisive moment was reached in the summer of 1959 as Mather was working
for legislative approval of a bill to increase faculty salaries. The proposal had
wide support and seemed close to passage when it was suddenly and summarily
killed by the Senate president, with whom Mather had an especially bad relationship. Enraged, Mather resigned, insisting that he could not remain in office
when the state's political system allowed such arbitrary uses of power.

The political fallout from Mather's resignation was considerable. The press
had a field day; *Time* magazine did a story; and the adverse publicity contributed to the Senate president's failure to win election as mayor of Boston. At its
next session, the legislature reconsidered and easily passed the pay-raise bill.
In this context, rumors spread that the trustees had agreed to replace the president in exchange for support on Beacon Hill. Mather vigorously denied being
forced out, but the story stuck, undoubtedly because, whatever the truth of the
matter, it accurately reflected legislative attitudes toward the university's
aggressive and outspoken leader.[18]

The view that resentment against Mather limited support for the university
in the 1950s has an immediate plausibility given the intensely personal character of Massachusetts politics. But structural factors were also at work that
would have made it difficult for any president to succeed with Mather's ambitious program. The mid-1950s were basically conservative years in the nation
and in Massachusetts. Governor Herter, despite his solicitude for the university, was not oriented as much toward building social programs as toward
improving the administrative operations of the state. The Massachusetts econ-

omy, only beginning to evolve away from its dying industrial base, was sluggish, and state revenues were limited for all purposes.

Moreover, the major effect of the postwar tidal wave of young people was still a planner's projection in the mid-1950s. Mather's arguments about accelerating demands for higher education were sound, but the political impact of the demographic pressures was not yet strongly felt among politicians. At the same time, the state's private schools were just beginning, in the mid-1950s, to recover from the uncertainties of the early postwar years. While Mather obtained useful assistance in some of his battles from leaders of elite institutions like Amherst College, Harvard, and Tufts, the mass-market private campuses of the Boston area, especially Boston University and Northeastern, remained wary of an expanded public system.[19]

The depth of political resistance to a major expansion of public higher education became particularly clear during the four-year administration of Herter's successor, Foster Furcolo, between 1956 and 1960. A liberal Democrat from Springfield who understood the need for new educational facilities, Furcolo was more ready than his predecessor to use public funds for this purpose. The new governor sponsored an "audit of state needs" by a special commission, which reported in early 1958 that Massachusetts faced a "crisis in higher education." Echoing similar calls from earlier legislative panels, the commission urged a massive expansion of existing public campuses, the creation of a network of regional community colleges, generous increases for the University of Massachusetts, and more scholarships for state residents attending private institutions. Furcolo embraced this program and proposed a sales tax to finance it. But the new governor achieved only limited success in rallying support for his recommendations and was defeated on his tax proposal. His only major accomplishment was the establishment, with modest funding, of a rudimentary community college system.

Furcolo, to be sure, had particular problems as a political leader. He did not develop a reputation as an effective executive, and by his second term, his administration was so tainted by scandal that he was weakened even within the Democratic party; he was in no position to mobilize broad enthusiasm for major policy initiatives. The central difficulty in advancing proposals to strengthen higher education, however, lay more in the character of the legislature than in the personalities of leaders like Furcolo, Herter, or Mather.[20]

For most of the 1950s, Massachusetts politics was in the last stage of the transition from the Yankee, Republican dominance that had lasted, virtually uncontested, into the 1920s to a period of ethnic, Democratic hegemony. The two major parties possessed nearly equal strength in both houses of the General Court, with the Republicans maintaining their traditional control of the Senate and the Democrats dominating the House. The situation was further complicated by serious divisions within the parties, especially on the Democratic side where little cooperation was possible between members from the urban enclaves of Boston and representatives from "out state." This fragmented situation presented problems of coalition building for anyone wishing to pursue a well-defined program, as Furcolo learned when many Democrats failed to endorse his educational and fiscal proposals.

In a fundamental sense, moreover, the balance of power in the legislature was tilted against public higher education, despite the presence of strong advocates like Senator Mahar. Herter notwithstanding, the Republican party, tied as it was to the state's Yankee elites and rural yeomanry, had never supported a broad program of public higher education. Among the Democrats, the center of strength still lay with representatives from the Boston area who had shown little interest historically in public higher education and harbored, as Mather learned to his sorrow, deep suspicions about the University of Massachusetts.

There were forces in the environment pointing toward change. The growing political importance of the suburbs around Boston was diminishing the significance of the city in state-wide elections—a phenomenon that played a crucial role in Herter's defeat of Paul Dever in 1952. A new generation of Democratic politicians, some of them "westerners," were rising to power in the Democratic party. Many Democratic families that traditionally would not have considered college for their children were being affected by the postwar atmosphere of democratization in higher education. These shifts contained important implications for public policy on higher education, as developments of the 1960s would demonstrate. In the mid-1950s, however, the historic forces and divisions that long had checked the growth of public higher education in Massachusetts continued to hold sway. David Riesman and Christopher Jencks, studying UMass in these years in preparation for writing *The Academic Revolution,* characterized the campus as

> a kind of educational New Deal, assuming those residual functions that the private system cannot, or will not, fulfill. It is hard to find a single area in which the university has entered into serious competition with the private sector . . . solely to make the University of Massachusetts an academically outstanding institution of which the state might be proud. The contrast with California and Michigan is obvious.[21]

Institutional Development in the 1950s

With Mather's energies focused on the campaigns for expansion and administrative freedom, academic change at UMass continued trends initiated with the shift to university status in the early postwar years. The College of Arts and Sciences was finally unified under a single dean. The nursing program was organized as a separate division. The Department of Education became a free-standing school, as did the Division of Physical Education. Academic subjects such as art, which historically had been based in landscape architecture, were removed from traditional moorings in applied fields and made into independent departments in the College of Arts and Sciences.

New themes of change reflected a heightened emphasis on university values. This orientation was encouraged by a new generation of faculty, many with

Ph.D.'s from Ivy League universities, that came to Amherst as part of the expansion. Particularly striking was the increased focus on graduate education and research, activities that had received minimal attention under Mather's predecessors. Between 1955 and 1959, graduate enrollments grew by 131 percent—from 8 percent to 13 percent of the student body—while the number of undergraduates increased by only 35 percent.

Mather and his colleagues made self-conscious efforts to foster a stronger academic culture while downplaying themes associated with agricultural or "state-school" education. In a move laden with symbolic significance, Mather sold a celebrated group of Percheron horses to obtain funds for the instructional program. Athletics was deemphasized and drinking was banned. On the initiative of a group of faculty and alumni/ae, the university sponsored a journal of the humanities, the *Massachusetts Review*. In his public statements, Mather stressed that purely academic criteria should govern the admission process, and he sought to abandon the tradition of seeking a distribution of students from all parts of the state and giving special treatment to applicants from small towns. Mather also advocated higher academic standards and publicly praised a presidential colleague for flunking large numbers of undergraduates.[22]

Although Mather complained that the university was not expanding rapidly enough, the restricted pattern of development contained academic as well as political advantages. The conjunction of slow growth with rising demand for admission caused UMass to become progressively more selective, and Mather was quick to claim the plaudits. In his 1957 report, he boasted that the Amherst campus had the most competitive admission program of any state university and noted that freshman scores on the College Qualification Test were well above national averages, dramatically so in quantitative subjects. Slow growth also protected Mather from members of the campus community who did not wish to see UMass evolve into a massive state university, though he still received criticism for overemphasizing the building program. Conditions of the 1950s thus allowed Mather simultaneously to trumpet the university's academic strength on the basis of its selectivity while pushing as hard as possible for more rapid expansion.[23]

Riesman and Jencks concluded that the Amherst campus in the late 1950s was midway in a transition that had yet to assume a clear direction. The major academic strengths continued to be in agriculture and related sciences. The social sciences and humanities as well as the elite professional fields were poorly developed. The student body, though talented, was overwhelmingly lower middle class and "western," and UMass was still regarded by cosmopolitan eighteen-year-olds from the Boston area as a "hick school." The faculty contained numerous individuals inclined to resist the entire pattern of change since the end of the war. Many, for example, believed that the university should persist in its historic orientation toward technical and occupational education at the undergraduate level.

It was clear, however, that the campus already had moved far beyond its earlier role. Many younger faculty members, especially in Arts and Sciences, together with some ambitious chairs were pressing a conventional idea of academic success for a state university. They wanted to expand, build graduate programs, stress research, and assign lower-division, non-honors instruction to teaching assistants. Others, also well represented in Arts and Sciences and undoubtedly influenced by the collegiate traditions of the Amherst campus, wanted to focus on undergraduate education and to increase the scholarly productivity of the faculty.

"Up to the present," Jencks and Riesman noted, "the University of Massachusetts has not had to decide what its particular educational mission is, since it can continue to battle against the indifference of the public and the undercover jealousy of private competitors." But the future might be strikingly different from the past. The rapidly approaching tidal wave of high school students would reduce interinstitutional competition for enrollments while intensifying public demand for access to good quality colleges. In this new context, Jencks and Riesman guessed, the public authorities of Massachusetts might finally prove ready to support a university of genuine quality. The character of that quality, if the hoped-for period of opportunity actually arrived, remained undetermined as the Mather years came to an end.[24]

UMass in the 1960s

A New Political World for Public Higher Education

In the 1960s, the forces that traditionally had retarded the development of the University of Massachusetts finally were overcome, and state authorities began providing the kind of financial support for which successive presidents had pleaded, with only marginal success, since the Depression. Appropriations for operating expenses, which had risen by an average of 8.5 percent a year during the Mather administration, grew by 12.8 percent annually between 1960 and 1965 and by 23.8 percent between 1965 and 1970. Between 1960–1961 and 1969–1970, enrollments at Amherst jumped from 6,300 to 17,800, thereby doubling in a single decade the scale of growth achieved in the entire preceding century. Additional students at the Boston campus pushed total enrollments in the statewide university to nearly twenty-two thousand by decade's end, with the Medical School in Worcester just opening its doors. Impressive building programs accompanied development at all three locations. Annual appropriations for capital projects, which had averaged $3.6 million between 1953 and 1960, averaged $8.2 million in the five years from 1961 to 1965 and $50.6 million between 1965 and 1970. Plans for the $350 million Boston campus represented the largest public construction project in the history of the commonwealth.

Breaking the problematic pattern of earlier periods, the state supported academic improvements at levels commensurate with numerical and physical growth. UMass was able to add a new faculty member for every fifteen additional students and to pay salaries competitive with those of the nation's leading institutions. The average salary at Amherst more than doubled during the decade, while the pay scale at Boston was exceeded only by Harvard, M.I.T., and Brandeis among schools in the metropolitan area. In a crucial break with long-established practice, the university was authorized to award salary increases to faculty based on a merit review of their achievements.[25]

The university's growth during the 1960s was part of a broader expansion of the state's entire system of public higher education. The community college program, given a shaky start during Furcolo's second term, took off in the early 1960s, and ten years later fifteen such schools enrolled over fifteen thousand students at facilities across the state. During the same years, the antiquated network of eleven teachers' colleges, renamed "state colleges" and authorized to award undergraduate degrees in arts and sciences, tripled their enrollments from 7,200 to 21,800. The commonwealth also created a new university at Dartmouth in the southeast out of two recently combined technological institutes and initiated expansion at the state college and technological institute in Lowell that ultimately led to their merger as an additional university. Total enrollments at the two regional universities grew from 2,500 in 1960 to 8,000 in a decade. Altogether the state's public campuses expanded from 16,000 to 66,000 during the 1960s, though, at the end of the period, they still accounted for less than 40 percent of all postsecondary enrollments in Massachusetts.

State appropriations for operating budgets for public higher education increased even more rapidly than funds for the university: 477 percent over the ten-year period compared with 386 percent. This growth rate placed Massachusetts in the historically unusual position of supporting higher education at levels above national norms: during the 1960s, aggregate financing by all state and local governments for the operations of public campuses increased by 330 percent. Perhaps the most significant indicator of the transformed position of public higher education in Massachusetts was the fact that spending for these institutions increased steadily as a proportion of total state expenditures: from 4 percent in 1960 to 6 percent in 1965, to 7 percent in the early 1970s. At one crucial juncture early in the decade, as the surge of educational growth was gathering momentum, the legislature authorized salary increases for academics double those approved for all other state employees.[26]

No single factor can explain the shift in the politics of higher education in Massachusetts in the 1960s. Admission pressures at the university and at all the state's public colleges increased, of course, year by year, driven, as in other regions, by a burgeoning youth population and an accelerating rate of college attendance. Other forces, however, some of them specific to Massachusetts, gave additional significance to demographic change.

New attitudes toward higher education within the state's dominant Catholic community were especially important. Traditionally, middle- and working-class Catholics sent a small percentage of their children to college, and those that did go were generally urged by parents and clergy to attend sectarian campuses. Both these patterns had been changing since World War II, as the power of the church weakened and Catholics increasingly wanted the same educational opportunities as other groups. By 1960 young Catholics were attending postsecondary institutions in the same percentages as Protestants.

Since the historic association of private higher education in Massachusetts with Protestant power had left a legacy of skepticism toward these schools among Catholic parents, many were inclined to turn to public colleges. This phenomenon heightened the impact of the baby boom on a legislature in which many representatives harbored doubts about the state's private institutions that mirrored those of their constituents.

The intensified public demand for educational opportunities came at a time when the private colleges and universities of Massachusetts were flooded with applications and were generally inclined to use the new situation to upgrade their student bodies with out-of-state and academically advantaged students. Thus, while political aid for the university in the 1950s had come chiefly from presidents of elite institutions, conditions of the 1960s made it possible for leaders of Boston College and Northeastern also to endorse an expansion of the public system. The perspective of B.C.'s Father Walsh provided a complex and poignant example of the dominant attitude. Eager to turn his traditionally locally oriented institution into a national center for Catholic thought and an educational competitor of Notre Dame and Georgetown, Walsh endorsed the development of UMass/Boston to ensure opportunities for the urban Catholics who would no longer have access to B.C.[27]

Broad economic and political trends of the 1960s also were conducive to the growth of public higher education. By this time, the slow transition of the state's economy from its historic reliance on manufacturing in fields like leather and textiles to a new emphasis on technology, especially electronics, and on services was having important effects. A string of sophisticated enterprises along Route 128 outside of Boston, many of them linked to defense-related scientific work at M.I.T., was producing growth and prosperity in the metropolitan suburbs. Even the capital city, despite losses in population, was mounting a program of urban renewal after four decades of stagnation. These changes brought greater pressures for educational facilities that could produce well-trained employees and educate the children of upwardly mobile suburban residents. Higher levels of employment and income increased tax revenues available for governmental projects.

Economic change was accompanied by a political climate receptive to social spending. At the national level, Democratic ascendency brought a revival of governmental activism, while watershed events like the *Sputnik I* crisis and the civil rights movement directed attention to the need to improve education. The local impact of these circumstances was increased by the leading role that representatives of Massachusetts were playing in the country's affairs. Harvard and M.I.T. became deeply involved in national efforts in science and education, and numerous members of both institutions took positions in the Kennedy and Johnson administrations. The fact that, for the first three years of the decade, the president himself was from Massachusetts, the oldest living son of the state's leading political family, guaranteed that his call for new social initiatives in higher education and in other fields would be heard on Beacon Hill.[28]

Latent concerns about education were given focus for Massachusetts residents in the fall of 1961 by a stinging series of articles in the *Boston Globe*. Referring to the commonwealth's growing school-age population, reporters Ian Menzies and Ian Forman identified numerous inadequacies in state programs at every academic level. They were particularly concerned about higher education, where Massachusetts was falling far behind states like New York and California. Menzies and Forman especially faulted the General Court, which, in their view, had shamefully neglected its public campuses, partially because of historic but outdated ethnic and religious resentments.

Not surprisingly, given the atmosphere of the time, the *Globe* articles triggered a public outcry, and in the spring of 1962, the General Court appointed a special commission to review state education policies, an idea lifted from Menzies and Forman. Over the next three years, under the leadership of Senator Kevin Harrington and staff director Benjamin Willis, the commission held dozens of hearings, consulted widely with experts, and in June 1965 published a thick report advocating a massive increase in the commonwealth's educational efforts. Such appeals had issued from legislative commissions with some regularity since World War II and had produced only modest results. This time, however, things were different. Even before the Willis–Harrington report was released, the commonwealth had begun to expand and upgrade all levels of public higher education. After 1965 state support moved to an entirely new level and remained there for the rest of the decade.[29]

The modification of public policies on higher education, so discontinuous with previous history, expressed not only broad trends in the socioeconomic character of Massachusetts but also specific political developments. The most important changes occurred within the state Democratic party and the General Court. In the 1958 elections, the Democrats retained their advantage in the House and wrested the Senate from the Republican majorities that had been dominant throughout the twentieth century. In succeeding years, Democratic majorities in both houses increased steadily, and by the mid-1960s two-party contention for control of the legislature, a phenomenon of state politics since the late 1940s, had been replaced by one-party rule.

Democratic hegemony in the legislature coincided with shifts within the party and its leadership. Continuing patterns of the 1950s, the importance of the state's traditional urban enclaves, especially Boston, whose legislative representatives historically had posed problems for higher education and particularly for UMass, declined steadily. At the same time, the metropolitan suburbs experienced rapid growth. In 1962 the Democratic nominee for governor was, amazingly, a liberal, Yankee Protestant named Endicott Peabody, whose election signaled a new significance for the middle-class, managerial suburbs in Democratic politics. This emergent constituency was far more inclined to support public spending for higher education than the party's traditional, blue-collar, urban adherents.

As the dominance of Boston over the state party declined, leadership increasingly came from the "out-state" wing of the party, and during the 1960s, a generation of western "populists," strongly oriented toward higher education, moved into key positions on Beacon Hill. For the first several years of the decade, the House speaker was John Thompson of Ludlow, a good friend of the university, and at the end of the decade, the speaker was David Bartley of Holyoke, a UMass alumnus. In the Senate, the key figure was Maurice Donohue, also from Holyoke, who was elected majority leader in 1958 and Senate president in 1964. Such men provided reliable support for public higher education and UMass within the legislative leadership throughout the decade. Many members of both houses, moreover, realizing that higher education was now good politics, were ready to be helpful. The new atmosphere was especially apparent in the attitudes of elected officials from traditional Democratic strongholds, like Robert Quinn of Boston, who served briefly as House speaker in the mid-1960s, and John Powers of Boston, who had summarily killed Mather's salary bill in 1959 but who, in the early 1960s, was ready to assist the university.

The politics of higher education in the 1960s reversed the patterns of the previous decade. Throughout the 1950s, the most important allies of UMass had been governors, first Herter and then Furcolo, and the legislature had tended to present problems. Now it was the legislature that took the lead, while the governor was, at best, a somewhat reluctant follower. For all but four years during the 1960s, the governorship was held by Republican John Volpe, who was not inclined during the early part of his term to stress higher education but was ready to listen on particular issues, as on the bill to create a state medical school. Not infrequently, legislative appropriations for higher education exceeded those recommended by the governor. In the middle of the decade, however, Volpe pressed hard and successfully for new taxes partially to fund the recommendations of the Willis–Harrington report.[30]

With the legislature in friendly hands, a governor who could be approached and persuaded, strong public interest in higher education, and an expanding state economy, the 1960s were a time of opportunity for the University of Massachusetts. And the university, following the turbulence of Jean Paul Mather's final years, led by an unusually strong Board of Trustees, had positioned itself to take advantage of the time.

A New President and the Advent of "Fiscal Autonomy"

In choosing presidents, academic institutions tend often to correct for the difficulties or excesses of previous administrations. If, for example, an outgoing president has been political and external and has neglected the inner workings of the institution, there is a natural inclination to seek a replacement of more academic or managerial bent, and vice versa. In this context, it is not surprising that the trustees of the University of Massachusetts, in replacing the sharp-tongued and freewheeling Mather, chose John William Lederle of the University of Michigan, a lawyer turned political scientist and a mild man who sought his ends through conciliation and quiet persuasion.

Lederle proved perfect for the times. With the need to strengthen public higher education gaining acceptance within state government, political leaders were prepared in the early 1960s to respond to reasonable appeals from an

advocate they could like and respect. The new president, who enjoyed inter-
acting with legislators, was just such a man, and his passionate, midwestern
commitment to public higher education gave force and persistence to his gentle demeanor. There is no reason, Lederle constantly told state officials in cor-
dial tones, why Massachusetts could not have a state university as eminent as
its outstanding private institutions or the great public universities of the West.

Lederle's political talents were by no means limited to his easygoing manner. He had extensive experience in both state and federal government. He
understood the political process and established an effective system of liaison
with Beacon Hill, personally cultivating the legislative leadership. He quickly
saw the political significance of Amherst's reputation an an anti-Catholic bastion and took steps to change this situation, recruiting Catholics to his staff,
reaching out to the church hierarchy, inviting Father Walsh of B.C. to be his
first commencement speaker, and establishing a Newman Center on campus.
He made contact with other influential constituencies ranging from labor to
private colleges and universities, to citizens' groups like the League of Women
Voters. He knew how to form coalitions and lobby state officials without badg-
ering them. He developed printed materials that laid key issues before the voters in simple, straightforward terms, and he turned the ritual annual report
into a public relations document.

It is difficult to say how the university would have fared during the 1960s
had the president proceeded in a manner less skillful or acceptable to political
leaders. The strong forces that were pushing the institution forward would
have been there in any case, but it would be a mistake to underestimate the
difficulties that might have arisen had the new president stirred hostility on
Beacon Hill or attempted to preserve the old collegiate atmosphere at Amherst
by resisting expansion. That major difficulties did not arise—that, indeed, the
university enjoyed good relations with state government throughout the decade—was Lederle's primary achievement. When he left office in 1970, the
members of the legislature honored him at a special session of the General
Court. For the previous ten years, they gave him, and the university, steady and
unprecedented support.[31]

The new atmosphere of cooperation between the university and the legislature became apparent early in Lederle's term in discussions of administrative
relationships between UMass and state government. This problematic topic
had given rise to persistent tensions between presidents and public officials
and had been the focus of Mather's campaign for the Freedom Bill in 1955.
Lederle was well-equipped to understand the difficult position of the university. He was a student of public administration and had been an expert consultant to the Eisenhower committee in the 1950s. He was convinced that a
public university could achieve excellence only if given a substantial degree of
independence from nonacademic authorities, and he regarded the Freedom
Bill as affording only minimal relief from the network of controls that constrained the operations of UMass. During his pre-appointment interviews, he
told the trustees that change in existing administrative arrangements was a pre-

requisite for institutional development, and he accepted the presidency only when convinced that such change was possible.

Lederle elected to test the possibilities for administrative reform as the first major initiative of his presidency. During the summer of 1961, he approached Speaker Thompson, who made clear his willingness to help, as did Senate president Powers. After that, the going was relatively easy. A friendly commission was appointed with Donohue as chair, a UMass alumnus as vice chair, and a Lederle aide as staff. The commission's January 1962 report urged that the university be granted much greater autonomy in financial affairs, the power to purchase most items and issue printed materials without going through the state purchasing agent, and authority over out-of-state travel by employees. In the area of personnel, the commission went far beyond the Freedom Bill, recommending that the university be allowed to establish salaries, grades, and titles for professional employees within the overall limits of state salary schedules. The commission capped its specific proposals by urging that the status of UMass be changed from a subordinate division of state government to an independent agency governed by its board.

These far-reaching recommendations, which changed half a century of administrative practice and eliminated numerous opportunities for political leaders to influence university affairs, proved remarkably uncontroversial in the legislature. Though there was some opposition from other public institutions to special treatment for UMass, Lederle and his colleagues were able to win endorsements of the "fiscal autonomy" bill from leaders of private colleges and universities, the press, and key citizens' groups like the League of Women Voters. It was easily approved by the General Court and by Governor Volpe. Lederle was ecstatic. "With the University's new birth of freedom," he wrote, "the Commonwealth must now see the opening of a new page of excellence . . . in the state's chief facility of higher education."[32]

Balancing Democratic and Elite Values in Institutional Change

John Lederle brought two primary—and to some extent conflicting—goals to his presidency: he wanted to enhance the role of UMass in meeting the state's needs for educational services, and he wanted to raise the standing of his institution in national academic rankings. His view of the ways in which the university might better serve the commonwealth was expansive, including a strong continuing emphasis on baccalaureate-level teaching, concern for the values of good citizenship, heightened attention to public service by the faculty and to continuing education, and significant growth of the undergraduate population. This last commitment seemed especially important to Lederle. Faced with rising numbers of high school graduates who wanted to attend college in a state with limited facilities for public higher education, he had little patience with those who hoped to maintain the old, small college atmosphere of Massachusetts State.

Lederle's interest in raising the academic standing of UMass was equally strong. His association with Michigan had convinced him that a public university could achieve prestige comparable with the best private institutions, and he wanted to replicate the Michigan model in Massachusetts. He even dreamed of moving UMass into the "top ten" among public universities. Lederle knew what was required to raise his institution's standing: a more cosmopolitan and academically well-prepared student body would need to be recruited and graduate programs expanded; faculty members with degrees from leading universities and high scholarly potential would need to be hired; teaching loads would have to be reduced, and facilities for research enhanced.[33]

The new president was well aware of the tension between the two sides of his plans for UMass. Indeed, from the beginning of his presidency he wrote and spoke feelingly about the danger of pursuing elite academic goals too vigorously lest democratic commitments be weakened. He especially feared the potential for neglect of undergraduate teaching as the faculty became more oriented toward research and advanced instruction. Yet he believed that UMass could maintain an appropriate balance. In his inaugural address, for example, he focused on the interplay between quality and size:

> We have the demand of a democratic society to give each student all the education of which he is capable. We have the equally insistent demand for the well-being and advancement of a democratic society to produce graduates of excellence . . . Increasingly we must be a great and continuing laboratory for testing out the limits of accommodation . . . between the demands of quantity and the need for high quality.

Lederle had a practical reason, as well as a philosophical one, for stressing democratic commitments while pursuing prestige. He knew the legislature was chiefly interested in providing educational opportunities for the young people of the state and that it had little interest in scholarship. To promote research and graduate education at the expense of undergraduate instruction was to place the university's political base at risk.[34]

Articulating the complexities of UMass was one thing, actually achieving the desired balance of emphases as the campus grew was quite another. The president and his colleagues made several attempts to define priorities. A long-range planning committee, appointed by Lederle early in his term, issued an interim report in 1962 and then disbanded. A new attempt at comprehensive planning was initiated within the administration in the middle of the decade, but none of the drafts produced by various offices was ever acted upon. In 1970 yet another long-range planning committee, reviewing the work of its predecessors, noted that the campus had been unable to produce a master plan and that academic change during the decade had been "sporadic, uncoordinated and fragmented."

While UMass seemed unable to adopt a scheme to guide campus growth, the successive planning efforts revealed a high degree of consensus among administrative and faculty leaders on two central points: first, that Amherst must grow substantially at the undergraduate level to accommodate expanding demand for admission; second, that Amherst should stress Ph.D. programs and encourage research in order to consolidate a preeminent position among the state's public institutions while also attaining national recognition. In practice, these twin policies were the primary developmental concerns of Lederle and his colleagues during a decade of exceptionally rapid change.

To concentrate on just two aspects of Amherst's evolution in the 1960s is, inevitably, to ignore a number of significant activities. By this period, the old state college had mushroomed into a large and multidimensional enterprise, and each of the draft long-range plans acknowledged the complexity, urging attention to public service, continuing education, and the undergraduate curriculum with varying degrees of enthusiasm. Indeed, important steps were taken in all these areas during the decade. Lederle worked particularly hard to build continuing education. New dormitory-based living/learning centers and a special program for black students represented important initiatives in the undergraduate program. The University of Massachusetts Press was established along with a chapter of Phi Beta Kappa, and cross-registration policies were worked out with nearby colleges—Amherst, Smith, and Holyoke—to bring UMass students into contact with more sophisticated peers. Influenced by his Michigan experience, Lederle even tried to promote big-time football.[35]

In the end, however, these initiatives were far less important in defining the character of change at UMass/Amherst than were expansion of undergraduate enrollments and the strengthening of doctoral programs and research. If we are to assess the efforts of Lederle and his colleagues to balance democratic and elite goals, it is appropriate to focus on the implications of these two areas of change.

Lederle was immensely proud that Amherst grew from under 6,000 to over 15,000 undergraduates during his presidency. Making provision to house, educate, and otherwise care for 1,250 additional students each fall—the annual increment during the 1960s—was an administrative accomplishment that Lederle likened to adding a new Amherst College every year. It is difficult to see how UMass/Amherst could have done more to enlarge the state's educational facilities.

Even with this growth, Amherst was not able to keep pace with the increased pressure on admissions, and the campus was constrained, year by year, to accept progressively smaller percentages of its applicants. For the fall of 1962, for example, UMass/Amherst accepted 50 percent of those who applied. Five years later, it accepted only 42 percent, causing it to reject more qualified applicants, according to Lederle, than any other major educational institution in the nation. As admissions became more competitive, test scores of entering freshmen rose steadily, along with high school class rank. About half the entering freshmen in the fall of 1962 were in the top 20 percent of their high school classes, compared with 64 percent five years later. In 1963 Lederle wrote enthusiastically of a "quiet revolution" in which highly qualified students, who in years past would have opted for a private university or an out-of-state public campus, were coming to UMass as a first choice.[36]

The changing character of the undergraduate student body illuminated the difficulty of balancing democratic and elite commitments at an upwardly mobile institution under conditions of excess demand for admission. Although a central purpose of the campus was to ensure educational opportunities for young people unable to afford private tuition, the students became steadily more affluent. Between 1966 and 1970, for example, the percentage of entering freshmen from families in the lowest third of the state's income rankings declined from 31 percent to 23 percent. By the end of the decade, only 19 percent of freshmen from the Boston area entering UMass/Amherst came from families in the state's lowest income quartile, while the major private universities in Boston enrolling Massachusetts residents—B.C., B.U., and Northeastern—collectively took 23 percent of their Boston-area freshmen from the lowest-income group. Amherst also enrolled a higher percentage of students from the top income quartile than did the grouping of B.U., B.C., and Northeastern, or B.U. and B.C. as a pair.

Amherst was, of course, a residential institution that historically had enrolled more affluent students than its urban, private counterparts. But during the 1960s, both B.U. and B.C. were turning themselves into residential campuses and attracting more middle- and upper-middle-class students than they traditionally had done. In fact, Amherst increasingly drew students who had alternative means of obtaining an education. Though the campus became more selective, decreasing percentages of those it admitted actually enrolled.

By the late 1960s, the changing character of the student body began to worry some campus leaders. The 1970 long-range planning committee criticized admission policies as focusing excessively on conventional indicators of academic ability, which tended to correlate with family income. Asserting that the University of Massachusetts "cannot adopt an educational philosophy of exclusivity," the committee urged the campus to "develop new and innovative educational techniques in order to serve the broad public which supports it." A similar conclusion was reached by a special committee of nonacademics that reviewed the three-campus system in 1971.

Lederle himself was concerned about the impact of institutional change on admission policies. Though pleased that undergraduate qualifications were improving, he was critical of many faculty who "wanted to limit the number of students" and enroll an "elitist student body." He fought to keep tuition down and supported special efforts to enroll low-income students, including expanded scholarships and the program for black students. It was clear, however, that such efforts affected only marginally the broad thrust of admissions in the 1960s.[37]

In the end, confronted with more students than it could accommodate, UMass/Amherst did what came naturally for an academically ambitious university, public or private. With limited exceptions, it admitted the best-prepared applicants. In so doing, it found itself catering to a more socially and economically well-positioned clientele. Lederle and his colleagues did not consciously seek this outcome, but it was consistent with—indeed the inevitable result of—the policies that guided the development of the Amherst campus during the 1960s.

The growth of doctoral programs proceeded in tandem with undergraduate expansion and dominated curriculum development during the decade. Thirty-four new Ph.D.s were established, covering most disciplines of the arts and sciences and most professional fields. Graduate enrollments actually grew at more than double the rate of undergraduates, though the scale was far smaller. To staff the advanced programs, faculty recruitment stressed research-oriented scholars, and many of the older faculty, who had concentrated on teaching for many years, were urged to mount research programs. These initiatives produced impressive results in qualitative terms. The A.C.E.'s 1969 survey of graduate programs ranked two UMass doctorates in the top twenty nationally and rated five others as "superior," a better record than B.C., B.U., or Tufts, all of which were stressing graduate work in these years. In 1971 UMass/Amherst ranked eighty-seventh in the nation in total federal dollars for sponsored research and outstripped all universities in Massachusetts except M.I.T. and Harvard in nonmedical federal research funding.

The impulse to add doctorates remained strong among campus leaders at the end of the decade despite indications that the nation's—as well as the state's—universities were overbuilding at this level. Lederle and his colleagues were also concerned that UMass/Amherst lacked a graduate professional school in any of the traditional high-status fields. In this context, the trustees' decision to locate the Medical School in Worcester was a serious blow, and planning now centered on obtaining approval for a law school.[38]

The focus on research and graduate development worked in complex harmonies with undergraduate expansion. The heightened intellectual intensity and improved standing that came with the advanced functions were obvious benefits for ambitious undergraduates. By the end of the decade, however, doubts were growing within the campus community about the compatibility of Amherst's two primary goals. The 1970 long-range planning committee, for example, worried that the undergraduates were being shortchanged:

> Despite the trend toward universal higher education and the resultant expanding number of students whose needs are changing; despite the changing roles of educational institutions in society, and despite the broad concern about higher education, major academic reforms have been slow in evolving . . .

While the committee approved the new graduate programs and urged their further expansion, it observed that the undergraduate curriculum had become more and more specialized. "In keeping with our concern . . . that a public university must provide diverse opportunities to its constituency," the committee reported, "we must . . . consider programs beyond the scope of narrow disciplines." The committee expressed special regret that UMass/Amherst had ignored the recommendation of the Willis–Harrington commission that it train teachers for community colleges. It suggested a Doctor of Arts program. It also advocated much greater efforts in public service, arguing that "a proper balance has not yet been reached" between this traditional public university function and more academic efforts in teaching and research.[39]

Lederle shared many of these reservations. Though he was proud of

UMass/Amherst's academic progress, by the end of his term he thought his campus had "moved too far in the graduate research emphasis."

> You start with the situation we had . . . where people . . . had gotten tenure . . . and had no interest in research . . . But as you bring in new people and they are trying to put this emphasis on research and graduate instruction, the thing begins to swing the other way . . . Toward the end of my period . . . the faculty . . . was arguing quantity or quality . . . They didn't want to keep taking on these kids . . . [they] only want[ed] to deal with an elitist student body, in restricted numbers and primarily at the graduate level, and often only those at that who were going on in graduate work. And you had the students saying we're getting the shaft at the undergraduate level.

Lederle tried corrective steps. He instituted an outstanding-teaching award. He exhorted chairs and senior faculty to pay attention to teaching. He even thought of forming a special college that would stress undergraduate education and compete with the regular departments, but this idea made little headway. In the end, Lederle did not think he had done much to reassert the importance of undergraduate teaching.[40]

Lederle's frustrations were the product of his own priorities. The faculty members whose disinterest in undergraduates he found distasteful were often the same research-oriented scholars the campus had brought in to staff its graduate programs. Consumed largely by external and legislative relations, Lederle relied heavily on key subordinates to guide recruitment and academic development. He had the good fortune to make a number of key appointments early—a new provost and deans of Arts and Sciences, Agriculture, and Home Economics in 1961; a second provost in 1964—and in filling these posts, he sought people who could raise Amherst's sights. "We had to shake this place up," he later recalled; "if we were going to build a great university, we had to have some different characters here . . . who'd been contaminated by being at institutions of excellence . . ."

Undoubtedly, the most important person to join Lederle's administration was Oswald Tippo, an alumnus and well-known botanist, who had a named professorship and served as department chair at Yale, and had held senior administrative posts at Illinois, Colorado, and N.Y.U. In offering him the provostship, Lederle told Tippo that his job was to attract more sophisticated students and "infus[e] the instructional staff with first-class, high-level outside personnel." Tippo proved an outstanding choice. Assisted by a new cadre of deans, he seized the opportunity offered by expansion to make a series of important appointments. The Math Department was an example. Amherst recruited senior men from Chicago and Harvard, both former chairs, and used them to attract exceptional younger people. The results were impressive, but the price, Lederle concluded, was reduced attention to undergraduates.[41]

Lederle's disappointment illustrated the difficulty of balancing democratic and elite commitments. To do more, for example to protect more aggressively the quality of the undergraduate program or to ensure a more egalitarian mix of students in socioeconomic terms, Lederle and his colleagues would have had to compromise the university's rising academic reputation. Instead, they pursued a model of academic excellence well established in public higher education: a massive undergraduate program utilizing large classes and armies of graduate assistants supporting a selective graduate school and research enterprise. By doing so, they gave the commonwealth something it historically had lacked: a major public campus that, while not yet in the first rank, was equal to many of the nation's good state universities.

Change at UMass/Amherst in the 1960s constituted a clear victory for one of the three campus subcultures that Jencks and Riesman had identified at the start of the period, and a defeat for those who aspired to maintain a focus on undergraduate education or on technical, scientific, and occupational programs. Like campus subgroups elsewhere who sought to resist the dominant values of the golden age—we have observed them, for example, at M.I.T. and at B.C.—these groups were weak not because their educational concerns lacked substance but because their arguments were overwhelmed by the impulse toward upward mobility, a goal against which it was difficult for any member of a campus community effectively—or unambivalently—to argue.

The Founding of UMass/Boston

The pressures of the early 1960s to expand public higher education revived long-standing questions about the need for a state university in the Boston area. This issue had arisen after World War II in connection with the education of veterans and had surfaced periodically in subsequent years, often through the advocacy of the C.I.O. Such proposals traditionally had worried leaders at Amherst, who feared that a campus located near the state's capital and population center would divert attention and resources from their badly undersupported institution. Both Van Meter and Mather had had occasion to combat the idea of a university campus in Boston. It seems quite probable, indeed, that a major consideration for Mather in rejecting the arguments of those who wished to maintain a small college atmosphere at Amherst was that such a course would guarantee the creation of competing public institutions.

Consistent with this history, the 1962 long-range plan, written by a committee of faculty and administrators at Amherst, rejected a Boston "branch" and endorsed service centers around the state to provide points of contact with the university. As Lederle became familiar with Massachusetts during the early 1960s, however, he grew doubtful about Amherst's resistance to a Boston facility. Demographic projections were making it clear that no conceivable program of expansion at Amherst would be adequate; nor could a western, rural campus accommodate the needs of low-income, urban students, especially in the context of limited state scholarships. The Willis–Harrington commission, concerned about disadvantaged and minority students, focused attention on the question of a university campus in the Boston area, and raised the possibility of an initiative in this direction outside the control of UMass. Moreover, Lederle was increasingly conscious of the political gulf between the eastern and western parts of the state. Finding it difficult to interest Boston-area legislators in the needs of Amherst, he reasoned that a campus with close ties to the city could be an asset rather than a liability. Early in his term, Lederle became convinced that the University of Massachusetts "had to get into Boston."[42]

The forces moving toward establishment of a Boston campus came to a head in the spring of 1964. In April, Lederle informed the Senate Ways and Means Committee that the university would need to reject eight thousand of the twelve thousand applicants for freshman admission. A week later, the Legislative Research Council reported that a state university was needed in the Boston area. There was talk that Boston State College, the traditional teacher-training college of the city, might be upgraded to university status. In late April, a committee of the UMass trustees discussed the importance of quick action and considered possible legislative allies. The following week Senate president Donohue announced his support for a Boston campus of the university and followed up by sponsoring an appropriate bill.

Potential opponents were taken by surprise. Leaders of the state colleges expressed opposition to Donohue's proposal. Case of B.U. argued for delay and further study. Knowles of Northeastern threatened to resign from the Willis–Harrington commission, since he believed there had been an unwritten agreement that no public university would be built in Boston in the immediate future. In the end, however, the city's major private institutions, busy in these years becoming regional and national in character, were not well positioned to prevent the expansion of the public system, and the state colleges were not a credible alternative. The intrinsic case for the Boston campus was strong, and the political sponsorship was irresistible. Donohue's bill was enacted in a matter of weeks.[43]

Despite the wave of legislative support, the effort actually to establish the new campus proved difficult. Part of the problem derived from the same sense of urgency that was so helpful politically. With large numbers of students seeking immediate admission to the university, it was assumed that UMass/Boston would open its doors quickly. The earliest feasible date was September 1965, fifteen months after the General Court had acted, and university authorities committed themselves to enrolling a thousand students by that date. Under these circumstances there was no opportunity to mount a deliberate planning process to determine the character of the new campus such as the one that preceded the opening of the Medical School. Discussions among the trustees assumed that UMass/Boston "would be a complete activity in every way paralleling the work on the campus at Amherst," and Lederle informed the board that he envisioned "a quality institution which eventually, like U.C.L.A., may grow to 20,000 or 25,000 students." Beyond such general statements, however, there was no opportunity for serious thought about the character of the new campus.

The pressures of time dictated a pragmatic decision about program: the first students would be entirely freshmen enrolled in basic courses in the arts and sciences. This plan kept the start-up task manageable and allowed most effort to go into the practical work of getting the place open. Responsibility for administrative arrangements, including finding facilities in downtown Boston on short notice, fell to an *ad hoc* group of administrators from Amherst assembled by Lederle in the summer of 1964. Academic planning, particularly the job of recruiting—in the most pressured labor market in the history of American higher education—the dozens of faculty that would be needed to offer courses for a thousand students, was done by a small group of Arts and Sciences faculty from Amherst during the early spring of 1965. A senior administrative officer—the title of chancellor was chosen—was named in February 1965, only six months before the projected opening. The job went to John A. Ryan, who had been one of Lederle's early staff appointments and had subsequently moved to Arizona as academic vice president.

It was, everyone agreed, a remarkable way to start a university. "To the best of our knowledge," reported the administrative task force, "no other academic institution has ever been charged with the responsibility of mounting a new program of this magnitude with such short deadlines." The pressures did not abate in succeeding years. With a new cadre of students to be admitted each fall as a new layer of program was added to meet the needs of earlier classes, the tasks of faculty recruitment and organizational development were unending.[44]

The cramped schedule for starting the new campus was made more difficult, from the beginning, by limited resources. The first sign of difficulty occurred early when no special funds were made available to support the frantic planning process. It soon became clear that political enthusiasm for the venture was highly circumscribed. Governor Volpe, who had not been an important participant in the decision to establish UMass/Boston, proved a grudging provider. His annual budget recommendations were consistently below the amounts requested by the trustees. Groups to which the new university might have looked for help—for example, the Boston business community, municipal authorities, and city politicians in the state house—were divided and lukewarm about the campus. Important representatives of all these constituencies were concerned that Boston already contained too many tax-exempt institutions and that the rapid expansion of existing universities was having negative impacts on the city's economy, housing stock, and living environment. Meanwhile, of course, those that never wanted UMass to build in Boston—major private universities and champions of the Amherst campus and of the state colleges—continued to create problems as opportunities arose.

UMass/Boston's political disadvantages became particularly evident when university authorities sought a site for the new campus. Powerful, competing interests were everywhere. At one point, for example, the university hoped to utilize undeveloped space at a turnpike cloverleaf near Copley Square but encountered strong opposition from the Christian Science church and the John Hancock insurance company, which had their own plans for the area. The fact that Hancock's top executive was also board chairman of Northeastern, which was located a few blocks from the proposed site, did not help. In the end, the only place available was an abandoned garbage dump and landfill on the southern rim of the city adjacent to Boston's most troubled housing project.

UMass/Boston's only reliable allies in the early going were the political leaders who had sponsored the enabling legislation. Each year the General Court restored some of the cuts in the campus budget recommended by the governor, but legislative support—by its nature linked to the broad political environment—was insufficient to overcome the problematic forces that lay everywhere around. Thus, year after year in the late 1960s, the new campus struggled to establish itself in rented quarters in Park Square with operating budgets that met only minimal needs for faculty and scientific facilities.[45]

As this pattern took shape, the vision of creating a major university campus like U.C.L.A. seemed progressively more remote. In early 1968, after Governor Volpe proposed a budget for fiscal year 1969 that reduced by 40 percent—from eight million to five million dollars—the amount the trustees had requested for UMass/Boston, the board considered a despairing analysis of the financial situation. Summarizing the poor support that had characterized the project from the beginning, this assessment concluded: "Among all of the new campuses of major state universities which have come into being in recent years, the one at Boston is the only one in present danger of collapse." Lederle's hope that building a campus in Boston and appointing an Irishman to the chancellorship would arouse strong local support was thus disappointed. Discouraged about the lack of progress, Ryan left his position after three years for a job in the Midwest.[46]

Despite early difficulties, UMass/Boston grew steadily in the late 1960s: from the initial thousand freshmen in the fall of 1965 to four thousand undergraduates by the fall of 1970. All commuters, these students were drawn mostly from the city and its immediate suburbs. Though some adventurers came to be associated with something new, most, inevitably, were individuals who could not afford a residential college experience, even one subsidized by the state. A large number were high school graduates from low- and moderate-income families. Many others were older than traditional college students and self-supporting. Most, needing income to provide for self or family and to pay college bills, combined classes with jobs.

The students began to give the Boston campus a distinctive character in terms of social class. From the beginning, UMass/Boston enrolled individuals from families of more-modest financial and educational attainments than their counterparts at UMass/Amherst or the private universities that historically had served the city. A study of 1969 high school graduates found that 40 percent of those enrolled at UMass/Boston came from the state's lowest-income quartile, compared with 19 percent from this group at Amherst. Boston also enrolled a larger percentage of minority students than Amherst: 7 percent versus 4 percent in 1970. Thus, as UMass/Amherst, B.U., and B.C. strengthened their academic positions during the 1960s by catering to more affluent students, UMass/Boston—complemented by Northeastern—emerged as the area university most concerned with educating the least-privileged members of the commonwealth's population. UMass/Boston authorities embedded this democratic orientation in their admission policies by regularly seeking to enroll 40 percent of their students from the city itself.[47]

As enrollments grew, the academic program evolved. By 1969 UMass/Boston offered a full four-year curriculum in the arts and sciences and possessed a faculty of approximately 250 persons. In the absence of defined plans for the new campus, the character of this faculty, essentially a by-product of the rushed early decision to begin with a general program for freshmen, proved the crucial factor in setting programmatic directions. Indeed, once the campus was established, both Lederle and the trustees, preoccupied with pressing problems at Amherst, the founding of the Medical School, and the location of a permanent home for Boston, left questions about the program in the hands of the emergent local leadership. Since Ryan concerned himself chiefly with external affairs, responsibility for institutional planning fell, essentially by default, to the faculty. Key leaders of this group, including the first dean, historian Paul Gagnon, had migrated to Boston from Amherst, in part because they were among those who had sought unsuccessfully to preserve the traditional collegiate atmosphere of the old state college, with its emphasis on undergraduate education, in the face of efforts to turn the campus into a large, conventional state university.

The faculty planners of UMass/Boston conceived an institution that reflected their personal ideals and enthusiasms, particularly their love of the small New England college. Drawing on contemporary ideas about breaking up large campuses into manageable units, such as the experiment at the University of California, Santa Cruz, faculty leaders decided that UMass/Boston would be organized into six undergraduate colleges of two thousand students each. In time, five hundred graduate students would be associated with each college, making a total population of fifteen thousand students when the new campus reached full size in 1980. The colleges would be relatively independent and self-contained and would emphasize small classes and close faculty-student relationships. Undergraduate teaching would be stressed, and standards for admission and performance would be relatively high.

By far the most unusual element of the academic plan, again reflecting the model of the small New England college, was that all six units would be devoted chiefly to the arts and sciences. There would be no undergraduate professional schools, although professional courses would be offered in such fields as education and business within the framework of more academic subjects, an ironic revival of the pattern of combining academic and practical fields that had characterized the Amherst campus before World War II. Graduate programs would be developed in both the arts and sciences and in selected professional fields, although there was disagreement within the faculty about the nature and importance of graduate work. The trustees approved the plan for UMass/Boston in 1969.[48]

The idea of creating a campus for urban commuting students that focused on high-quality undergraduate education in the arts and sciences was both idealistic and radical. At its heart was the belief that young people who were constrained by circumstances to seek education in a public, urban university should have access to programs comparable to those offered by the nation's top residential colleges. The plan for UMass/Boston thus departed not only from the standard model for large state institutions that had been adopted at Amherst but also from patterns traditionally associated with the nation's urban and municipal universities, both public and private. These campuses, like B.U. in Boston during the 1920s and 1930s or City College in New York in the 1930s and 1940s (despite its mythical image as a school focused on the arts and sciences) or the new urban publics of the postwar years, tended to stress practical programs bound to be important to upwardly mobile students. They also typically offered their courses in the evening for part-time and adult students unable to attend classes during the day, and they eased arrangements for transfer students, especially those from nearby community colleges. The planners of UMass/Boston rejected not just the programmatic orientation but also the organizational practices of these institutions. Students at UMass/Boston were expected to enroll as freshmen and pursue their studies of the liberal arts during the day in patterns similar to their counterparts at residential institutions.

There was in all this an unrealism that seriously compromised the educational aspirations of the founders. Inevitably, the program conceived for UMass/Boston would not seem interesting or attractive to many of the students the campus hoped to serve. Inevitably, many such students would be unable to attend classes on the terms being offered. It is indicative of the inherent difficulties of the plan that it resembled so closely the initial scheme for Brandeis, created twenty years earlier for an elite, residential student body. If it was predictable, in the 1950s, that UMass/Amherst would grow into a large state university despite the inclinations of some faculty members, it was also certain that the initial vision of UMass/Boston would be modified, despite the elegant dreams of faculty proponents.

The plan for UMass/Boston turned the mix of democratic and elite commitments evolving at Amherst on its head: there, on a campus that offered a wide range of programs appealing to diverse interests and needs, the student body was becoming selective and affluent; at Boston, where the student profile was far more democratic, the academic program was limited to offerings associated with elite institutions.

From the beginning, some members of the university hierarchy, Lederle among them, felt doubtful about the evolving character of UMass/Boston. There was division among the trustees. The faculty leadership had strong support from some board members, particularly the powerful chair of the Committee on Faculty and Educational Policy, M.S.C. alumnus Frederick Troy, who shared the founders' affection for the old state college as well as their aversion to occupational programs. Others were less enthusiastic. By 1970 trustee doubts became strong enough to prompt an expression of concern that the new campus was not living up to its mandate to become an urban university.

The need for a more complex vision of UMass/Boston was articulated most clearly by Ryan's replacement, Francis L. Broderick, a historian, former Peace Corps executive, and academic dean at Lawrence University in Wisconsin. Arriving in Boston in late 1968, Broderick found an institution deserving admiration but needing to change. He shared the founders' belief in the importance of teaching and undergraduate education, and he applauded their resistance to the conventional impulse of academic institution builders of the 1960s to stress research and graduate programs. Broderick believed, however, that in their zeal to provide disadvantaged students with the best in higher education, UMass/Boston's leaders were isolating the campus intellectually and culturally from large parts of the urban community. Convinced that a new direction was needed, Broderick initiated programs to connect with important external agencies, like an institute to work with the public schools and service centers in communities adjacent to the new campus. He also brought the planning of additional liberal arts colleges to a halt, announcing that the next major program would be a College of Public and Community Service.[49]

Academic Organization and Political Systems

Edging Toward University Organization at Amherst

Although the campus at Amherst was formally designated as the University of Massachusetts in 1947, it operated throughout the 1950s and 1960s with organizational patterns more closely associated with its history as an agricultural college than its status as a modern university. Three mutually reinforcing factors retarded organizational change. In the first place, between 1947 and 1962 the campus remained in its prewar position as a subordinate department of state government. This anomalous situation required UMass to conform to the systems and procedures of the state bureaucracy in areas where most universities, even public ones, enjoyed a high degree of autonomy.

Secondly, patterns of growth at the university following World War II had a "boom or bust" quality that also worked against orderly organizational change. During periods of rapid development, as in the late 1940s and mid-1960s, campus leaders were necessarily preoccupied with immediate problems. The in-between years of the mid-1950s were dominated by Mather's colorful struggle to win greater institutional freedom. Though some specific organizational changes occurred, such as the establishment of the new posts of provost and treasurer in the early 1950s, there was little opportunity to think through the structural and procedural reforms needed to keep pace with the changing character of the institution. The first comprehensive reviews of the organizational requirements of UMass as a full university did not occur until the late 1960s.

A third factor inhibiting organizational change at Amherst was the tradition of academic administration that had taken root during decades of operation as "Mass Aggie." As we have seen in the cases of M.I.T. and Northeastern, institutions devoted to technical education tended to be dominated by administrative officers and bureaucratic controls, as distinct from the collegial modes of decision making based on the professional authority of the faculty commonly associated with the arts and sciences.

At Amherst, administrative power was historically concentrated in a hierarchy involving trustees, president, and department and divisional heads—and later deans, as separate schools and colleges were formed. Heads and deans were appointed by the president with no requirement of consultation with the faculty, and they exercised, under the president, full authority over their units. Budgets were requested and allocated through interactions among heads, deans, and president. Matters of academic personnel, including initial appointments and tenure, were handled in the same fashion.

There was no formal requirement of faculty involvement in any of these matters and no published criteria guided or constrained administrative authority. The chief deliberative body for the campus, called the Educational Policies Committee, was dominated by senior administrators, although it also included some elected faculty representatives. The E.P.C. dealt with crucial educational issues, such as requirements for admission and degrees and the approval of new programs. Committees of the faculty were appointed by the president to concern themselves with various aspects of campus affairs, but these groups possessed little delegated authority beyond the power to make recommendations to the E.P.C. As Jean Paul Mather put it, characterizing the governance of UMass when he arrived in 1953, "there was a practical, complete lack of communication between the administration and the faculty. They learned of things through the *Springfield Union* [and other papers] after the fact . . ."[50]

Mather enjoyed power, and he made full use of the discretion afforded him by campus administrative culture. In setting goals for growth during the 1950s, for example, Mather worked out an understanding with the chairman of the trustees, then announced his plan to the campus community. Though the faculty was seriously divided about how their campus should develop, there was no expectation that disagreements would be debated and resolved before initiatives were taken. Mather's efforts to turn his institution into a full university implied, however, major shifts in the distribution of power and patterns of decision making. The Ph.D.s from leading research universities whom Mather sought to recruit were not likely to be comfortable in Amherst's anachronistic organizational atmosphere. Changes began to be evident by the late 1950s. For example, an independent, elected faculty Senate was established in 1957.

The slow process of organizational change was given impetus by the advent of fiscal autonomy in 1962. In granting UMass full control over its own affairs in academic personnel, this legislation required the campus to establish a system for making decisions about the appointment, retention, and promotion of faculty. The first such policy, enacted by the trustees in 1963, established the requirement that administrators—department heads and deans—engage in "appropriate consultation" with faculty before making recommendations on personnel matters. The mode of consultation, however, was not specified. The first elected personnel committee was established by the faculty Senate in 1964, but this group had no regular recommending role and was authorized only to consider appeals by aggrieved faculty members and to review instances involving the dismissal of tenured professors.

Throughout the 1960s, in fact, department heads, who continued to be appointed by deans and president and to serve at the pleasure of their administrative superiors, exercised "full authority" in the area of academic personnel. This authority was somewhat qualified, especially in the College of Arts and Sciences, by the existence of departmental personnel committees through which the faculty were consulted. In many instances, however, these committees were appointed by heads rather than elected, since university policy only assured faculty the right to have such committees, not the opportunity to choose them. As the 1960s ended, a number of departments at Amherst never had formed personnel committees.

The character of campus personnel practices and the power of administratively appointed department heads were symptomatic of the modest pace of organizational change at Amherst during the 1950s and 1960s. The new faculty Senate did little to modify a campus culture in which administrative officers exercised a high degree of discretion. The president served *ex officio* as chair of this body and approximately 20 percent of the seats were held by administrators. Throughout the 1960s, in fact, the Senate was compliant and reactive, rarely challenging administrative initiatives and playing no effective role in long-range planning. There was, moreover, no organized student involvement in campus decision making. By the end of the decade, there were rumblings that dramatic changes would be demanded. In 1969 a faculty committee recommended more professorial involvement in matters of budget, planning, departmental organization, personnel, and the selection of senior administrators.[51]

All these changes, familiar components of university organization elsewhere, would come soon to Amherst. During the years of rapid expansion from the mid-1950s to the late 1960s, however, the campus administration (first Mather, then Lederle and Tippo) was able to move rapidly with major actions—including senior appointments and new programs—that might have proved politically difficult in a more highly evolved university community.

Beginnings of the Three-Campus System

The establishment of new campuses in Boston and Worcester introduced a powerful force for organizational change at UMass. The impact was initially most apparent among the trustees, but before long intercampus tensions were evident at all levels of the university community.

The need to choose a location for the Medical School in early 1964 produced the first serious regional division on the board, although the sources of conflict long predated this particular debate. The idea of a state-supported medical school linked to UMass was, in fact, a venerable political hot potato that catalyzed deep conflicts within Massachusetts society: Democrat versus Republican; east versus west; urban versus rural; middle and upper class versus working class and labor; and public versus private higher education. Proponents of a medical school, arguing that individuals from modest backgrounds lacked access to private medical education or to adequate health care, had been advancing their plans since the late 1940s. These forces were chiefly allied with the Democratic party and organized labor—the notion first surfaced during the Dever administration—and they favored building the school in Boston. Opposition centered in the private medical schools—Harvard, Tufts, and B.U., all Boston based—and the state's medical establishment, both of which had strong Republican ties.

In the politically divided circumstances of the state in the 1950s, a series of Democratic initiatives were beaten back. The wave of support for expanding public higher education in the early 1960s, however, combined with Democratic ascendancy in the legislature to revive the idea. An authorizing bill was passed in 1962, although it was necessary to leave the location unspecified and to mount a major campaign—proponents obtained active support from labor and the Catholic church—to avoid a gubernatorial veto.

The legislature's action bumped the issue of location to the university's trustees, who began serious consideration of the problem in early 1964, simultaneously with the effort to establish the Boston campus. The board was deeply divided. A strong Boston faction, including individuals who had been active on the issue since the late 1940s, pressed hard. Champions of Amherst, joined by Lederle, were equally vigorous. Outside consultants concluded that a western site—Amherst or Springfield—made the most sense in terms of public need, with Boston a less desirable alternative, and Worcester least useful of all. In the end neither the Boston nor western factions could muster a majority, and the decision went to Worcester when the Boston group settled for an urban location in the middle of the state. Lederle subsequently recorded his extreme discomfort with the entire process. For the first time, he found himself in opposition to his own trustees, and the trustees themselves unable to reach consensus.[52]

The new units in Worcester and Boston quickly developed organizational cultures quite distinct from Amherst. Indeed, administrative patterns at Boston were strongly affected by the aversion felt by some of the founding faculty, migrants from Amherst, to the atmosphere of bureaucratic control they had experienced at their former campus. From the beginning, Boston operated with a minimum of professional administration. While Chancellor Ryan concentrated on external affairs, an elected faculty Senate, established in the second year of operations, assumed the leading role in planning the academic program and designing the campus.

Initially, faculty power was concentrated in the senior ranks led by the influential first dean, Paul Gagnon. Senior faculty dominated the Senate. A divisional form of organization, comparable to the pattern utilized at Brandeis in the early years, was adopted, and Ryan and Gagnon appointed strong divisional chairs who controlled budgets, faculty recruitment, and program development. Gagnon and the divisional chairs also held *ex officio* seats on the Senate and were able to play central roles in the deliberations of that body. Within each division, academic departments were organized under appointed chairs, who were granted broad power, subject to review by divisional chairs. In choosing chairs, the dean was obligated only to consult with senior professors.

These arrangements enabled a core group of founding faculty to exercise tight control over the campus, and to maintain a clear focus on establishing a high quality, traditional, undergraduate program in arts and sciences. Proposed initiatives to broaden ties to the city's population, by scheduling evening classes for part-time students or working with teachers in the city's schools, made little headway. Suggestions for curricular innovation, such as an interdisciplinary program in urban studies, were regularly defeated in the Senate.[53]

In contrast to Amherst, organizational change came quickly at Boston. Several forces coalesced. This was the 1960s, and egalitarian modes of decision making were in the air. Younger faculty members, many of whom had been politically active as graduate students and did not share the strict traditionalism of the founders on matters of curriculum, soon grew restive under the initial regime. Students sought a role in institutional governance. Ryan's successor, Francis Broderick, realized early in his term that the existing system of governance was an obstacle to his hopes for changing the direction of the campus.

Broderick joined forces with junior faculty and students, as well as some disaffected senior faculty, to promote a combined faculty-student Senate with a fixed percentage of seats for junior faculty. It was this new body that approved Broderick's plan for a College of Public and Community Service, despite opposition among the founders. The new constitution abolished the divisional system and mandated that departments be headed by chairs elected by all full-time faculty. Broderick also seized upon the collegiate plan of organization as a means to contain the power of the initial faculty in established units while innovative ideas could be tried out in new colleges with new casts of characters. Thus at Boston, the extension of power to additional segments of the community proved essential in fostering change, while at Amherst, concentration of power facilitated campus development.[54]

There was, however, a contradiction in the Boston pattern. Over extended periods, it seemed likely that a participatory mode of academic decision making would obstruct rather than ease institutional change. It remained to be seen whether the system of governance installed at Boston in the late 1960s would prove compatible with continuing needs to develop new programs in a diverse array of fields to respond to the complex pressures of an urban constituency.

As UMass/Boston took form during the late 1960s, leaders at Amherst grew concerned about the potential power of the university's new unit. With the question of preventing a campus at Boston now moot, attention shifted to limiting its scope while ensuring Amherst's role as the state's leading public campus. The 1966 long-range plan drafted by one of Lederle's top aides argued that doctoral programs and high prestige professional schools should be concentrated at Amherst and that Boston should stress undergraduate education. The 1970 plan, while criticizing the impact of graduate education and research on undergraduates, stressed the importance of consolidating Amherst's position at the apex of public higher education.

During the mid-1960s, Lederle and the trustees attempted to manage their rapidly growing, three-campus system with only modest change in the overall structure of the university. Lederle continued to focus on Amherst, where he also resided. Administrative arrangements treated the new units to some degree as branches of the older campus, and many functions, including academic appointments, payroll, accounting, and purchasing, were channeled through the Amherst bureaucracy. Inevitably, relationships became strained as Boston and Worcester sought to establish their independence, administratively parallel to Amherst rather than subordinate to it. By the late 1960s, it was clear to the trustees that the university had outgrown the *ad hoc* organizational forms that had been put in place as the new units were launched and that major changes were needed.[55]

Coordinating the Growth of Public Higher Education

While the University of Massachusetts was learning in the 1960s to live with internal tension among multiple campuses, rapid growth among the state colleges, community colleges, and regional universities produced additional centers of competition for resources and political support. Like the university, all of these institutions had enormous financial needs, either to overcome histories of legislative neglect or to establish themselves as new entities. Their leaders realized that the times presented exceptional opportunities and links with regional constituencies gave them standing with the legislature. The pie was growing larger, but there were also more seats at table. It was not clear that everyone's appetite could be satisfied.

From the perspective of the university, there was much to welcome in the general strengthening of state-supported campuses. Lederle and his associates were, after all, committed philosophically to public higher education, and an improved state system would reflect well on all public institutions, helping each to attract students, faculty, and support. There were specific benefits to the university as well, including heightened—and prescreened—demand for baccalaureate degrees for graduates of the community colleges and for graduate programs from alumni/ae of the state colleges. Lederle also understood that an expanded public system would reduce the pressure on UMass to accept poorly prepared students.

Despite such benefits, the leadership of UMass feared the self-aggrandizing impulses of other public campuses. Lederle was dismayed, for example, by the efforts of Lowell Tech and some of the state colleges to prevent the university from winning fiscal autonomy. In his 1964 report, Lederle expressed alarm that some of the four-year institutions were seeking university status. In the rough and tumble political world of higher education in Massachusetts, however, the university was in no position to dictate growth patterns for other public colleges. For this reason, Lederle urged the legislature to grant UMass legal status as the commonwealth's only public university, with exclusive control over doctoral degrees, and to fix by statute the missions of all state institutions. He also advocated a suprainstitutional coordinating agency that would be strong enough to establish a framework of rational planning and keep other campuses within appropriate boundaries but too weak to seriously constrain the expansion of UMass. "The problem," he wrote, "is that everybody wants to be a university . . . We have got to have some agency that keeps community colleges . . . from becoming four-year institutions; four-year institutions becoming universities . . ."[56]

The need for greater coordination within public higher education was, from the beginning, a central concern of the Willis–Harrington commission, and Lederle worked hard and successfully for recommendations that would serve the interests of the university. The commission proposed legislation guaranteeing UMass the exclusive role as a university that Lederle sought and also suggested a statewide Board of Higher Education along the lines Lederle advocated. Although the new B.H.E. would have exclusive power to authorize new programs and degrees, it was not intended to be a powerful governing body comparable to those established in some other states. The commission projected a small planning agency with no control over campus budgets. Its board was to include *ex officio* representatives of the various public segments. Under the commission's recommendations, the university's position would be secure.

Once submitted to the General Court, however, the Willis–Harrington report became subject to the pulls and tugs of institutional politics that always accompanied educational developments in Massachusetts. After various institutional constituencies had been heard from, the bill finally passed by the legislature opened the way for other campuses to become universities by redefining the role of UMass as the "sole *general* state university" and shifting jurisdiction over doctoral degrees from the university to the new B.H.E.[57]

Formally created in 1965, the Massachusetts Board of Higher Education was able to exercise only modest influence. As Lederle had hoped, the board did sponsor useful technical studies, but political power continued to rest with the institutions. Between 1965 and 1970, the board routinely approved the university's proposals for programs and degrees. The legislative leadership, moreover, for reasons of their own, showed little interest in enabling the B.H.E. to make maximum use of its statutory authority. Budgets were minimal, and the new chancellor's salary was fixed by law at a low level. It took champions of Southeastern Massachusetts Technological Institute only a few years to win legislative designation as a free-standing university, thus breaking the UMass monopoly that Willis–Harrington had recommended. A few years later, advocates from the northeastern part of the state won the same status for a new entity created by merging Lowell Tech and Lowell State College.

Efforts of the B.H.E.'s chancellors to provide leadership on state policy were quickly defeated in this environment, and a succession of appointees served short, ineffectual terms and departed in frustration. By the end of the decade, political leaders were discussing another reorganization of public higher education to establish more effective control of the state system. The missing ingredient, however, was not structure but a lack of political will on the part of any major participant—especially institutions and legislators—to significantly modify a ramshackle system that served everybody's interests well enough.[58]

The Privates Get Organized

The growth of public higher education in the mid-1960s was uncomfortable for leaders of the state's private colleges and universities. For a number of these campuses, particularly those that traditionally enrolled large numbers of Massachusetts residents, public sector expansion was inherently threatening. At the same time, key private presidents, especially at B.U., B.C., and Northeastern, were eager to expand out-of-state enrollments and knew they could not meet the growing demand for admission from graduates of the commonwealth's high schools. The regional and national orientations of their own plans combined with the scale of projected in-state needs and the political momentum behind public expansion explain the otherwise puzzling failure of private presidents to advocate state-aided private-sector growth as an alternative to enlarging the public system.* Instead, private presidents watched nervously as public campuses grew. They were ready to cooperate with state authorities up to a point but hopeful that this development could be contained within acceptable limits.

The perception among private presidents that public sector growth was inevitable did not imply that independent institutions could not benefit from increased state expenditures for higher education. On the contrary, it was clear that, even with an ambitious program to expand public campuses, Massachusetts would need help from its private colleges and universities to accommodate projected enrollments. Recognizing this reality, the Willis–Harrington commission recommended more state scholarships to help residents attend private colleges. It was also clear to private leaders, however, that the character and extent of state assistance would be determined by the year-to-year machinations of the Massachusetts political system, an uncertain and alien source of aid. In this promising but volatile context, independent leaders recognized a need for an improved means of exercising political influence.

Leadership came from Walsh of B.C., joined by Knowles of N.U. and Case of B.U. Borrowing a model from other states, these men proposed to organize the commonwealth's private institutions into an Association of Independent Colleges and Universities in Massachusetts (A.I.C.U.M.). The new association would not limit the autonomy of members but would utilize their collective power to affect public policy. The founders were particularly eager to forge a working alliance with the B.H.E., which they believed would be the focal point for directing future developments in the public sector.

An organizational meeting, chaired by Walsh, was held at B.C. in March 1967. Walsh reported that B.H.E. chancellor Richard Millard had given his blessing to the new organization. Within weeks A.I.C.U.M. had enrolled fifty-

---

*Private-sector presidents were aware of the constitutional barrier to state aid for private higher education presented by the 1918 amendment to the Massachusetts constitution—see pp. 43 and 341—but this legal constraint was probably not a primary reason for private leaders not to urge expansion of their own institutions as an alternative to public sector expansion. In the late 1960s, as they became conscious of their growing financial problems, the private presidents launched a successful campaign to repeal the anti-aid amendment.

one of fifty-three eligible institutions, including nationally oriented campuses like Harvard and M.I.T. The core of the new organization, however, was made up of poorly endowed colleges and universities that relied heavily on in-state students. Financial support was secured from a local foundation. By the fall, an association office was established at Boston College, and an executive director, freed from other duties on the staff of B.C., was in place.[59]

Initially, the new association gave top priority to state scholarships, working collaboratively with the B.H.E. The results were encouraging. For fiscal year 1968, the scholarship appropriation was $500,000, having risen gradually from $100,000 in 1960. In 1969, however, the figure jumped to $2 million, and the following year to $3.5 million. Meanwhile, leaders of the new association worked with Millard and his staff to mount studies of the state's educational needs and to establish a regional planning process for the Boston metropolitan area.

In mid-1968, with Christ-Janer succeeding Walsh as president, the leaders of A.I.C.U.M. became aware of a new possibility for financial assistance from the commonwealth. Inspiration came from New York, where a gubernatorial commission headed by former Harvard dean McGeorge Bundy had recommended direct state grants to private institutions. Similar plans were under discussion in California, Illinois, Texas, and Oregon. The notion of Bundy-type aid had obvious appeal, and consultations with Millard promised support from the B.H.E. In the spring of 1969 A.I.C.U.M. persuaded the Republican governor, Francis Sargent, to appoint a Select Committee to study the matter, with a charge and membership that closely followed the association's recommendations. Predictably, the committee's January 1970 report proposed direct state subsidies to private colleges and universities based on enrollments of Massachusetts residents.

From A.I.C.U.M.'s perspective, the work of the governor's Select Committee could not have been more satisfactory, but realization of the grants program required repeal of the 1918 constitutional amendment forbidding state aid to private institutions. During 1970 A.I.C.U.M.'s leaders took the first steps down the lengthy road of constitutional change. Though they achieved some initial successes, they also encountered legislative doubts about the readiness of private campuses to accept Massachusetts residents—an echo of the commonwealth's historic class, ethnic, and religious conflicts. There were also worries about diverting resources from public institutions. In late 1970, the governor decided against further action on anti-aid repeal in that year's legislative session.

The failure of A.I.C.U.M.'s first serious attempt to change public policy in Massachusetts taught several important lessons. The private presidents uncovered considerably more political opposition to their cause than they had anticipated. They also learned that support from the B.H.E. did not count for much when important institutional interests were involved. It was now clear that success in the campaign for direct aid from the commonwealth would require a much greater effort than had been mounted so far.[60]

Higher Levels of Organization at the
University of Massachusetts

The rapid growth of colleges and universities in Massachusetts during the 1960s pushed all parts of higher education toward more complex and aggregated modes of organization. This pattern was evident at the institutional level as leaders of both public and private campuses, needing to manage swollen student bodies, bigger budgets with multiple sources of revenue, more diversified programs and expanded facilities, enlarged and redesigned their bureaucracies. A similar phenomenon, at the next higher level of organization, prompted state government to establish the new Board of Higher Education to coordinate growth within the public system and the privates to counter with A.I.C.U.M.

Thus, a logic of countervailing powers, in which each increase in organizational capacity in one part of the system produced a competing response elsewhere, seemed to operate among the state's colleges and universities. This logic was evident not only at the interinstitutional level but also within campus communities, where increases of bureaucratic capabilities tended to occur simultaneously with heightened efforts by particular constituencies, especially faculties, to ensure their influence through enhanced modes of organization. Both patterns—the movement toward higher levels of administrative organization and the emergence of countervailing faculty responses—occurred at the University of Massachusetts during the late 1960s and early 1970s.

Organizational change at UMass was, in any case, inevitable, made so by the inauguration of the three-campus system during the early years of the Lederle administration. By the late 1960s, the university was operating with an outmoded form of administration that had grown up through a series of *ad hoc* adjustments rather than a planned review of new needs. Lederle's decision in the spring of 1969 to resign after completing his tenth year the following June coincided with a growing interest among the trustees in rethinking the university's organization. The moment was made more propitious for change by the simultaneous resignation of longtime board chairman Frank L. Boyden, the fabled headmaster of Deerfield Academy, whose leadership was associated more strongly with the western, rural, Amherst-oriented traditions of the university than with its new, statewide role.

The Executive Committee of the board, now led by a politically well-connected banker from Boston, Joseph P. Healey, commissioned a senior member of the Amherst administration, associate dean of engineering Joseph Marcus, to study patterns of organization among the nation's multicampus universities and make recommendations. Marcus found that universities composed of several campuses, whatever their initial mode of organization, tended to evolve toward a common model: a strong president under a single board supervising the work of relatively autonomous campuses. This pattern was preferable to a weak-president/strong-campus arrangement because it provided maximum leverage for the institution in approaching the legislature, while also facilitating a coordinated approach to state educational needs. It was preferable to a main-campus/branch-campus pattern because it allowed each unit the opportunity to flourish.

Marcus proposed a strong, system-wide presidency supported by several vice presidents. He urged that the new office be located in Boston for ease of communication with state political authorities, but be separate from the Boston campus to ensure equitable treatment of all three units. Marcus also stressed the importance of autonomy for the campuses, which would be led by chancellors. The crucial distinction was between policy and operations. The president would establish policy contexts, determine budgetary priorities, coordinate system-wide planning activities, and represent the university to external constituencies. The chancellors would be relatively free to administer internal campus affairs. To strengthen the campuses, Marcus suggested that the vice presidents be viewed as staff officers and that chancellors report directly to the president.[61]

During 1969–1970, the trustees took the first steps toward establishing the new "university system." A search committee sought a leader who could inaugurate the reconceived presidential office at a high level of visibility and political effectiveness. Meanwhile, the respected provost at Amherst, Oswald Tippo, who had grown restive toward the end of the Lederle administration—on one occasion he had submitted his resignation—was elevated to the position of chancellor, a title already held by Broderick at Boston. In the spring of 1970, the trustees announced a choice for the presidency who seemed perfectly matched to the job. He was Robert C. Wood, a well-known political scientist and department chairman at M.I.T. who was also chairman of the Massachusetts Bay Transportation Authority and director of the Harvard-M.I.T. Joint Center for Urban Studies.

Wood's career had followed an unusual path for a scholar. With degrees from Princeton and Harvard, a widely read book on suburbia, and a senior appointment at a major institution, he possessed flawless academic credentials. Throughout his career, however, he had been active in liberal Democratic politics at state and national levels; from 1966 to 1969, he was under secretary and secretary of Housing and Urban Development in the Johnson administration. An eastern, cosmopolitan figure with national visibility, Wood had in excess all the qualities needed to reposition UMass as a major public university with statewide concerns rather than a somewhat overgrown state college "out west." He also seemed well-suited to negotiate the political thicket he was certain to encounter—among wary, campus-oriented academics threatened by a powerful new executive office; and among an array of external forces concerned about the expansion of the state university. Though an intellectual, Wood was exquisitely attuned to the uses of power. He understood it, and he enjoyed exercising it.[62]

In the fall of 1970, Wood opened the presidential office in the heart of Boston's financial district, a short walk from the state house. He appointed vice presidents for administration, especially for budget and for development, while deferring action on an academic vice presidency. He asked for and received supervisory authority over the treasurer and secretary of the trustees, steps not clearly anticipated by Marcus that gave him control over two officers who otherwise might have provided the board with independent staff capabilities. To strengthen ties to key political constituencies, he created two new public service institutes, one for labor affairs and one for local government, turning for the directorship of the latter to former Senate president Maurice Donohue. To smooth relations with the privates, he brought in Franklin Patterson, founding president of Hampshire College, member of the Willis–Harrington commission, and a man widely associated with efforts to promote interinstitutional cooperation. To connect with the Catholic church, A.I.C.U.M., and the Catholic political community, he hired Father Walsh, who had done a short stint as president of Fordham after leaving B.C.

Perhaps most important of all, through force of personality, public prominence, careful cultivation of the media, and intense, restless energy, Wood immediately established himself as the visible voice and leader of the university in the press and among state officials. While initially cautious about asserting operational authority over the internal affairs of the institution—his staff functioned more as troubleshooters than administrative officers—he made clear from the start his intention to exercise complete control over external and political relations.[63]

Wood's activities were bound to stir conflict with the campuses, especially Amherst, where leaders were accustomed to operating autonomously and dealing directly with the legislature. The potential for difficulty was increased by the fact that Wood's appointment occurred during a period of internal organizational change at both Amherst and Boston. At the older campus, the faculty had grown increasingly restive with administrative practices little changed since the early postwar years. In the spring of 1970, only months before Wood's appointment, the trustees approved a statement on governance, based on the work of a group of Amherst faculty, that greatly increased the professorial role in campus affairs. A year later, the Senate constitution was revised to assert faculty control over committee appointments. Parallel changes were occurring at Boston in association with the governance reforms sponsored by Broderick. Thus, political forces on both campuses were promoting the diffusion of organizational power to representative and especially faculty bodies at precisely the same moment that a new system president was asserting the authority of his office. The combination of events was a political crisis waiting to happen.

The stresses inherent in the new organizational arrangements expressed themselves initially and most dramatically at the level of the chancellors. These individuals, who, as heads of campuses, occupied positions traditionally associated with great importance and prestige in American higher education, found their power eroded from above and below. The structural conflicts were exacerbated by personal tensions that quickly developed between Wood and both Tippo and Broderick. During the fall of 1971, Wood took a number of steps to increase his managerial role, especially in the areas of budget and academic personnel. Both Tippo and Broderick objected, and in October Tippo resigned, the second time he had done so in two years.

Tippo's action reinforced the worries of an Amherst community disposed toward suspicion of the university's aggressive new executive. A "Committee of Concern" composed a series of questions about trustee intentions with respect to university organization. The Amherst Senate called upon the trustees to endorse A.A.U.P. guidelines on campus government. Tensions built somewhat more slowly at Boston, but Wood and Broderick found it increasingly difficult to work together. In the spring of 1972, after a series of skirmishes and only eight months after Tippo's resignation, Wood forced Broderick from office.[64]

By 1972 the struggle for organizational power between the president's office and the campuses, and between the faculty generally and the administration, had become sufficiently acrimonious to require trustee action. Questions of student power were an additional but secondary concern. In June the trustees established a committee of faculty, students, and administrators from each of the campuses to review the university's new system of organization and recommend improvements.

At the heart of the committee's proposals were the principles of "joint effort" and "primary responsibility," which meant that administrative power must be shared and that key subgroups, particularly faculty and students, should have the right to initiate recommendations in areas where they had professional expertise or special interests. The committee's report also included ground rules for administrative responses to actions by campus governance bodies and suggested two new multicampus committees, budget and long-range planning, to provide settings in which faculty, students, and administrators from each campus could interact with the president on central questions of university policy.

Adopted in the spring of 1973, the policy on university governance diffused, for the moment, the tensions that had been building since the establishment of the new system office. But these problems were rooted in struggles for control that were not likely to be resolved by a broad statement of intent, especially one that, in the end, did little to change the real distribution of power. One indication of future difficulties was a growing interest among the faculty members in collective bargaining. Though unionization was defeated in an initial vote in 1973, the sudden strength of this movement made it clear that the principle of countervailing powers could carry UMass to yet another level of organizational aggregation if the faculty felt threatened by increasingly remote and powerful administrative centers.

By this time, too, conflicts within the university involved much more than structural rifts associated with Wood's new office. UMass was beginning to feel the effects of the far more skeptical public and legislative attitudes toward higher education that had been building in Massachusetts and around the country since the late 1960s.[65]

From Rapid Growth to Steady State

Robert Wood and the "Future University"

By disposition, Robert Wood was a builder and an innovator. As a liberal intellectual, he had participated in the debates of the 1960s about the problems of American universities, and he was sympathetically attuned to the litany of reform proposals emanating from the study commissions of this period. Wood was especially critical of the impulse shown by universities during the golden age to reproduce the educational patterns of well-established, high-status institutions, and he used his inauguration in December 1970 to encourage fresh thinking. "It is my conviction," he told his listeners, "that new patterns, new models must be found for university education in the Commonwealth. Our liberal arts education derives from the days of Cardinal Newman and the idea of training for a leisure class . . . Our preoccupation with graduate studies and graduate schools comes from a venerable tradition of scholarly elitism . . ."

Wood questioned the need for additional graduate programs and argued for renewed attention to undergraduate work. Just shifting the focus, however, would not be enough. Noting that most UMass students came from moderate-income families and wished to improve their economic prospects, Wood urged curricula that would give undergraduates practical skills, especially courses that would help them "become aware of society's needs and capable of responding to them." This last point revealed Wood's strong interest in the public service potential of the university, which he emphasized even more clearly in talking about the scholarly work of the faculty. "In field after field," Wood stated, the knowledge we have has out-run our ability to use it." It was time for the state university to focus its energies on the absorption and utilization of knowledge rather than its generation.

Wood's speech challenged central themes of recent development at both Amherst and Boston. The established western campus had spent the 1960s building just the kinds of graduate programs and research capabilities that Wood questioned, and the new urban campus had evolved as a traditional undergraduate arts and sciences institution. Wood made it plain, moreover, that he intended to turn his rhetoric into concrete plans for change. As the centerpiece of his inaugural, he announced the formation of an external planning committee, composed of highly regarded leaders from business, the professions, and academia, to help him chart new directions. He called the group the Committee on the Future University of Massachusetts.[66]

Wood's belief that he could lead UMass into a period of educational innovation was based on the assumption that the growth patterns of the 1960s would be sustained for the foreseeable future. In an early review of policy issues for the Board of Trustees, the new president argued that current plans to build the three-campus system to a total of fifty thousand students by 1980 were too restrained. Noting that the university's enrollment targets were derived from projections of student demand produced by the Board of Higher Education in 1969, Wood argued that the B.H.E. analysis failed to consider a number of important factors, including the inability of the state's private institutions to absorb their assigned share of statewide growth.

Wood's assessment was echoed in the report of his Future committee, issued in December 1971. While acknowledging that "the era of burgeoning expansion is over for most public universities," the committee noted that UMass, "having developed late, is still growing" and was slated, in B.H.E. plans, to double in size over the next ten years. In the committee's view, however, merely doubling enrollments would not be adequate, even though the B.H.E. probably had overestimated future demand for higher education in the commonwealth. Wood and the trustees, the Future committee concluded, should plan to add facilities—especially at Boston, Worcester, and a series of satellite centers around the state—for fifteen thousand to twenty thousand part-time students in addition to the fifty thousand full-timers already anticipated.[67]

Even before the Future committee issued its report, Wood was promoting new programs on the campuses. His most ambitious initiative involved a university law school, a goal of Lederle and his associates at Amherst for some time. In the spring of 1971, Wood appointed a study committee, containing representatives of the state's private law schools and chaired by former House speaker, now attorney general, Robert Quinn, to consider the potential need for UMass to move into this field. A year later, this group recommended a law center at Amherst, combining the new law school with additional programs in allied fields, and Wood established a campus-based planning group to turn the proposal into a concrete plan.

Wood conceived a parallel expansion at Worcester. He wanted this campus to move beyond medical education and create an array of programs in the health sciences, thereby serving a larger and more diverse student body than anticipated in existing plans. At Boston, Wood encouraged Broderick to proceed with the College of Public and Community Service, and he also urged the campus to think of expanding beyond Columbia Point, possibly by acquiring adjacent properties, possibly through dispersed facilities at multiple locations in the metropolitan area.

The Future committee weighed in with its own set of recommendations: an expanded admissions effort oriented toward low-income and minority students, supported by new financial aid and skill-development courses; a technology-based "open university" to bring educational opportunities to individuals unable to reach the campuses; innovative instructional programs, including problem-centered units and field-based courses; "vastly expanded" advising and counseling facilities; and increased efforts in public service.[68]

Both Wood and his committee knew their recommendations would require more financial support. Wood focused on the need for larger budgets in his initial policy review for the board, arguing that the commonwealth was capable of doing more for higher education, especially in the context of tax reform. The Future committee estimated that its recommendations would add six to seven million dollars to the university's fiscal year 1973 budget.

As the Future committee was readying its report for publication in late 1971, financial planners in the governor's office were formulating the state's 1973 budget for submission to the legislature. Governor Sargent's fiscal message, issued in early 1972, suggested a far different financial climate than the one envisioned by Wood and his planning committee. Drawing attention to the new sluggishness in the economy, rising inflation, and heightened pressures on state revenues, the governor recommended restricted support for most state agencies and actual cuts for some. For the University of Massachusetts, which had grown accustomed to large annual increases, the governor proposed a modest increment over the previous year's funding. This was, as Wood noted, a "standstill" budget, hardly a basis for the panoply of initiatives that he and his planning committee hoped to launch. The governor's fiscal year 1973 budget proposals were the first clear signal that the economic and political conditions that had enabled the University of Massachusetts to prosper during the 1960s were changing.[69]

The New Context of Higher Education

In truth, political support for expanding the University of Massachusetts at the rate of the mid-1960s was eroding even before Robert Wood assumed his duties. During the final years of his administration, Lederle found it progressively more difficult to win large annual increases in the university's appropriation. Though the financial growth of the mid-1960s continued to the end of the decade in terms of yearly budgetary increments, the tone had changed, and Lederle sounded the alarm. In 1968 he issued a glossy pamphlet titled "Massachusetts Must Do Better" faulting the commonwealth's commitment to higher education and drawing unfavorable comparisons between Massachusetts and other states. In his 1969 annual report, and again in his letter of resignation, Lederle expressed concern about loss of momentum in the university's development as a result of diminished support.

To some extent, of course, the new financial pressures felt by UMass involved changes in the national environment of higher education, especially federal policy, that were affecting many academic institutions. As government funding for scholarly work became more difficult to obtain in the late 1960s, states and institutions felt greater pressure from their faculties to provide resources locally. Thus, perceptions of the university's financial situation within the UMass community tended to exaggerate the slackening of state support. Still, the political atmosphere of higher education in Massachusetts clearly had changed by the beginning of the Wood administration. In early 1971, Broderick spoke at length to the Boston faculty about the altered circumstances of the university, warning that the bounty of the recent past "is unlikely to come again except in our dreams."[70]

Two broad forces converged in the late 1960s and early 1970s to create financial problems for public higher education. The most fundamental difficulty was economic. These were years of declining business vitality in the state.

348

Prices were rising; growth was weak; unemployment was growing. At the same time, some chickens of the 1960s were coming home to roost. During a decade of economic expansion—and expanding social programs—state tax revenues had increased steadily as a percentage of gross state product, so that political leaders became concerned about the state's reputation as "taxachusetts." New taxes were thus an unlikely source of increased revenue—Wood's hopes notwithstanding—as the taxpayers demonstrated in defeating a referendum on a graduated income tax in 1972.

Claims on state revenues, however, had grown from a number of directions, particularly the commonwealth's assumption of local welfare costs in 1969. With the economy stagnant and no chance for significant new revenues, it was apparent that the funding prospects for all state agencies in the early 1970s were extremely poor. As Broderick put it in his 1971 address: "The State House will be scrutinizing our budget more demandingly than ever, not because of any faltering of enthusiasm for UMass/Boston, but because dollars will be scarce."[71]

Unfortunately, enthusiasm *was* faltering for public higher education. Several factors contributed to the change. In Massachusetts, as in other states, the attitudes of citizens and politicians were adversely affected by the rash of highly publicized student demonstrations. The altered mood did not especially reflect problems at the University of Massachusetts. Indeed, the three UMass campuses were less active centers of student unrest than many other institutions, despite the occurrence of several incidents at Amherst and Boston, one of which required intervention by the state police. But feelings for UMass inevitably were influenced by the general souring of attitudes toward students, educators, and academic institutions that resulted from the student protest movement.

As the base of support for UMass weakened, negative political forces became more important. Lederle was convinced that the rapid growth of the university in the mid-1960s had produced resentment in other segments of public higher education and in other regions of the state. He believed these feelings began to affect the atmosphere in the legislature by the end of the decade, especially among key supporters, like Maurice Donohue and David Bartley, who had statewide political ambitions. Pressures from the state's independent colleges and universities to constrain public sector growth also took a sharp upswing in these years, as private presidents became concerned about their own financial problems. The new president of Boston University, John Silber, was particularly aggressive in challenging the need for continued expansion of public higher education.

In the early 1970s A.I.C.U.M. abandoned the policy of cooperation with the public sector that it had followed in its early years. The association began advocating increased tuition charges at public institutions in order to equalize the competition for students between public and private campuses and pressed the state to contract with private schools for academic programs in specific fields instead of building new capacity within the public system. In this context, Wood's proposal to build a law school on the UMass/Amherst campus encountered a firestorm of criticism from private institutions and the state bar association, which issued a statement opposing the initiative.[72]

The receptivity of state officials to the negative political pressures of the early 1970s was intensified by growing skepticism about the need to continue expanding public higher education. The buildup of the 1960s had reflected widespread belief among policymakers that there existed a large demand for access to college by state residents that could not be met by existing institutions, a circumstance confirmed by the Board of Higher Education's estimates in 1969. The B.H.E.'s projections, however, had been suspect on methodological grounds from the beginning—Wood's Future committee concluded they greatly overestimated likely enrollments—and as time went by, the criticisms and doubts grew stronger.

Reports from around the country of diminished pressures for growth, curtailment of expansion plans by other states, and the collapse of the market for Ph.D.s reinforced questions about the need for Massachusetts to extend its own program of institutional development. By 1972 the B.H.E. was convinced that revised projections were needed, particularly in view of the potential for using new demographic data collected in the 1970 census. For advocates of additional public sector growth, the new enrollment study, published in 1973, was devastating. It found that the state was likely to need two hundred thousand fewer undergraduate places in 1980 than the B.H.E. had projected in 1969.[73]

The combination of tight revenues, weakened enthusiasm for higher education, and doubts about the need for continued expansion radically altered the political environment for the commonwealth's public colleges and universities. Realizing that a revised basis for state policy was needed, the chancellor of higher education, Patrick McCarthy, joined by the governor's secretary of education, Joseph Cronin, initiated three major studies by external groups. The Academy for Educational Development, a respected New York consulting firm, undertook a comprehensive assessment of state needs in higher education. A local group, University Consultants, reviewed the area of adult and continuing education. A second local firm, the Organization for Social and Technical Innovation (O.S.T.I.), began a detailed, institution-by-institution study of the state's colleges and universities, public and private.

By 1973 these reports were in the hands of state policymakers and were sounding common themes. There was no basis for a continuing emphasis on expansion either in terms of enrollments or physical facilities. Several of the state's most important private institutions were already in financial trouble and were likely to experience difficulty maintaining enrollments when the state's youth cohort began to shrink. Future public policy should take into account the capabilities of both public and private institutions, viewing the two sectors together as a comprehensive system for meeting the state's academic needs.[74]

Taken together, the policy reviews of the early 1970s signaled a resurgence of the traditional academic politics of Massachusetts in which the substantive and political strength of an established private system tended to confine the public sector within relatively narrow boundaries. Clearly, the balance of power between public and private higher education had shifted in favor of the publics in recent years. What had happened would not be undone and would probably provide a base for some future growth. But it was equally certain that the era of rapid expansion was over for state-supported higher education in Massachusetts. The implications of the new situation were particularly important for the University of Massachusetts, which was engaged in major building programs on all three campuses, two of which had opened only recently.

Cutting Back

The UMass leadership realized that a change of course was needed well before the policy reviews sponsored by the state B.H.E. were completed. The clear message contained in the governor's budget proposals in early 1972 was followed, later that year, by B.H.E. refusal to endorse the law center at Amherst, the first major defeat that the board had administered to UMass. By early 1973, Healey and Wood were recommending that the university reduce the enrollment goals which only a year earlier had seemed too modest. Plans for the Boston campus were scaled back to 12,500 full- and part-time students, then further cut to 10,000. The idea of multiple locations was quietly abandoned. Plans to expand the program at Worcester beyond medical education were shelved.

Wood's 1973 report, the second of his presidency, formally announced the shift of emphasis: "The strategy of growth that had characterized the past . . . has in the opening years of the new decade changed perforce to a strategy of consolidating the University and assuring its excellence." With this realization, the central challenge of Wood's still-young presidency was transformed: the innovator-builder oriented toward the expansive conditions of the 1960s was now called upon to manage a partially developed institution with little hope of significant new resources.[75]

PART THREE

Patterns

CHAPTER SEVEN

The Institutional Complex and Academic Adaptation, 1945-1980

Change among universities in Massachusetts during the golden age illustrated the pervasive tendency of academic institutions, linked as they were to historic social divisions, to seek higher status. With essential resources readily available, these campuses converged from disparate prewar positions toward the functions and values of the research university, the dominant model of excellence in the postwar period. The inclination to pursue common goals was circumscribed, however, because the circumstances of change were always specific and resources were never infinite. Local variations in competitive conditions combined with other elements of the institutional complex—academic ideas and organizational dynamics—to channel campus ambitions and preserve elements of diversity.

The new conditions of the 1970s further demonstrated the relationship between competition and diversity while testing the durability of initiatives launched in years when growth was easy. With resources now more constrained, universities were compelled to craft their strategies of change more carefully and pay closer attention to their particular strengths and characteristics. Still, campus priorities in the decade following the golden age revealed the extent to which institutional ambitions tend to take precedence over educational ideas. Efforts to pursue the most important reform proposals of the late 1960s and early 1970s were repeatedly subordinated to the protection of institutional interests in the face of new and challenging competitive pressures.

The Institutional Complex in Action: 1945-1970

Upward Academic Mobility—the Institutional Imperative

In the closing section of Chapter 2, we considered the forces that produced change among universities in the golden age as understood by commentators at the end of the period. These accounts stressed two phenomena: the increased demands of society for academic services and the enlarged power of the academic professions. In the face of these nonacademic and extrainstitutional pressures, it was widely argued, individual universities were largely reactive, more carried by currents they could not control than aggressive in shaping their own futures.

The postwar histories of universities in Massachusetts, as we have encountered them in the last four chapters, demonstrated the importance of macro-level causes of institutional change but also focused attention on the initiative exercised by campus leaders within an academic marketplace still dominated by interinstitutional competition. There were differences among these campuses in the degree to which their leaders tried to manipulate environmental circumstances for institutional ends, as well as in the success of such efforts, but in most cases, discretionary choices at the campus level were major factors in shaping patterns of development.

Responses to the pressure for undergraduate expansion illustrated the importance of institutional choice. Growth was the most insistent social demand of the golden age, as an expanding youth cohort sought college places in larger and larger proportions. Late 1960s' observers consistently cited the impact of increased applications in reshaping the nation's system of higher education, while academic leaders credited themselves with opening their gates to the generous democratic impulses of the postwar years.

Among universities in Massachusetts, however, policies on admission and enrollment were driven more by institutional priorities than by social demands. Universities that could afford not to expand because they were not heavily dependent on tuition for working capital—Harvard, M.I.T., and Brandeis—largely resisted pressures to grow at the undergraduate level. Those that stressed expansion—B.U., B.C., and Northeastern—had a financial interest in doing so. The clearest exception to the rule that internally defined institutional interests governed enrollment policies occurred, not surprisingly, in the public sector. During the 1950s, the University of Massachusetts was forced by the legislature to expand more rapidly than campus leaders thought was wise.[1]

The circumstance most likely to persuade campus leaders to expand beyond a preferred size was not the social appeal for more spaces but the institutional need for more revenues, as the case of Tufts illustrated. In fact, throughout the period, enrollment policies were often inversely related to demand: restrictive policies were adopted by universities with the most applications in relation to seats, while expansion was pursued eagerly by those under the least pressure to grow.

Enrollment policies were rarely just a matter of money. Leaders of universities that embraced growth—Mather and Lederle at UMass, Knowles at N.U., and Case at B.U.—expressed a dedication to making their institutions accessible that was rooted in genuine value commitments. It remained true, nonetheless, that social considerations did not produce undergraduate growth in the absence of economic incentives. Indeed, once the analysis is discounted for finances, the most common response to demands for increased access was not more seats but greater selectivity.

From an institutional perspective, the chief significance of applicant pressure was that it allowed campuses—in most cases for the first time—to determine the nature of their student bodies. Though there were exceptions and countercurrents—the most important being efforts to enroll African Americans—the choices universities made in this new situation chiefly reflected an eagerness to improve their academic standing and financial security. The tendency was to enroll those applicants most likely, through their future achievements, to return reputation, influence, and wealth to the campus that nurtured them.[2]

Such students could be characterized, of course, as especially deserving of admission. It is hard to believe, however, that a reluctance to deny opportunities to talented young people was a dominant motive in shaping admission policies, since universities competed most vigorously for candidates with the greatest range of choices. This was particularly true at schools that restricted undergraduate numbers and pursued selectivity. Similar priorities appeared at the rapid-growth institutions as they approached the size that their leaders considered optimal or maximal. Such practices readily account for the increase in the class stratification of student bodies that occurred among universities in Massachusetts and around the country during the golden age.

The environment, of course, placed limits on the degree to which even selective universities could shape their student bodies. Harvard, with its broad appeal, had few externally imposed constraints, although there was a problem for much of the period in attracting Catholics. At M.I.T., by contrast, the boundaries were severe. Despite its high selectivity the Institute was no more successful in appealing to applicants whose primary focus lay outside math and science than was Brandeis in drawing non-Jews.

Policies on program development and faculty recruitment, like those on admission and enrollment, were decisively shaped by the desire of campus leaders to raise the status of their institutions. The universities that restricted undergraduate expansion built high-status and expensive doctoral programs and clusters of research-oriented scholars even when societal demand for such emphases was questionable. The national needs for more Ph.D.s and better research were evident for much of the period, of course, and provided the basis for elite institutions, like Harvard and M.I.T., to freeze undergraduate numbers and build the advanced functions. At Brandeis and Tufts, however, the development of graduate programs and the recruitment of research-oriented faculty reflected strategies of upward mobility much more clearly than responses to societal requirements.[3]

The mass-market institutions adopted more complex policies, since they were compelled to expand their undergraduate programs and their teaching faculties to accommodate enlarged numbers of undergraduates. Each of them also sought ways, however, to incorporate the functions of research universities as part of explicit strategies of upgrading. Lederle hoped to recast the Amherst campus of UMass in the image of the University of Michigan. Walsh aspired to outdistance Notre Dame as the nation's leading Catholic university. Case wanted to transform B.U. from a service-oriented school for local commuters into a residential university with regional or national influence. Knowles sought for Northeastern "a place at the head table of academic respectability." If, in the effort to build advanced programs, upwardly mobile institutions could meet important social needs—in the training of skilled professionals, the advancement of understanding, or the solution of important problems—they were disposed to shape their initiatives accordingly. If not, however, they pursued such priorities anyway. Long after it became clear that the nation and state had created more Ph.D. programs than were needed, the leaders of the University of Massachusetts pressed for doctoral expansion. They showed no interest, however, in designing graduate programs for community college teachers, despite the urgings of a legislative commission.

The impulse of campus leaders to raise the positions of their institutions in the academic hierarchy was hardly new in the golden age. On the contrary, we observed the same phenomenon as it was expressed under different market conditions during the decades before World War II. So powerful was the drive for upward repositioning that it produced generalized patterns of development over extended periods to which all universities in Massachusetts conformed.

They began as limited-purpose campuses, dedicated to a particular form of education for a specified, typically local constituency. Under the dual pressures of the academic marketplace, they diversified off the original base, if necessary adding programs to increase enrollments and earn revenues, if possible adding functions to achieve academic goals or enhance prestige. Diversification policies tended to follow either a "low road" or a "high road." Universities least able to obtain private funds and build endowments—Tufts in the nineteenth and early twentieth centuries, B.U. for much of the twentieth century, and B.C. and Northeastern in the postwar years—pursued the low road, expanding horizontally with new undergraduate programs, often practical in character, for local commuters, growing large, and retaining unselective admission policies.

Those institutions that could attract large donations—Harvard, M.I.T., and Brandeis—pursued the high road, evolving as limited-purpose, selective, residential campuses for national constituencies at the undergraduate level and diversifying vertically with graduate programs and clusters of distinguished scholars. Campuses that followed the high road based claims to status on the quality of their offerings, their students, and their faculties. Campuses that followed the low road sought prestige in size. The proudest boast of Asa Knowles, the chief exponent of low-road functions among local universities, came in 1967 when he reported that Northeastern had become the largest private university in the United States.[4]

Low-road campuses tended eventually to use the revenues earned by their inexpensive undergraduate programs to shift toward high-road functions—building residential campuses, adding more costly and prestigious programs, upgrading their student bodies, and, ultimately, attracting private financial support, in part from the constituencies they had cultivated through unfashionable technical offerings. The golden age provided unique opportunities for such shifts. Tufts committed itself to an elite strategy in the 1920s, made halting progress in the 1940s and 1950s, and finally succeeded in the 1960s. B.C.

and B.U. shifted priorities toward high-road functions during the second half of the golden age.[5]

As upwardly mobile universities adopted more advanced functions, they often cast aside the low-status programs on which they had depended at an earlier stage. Boston College historically provided educational opportunities for commuters from the city's ethnic neighborhoods, but the order's ambitions for the campus, carried out by Walsh in the 1960s, left this population behind. Similarly, as soon as their circumstances permitted it, leaders of Tufts abandoned the affiliated-schools programs that had kept them solvent during the Depression, the war, and the early postwar years. By this process, local constituencies were "bumped down" to lower-status, often newer institutions. Some of the programs dropped by Tufts were picked up by Northeastern. Low-income commuters turned from Boston College to the Boston campus of UMass and to other public campuses.

To speak of long-term patterns of change is not to suggest that these directions were planned or even articulated in their full implications. Indeed, universities in Massachusetts engaged in remarkably little long-range planning during the central years of the golden age, and the plans that were made rarely transcended particular administrations. Moreover, trajectories of development were subject to diversion as a result of changes in leadership or deterioration in the resource environment. Such contingencies make the basically linear evolutionary patterns that we have observed especially notable. Each university's evolutionary course seemed simply to occur, without explicit design, as successive generations of leaders, some of them quite ignorant of their institutions' histories and their predecessors' achievements, sought to advance the positions of their campuses.

Thus, there occurred a ratcheting up of institutional ambitions from one regime to the next. Maxwell of B.C. aspired to lead the top Catholic university in New England. Walsh, believing this goal achieved, sought to challenge the leading Catholic campuses nationally. Ell of Northeastern sought stability and acceptability within a circumscribed programmatic framework and a commitment to local service. Knowles added the idea of horizontal and vertical diversification and sought national recognition.

There was an irony in these upward spirals. At any given stage, campus leaders were inclined to believe that their ambitions would serve the interests of their current constituencies. Those who advocated building UMass/ Amherst into a major public university did so in the name of improving opportunities for the moderate-income students whom the campus traditionally enrolled. As a result of institutional progress, however, UMass attracted more students capable financially of attending private colleges who squeezed out many of the less-affluent students whose needs had justified change. Similarly, Walsh of B.C. sought to raise the academic standards of his campus as a means of enhancing its contributions to Catholic life in the region. The process of upgrading, however, built into the university forces far less concerned than he with Boston and New England, and in his later years he regretted the indifference of his successors to the community from which B.C. had sprung.

The consistency with which universities sought upward academic mobility draws attention to a particular limitation on the discretion available to campus leaders. There was, indeed, a compulsory quality to policies of institutional change that is not difficult to understand. What leader, in an atmosphere of rapid institutional development by competitors on every hand, could survive politically while opting out of the race? How many would even be tempted to do so? If, moreover, in the new scheme of academic values, maintaining the appearance of quality required the presence of research-oriented scholars and if such faculty could not be attracted, retained, and helped in their work without doctoral programs, what campus leader would reject the dominant institutional paradigm?[6]

Harvard, in recognizing the inevitability of dependence on federal funds, no less than Northeastern in accepting the necessity of doctoral programs, acknowledged that securing its position in the academic hierarchy constituted a primary claim on the efforts of institutional leaders. Presidents who attempted to assert traditional, college-centered values against the priorities of the research university—Van Meter at UMass/Amherst, Pusey at Harvard, or Stratton at M.I.T.—were mostly frustrated in intramural policy debates. The external conditions that determined institutional prestige empowered internal representatives of the ascendant value system.

The imperatives of upward mobility constrained but did not eliminate the discretion available to campus leaders. The development policies of universities in Massachusetts expressed, in fact, quite different relationships to the dominant paradigm of the age. Sachar of Brandeis embraced the research model because he was primarily interested in raising his university's status. Others, like Wessell of Tufts or Walsh of Boston College, worked to balance the claims of the research ideal with more particular institutional values— Catholicism at B.C. and liberal learning at Tufts. Knowles of Northeastern represented still another possibility. He was interested in undergraduate education in practical fields and skeptical about the dominant emphasis on basic disciplines, graduate work, and research. He made the accommodations he felt necessary to promote his campus but maintained a primary focus on N.U.'s distinctive functions. Thus, in a central dialectic of the institutional complex, specific commitments often intersected the conformist pressures of upward mobility, causing universities to nurture their special qualities at the same time they adopted elite conventions.

Institutional Mobility and Social Mobility

To observe the mandatory character of upward institutional mobility is not, of course, to explain the pervasiveness of this phenomenon. Why, ultimately, were universities in Massachusetts so profoundly oriented toward improving their positions in the academic hierarchy? Each was, after all, doing useful work and doing it well in the years before World War II, and important subpopulations wanted to continue those missions, subject only to the requirements of modernization and renewal. Yet none of these institutions chose to retain its established domain once presented with the opportunity to shift to high-road activities. Why were conservative institutional forces so consistently overwhelmed by advocates of upward mobility? And why, ultimately, did conservatives offer so little fight and stand aside so willingly while others took the lead in transforming their campuses? At this point, the documentary record fails us, and we are forced to speculate, with all the risks that entails. Still, confronted with long-term patterns of change at eight universities, it is hard to avoid the conclusion that a powerful and largely unacknowledged value was being expressed: the deeply held American commitment to social mobility.

There was ample reason, as we observed in Chapter 1, to link the early histories of the state's universities with broader societal patterns of stratification and conflict. From the beginning, social prestige conferred academic prestige, and social prestige involved both occupation and wealth. Thus, colonial Harvard, in training the next generation of ministers for a community dominated by religion and in enrolling the sons of leading families, was tied, from its inception, to the social elites of Massachusetts. The college worked hard to retain this association in subsequent periods by continuing to attract both the academically talented and the socially influential. The genius of Charles Eliot was his understanding that a new form of education was needed to train the leaders of post-Civil War America and that Harvard risked its position by clinging to the classical curriculum inherited from its Congregational founders.

Academic prestige also conferred social prestige. Thus, other groups—Universalists, Methodists, Catholics, and farmers—intensely conscious of Harvard and its social functions, sponsored colleges not only to educate their young but also to raise their own status. These communities were inevitably disposed toward projects that would raise the standing of their institutions, which typically meant making them more like Harvard. The pattern was by no means simple or unilinear, however; we have seen how devout Catholics, loyal Universalists, and narrowly focused farmers sometimes resisted measures intended to raise institutional prestige at B.C., Tufts, and Massachusetts Agricultural College.

The link between academic and social prestige was reinforced in the late nineteenth and early twentieth centuries as colleges assumed the task of identifying the most talented young people for movement into leading positions in business, government, and the professions. As the numbers seeking higher education expanded, middle- and working-class students were drawn to campuses that could most effectively promote their economic and social ascent.[7] Thus, historically, the ambitions of educators, the aspirations of nonacademic communities, and the hopes of students conspired to push universities toward patterns of development that would enhance their power and prestige in comparison with other institutions.

In the years following World War II, the landscape of higher education changed, yet the association of academic institutions and social mobility remained strong—probably stronger than ever. There were puzzling aspects to this continuity. One might have expected, for example, that the weakening of ties between campuses and nonacademic sponsoring communities that occurred at all the state's upwardly mobile universities would reduce pressures to raise status, since the social resentments of these constituencies had historically provided an incentive for institutional advance. But, as we have seen, the opposite occurred. Universities pursued strategies of upward mobility more vigorously than ever, and the inclinations of traditional sponsors to retain functions reflective of their particular values—like moribund divinity schools at Tufts and B.U. or archaic requirements in philosophy and theology at B.C.—were often perceived by academic leaders as impediments to progress.

To a substantial degree, the postwar intensification of efforts by institutions to raise their positions reflected long-standing ambitions expressed in the unusual conditions of the golden age. But something else occurred also: as universities cut loose from traditional sponsoring communities their roles were strengthened as vehicles for the social ambitions of their members—trustees, administrative leaders, and faculty, as well as students. The social tensions they embodied became less the original conflicts between religious groups and regions and more those of social class and occupational status. Members of governing boards were now selected less because of their ethnic and religious backgrounds and more because of their social and economic standing. The highest-ranking universities had that most impressive rosters of trustees. Academic leaders seeking to upgrade their institutions—Sachar, Wessell, and Walsh were examples—often sought to replace board members from traditional constituencies with more cosmopolitan individuals who could link them to important centers of influence and wealth. Board members, in turn, often viewed their roles as opportunities for personal advancement as much as for service to a campus to which they were devoted.

Administrative leaders themselves decreasingly lived out their professional lives within single institutions and increasingly viewed their positions as stepping stones toward higher positions at a "better" place. A parallel evolution was evident among faculties, which also became less reflective of traditional sponsoring communities, more tied to nationally organized, discipline-based professional societies. Few of this newer breed would reject Harvard to take a job at Tufts, or turn down Tufts for Northeastern, because they admired the particular commitments of the lower-status institution. Most faculties were disposed toward proposals that would narrow the professional and social distance that separated them from better-situated colleagues.[8]

Social prestige, moreover, still conferred academic prestige. Here lay the magnetic appeal of the new elite model of academic excellence, which mirrored an altered set of social concerns. As Alain Touraine has observed, the priorities of the postwar years represented "a complete reversal."

> The education theme was once aristocratic, while the technical-professional theme was the "democratic" one; now it was just the opposite. The highest type of activity (research) linked the university to the social and political elite, while the education theme became a grass-roots demand . . .[9]

The connections between scholarship, status, and power were of fundamental importance in driving the postwar preoccupation with research and graduate education and also help to explain the intensified pursuit of academic prestige. As Touraine points out, the social significance of academic work before the war lay primarily in the identification and grooming of future leaders, not the instrumental value of knowledge. In the postwar period, however, as scholarly activities became essential elements of economic, military, and technological progress, universities became significant institutional actors at the highest levels of political and economic life.

The academic stakes were thus greatly raised, and those who sought roles in this drama saw universities as stages for their performances. Although his own institution retained strong ties to its traditional sponsor, the Society of Jesus, Walsh of B.C. understood this new world with particular clarity: "Never in history has there been an educational institution so . . . powerful to shape its time as the modern American university . . . The purpose of the American Jesuit university therefore is to become an ever stronger factor in this shaping of society *ad majorem Dei gloriam.*"[10]

Ironically, despite the efforts of academic leaders to raise the status and improve the quality of their institutions, their relative standing changed very little, especially in the perceptions of nonacademic observers and potential students. A rough ranking of universities in Massachusetts in 1940 in terms of perceived prestige would have put Harvard and M.I.T. (in that order) at the top, Tufts and BU in a middle group, and UMass (M.S.C.), B.C., and Northeastern in a bottom category. A similar ranking at the beginning of the century would have produced similar results, with allowances for the fact that Northeastern had barely opened. As late as 1970, notwithstanding the enormous developments of the postwar years, very little had changed in their relative positions. In the broader arenas in which they functioned—other Ivy League and research universities for Harvard, other technical institutes for M.I.T., other Jesuit colleges for B.C., and other public campuses for UMass—a similar phenomenon prevailed, although these older, eastern schools often struggled to maintain their positions as younger western institutions grew with their regions. In this context, the accomplishment of Brandeis, in achieving recognition so quickly, was especially impressive.[11]

There was, for all the reasons we have discussed, more elasticity of reputation among academic professionals, especially within particular fields, based chiefly on the reputations of faculties. Despite its modest standing among lay observers, for example, UMass/Amherst built several nationally distinguished departments. Eventually, such changes did modify public notions of status, and there was evidence that this was occurring for UMass as well as B.C. in the 1960s. In general, however, a profound conservatism in lay and even professional perceptions of institutional standing prevailed. Brandeis, for all its academic successes, never attracted a strong pool of undergraduate applicants among non-Jews.

Two phenomena account for the rigidities of the academic hierarchy. The first involved the elusive basis of institutional reputations. The difficulty of measuring the quality of academic work built conservatism into the system. Once established, a university's image acquired independent life and tended to remain in place. This reality was compounded by the ignorance of most people, even most academic professionals, about campuses they had not directly encountered. The resilient nature of academic reputations became, in turn, a powerful aid to established universities in attracting students, faculty, and financial support—and a problematic barrier to upwardly mobile institutions trying to do the same. Reputation, therefore, reinforced substantive quality.[12]

Something other than substantive quality was clearly involved, however. Harvard could neglect undergraduate education while Tufts labored over it, and applicants almost invariably chose Harvard anyway. Why? The answer, ultimately, had more to do with the relationship between universities and social standing than with academic realities. Everyone understood the difference between Harvard and Tufts in terms of prestige. Young Americans and their parents, no less than trained professionals, sought to gain by institutional association the status that their fragmented, mobile society offered few means to obtain. This, more than learning, for many applicants was what a university was uniquely able to confer.

Academic Ideas, Change, and Power

We have observed that the conformist tendencies of upward mobility among universities were sometimes offset by the claims of particular institutional values. But notions of distinctive campus missions were only one of four categories of academic ideas—normative conceptions about what a university should be and do—that shaped patterns of change. Professional, intellectual, and cultural conceptions also contributed to the dynamic.

Professional values expressed the expectations and commitments of the faculty as advanced by nationally organized learned societies and academic associations. Intellectual commitments derived from the orientation toward truth seeking inherent in any modern scholarly enterprise. Cultural concerns emanated from outside academia and mirrored the political and social preoccupations of the period. Each kind of idea, like the impulse to upward mobility itself, entered the institutional complex through the advocacy of one or another campus constituency. Interactions between the imperative of upward mobility and the claims of academic ideas were inevitably enacted—either as conflicts or alliances—through the processes of campus decision making.

Historically, institutional values tended to reflect the concerns of nonacademic sponsoring groups that were heavily represented on governing boards, in administrative hierarchies, and, to a lesser extent, among faculties. As the formal links between external groups and universities weakened and institutions became more independent and complex, particularistic conceptions of mission remained, typically in an amended and secularized form, and found adherents in individuals, in all campus constituencies, with long-standing ties to the university, the sponsoring group, or both. For example, Tufts's focus on undergraduate teaching in the liberal arts derived from earlier Universalist preoccupations with transmitting liberal values to their children.

Presidents were often the primary exponents of institutional values since it fell to them, as to no one else, to articulate the purposes of their schools and relate current priorities to established traditions. We have noted the seriousness and effectiveness with which Wessell sustained Tufts's distinctive qualities, as did Walsh at B.C. and Knowles at Northeastern. The policy implications of institutional values could be extensive. In the case of Boston College during the 1960s, priorities on student and faculty recruitment, the emphasis on undergraduate education in arts and sciences, the character of curriculum reform, and the late-appearing focus on social engagement all expressed a dedication to shaping a specifically Catholic university in a modern academic context.[13]

Not all universities displayed the preoccupation with institutional values that was evident at Tufts, B.C., and N.U. Large, comprehensive institutions like Harvard, Boston University, and the Amherst campus of UMass—institutions that approximated Kerr's multiversity—were at a disadvantage in this respect since they lacked an organizing principle that could relate their various functions and guide new development. Even among these universities, however, institutional values could be an important force in directing change.

Harvard, with its historic emphasis on decentralization, needed to be understood chiefly in terms of faculties, schools, and individual departments. But the dedication to the values of the academic culture at a high intellectual level that gradually supplanted Yankee traditions did provide a common theme or standard against which the entrepreneurial efforts of the university's many parts were judged. The dominance of these values at Harvard by the 1950s was demonstrated by the ascendancy of research and graduate work even though important individuals, Pusey included, wanted to direct energy toward undergraduate education. The public character of the University of Massachusetts was evident in a continuing emphasis on accessibility at the undergraduate level. The outstanding example of an institution that lost a sense of specific purpose was Boston University. In their concentration on building the Charles River campus, the leaders of B.U. allowed their university to grow large, shapeless, and directionless.

Professional values were typically strong in inverse relation to institutional values. It was no coincidence that B.C. and Northeastern, which possessed clear conceptions of mission, were also among the least advanced in professional terms. Harvard was the most professionalized university in Massachusetts. By the 1960s, Harvard was so much dominated by the concerns of the disciplines it housed that it had become a kind of holding company for a collection of professional interests. But professional values were prevailing everywhere in the golden age and were expressed most clearly in increased professorial control of academic affairs and in heightened faculty interest in scholarly activities as distinct from institutional work. Institutional and professional values were by no means inherently contradictory, but they were different, and clashes between them, typically expressed as conflicts between administrators and faculty, were a standard source of intramural tension within upwardly mobile universities.

Intellectual commitments—rooted in a dedication to learning—were closely tied to professional interests and exerted the strongest influence for change among universities most focused on research and graduate education. In making the advancement of knowledge a primary function, both Harvard and M.I.T. were compelled to follow intellectual inquiry where it led and to adjust their programs and structures accordingly. Elting Morison has noted that M.I.T. "was being constantly shaken up not only intellectually but also structurally" by scientific progress.

The evolution of the life sciences illustrated Morison's point. In the 1940s, reflecting advanced scientific opinion of the time, Compton decided to invigorate the Institute's uninspired work in biology by separating it from Food Technology and introducing scholarly strength from the physical sciences. Subsequent appointments in biophysics, biochemistry, and bioengineering created the basis by the 1950s for a reconstituted department focused on molecular biology. Out of this shift came top-ranked doctoral programs in biochemistry, microbiology, cellular and molecular biology, and, eventually, the Center for Cancer Research and the Whitehead Institute for Biomedical Research. Thus did a stream of educational and research activities with associated organizational changes flow from the impulse to make sure the Institute's work in biology remained at the leading edge of the field.[14]

Intellectual progress produced change in two other ways. First, upwardly mobile universities seeking to build programs of graduate education and research frequently sought emerging subfields in which established institutions had not yet achieved dominant positions. This was the story of biochemistry at Brandeis. Similarly, in adding doctoral programs in the social sciences, M.I.T. looked for areas in which Harvard had not built strength. Second, the progress of knowledge changed all universities. Once new arenas of inquiry entered disciplinary mainstreams, institutions needed to adapt their offerings to remain current. By this process, universities underwent constant, and largely invisible, change—department by department and appointment by appointment. This process was basically independent of institutional values, except as these values affected the programmatic emphases of individual campuses.

Cultural concerns, like intellectual values, penetrated universities and exerted influence for change with only modest relationship to distinctive institutional characteristics. Cultural concerns entered schools through multiple pathways. In the early postwar years, campus leaders—presidents and trustees, as well as faculties—were inspired by the patriotism stirred by World War II to institute programs of general education, international relations, area studies, and foreign languages. The funding priorities of government agencies and foundations provided additional incentives to address current policy concerns, a phenomenon illustrated by the emergence of M.I.T. as a research arm of the Pentagon.[15]

In the 1960s, the shift of public attention to issues of domestic social justice had a comparable impact. Most universities in Massachusetts were moved by this atmosphere to recruit more blacks. Once in place in sufficient numbers, however, African-American students themselves became an important force for change. The demands of blacks were a major factor in crises at Harvard, Brandeis, and Northeastern in the late 1960s. In these years, in fact, student bodies were undoubtedly the major carriers of cultural concerns into the decision-making processes of universities. Aroused and socially aware students pressed campus administrators to become more involved with local communities and to attend to pressing political questions about civil rights and the war in Vietnam.[16]

The relative significance of each kind of academic idea—institutional, professional, intellectual, and cultural—for each university was subject to change. In general, institutional values grew weaker during the golden age while professional and intellectual commitments grew stronger. Cultural concerns were important in the early postwar years and the late 1960s and less prominent in between. But universities differed in their propensity for value change and in the characteristics of the changes that did occur.

Burton Clark has written interestingly on the durability of institutional values. "Secure" values, those most likely to persist according to Clark, are those that are widely shared within an organizational community, have a high priority in comparison with other values, relate closely to the basic mission of an organization, and are strongly affirmed by external constituencies. "Precarious" values, by contrast, are more tenuously linked to the centers of institutional life. It is the nature of precarious values to be less reflective of core organizational characteristics than of transitory social movements or the personal commitments of individual leaders or even opportunistic competitive strategies.[17]

Clark's distinction illuminates the different significance of institutional values from school to school. Universities where ideas about mission were well-defined, widely shared, and deeply embedded tended to be stable in this respect, to possess, to use a parallel term, a strong institutional culture. Northeastern, M.I.T., and Boston College all could be characterized in these terms in the 1960s. Among these schools, change tended to be continuous with established value systems. Not surprisingly, such institutions often manifested a high degree of continuity in leadership positions and selected presidents who had long associations with the campus.

Where universities possessed a weak culture—where purposes were poorly defined, not widely shared, and not organizationally embedded—change was more likely in general and more likely to be discontinuous with existing patterns. Boston University and the University of Massachusetts were in this category in the 1960s. These institutions tended to import leaders from outside who brought their own values and priorities with them, subjecting the campuses to potentially erratic and inconsistent shifts of self-definition. The revolutionary impact of student protests at Harvard in the late 1960s revealed the weakness of Harvard's culture at the campus level, a fact that had remained invisible for years because coordinated action across the entire university was so rarely necessary.

When different subpopulations in schools with weak cultures were committed to conflicting values, patterns of change were accommodations among competing groups and were crucially shaped by the internal distribution of power. At UMass/Amherst, for example, the state college types, the "ag school" types, and the new professionals pulled in different directions in the 1950s. The ultimate triumph of the latter group was dictated by their growing numbers during a period of expansion, the fit between their emphasis on growth and the demands of the political environment, the attitudes of presidents, and the conformity of their values with the dominant paradigm of the period. At the same time, the residual power of those displaced ensured that traditional values would not be entirely neglected, a fact that limited the homogenizing impact of upward mobility and promoted continued diversity.

Value conflicts could also occur, of course, at universities with strong cultures when a force for change was introduced, often as the result of a conscious board decision. Such a situation arose at B.C. with the appointments of Maxwell and Walsh in the 1950s, just as it had at M.I.T. with the selection of Compton in 1930. For presidents charged to transform deeply rooted cultures, the existence of conflict provided room to maneuver. Both Maxwell and Walsh used the academic commitments of lay faculty to overcome resistance to modernization among conservative Jesuits.

As the cases of M.I.T. and B.C. suggest, over extended periods of time all campuses experienced internal conflict, no matter how strong their cultures. The reason for this is implied by the first premise of the institutional complex: the most important force for change is, ultimately, the competition for prestige and resources. The external conditions that produced these two scarce "goods" evolved continuously, however, and power flowed toward those best able in the altering context to attract resources or to enhance prestige or both. It was inevitable that M.I.T. would strengthen science, that Northeastern would build up the liberal arts, and that Tufts and Brandeis would stress graduate development—provided that needed resources could be obtained. This phenomenon allows us to amend Clark's analysis of secure and precarious values by observing that, in the long run, those values that most support efforts to acquire prestige and resources will be most secure.

This last observation helps us see why cultural concerns tended to be ephemeral in their impact. The changes engendered by current political and social pressures rarely provided continuing benefits in the crucial categories of the institutional complex. The short-lived fascination with general education in the 1950s illustrated this reality. Even more provocative was the interest in minority recruitment in the 1960s. Such efforts enjoyed wide support at the time they were implemented but were problematic in terms of both resources and prestige. Programs for disadvantaged blacks were costly, did not bring to campus large numbers of students likely to enhance academic reputation, and did not reflect deep commitments from any crucial financial constituency. Similar problems, in fact, attended efforts to enroll nonminority students from disadvantaged backgrounds. Little wonder, then, that campus after campus in Massachusetts, given the opportunity to do so, moved away from local, low-income students as a primary service community.[18]

Organizational Dynamics and Institutional Change: The Continuing Significance of Presidential Leadership

We have observed that general studies of organizational change at the end of the golden age stressed the disintegration of institutional communities and the decline of administrative authority. A close examination of universities in Massachusetts, however, suggests two qualifications to these themes. The most significant changes were often more reflective of converging interests among campus constituencies than of conflict among them. Also, administrative leadership—especially by presidents—while less likely than in an earlier era to assume heroic forms, remained indispensable for the most important forms of change.

The widely noted fragmentation of university communities was both structural and political. As campuses became larger and more diversified, component parts grew distant from organizational centers and tended to pursue their work in relative isolation. Intellectual specialization, born of the explosive growth of knowledge, compounded the problem by decreasing the likelihood of shared perspectives, interests, or expertise among subunits. The ascendant professionalism of the faculty contributed another centrifugal force. Finally, the politicization of academia at the end of the period, entering institutional arenas in which bonds of common purpose were already frayed, dealt a *coup de grâce* to old-fashioned notions of scholarly collectivity.

Late 1960s observers typically characterized universities as atomized into antagonistic interest groups: faculties pursuing their specialties with minimal awareness of institutional settings; students demanding more attention from professors and administrators and more social engagement from institutions; trustees trapped between external demands for responsiveness and faculty insistence upon autonomy; and increasingly bureaucratized administrations entrenched in their own insular culture, equally distant from faculty and students.[19]

We have observed all these disintegrative forces among universities in Massachusetts. Campuses like M.I.T. and Northeastern with long traditions of tight-knit organization struggled to maintain a sense of coordinated enterprise, while comprehensive, decentralized schools like Harvard and B.U. became more Balkanized than ever. There was no shortage of political conflict. Legislators, state bureaucrats, trustees, and administrators battled for control of the University of Massachusetts, while faculty factions at Amherst and Boston contended for intramural dominance. Sachar engaged in running battles with faculty, students, and some trustees. Jesuit academics wrestled with the order's hierarchy for control of Boston College, while reformers and conservatives among the religious faculty vied with each other and their lay counterparts over the character of change. At the end of the period, moreover, most of these universities erupted in protest. At five of the eight, presidents were forced from office or resigned in troubled circumstances between 1969 and 1972.

Despite fragmentation and conflict, however, the most notable fact about the universities we have examined was how little discord—or even serious debate—attended major changes during the golden age. Harvard experienced no battles over academic policy as fractious as those of the early Conant years; M.I.T. and Tufts accomplished major transitions with less contention than either displayed in the early years of the century; and jostling between Jesuit academics and the order's hierarchy was less divisive at B.C. than in the 1920s.

External conditions helped greatly, of course. Given pervasive growth, victory for one group did not imply substantive harm to others, and the truly disaffected could usually withdraw into departmental or individual enclaves to pursue their preoccupations in peace. Equally important, however, was the support in all constituencies for policies of academic strengthening and upward institutional mobility. Indeed, though conservatives questioned movements toward the values and functions of research universities at every campus in Massachusetts, nowhere did they mount effective, or even very spirited, opposition. Power struggles remained, of course, a universal fact of organizational life. But most policy-oriented disagreements represented not fundamental differences about directions of change but efforts of one or another constituency to ensure outcomes, within broadly supported evolutionary patterns, that most closely reflected their preferred balance of institutional, professional, and intellectual values.

The altered position of trustees illustrates the dynamic of change. Commentators at the end of the golden age emphasized the success of faculties in wresting power from administrators and trustees in order to impose homogenizing professional priorities on previously distinctive institutions. To note the declining role of external, nonacademic sponsoring communities—something that clearly occurred in Massachusetts—is not, however, to demonstrate that development policies expressed basic conflicts between governing boards and internal institutional communities. It was not uncommon, in fact, for trustees to play active roles in severing ties to external groups, as we have seen in the cases of Northeastern and UMass.

Boards also initiated programs of academic modernization in a number of institutions. This was the case not only at Harvard and M.I.T., where Corporation decisions to appoint Conant and Compton in the 1930s marked decisive breaks with the past, but also at B.C., where the order's hierarchy began appointing academically oriented presidents in the 1950s, and at UMass, where the board gave power to an aggressive young provost intent on overturning that institution's small-college traditions. The professionalization of universities in Massachusetts was more often the outcome of trustee decisions than of political triumphs by the faculty.

Boards were rarely conscious, of course, of the full implications of modernization, and it was not uncommon for tensions between trustees and internal communities to develop as the process of upgrading continued. Both Sachar and Wessell, charged to raise the academic sights of their campuses, soon perceived conservative trustees as obstacles to progress. Both acquired sufficient power to change the character of their boards in ways that would ensure support for continued development. A parallel situation occurred at B.C., where Walsh, having been charged by the order to build academic strength, joined other Jesuit presidents in maneuvering for independence from the hierarchy. These transitions were part of the long-term heightening of campus ambitions. Of all the organizational changes that occurred in the golden age, shifts in the character of the governing authority were among the most profound, since they institutionalized new value systems.

A similar phenomenon of alliance evolving toward tension occurred between modernizing presidents and their faculties. Executives intent on upgrading invariably recruited professionally oriented Ph.D.s as agents of reform. To create conditions attractive to top scholars, these presidents often invited faculty participation in decision making. On this basis, Lederle of UMass, Knowles of Northeastern, Wessell of Tufts, and Walsh of B.C. promoted faculty roles in academic personnel decisions and in broader areas of governance. Such events complicate the conventional picture of postwar change, which stresses conflicts between professors demanding power and administrators protecting prerogatives.

Ultimately, however, just as ambitious presidents sometimes pursued change beyond the bounds contemplated by their boards, empowered faculties often pressed policies not fully anticipated by their presidential sponsors. At Northeastern, Knowles recruited Ph.D.s in the liberal arts to achieve respectability, then resented their insistence on creating graduate programs. Stratton of M.I.T., who encouraged new doctorates, later worried that these activities careened out of control and undermined other priorities. Sachar, Lederle, and Wessell, all eager to attract outstanding scholars, complained that their faculties became focused unduly on research. Such grumbling rarely led to significant action, however. Presidents were too aware that the abuses of which they complained were extensions of the changes they advocated.[20]

Presidential acknowledgment of the difficulty of controlling faculty activities, like similar comments on the irresistibility of external demands, encouraged the perception that diminished administrative authority was an inevitable consequence of academic modernization. The grounds for such observations were clear enough, especially the declining ability of a president, provost, or dean to make substantive judgments on academic issues. As institutions became more complex, the capacity of university-level officers to coordinate the component parts was curtailed. As noninstitutional funds became available to individuals, institutes, departments, and schools, a fundamental tool of administrative control diminished. As professional values eroded institutional concerns, presidents were decreasingly able to articulate common purposes as a basis for concerted action.[21]

Rapid growth thus seemed to overwhelm existing coordinating structures, and students of academic organization increasingly saw institutional change as the aggregate consequence of unrelated entrepreneurial initiatives at all levels. Notions of planned change—organized efforts reflective of university-wide priorities developed by campus leaders—seemed hopelessly old-fashioned, the stuff of presidential fantasies and outdated textbooks.

Perhaps the most widely cited picture of the weakened president at the end of the golden age was provided by Cohen and March, who wrote:

> The . . . presidency is a reactive job . . . They see themselves as trying to reconcile the conflicting pressures on the college. They allocate their time by a process that is largely controlled by the desires of others . . . The Presidency is an illusion . . . Decision making in the university seems to result extensively from a process that decouples problems and choices and makes the president's role more commonly sporadic and symbolic than significant . . . The president has modest control over the events of college life. The contributions he makes can easily be swamped by outside events or the diffuse qualities of university decision making . . . It is probably a mistake for a college president to imagine that what he does in office affects significantly . . . the long-run position of the institution . . .[22]

When the Cohen/March assessment of the presidency, administrative leadership, and development process is considered in relation to the detailed institutional histories we have reviewed, we can see its force. Presidents were quite open about their inability to dominate their universities in the manner of their turn-of-the-century predecessors. Nonacademic Morris Abram learned this reality the hard way during his brief tenure at Brandeis.

Most presidents, however, despite their complaints, recognized their altered position as the result of intellectual and institutional progress. Indeed, at every university in Massachusetts, numerous instances of change—often significant—occurred in precisely the uncoordinated, disjointed manner frequently described. At some universities, this type of change was predominant in the 1950s and 1960s. Elsewhere, however, it was not. These latter instances can help us understand the continuing potential for presidential leadership in the conditions presented by modern universities.[23] They dramatize also the limited validity of generalizations like those offered by Cohen and March.

This is not the place for an extended discussion of leadership, which remains an elusive concept despite the efforts of scholars to define and analyze it. For present purposes, the term will be used to denote the effectiveness of a president, through whatever processes of planning, decision making, and implementing are appropriate in a particular setting, in changing an institution in specified and intended ways: functions performed, clients served, or standards maintained. This definition of leadership involves precisely the "long-run position of the institution" that Cohen and March most question.

This definition also implies a bias for change over stability. Clearly, there are circumstances in which maintaining a campus at an established level of activity and quality represents a challenge, others where even maintenance is not feasible, and others where keeping the peace is as much as can be hoped for. Mostly, however, change is the goal of leadership, no less in bad times than in good. In the golden age, growth was pervasive and change almost unavoidable. The challenge lay in guiding it wisely.

Among universities in Massachusetts, Harvard under Pusey and B.U. under Case came closest to the image of random, undirected change. Both men were content to preside over institutional development rather than lead it, Case because he was preoccupied with the Charles River campus, Pusey because he saw his role in ambassadorial terms. Such presidents could make important contributions in the conditions that existed from the mid-1950s to the late 1960s because they could represent their institutions well to external, resource-providing constituencies while fostering an internal atmosphere of relative harmony.

These presidencies also illustrated the significance of organizational capability in the change process. Harvard achieved incremental, unit-by-unit, scholarly strengthening because it possessed an entrenched, decentralized organization of highly competent leaders and members, and Pusey understood the importance of middle-level roles, especially the deanships. By contrast, Boston University drifted academically because it lacked the organizational depth to achieve significant progress in the absence of effective leadership. Both institutions tended to replicate and expand what they already were: strong units added strength, weak units reproduced weakness, while the aggregate grew larger, more complex, and less coherent.

Much good occurred through such processes, and in the golden age the adverse consequences were minimal. By 1970, however, the cumulative implications of unconsidered and uncoordinated change had become apparent on both campuses. Under pressure, the government of Harvard simply collapsed, while leaders at B.U. realized they had stumbled into a position where radical, possibly disruptive change was essential.

Universities that achieved more coherent programs of change typically had presidents who worked hard for this outcome. M.I.T. and Northeastern went through major transformations of function guided by thought-through conceptions of institutional purpose linked to operational priorities. Picking up where Compton left off, Killian helped a campus focused almost entirely on science and engineering become a diversified research university. Building on the base Ell established, Knowles turned a limited, local institution into a comprehensive university with a national role in its area of special expertise.

Other universities changed less dramatically, not through a transformation of function but a deepening and extending of new values within a largely established configuration of programs. Tufts under Wessell and B.C. under Walsh could be characterized in this way. Both men institutionalized the intensified intellectual values of modern academic culture while preserving distinctive missions. In some ways, the most remarkable case of all was Brandeis, where Sachar turned a defunct medical school into a nationally recognized research university in twenty years.

Though presidents typically provided direct, personal leadership to the development process, they rarely functioned independently. Sachar's autocratic propensities notwithstanding, most presidents relied upon the work of subordinates—deans, vice presidents, and staff members—whose efforts they directed and coordinated. Some of the most important developments at Brandeis occurred during years when Sachar worked closely with his first provost, Cohen. The significance of the leadership team is particularly underscored by the history of UMass/Amherst during the 1960s. Lederle, the president, viewed his role in ambassadorial terms, but he appointed and supported a highly effective provost, Tippo, who orchestrated a campus-wide program of academic upgrading.

The histories of M.I.T., Northeastern, Tufts, B.C., Brandeis, and UMass in the golden age demonstrate the potential for coordinated programs of institutional change despite the complexity of modern universities. In none of these institutions were the most important changes of the period the result merely of unrelated entrepreneurial efforts by individuals and subunits, though such activities played indispensable roles. Equally important, however, was the existence of a general framework of policy and direction, more or less elaborated, provided by a president and a leadership team within which individual efforts could occur, priorities could be set, and choices could be made.

It is, in fact, impossible to believe that changes of the magnitude and character that we have observed could have happened without such coordination at the campus level. As the concept of the organizational complex makes clear, multiple forces incessantly pull universities in conflicting directions. For even moderately orderly change to result, as it did among these universities, a coordinating mechanism is essential. The president, by structural necessity, was the key to that effort, typically through direct leadership, if not through delegation to someone who could play that role.

Twenty-six presidencies occurred among universities in Massachusetts from the onset of the Depression to the end of the golden age. Of these, at least eight unquestionably had a significant long-term impact on the positions of their campuses: Conant at Harvard, Compton and Killian at M.I.T., Sachar at Brandeis, Wessell at Tufts, Ell and Knowles at Northeastern, and Walsh at B.C. It is hard to imagine anyone who participated in the work of these universities during these years, or who has closely studied the histories of these institutions, arguing that the leadership provided by these individuals was not a major factor in the transformations they achieved.

Strong cases could also be made for several other presidents among those we have studied, but the group of eight seems sufficient to make the point. The presidency of universities, no less than top positions in industry and government, lost much of its mythic quality in the middle decades of the twentieth century, but it continued to be a role in which talented and dedicated individuals made contributions of lasting significance. When effective leadership was not present, moreover, institutional communities knew it—and suffered as a result. Our histories contain no instances in which a campus accomplished a major transformation without deliberate organization by a campus administration.

The Strategic Balance: Integrating Institutional Ambitions,
Academic Values, and Organizational Dynamics

Although several of the universities we have reviewed accomplished impressive development programs during the golden age, none avoided problems. A common source of trouble involved the relationships contained within the institutional complex. Those relationships, in fact, constituted a set of implicit questions, an institutional conundrum, that needed to be understood and resolved by leaders eager to promote change.

The first premise of the institutional complex—that universities are driven by a continuous competition for prestige and resources—suggests an essential starting point in conceiving a coherent program of campus development. To succeed, the plans of academic leaders must inspire enthusiasm within a campus community. Proposals that offer an improved position in the academic hierarchy are most likely to win such support. At the same time, such plans must attend to the changing realities of the academic marketplace. The university must be able to acquire the dollars, students, and faculty necessary to sustain its new self-definition.

The second element of the institutional complex involves academic ideas, including conceptions of campus mission—institutional values—that are rooted in history and have support within the existing university community. Proposals for change are most likely to stir enthusiasm among internal and external constituencies, and maintain coherence among functions, when they build on current commitments.

Institutional values, however, are closely linked to the third element of the institutional complex: organizational dynamics. In both planning and implementing change, academic leaders must obtain whatever level of internal political support is needed given local decision mechanisms, consider the implications of their proposals for future intramural relationships, and ensure a fit between revised functions and existing organizational capabilities. Building on established programmatic and faculty strengths has traditionally been a way to accomplish these things while honoring institutional values. For this reason, a classic approach to upward mobility has been to add research and graduate programs in basic disciplines linked to previously established technical and service activities.[24]

The postwar histories of universities in Massachusetts, for all their impressive achievements, amply demonstrated the problematic consequences of inattention to relationships within the institutional complex. For example, few campus leaders had difficulty defining a desirable future domain, but many encountered problems integrating proposed changes with established functions and values.

One common problem involved relationships between the new priorities of graduate education and research—and of faculty committed to them—and established missions in undergraduate education. On every campus in Massachusetts, academic leaders came to believe that building the advanced functions exacted a price from baccalaureate-level instruction. This fact qualified the widespread perception that modern universities were such loose collections of independent units that activities could be added or subtracted with minimal impact on other commitments. Horizontal diversification largely confirmed this generalization: the addition of new undergraduate programs at N.U., B.U., and UMass/Amherst created predictable problems of supervision, resource diffusion, and political rivalry but few operational problems between units. Vertical diversification, the addition of new activities in graduate education and research, was more troubled.

The development of advanced functions was least problematic at selective universities where undergraduates could adapt readily to the expectations of research-oriented faculty, a relationship that Compton understood fully. Even at places like Harvard and Tufts, however, campus leaders perceived a loss to undergraduate teaching as the research/graduate paradigm grew stronger, and Wessell worked consistently, through exhortation and policy, to offset this tendency.[25]

The problem of vertical integration was especially acute at unselective universities that sought upward mobility by adding high-quality research teams and doctoral programs. Lederle of UMass/Amherst became convinced that undergraduates were "getting the shaft" as they were increasingly instructed in large classes and had contact chiefly with graduate students, while faculty concentrated on advanced undergraduates, graduate students, and their own scholarship. Yet neither Lederle nor his counterparts at other mass-market universities found effective means to correct these difficulties. Their unwillingness or inability to do so represented the greatest failure of educational leadership among universities in Massachusetts during the golden age.

Several universities experienced problems matching their aspirations to the realities of the academic marketplace. Tufts and B.C. created doctorates in fields where they lacked the scholarly strength to compete and were forced to dismantle new programs after a short period. B.C. adopted the financial practices of high-cost institutions without the tuition level, endowment base, or giving capability to sustain it and fell into financial crisis. B.U. starved its academic program to build a new campus, then discovered that its quality was too low to rival private residential universities and its price too high to compete with the public sector. M.I.T. and Brandeis were unable to achieve their goals with respect to the character of their undergraduate students.

A particularly dramatic problem of matching aspirations with practical possibilities occurred at UMass/Boston. The early leaders of this campus imagined an institution for low-income, urban, commuting students on the model of elite, residential, New England colleges: admission standards and academic requirements were to be kept high and undergraduate work was to focus almost exclusively on the arts and sciences. This conception, however educationally idealistic, had little to do with the interests of the campus's natural student or public constituencies. The only niche available to the new urban campus in the crowded academic world of Boston, and the only mission likely to gain wide political support, was to provide a diversified set of offerings, including occupational and professional programs, for local students from modest academic backgrounds. UMass/Boston experienced a wrenching internal debate as its leaders faced the necessity of radically altering the initial conception of the campus.[26]

The most neglected relationship within the institutional complex was the one between academic plans and formal organization. Few universities followed the corporate pattern of designing new structures in advance for the purpose of undertaking new functions. While there were exceptions to this general rule—M.I.T. and Northeastern, for example—the common approach was to move into new areas in relatively *ad hoc* ways, grafting new functions onto existing structures, and to attend to matters of organization only when problems of coordination or control occurred. Perhaps the outstanding example of this tendency was Harvard, where Pusey took pride in retaining the organization in place at the time of his appointment despite massive growth in most areas of campus life—with highly problematic results. Sachar at Brandeis was equally indifferent to many aspects of organization. His campus was in political turmoil for much of his term and was evaluated by outside consultants as one of the most poorly administered universities they had ever observed.

Not all developmental problems represented inattention to relationships within the institutional complex. Sachar, for example, had highly evolved views about the importance of presidential authority in the early years of campus development. He believed that conflict was a small price to pay for rapid upward ascent in the status hierarchy. Brandeis's history during the golden age stands as a monument to both the potential and the limitations of his perspective. Similarly, Wessell's failure to install policies on recruitment, promotion, and compensation that would ensure maximum upward progress reflected the importance he attached to Tufts' traditions of community, harmony, and decency. Wessell wanted to share the abundance of the golden age with faculty who had devoted themselves to Tufts, and he was ready to pay a price in terms of scholarly progress and reputation. Other leaders at either institution might have proceeded differently.[27] There existed, therefore, different ways to balance the elements of the institutional complex, with different costs and benefits. Sometimes a less than optimal outcome along one dimension was essential to accomplish important objectives in other areas.

Among universities in Massachusetts, leaders at M.I.T. consistently demonstrated the most comprehensive awareness of the multiple implications of change. The two most important postwar presidents, Compton and Killian, were typical in their emphasis on maintaining the Institute's special character or, to use Killian's term, its "personality," which derived from its historic focus on the practical uses of scientific knowledge at the highest intellectual level. In leading the campus through major transitions, both men referred constantly to this core, while pressing for changes that would enhance M.I.T.'s role and status. The evolution from Rogers's founding vision to Maclaurin's "scientific university" to Killian's "university polarized around science" was explicit and self-conscious.[28]

Compton's efforts in the 1930s and 1940s to elevate science by making it independent of engineering while also stressing research and graduate education illustrated the Institute's approach to development. Compton was convinced that the shifts he proposed were indicated by intellectual changes in both basic and applied work and in the relationship between them. He also perceived a moment of opportunity at the end of World War II.

Compton gave his colleagues a chance to consider, digest, and amend his policies through the work of the Lewis committee. At the same time, he installed a series of organizational innovations to accommodate the Institute's altered functions. The interdisciplinary centers, established during the war, were retained as primary vehicles for research and technical innovation. The "four-school concept" gave the disciplines independent homes. The undergraduate program was made more compatible with research and graduate work. On the financial side, the Institute exploited its advantaged position with respect to federal dollars and nurtured ties to the national security apparatus. At the same time, M.I.T. installed mechanisms to regulate sponsored projects and launched a capital campaign to offset dependence on the government.

Killian displayed an equal grasp of the complexity of change in promoting diversification in the 1950s. His dedication to building the social sciences and humanities reflected his awareness of the public significance of technology and his belief that a broader program would enhance the Institute's stature and attract better students. In promoting new fields, however, he stressed subdisciplines that connected most naturally to science and technology. He also paid consistent attention to the relationship between organizational change and functional development, installing a less-centralized administrative structure and creating new coordinating mechanisms.

Of what value was M.I.T.'s emphasis on campus-level coordination of the change process? Institute leaders claimed that their policies of building on strengths and concentrating resources in a limited number of fields explained their success in intellectual innovation. The results were hard to fault in competitive terms. M.I.T. retained its leading national position in engineering, achieved top rankings in all the basic sciences, and attained eminence in several nonscientific fields, especially in the social sciences. The transitions that we have described were accomplished, moreover, with minimum cost to the Institute's historically strong culture and with remarkably little conflict.

Despite its successes, M.I.T. did not entirely escape developmental difficulties. While the Institute's leaders understood the importance of their core strengths, they did not always appreciate the limits imposed by these characteristics, as evidenced in their failed attempts to broaden the undergraduate applicant pool. The problems encountered in integrating the humanities further expressed M.I.T.'s difficulty in resolving the tension between the impulse to remain focused on science and technology and to become a more general university. The evolution of Killian's famous phrase from the initial "university polarized around science, engineering and the arts" to the more widely remembered truncated version undoubtedly mirrored the president's deepening awareness of his university's boundaries. Even at an institution as committed to the systematic planning of new development as M.I.T., trial and error was an important factor in setting directions.

The decision to rely heavily on military support was another area of chronic concern and a policy choice that ultimately generated problems, as the changes of the late 1960s acknowledged. In most respects, however, the remarkable thing about the Institute's dependence on government contracts, many of them for classified work, was the lack of negative impact on its simultaneous development in basic science.

For M.I.T., however, as for other universities in Massachusetts, the most important test of the development policies of the golden age could not occur while the years of expansion continued. During the 1950s and 1960s, almost any approach to institution building worked—more or less. Maintaining the new campus configurations under the altered conditions of the 1970s represented a much more serious challenge. Would M.I.T. be able to sustain its new mix of functions as federal financial support diminished? Would B.C. and Tufts keep their upgraded undergraduate admission standards after the baby-boom generation completed college? Would Brandeis find a viable second act following the retirement of Sachar? We can learn more about the dynamics of institutional change by examining the way universities managed the transition from a period of abundance to a time of constraint.

Adaptations of the 1970s

The Three Revolutions
Revisited—and a Counterrevolution

During the 1970s, the changed circumstances of higher education that marked the end of the golden age evolved into a fundamentally altered context for institutional development. The turbulent atmosphere associated with student protests was replaced by a general calm, only occasionally interrupted by new incidents, but the expansive atmosphere of the 1960s was gone. The confident anticipation of growth fostered by rising levels of student demand and financial support gave way to a preoccupation with enrollment declines and fiscal pressures. The political position of faculties, which had grown steadily stronger during the golden age, was challenged by new administrative emphases on management and planning. Simultaneously, an array of external controls restricted the institutional autonomy that had long been the dominant characteristic of the nation's academic system.

A curious duality characterized conditions with respect to student demand during the 1970s. The expectation voiced by the Carnegie commission in 1971—that the rate of enrollment growth would decrease to zero and be replaced in the 1980s by stable overall numbers and fewer traditional students—haunted colleges and universities. The apprehensions were particularly acute in Massachusetts, where enrollments were imperiled by a greater than average anticipated shrinkage of the eighteen- to twenty-four-year-old age group. In 1975 the state's Board of Higher Education predicted actual declines during the 1980s for both public and private universities. Throughout the decade, worries about the future overshadowed the reality of continued growth, across the country and in Massachusetts. Expansion was especially robust at the national level where total enrollments increased by 3.5 million students, 41 percent, between 1970 and 1980. Locally, as anticipated, the gains were more modest: total enrollments increased by 38 percent over the ten-year period, and showed very little growth during the last years of the decade.[29]

Two kinds of changes worked against the anticipated declines. The first involved the composition of the college-going population. During the 1970s, "non-traditional" students of all kinds—minorities, women, and older individuals—sought out college more actively than in earlier years, and institutions, partially because of enrollment worries and partially because of broadened values, proved receptive to them. A marked increase in the percentage of students attending on a part-time basis was one measure of the altered situation. These new clienteles opened up vast and upredictable territory for higher education and called into question projections based on past patterns or the demographics of the youth population. With respect to minorities, however, the trend reversed in the mid-1970s, and the last years of the decade witnessed a decline in the percentage of black and Hispanic high school graduates going to college and an absolute reduction of enrollments from these groups in graduate schools.

A second new factor in the enrollment picture was modified institutional behavior. Many schools developed aggressive and highly professional programs of student recruitment, supplemented by expanded scholarship offerings. Administrators paid so much attention to student interests in designing programs and shaping academic policies that some observers worried about a new age of "consumerism" in higher education. At the end of the decade, 60 percent of the nation's colleges and universities reported that they had grown over the past ten years, while only 30 percent had lost students. Still, fears of reduced student numbers dominated the academic imagination. A group of college presidents surveyed by the Carnegie council in 1978 listed "decreasing enrollments" as their second most important concern.[30]

The greatest worry was finances, as it had been eight years earlier. Here, too, academia's situation was paradoxical. By most objective measures, the 1970s were comfortable years. The "new depression" detected by Cheit in 1971 proved short-lived. In 1973 Cheit reviewed financial data from his original set of institutions and found a "fragile stability." William Bowen, whose cost studies in the late 1960s heralded the changing financial atmosphere, came to similar conclusions in 1975, finding that most private schools he studied were "solvent but not highly prosperous." In Cheit's view, the improved picture resulted more from improved management than increased revenues, but revenues also were more resilient than many anticipated. Total national income for higher education doubled from $16.2 billion in fiscal year 1970 to $32.3 billion in fiscal year 1977, and instructional expenditures per student remained steady in constant dollars.

While the greatest financial worry of the early 1970s—declining federal support for research—remained a problem for much of the decade, government aid to students grew dramatically, so that overall federal funding expanded in real terms. So did state support, which provided a greater share of total funds to academia in 1977 than in 1970. The proportional contributions of tuition, endowment, and gifts also remained quite steady, with tuition becoming slightly more important and endowment less so across the period. As the Carnegie council put it in 1982: "The 1970s was a good decade for higher education . . . possibly the best decade in all of history . . . except for the 1960s."

Persistent apprehensions about finances despite continued support expressed underlying economic concerns. The inflation of the 1970s was particularly threatening to colleges and universities—with their high personnel costs and limited ability to increase productivity. Level budgets in the context of rapidly escalating fuel prices translated into reduced instructional expenditures for many institutions. Two national recessions added to the gloom, one at the beginning of the decade and a second, the worst since the 1930s, in the mid-1970s. Then, as the national economy began to emerge from its doldrums, a ground swell of anti-tax sentiment, beginning with the campaign for Proposition 13 in California, created new constraints, especially on state support.[31]

Just as faculties grew stronger and more prosperous during the years of growth, their circumstances deteriorated both materially and politically in the 1970s. As institutions became more cautious about hiring and rates of enrollment growth diminished, the labor market for full-time faculty collapsed and the use of part-timers grew. In 1968 a young Ph.D. from a good university could expect offers from several respectable institutions. Five years later 1,402 new graduates in English competed for 139 openings. Only one freshly trained historian in six found a position that year. Few fields were exempted from the altered situation. Net annual additions to the full-time faculty declined from 21,000 in the late 1960s to 19,800 in the early 1970s, to 7,000 in the late 1970s, and to zero at the end of the decade.

The "Ph.D. glut" had several effects. Faculty quality improved, as low-status institutions were able to attract applicants from leading universities. Academic salaries, which had not only grown faster than inflation during the golden age but had improved relative to other civilian fields, advanced less rapidly than the cost of living. Working conditions also declined. For example, faculty-student ratios increased and average work loads grew, reversing two important trends of the 1960s. Standards for promotion crept upward, as institutions became more cautious about permanent commitments and more confident about their ability to replace those not retained.[32]

To some extent, the new conditions empowered administrators at the expense of faculties—as tougher standards and heavier work loads attested. In an atmosphere of economic apprehension, trustees and senior administrators felt compelled to husband resources more carefully, and faculty members resisted from a weakened position. The decline in federal research support reinforced this trend, just as the availability of noninstitutional grants had been a source of scholarly power during the golden age. In the 1970s, professional management and strategic planning became fashionable in higher education.

Given the abruptness and severity of these changes, it is hardly surprising that the professoriate sought new means of protection, of which collective bargaining was the most visible. In 1969 the faculty of the City University of New York made news by voting to unionize. Within a few years, what had been a marginal phenomenon became a national movement. In 1972 the A.A.U.P. embraced collective bargaining, and by 1976 430 colleges and universities had elected agents.[33]

The rise of regulatory control over the affairs of colleges and universities by agencies of state and federal governments was the most distinctive development of the 1970s. For the public sector, the most important manifestation of this trend was the delegation of broad controls over institutional development to statewide coordinating boards. This pattern began in the 1950s, accelerated in the 1960s, and continued, with increasing centralization, in the 1970s. By 1979 thirty-eight states had established powerful regulatory boards or consolidated statewide governing authorities. Few public campuses continued to be ruled chiefly by their own trustees.

At the federal level, the 1970s was the decade when the fears of the early postwar years—that federal support would bring federal intervention—began to be realized. As the political position of higher education weakened, federal regulation grew—in financial management, hiring and employment practices, student rights, safety, and research involving human subjects or affecting public health. By the late 1970s, academic leaders worried that the proliferation of external controls was transforming a system of autonomous campuses into a "regulated industry."

There was no question about the direction of change, but Burton Clark, reviewing systemic developments of the 1970s as part of an international comparative study, concluded that "the market conditions under which institutions have traditionally operated still prevail." Indeed, the various ways in which universities in Massachusetts negotiated the altered conditions of the 1970s illustrated how much room there was for institutional maneuver within the broad framework of national trends.[34]

The Resiliency of the Research University

In the early 1970s, as in the early 1930s, both Harvard and M.I.T. needed presidents. On the latter occasion, as on the former, the transitions in leadership coincided with sudden and adverse changes in the resource environment, but internal conditions differed markedly from the earlier era. In the 1930s, both Corporations had perceived a need for fundamental shifts of institutional emphasis and had appointed scientist-presidents committed to a new academic order. Forty years later, Harvard and M.I.T. had been reconstructed in accordance with the values of Conant and Compton and had just completed two decades of rapid, ultimately tumultuous, growth and change. There was little appetite on either campus for innovation. The clearest need was peace.

The two searches proceeded in tandem in the fall of 1970, with images of student protests and embarrassing headlines fresh in everyone's memories. In this atmosphere, the Harvard board conducted the most public and political selection process in that university's history, consulting widely for nominations and advice. However, from the beginning, the leading contender was the young Law dean, Derek Bok, who had won plaudits for his handling of a protest incident at his own school and had advised Pusey against using force in April 1969.

As a faculty member, Bok had been regarded as competent, though not brilliant, but he had flourished in the deanship. Accessible and open to change, he had promoted affirmative action, forged interdisciplinary links to other parts of Harvard, encouraged curriculum reform, relaxed grading standards—and won impressively broad-based support. His cautious, balanced manner seemed more likely to settle Harvard down than shake it up, an advantage under the circumstances. Other assets included the social connections and graces that he had inherited as the offspring of two wealthy and well-established families. In January 1971, Hooks Burr of the Corporation announced Bok's selection, acknowledging that "if [the choice] isn't met with euphoria, we hope it will meet at least with general acceptance."[35]

The M.I.T. Corporation, with its history of valuing continuity in leadership roles, was even less inclined than its Harvard counterpart to look beyond the small circle of incumbent senior officers. The search was brief and focused from the beginning on Johnson's widely respected provost, Jerome Wiesner. The selection process was complicated, however, by the Corporation's decision to accept Johnson's advice and divide executive authority between a president and chancellor. The need to appoint a team pushed matters even more firmly toward internal candidates, and, indeed, the ultimate decision paired Wiesner with his former associate provost, now dean of Engineering, Paul Gray. The two men appeared to complement each other beautifully. Wiesner was a celebrated scholar, an engineer who had headed the School of Science, and a policy intellectual who had advised President Kennedy. Gray, also an engineer, was a gifted teacher and administrator who had made his way as an Institute insider.[36]

For Wiesner and Gray, organizational and financial restructuring were unavoidable priorities. The new team at M.I.T. had to translate a generalized conception of shared responsibility into a practical division of labor. The arrangements that evolved were the expected ones: Wiesner concentrated on planning and resource acquisition; Gray supervised programs and operations. The situation was made even more complex by the prominence of two other positions—the chair of the Corporation, now occupied by Johnson, and the provostship, to which Wiesner appointed biophysicist Walter Rosenblith. More than ever before, M.I.T. was governed in the 1970s by a team rather than an individual.

A deeper institutional question involved the ability of M.I.T.'s structure of schools, departments, centers, and labs, which had thrived during the golden age, to adapt to the new conditions of the 1970s. True to the Institute's tradition of linking academic and organizational change, Wiesner and Gray charged a Committee on Research Structure, headed by Frank Press, to consider the issue.

Bok's organizational problems were equally complicated. Despite Harvard's venerable age, the presidency was not well-defined. Conant had surrendered the traditional duty of heading Arts and Sciences, but Pusey had not clearly established an executive function appropriate for the university's decentralized mode of operation. While Bok wrestled with the ambiguities in his own position, he was also required to reassemble the shattered administrative mechanism he had inherited from his predecessor. In 1972 Bok created four vice presidencies—for administration, finance, government and community affairs, and alumni and development—and appointed to these positions a group of nonacademic operatives. Bok thus brought to Massachusetts Hall the hard-edged, bureaucratic style of modern academic management that Pusey had doggedly resisted. For longtime Harvardians, the restructuring marked the end of an era. Their comfortable, familiar, informal world was gone forever. Bok preserved one essential element of Harvard's organizational tradition, however: academic affairs were not centralized. There would be no provost. Harvard would continue to be, in essence, not one university but a collection of ten schools.[37]

Organizational issues were closely tied to financial ones. Both Harvard and M.I.T. incurred deficits in the early 1970s as federal research funds fell while inflation continued. Bok's administrative structure was intended to make Harvard more efficient, and it was accompanied by new cost controls and budgeting procedures. A less-widely advertised but financially more significant change was the division of the treasurer's office to create an independent subsidiary, the Harvard Management Company, with the sole function of husbanding Harvard's endowment. This new operation, staffed by professional money managers and located in Boston's financial district, was intended to tighten the connection between Harvard's investment strategies and overall institutional needs. The Management Company kept annual contributions of fund income to operating budgets stable during the 1970s.

Despite the administrative reforms, Bok's first decade was a period of continuing financial pressure. Federal support in real terms continued its downward trend. By 1978 government dollars for research and training accounted for only 26 percent of Harvard's budget, compared with 38 percent in 1968. The constant-dollar value of annual giving for capital and current use also diminished. A financially disastrous investment in a new power plant added to the fiscal woes. With the value of other revenue sources falling, Harvard increased tuition by nearly 8 percent per year in the 1970s, a sharper rise than the consumer price index and per capita annual income. Between 1968 and 1978, tuition rose from 20 percent to 30 percent of the annual budget. Still, faculty salaries lost ground in relation to inflation, and in mid-decade the teaching staff had to be reduced. Bok and his associates became convinced that increased support from private donors was the only solution. In 1979 they announced a major capital campaign linked to Harvard's 350th anniversary in 1986.[38]

M.I.T., with its heavy dependence on sponsored projects, was even more vulnerable to changes in federal policy than Harvard. The 1 percent annual average decline in constant-dollar government support for Institute research between 1969 and 1975, combined with drastic reductions in federal sponsorship of graduate students, threatened the financial basis on which the old engineering school had become a major university. The use of unrestricted gifts to cover operating deficits, a practice begun with the decline of federal support in the late 1960s, increased in the 1970s. In this context, M.I.T., like Harvard, undertook an assortment of measures to control costs and increase revenues. Tuition rates doubled between 1971–1972 and 1979–1980, and enrollments were enlarged. By the end of the decade, student charges contributed 12 percent of the annual budget compared with 10 percent ten years earlier. The Industrial Liaison and M.I.T. Associates programs were expanded, and continuing education for mid-career professionals became a new and profitable activity. A capital campaign raised over $250 million.

The Institute's most characteristic response to the altered financial environment was to encourage new configurations of research expertise to take advantage of shifting priorities among funding sources—a course strongly urged by the Press committee. The life sciences prospered in the 1970s because federal interest in this area remained strong, and the Institute was ready to redirect its energies accordingly. Even more striking was the heightened emphasis on corporate funding. The 1970s witnessed a new generation of privately financed centers, labs, and programs, like the Polymer Processing Program, in which, as Wiesner and Gray noted, industrial sponsors "share in its guidance, involve their own staff members in the work as a regular practice, and seek to apply the results." As a result of these entrepreneurial adaptations, sponsored research declined only slightly—from 73 percent of the operating budget in 1971 to 71 percent in 1980—and the nonfederal portion of these revenues increased steadily, from 14.6 percent in 1972 to 17.1 percent in 1976. A 1977 review of the impact of government cutbacks on M.I.T. concluded that most departments "have managed to adjust to recent changes . . . without undue hardship." A similar finding would have been appropriate for Harvard. As Cheit and Bowen found, the 1970s were more important in demonstrating the resilience than the vulnerability of private research universities.[39]

As organizational and financial stability returned to Cambridge, the new presidents of the state's leading universities were able to focus on academic issues. For Bok, a reflective, intellectual man, this was always the central interest. His reorganization did not include a provost partly because he wanted to be Harvard's academic leader. In his early reviews of departmental recommendations for senior appointments, he established himself as a demanding and fundamentally conservative guardian of his university's academic position. True to the values of post-Conant Harvard, he denied promotion to several popular teachers because they lacked outstanding scholarly credentials. He was less clear, however, about new directions. Unlike Eliot, Lowell, or even Conant, he came to the presidency with no agenda for reform. "To be blunt," he wrote in 1971, "there is no proven model for a radically changed university

. . . [The best] course for Harvard is . . . patient, systematic work on a number of fronts"—like improving teaching, promoting interdisciplinary activities, and making better use of technology.

Bok's first clear focus emerged in his second report, an extended analysis of the deterioration of the collegiate curriculum. When Dunlop left the deanship of Arts and Sciences in 1973, Bok charged his replacement, economist Henry Rosovsky, to lead a full-dress review of undergraduate education. A second emphasis of the new president—Harvard's role in strengthening public and professional life in America—evolved more gradually. One early expression was the expansion and upgrading of the Kennedy School of Government as a center for training high-level public officials. In serial reviews of Harvard's other graduate schools, Bok advocated the extension of central elements of the Kennedy School's program, particularly the concern with social responsibility and applied ethics, to law, business, and medicine. In the late 1970s, he brought his concern with public service to the university itself, issuing a series of papers on Harvard's social role.

As the academic themes of Bok's presidency evolved, so too did his conception of his office. Bok defined himself as neither a domineering executive nor a passive representative but a consensus builder and friendly critic who would use his pulpit to question the orthodoxies of Harvard's various units, reason through difficult issues like the relationship of investment policies to social values, and encourage moderate change on a case-by-case basis.[40]

The substantive emphases of the Wiesner/Gray administration displayed a remarkable symmetry with those of their Harvard counterpart, as had been true of Compton and Conant in the 1930s. Like Bok, they were more oriented toward continuity than change. As Wiesner noted, both he and Gray had been part of the Institute's leadership prior to their appointments. They were not inclined to redirect what they had helped shape. Under the constrained conditions of the 1970s, moreover, the central challenge was maintaining the vitality and position of established activities.

There was some room for change, however. Wiesner had a special interest in the social implications of technology, and he promoted the organization of M.I.T.'s resources in science, engineering, social sciences, and humanities into centers and programs to address "sociotechnical dilemmas" in fields ranging from energy and environmental protection to health care and housing to industrial productivity and arms control. Gray continued his long-standing interest in educational reform. The team's annual reports included a steady emphasis on efforts to encourage independent learning, promote curricular flexibility, strengthen liberal education, and improve engineering instruction.

What was striking about the academic interests of Bok and of Wiesner and Gray was the extent to which they addressed two of the most prominent criticisms of higher education to emerge from the reassessments of the late 1960s: disinterest in undergraduates and confusion about the social functions of academia. The actions of both administrations contained an implicit question about the ability of leading research universities to somewhat reorder their priorities while also protecting the scholarly strengths that had earned them national prominence. It was, Wiesner and Gray noted in classic M.I.T. fashion, like "trying to solve a set of simultaneous equations."[41]

The Vulnerability of the College-centered University

The 1970s were a more difficult period for the state's two college-centered universities than for its major research institutions. Both Tufts and Brandeis had made the transition from college to university on the rising tide of the golden age, but neither had the depth of financial resources nor strength in student markets to maintain their positions comfortably when the flood began to recede. Both had limited flexibility to adapt to the changing student markets of the period, especially the declining interest in the liberal arts. Both were led by presidents, moreover, whose strengths lay more in restoring stability after the dislocations of the 1960s than in fostering institutional creativity in cramped conditions.

Like a latter-day, small-town Lawrence Lowell, Burton Hallowell, Wessell's replacement at Tufts, called for a reversal of what he perceived to be his university's drift toward the research ideal even before external conditions made some consolidation unavoidable. From his inaugural in 1967 to his final report in 1976, Hallowell emphasized Tufts's core commitment to undergraduate education and disparaged tendencies toward professionalism and specialization that he saw as the enemy of liberal learning. He wanted to focus on "man, not knowledge," and he was critical of the way graduate programs in arts and sciences diverted universities, Tufts included, from what he saw as their central goal. To offset such tendencies he tried to refocus Tufts's graduate offerings toward interdisciplinary configurations that would reinforce collegiate values. He also urged the professional schools—the Medical and Dental schools as well as Engineering and Fletcher—to stress humanistic concerns.

Hallowell's central focus was reform of the collegiate curriculum. He wanted to restore coherence by building connections among Tufts's academic and professional departments. He hoped to supplement intellectual training with the cultivation of humane sensitivity, moral awareness, and social skills so that a Tufts graduate could "live and act as an integrated person." He admired Wessell's Experimental College because it provided courses outside normal disciplinary boundaries. In support of his "vision" for a "new environment" within the university, Hallowell and his provost, Albert Ullman, encouraged a series of innovations. The Plans of Study, adopted in 1968, allowed students to design interdisciplinary majors, while a new crop of joint majors offered ready-made alternatives to conventional areas of concentration. The College Within, created in 1971, allowed small groups of students to pursue programs organized around themes.[42]

The initial years of Hallowell's presidency were a time of weakening in Tufts's financial position. Still, between 1967 and 1971, despite accumulating deficits, moderate enrollment growth combined with rapid tuition hikes—a jump of 50 percent in four years—to permit some budgetary expansion. The number of full-time faculty increased at approximately the same rate as enrollments, and salaries, despite some slippage relative to national norms, retained their A.A.U.P. rankings at the senior levels. By 1971, however, Hallowell was observing that the new decade "may prove to be the most important in the history of Tufts University" because financial pressures could jeopardize academic progress.

That year's annual report contained an extended description of the college-centered university in which Hallowell insisted that his priorities were compatible with Tufts's changing circumstances. Greater attention to undergraduate education would keep the campus attractive in the heightened competition for students. The deemphasis of doctoral programs was both appropriate, given the Ph.D. glut, and financially helpful. Hallowell proposed two committees to identify ways to "consolidate the gains" of the recent past. A Committee on Undergraduate Education (C.U.E.) was charged to review the collegiate curriculum and seek new approaches to coherence. A University Steering Committee (U.S.C.) was asked how Tufts could bring all its resources—academic, professional, and organizational—to bear on its primary mission in undergraduate education.[43]

Hallowell got what he wanted from his study groups. Both produced long, thoughtful statements that echoed his educational philosophy. The C.U E. proposed "focal programs" of courses from multiple disciplines based on topics—like "the city"—as an alternative to the existing distribution requirement. The U.S.C. endorsed the focal programs and advocated additional measures to accomplish Hallowell's goals, including a 33 percent reduction in graduate enrollments. The fact that two groups of faculty leaders could ratify Hallowell's program so firmly was further evidence that enthusiasm for the more academically ambitious aspects of Wessell's agenda had been limited. Indeed, in recommending higher standards for promotion and tenure, the U.S.C. complained that published research had too often been used in the recent past as the primary indicator of faculty quality. The reports contained a significant caveat, however. Both the C.U.E. and the U.S.C. believed Tufts needed to add faculty and staff to implement their recommendations. The U.S.C. proposed that funding be obtained from further undergraduate expansion combined with improved annual giving.

Unfortunately, the second half of Hallowell's term brought additional erosion of Tufts's financial position. No major fund drive was organized, and private giving remained level—at 4 percent—as a proportion of the annual budget. The recommended growth of enrollments occurred, but increased financial pressures prohibited faculty expansion. Tufts's faculty-to-student ratio jumped—from under seventeen to one in the early 1970s to nearly nineteen to one by 1975—and the academic preparation of entering classes declined, as Tufts became less selective. At the same time, in the pressured academic labor market of these years, standards for promotion edged upward in scholarly terms. Hallowell was in the position of asking his faculty to undertake new instructional tasks while accepting higher work loads, less-prepared students, and heightened scholarly expectations. It was a difficult context for educational reform.[44]

The atmosphere at Brandeis in the 1970s was even more strained. Marver Bernstein, Schottland's replacement in the presidency, assumed his duties in the fall of 1972, five years after Hallowell began at Tufts. Bernstein, a political scientist from Princeton and a former dean of the Woodrow Wilson School, was, like Hallowell, eager to focus on questions of undergraduate education. He also wanted to modify Sachar's legacy by making more explicit Brandeis's identity as a Jewish institution through new programs of education and research as well as service. As a professional administrator, moreover, Bernstein was appalled by the Byzantine bureaucratic atmosphere of Brandeis. Determined to bring directness and collegiality to his administration, he appointed a faculty-based Academic Planning Committee and instituted more open forms of budgetary management and financial reporting.

Brandeis's new president, unlike his counterpart at Tufts, enjoyed no period of prosperity in which to pursue either his organizational or his academic ideas. By the time he arrived, the financial pressures of the new decade were already being felt at the Waltham campus. In the spring of 1972, for example, Schottland had proposed eliminating three graduate departments and laying off forty employees for lack of funds, and Bernstein soon discovered that the cumulative deficit was much larger than even the trustees understood. Conditions worsened in the middle 1970s, forcing attention to questions of consolidation. During 1973–1974 and again in 1974–1975 Bernstein proposed reductions in instructional staff to ease budgetary pressures but quickly became locked in acrimonious confrontations with the faculty, especially the Academic Planning Committee that he had created to promote good relations between the administration and the professors. In the end, having no stomach for sustained conflict, he withdrew many of his recommendations.[45]

Brandeis's financial problems had deep roots. To some extent, they began with the new university's extraordinary monetary success under Sachar, which would have been difficult to sustain under any circumstances. There were also some specific hitches in Sachar's legacy. The founding president had raised impressive amounts for construction but had made little provision for upkeep, and by the 1970s maintenance costs were an expanding claim on the annual budget. The phasing out of Ford funds added to the pressure. Though annual giving remained strong between 1968 and 1972, the level did not rise enough to offset the withdrawal of grant support. In the early 1970s, Brandeis began borrowing to meet its current obligations. The accumulated deficit at the time of Bernstein's appointment exceeded eight million dollars.

The new president, though well connected in Jewish circles—he had chaired the National B'nai B'rith Hillel Commission and served as state comptroller of Israel—was not an experienced or gifted fund-raiser, and the early 1970s were a difficult time for Brandeis to find money. The Yom Kippur War diverted the attention of Jewish philanthropists, and the radical reputation of the campus, reinforced by the disruptions of the Abram years and continuing protest activity under Bernstein, added a further impediment. There was, in any case, no well-developed alumni/ae giving program to offer significant help. Annual donations fell steadily: from fourteen million dollars in 1973 to twelve million in 1974 and to ten million in 1975, while inflation reduced the value of each dollar.

In this context, Brandeis turned to its students to make up for losses elsewhere and minimize the necessity for cutbacks. The size of the entering class jumped from 600 in the fall of 1972 to 675 the following year and rose steadily through 1976, when it reached 800. Student payments went from 25 percent of current income in Sachar's last year to 32 percent in 1970 to 40 percent in 1978.

Changes at Brandeis in the areas of finance and enrollment—the reduced value of gift income, the reluctant expansion, and the greater reliance on student payments—generally paralleled those at Tufts. Nonetheless, the loss of financial momentum was especially severe—and damaging—at the state's youngest private university. One comparison was especially telling. Between 1958 and 1968, Brandeis expanded its total annual revenues by 398 percent, compared with 219 percent at Tufts; between 1968 and 1976, yearly income at Brandeis grew by only 51 percent, compared with 90 percent at Tufts, which was itself struggling in these years.[46]

To make matters worse, Brandeis, much more than Tufts, was attempting to be a major research institution on a limited overall base. Its departments were not large, so even modest limits on hiring were threatening. A marked drop in graduate enrollments reduced the numbers of research and teaching assistants and further jeopardized the scholarly environment. With new appointments restricted, undergraduate classes expanding, and graduate numbers declining, the teaching loads of Brandeis faculty became both heavier and more concentrated at the college level. In 1970–1971, the average professor taught thirty-two undergraduates per term; by 1975–1976 the figure was forty-four.

Student quality, moreover, fell in association with Bernstein's expansion. The new university's inability to reach beyond a narrow segment of the Jewish community was painfully evident in these years. The ratio of applications to matriculants dropped from 5 to 1 in 1972 to 3.4 to 1 in 1976, as the numbers seeking admission declined while the total accepted rose. Average S.A.T. scores, which had slipped sharply in the late 1960s and early 1970s, took another plunge. The student body became more heavily Jewish than ever. Once again the comparison with Tufts is helpful. In 1972 the average verbal S.A.T. score of Brandeis freshmen was 10 points above their Tufts counterparts; by 1976 the scores were identical. Some new students needed precollegiate work.

There were indications of declining faculty quality as well. Several established stars departed as financial conditions deteriorated. Others reached retirement age. Those who left were often not replaced with comparable appointments or not replaced at all. The Academic Planning Committee expressed concern that standards for tenure were slipping.

The developments of the early Bernstein years would have been disturbing to any faculty. For Brandeis's ambitious professoriate—which had little of the ambivalence toward the advanced academic functions of their Tufts counterparts, and little of their colleagues' tendency toward self-deprecation—they were especially so. As Bernstein put it: "we have many faculty members whose only experience was growth . . . To them, any kind of austerity . . . seems almost immoral." Indeed, the Academic Planning Committee took the posi-tion that economic considerations were not a legitimate basis for decisions on staffing.

In 1976 Bernstein's dean of faculty, Jack Goldstein, circulated among the faculty a long letter to the president, cataloging the declining academic situa-tion and stressing the need for more effective planning. Goldstein described the atmosphere on campus as follows:

> . . . morale is, at best, uneven. The Faculty does not, in 1976, have a clear sense that its collective purpose is achievable. Instead, we find ourselves adopting con-servative postures in our attempts to deal with threatening financial conditions . . . We are troubled about whether we can, indeed, remain a liberal arts insti-tution of the highest quality.[47]

Bernstein stayed in the presidency until 1983. During the late 1970s, there was a modest improvement in conditions. Annual giving turned upward, but Brandeis, unlike Harvard and M.I.T., did not mount the kind of campaign that could produce a large infusion of new funds. Admissions statistics also improved temporarily but slipped again in the early 1980s. The second half of the Bernstein presidency thus evolved into a plodding, difficult, frustrating period for faculty and administration alike.

Although Brandeis's standing remained high—in 1981 a rating by *Change* magazine placed the campus in a select group nationally as having top under-graduate programs in key fields—it was a reputation increasingly based on the past. Media testimonials during the thirtieth anniversary in 1977–1978 evoked the glory of the early years under Sachar more than recent accomplishments. Indeed, Sachar, still active and vigorous, remained the most visible public face of Brandeis. In the 1970s, more than a decade after the founder had left the presidency for the chancellorship, the university he had created, and the board charged with its stewardship, had yet to devise a successful second act.[48]

The Adaptability of the Urban University

The most surprising pattern of change during the 1970s occurred among the state's private, urban universities: Boston University, Boston College, and Northeastern. As the decade began, these three institutions—with their dependence on student payments and in-state enrollments in the context of high inflation, increased competition for applicants, and growth in the public sector—seemed especially vulnerable. As the decade unfolded, however, each found ways to prosper. Indeed, for the two campuses that were most troubled at the beginning of the period—B.U. and B.C.—the 1970s proved to be years of impressive development. Northeastern's more cautious policies during the golden age were repaid by stability amid the generalized angst of higher edu-cation.

Knowles remained in the N.U. presidency until 1975, long enough to see the worries of a few years earlier gradually abate. While there were no major initiatives during the final part of his term, there were few cutbacks either. Enrollments, aided by continued growth in state scholarships, an influx of foreign students, the special appeal of co-op, and the recently diversified portfolio of offerings, held steady during the early 1970s and in 1974 jumped upward, initiating a period of moderate expansion that would last through the end of the decade.

The Diamond Anniversary Development Program was completed successfully, with its increased target of sixty-five million dollars surpassed. Especially significant was a continued rise in the proportion of private giving, as distinct from the government grants that initially had dominated the campaign. Knowles was able to leave the presidency on a note of celebration and achievement, something that few of his colleague-presidents during the 1960s accomplished. In May 1975, the trustees expressed their confidence in N.U.'s position by naming Knowles's executive vice president, Kenneth Ryder, as his successor.[49]

The most important area of tension at the time of Knowles's retirement was the unresolved question of collective bargaining. The union movement at Northeastern had its roots in the political activism of the late 1960s, which had stirred a new aggressiveness in the university's historically passive faculty, and the financial worries of the early 1970s, which had led Knowles and the trustees to place controls on tenure and salaries.

With the election scheduled five months after his appointment—and one week after his inaugural—Ryder persuaded his board to drop the tenure quota and award raises to all full-time faculty members. The gesture was transparent, but it was also a signal that the new president intended to be more conciliatory than his domineering predecessor and that the university itself was financially strong. Ryder's initiative may have tipped the electoral balance. In a two-stage process—the first ballot proving inconclusive—unionization was defeated by five votes.[50]

Boston University also held a union election in the 1970s, but with dramatically different results. In May 1975, six months before the Northeastern vote, 60 percent of the B.U. faculty voted for collective bargaining, with 75 percent of those eligible participating. The contrasting outcomes could not be attributed to intrinsic characteristics of the two institutions. In most respects, B.U.—with its deeper scholarly traditions and higher academic aspirations— was a less likely arena for unionization than the quasi-industrial Northeastern. What seemed to count at the polls, however, was the way campus leaders negotiated the transition into the 1970s. While Knowles guided N.U. with minimum disruption and Ryder promised an era of collegiality, B.U.'s Silber went out of his way to promote crisis and confrontation.

Silber had made no effort prior to his appointment to disguise his ambitions for B.U. or his abrasive personality. He was attracted to the sprawling, ill-managed campus, in fact, because he felt it possessed great "upside potential" to respond to his aggressive brand of leadership—and carried a "downside risk" of bankruptcy if it continued to drift. He was also clear about what needed to be done. B.U., in Silber's view, could not "compete on price" with the state's public universities, so it had to "compete on quality," chiefly by adding top-flight faculty and forcing out those who were tired or mediocre.

Since Silber thought B.U. was "terribly understaffed," the new president identified units where a core of solid people justified adding resources. He approved a stream of appointments—generally of high quality, some truly distinguished, many at the senior level—in Law, Medicine, Dentistry, and Fine Arts. He sponsored showcase initiatives, like the University Professors Program, which housed prominent academic stars whose work cut across disciplinary lines, and the Center for Latin American Development Studies, built around a former M.I.T. economist. He encouraged a host of programmatic initiatives, especially interdisciplinary offerings that linked professional courses and the arts and sciences. Simultaneously, Silber made dollars available to encourage the retirement of unwanted older faculty members, and he was characteristically blunt in letting chairs and individuals know who should go. Reports of the new president's brutality in harassing faculty he wanted to push out became standard themes of gossip in the Boston academic community. For schools that needed to be built up—Management, Education, and Arts and Sciences—the president recruited a cadre of talented deans.[51]

All of this cost money, and before Silber's first year was over, the financial alarms were ringing. B.U. incurred a 2.4 million dollar deficit for fiscal year 1971, and Silber projected an even larger one for the next year. In the fall of 1971 the new president proclaimed a financial crisis, telling a special faculty meeting that B.U. was "going to go broke" and announcing a tuition increase and a postponement of student aid. Between 1971 and 1974, B.U.'s prices rose more rapidly than those of any university in the area, moving from a level below Boston College and above Northeastern, to a position just below Harvard and M.I.T. The president defended the increases on academic as well as budgetary grounds: if B.U. were going to compete on quality, it needed to spend and charge accordingly.

Silber also recruited a new vice president for finance, who installed professional practices in the area of money management. Additional help came from improved grant income, spurred by the wave of new appointments. By the mid-1970s, the budget was again in balance, and Silber claimed credit for a dramatic rescue operation. The achievement was real enough, but the president could not resist exaggeration. Individuals familiar with B.U.'s finances pointed out that the deficit of fiscal year 1971 was both modest and fully anticipated and that Silber's basic solution—hiking tuition as opposed to raising private funds—was precisely that of his predecessors.

Silber's tuition increases solved one problem but contributed to another. Between 1971 and 1974, freshman applications declined from 17,000 to 11,000, and numbers of entering freshmen fell also—from 3,300 in 1971 to 2,600 in 1975. The pattern appeared to confirm the fears of the late 1960s—that B.U. lacked the reputation to attract adequate enrollments if it significantly raised its charges. Faced with declines even before the demographic downturn predicted for the 1980s, Silber and his associates anticipated reduced operations, concluding that B.U. would shrink from 19,000 students to 15,000 by the end of the decade. The financial implications of these plans were daunting, however. When nonstudent income was held constant in the university's calculations—the assumption most consistent with recent history—the projected deficit reached $30.6 million in six years. In this context, the new president changed his emphasis from expanding the faculty to scaling it back. In the fall of 1974, Silber announced that B.U. would have to eliminate 150 positions over the next several years.[52]

Silber's intimidating leadership style was hard enough for administrative subordinates and faculty to accept in a time of growth; in the context of contraction it was terrifying. The union movement took off in the fall of 1974. Several deans were infuriated by the manner in which budgetary discussions were conducted during 1975–1976. The gathering pressures came to a head in the spring of 1976. Disgruntled faculty aired their grievances to a trustee committee conducting a routine presidential review. Ten deans asked the review committee to recommend Silber's removal. The faculty Senate passed a no-confidence vote, and the full faculty overwhelmingly endorsed a call for Silber's removal.

When the issue came to the trustees, however, the president had the votes to defy the rebellion that boiled around him. The board had known he would not be popular when they hired him, and Silber had worked hard to retain their support. Following the crisis, dissident deans, vice presidents, and even trustees departed, leaving Silber and his allies to consolidate their power. The bloodiest bureaucratic battle in the modern history of Massachusetts higher education was over.[53]

The final years of the 1970s brought a remarkable resurgence for B.U.—and an implicit exoneration of Silber's methods. The decline in applications was reversed in 1975, after which freshman enrollments grew steadily and total enrollments increased even more rapidly as emphasis shifted toward upper-division and graduate work. The improved numbers were partially attributable to a sophisticated marketing campaign carried out by a reorganized admissions office. Equally important was the rising reputation of B.U. itself, propelled partially by new faculty appointments but mostly by the visibility of the charismatic president. Silber's readiness to challenge the liberal conventions of the 1960s, to face down the faculty and students who had defeated so many academic leaders only a few years earlier, made him a folk hero for many Americans and projected an image of traditionalism and excellence.

With the student body growing as tuition remained high, the financial pressures of the mid-1970s lessened. The much feared layoffs never occurred, and at decade's end the faculty was larger than it had been in 1971 by just the two hundred positions that Silber had projected ten years earlier. In 1981 he issued a glossy and self-celebrating account of how, through brilliant hiring—including 274 faculty at the senior level—and tough-minded management, he had transformed a flabby, mediocre institution into a top-flight university. Silber's claims lacked modesty, but the changes—in academic reputation, student selectivity, program initiatives, and financial soundness—were impressive. It was far from clear that a less ruthless leader could have produced such results.[54]

The turnaround at Boston College was at least as impressive as at B.U. but was carried out in a much different atmosphere. Once again, the president was an essential variable in the equation. B.C.'s new leader, appointed in the fall of 1972, was Father J. Donald Monan, S.J., an Aristotelian philosopher and the former academic dean of LeMoyne College, a Jesuit institution in Syracuse, New York. The choice broke with tradition in two ways. Monan was the first campus executive selected in conventional fashion by a representative search committee rather than in secret by the provincial and general. He was also the first from outside of New England. These innovations reflected B.C.'s urgent need for effective, unifying leadership following the turmoil of the Joyce years. Monan brought with him a reputation for level-headed administrative competence. He had maintained good relationships with various campus groups during the uproars of the late 1960s. His measured, gentle manner projected confidence and calm. He had strong support, moreover, from Walsh, who promoted his selection and later served on his board.[55]

Monan was a rationalist and planner who brought the logic of his discipline to questions of institutional policy. Focusing initially on the deficit he had inherited from Joyce, Monan strengthened B.C.'s administrative capacities by naming an executive vice president and adding professionals to the development office, while also appointing a Long-Range Financial Planning Committee. Since B.C., like B.U., depended largely upon student payments, budgetary discussions centered on enrollments. Monan and his colleagues concluded that B.C., with its specialized appeal, could maintain its size despite general predictions of decline and could achieve balanced budgets through tuition increases and improved financial management. These projections proved conservative. Between 1972 and 1978, freshman applications rose from 7,300 to 12,400, and full-time undergraduate enrollment, from 7,700 to 9,100. The number of part-time students also grew.

Two phenomena accounted for B.C.'s vibrant statistics. First, a gifted dean of admissions, Jack McGuire, developed a program of "enrollment management" that combined well-conceived recruiting with a heightened emphasis on retention and a new readiness to admit transfers. Second, coeducation, introduced tentatively under Walsh and Joyce, blossomed under Monan. Women accounted for all the undergraduate growth of the 1970s, as male enrollments actually declined, and undergraduate women came to outnumber their male counterparts. A major factor in the expansion of female enrollments was B.C.'s takeover of financially troubled Newton College of the Sacred Heart in 1974, a move that the university's historian argues "may rank in importance with Father Gasson's 1907 decision to move Boston College from the South End to Chestnut Hill." As B.C. became more selective, reduced attrition and more transfers led to steady growth, even though the freshman class expanded only marginally. Higher charges turned the enlarged numbers into a 63 percent increase in tuition income during Monan's first five years.

Two other factors helped the financial picture. Monan reined in the development of expensive graduate programs that Walsh and Joyce had stressed. The crucial fact, however, was that faculty numbers remained stable as the student body grew. Monan initially had thought he would have to cut the instructional staff that the freewheeling Walsh had enriched so luxuriantly, but higher enrollments spared him this painful possibility. By 1976 the deficit had been eliminated, and the budget was in balance. Meanwhile, successful fund-raising supported physical improvements and new dorms, which aided the admissions effort. Faculty salaries mirrored B.C.'s improved position. Compensation at the senior ranks, which stood at middling levels in 1972, improved greatly under Monan, while pay for junior faculty, high at the start of the period, was maintained. Monan's five-year report, issued in 1977, was a slick declaration of prosperity.[56]

As financial and political stability were restored in the mid-1970s, Monan turned his attention to academic issues. In 1973 he constituted the University Academic Planning Council as a successor to Joyce's Priorities Committee and appointed that committee's former chair, Father Charles Donovan, as director. Not surprisingly, the new committee reasserted the themes of its predecessor, calling for a restoration of values that had been neglected during the 1960s. A summary of institutional goals stressed the "distinctively Catholic" nature of B.C. as well as the school's primary commitment to undergraduate, liberal education. Research and graduate training were downplayed. Public service was given even shorter shrift.

Monan endorsed the recommended modifications in B.C.'s priorities, as indicated by his decision to retain Donovan as academic vice president and his affirmation of the U.A.P.C.'s goals in his own five-year report. Monan's revitalized Boston College thus departed from both the secular academic professionalism that was ascendant under Walsh and the pastoral concern with Boston's Catholic neighborhoods that dominated B.C.'s early history. Monan's B.C. evolved as a relatively selective, relatively expensive, residential, college-centered university with a strong Catholic presence and as national a student body as could be achieved. As statistics on enrollments, budgets, and annual giving amply demonstrated, this was a resolution of the forces impinging on B.C. admirably suited for the conditions of the 1970s.[57]

The Roller Coaster of Public Higher Education

The weakening of student demand and slackening of public support that characterized higher education nationally in the 1970s were registered with particular vengeance at the University of Massachusetts. Enrollments at Amherst, which had increased by 1,250 per year during the 1960s, grew by only 700 annually between 1973 and 1975, then began to decline. The new campuses at Boston and Worcester continued to expand, but at rates far below those initially projected. In 1977–1978 UMass/Boston's student body was only half the 15,000 originally planned for 1980, and enrollments at the Medical School, always intended to be small, stood at 364 after eight years of operations.

In the context of a troubled regional economy and a drop in state revenues, funding also plummeted. The legislatively appropriated operating budget, which had grown by 23.8 percent annually between 1965 and 1970, was frozen in place. Limited increases in fiscal years 1974 and 1975 mostly allowed the opening of facilities planned years earlier. In 1976, with revenues below expectations, newly elected governor Michael Dukakis imposed an unexpected tax hike and reduced support for state programs. Both Amherst and Boston absorbed absolute cuts, which were barely restored in deflated current dollars over the next two years, and public sector faculties endured three years without salary increases. The latter part of the decade brought the beginnings of the "Massachusetts miracle," driven by the success of technologically oriented industry, along with a well-organized campaign against taxes that culminated in a statewide limit on real estate levies in 1980. As conditions improved, the state increased scholarship support significantly, but public colleges and universities did not recover their prior level of funding. Indeed, while overall state expenditures for higher education rose by nearly 300 percent between fiscal years 1969 and 1979—partially as a result of expansion, partially because of the opening of new facilities—real support per student declined by 15 percent over the period, and higher education's share of the state budget fell from 7.5 percent in fiscal year 1973 to 5.65 percent in fiscal year 1980.

The abrupt change in the circumstances of public higher education after 1973 was consistent with the "boom-bust" pattern that historically had plagued public higher education in Massachusetts. When student demand was strong, as in the 1930s, the late 1940s, and middle 1960s, government funds flowed into the university at rates that were difficult to absorb. When demand weakened and public interest turned elsewhere, as in the 1920s or early 1940s or mid-1950s, political support collapsed.[58]

The new conditions fostered intramural tensions. Amherst, for example, had grown in all directions in the 1960s—graduate and undergraduate, academic and professional, traditional and innovative—as abundance had allowed administrators to satisfy divergent priorities within the campus community. Now it was necessary to reduce support for some functions to maintain or strengthen others.

The new chancellor, former faculty member and student-affairs vice chancellor Randolph Bromery, elevated to the top position in 1971 following Tippo's resignation, sponsored several efforts to establish a basis for choice. First the graduate dean undertook an encyclopedic review of Amherst's work at the advanced level. Then a Commission on Goals tried to clarify UMass/Amherst's role within the state's public system. Neither effort settled very much. Finally a new provost, Paul Puryear, drafted a detailed plan for redistributing resources from Arts and Sciences, where enrollments were falling, to professional fields, where demand was strong, but Puryear's proposals enraged the faculty, and he was quickly forced from office.

Bromery himself decided to leave shortly thereafter, by which time the provostship and four of the ten deanships were filled on an acting basis, and a fifth deanship was in transition. A reaccreditation committee, visiting the campus that year, viewed the administrative instability as a sign of organizational failure. The campus had been "unable or unwilling," the committee noted, "to arrive at a plan of resource reallocation which would better fit the limited funds available."[59]

The Boston campus was as stymied by internal conflict as Amherst. Broderick's replacement in the chancellorship, Carlo Golino, a former vice chancellor in the California system, had hopes of building a Berkeley or a U.C.L.A. in the imposing new facility on Columbia Point to which UMass/Boston moved shortly after his arrival in 1973. Golino had little interest in the efforts of the founding faculty to create a high-quality undergraduate institution or in later pushes toward public service and practical education. Indeed, he set out to dismantle the system of semiautonomous colleges established under the 1969 master plan, while advocating graduate studies and traditional forms of research.

The chancellor's priorities stirred opposition from faculty committed to earlier emphases and did not win much support from either the president or the trustees. The fact that at Boston, as at Amherst, new programs needed to be nurtured by reallocating resources added to Golino's difficulties, as did resentment of his autocratic style. He did accomplish a few of his goals, however, including merger of the two arts and sciences colleges and a modest spurt of development at the master's level. Golino also did what Bromery could not do: he removed faculty positions from the first two colleges to allow the growth of two career-oriented units. But these steps further weakened his position with the faculty, which was soon devoting as much energy to resisting his alien vision as to building their fledgling campus. Administrative turnover symbolized the conflict. Golino forced out the provost, both sitting deans of Arts and Sciences, and the director of student activities before the opposition coalesced sufficiently to persuade the trustees to remove him, less than five years after his arrival.[60]

Internecine struggles at the campus level were part of a crippling pattern of political and financial skirmishing that swirled around the central office of the university in the middle 1970s. The trustees had reshaped the presidency in 1969 to rationalize the evolution of UMass as a multicampus system, but by 1973 the first incumbent, Robert Wood, was perforce more concerned with cutting back than elaborating previously approved plans for growth. His efforts involved him in a series of internal battles, while the broader pressures of the period fostered conflict with the political hierarchy of the state and with other institutions of higher education.

In the first years of his presidency, Wood had focused chiefly on relations with the legislature and governor and on the budget, leaving the campuses relatively free to manage their internal affairs. Under pressure to limit growth and control costs in the mid-1970s, however—and convinced that UMass, like most academic institutions, suffered from inadequate machinery for planning and decision making—the president asserted more direct operational control.

In 1973 Wood established new vice presidencies in academic affairs and planning. The first began to oversee the university's activities in academic personnel and curricular change, while the second took charge of physical development. At the same time, Wood moved the Office of the Secretary, the staff office of the trustees, from Amherst to Boston, and replaced the secretary, an old Amherst hand. Shortly thereafter, following a consultant's review of university organization—and a scandal in the management of federal funds by Amherst's School of Education—he created a vice presidency for management and business to supervise administrative systems that previously had reported to the chancellor at UMass/Amherst. These moves aggravated the structural tensions between chancellors and president that had been apparent from the early days of Wood's term. The new vice presidents, though formally conceived as staff in the system office, tended inevitably to claim supervisory status over their functional counterparts on the campuses, thus intersecting established relationships between vice chancellors and chancellors and between chancellors and the president. Both the president's office and campus hierarchies expended considerable energy between 1973 and 1977 wrestling over their respective roles.[61]

Though much of the bureaucratic maneuvering at the top of the university's pyramid had little effect on life in the classroom and library, some of it did, and much of the rest engaged the interest of highly politicized academic leaders on both campuses. Faculty at Amherst, accustomed to ascendancy within the university, felt especially threatened by encroachments on the authority of their chancellor and tended to support campus officials in struggles with the president. Scholarly anxieties were heightened when presidential involvement in academic planning seemed to jeopardize Amherst's upward progress in the status hierarchy, as when Wood rejected two proposed Ph.D. programs that would have edged the campus past Berkeley in total doctorates. The president's support of Puryear's reallocation plan prompted one of four votes for his removal by the Amherst faculty.

At Boston, professorial reactions to Wood followed a somewhat different course, partially because of his obvious interest in building the new urban campus and partially because many faculty felt closer to his educational ideas than to Golino's. Still, Wood's use of presidential power stirred a generalized distaste for authority unrelated to substantive questions. On both campuses, resentments toward the president, reinforced by diminished resources and frozen salaries, led to the formation of a faculty union in 1977. Long and acrimonious negotiations over an initial contract added to the university's preoccupation with political struggle.[62]

While fighting to establish the authority of his office within the university, Wood was engaged in an even more demanding tangle with Governor Dukakis. The state's new chief executive, a graduate of Swarthmore and Harvard, had never been a champion of public higher education, had little use for the independent, free-wheeling Wood, and faced, in any case, a severe deficit. Dukakis not only cut the UMass budget but tried to stop the Medical School from occupying new facilities in Worcester, impounded funds that had been appropriated for construction at Boston, and imposed restrictions on the university's authority to manage its budget and fill vacant positions. Seeing little hope of compromise, Wood fought back. With the help of allies in the legislature, he won a measure of budgetary relief from the governor's austere regimen. He went to court to obtain the release of appropriated dollars and reassert the fiscal autonomy granted by statute in 1962.

The battle between Wood and Dukakis became intense, personal, and public, to the delight of the state's leading media. The governor began a systematic effort to gain control of the university through appointments of lay trustees, the efforts of *ex officio* trustees from within his administration, and the exercise of his own role as a board member. Wood counterattacked by sponsoring, with Senate president Kevin Harrington, a plan to reorganize higher education by replacing the relatively weak Board of Higher Education with a strong "super board" and executive able to exert genuine control over the state's campuses while insulating the entire system from political intervention. The defeat of the Wood–Harrington proposal in the legislature left Wood essentially defenseless against the growing power of the governor.[63]

In his political struggles, Wood was hampered by rivalry among the state's colleges and universities, a historic phenomenon that had been muted during the 1960s but revived in the pressured circumstances of the new decade. The Wood–Harrington reorganization plan, for example, was weakened by opposition from the regional universities, whose leaders feared reduced freedom. Indeed, interinstitutional competition for support, and the inability of the Board of Higher Education to manage the public system effectively, was a growing source of frustration on Beacon Hill in the late 1970s. In 1980, dismayed by years of inconclusive discussion about how best to organize public higher education, the legislature approved a hastily conceived plan for a powerful Board of Regents as a rider to the annual budget.

Even more important was renewed antagonism from private universities, who responded to worries about enrollments and finances with intensified efforts to obtain state subsidies and limit the expansion of public campuses. While the Association of Independent Colleges and Universities pursued its campaign to repeal the constitutional prohibition on aid to private institutions, several prominent private leaders, most notably Silber of B.U., advocated increased public tuition to promote more equal competition between the two sectors.

Recognizing the dangers of intersectorial controversy, Wood made several efforts at accommodation. He set aside his personal belief in low-cost public higher education and advocated increased tuition at the university, a move also dictated by the state's fiscal problems. He joined with willing colleagues from private institutions in several attempts to build collaborative relations. Of these, the most significant was the "public-private forum," a congress of executives from the two sectors sponsored by the Board of Higher Education. The effort bore some fruit, especially the famous bargain in which the public presidents agreed to stop opposing anti-aid repeal and promote expansion of state scholarships and the privates called off their campaign for higher public tuition. Ultimately, however, the forces that drove the two sectors apart were far more powerful than the impulse to find common ground. The public-private forum disintegrated in a cross fire of recrimination.[64]

By 1977 Wood was embattled on several fronts—with the new faculty-staff union, with the governor, with his private-sector counterparts, and, increasingly, with his own board. He had survived for seven years and could claim some notable accomplishments, including the creation of an executive office for the three-campus system, the opening of the medical school facility and construction of the teaching hospital in Worcester, the location of the Kennedy presidential library at Boston, and the scaling back of unrealistic plans for growth.

In the end, however, the enervating atmosphere of perpetual conflict overwhelmed the potential for constructive activity, and Wood resigned in a mood of weariness and frustration. His final report noted that for the past two years he had been unable to attend to academic issues because

> our very survival sometimes seemed at stake. An institution wrestling with the question of meeting next week's payroll, considering the implications of temporarily closing a campus, or preparing lists of employees to lay off, cannot at the same time effectively develop a master plan, initiate innovative academic programs, or expand services to the public . . .

Outsiders to Massachusetts were sometimes baffled by the university's political helplessness. The 1978 accreditation report for Amherst observed that "one is taken aback by the fact that the University, which has existed in the Commonwealth . . . for so long has exercised relatively little in the way of political power."

But Wood's evolution from the optimism of the Future University committee to the disappointment of his final report was a familiar story. Among recent UMass presidents, Baker in the 1940s and Mather in the 1950s had come to Massachusetts determined to help the state's land grant university achieve its neglected potential and had departed in frustration. Only Lederle, the fortunate incumbent of the 1960s, had caught the roller coaster at a congenial moment. And as Wood prepared to leave, so too did chancellors on all three campuses. Still, the University of Massachusetts in 1977 was a much larger and more academically respectable institution than it had been in 1960, not to mention 1945. In the go-stop-go world of public higher education, progress was possible, though the cost was high.[65]

The Institutional Complex and the Reform Agenda

The critical consensus that emerged from reviews by national commissions at the end of the golden age contained a series of challenges for campus leaders. The issues were not new. Indeed, they involved the same questions that academia had debated after World War II. Who should go to college, and what sort of experience should they have there? How should graduate education and research be structured and supported? What limits should be placed on the social functions of colleges and universities? And how should the nation's academic system be organized and financed? During the 1970s, these fundamental issues were often displaced in campus debates by parochial worries about enrollments, money, and even survival. Yet the questions remained, and in reviewing the history of academic reform in these years, we shall learn more about the ways in which the workings of the institutional complex served the country's needs—or failed to do so.

Democratic Admissions and Interinstitutional Competition in the 1970s

At the end of the golden age, many academics were distressed to realize that higher education remained highly stratified by class and race despite the democratization of admission policies following World War II. Commission reports of the late 1960s and early 1970s urged redoubled efforts to enroll students from disadvantaged backgrounds, especially blacks. For most universities in Massachusetts, however, conditions of the 1970s clashed with egalitarian values. This phenomenon was especially apparent among upwardly mobile independent campuses like Tufts, Boston University, Boston College, and Brandeis, where fiscal pressures jeopardized the academic gains of the preceding two decades.

At the heart of the problem were trends in costs and prices. With inflation high and federal support constrained, private universities consistently asked their students to take up the financial slack. Tuition and fees increased rapidly, and income from these sources supplied a larger share of campus budgets than in the 1960s. Nowhere did expenditures for student assistance keep pace with rising charges. On the contrary, scholarship programs were a vulnerable expense for institutions struggling with deficits, as was demonstrated by B.U.'s decision to cancel aid payments in 1971. Independent universities in Massachusetts in the 1970s needed candidates for admission with sufficient resources to cover the escalating costs of their education.

It was probably to be expected, given the context, that the most striking feature of recruitment practices during these years was the introduction of professional techniques of marketing and public relations. The biggest admissions story of the period was the success of private campuses in attracting affluent students in sufficient numbers. In the 1970s, universities discovered that they could simultaneously raise prices and increase applications by seeking out carefully targeted groups of teenagers from prosperous circumstances. This insight was a crucial factor in the turnaround at B.C., which increasingly enrolled upper-middle-class Catholic women, and at B.U., which devised a sophisticated strategy to reach beyond the New England/New York area to "secondary" and "tertiary" zones identified through state-by-state analyses of the school's market potential. Tufts, too, shifted its focus toward wealthier students, and its percentage of freshmen from private secondary schools grew steadily during the 1970s.[66]

Leaders of independent universities acknowledged the difficulty of keeping their institutions open to applicants from modest financial backgrounds by campaigning for higher tuition at public campuses and for government-financed scholarships. They were especially worried about middle-class applicants who received little or no help from need-based federal aid programs, and they advocated changes in national policy to broaden the range of eligibility. Silber was especially outspoken on this topic and promoted a Tuition Advance Fund though which Washington would cover the college costs of participants in return for a promise of repayment linked to subsequent earnings. Within Massachusetts, A.I.C.U.M. won support for expanded state scholarships, but the commonwealth's program remained small in comparison with other states and had a limited effect on the accessibility of independent universities.

A staff report for the Sloan Commission on Government and Higher Education, analyzing income as a barrier to educational opportunity in Massachusetts in the 1970s, concluded that the primary guarantor of access was the low-cost public system. "Choice" among institutions—the ability of individuals to attend the college they preferred—remained, the report indicated, significantly dependent on family income. This was true even for the upper end of the public system, where, for example, UMass/Amherst continued its historic pattern of enrolling students from comfortable backgrounds.

Monetary impediments to admission were most evident at the state's independent universities. Among the latter, only Harvard and M.I.T. could afford large enough scholarship programs to offset costs for middle- and low-income applicants, and by the late 1970s these institutions were worried also. In 1978 the Harvard treasurer, drawing attention to recent jumps in undergraduate charges that had brought tuition to 70 percent of average disposable income, observed that "without new resources for financial aid, increases of this magnitude cannot continue without significantly affecting the composition of the student body in Harvard College." Even Bok became concerned about the tuition gap between public and independent universities.[67]

Academic economics of the 1970s particularly affected minorities, who were disproportionately represented in the lower financial tiers of the state's population. National studies detailing the decline in African-American and Hispanic enrollments after the mid-1970s, despite increasing rates of high school graduation among these groups, typically identified rising prices and restricted aid as the chief culprits. Patterns among universities in Massachusetts reinforced such analyses.

At both Tufts and B.U., minority percentages fell as financial pressures intensified, while the numbers at B.C. remained level but low. The most positive trends occurred at the ends of the institutional spectrum. Harvard, with its extensive student-aid funds, sustained stronger minority enrollments than other independent campuses, though its numbers also declined from the heights of the early 1970s. M.I.T., never able to achieve a high percentage of black or Hispanic students in its specialized programs, nonetheless was able to reverse a decline among these groups in the mid-1970s by expanding its scholarships.

For quite different reasons, minority numbers also remained relatively high at UMass/Boston and Northeastern. A philosophical orientation toward access played a role at both campuses, but the major difference between them and their upwardly mobile private counterparts was probably economic. With their low costs, low prices, and low status, these institutions needed to attract large numbers of undergraduates and were able to exercise only limited selectivity. Their admission policies would always tend to follow where the least-affluent portion of the student market led.

There was more, however, to the changing picture of minority enrollments than escalating costs. The often naive idealism associated with programs to achieve cultural diversity in admissions in the late 1960s was replaced, ten years later, with more awareness of the pitfalls of such efforts. Harvard, Northeastern, and Brandeis had learned through angry incidents that African-American students would not be content with mere acceptance at otherwise unchanged institutions. The decline of the Transitional Year Program at Brandeis illustrated the altered atmosphere. Abram viewed the T.Y.P. as a liberal sell-out to campus radicals, and Bernstein thought the program inappropriate for Brandeis and wanted to shut it down. Minority applicants were undoubtedly more guarded also. They had learned, through the experiences of older siblings and friends, that going to a white college could be a painful and alienating experience.[68]

The deterioration of access to college for low-income students during the 1970s was a predictable result of the hierarchy of values contained within the institutional complex. Universities bent on improving their standing in competition with other campuses and on obtaining the revenues necessary for that objective were not likely to emphasize egalitarian admissions when financial conditions forced a choice between higher tuition and lower costs. Quality and status were still directly linked to costs, and for universities, as for other large organizations in the nation's market-driven political economy, first things came first. The shift toward more affluent students did not, of course, lead necessarily to higher academic standards. On the contrary, the qualifications of entering students declined at both Brandeis and Tufts in the 1970s as both campuses solved financial problems by growing and grew by reaching deeper into their applicant pools. Such instances made it clear that, if status was a more important value than access for most universities, survival was more important than either.

The emphasis of academic leaders in Massachusetts on institutional interests did not imply indifference or cynicism about the openness of their campuses to students from diverse backgrounds. The records of Harvard and M.I.T., the two universities in the state with the fewest worries about enrollments, indicated that the reverse was true, and the financial aid programs of both campuses were reinforced by repeated public advocacy. In 1981 Bok published an open letter defending Harvard's efforts to attain racial balance in its student body, and Weisner's annual reports consistently stressed the need for progress in minority admissions. Similarly, as B.U. recovered financial strength in the late 1970s, Silber placed a renewed emphasis on enrolling blacks and Hispanics. The problem, in most instances, was not disinterest in attracting students from socially diverse backgrounds; the problem was the way in which this goal was qualified by institutional considerations.[69]

The firmest basis of democratic values in the admission policies of selective colleges, as the advocacy of James Conant revealed in the 1930s and 1940s, was the interest of these institutions in recruiting talent from all sectors of society in order to maintain high standards and stay connected with shifting centers of power and wealth in a highly mobile society. While elite universities would always seek some students from rich families, a campus accessible only to the affluent was at risk in competitive terms. This fact worked in favor of gifted students from modest circumstances, but given the correlation of academic achievement and social class, it offered limited consolation to most disadvantaged youth. Minorities were not likely, therefore, to achieve representation proportional to their numbers in the population in the middle and upper levels of the academic hierarchy until their academic accomplishments, as well as their economic and political power, rendered this orientation desirable in terms of fundamental institutional interests.

The value commitments of campus leaders sometimes pushed universities a step or two beyond the level of socioeconomic diversity dictated by economic or political pressures or meritocratic, competitive norms, but this factor made only a marginal difference in the overall accessibility of the system. As the staff report for the Sloan commission pointed out, students from modest backgrounds could count on access to higher education but had limited choice about the campus they attended. This was the achievement of American higher education in the years following World War II. It was an ambiguous outcome in a country dedicated to democratic values, but it provided a measure of opportunity for almost everyone, even as it failed to eradicate the unfair encumbrances of birth.

Patterns of access and choice reflected faithfully the central importance of social mobility as an organizing value in academia. Institutional communities on which the nation depended to improve the life chances of individuals were bound to be preoccupied with their own status as well. On balance, however, the self-interested behavior of universities in advancing their positions promoted opportunity by constantly challenging established schools as exclusive points of entry to the upper reaches of the country's social system.[70] At the same time, enlightened—and politically sensitive—public policies, such as federal and state scholarship programs and subsidized public campuses, introduced nonmarket forces into academia to counterbalance the raw effects of institutional competition. The combination was probably not capable of achieving perfection in terms of social justice, but it was difficult to imagine social arrangements that were likely to do better.

Reasserting Concern for Undergraduate Education

A common criticism of the golden age was that universities, in their eagerness to promote the advanced academic functions, devalued undergraduate education. Faculty members were widely perceived as scrimping on teaching to pursue research. Undergraduate curricula were faulted for retaining rigid, discipline-based categories reflective of professorial interests rather than student needs. Above all, general education was lamented as a neglected priority.

This litany was familiar territory to the academics who became presidents of universities in Massachusetts in the 1970s. In early policy statements, Bok, Silber, Hallowell, Wood, and Bernstein all stressed their intention to reemphasize baccalaureate-level work. Similarly, Gray was brought into the leadership of M.I.T. in part because of his interest in undergraduate education, and Monan announced that teaching and learning at this level were B.C.'s primary concerns. The undergraduate curriculum received renewed emphasis among universities in Massachusetts during the 1970s largely through the instigation of this new generation of campus executives. Noting the trend, Knowles of Northeastern, survivor of the sixties, expressed his satisfaction; he had never shared the enthusiasm of his fellow presidents of that period for graduate education and research.[71]

One theme of reform, especially evident in the early 1970s, involved efforts to introduce more flexible forms into the undergraduate curriculum. The state's two college-centered universities were especially active in this movement. Hallowell encouraged interdisciplinary work and joint majors and also promoted structures that allowed students to design their own programs. Bernstein, too, fostered interdisciplinary and problem-centered programs and wanted students to have more control over their education. Similar innovations were instituted at M.I.T., and one of the liberal arts colleges at UMass/Boston stressed interdepartmental clusters. Both Bok and Silber deplored the tyranny of the disciplines over collegiate programs and advocated new configurations of courses, especially ones that brought the arts and sciences into closer relationship to professional courses.[72]

Attempts to open up the undergraduate curriculum expressed the academic values of educators who believed their institutions had been insufficiently attentive to an important responsibility. The movement was also driven, however, by practical pressures. Presidents concerned about enrollments— and aware that tuition payments were becoming more important components of their budgets—inevitably worried about the attractiveness of their offerings. Hallowell defended his reformist exhortations on the ground that Tufts must project a special concern for undergraduate learning in order to prosper in the intensifying competition for students.

Academic leaders were also aware that the potential applicants to whom they wanted to appeal were more diverse in character than students of an earlier era. As universities welcomed minorities, women, and older students, they found themselves pressured to create programs of interest to the new clienteles. Student concerns also contributed to a new emphasis on career-oriented programs. Comprehensive universities like UMass/Amherst and B.U. found enrollments shifting from the liberal arts to professional schools as economic uncertainty made undergraduates more anxious about the future. Even liberal arts campuses like Tufts and Brandeis, undoubtedly influenced by altered student priorities as their admissions officers dipped lower into applicant pools, sought ways to introduce practical concerns into an academic framework.

UMass/Boston abandoned its exclusive early emphasis on the arts and sciences.[73]

The impact of academic values on the reform movement was particularly evident in a second wave of initiatives that, in fundamental ways, ran counter to the impulse to make undergraduate curricula more flexible. During the late 1970s, several area universities attempted to reassert the importance of structure in undergraduate work through the reintroduction of core requirements and general education programs. While there were pragmatic considerations behind this shift—especially the need to control costs by containing the proliferation of courses—the primary impetus came from the educational consciences of campus leaders. Reflecting current critiques of academic practice, many administrators and faculty argued that students deserved a more coherent introduction to intellectual life than was attainable in programs driven by student choice and professorial specialties.

Harvard's Rosovsky put the central question to his faculty in an open letter in 1974:

> Can we assume that students are sufficiently mature and responsible to benefit from untrammeled freedom, and that we will have done a great deal simply to engage them in serious intellectual work of some kind during their undergraduate years? Will the faculty be satisfied with a B.A. degree that is basically a certificate of attendance?

Rosovsky thought not. With Bok's support, Harvard's dean prodded the Faculty of Arts and Sciences through nearly ten years of committee work and general debate to put in place requirements that expressed, in Rosovsky's phrase, what it meant to be "an educated person in the latter part of the twentieth century." Other campuses went through similar exercises with less fanfare and comparable results. By the end of the decade, Tufts, Brandeis, and UMass/Boston had adopted new sets of core or distribution requirements for all undergraduates. M.I.T. and UMass/Amherst followed suit a few years later.[74]

It is not easy to assess the educational impact of curriculum reform in the 1970s. Detailed information about student experiences in the new structures is exceedingly difficult to obtain. To judge from superficial indicators like enrollments and formal structures, however, one would have to conclude that the results were constructive but modest. With the exception of a small number of experimental units (the College Within at Tufts, the College of Public and Community Service at UMass/Boston), the innovative curricular forms of the first part of the decade added elective options at the edges of traditional programs. Their primary contribution was to offer alternatives to the minority of students and faculty who wanted some relief from normal categories of teaching and learning.

The results of the core curriculum movement were also limited. The Harvard program, despite the publicity it received, was fundamentally a distribution requirement, as were the new structures at Brandeis and UMass/Boston. In forcing students to engage a range of subjects and perspectives, these initiatives accomplished some of the goals of general education, but the tendency to accept sponsorship of core courses by departments guaranteed that students' experiences in them would differ only marginally, if at all, from what they encountered in conventional courses.

Indeed, what the movement for curriculum reform mostly proved was the firmness with which the academic disciplines, based in departments and professional associations, controlled undergraduate education. Academic practice in this area was, in essence, the sum of the parts represented by disciplinary specialties, and the possibilities for reform seemed limited to changing the arrangements among these parts, making due allowance for the interests of each. The major, the primary concern of departments and disciplines, was left largely untouched, even uncriticized, by the reform movement.

There were real losses in the halfheartedness of curriculum change. Faculty members largely renounced the effort to provide their students with a framework for integrating perspectives from their various subjects or to judge the relative importance of various kinds of knowledge. They also gave up the effort to help students make clear connections between their studies and the non-academic world for which they were preparing. Realists recognized, however, that the meager results of the reform movement accurately reflected the state of academic knowledge, the organization of universities, and the training of most faculties.[75]

It is too easy, however, to explain the marginal impact of the reform movement on the basis of the knowledge explosion and the strength of academic professionalism. In the end, institutions and their leaders defined the limits of innovation, and campus policies, in the 1970s no less than the 1960s, were dominated by the interinstitutional competition for prestige and resources. In the first of these contexts, the undergraduate curriculum was far less significant than the strength of departments as assessed by professional peers or the scholarly records of individual faculty. This reality was symbolized by a 1981 *Change* magazine survey that rated the nation's universities in terms of their undergraduate programs; with few exceptions, the top-rated universities were all leading research centers.

The insignificance of actual institutional practice on the reputations of universities, even in the area of undergraduate education, limited the motivation of presidents, provosts, and deans to focus on substantive issues of learning and teaching or provide more than token resistance to the adverse impact of professional priorities on instructional activities. This unfortunate dynamic would not change until improved means could be found to measure and report institutional results with enough clarity to allow comparative educational accomplishments to become a basis for interinstitutional competition for status. By the late 1970s, indeed, critics of higher education, including government officials, were beginning to press for formal assessments of the outcome of college work, but this new movement had little immediate impact at the campus level.

One might suppose that the other dimension of interinstitutional competition—the battle for resources—would provide a counterforce against academic tendencies toward excessive deference to professional values. Students were, after all, an essential source of revenue at all institutions—the primary one at most independents—and students and their parents paid their bills in return for direct educational benefits. Unfortunately, however, undergraduates typically exerted only modest pressures for educational reform. Indeed, most students at universities that placed a primary emphasis on research, including Harvard and M.I.T., reported themselves satisfied with what they encountered.[76]

This fact reflected the basic purpose of education for most young Americans, who chose their colleges, after all, largely because of the social and economic value of the degree rather than the intrinsic merits of the education offered. Thus, if they were confident of their school's reputation, they were unlikely to complain very much, so long as their experience was fundamentally reasonable—which, at top-ranked schools was typically the case, even if their education fell short by the standards of idealistic champions of undergraduate programs. Tuition-paying parents constituted a potentially more critical constituency. For much of the 1960s and 1970s, leaders of elite campuses worried that rising prices might reduce their attractiveness to top students, but the applications kept increasing in number, sometimes, apparently, positively influenced by higher prices. At some point, however, it seemed inevitable that the rising costs of undergraduate education would produce a consumer revolt unless universities focused more attention on this aspect of their activities.

The passivity of students at upwardly mobile institutions was more troubling, but no less surprising, than that of undergraduates at elite campuses. Here, the preoccupation of academic leaders with promoting institutional status was especially threatening to education, since undergraduates at unselective campuses were far less able to teach each other or profit from distant contact with academic stars than their more privileged and talented counterparts. Students in such settings, however, were unavoidably anxious about their own social status and that of the university they had selected, undoubtedly with mixed feelings. They were probably disposed, in the end, to accept institutional norms that brought their alma mater as close as possible to the schools they would have preferred.

The hierarchy of values that dominated the movement to reform undergraduate education in the 1970s was symbolized by the actions of two presidents who made themselves articulate spokespersons for change, Bok and Silber. One represented the nation's most prestigious campus, the other an upwardly mobile urban university. Both were troubled by the devalued status of undergraduate teaching, and both took steps at the beginning of their presidencies to alter this situation. Bok established a special fund to encourage pedagogical innovation and created a Center for Teaching and Learning to promote faculty interaction on instructional questions. Silber offered awards for outstanding teaching and urged his senior faculty to involve themselves in introductory courses.

Such initiatives undoubtedly had an impact, but, once again, the effect could not have been more than marginal. At the point where it counted most, appointments and promotions of faculty, both Bok and Silber developed reputations chiefly for their insistence upon high standards in research. Bok did not alter in any significant way the criteria for making senior appointments that had obtained since the days of James Conant, and his most controversial early decisions involved his rejection of popular teachers whose scholarly work was judged inadequate. One of the B.U.'s stars during the Silber years, literary critic Helen Vendler, ultimately became disillusioned with her president for forcing out a significant number of dedicated teachers who were contributing greatly to the quality of undergraduate education but lacked scholarly luster.

There was ample room in all this for reformers to be discouraged. Bok himself admitted the limits of Harvard's new core requirements but stressed their benefits nonetheless—and especially of the debate that produced them. He was making the best defense that could be made of undergraduate reform in the 1970s. In terms of curricular change, the results were not radical, but neither were they trivial. The innovations of the period enriched and broadened the experiences of many students. In relation to the quality of teaching, the reform movement was probably even more important. Bok argued that Harvard's endless debate on the core had great value in focusing the faculty on undergraduate education, even if concrete outcomes were modest. This point should not be slighted.[77]

Indeed, while systemic pressures failed to give institutions and their leaders compelling reasons to pursue reform aggressively, individual professors and administrators took steps within their circles of influence and activity to do things differently. Here one encounters, in a positive way, the impact of personal and professional values on institutional life. For example, many younger faculty, who attended graduate school in the late 1960s and early 1970s, had absorbed the period's critiques of academic practice in undergraduate education and came to their classrooms determined to pay attention to their students. In this, they sometimes found common cause with older colleagues who had never adopted the values of the academic revolution.

Thus, beneath the disappointing surface of debates about curricular forms and despite the logic of policies on promotion and tenure, there clearly occurred a new intensity of interest in undergraduate education. This was true across the spectrum of universities in Massachusetts. In some instances, moreover—Tufts and UMass/Boston continued to be the best local examples—the commitment to education was shared by sufficient numbers, at enough levels of the hierarchy, to foster a true culture of teaching and learning that transcended, at least for a time, the logic of the competitive pressures that dominated long-term patterns of academic change.

Continuity and Innovation in Graduate Education and Public Service

The marketplace dynamics that limited efforts to strengthen undergraduate education in the 1970s also shaped institutional responses to reformist proposals in graduate education and public service. Both fields had been the objects of concern in commission reports at the end of the golden age. Graduate education, it was widely held, had been grossly overbuilt in relation to national needs, especially with respect to the production of Ph.D.s in basic disciplines. In addition, the programs that produced the nation's future professors were commonly criticized for being excessively focused on research and too little oriented toward preparing students for the work in which a majority of them would spend most of their time—college teaching.

Public-service activities came under scrutiny for different reasons. Many observers believed that in responding to outside calls for help during the 1960s—especially from government agencies and community groups—universities had compromised their political neutrality as well as their programmatic coherence. Commission reports at the end of the golden age urged a pulling back from indiscriminate external involvements toward the core academic functions that universities were uniquely equipped to perform.

As they were with respect to undergraduate education, presidents of universities in Massachusetts were well-briefed on the complaints about graduate education advanced by academic reformers. Bernstein, Hallowell, Wood, Monan, and Bok all expressed the view that their institutions had devoted too much energy in the 1960s to building research-oriented Ph.D.s in conventional fields, and all five took steps, early in their presidencies, to limit or altogether prevent the development of new programs. Both B.C. and Brandeis actually eliminated doctorates that had not established themselves on viable bases. The net impact of such efforts was to halt the expansion of graduate enrollments in arts and sciences among the area's universities, though patterns varied from campus to campus. Brandeis, UMass/Amherst, and N.U. experienced modest declines in the number of advanced students, but Tufts, B.U., B.C., and M.I.T. all reported some expansion. Only Harvard undertook major cutbacks, consistent with the recommendations of a 1968 review of the Graduate School.[78]

The propensity to maintain graduate enrollments in arts and sciences despite the collapse of the academic labor market perfectly reflected the dominance of self-aggrandizing institutional impulses over educational concerns within the institutional complex. Reformers could argue that students were ill-served by programs that could not ensure jobs upon completion of their degrees and that campus resources could be used to better purpose in other areas, but, for most institutions, systemic pressures worked against significant reductions at the doctoral level. Harvard was the exception that proved the rule. With its well-developed programs and secure position in the status hierarchy, the nation's oldest university could afford to scale back its graduate activities without eliminating programs or adversely affecting faculty work.

For upwardly mobile schools, however, Ph.D. programs were the prized tokens of progress during the golden age, and campus leaders were reluctant to give them up. For almost all area universities, moreover, doctoral students had become indispensable components of the academic production system. Aspiring Ph.D.s undertook large amounts of instructional work and provided crucial assistance for faculty research—all for subsistence wages. So long as adequately prepared applicants continued to seek entry, departments were going to want to admit them, and administrative leaders were not likely to raise serious objections—however irrational the resulting pattern in aggregate terms. Brandeis's Bernstein was a prime example of the phenomenon; he was convinced that his struggling university was overbuilt at the doctoral level but was simply not prepared to engage the fight that cutting back would have precipitated.

In the long run, of course, the market mechanism was likely to force change. Ambitious students would not continue to endure the extended deprivations of doctoral studies if the effort led nowhere in terms of careers. Shifts in federal funding policies were raising the costs to universities of advanced programs. In the 1970s, however, these forces were not sufficiently strong to produce more than a modest effect on the scale of graduate education in Massachusetts.

Calls to change the character of doctoral programs had even less impact than proposals to prune them back. This was an old story. In the early postwar years, the President's Commission on Higher Education had argued that more should be done to prepare advanced students for instructional work, but the commission's exhortations had had little impact on the expansion of graduate education that began in the 1950s. The most striking version of this recycled idea in the 1970s was the Doctorate of Arts, a new degree championed by the Carnegie commission as an alternative to the Ph.D. for future faculty inclined to emphasize teaching rather than research.

There was, in fact, good reason for distinguishing the training of apprentice researchers from that of college teachers more sharply than the conventional model of doctoral education allowed. Empirical studies during the 1970s found virtually no relationship between the scholarly productivity of college professors and effective teaching. Still, no university in Massachusetts instituted the D.A. Indeed, area institutions did not respond in any significant way to the argument that doctoral programs overemphasized research.[79]

The unhappy truth was that, though some local leaders (Bok among them) were critical of graduate training, the systemic pressures of the period worked against reform. There was, for example, no strong evidence of market demand for the products of graduate programs that stressed instructional training. Indeed, the oversupply of Ph.D.s in the 1970s allowed low-status, teaching-oriented institutions to upgrade their faculties by hiring products of research-oriented programs from top universities. Most institutions, eager to improve their standing in the academic hierarchy, took advantage of this opportunity. In the absence of external pressure for change, graduate faculties had little incentive to divert their energies—and the attention of their students—toward pedagogical reflections. The effort to restructure graduate education in the 1970s was doomed by the absence of links between the reform movement and institutional interests in the competition for prestige and resources.

Competitive pressures affected the public-service activities of universities in a different way. Late 1960s' critiques of academia as excessively responsive to external demands for help typically underestimated the self-interested, entrepreneurial impulses that drove such involvements. Universities took on consulting contracts and problem-solving activities largely because they were sources of revenue that could help support both faculty and graduate students. Calls for reducing such involvements were not likely, therefore, to have much salience at a time of intensified financial pressure. On the contrary, the correct expectation would have been that universities would pursue new avenues of external support in order to maintain and expand their capacities.

The impulse was best illustrated by M.I.T., the regional leader in deploying its expertise in revenue-producing service activities. The Institute had recast itself as a major university in the postwar years through shrewd exploitation of its ability to serve the interests of federal agencies. As government funds became more difficult to obtain in the 1970s, the Institute aggressively sought new clients, most notably in industry—which had been its chief source of outside support before the rise of federal funding. The report of the Press committee and the creation of industry-oriented research and development centers symbolized the transition.

Other universities in Massachusetts pursued similar ventures. B.U., UMass/Amherst, and Northeastern all created strings of soft-money institutes and centers in the 1970s. Simultaneously, non-degree, mid-career education emerged as a growth industry in response to the desire of practicing professionals to update their skills and improve their personal mobility. At Harvard, for example, mid-career programs were developed in the schools of Business, Government, and Education as well as the Medical School. Thus, while the market mechanism was muted in the area of doctoral education where issues of prestige fostered resistance to change, it was a vigorous source of innovation in service-oriented activities that were rooted in the ongoing effort to expand resources.[80]

Patterns of change in graduate education and public service during the 1970s revealed both the strengths and limitations of the market mechanism. On the positive side was the obvious fact that the pressures of the period channeled energy and creativity toward many useful ventures. At the same time, the decade revealed academia's unfortunate tendency toward overproduction and boom-bust cycles, especially in areas—like doctoral education and research—with intrinsic attractions to institutions and faculty. There was also the inevitable period of lag, while campus leaders adjusted to new conditions, when the policies of universities and the needs of the country were seriously out of alignment. There was, finally, the danger, illustrated most clearly by the new emphasis on industry-financed research projects, that institutions, in their eagerness for new sources of revenue, would compromise and weaken their basic educational and scholarly functions.

It is important to remember, however, in evaluating the consequences of the academic marketplace, that the problems of excess supply and overemphasis in the advanced academic functions that occurred in the 1970s were caused as much by federal policies of the 1960s as by the dynamics of the market. Indeed, Joseph Ben-David has argued that, in supporting research and graduate education at levels beyond those sustainable by market forces, public policy was the primary cause of distorted institutional priorities.[81]

The Persistence of Institutional Diversity

We come now to the basic question posed by this study: the implications of the institutional complex for the character of the nation's system of universities and especially for the diversity of campuses sustained by that system. The evidence of the golden age was ambiguous on this question, but observers at the end of the period worried that continuing variations might simply be "residual differences" destined for further erosion and ultimate extinction as universities devolved toward a single institutional model. The concern could be restated in terms of a scholarly debate that we encountered in the Introduction: did the tendency of universities to compete for prestige and resources imply an inevitable homogenization among campuses driven toward a common conception of status? or was competition a great engine of diversity that ensured an academic system responsive to the shifting needs of a pluralistic democracy?

Changes during the 1970s provided evidence on both sides of this long-running argument. Some trends toward greater similarity among institutions in Massachusetts continued during this decade. By far the most important such instance involved the further development of an academic professional culture as a pervasive force that linked faculties across institutional boundaries and was largely endorsed by campus hierarchies. On crucial questions about educational programs and scholarly work, there was nearly universal deference to the norms of the disciplinary societies and widespread acceptance of the claims to organizational power that academic departments made on the basis of professional authority. Apparent departures from collegial conventions—such as Silber's assertion of presidential prerogatives at B.U. or unionization movements at UMass, Northeastern, and B.U.—were mostly power struggles among groups and individuals with similar basic commitments.

The continuing significance of professional values was especially apparent in efforts to create new programs of general education. In the years before World War II, undergraduate, nonmajor requirements were one of the contexts in which these campuses displayed their intellectual, social, and even religious distinctiveness. Reform ideas of the 1970s, by contrast, exhibited a dreary uniformity. The new core curricula created by faculties at Harvard, Brandeis, and UMass/Boston differed from each other only in details, and all were shaped by current intellectual fashions within the disciplinary professions.

Similarly, despite real differences among campuses in attention paid to teaching, initiatives to promote greater faculty concern with matters of pedagogy and course design encountered parallel constraints at research universities and local-service institutions. A dean at Northeastern could read Derek Bok's descriptions of Harvard's experience in this area with complete understanding. Efforts to reshape doctoral programs in response to the conditions of the 1970s were another setting in which to observe the power of academic culture. Campus after campus clung to its portfolio of conventional Ph.D.s as tokens of stature and resisted the urgings of reforming commissions to experiment with modes of advanced study that departed from professionally approved norms.

The apparently inexorable movement of universities toward similar organizational patterns was extended in the 1970s into administrative hierarchies, where environmental pressures produced greater professionalization than had been true during the golden age. The new emphasis on managerial expertise in areas ranging from finance to public relations to admissions to planning was linked to the development in each of these areas of national professional societies complete with their own standards, networks, and journals.

Universities became increasingly standardized in structural terms. Harvard's movement away from informal, decentralized administration converged with Northeastern's abandonment of centralized, quasi-industrial patterns and B.C.'s rejection of Jesuit amateurism: by the late 1970s the organizational charts of the three campuses were scarcely distinguishable, and middle-level administrators could move comfortably from one to another as readily as could their faculty counterparts. The rise of external regulation contributed to the trend toward organizational conformity, as all campuses were compelled to adopt similar practices in areas like affirmative action, grant accounting, and campus safety.[82]

Despite continuing trends toward homogenization, students of academic change during the 1970s expressed much less concern about declining institutional diversity than had been the case at the end of the golden age. Two reviews of higher education during these years by the Carnegie Council on Policy Studies concluded that variability among campuses remained a vibrant reality. The scholarly literature contained a similar shift of emphasis, as illustrated in the work of Burton Clark, whose massive comparative study stressed the reliance of the United States on a relatively free market to guide academic development and the capacity of such a system to generate institutional innovation.

What united analyses stressing the revival of diversity was the realization that deteriorating economic conditions had caused an intensified competition for resources that, in turn, forced universities to design distinctive programs that would sell in the marketplace. Such perceptions help resolve confusion among scholars about the impact of competition on institutional diversity. When resources are abundant, it appears, competition tends to reduce diversity since it allows campus leaders to focus on increasing prestige. When resources are scarce, however, competitive pressures lead universities to look for distinctive market niches.

The Carnegie council put it this way in its 1982 final report, fittingly titled *Three Thousand Futures* to celebrate persistent variation among the nation's academic institutions:

> The road to survival now leads through the marketplace. A new "academic revolution" is upon us. In the 1960s the revolution consisted of many institutions trying to become research universities and mostly failing . . . In the 1980s and 1990s it will take the form of following the long-term example of the community colleges in adjusting to the market . . . Excellence was the theme. Now it is survival.

Universities in Massachusetts provided ample evidence of the link between heightened competition for resources and increased diversity. Efforts to ensure a steady flow of students contributed to B.C.'s decision to reemphasize its ties to the Catholic church and Brandeis its connections to the Jewish community. The same concerns led Tufts to stress its collegiate qualities, UMass/ Boston to promote practical programs of interest to commuting students, M.I.T. to create new aggregations of scholarly expertise for industrial projects, and Harvard to generate executive development programs. While some observers deplored the new orientation toward marketing in academia, David Riesman, the chief theorist of declining diversity in the 1960s, welcomed it, noting that intensified efforts to find students was forcing institutions to match programs more closely with the interests of various constituencies.[83]

It is important to note, of course, that much of the diversity fostered by the new competition for students and dollars involved variation within a commonly held institutional conception. By the 1970s, all the schools we have studied had become complex universities. Locally and nationally, the era of special-purpose campuses like the pre-World War II versions of Northeastern, Massachusetts Agricultural College, M.I.T., and Boston College appeared to be gone forever.

Diversity among area universities had become more subtle. It was now expressed in their participation in what Gross and Grambsch called different "leagues," subgroupings of universities—private versus public, research-intensive versus those that were less so, and high status versus all others—with relatively little competition among campuses in different groups. Continuing diversity was also displayed in differences within fields across campus boundaries. Every university, for example, possessed an English department and most housed an undergraduate program in business. While disciplinary conventions limited variability in any such field, there remained room for important distinctions of emphasis and approach, especially at the graduate level.

Despite such nuances, the evolution of universities toward more or less similar programmatic portfolios staffed by faculties with common professional affiliations led many students of higher education, like the members of the Carnegie council, to observe that diversity was now more evident within universities than between them. To such observers, differences in interests and values between campus subunits—colleges of business, arts and sciences, nursing, education, and engineering, as well as subdisciplines within these aggregates—now seemed more striking than variation among institutions. From this perspective, the competitive dynamics that had led institutions to converge toward a common organizational form ultimately helped preserve diversity in academia, though in a radically altered pattern from the pre-World War II period.[84]

While universities in Massachusetts illustrated the new patterns of diversity between campuses based on disciplinary emphases and within campuses based on divergences between schools and departments, they also demonstrated, once again, that generalizations derived from macro-level analyses of national trends leave out important local realities. For, beneath surface similarities of function and commitment, area universities continued to manifest distinctive cultural strains: the Catholic character of Boston College, the Jewish culture of Brandeis, the pragmatic, working-class atmosphere of Northeastern, the localistic qualities of UMass/Boston, the technocratic orientation of M.I.T., and the cosmopolitan, upper-middle-class sheen of Harvard.

These differences among campuses remained evident in the students they enrolled, the nonacademic communities on which they relied for support, and even—though to a lesser extent—the faculties they attracted and the emphases of their programs. This fact, in turn, reflected the reality that interinstitutional competition was only one of the forces driving academic change at the campus level. Ideas and values still mattered, and so did intraorganizational dynamics. In the 1970s, as in the 1930s, academic variation resulted from complicated interactions within the institutional complex that could only be understood in terms of the particularities of individual universities.

Boston College provided a rich example of the workings of the institutional complex in the 1970s. Monan's reassertion of Catholic themes was more than a marketing device for a school that needed to expand its enrollments. It reflected, rather, deep currents within the Society of Jesus and the Catholic church that were themselves part of a larger revival of religiosity following the secularizing trends of the 1960s. Policies at B.C. also expressed the determination of the Jesuits to dominate the intellectual and spiritual life of their campus while ceding formal power to a lay board. What Monan was seeking, therefore, was not simply a formula for B.C. that would ensure its survival but a strategic balance that would allow it to prosper as a Catholic and Jesuit university. A parallel expression of institutional culture was occurring at M.I.T. in the same years. Under pressure to develop new sources of revenue, the Institute's leaders relied on campus traditions of applied work and close ties to industrial sponsors, unlike Harvard which solved the same problem through increased charges to students and private fund-raising.

In contrast to B.C. and M.I.T., Boston University under Silber was profoundly reshaped on the basis of competitive considerations. This was possible because B.U. possessed a weak institutional culture at the time of Silber's appointment and because the new president was uniquely successful in imposing his will on his adopted academic community. Even here, however, academic ideas played a vital role, though the ideas that mattered most were Silber's, not those embodied in campus traditions or long-standing relationships with nonacademic constituencies. Indeed, an irony of B.U. in the 1970s—and a measure of Silber's influence—was the fact that a campus with Methodist roots that historically had stood for liberal academic and social values became a national symbol of conservatism. In effect, Silber was able to reinvent his institution's culture by changing its student constituency, capturing its governing board, installing like-minded lieutenants in key positions, asserting personal control over faculty hiring, and surviving in office for a long period of time.

In the end, of course, it is no easier for the 1970s than for earlier periods to separate the relative contributions of interinstitutional competition, academic ideas, and intraorganizational dynamics to directions of change among universities in Massachusetts. The genius of Monan's policies and of those of

Weisner and Gray was that they so effectively combined the three dimensions of the institutional complex: steps that worked in the marketplace also were compatible with institutional traditions that helped mobilize internal support. In a different way, Silber succeeded because his new formula for B.U. effectively integrated a competitive plan, a set of academic values, and domination of internal decison-making mechanisms.

All three campuses thus illustrated the dynamic mechanism that ensured continued diversity among the nation's universities. All three also illustrated the indispensability of presidential leadership in helping institutional communities assemble coherent strategies of change from the chaos of pressures, ideas, and interests that threatened constantly to break them into fragments.

Epilogue

As this book was being written, the academic community was engaged in yet another debate about its performance. Between 1980 and 1984, nearly two dozen reports on the state of American higher education—the third such wave of commentary since World War II—were produced by national commissions, government agencies, and individual observers. These documents wrestled with some new issues—like the increasing importance of "nontraditional" students, and the growing reliance on financial support from industry—and contained some new themes, like the tendency to blame the professoriate for many of academia's ills. The reports also revealed some new divisions, especially a sharp split between liberals and conservatives on questions about undergraduate curricula.[85]

For anyone who had reviewed the debates of the late 1940s and late 1960s, however, the overall tenor of the new reports, as well as many of the specific concerns discussed, was familiar territory. Once again, academia was scolded for not living up to its potentialities, especially in the area of undergraduate education. Once again, the demise of general education was lamented. Once again, faculty were criticized for being preoccupied with their narrow scholarly specialities, while neglecting the well-being of students. And once again, neither the professoriate nor institutional leaders seemed to take much notice.

By the end of the decade, however, outsiders to higher education were beginning to pay attention. Driven by national worries about elementary and secondary schools, public officials and corporate executives focused on the shortcomings of higher education as well. As they did so, it became clear that they were familiar with the complaints of academia's recent detractors, not to mention earlier critics at the beginning and end of the golden age. For those, like the author, who care about educational institutions, there was reason to welcome lay recognition that schools and colleges play an essential national role. There was also ground for worry, however, that politicians and business leaders, impatient with the slow pace of academic change, would try to force solutions on a reluctant and resisting academy. Indeed, by the early 1990s, several state legislatures had passed laws attempting to control the outcomes of undergraduate studies in public colleges.[86]

It is easy for a student of higher education to sympathize with the frustrations of nonacademics faced with the Byzantine workings of the academic system. The campus histories contained in this book, together with the summary assessments of national patterns, contain ample ammunition for critics and reformers. When I began work on this project in the mid-1970s, I was inclined to agree with those who argue that new structures of centralized authority (for example, statewide governing boards with enhanced powers) are needed to compel academic institutions to fulfill their diverse social functions.

However, my immersion in this project together with my direct experience in academic administration have changed my perceptions. I have concluded, for example, that many of the criticisms of higher education that have been most widely repeated—in the 1940s, the 1960s, and the 1980s—are exaggerated and oversimplified. In particular, the sweeping commentaries of national reports tend to neglect the existence of multiple emphases within complex academic institutions, not to mention the bewildering variety of activities represented by the entire post-secondary system. They also tend, I believe, to undervalue the significance of social, intellectual, and professional dedication among individual faculty and administrators. It is clear to me, for example, that even as universities in Massachusetts pursued self-serving strategies of upward mobility during the golden age, they sponsored activities that reflected admirable concern for the students and communities they served as well as the subjects they professed.

Even more important, through the workings of the institutional complex, the dynamics of the academic marketplace produce much greater variation and responsiveness among universities than is evident from the generalized accounts offered in many commission reports. Indeed, however much I have been inclined to fault universities for their preoccupation with institutional status and professional interests, it has been impossible for me to deny the net social benefit that has flowed from the interplay of market forces during the period chronicled in this book. On balance, the contributions of universities in Massachusetts to both the elite and democratic functions of higher education were greatly enhanced during the golden age.

By looking at institutions over an extended period of time, I also have acquired a heightened appreciation of the capacity of the academic system to moderate the excesses of one period through subsequent shifts of emphasis. In the 1970s, most universities in Massachusetts took useful, if circumscribed, steps to strengthen undergraduate education and encourage effective teaching. The shift of emphasis back toward students appeared to be continuing in the early 1990s, especially at elite institutions under pressure from parents who were paying large percentages of their annual incomes for their children's education.

In the end, this study has led me, somewhat to my surprise, to believe that the existing academic system, for all its faults and self-serving proclivities, is more likely than any other to serve the shifting array of social demands that Americans place on their universities. But this volume is not intended as an apologia for the status quo.[87] There is much truth in the frequently leveled crit-

419

icisms of academia, and one of the frustrations one experiences in reading the reports of the 1980s derives from recognizing that important concerns, so often reiterated, have not been adequately addressed. As in any market-oriented system, the need for reform is always present, as is the need for non-market interventions to channel institutional energies in directions that would otherwise be neglected.

The message in this study is that the most effective measures to promote change will build on the dynamic forces that drive institutions. The beating heart of academia is to be found in individual campuses, their constituent schools and departments, and in the academic professions, which connect with institutions through their component parts. It is simply not possible, ultimately, to force a faculty member to be an enthusiastic teacher or a department to be inventive in strengthening its offerings. We need to design positive incentives that will enlist the creative energies latent within institutional and professional structures, not to criticize academics for lacking the virtue of priests or to bludgeon the system into submission. The account of the insitutional complex contained in this book is intended to offer a way of thinking about the forces that drive universities for those who want to help them provide their maximum benefit to contemporary society.

Abbreviations

The following terms are used throughout the notes and bibliography to indicate institutional documents.

Boston College

BC	Boston College
BCA	BC archive
BCAR	annual report of president for the year indicated; the year in parenthesis here and in other abbreviations is the second half of a typical academic year.
BCB	BC Bulletin
BCFS	annual financial statement for a given fiscal year

Boston University

BU	Boston University
BUA	BU archive
BUAR	annual report of president
BUC	BU Catalog
BUTR	annual report of treasurer

Brandeis

BrU	Brandeis University
BrUA	BrU archive
BrUC	BrU Catalogue
BrUFS	annual financial statement

Commonwealth of Massachusetts

CM	Commonwealth of Massachusetts
MGC	Massachusetts General Court
SHL	State House Library
MBHE	Massachusetts Board of Higher Education
MACE	Massachusetts Advisory Council on Education

Harvard

HU	Harvard University
HUAR	annual report of president
HUA	HU archive
HUFAS	HU Faculty of Arts and Sciences
HCR	annual report of administrative officer
HUC	HU Catalogue
HUTR	HU annual report of treasurer
RC	Radcliffe College
HUO	HU Board of Overseers

Massachusetts Institute of Technology

MIT	Massachusetts Institute of Technology
MITA	MIT archive
MITAR	annual report of president
MITB	MIT Bulletin
MITR	annual report of administrative officer
MITTR	annual report of treasurer

Northeastern

NU	Northeastern University
NUAR	annual report of president
NUA	NU archive
NUC	NU Catalog

Society of Jesus

SJ	Society of Jesus
JEA	Jesuit Educational Association
NEP	New England province of Jesuit order
CHA	Campion Hall, Weston, Jesuit archive

Tufts

TU	Tufts University
TUA	TU archive
TUAR	annual report of president
TUR	annual report of administrative officer
TUTR	annual report of treasurer

University of Massachusetts

MAC	Massachusetts Agricultural College
MSC	Massachusetts State College
UM	University of Massachusetts
UM/A	Amherst campus of UMass

UM/B	Boston campus of UMass
UM/W	Worcester campus of UMass
UMAR (or MACAR or MSCAR)	annual report of president
UMR (or MACR or MSCR)	annual report of administrative officer
UM/AAR (or UM/BAR)	annual report of UM/A (or UM/B) chancellor
UM/AR (or UM/BR)	annual report of UM/A (or UM/B) administrative officer
UM/AA	UM/A archive
UM/BA	UM/B archive
UM/BC	UM/B Catalog
UMSO	UMass system office

Notes

INTRODUCTION

1. Many observers have identified the years between 1945 and 1970 as constituting a distinctive period of growth and development in American higher education. As Clark Kerr wrote in 1963: "The American university is currently undergoing its second great transformation. The first occurred during roughly the last quarter of the nineteenth century . . . The current transformation will cover roughly the quarter century after World War II." See Clark Kerr, 1963, p. 86. For general reviews of the period see: David Henry, 1975; Nathan Pusey, 1978; Harold Hodgkinson, 1971; Alain Touraine, 1974; Robert Nisbet, 1971. The current volume, like Henry's and others, includes material on the decades immediately before and after the period of postwar growth in order to consider the impact of fundamentally changed circumstances on academic institutions.

2. The variety, of course, extends far beyond the institutions discussed in this volume and includes other universities like Clark in Worcester and Suffolk in Boston. This book does not set out, however, to provide a definitive history of higher education or even of universities in Massachusetts in the postwar years. Its purpose is to draw selectively on material about the state's academic community to advance our general understanding of the development of universities. The eight selected campuses seemed sufficient for this purpose.

3. For a discussion of the similarity of postwar change among geographic regions, see H. Hodgkinson, 1971, p. 79; see also 84.

4. For Kennedy reference, see D. Henry, 1975, pp. 127–28.

5. For characteristic statements, see the following volumes: Abraham Flexner, 1930; Robert M. Hutchins, 1936. Thorstein Veblen, 1918, reissued 1954.

6. Joseph Ben-David, 1972, pp. 5, 9, 25, 31–32, 35, 41. Burton Clark, 1983, pp. 137–39, 162; see also Chapt. 6. Martin Trow, 1974; Martin Trow, Autumn 1976; Martin Trow, 1987. Laurence Veysey, 1965, pp. 330, 333, 338–41. David Riesman, 1958. In *Maintaining Diversity in Higher Education,* 1983, Robert Birnbaum provides an excellent summary of recent literature on diversity and change in relation to system characteristics; see especially Chapt. 1.

7. Victor Baldridge, 1971; Victor Baldridge et al., 1978. Karl Weick, March 1976, pp. 1–19. For a review of this literature see Marvin Peterson and Lisa A. Mets, eds., 1987.

8. For importance of external forces, see C. Kerr, 1963; for an alternative perception, however, see B. Clark, 1983, who argues that developments since Kerr's book was published have underscored the significance of internal forces in producing change—

see pp. 184–86. For role of faculty power, see Christopher Jencks and David Riesman, 1968. For leadership, see Michael Cohen and James March, 1974. Birnbaum's 1983 study reviews recent literature on the extent to which academic change derives from the decisions of institutional leaders or the pressures of the external environment and argues that, over the long run, environmental pressures are the primary source of academic change; see especially pp. 22ff.; see also Ellen Chaffee, 1985.

CHAPTER I. ACADEMIC DEVELOPMENT AND SOCIAL CHANGE: HIGHER EDUCATION IN MASSACHUSETTS BEFORE 1945

1. James B. Conant, speech at Northeastern's 50th anniversary, Oct. 2, 1948. See also Everett C. Marston, 1961, p. 90.

2. On colonial colleges in general, see Richard Hofstadter, and C. DeWitt Hardy, 1952, Chapt. 1; see also Frederick Rudolph, 1962, Chapt. 1. For Harvard from 1636 to 1869, I have relied chiefly on Samuel E. Morison, 1942, Chapts. 1–13; see also George G. Bush, 1891, Chapts. 2–8; Seymour Harris, 1970; Ronald Story, 1980.

3. My account of the Eliot years depends chiefly on the following: S. Morison, 1942, Chapts. 14–15; Hugh Hawkins, 1972; Bruce Kuklick, 1977; Seymour M. Lipset and David Riesman, 1975, pt. I, Chapt. 4; R. Story, 1980; S. Harris, 1970; Richard N. Smith, 1986, Chapt. 1. For general accounts that cover the significance of Eliot's presidency, see Burton Bledstein, 1976; Roger Geiger, 1986; L. Veysey, 1965.

4. On financial problems, see S. Harris, 1970; Special Committee of the Board of Overseers on the Financial Requirements of the University and the Deficit Incurred During Recent Years, 1904. On enrollment problems, see HUAR (1908).

5. My account of the Lowell years relies chiefly on the following: S. Morison, 1942, Chapt. 14; S. Lipset and D. Riesman, 1975, pt. I, Chapt. 5; S. Harris, 1970; R. Smith, 1986, Chapt. 2. H. A. Yeomans, 1948; A. Lawrence Lowell, 1934; Arthur G. Powell, 1980; James B. Conant, 1970; E. J. Kahn, 1969; Special Committee, 1939. For general accounts that also cover Lowell, see R. Geiger, 1986; L. Veysey, 1965; Marcia G. Sinnott, 1979.

6. On criticisms of Lowell, see: S. Lipset and D. Riesman, 1975, pp. 153–54; De Voto quote is on 154.

7. For general accounts of the college movement, I have relied on the following: R. Hofstadter and C. Hardy, 1952; F. Rudolph, 1962; Donald G. Tewksbury, 1965; Colin G. Burke, 1982. For estimates of numbers of colleges founded and survival rates, I have relied on Burke, who challenges Tewksbury's account on this score. See also Walter P. Metzger, 1987, pp. 127–30. For the founding of Tufts, I have followed Russell E. Miller, 1966.

8. For the early history of Catholic and Jesuit higher education, I have relied on David R. Dunigan, 1947, Chapt. 1; see also F. Rudolph, 1962; C. Burke, 1982; William F. Kelley, 1966; Allan P. Farrell and Matthew J. Fitzsimons, 1958, pp. 70ff. For the founding of BC, I have followed Dunigan.

9. My account of Tufts from 1852 to 1905 relies on R. Miller, 1966; quote is on 59.

10. For Cousens era, see R. Miller, 1966. I also used Cousens's annual reports, speeches, memos, and correspondence, as well as the Tufts *Graduate,* all in TUA. Cousens's reorganization plan is discussed in Miller, 1966, pp. 521–23; quote is on 521; see also J. A. Cousens, June 1921, Cousens papers; see also Cousens's speeches of June 1924 (to faculty); Oct. 31, 1925; Jan. 20, 1926, Cousens papers; *Graduate* (June–Aug., 1924); (Dec. 1925–Feb. 1926). For broader discussion of movement to divide universities into lower and upper divisions see David Levine, 1986, pp. 99–100, 167–68.

11. For early history of BC I have followed D. Dunigan, 1947.

12. On Gasson, I used Dunigan, 1947; quote is on 185–87; also *Stylus,* vol. 20, no. 9 (June 1907): 23, 31–32; David Riesman and Christopher Jencks, in Nevitt Sanford, 1962, p. 149. I also profited greatly from my interviews with Father Michael P. Walsh, S.J., on the modern history of BC.

13. On traditions of Catholic and Jesuit higher education, I relied on D. Dunigan, 1947; Andrew M. Greeley, 1967; Walsh interviews.

14. On reform movement, see Paul A. Fitzgerald, 1984, Chapt. 1. On addition of graduate work at BC in 1920s, see D. Dunigan, 1947. On movement toward secularization and professionalization among Catholic universities in 1920s, see D. Levine, 1986, p. 77.

15. For the attack on antebellum colleges, see R. Hofstadter and C. Hardy, 1952; C. Burke, 1982, Chapt. 2, persuasively challenges the enrollment figures cited by Hofstadter and Hardy. For enrollment growth from 1870 to 1910, see Hofstadter and Hardy, 1952, p. 141; also Newton Edwards and Herman G. Richey, 1963, p. 503.

16. Best general account of age of the university is L. Veysey, 1965; see also R. Geiger, 1986; R. Hofstadter and C. Hardy, 1952; F. Rudolph, 1962. On founding of W.P.I. and Clark, see G. Bush, 1891, Chapts. 14 and 18; Albert B. Hart, 1927–30, vol. 5, pp. 257, 261.

17. For founding and early development of MIT through 1909, I have relied chiefly on Samuel C. Prescott, 1954. See also Committee on Educational Survey, 1949; P. J. Ladd, Sept. 1947. Former President Julius Stratton, also a historian of MIT, stated in an interview that Prescott exaggerates Rogers's role in the founding, that the driving force was a group of local industrialists who persuaded Rogers to take the lead. "Forward looking" quote from Ladd, Sept. 1947, p. 1. Rogers's quote that MIT had taken "first place" from Prescott, 1954, p. 74; for additional discussion of MIT's national standing, see Prescott, 1954, pp. 69, 74–75, 129, 146–50. For early financial history of MIT, see R. Geiger, 1986, p. 39ff.

18. On narrowing of focus in late nineteenth century, see Committee on Educational Survey, 1949, pp. 11–12; also S. Prescott, 1954; Stratton interview. On Maclaurin appointment and views, see Henry G. Pearson, 1937; also Prescott, 1954; also P. Ladd, Sept. 1947. On development of links to industrial elite see Pearson, 1937, Chapt. 6, pp. 151–57; Prescott, 1954, Chapt. 12. On Technology Plan, see Pearson, 1937, pp. 276–77; C. L. Norton, 1924; Committee on Educational Survey, 1949, p. 44; David F. Noble, 1977, pp. 140–42; letter from Alfred D. Chandler.

19. On MIT in twenties, see Committee on Educational Survey, 1949; C. Norton, 1924; D. Noble, 1979; R. Geiger, 1986, pp. 177–87; interviews with Samuel Stratton and Elting Morison. Material in MITA on Technology Plan in twenties in president's files 1897–1932 and 1930–1958 under Division of Industrial Cooperation. See also James R. Killian, 1985, pp. 254ff.

20. My account of MAC in nineteenth century generally relies on Harold W. Cary, 1962; also Frank P. Rand, 1933; D. Riesman and C. Jencks, 1962, p. 133.

21. On MAC from 1900–30, see H. Cary, 1962; F. Rand, 1933. For accounts that stress positive features of this period see Frederick S. Troy, 1982, p. 2; D. Riesman and C. Jencks, 1962, p. 133. On strong record of MAC in preparing students for graduate work in science, see MACAR (1951), 7–8; Mather, oral history interview, 9. On role of state government see A. Hart, 1927–30, vol. 5, p. 261. On student body in 1930, see D. Levine, 1986, p. 131. Quote on curriculum in 1931 is from Cary, 1962, p. 151.

22. My account of BU in nineteenth century relies on Warren O. Ault, 1973; also G. Bush, 1891, Chapt. 15. On the problem of feminization, see D. Levine, 1986, p. 124.

23. On BU in the twentieth century, see W. Ault, 1973. See also BUAR (1945), 6; (1950), 5, 24. On size of BU in twenties, see A. Hart, 1927–30, vol. 5, pp. 255, 257. Also NU, "An Opportunity for Investment" Jan. 1931, p. 6. On rise of "municipal" and "urban" universities early in twentieth century, see D. Levine, 1986, Chapt. 4. On changes in Methodist universities in the Progressive period, see Levine, 1986, pp. 76–77.

24. For general discussion of education for women, see F. Rudolph, 1962, Chapt. 15. On Massachusetts, see A. Hart, 1927–30, vol. 5, pp. 206ff., 257.

25. For HU, see H. Hawkins, 1972, pp. 195–96. For TU, see R. Miller, 1966, Chapt. 6. For MAC see W. Cary, 1962, pp. 114, 134ff. For MIT, see S. Prescott, 1954, pp. 53, 99; also Morison interview.

26. For general discussion of Progressivism in higher education, see F. Rudolph, 1962, Chapt. 17.

27. On extension at MIT, see S. Prescott, 1954, p. 52. On Lowell's consortium, see Edward Weeks, 1966, p. 125.

28. For Simmons and Suffolk, see A. Hart, 1927–30, vol. 5, pp. 109, 208. On NU, see E. Marston, 1961; also Antoinette Frederick, 1982.

29. On early history of NU, see E. Marston, 1961; also A. Frederick, 1982. On evolution of YMCA schools into colleges, see Tyrus Hillway, 1958, p. 51.

30. On NU in twenties, see E. Marston, 1961; Rudolph Morris, 1977.

31. For early finances at HU, see S. Morison, 1942, pp. 14–17, 153–60, 218–220; S. Harris, 1970, pp. 238ff.

32. For general discussions of competition in higher education in nineteenth century, see L. Veysey, 1965, pp. 324ff., 339–41; J. Ben-David, 1972, Chapt. 3.

33. For percentage going to college in 1922, see MGC, Commission for an Investigation, 1923, p. 293. On HU enrollments in 1929–30, see HCR, Committee on Admission (1930). For MIT, see MITR, Registrar (1930).

34. Capen quote from Miller, 1966, p. 142.

35. On Catholic preferences for Catholic schools, see Stephan Thernstrom, 1973, p. 174; also Herbert J. Gans, 1962, p. 131. On enrollment pressures as impetus to diversification, see C. Jencks and D. Riesman, 1962, p. 113; J.B.Lon Hefferlin, 1969, pp. 140, 245–46; J. Ben-David, 1972, p. 30. For Harvard vs. Tufts on medicine, see R. Miller, 1966, pp. 210–11.

36. On state aid to private schools in 19th century, see A. Hart, 1927–30, vol. 5, p. 239; John P. Whitaker, 1991, p. 42. On Harvard, see S. Morison, 1942, pp. 14–17, 153–60, 219–20. On Tufts, see R. Miller, 1966, pp. 96–98. For development of public higher education in 19th century, see F. Rudolph, 1962, pp. 275–80. For lack of political support in Massachusetts see D. Riesman and C. Jencks, 1962, pp. 133–37. For Catholics and public higher education, see John Whitaker, unpublished paper, University of Massachusetts, Dec. 1985. For Eliot, see Rudolph, 1962, p. 278; H. Hawkins, 1972, p. 153.

37. On Board of Education proposal, see MGC, Staff of Special Commission Established to Make an Investigation, 1962–65, Appendix 2. On 1922 commission, see ibid., Appendix 2; MGC, Commission for an Investigation . . . , 1923; A. Hart, 1927–30, vol. 5, p. 235. For income as a barrier to college attendance in Massachusetts in 1920s, see ibid., 246. For Cousens on community colleges, see letter to Tufts *Graduate* (Nov. 9, 1921); speech to Tufts Teachers' Association, Nov. 10, 1923, Cousens Papers. For BU/BC see D. Dunigan, 1947, pp. 244–47. For extension program, see A. Hart, 1927–30, vol. 5, p. 248.

38. On Tufts, see R. Miller, 1966, p. 380. On tendency of fund-raising pressures to

produce blandness, see L. Veysey, 1965, pp. 342ff.; J. Ben-David, 1972, p. 26.

39. For HU/Eliot, see S. Lipset and D. Riesman, 1975, pp. 96, 118. For a recent study asserting that financially independent institutions are the least likely to change over time, see J. Hefferlin, 1969, p. 149.

40. On HU-MIT merger, see S. Prescott, 1954, pp. 71–82, 249; H. Pearson, 1937, pp. 95–96, 101, 113, 186–88; P. Ladd, Sept. 1947, pp. 10–11; H. Yeomans, 1948, pp. 260ff.

41. For BU-MAC and MIT, see G. Bush, 1931, p. 357; W. Ault, 1973, p. 16. For BC-MIT and TU, see D. Dunigan, 1947, p. 160; Walsh interview. For HU-MIT, see S. Prescott, 1954, pp. 285–93; H. Pearson, 1937, pp. 125, 140, 210; P. Ladd, Sept. 1947, p. 13. For TU-BU, see R. Miller, 1966, pp. 577–79; BUAR (1920). On NU, see E. Marston, 1961, pp. 31–32, 60; NUAR (1959), 19.

42. For Eliot inaugural, see S. Morison, 1942, p. 330.

43. On Massachusetts as highly stratified, see S. Thernstrom, 1973, pp. 78–79, 112–13, 143, 171; see also (generally) E. Digby Baltzell, 1979; Peter Schrag, 1967, Chapt. 2. On social tension in relation to higher education, in Massachusetts and also nationally, see D. Riesman and C. Jencks, 1962.

44. On HU ties to elite and class conflict, see E. Baltzell, 1979, pp. 250, 274; Martin Green, 1967, pp. 29, 70; S. Lipset and D. Riesman, 1975, pp. 27–29, 41–44; Ronald Story, Spring 1975, pp. 94–121. Morison quote in S. Morison, 1942, p. 185. On Amherst/Williams, see Story, 1975; also R. Story, 1980, p. 139; D. Riesman and C. Jencks, 1962, pp. 89, 95. On TU, BU, MIT, and MAC, see Story, 1975; Story, 1980, p. 179; H. Cary, 1962, p. 38; S. Prescott, 1954, p. 336. On sectarian feeling and higher education, see A. Hart, 1927–30, vol. 5, Chapt. 15; Riesman and Jencks, 1962, p. 89.

45. On MIT students, see S. Prescott, 1954, p. 140. On MAC, see D. Riesman and C. Jencks, 1962, p. 137–38.

46. On HU students in twenties, see D. Levine, 1986, pp. 128, 146. For Lowell's views on admissions, see H. Yeomans, 1948, pp. 68, 168–70, 182, 200, 205–8, 336, 380; M. Sinnott, 1979, pp. 13–20, 92, 106–7; S. Lipset and D. Riesman, 1975, pt. I, 146–48; Penny Feldman, unpublished thesis, Harvard College, 1975. On enrollment limitation, see Sinnott, 1979, pp. 110–12. On tuition policy, see Yeomans, 1948, pp. 249–50; S. Harris, 1970, pp. 47–48, 55–61, 100. On narrowing of HU student body, see J. Conant, 1970, p. 135.

47. On TU students, see TUR, Dean of Admissions (1932); also, TUAR (1933). On Jews at TU, see TUAR (1933); (1934), 4, 17, 29–30; (1936), 21–22. On BU students, see W. Ault, 1973, p. 115; BUAR (1930), 17; Harold Case, 1957, p. 13; Nora Ephron, Sept. 1977, p. 137. On NU, see R. Morris, 1977, pp. 120–21.

48. On anti-Catholic feeling in Mass., see D. Dunigan, 1947, Chapt. 1, pp. 108, 153, 213. For a discussion of difference between popular legend and reality, see R. Higgins, 1988, p. 27. On BC and HC charters, see R. Miller, 1966, p. 39. For law school list, see H. Hawkins, 1972, pp. 187–89.

49. On anti-aid amendment, see A. Hart, 1927–30, vol. 5, pp. 239, 637; Augustus Loring, 1933, pp. 25–36; J. Whitaker, 1991, p. 39–54. On new campus, see Walsh interview. On social class of BC students, see D. Dunigan, 1947, p. 111; Powers interview; D. Riesman and C. Jencks, 1962, p. 149; William F. Whyte, 1943, pp. 56, 105–6.

50. For BC reactions to Eliot, see D. Dunigan, 1947, pp. 192ff.; Timothy Brosnahan, S.J., Jan. 13, 1900; also editorial in ibid. For Cousens, see speech to Boston Tufts Club, Jan. 20, 1926, Cousens Papers; also TUAR (1934), 6–7. On general pattern of academic prestige following social prestige, see J. Ben-David, 1972, pp. 39–41.

51. For a discussion of the frequently oppressive nature of the control exercised

over colleges by sponsoring groups, see R. Hofstadter and C. Hardy, 1952, pp. 123ff.; for an account that gives the early colleges more credit for creativity in responding to changing social conditions, see C. Burke, 1982, Chapts. 1 and 2. On BU trustees revoking faculty authority, see W. Ault, 1973, p. 75; BUAR (1916), 11. On alumni and coeducation at HU, see H. Hawkins, 1972, p. 195.

52. For Eliot, see B. Kuklick, 1977, pp. 233ff.

53. A Lowell example was the decision to build residential houses for upperclassmen; see S. Morison, 1942, pp. 476ff. On financial role of Tufts president, see R. Miller, 1966, pp. 467–68. For a general discussion of power in nineteenth-century colleges see F. Rudolph, 1962, Chapt. 8; for presidential power see ibid., pp. 164ff.

54. On role of trustees in traditional colleges, see F. Rudolph, 1962, Chapt. 8, esp. pp. 173ff.

55. On faculty in traditional colleges, see ibid., Chapt. 8, esp. pp. 157ff. See also D. Riesman and C. Jencks, 1962, pp. 5–6.

56. For HU, see R. Geiger, 1986, pp. 50–53. For BC see D. Dunigan, 1947, Chapts. 15 and 16.

57. On development of professionalism, see Walter Metzger, 1987, esp. pp. 134–36; R. Geiger, 1986, pp. 20ff.; see also, generally, B. Bledstein, 1976; Robert H. Weibe, 1967, esp. Chapt. 5; Harland G. Bloland and Sue M. Bloland, 1974.

58. H. Bloland and S. Bloland, 1974, p. 16; L. Veysey, 1965, pp. 264–68; F. Rudolph, 1962, Chapt. 20.

59. For HU and Eliot, see R. Geiger, 1986, pp. 35–36; see also B. Kuklick, 1977, esp. Pt. 5. For establishment of schools at MIT, see MITAR (1932), 12–13. For role of president at TU see below, Chapt. 4, "Organization, Leadership, and Institutional Change"; at MAC, see Chapt. 6, "Academic Organization and Political Systems"; at NU and BC see Chapt. 5, "Institutional Mobility and Organizational Form."

60. On professionalization and organizational power, see L. Veysey, 1965, pp. 355–56. On AAUP, see W. Metzger, 1987, pp. 167–70. For AAUP as labor union, see R. Miller, 1966, p. 490.

61. On forces producing accreditation, see William K. Selden, 1960, pp. 25–28, 30–34; R. Geiger, 1986, pp. 17–18; F. Rudolph, 1962, pp. 436ff. On professional accreditation generally, including medicine, see Selden, 1960, Chapt. 6. On TU-medicine, see R. Miller, 1966, pp. 251–82, 507–18; also TUAR (1934), 27; (1935); (1936), 78; (1938). For TU-engineering, see Miller, 1966, pp. 529–34, 661; TUAR (1936), 24–25; also TUR, Dean of Engineering (1936). For TU-dentistry, see Miller, 1966, 518–20. For TU-education, see TUAR (1932), 7; (1933), 8.

62. For NU-engineering, see A. Frederick, 1982, pp. 136–37; E. Marston, 1961, pp. 84–85; R. Morris, 1977, p. 130; Carl Ell, Jan. 23, 1937, p. 3; for Engineer's Council see George S. Emmerson, 1973; Engineer's Council for Professional Development, annual reports, 1933–39. For BC, see Walsh interview. For Cousens, see TUAR (1935), esp. 25.

63. On importance of HU being free of state control, see S. Morison, 1942, p. 326; S. Lipset and D. Riesman, 1975, pp. 96, 118. On NU, see Carl Ell, speech to Newcomen Society, May 24, 1956.

64. For Compton appointment, see D. Noble, 1977, p. 144; Vannevar Bush, 1970, p. 32; R. Geiger, 1986, pp. 181–83; J. Killian, 1985, Chapt. 9, and Appendix p. 421; Morison interview. For Conant appointment, see J. Conant, 1970, Chapt. 8; S. Lipset and D. Riesman, 1975, pp. 153–55; Geiger, 1986, p. 196. For America's potential role in science, see K. Compton, in Committee on Financing Development: "M.I.T.—A New Era," 1948.

65. D. Noble, 1977, p. 130.

66. For MIT as top engineering school, see MITAR (1931), 21–22; (1933), 15; (1935), 18–19; (1936), 22. For importance of science, see MITAR (1947), 16; P. Ladd, Sept. 1947, pp. 18ff.; Committee on Educational Survey, 1949, p. 37. For importance of research, see MITAR (1931), 21–22; (1934), 28–29; (1935), 16–25; quote from 1936, p. 23. For early initiatives, see *Technology Review* (July 1930) 451; MITAR (1931), 21ff. For "deadwood" see J. Killian, 1985, p. 160. For graduate education, see MITAR (1931), 1off., 21–22; (1932), 13; (1936), 22; quote from 1931, p. 13. On undergraduate education and admissions, see MITAR (1932), 15; (1933), 12; (1935), 15–16, 21; (1939), 15; "leaders" quote from 1937, pp. 10–11; see also Ladd, Sept. 1947, p. 19.

67. For analogy to HU/Chicago, see MITAR (1947), 12. For internal disagreements at MIT, see Committee on Educational Survey, 1949, pp. 131–32.

68. For "eminent scholars" quote, see J. Conant, 1970, p. 83. For "filling up ranks," see ibid., 82. For "young gentlemen," see ibid., 368. For Conant on student changes in 1920s, see ibid, Chapt. 12. For "intensification," see HUAR (1940), 22.

69. For the personnel crisis, see J. Conant, 1970, Chapts. 14 and 15; HUAR (1952), 9–12. For faculty review see Special Committee, 1939. See also S. Lipset and D. Riesman, 1975, pp. 167–68, 308–9; R. Geiger, 1986, pp. 226–27; R. Smith, 1986, pp. 132ff., 155ff.

70. For Conant on undergraduate admissions, see HUAR (1952), 9–10, 17, 19; for quote, see ibid, 18; see also S. Harris, 1970, p. 4. For National Scholarships, see J. Conant, 1970, Chapt. 10; see also R. Geiger, 1986, pp. 217–18; M. Sinnott, 1979, p. 203; S. Lipset and D. Riesman, 1975, pp. 308–9. For actual change in students, see HCR, Committee on Admission (1930); (1940); (1952). For Conant's efforts to nationalize HU, see R. Smith, 1986, pp. 173ff.

71. For impact of Depression on MIT, see MITAR (1932), 14, 16, 18; (1934), 25, 28–29; (1935), 12, 25; (1936), 17–18, 20; (1938), 27–29; (1939), 11–15, 31; (1941), 29; see also R. Geiger, 1986, pp. 228–33. For Compton's cutbacks in weak programs, see J. Killian, 1985, p. 160. For HU, see HUAR (1952), 5–12; J. Conant, 1970, pp. 118–19; S. Harris, 1970, p. 125.

72. On need for federal aid, see K. Compton, April 12, 1935, pp. 347–55; MITAR (1939), 31. For Science Advisory Board, see R. Geiger, 1986, pp. 255–64; Alice Rivlin, 1961, p. 30. On lack of public support for scholarship, see ibid., 24–28; D. Henry, 1975, pp. 123–24; Joseph Ben-David, 1977, Chapt. 5; John S. Brubacher and Willis Rudy, 1976, p. 196; US President, Commission on Higher Education, 1947, p. 92; Commission on Financing Higher Education, 1952, p. 180; Carl Kaysen, 1969, p. 17; F. Rudolph, 1962, pp. 462–63. For Compton on anti-intellectualism, see MITAR (1935), 16; for Conant, see J. Conant, 1970, p. 655.

73. For Harvard during war, see HUAR (1940–45); see also J. Conant, 1970, Chapt. 18; for quote, see ibid., 363. For MIT during war, see MITAR (1940); (1942), 5–6; (1943), 6. For "long pause," see Conant, 1970, p. 76.

74. For impact of war and Depression on Tufts, see R. Miller, 1966, pp. 620, 649, 695ff.; TUAR (1940), 14; (1941), 22; (1942); (1945), 8–12; (1952), 12; TUR, Dean's Report (1943), 25. On BU, see BUAR (1941), 4, 19ff.; (1942), 4, 11–12, 17ff.; (1943), 1off.; (1944), 3; see also W. Ault, 1973, pp. 93, 102, 108, 115, 118–19, 141. On BC, see D. Dunigan, 1947, pp. 263–64, 269, 301ff.; JEA, Report of Executive Director to Fathers Provincial (1941), 4; JEA, Board of Governors, May 13, 1941, pp. 4–5; Walsh interview. On NU, see A. Frederick, 1982, pp. 15–16; NUAR (1942), 10; (1943), 3, 8; (1944); (1946), 4. For new focus on national policies at TU, see Miller, 1966, pp. 634–38; 707; TUAR (1934), 37; (1941), 12–13; (1942), 1–2; (1952), 14. At BU, see Ault,

1973, Chapt. 6; BUAR (1940), 18; (1941), 14; (1942), 6. At BC, see Dunigan, 1947, Chapt. 24. At NU, see NUAR (1941), 10–11; (1942); (1943); (1944), 14ff.; (1945), 4–5. At national level, see D. Henry, 1975, pp. 40–41, 43–46; J. Conant, 1970, Chapts. 24 and 25; US Congress, House, 1945.

75. For TU, see R. Miller, 1966, pp. 625–33. For BU, see Faculty Manual, 1950, pt. VI and VI-B. For NU, see R. Morris, 1977, p. 152.

76. For Cousens's shift on enrollment policy, see R. Miller, 1966, pp. 497–98. For Fletcher, see ibid., Chapt. 14; quote on 592; see also TUAR (1936), 70.

77. For Carmichael appointment, see R. Miller, 1966, Chapt. 15. For Carmichael's views, see TUAR (1939); (1941), 21, 23, (1951), 7.

78. For space problems, see W. Ault, 1973, pp. 113ff. For organizational problems, see BUAR (1945), 5–6. For Marsh appointment, see Ault, 1973, pp. 102–3. For new campus, see BUAR (1950), 22ff.

79. For Marsh goals, see BUAR (1950), 5–6. For Marsh on BU as national leader, see BUAR (1937), 12–13; (1940), 7; (1941), 8. For efforts to build faculty in 1930s, see BUAR (1941), 10; (1942), 12. For campus in 1930s, see BUAR (1938), 10–13; (1939); (1940), 13; (1945), 19–20; (1950), 22, 24.

80. For general position of Catholic and Jesuit higher education in 1930s, see Peter G. Rossi, "Preface" to Andrew Greeley, 1967, p. v; also ibid., 29; see also Robert J. McNamara, in JEA, "The Society of Jesus and Higher Education," Oct. 1964, pp. 37ff. For developments of 1930s, see P. Fitzgerald, 1984, Chapts. 2, 3, and 4; father general quote on 37–38; see also D. Dunigan, 1947, Chapts. 21, 22, 23, and 24. Edward B. Bunn, in JEA, "The Society of Jesus and Higher Education," Oct. 1964, p. 29; Walsh interview; Fitzgerald interview.

81. For O'Connell review, see P. Fitzgerald, 1984, Chapts. 3 and 4. For Special Studies, see JEA Executive Committee, Minutes of Meetings, Dec. 12, 1937; April 22, 1938; and Oct. 5, 1942; see also Fitzgerald, 1984, pp. 96, 98–101; also JEA, Executive Director, May 13, 1941 and May 6, 1942. For change at BC in thirties, see D. Dunigan, 1947, Chapt. 22; BC, "Report to the Commission . . .," Feb. 1976, p. 21; BC, "Jesuits at Boston College," 1974; Walsh interview.

82. For reorganization on NU in thirties, see E. Marston, 1961, pp. 60–62; NUAR (1959), 19. For campus development in thirties, see NUAR (1942), 14–15; (1944), 23; (1950), 22; (1959), 15. For Ell appointment and views, see Marston, 1961, pp. 43ff.; A. Frederick, 1982, pp. 11ff.; R. Morris, 1977, p. 25. For view that expansion was over, see Morris, 1977, p. 133; also Advisory Committee on Education, 1938, pp. 8–11; John Millett, 1952, p. 270; BUAR (1938), 9. On liberal arts at NU, see Frederick, 1982, pp. 166–70; Morris, 1977, pp. 115, 118.

83. For Wriston quote, see "Blazing a New Trail in Higher Education," 1935. For NU brochure, see "An Opportunity to Invest," 1931, pp. 1–3.

84. For admissions growth in thirties, see MSCAR (1940), 6–7; see also (1938), 4; (1939), 7; (1941), 11–12; (1942), 7; (1951), 8; W. Cary, 1962, pp. 154, 165–66. For university movement, see Cary, 1962, pp. 161, 163–64; MSCAR (1940), 10. For New Deal and public higher education, see D. Levine, 1986, Chapt. 8; J. Millett, 1952, Chapt. 19; R. Geiger, 1986, pp. 247–48; *Shepard's Acts*, 1986. For New Deal and MSC, see Cary, 1962, pp. 160ff.

85. For WWII and MSC, see MSCAR (1941), 3ff.; (1942), 2; (1944), 1–2, 6–7, 24, 28–29; W. Cary, 1962, pp. 165–67. For university movement in thirties, see Cary, 1962, pp. 154ff.; also Frederick Troy, letter to author. On agriculture, see MSCAR (1943), 8; (1944), 24–25; (1945), 5, 7, 17–18; (1951), 9; also Mather oral history interview, 7. On private sector, see MSCAR (1939), 8; (1941), 3; see also BUAR (1938), 9. For Baker,

see MSCAR (1937); (1938); (1940); (1941); see also F. Rand, 1933, pp. 188–89; Cary, 1962, pp. 159–60, 181; Troy interview. For conservatism of faculty/staff, see MSCAR (1946), 25.

86. On lack of legislative interest, see MGC, Staff of the Special Commission Established to Make an Investigation, 1962–65; Duane Lockhard, 1959, p. 163. On budgets, see MSCAR (1939); (1941), 2–3. On building authority, see W. Cary, 1962, p. 161; UMAR (1948), 3–5. On administrative controls, see Mather oral history interview, 8–9.

87. On early history of Jews and higher education, see Abram L. Sachar, 1)76, Chapt. 1; see also Dean Richlin, unpublished thesis, Wesleyan University, 1974, pp. 99ff. For Hebrew Teacher's College, see L. Medalia, 1957, p. 2; "The Family Remembers" in *Hebrew College Bulletin,* 1975, p. 18.

88. For a general account, see A. Sachar, 1976, pp. 8–11. For Newman, see Alfred Werner, 1948, pp. 10–18; Israel Goldstein, 1951, pp. 3–4, 7–9; Goldstein interview with Richlin; D. Richlin thesis, 1974, pp. 99ff.; "A New University Under Jewish Auspices? Present Status of the Idea," *Jewish Post* (June 22 and 29, 1945), reprinted in Louis Newman, 1946. On B'nai B'rith, see Sachar, 1976, p. 11; Sachar interview; Richlin thesis, 1974, p. 32.

CHAPTER 2. THE WORLD TRANSFORMED: A GOLDEN AGE FOR AMERICAN UNIVERSITIES, 1945-1970

1. On new social orientation of academics, see D. Henry, 1975, Chapt. 3 and pp. 69, 86; Oscar Handlin and Mary F. Handlin. 1970, pp. 74–75; J. Brubacher and W. Rudy, 1976, p. 295; A. Powell, 1980, pp. 231–32. For Massachusetts examples, see NUAR (1943), 17; (1944), 6; (1949), 3–6; BUAR (1941), 22; Boston College Building Fund Committee, 1946, p. 20. Quote from BUAR (1951), 15.

2. For perception of changed public attitudes, see O. and M. Handlin, 1970, pp. 74–75. For Baker quote, see MSCAR (1942), 4–5. For Carmichael, see TUAR (1942); R. Miller, 1966, p. 707. See also MITAR (1941), 6–7; (1944), 30. For view that federal research support would probably decline after the war to prewar levels, see MIT, Committee on Educational Survey, 1949, p. 55. Not all institutional leaders thought public subsidies were a good idea; see, for example, Ell's perspective in NUAR (1947), 8–9.

3. On NDRC and OSRD, see J. Conant, 1970, Chapt. 19; V. Bush, 1970, pp. 31ff.; N. Pusey, 1978, pp. 61ff.; R. Geiger, 1986, pp. 264–65; MITAR (1940), 13.

4. For Bush report, see Vannevar Bush, 1945; V. Bush, 1970, p. 64; see also A. Rivlin, 1961, p. 37; N. Pusey, 1978, pp. 67–70. For Scientific Research Board, see President's Scientific Research Board, 1947, recommendations are on 6–7. For Compton, see MITAR (1941), 16. For MIT/HU in OSRD, see V. Bush, 1970, pp. 32, 48–53; J. Conant, 1970, p. 242; John E. Burchard, 1948, p. ix; MITAR (1940), 13.

5. For general discussion of GI Bill, see Keith W. Olson, 1974; Davis R. B. Ross, 1969; D. Henry, 1975, Chapt. 4. For Congressional Hearings, see US Congress, House, 1943; US Congress, Senate, Committee on Education and Labor, 1943. For wartime estimates of participation, see Henry, 1975, pp. 59–60.

6. For MIT, see J. Burchard, 1948, p. 315. For overall participation, see D. Henry, 1975, pp. 62–63. For HU, see R. Smith, 1986, p. 60. For Conant, see HUAR (1946), 5. For national patterns in accommodating vets, see Henry, 1975, pp. 61–68. For Massachusetts examples, see HUAR (1952), 14–15; NUAR (1944), 12; (1946), 8–10; Bur-

chard, 1948, p. 316; MITAR (1946); K. Olson, 1974, p. 36: TUAR (1944), 4; (1946), 1–2; BUAR (1946), 7–8.

7. For background of commission, see Diane Ravitch, 1983, p. 15. For report, see US President, Commission on Higher Education, 1947–48, 6 vols.; report is excerpted in Gail Kennedy (ed.), 1952. For biographical information on commission members, see *Who's Who*, 1946–47. For pre-WWII sentiment on expanding educational opportunity, see J. Brubacher and W. Rudy, 1976, pp. 234, 241–50, 258. For influence of progressive education, see F. Rudolph, 1962, Chapt. 22; Ravitch, 1983, Chapt. 2.

8. For campus-level planning activities in Massachusetts, see as follows: for HU, see references to Committee on General Education in a Free Society (below, n. 15); for BU, see discussion of Committee on the University in the Postwar World, BUAR (1942), 30; for MIT, see Committee on Educational Survey, 1949; for NU, see discussion of General Committee on Postwar Planning, NUAR (1943); for MSC, see discussion of Faculty Defense Council and Subcommittee on Postwar Planning, MSCAR (1941), 3, 15; for Jesuits, see discussion of Committee on Postwar Jesuit Education in JEA, Executive Committee, Minutes, Nov. 5, 1943; April 8, 1944; Oct. 7, 1944; and Oct. 17, 1944; also JEA, Executive Director, 1943 and 1944. For national patterns, see D. Henry, 1975, pp. 46–54; 70–71. For Carnegie quote, see Henry, pp. 1975, p. 70.

9. For Rockefeller, see Commission on Financing Higher Education, 1952. For comparison of Zook and Rockefeller, see D. Henry, 1975, pp. 80ff. For background on Rockefeller, see Exploratory Committee on Financing Higher Education and Research, Rockefeller Foundation, Aug. 17, 1948.

10. For discussion of enrollments, see US President, Commission on Higher Education, vol. 1, 1947, Chapt. 2. Quote is from ibid., 41; also G. Kennedy, 1952, p. 13, and O. and M. Handlin, 1970, p. 76.

11. Commission on Financing Higher Education, 1952, pp. 12–15, 45–54, 158.

12. For Conant on admissions, see James B. Conant, 1948, pp. 195–98; also "Education for A Classless Society: The Jeffersonian Tradition," May 1940, reprinted in G. Kennedy, 1952. For Conant on curriculum, see Conant, 1948, pp. 153–63, 195–203. For Marsh on Zook, admissions, see BUAR (1948), 6–12; (1950), 15. On BU curriculum, see Committee on the University in the Postwar World, reprinted in BUAR (1944), 13ff. For Ell on Zook, admissions, see NUAR (1949), 7–8; (1950), 6. For Ell on curriculum, see NUAR (1946); quote is on 7; also (1948), 6.

13. For general education in twenties and thirties, see Frederick Rudolph, 1977, pp. 252ff.; F. Rudolph, 1962, pp. 455ff.; C. Jencks and D. Riesman, 1968, pp. 493–504; Daniel Bell, 1968; J. Brubacher and W. Rudy, 1976, pp. 259–60, 265, 271–78. For Massachusetts examples of these movements, see following references: for Tufts, TUR, Dean of Liberal Arts (1939); TUAR (1941), 1–8; R. Miller, 1966, pp. 618–21. For MSC, MSCAR (1938), 14–15; (1939), 6.

14. For general education after WWII, see F. Rudolph, 1977, pp. 256ff.; C. Jencks and D. Riesman, 1968, p. 494. For Zook, see US President, Commission on Higher Education, vol. 1, 1947, pp. 23–31. For Rockefeller, see Commission on Financing Higher Education, 1952, pp. 15–19.

15. For discussion of Redbook, see F. Rudolph, 1977, p. 257–59; Phyllis Keller, 1982, Chapt. 1; N. Pusey, 1978, pp. 16off.; S. Lipset and D. Riesman, 1975, pp. 347, 376, 385–86; R. Smith, 1986, pp. 16off. For Conant on Redbook, see J. Conant, 1970, Chapt. 27; HUAR (1942), 12ff.; (1944), 11–12; (1945), 10–14; (1952), 25; see also A. Powell, 1980, p. 207; quote is from Harvard Committee, 1945, pp. vi, x.

16. For impact of Redbook, see F. Rudolph, 1977, p. 257. For Harvard, see S. Lipset and D. Riesman, 1975, pp. 347–48. For Tufts, see TUAR (1952), 16. For other Mas-

sachusetts examples, see following references: for BU, BUAR (1946), 12; (1950), 10; W. Ault, 1973, pp. 143ff., 172. For MIT, Committee on Educational Survey, 1949, pp. 81ff. For NU, NUAR (1946), 6.

17. For international emphasis, see US President, Commission on Higher Education, vol. 1, 1947, pp. 14–20; N. Pusey, 1978, pp. 38ff.; HUAR (1946), 20–21; BUAR (1943), 8–10; (1944), 9ff.; (1947), 22. For religion, see D. Henry, 1975, p. 102; Harvard Committee, 1945, pp. 76ff.; BUAR (1951), 15ff.; MITAR (1953), 29; (1954), 29ff.; Wilfred M. Mallon, "Proceedings on the Institute . . . ," Aug. 3–13, 1948, pp. 4ff. On student life, see BUAR (1950), 15ff.; MSCAR (1945), 10–11; UMAR (1951), 4–6. For MIT, see MITAR (1947), 17ff.

18. Commission on Financing Higher Education, 1952, Chapt. 4; Exploratory Committee on Financing Higher Education and Research, 1948, pp. 53–54.

19. For Rockefeller on research, see Commission on Financing Higher Education, 1952, pp. 21–24, 176; quote is on 163; for Zook on research, see US President, Commission on Higher Education, vol. 1, 1947, pp. 92ff. For Office of Naval Research, see J. Killian, 1985, p. 61.

20. For MIT, see MITAR (1944), 25ff.; Committee on Educational Survey, 1949, Chapt. 4 and p. 60; John E. Burchard (ed.), 1950. For HU, see HUAR (1946), 244–45; (1952), 15–16; J. Conant, 1970, pp. 244–45; J. Conant, 1948, p. 171; McGeorge Bundy, Summer 1970, p. 536.

21. For pre-WWII status of graduate education, see Everett Walters in Lewis Mayhew, 1967, pp. 131ff.; Bernard Berelson, 1960. For Conant, see HUAR (1946), 9–10; also J. Conant, 1948, pp. 197–98. For MIT, see Committee on Educational Survey, 1949, Chapt. 2. For Zook, see US President, Commission on Higher Education, vol. 1, 1947, pp. 75–90; G. Kennedy, 1952, p. 21. For Rockefeller, see Commission on Financing Higher Education, 1952, Chapt. 1. See also N. Pusey, 1978, p. 62–65; Dael Wolfle, 1954.

22. For Zook, see US President, Commission on Higher Education, vol. 1, 1947, Chapt. 4. For a characteristic Compton statement on relation of undergraduate and graduate education, see MITAR (1931).

23. For Science Board, see President's Scientific Research Board, vol. 1, 1947, Appendix 1. For Zook charge, see US President, Commission on Higher Education, vol. 1, 1947, "letter of appointment." For Zook quote, see ibid., pp. 5–6, 91.

24. For controversy stirred by Zook, see G. Kennedy, 1952, esp. essays by Farrell and Hutchins; see also D. Henry, 1975, pp. 73ff. For Rockefeller, see Commission on Financing Higher Education, 1952, pp. 26–27 ("trained experts"), 25–26 ("still be done"), 27–30.

25. For Zook on diversity, see, for example, US President, Commission on Higher Education, vol. 1, 1947, pp. 44–46 and vol. 3, 1947, pp. 1–2; see also D. Henry, 1975, p. 74. For Rockefeller on diversity, see Commission on Financing Higher Education, 1952, pp. 31–32, 157–64.

26. For impact of Zook, see D. Ravitch, 1983, p. 18.

27. For Conant, see HUAR (1946). For Baker, see MSCAR (1944), 26; (1946), 12. For Ell, see NUAR (1950), 18. For USOE projections, see NUAR (1947), 6; MITAR (1947), 8. For other perspectives on enrollments, see US President, Commission on Higher Education, vol. 1, 1947, pp. 1–2; O. and M. Handlin, 1970, p. 74; Commission on Financing Higher Education, 1952, pp. 77ff.

28. For debates on draft, see D. Henry, 1975, pp. 85–88; J. Conant, 1970, Chapts. 26 and 38; Commission on Financing Higher Education, 1952, pp. 81ff.; TUAR (1951), 5; UMAR (1950), 2, 14–15. For Conant, see HUAR (1952), 20.

29. US Office of Education, 1956. See also J. Millett, 1952, pp. 68–70, 271.

30. For Van Meter, see UMAR (1951), 3, 15; (1952), 2–3. For national figures, see US Office of Education, 1956, p. 2; US Bureau of the Census, 1975, Series H700–715, p. 383; US Bureau of Census, 1985, Table A-6, p. 52. For consensus on new conditions see D. Henry, 1975, pp. 99–100; N. Pusey, 1978, pp. 56–62.

31. For increased attendance rates, see O. and M. Handlin, 1970, pp. 72–73; Commission on Financing Higher Education, 1952, p. 133; J. Brubacher and W. Rudy, 1976, pp. 257–58; D. Henry, 1975, pp. 99–103.

32. For statistics on growth, see US Bureau of Census, 1975, Table H700–715, p. 383; US Bureau of Census, 1985, Table A-6, p. 52; John A. Dunn, "Some Trends in Higher Education in the 1960's and 1970's" in "Tufts: The Total University," 1973, Appendix C, 11–16.

33. Gardner cited in D. Henry, 1975, p. 112.

34. For financial problems of higher education, see J. Millett, 1952, pp. 132, 136; US President, Commission on Higher Education, vol. 5, 1948, pp. 13, 26; Commission on Financing Higher Education, 1952, esp. Chapt. 3. For Rockefeller quote, see Commission on Financing Higher Education, 1952, p. 114.

35. For general discussion of endowments and annual giving, see J. Millett, 1952, Chapts. 16 and 18; Commission on Financing Higher Education, 1952, pp. 139–42, 165–84; US President, Commission on Higher Education, vol. 5, 1948, pp. 30–31, 48. For Rockefeller quote, see Exploratory Committee on Financing Higher Education and Research, Aug. 1, 1948, pp. 7, 20. For HU, see HUAR (1945), 14–16; (1947), 9; (1952), 7, 15; HUTR (1930); (1948). For TU, see TUAR (1952); TUTR (1930); (1948). For MIT, see MITAR (1947), 19–20; see also (1948), 7–12.

36. On trends in student payments, see J. Millett, 1952, Chapt. 15; see also N. Pusey, 1978, p. 102. BU and BC exemplified the national trend among Massachusetts institutions.

37. On publics vs. privates, see Commission on Financing Higher Education, 1952, pp. 64, 86; J. Millett, 1952, pp. 256–57; R. Geiger, 1986, p. 61. On growth of public funding after war, see N. Pusey, 1978, pp. 105ff.; Malcolm Moos and Francis Rourke, 1959, p. 11, Fig. #1; R. Geiger, Dec. 1986, draft Chapt. 2, pp. 62–63. For MSC in 1940s, see MSCAR (1952), 2. For MIT, see MITAR (1947), 7–14; (1948); quote from 1948, p. 11; see also Committee on Educational Survey, 1949, pp. 16, 18.

38. Excellent general treatments of postwar trends in federal funding for academic research can be found in the following: A. Rivlin, 1961; Chester E. Finn, 1978; Bruce L. R. Smith and Joseph J. Karlesky, 1977. See also D. Henry, 1975, pp. 123ff.; Commission on Financing Higher Education, 1952, Chapts. 4 and 5; N. Pusey, 1978, pp. 72ff.; A. Touraine, 1974, pp. 133–35; J. Ben-David, 1977, p. 117; MITAR (1952), 29; (1956), 5.

39. On nonresearch support, see A. Rivlin, 1961, Chapt. 4; C. Finn, 1978; for table summarizing allocation of federal funds among categories of aid in 1968 and 1977, see Finn, 1978, p. 12; see also D. Henry, 1975, pp. 12ff.; J. Brubacher and W. Rudy, 1976, p. 249; MITAR (1956), 2–4; N. Pusey, 1978, p. 107.

40. For general patterns, see C. Finn, 1978, esp. Chapt. 1; Frank Newman et al., 1973, Chapt. 5. For aggregate federal support as percent of current funds, see Finn, 1978, p. 14.

41. Statistics on state spending, voluntary giving and student payments from: US Bureau of the Census, 1975, Series H 716–727; US Dept. of Education, Office of Educational Research and Improvement, 1988, Tables 226 and 227.

42. For aggregate expenditures, see US Bureau of the Census, 1975, Series H 728–738. For expenditures in relation to GNP, see C. Jencks and D. Riesman, 1968, p. 111n.

43. For PhD shortage, see Allan M. Cartter, 1976, Chapt. 2; quote is on 13. See also D. Henry, 1975, pp. 105ff.; C. Jencks and D. Riesman, 1968, p. 13; W. Metzger, 1987, pp. 150ff. For Pusey, see below, Chapt. 3, n. 40.

44. For faculty in 1952, see D. Henry, 1975, p. 105. For 1970, see H. and S. Bloland, 1974, p. 11. For myth of PhD shortage, see A. Cartter, 1976, Chapt. 2; see also C. Jencks and D. Riesman, 1968, pp. 113–14; for studies that repeat myth of shortage, see L. Mayhew, 1967, p. 5; J. Brubacher and W. Rudy, 1976, p. 214. For annual production of PhDs, see Cartter, 1976, pp. 83, 129. See also Seymour Harris, 1972, pp. 317, 379; National Science Board; 1969.

45. For impact of external funding, see R. Nisbett, 1971, Chapts. 5 and 6; A. Touraine, 1974, pp. 137–39; C. Kaysen, 1969, p. 26.

46. For professional associations, see H. and S. Bloland, 1974, Chapt. 2. For rise of professionalism generally, see C. Jencks and D. Riesman, 1968; O. and M. Handlin, 1970, pp. 74–75; A. Touraine, 1974, Chapt. 4; Logan Wilson, 1979.

47. For AAUP, see Louis Joughlin (ed.), 1967.

48. For BU, see BUAR (1947), 13ff.; also Faculty Manual for following years: 1950, 1957, 1962, 1967, 1970. For NU, see Faculty Handbooks for following years: 1957, 1961, 1962, 1966, 1967, 1971.

49. For MIT, see below, Chapt. 3, "Organizational Dimensions of Academic Change." For a general discussion of faculty vs. administration on control of academic appointments, see Peter Blau, 1973, Chapt. 7.

50. For BU, see Faculty Manual for 1950, VI-1. For UMass see below, Chapt. 6, n. 51. For NU, see below, Chapt. 5, n. 55. For general role of senates, see J. Brubacher and W. Rudy, 1976, pp. 375ff. For AAUP, see L. Wilson, 1979, p. 104; L. Joughlin, 1967, pp. 90ff.

51. Earl F. Cheit, 1971. For national projections, see forward to Cheit by Clark Kerr, ix–x. For general review of financial crisis, see C. Finn, 1978, pp. 23ff.

52. For reviews of student protests by major commissions, see President's Commission on Campus Unrest, 1970; Special Committee on Campus Tensions, 1970. For additional studies, see D. Ravitch, 1983, Chapt. 6; David Riesman and Verne Stadtman (eds.), 1973; *Daedalus*, vol. 99, no. 1, "The Embattled University" (Winter 1970); vol. 99, no. 3; "Rights and Responsibilities, The University's Dilemma" (Summer 1970); vol. 103, no. 4, "American Higher Education, Toward an Uncertain Future/I" (Fall 1974); vol. 104, no. 1, "American Higher Education, Toward an Uncertain Future/II" (Winter 1975); Immanuel Wallerstein and Paul Starr, 1971; Peter Blau and Ellen Slaughter, Spring 1971; *Public Interest*, no. 13, (Fall 1968); J. Ben-David, 1977, Chapt. 6; R. Nisbet, 1971, Chapt. 11; J. W. Scott and Mohammed El-Assai, Oct. 1969, pp. 702–9. For accounts of protests at Massachusetts universities, see below as follows: BrU (Chapt. 4, "Dilemmas of the College-Centered University"); NU (Chapt. 5, "The Good Times End"); MIT (Chapt. 3, "The Old Order Changes"); BC (Chapt. 5, "The Good Times End"); and HU (Chapt. 3, "The Old Order Changes").

53. For political impact of protests, see Special Committee on Campus Tensions, 1970, p. 32; Assembly on University Goals and Governance, 1971, p. 32. On change in federal funding after 1968, see B. Smith and J. Karlesky, 1977, Chapt. 2.

54. For new national projections, see Carnegie Commission on Higher Education, *New Students*, 1971, pp. 60–61; Carnegie Commission on Higher Education, *Priorities for Action*, 1973, pp. 4–5 and Technical Note A. For new Massachusetts projections, see

Organization for Social and Technical Innovation, *A Master Planning Process*, Oct. 1973, p. 42. See also Ivar Berg, 1971.

55. Jacques Barzun, 1968; R. Nisbet, 1971; Paul Dressel, 1971; Adam Ulam, 1972. For "triumphalism,"see Malcolm G. Scully, "American Universities' 'Triumphal' View Disputed," *Chronicle of Higher Education*, Nov. 24, 1975, p. 7.

56. For evolution of Carnegie, see Carnegie Commission on Higher Education, *Priorities for Action*, 1973, p. 75. For a discussion of Carnegie, see Robert C. Wood, Winter 1975. For AAU, see Association of American Universities, Apr. 1968. For ACE, see American Council on Education, 1969. For National Science Board, see *Graduate Education*, 1969, and *Toward a Public Policy*, 1969. For Linowitz, see Special Committee on Campus Tensions, 1970. For President's task force, see President's Commission on Campus Unrest, 1970. For Hester, see President's Task Force on Higher Education, 1970. For Newman, see US Department of Health, Education and Welfare, 1971. For Assembly, see Assembly on University Goals and Governance, 1971.

57. On the fundamental shift of thinking on admissions after World War II, see Carnegie Commission on Higher Education, *Less Time*, 1971, p. 5. For a more scholarly discussion of changed admissions practices, see M. Sinnott, 1979, p. xix. On triumph of Zook's recommendations, see Carnegie Commission, *Less Time*, 1971, p. 81. On impact of expanded admissions on mental ability see Paul Taubman and Terence Wales, 1972.

58. On need to increase access, see Carnegie Commission on Higher Education, *A Chance*, 1970; see also US Department of Health, Education and Welfare, 1971, p. 8; F. Newman et al., 1973, p. 43; Assembly on University Goals and Governance, 1971; Carnegie Commission on Higher Education, *A Learning Society*, 1973. On special needs of minorities, see Carnegie Commission on Higher Education, *A Chance*, 1970, p. 18; Assembly on University Goals and Governance, 1971, p. 11; US Department of Health, Education and Welfare, 1971, pp. 44ff., quote is on 79.

59. On increased class stratification, see C. Jencks and D. Riesman, 1968, pp. 132, 135. On correlation of test scores and income, see ibid., 103, 117–19, 122; A. Morrison and D. McIntyre, 1971, p. 50; Daniel P. Moynihan and Frederick Mosteller, 1972, pp. 23, 24.

60. For TU, see below, Chapt. 4, "The 1960s at Tufts." For BC, see Chapt. 5, "'Bonanza Years' at Boston College." For BU, see Chapt. 5, "The 1960s at Boston University." For NU, see Chapt. 5, "'The Blooming' at Northeastern." For UM, see Chapt. 6, "UMass in the 1960s."

61. For HU, see below, Chapt. 3, "Undergradaute Education in the Research University."

62. For increased focus on research and impact of federal funding, see Harold Orlans, 1968, esp. pp. 53ff. For increased use of graduate students as teachers, see John L. Chase, 1970. On economic revival in Massachusetts, see Martin Meyerson and Edward C. Banfield, 1966, p. 54; Walter Whitehill, 1966, p. 37; J. Ben-David, 1977, p. 154. On MIT role in economic development, see Christopher Rand, 1964, pp. 3–26, 32–33, 65; J. Killian, 1985, p. 378; Second Century Program, "In Common Cause," 1961, pp. 1–4. For quote, see Association of American Universities, Apr. 1968, pp. 8–9. For a contrary view on economic impact of university-based research, see C. Kaysen, 1969, p. 55.

63. For impact of federal funding, see Eric Ashby, 1971, pp. 82–84; L. Mayhew, 1967, p. 6; J. Brubacher and W. Rudy, 1976, p. 305; N. Pusey, 1978, pp. 83–84; quote is on 76. For HU and MIT, see below, Chapt. 3, "Consolidating the New Focus."

64. For ACE Commission, see Special Committee on Campus Tensions, 1970, pp. 40, 41. For Assembly, see Assembly on University Goals and Governance, 1971, pp. 8, 9, 16, Thesis 23.

65. For general discussion of graduate expansion, see L. Mayhew, 1967, p. 127ff. For Wilson, see L. Wilson, 1979, Chapt. 1. For need to stress teaching in graduate education, see E. Ashby, 1971, pp. 43ff.; President's Task Force on Higher Education, 1970, p. 16; C. Jencks and D. Riesman, 1968, pp. 239ff., 503; J. Brubacher and W. Rudy, 1976, pp. 214–15; Assembly on University Goals and Governance, 1971, p. 20, quote is on 9. For DA, see Carnegie Commission on Higher Education, *A Digest*, 1974, p. 7.

66. For Assembly, see Assembly on University Goals and Governance, 1971, Thesis 23. For additional discussion of teaching/research issue, see HUAR (1952), 26; R. Nisbett, 1971, Chapt. 6; David S. Webster, 1985, pp. 60–62. For a quantitative analysis, see P. Blau, 1973, p. 32.

67. For TU, see below, Chapt. 4, "Dilemmas of the College-Centered University." For UM/B, see Chapt. 6, "UMass in the 1960s." For BrU, see Chapt. 4, "Dilemmas of the College-centered University"; for quote, see ibid., n. 63.

68. For evolution of Carnegie perspective, see Carnegie Commission on Higher Education, *A Digest*, 1974, pp. 12, 78, 117, 160. See also President's Task Force on Higher Education, 1970, p. 13.

69. Quote is from US Department of Health, Education and Welfare, 1971, pp. 1, 3.

70. On problem of "involuntary students," see ibid., 4–7; Martin Trow, Winter 1970; Assembly on University Goals and Governance, 1971, pp. 7, 13. On need to sever link of education and jobs, see Carnegie Commission on Higher Education, *A Digest*, 1974, p. 45; US Department of Health, Education and Welfare, 1971, pp. 38ff.; Assembly on University Goals and Governance, 1971, pp. 7, 13, quote is on 8.

71. On convergence on single model, see President's Task Force on Higher Education, 1970, p. 10; US Department of Health, Education and Welfare, 1971, pp. 13, 63. On need for more program diversity, see Carnegie Commission on Higher Education, *Less Time*, 1971; Carnegie Commission on Higher Education, *Reform*, 1972, p. 125; Carnegie Commission on Higher Education, *The Campus*, 1972, "Access is Not Enough"; President's Task Force on Higher Education, 1970; Assembly on University Goals and Governance, 1971, pp. 8, 12; US Department of Health, Education and Welfare, 1971, p. 64; F. Newman et al., 1973, pp. 2–3.

72. For NU, see below, Chapt. 5, "'The Blooming' at Northeastern." For BrU, see Chapt. 4, "Founding of Brandeis" and "Institutional Mobility in the Early Golden Age." For UM/B, see Chapt. 6, "UMass in the 1960s."

73. Quote from Carnegie Commission on Higher Education, *A Digest*, 1974, p. 130. For other references to failure of general education, see Assembly on University Goals and Governance, 1971, p. 18; E. Ashby, 1971, pp. 39–40. For a contrary assessment, see J. Ben-David, 1977, p. 79.

74. On HU, see Phyllis Keller, 1982, p. 55. Office of the Dean, Oct. 1974, pp. 8–9. For MIT, see below, Chapt. 3. "Undergraduate Education in the Research University." For BC, see below, Chapt. 5, "'Bonanza Years' at Boston College." For reviews of general education after WWII, see C. Jencks and D. Riesman, 1968, pp. 493ff.; F. Rudolph, 1977, pp. 252–64; Carnegie Commission on Higher Education, *Priorities for Action*, 1973, p. 25.

75. For social change and general education, see Lawrence Cremin, 1961, p. 351;

see also D. Riesman, 1958, Chapt. 3. For Carnegie Commission on Higher Education on changed ideas about citizenship, see *A Digest,* 1974, pp. 181, 183.

76. On view that protests caused demise of general education, see Gerald Grant and David Riesman, 1978, pp. 188–89. On intellectual doubts about general education, see Carnegie Commission on Higher Education, *Priorities for Action,* 1973, p. 25; see also J. Brubacher and W. Rudy, 1976, pp. 303–34. For MIT, see Committee on Curriculum Content Planning, May 1964, p. 12.

77. In its final report, *Priorities for Action,* 1973, for example, the Carnegie Commission on Higher Education both disclaims the possibility of general education under current circumstances (p. 47) and stresses its importance (pp. 89–90). See also Assembly on University Goals and Governance, 1971, p. 18; Stephen Graubard, in *Daedalus,* vol. 103, Fall 1974, p. 6.

78. For consortium study, see SDL, Systems Research Group, Feb. 1974. For MIT, see below, Chapt. 3, "Consolidating the New Focus." For Brandeis, see Stephan Thernstrom, 1969, pp. 8–18. For NU, see Dan Waldorf, 1973. For Harvard's community activities, see Committee on the University and the City, Dec. 1968; HUAR (1971), 8.

79. On theme of reducing external involvement, see Assembly on University Goals and Governance, 1971, Thesis 46, p. 23; President's Commission on Campus Unrest, 1970, pp. 208, 210. For President's Commission see ibid., pp. 187–88; also 74–76. For intensified social involvements, see Carnegie Commission on Higher Education, *Governance,* 1973, pp. 17ff.; see also A. Touraine, 1974, Chapts. 3 and 4; David Apter, in *Daedalus,* vol. 103, Fall 1974, pp. 88, 101. On external demands as cause of academic change, see John Corson, 1975, pp. 3–20; Edward Gross and Paul V. Grambsch, 1974, p. 204; J. Hefferlin, 1969, p. 146; Derek Bok, 1982, Chapt. 3; D. Henry, 1975, p. 142. For a contrary view, see P. Blau, 1973, p. 201ff. For external involvements as cause of internal conflict, see Harold J. Leavitt, William R. Dill, and Henry B. Eyring, 1973, p. 205.

80. For universities as closed systems, see Daniel Katz and Robert Kahn, 1966, p. 91; A. K. Rice, 1970, p. 4; Barry M. Richman and Richard N. Farmer, 1974, pp. 5, 33. On transition from closed to open systems, see M. Peterson and L. Mets, 1987, pp. 12–13; Richman and Farmer, 1974, pp. 11, 33; Robert H. Miles, 1980, p. 11. For Kerr, see C. Kerr, 1963, pp. 49, 94ff., 105. For open systems perspective, see Burton Clark, June 1956; Francis E. Rourke and Glenn E. Brooks, 1966, p. 115; J. Hefferlin, 1969. Kerr quote is from D. Henry, 1975, p. 164. See also J. Corson, 1975, Chapt. 2, esp. 19, 50; Charles Frankel, in *Daedalus,* vol. 103, Fall 1974, p. 30; also C. Vann Woodward, in *Daedalus,* vol. 103, Fall 1974, 33ff.

81. Carnegie Commission on Higher Education, *Digest,* 1974, pp. 185, 187, 189–90. See also Assembly on University Goals and Governance, 1971, Theses 42, 43, 44.

82. For Newman quote, see US Department of Health, Education and Welfare, 1971, p. 5; see also ibid., Preface, p. vii; Albert Shanker, "Where We Stand: Wide Gulf Between Leaders, Public" in the *New York Times,* Feb. 28, 1982, section IV, p. 7. For a contrary view, see J. Corson, 1975, p. 99.

83. C. Jencks and D. Riesman, 1968. Research on faculty goals supported Jencks and Riesman by showing their convergence despite different institutional settings; for references, see E. Gross and P. Grambsch, 1974, p. 51; also B. Berelson, 1960, p. 116. For quotes, see Carnegie Commission on Higher Education, *Reform,* 1972, p. 35; US Department of Health, Education and Welfare, 1971, p. vii; Assembly on University Goals and Governance, 1971, p. 8. See also Carnegie Commission on Higher Education reports on specific institutional types: H. Hodgkinson, 1971; E. Alden Dunham, 1969;

C. Robert Pace, 1972; reports summarized in Carnegie Commission on Higher Education *Sponsored Research,* 1975, pp. 75ff. See also, Association of American Universities, 1968; Talcott Parsons in "Introduction" to Assembly on University Goals and Governance, 1971, p. 4; US Department of Health, Education and Welfare, 1971, pp. x, 12–16, 82. R. Birnbaum, 1983, concludes that most studies of academic change in the 1960s found declining diversity; see esp. Chapt. 3. On contradiction between rise of external pressures and rise of professionalism, see F. Rourke and G. Brooks, 1966, p. 8; A. Touraine, 1974, p. 161.

84. For calls for more diversity see Carnegie Commission on Higher Education, *Reform,* 1972, p. 129; US Department of Health, Education and Welfare, 1971, pp. 61–66; F. Newman et al., 1973, p. 82; Assembly on University Goals and Governance, 1971, pp. 9, 29; President's Task Force on Higher Education, 1970, p. v; Association of American Universities, 1968, p. 6.

85. On agreement about needed reforms, see US Department of Health, Education and Welfare, 1971, pp. 61–62. See also Special Committee on Campus Tensions, 1970, p. 37; Assembly on University Goals and Governance, 1971, p. 41.

86. On passivity of academia in face of new pressures, see J. Hefferlin, 1969, pp. 142ff.; B. Clark, 1956; F. Rourke and G. Brooks, 1966, p. 115; D. Bok, 1982, Chapt. 3; D. Henry, 1975, p. 142; for a contrary view, see B. Clark, 1983, p. 234. On breakdown of university government and need for strengthening, see President's Commission on Campus Unrest, 1970, Chapt. 6; the Special Committee on Campus Tensions, 1970, put it this way: "If colleges and universities cannot govern themselves, they will be governed by others." (p. 5); see also below, Chapt. 7, "The Institutional Complex in Action." For scholarship on internal disorganization, see V. Baldridge, 1971; M. Cohen and J. March, 1974, K. Weick, 1976.

87. On pursuit of prestige as driving force for change in golden age, see Assembly on University Goals and Governance, 1971, Theses 76, 77, 78; US Department of Health, Education and Welfare, 1971, p. x; F. Newman et al., 1973, p. 87; D. Riesman, 1958; B. Clark, 1983, pp. 165ff.; Walter F. Abbott, 1974. See also below, Chapt. 7, "The Institutional Complex in Action." For more general discussions of prestige as a motivation for organizational change, see J. Eugene Haas and Thomas E. Drabek, 1973, p. 204; Charles Perrow, 1961. For emergence of research model, see J. Ben-David, 1972, p. 47; J. Ben-David, 1977, pp. 61, 65; A. Touraine, 1974; T. Parsons and G. Platt, 1973, Chapts. 2 and 3, esp. pp. 45–55. For "leading sociologist," see P. Blau, 1973, pp. 250–58; for a parallel characterization, see Theodore Caplow and Reece J. Magee, 1958, pp. 232–33.

88. For the Brandeis story, see below, Chapt. 4, "Dilemmas of the College-centered University."

CHAPTER 3. EMERGENCE OF THE MODERN RESEARCH UNIVERSITY: HARVARD AND M.I.T., 1945–1970

1. For Conant quote, see HUAR (1943), 12. For Compton quote, see MITAR (1944), 30. For additional material on Compton's anticipation of development after the war, see MITAR (1941), 5–18, 29–30.

2. For Conant's anticipation of higher demand, see HUAR (1946). For policy of nonexpansion, see HUAR (1947), 8.

3. For need for subsidies for advanced education, see HUAR (1952), 36–37. For "it seems to me clear," see J. Conant, 1948, p. 171. For need for federal support, see J.

Conant, 1970, pp. 244–45. For "the first duty," see HUAR (1946), 10. For "best brains," HUAR (1944), 9–10.

4. For impact of war, see J. Burchard, 1948, pp. 313–14; J. Killian, 1985, pp. 400–404, 414; Morison interview; MITAR (1943), 6–13. For "super institute," see MITAR (1941), 16ff. For Compton quote, see MITAR (1943), 17ff. For reviews of postwar plans, see MITAR (1943), 17–23; (1944), 9–31; (1949), 8–9. For RLE decision, see Killian, 1985, pp. 46ff. For Compton on MIT's continuing close ties to military, see MITAR (1950), 7–10; (1951), 7, 22.

5. For Conant's postwar career, see J. Conant, 1970, Pt. V. For provost role, see HUAR (1952), 13–14.

6. For a general review of postwar change, see HUAR (1947), 8ff.; see also (1963), 7ff. For enrollment figures, see HCR, Committee on Admission (1947); (1952). For Russian Research Center, see R. Smith, 1986, p. 171; N. Pusey, 1978, p. 22. For lack of fund-raising in Conant's last years, see HUAR (1963), 15; Kistiakowski interview. For HU financial position, see HUAR (1945), 14–15; (1947); see also HUAR (1963), 12–13. For Conant on federal funding, see HUAR (1952), 15ff.

7. For general discussion of postwar admissions, see HUAR (1952), 17ff.; Conant quote is on 18; see also S. Harris, 1970, pp. 117–18; E. J. Kahn, Jr., 1969, pp. 33ff. For women and veterans, see S. Lipset and D. Riesman, 1975, p. 306; J. Conant, 1970, Chapt. 28; HUAR (1952), 30. For tuition policy, see S. Harris, 1970, pp. 58–59. For organizational changes, see HUAR (1952), 18; HCR, Committee on Admission (1948), 157–58; (1960), 234–39. For student characteristics, see HCR, Committee on Admission (1930), (1940), and (1960).

8. For postwar change in graduate schools, see HUAR (1952), 31ff.; see also (1963), 5–6.

9. For School of Education, see J. Conant, 1970, Chapt. 29; A. Powell, 1980, Chapt. 9.

10. For appointments of Jewish refugees, see J. Conant, 1970, p. 213. On Corporation appointments, see R. Smith, 1986, pp. 173–74

11. For postwar atmosphere, see J. Burchard, 1948, p. 314. For Killian quote, see ibid., 314.

12. For faculty appointments, see ibid., 323–24; Zacharias interview. For staff expansion, see MITR, Registrar, (1945), (1946), and (1947). On 1947 budget, see MITTR (1947). For facilities, see MITAR (1944), 28ff.; J. Burchard, 1948, pp. 315, 321, 322. For Mid-Century Convocation, see J. Killian, 1985, pp. 94ff.; also J. Burchard (ed.), 1950.

13. For origins of Lewis, see J. Killian, 1985, Chapt. 4; P. Ladd, Sept. 1947, pp. 20–21; MITAR (1946), 11–12. For quote on committee charge, see Committee on Educational Survey, 1949, p. 3. For Lewis on general education, see ibid., 21, 26, and Chapt. 3. For Compton reaction, see Killian, 1985, p. 83. For Morison quote, see Morison interview.

14. For financial worries, see MITAR (1944), 29; (1947), 19–20; (1948), 7–13; see also James R. Killian, "Funding M.I.T.'s Independence" in Committee on Financing Development: "Funding M.I.T.'s Independence," 1948. K. Compton, in Committee on Financing Development, "MIT—A New Era," 1948. For endowment, see R. Geiger, 1986, pp. 276–77. For capital campaign, see MITAR (1948), 7–8; (1949), 10; Compton, in Committee on Financing Development, "Era," 1948, pp. 5, 8–9; Killian in Committee on Financing Development, "Funding," pp. 3, 6–7; Committee on Financing Development, "Statement," 1948. For Compton quote, see MITAR (1948), 11–12. For Industrial Liaison Program, see MITAR (1949), 11–12; J. Killian, 1985, Chapt. 12.

15. For Compton retirement, see J. Killian, 1985, pp. 84ff. For Defense Department role, see Roslyn Romanowski, 1939–54.

16. For policy on vets, see MITAR (1943), 17–19; J. Burchard, 1948, p. 315. For enrollment/admission policies, see MITAR (1951), 18; (1952), 9–10. For enrollments/applicants, see MITR, Registrar (1948) and (1951); MITR, Director of Admissions (1948), 62–3. For tuition, see MITB (1948) and (1949).

17. For success of fund drive, see MITAR (1951), 23. On change in applications, see MITR, Director of Admissions (1953)

18. For Killian background, see J. Killian, 1985, Chapts. 1 and 5. For Killian's view of Compton's legacy, see Killian, 1985, Chapt. 9.

19. For discussion of shift in priorities from Compton/Bush era to Killian/Stratton, see Commission on MIT Education, Nov. 1970, p. 5. For Killian on MIT purposes, see MITAR (1952), 11; (1953), 6ff. For Management, see MITAR (1951), 10; J. Killian, 1985, pp. 194ff. For Humanities and Social Studies, see MITAR (1951), 7, 10–15; (1952), 11; (1953), 11ff.; "Liberal Education at the Massachusetts Institute of Technology," 1952. For "a great university," see Killian, 1985, p. 147. For atmosphere of early 1950s, see interviews with Morison, Rosenblith, and Chandler. For "a university polarized," see Killian, 1985, p. 107, and Chapt. 15.

20. For Pusey background, see R. Smith, 1986, pp. 197–201. For Pusey view of Harvard needs, see Pusey interview. For Corporation members on appointment, see R. Smith, 1986, p. 187.

21. For Pusey views, see Pusey interview.

22. For "if there has been," see Nathan Pusey, 1964, p. 160. For "simply stated," see HUAR (1966), 23–24. For "it is difficult," see N. Pusey, 1978, pp. 76. For "the graduate school," see Pusey, 1978, pp. 84–85. For "what encouraged," see Pusey, 1978, p. 77. For a general discussion of Pusey's view of postwar change, see HUAR (1963), 33ff.

23. For discussion of undergraduate expansion, see HUAR (1953), 6–7; (1954), 19. For faculty committees, see HCR, Dean of Arts and Sciences (1956), 44–45; Special Committee on College Admission Policy, 1960, p. 28. For applicant, admission and enrollment statistics under Pusey, see HCR, Committee on Admission (1954); (1969); see also (1960), 217; Committee on the Future of the Graduate School, 1969, p. 12; HCR, Dean of Arts and Sciences (1955), 54. On need for college teachers, see HUAR (1954), 8–9; (1955), 23.

24. For priority on Education and Divinity, see HUAR (1955); (1963), 7. For efforts to help Divinity, see R. Smith, 1986, pp. 185, 202. For "Queen of Theology," see ibid., 202. See also E. Kahn, 1969, p. 272. For federal funding, see: N. Pusey, 1978, pp. 79ff.; N. Pusey, 1964, p. 177. For efforts to offset impact of federal funds through private support, see HUAR (1962), 27–28; Nathan Pusey, Sept. 1961, Exhibit VII. For restrictions on use of outside funds, see HUAR (1952), 10; Pusey, 1978, pp. 154–55. For quote, see M. Bundy, 1970, pp. 535–36. For statistics on Harvard's budget, see HUTR (1952); (1957); (1962); (1967); see also "Growth and Change at Harvard: Ten Years in Statistical Summary," 1964. For Pusey on *Sputnik I*, see HUAR (1957), 14ff.

25. For Killian quote, see MITAR (1953), 14. For new labs, see: MITAR (1949), 8; (1952), 29; (1961), 14; J. Killian, 1985, pp. 71ff.; J. Burchard, 1948, pp. 317–18. For federal support 1945–52, see MITAR (1952), 29.

26. For national security crisis, see MITAR (1953), 14. For financial figures, see MITTR (1953); (1958). For summer studies, see J. Killian, 1985, pp. 63–64. For Killian appointment, see MITAR (1958), 1; Killian, 1985, pp. 266ff.; N. Pusey, 1978, p. 74.

27. For Stratton appointment, see J. Killian, 1985, pp. 267–68. For financial fig-

ures, see MITTR (1940); (1968). For interdisciplinary labs, see Commission on MIT Education, 1970, p. 2; see also, MITAR (1959), 17ff.; (1961), 12; (1962), 18–20; (1963), 17ff. For CIS, see MITAR (1952), p. 17; Geiger, draft manuscript, Dec. 1986, Section 2.3b.

28. For problems with federal funds, see MITAR (1956), 5; (1961), 14–22; Committee on Educational Survey, 1949, pp. 16, 50ff., 60. For private fund-raising, see J. Killian, in Committee on Financing Development, "Funding Independence," 1948; MITAR (1960); (1964), 33–34; J. Killian, 1985, pp. 288ff.; Committee on Educational Survey, 1949, p. 64.

29. For research growth fueled by federal support, see MITAR (1959), 36; (1963), 11ff.; see also Commission on MIT Education, 1970, p. 38; Planning Committee for the Work of the Commission on Nature and Purposes, Aug. 4, 1969, p. 13. For continuing concerns, see MITAR (1966), 5–6; R. Geiger, draft manuscript, Dec. 1986, pp. 141–43. For financial data, see MITTR (1953); (1958); (1963); (1968). Note that the 32 percent figure in 1968 salary support includes federal and nonfederal funds. See also David Garvin, 1977, pp. 41–81.

30. For undergraduate admissions, see MITAR (1952), 7–9; (1953), 20; (1954); (1959), 4–5; (1963), 5; see also Ad Hoc Committee on Enrollment, Feb. 23, 1956; Planning Committee for the Work of the Commission on Nature and Purposes, Aug. 4, 1969, p. 10. For growth of graduate education, see MITAR (1958); (1960), 29–30; (1961); (1964), 38; see also MITR, Registrar (1948); (1958); (1961); (1966); J. Killian, 1985, p. 222; Committee on the Future of the Graduate School, Feb. 7, 1958, p. 4; for summary statistics, see MITAR (1974), 14.

31. For federal support of graduate education, see D. Garvin, 1977, p. 49ff.

32. For evolution as research university, see MITAR (1960), 1–4; (1966). For standing of MIT Programs, see Kenneth Roose and Charles Anderson, 1970; Rebecca Zames Margulies and Peter M. Blau, Nov. 1973, p. 21ff.

33. For Federal Grant University, see C. Kerr, 1963, Chapt. 2; A. Touraine, 1974, p. 136. For MIT as model, see J. Killian, 1985, p. 55ff.; MITAR (1957), 16; Morison interview; Committee on Educational Survey, 1949, p. 61; Ad Hoc Committee on Outside Commitments, Feb. 15, 1970; Commission on Financing Higher Education, 1952, pp. 71ff.

34. For financial data, see HUTR (1953); (1958); (1968). For 1960 review, see: HUAR (1960), 18ff.; (1961); N. Pusey, Sept. 1961; N. Pusey, 1978, p. 155. For programmatic change, see HUAR (1963), 8, 22–25; (1967), 5ff.; (1968), 7ff.; R. Smith, 1986, p. 212; P. Keller, 1982, pp. 19, 29.

35. For "ivory towers," see HUAR (1967), 5, 11. For balance among fields, see Committee on the Future of the Graduate School, 1969, p. 3, section V.

36. For CIS, see R. Geiger, draft manuscript, Dec. 1986, pp. 133–34. For compatibility of policy with research interests, see Robinson interview. For individual participation in classified work, see University Committee on Governance, Nov. 1970, p. 9; Brown letter to author. For impact of federal funds, see "The University and Its Resources," 1968, pp. 15ff.; S. Harris, 1970, p. 210; N. Pusey, 1978, p. 79; A. Powell, 1980, pp. 273–78; William R. Galeota, unpublished thesis, Harvard College, 1970, Chapt. 2. For quote, see HUAR (1975), 3.

37. For growth of graduate programs, see HUAR (1954), 9; (1955), 19; (1963), 17–19; Committee on the Future of the Graduate School, 1969, p. 1; Committee on Recruitment and Retention of Faculty, May 1968, p. 25; A. Powell, 1980, Chapt. 10. For federal support, see N. Pusey, Sept. 1961, pp. 7–8.

38. HU data derived from HUTR (1953); (1968); HCR, Committee on Admission

(1953); (1968). MIT data derived from MITTR (1953); (1968); MITR, Registrar (1953); (1968). NB: The technical term "Departmental Instruction and Research" (DIR), as distinct from a more general phrase like "educational and research activities," is used extensively in this section and elsewhere in the text and should be defined. The author hastens to acknowledge, however, that he is neither an accountant nor an economist and has attempted only to develop reasonably accurate figures that fairly represent broad financial developments. As used here, the term DIR encompasses expenditures, including both direct and indirect costs, of academic departments offering educational programs to students and excludes research expenditures supported by outside sponsors. The figure also includes the cost of the university's central administration. DIR excludes expenses associated with self-liquidating auxiliary services and activities like dormitories and dining halls as well as the costs of museums and other academic facilities not responsible for educational programs or receiving tuition.

39. For "the costs of educating," see "The University and Its Resources," 1968, p. 13. For increase in undergraduate courses and decline in enrollments, see Office of the Dean, Oct. 1974, 15. For Conant quote, see HUAR (1952), 29.

40. For salaries under Conant, see Committee on the Recruitment and Retention of Faculty, 1968, pp. 3–4. For compensation under Pusey, see HUAR (1963), 22; Committee on the Recruitment and Retention of Faculty, 1968, Chapts. 2 and 5, pp. 52ff.; N. Pusey, Sept. 1961, p. 17; "The University and Its Resources," 1968, pp. 10–11, 15; R. Smith, 1986, p. 211; HUTR (1953); (1968). For expansion of facilities and support, see "The University and Its Resources," 1968, pp. 10–11, 13; HUAR (1963), 29; Nelson W. Aldrich, Jr., March 1976, p. 42. For Pusey quote, see "The University and Its Resources," 1968, p. 13.

41. For salaries, see Committee on Staff Environment, 1949, p. 142; Committee on Financing Development, "Funding," 1948, p. 3; MITAR (1949), 22; American Association of University Professors: *Bulletin,* Winter 1957; Summer 1968. For teaching loads, see Committee on Educational Policy, 1964, pp. 5–6.

42. For Pusey quote, see letter to author.

43. For investment firm, see J. Millett, 1952, p. 314; HUAR (1963), 26ff. For campaigns under Pusey, see HUAR (1958), 14–16; (1960), 1; (1961), 16; (1963), 9–10; (1966), 18ff.; E. Kahn, 1969, pp. 331–33; "The University and Its Resources," 1968, pp. 19–20; "Growth and Change," 1964; HUTR (1968); N. Pusey, 1978, pp. 114, 119–20. NB: The $350 million figure in total capital includes funds for construction as well as endowment. For gifts for current use under Pusey, see "Growth and Change," 1964; "The University and Its Resources," 1968; HUTR (1968); HUAR (1963), 12ff.; (1969), 24; N. Pusey, 1978, p. 116. For foundations and corporations, see HUAR (1955), 24–25; (1957), 6; N. Pusey, 1978, p. 117. For fund-raising summaries, see HUAR (1963), 15; E. Kahn, 1969, p. 277. For decentralization, see University Committee on Governance, Nov. 1970, p. 26.

44. For Pusey on tuition, see N. Pusey, 1978, p. 102ff.; HUAR (1963), 26; S. Harris, 1970, p. 56; W. Galeota, 1970, p. 59–61. For quote, see Pusey letter to author. For tuition data, see S. Harris, 1970, p. 56; for 1968, see Otis Singletary (ed), 1968, p. 666; see also Harris, 1970, pp. 45, 111.

45. For criticisms and responses, see Pusey letter to author; HCR, Admission and Scholarship Committee (1960), 244; W. Galeota, 1970, pp. 59–61. For quotation, see Office of the Dean, Oct. 1974, p. 3. For general discussion on subsidizing graduate programs with undergraduate tuition, see June O'Neill, 1973, pp. 10ff.

46. For fund-raising efforts, see MITAR (1951), 24; (1952), 31–33; (1955), 20; (1956); (1964), 34; Committee on Financing Development, "New Era," 1948; Second-

Century Program, "From Strength to Greater Strength," 1961; "Policies and Procedures," 1966, pp. 70–71. For data, see MITTR (1953); (1958); (1963); (1968).

47. For Harvard statistics, see HCR, Admission and Scholarship Committee (1960); (1968); see also S. Harris, 1970, p. 118; HUAR (1963). For Bender quote, see HCR, Admission and Scholarship Committee (1960), 233. For selective admissions at HU, see P. Keller, 1982, p. 35; N. Aldrich, March 1976, p. 46; HUAR (1961), 18; Robert Trumbull: "Talent Edges Out Wealth at Big Three," in the *New York Times,* March 14, 1964. For MIT statistics, see MITR, Registrar (1953); (1968). For comparisons between beginning and end of period, see HCR, Admission and Scholarship Committee, 1960; Committee on Educational Policy, 1964, p. 2.

48. For advanced standing, see S. Lipset and D. Riesman, 1975, p. 350–52; P. Keller, 1982, p. 24–26. For MIT, see Ad Hoc Committee on Enrollment, 1956, pp. 3–4; MITAR (1958), 7–10; (1959), 6–7, 11–15; (1960), 43.

49. For decline in faculy interest in general education at HU, see S. Lipset and D. Riesman, 1975, p. 350ff.; Office of the Dean, Oct. 1974, p. 12–14; F. Rudolph, 1977, p. 259ff. For Killian and Stratton, see MITAR (1953), 7–8, 29; (1955), 9; (1958), 5–10; (1961), 14–24; see also Committee on Educational Policy, "Faculty Survey," 1964, p. 10; Ad Hoc Committee on Enrollment, 1956, p. 3. For freshman seminars, see S. Lipset and D. Riesman, 1975, p. 350. For UROP, see J. Killian, 1985, p. 177.

50. For Zacharias, see Committee on Curriculum Content, May 1964; MITAR (1963), 28–30; (1964), 26–31; (1964), 26; (1979), 3. For Stratton quote, see MITAR (1964), 2. For Zacharias quote, see Committee on Curriculum Content, 1964, pp. 3–4, 12.

51. For Doty, see Special Committee to Review the Present Status and Problems of the General Education Program, May 1964; HUAR (1964), 7; (1965), 11; (1966), 5ff. For quotes, see P. Keller, 1982, pp. 25, 38.

52. For reforms of 1960s, see S. Lipset and D. Riesman, 1975, p. 385; Office of the Dean, Oct. 1974; HUAR (1971), 9; Commission on MIT Education, 1970, p. 11, Chapt. 2, Minority Report, p. 129. For Conant quote, see J. Conant, 1970, p. 366.

53. For changes at HU, see S. Lipset and D. Riesman, 1975, pp. 218, 341–44, 376; P. Keller, 1982, p. 55; Office of the Dean, Oct. 1974, pp. 38ff. For MIT, Johnson, see MITAR (1971), 5. For quote, see Commission on MIT Education, 1970, p. 13.

54. For HU debates, see P. Keller, 1982, pp. 22ff.; R. Smith, 1986, p. 214ff.; N. Aldrich, March 1976, p. 50; E. Kahn, 1969, Chapt. 2; Special Committee on College Admission Policy, 1960, p. 30. For Bender quote, see P. Keller, 1982, 22.

55. For Ford committee, see Special Committee on College Admission Policy, 1960; for quotes, see ibid., 9–11, 36; see also Franklin Ford private communication. For Bender, see HCR, Admission and Scholarship Committee (1960); for quotes, see ibid., 243–45. For decline in accessibility in 1950s, see P. Keller, 1982, p. 23; HUTR (1978), 11–13. For changes after 1960, see Keller, 1982, pp. 2–3, 23, 33, 41; HCR, Admission and Scholarship Committee (1967); HUAR (1968), 14; (1971), 7; R. Smith, 1986, p. 216.

56. For special committee, see Committee on Undergraduate Admissions and Student Aid, Oct. 10, 1969. See also MITR, Committee on Undergraduate Admissions and Student Aid (1968), 589; MITAR (1957), 13.

57. For Riesman quote, see S. Lipset and D. Riesman, 1975, pt. II, Chapt. 2.

58. For traditional organization of HU, see University Committee on Governance, March 1971; HUAR (1952); HUC (1973), section on "History and Government"; Peter French, 1962, p. 190. For quote, see University Committee on Governance, March 1971, p. 44.

59. For traditional MIT organization, see "Rules and Regulations of the Faculty,"

1930; "Policies and Procedures," 1939, pp. 7–11; "By-laws of the Corporation," 1934; Commission on MIT Education, 1970, Chapt. 4.

60. For change under Compton, see MITAR (1940), 23; (1946), 22; Committee on Educational Survey, 1949, pp. 26, 43–44, Chapt. 5; Commission on MIT Education, 1970, p. 59.

61. For change under Conant, see HUAR (1952), 13ff.; 22ff.; 35; J. Conant, 1970, p. 381; M. Bundy, 1970, pp. 531ff.; S. Lipset and D. Riesman, 1975, p. 357; J. Millett, 1952, p. 230; University Committee on Governance, Nov. 1970, p. 6.

62. For Killian background and orientation, see J. Killian, 1985, Chapt. 1, pp. 126ff. For Pusey orientation, see University Committee on Governance, March 1971, pp. 46ff.; P. French, 1962, Chapt. 16; R. Smith, 1986, p. 235; Carl A. Vigeland, 1986, p. 8.

63. For changes under Killian, see MITAR (1949), 21; (1951), 25–26; (1952), 34; (1953), 25–26, 35–36; (1954), 35, 41; (1955), 27; (1956), 17; (1957), 15; J. Killian, 1985, pp. 115, 127ff., 402; Commission on MIT Education, 1970, pp. 59, 62–63. For Stratton, see MITAR (1963), 25–26. For Johnson, see MITAR (1968), 7; F. Rourke and G. Brooks, 1966, p. 17.

64. For change under Pusey, see University Committee on Governance, March 1971, pp. 46ff.; HUAR (1963), 10ff.; P. French, 1962, Chapt. 16; Committee on the University and the City, Dec. 1968, pp. 23–24; R. Smith, 1986, pp. 235; W. Galeota, 1970; Office of the Dean, Oct. 1974, pp. 3, 4. For "If there was a criticism," see C. Vigeland, 1986, p. 8. For Andrews quote, see University Committee on Governance, March 1971, p. 47. For "major questions demanding," see ibid., 37.

65. For evolution of MIT policies, see "Policies and Procedures," 1945; 1947; 1952; 1957; 1961; 1966; see also Committee on Faculty Responsibility, Jan. 1963; for quote, see ibid., 7; Ad Hoc Committee on Outside Commitments, 1970; MITAR (1959), 17–22; (1962), 18–20; (1963), 33ff.; J. Killian, 1985, pp. 133ff. Note: an exception to the loosening of controls on grant-getting involved the special defense labs, which continued to be closely supervised.

66. For evolution of MIT policies, see MITAR (1959), 16; (1963), 5–7; (1966), 17; Committee on the Future of the Graduate School, Feb. 1958; for quote, see p. 5. For Stratton quote, see MITAR (1966), 17. For HU policies, see Committee on the Future of the Graduate School, 1969, pp. 6, 30.

67. For growth of PhDs at MIT, see MITAR (1963), 17. For "best man available," see S. Lipset and D. Riesman, 1975, pp. 309, 314; "Policies and Procedures," 1966. For competition for faculty, see HUAR (1976), 4–5. For fragmentation of faculty, see N. Aldrich, March 1976, pp. 47–48; note also comparison of Committee on Educational Survey, 1949, with Commission on MIT Education, 1970, on this point. For changes in MIT personnel policy postwar, see "Policies and Procedures," 1945; 1947; 1952; 1957; 1961; 1966; MITAR (1953), 15, 20; J. Killian, 1985, pp. 132–33. For loss of power by central administration at MIT, see Commission on MIT Education, 1970, pp. 23, 64; Morison interview; Ad Hoc Committee on Outside Commitments, 1970, pp. 25–27.

68. For growth of nonfaculty personnel, see Committee on the Recruitment and Retention, 1968, p. 42; "Policies and Procedures," 1952. For difficulties in maintaining communication, see University Committee on Governance, March 1971; C. Vigeland, 1986, p. 132; Commission on MIT Education, 1970. For HU as Christian institution, see E. Kahn, 1969, p. 272; R. Smith, 1986, pp. 210–11. For deterioration of ties to Boston students, see Special Committee on College Admission Policy, 1960, pp. 37–38, 235. Committee to Consider Aspects of the Harvard-Radcliffe Relationship that Affect

Administrative Arrangements, Admissions, Financial Aid and Educational Policy, Feb. 1975, A2–4. For general discussion of cultural change at HU, see N. Aldrich, March 1976, pp. 39–52.

69. For strength of academic culture in 1950s and early 1960s, see M. Bundy, 1970, pp. 541–42; O. and M. Handlin, 1970, "Discipline of Scholarship"; Morison interview; S. Lipset and D. Riesman, 1975, pp. 190–91. For increasing focus on research, see ibid., 388–89; MITAR (1966), 5–6; "Policies and Procedures," 1939 compared with 1945. For convergence of HU and MIT on common values and activities, see R. Smith, 1986, p. 220; MITAR (1951), 13; (1956), 4, 27; (1959), 31; (1970), 4; J. Killian, 1985, p. 219.

70. For continuing limits on faculty role in governance at MIT, see MITAR (1963), 23, 35. For an instructive comparison of Harvard and MIT, see two unpublished theses on budget process: W. Galeota, 1970, stresses HU's inefficiency and lack of central control; M. Gutierrez, 1977, stresses close control by Academic Council, president and Corporation at MIT. For Pusey quote, see R. Smith, 1986, p. 231. For Morison quote, see J. Killian 1985, pp. 399–400.

71. For Pusey, see HUAR (1967), 20ff., 28. For Johnson, see MITAR (1968), 5–6.

72. For HU's growing financial problems, see HUAR (1969), pp. 21–23; (1971), 12–13; see also John T. Bethell, March–Apr. 1979, p. 27; E. Cheit, 1971, p. 6; "The University and Its Resources," 1968, pp. 20ff. For Bator/Allison, see University Committee on Governance, Nov. 1970. For quotes, see ibid., 10, 13, 14–15.

73. For impact of altered federal policies, see D. Garvin, 1977, pp. 49–57, 60–61. For deficit, see Commission on MIT Education, 1970, p. 43. For Johnson, see MITAR (1968), 8–9; (1970), 1; (1971), 8–9; for quote, see MITAR (1971), 9.

74. There are numerous accounts of events at Harvard in the late 1960s, and I have not undertaken a comprehensive review of this literature. Rather, I have relied on several authoritative sources, including HUAR (1967); (1968); (1969); (1970); R. Smith, 1986, Chapt. 7; A. Ulam, 1972, 128ff.; S. Lipset and D. Riesman, 1975, pt. I, Chapt. 8; P. Keller, 1982, pp. 30ff.; J. Bethell, March–Apr. 1979. For "no widespread alienation," see Committee of Fifteen, June 9, 1969, p. 2. For "Walter Mittys," see HUAR (1967), 22. For undercurrents of disaffection, see Committee on the Future of the Graduate School, 1969, esp. 2, 24–26, 64ff.; R. Smith, 1986, pp. 242–43; HUAR (1968), 17ff.; Committee on the Recruitment and Retention of Faculty, 1968, esp. pp. 36ff., 99. For liberal, conservative caucuses, see Henry Rosovsky, 1990, p. 25. For challenge to view that student dissatisfaction with Harvard was important, see Marshall Meyer, in D. Riesman and V. Stadtman, 1973, pp. 127ff.

75. My account of the bust and strike relies on the sources mentioned above (n. 74). For Rosovsky quote, see J. Bethell, March–Apr. 1979, p. 24.

76. For committees, see Committee on the Organization of the Faculty of Arts and Sciences, Oct. 17, 1969; Committee of Fifteen, June 9, 1969; University Committee on Governance. The latter committee issued a number of reports; its most important account of the crisis occurs in Jan. 1971. For account of Committee of Fifteen, see June 9, 1969, pp. 2–15; quotes are on 14. For Cox, Dunlop, and administrative operations in wake of bust, see R. Smith, 1986, p. 252; O'Brien interview. For chaplain quote, see Smith, 261.

77. For Stratton, see MITAR (1966), 1–21; for quotes, see 10, 13; for graduate committee, see 17. For rising tensions of late 1960s, see MITAR (1968); (1969); Commission on MIT Education, 1970, p. 57; Graduate School Study Committee, 1968; Committee on Educational Policy, 1964, esp. pp. 14–16.

78. For Pounds committee, see MITAR (1969), 5, 675ff.; (1970), 427ff. For Hoff-

man committee, see MITAR (1969), 6; (1970), 4; Planning Committee for the work of the Commission on Nature and Purposes, Aug. 1969; quotes are from ibid., 3, 5.

79. For November Action, see Benson Snyder, in D. Riesman and V. Stadtman, 1973, pp. 155ff.; see also *Technology Review* July–Aug. 1970; Commission on MIT Education, 1970, pp. 68–69; Thomas Tatlow, student paper, 1987.

80. For divestment decision, see MITAR (1970), 5, 430ff.; J. Killian, 1985, pp. 276ff.; D. Garvin personal communication.

81. For Pusey's resignation, see R. Smith, 1986, pp. 247, 268, 269; C. Vigeland, 1986, p. 5. For Johnson, see *Technology Review*, Oct.–Nov. 1970, p. 96A.

CHAPTER 4. EVOLUTION OF THE COLLEGE-CENTERED UNIVERSITY: TUFTS AND BRANDEIS, 1945–1970

1. For opportunities presented by WWII, see, generally, TUAR (1941); (1942); (1943); (1945). For NROTC, see TUAR (1941), 10–11; (1942); (1952), 14. For "it is not too early," see TUAR (1943), 6–7. For "every effort is being made," see TUAR (1945), 9–10.

2. For Carmichael's view of TU, see above, Chapt. 1, "The Long Pause." The best summary of TU's position in the 1940s can be found in R. Miller, 1966, esp. Chapt. 16; see also TUARs for this period. For issues of research and graduate development, see TUAR (1939), 13; TUAR (1946), 4–5; Miller, 1966, pp. 639, 710.

3. For Carmichael's wish to limit enrollments, see TUAR (1946), 9; (1948), 2–3; (1949), 5–6; for "may the postwar period," see TUAR (1946), 9. For initiatives in admissions, see TUAR (1947), 2–3; R. Miller, 1966, p. 645. For veterans at Tufts, see TUAR (1943), 8–9, and subsequent annual reports; Miller, 1966, p. 642. For data on applications and enrollments, see TUAR (1940); (1948); (1952). For "not a source of satisfaction" and "better not bigger," see TUAR (1952), 13.

4. For financial pressures of postwar period, see TUAR (1947), 4; (1948), 6; R. Miller, 1966, pp. 650–56, 709–11. For Second-Century Campaign, see TUAR (1946), 9; (1948), 8; Miller, 1966, pp. 707–8. For Carmichael on federal aid, see TUAR (1947), 4–5; (1948), 9. For tuition increases, see Miller, 1966, pp. 706–7; TUAR (1947), 4. For tuition revenues, see TUTR (1940); (1948); (1953). For "how to reduce student numbers," see TUAR (1948), 3.

5. For admissions data, see TUAR (1940); (1953). In his final report—TUAR (1952)—Carmichael claimed that TU's student body was "better selected than previously," but statistics on applications and acceptances indicate no significant change in selectivity. For growth of affiliated schools, see TUAR (1947), 9; (1952), 12; R. Miller, 1966, pp. 695ff.; "Report of a Visiting Committee to Re-evaluate Tufts University," Nov. 1, 1959, p. 41. Information on financial role of affiliated schools from TUTRs for postwar years.

6. For growth of federal research contracts, see TUR, Research Coordinator (1953); TUAR (1946), 8; (1948), 8; (1952), 9. For "made over our institution," see TUAR (1952), 9. For faculty growth, see TUAR (1952). For lack of broad emphasis on research, see TUR, Research Coordinator, (1953), esp. 1; see also interview with Miller. For steps needed to upgrade faculty, see TUAR (1946), 4, 6; (1952), 7; R. Miller, 1966, pp. 630–31.

7. For development of Graduate School, see R. Miller, 1966, p. 710; TUAR (1948), 4.

8. For Carmichael's review of his presidency, see TUAR (1952); see also R. Miller,

1966, esp. Chapt. 16. For additional expressions of apprehension about future, see TUAR (1950), 1–4; (1951), 1–2. For proposed name change, see TUAR (1951), 8. For "future usefulness of Tufts," see TUAR (1952), 17.

9. For background on selection of Brandeis name, see I. Goldstein, 1951, Chapt. 7. The story of Goldstein's efforts to establish BrU can be found in ibid., esp. Chapts. 2 and 3; see also A. Sachar, 1976, Chapt. 2; D. Richlin, 1974, Chapt. 1. A profile of Goldstein can be found in ibid., 8–11. I also benefited from the opportunity, generously arranged by Mr. Richlin, to listen to several interviews he taped in 1973 with principals in the BrU story, including Otto Nathan, Abram Sachar, Ruggles Smith, George Alpert, Israel Goldstein, and Clarence Berger. "Essentially Zionist purpose" quote is from Goldstein interview.

10. For Goldstein's contacts with Middlesex and formation of the committee of New Yorkers, see I. Goldstein, 1951. For "what a glorious place" and "intrinsically worthy of becoming," see ibid., p. 20. For Goldstein's early contacts with Einstein, see ibid.; also Richlin interview with Goldstein; D. Richlin, 1974, p. 52.

11. Accounts of the period between the acquisition of Middlesex and the opening of Brandeis told by several principals (especially, Sachar, Goldstein, Alpert, and Einstein's associates) differ in significant ways, and it has not been possible to sift through the claims and counterclaims, charges and countercharges made by these men. Hence the somewhat generalized nature of my account, which uses the following: D. Richlin, 1974; Richlin's interviews with Alpert, Goldstein, and Nathan; I. Goldstein, 1951, Chapts. 4–10; A. Sachar, 1976, Chapt. 2.

12. My interpretation of the conflicts between Goldstein, Einstein, and Alpert, especially the links between each of these men and important currents in the American Jewish community, relies heavily on D. Richlin, 1974, who outlines his essential thesis in his introduction, 6–7; see also A. Werner, 1948, pp. 24–27; Richlin interviews with Berger and Goldstein, 1973.

13. For story of Alpert/Sachar negotiations, see A. Sachar, 1976, Chapts. 2 and 3; author interview with Sachar; D. Richlin, 1974. For Sachar background, see Richlin, 1974, pp. 6, 31ff.; Sachar, 1976, p. 62; author interview with Sachar; "Materials Submitted to Massachusetts Pre-Medical Approving Authority," Schedule 5e, 1951. I. Goldstein, 1951, p. 60.

14. For Brandeis as symbol, see A. Sachar, 1976, p. 39; author interview with Sachar. For "if they [the Jews] are going to create," see author interview with Sachar. For early thinking about Brandeis in terms of academic quality, not Jewish issues, see Sachar, 1976, pp. 26–28, 246; author interview with Sachar; D. Richlin, 1974, p. 87; Richlin interview with Berger. For role of Jewish themes, see Sachar, 1976, Chapts. 15 and 19; author interview with Sachar. For opposition to innovation and professionalism, see Sachar, 1976, p. 122; author interview with Sachar; Richlin interview with Berger. For Redbook and accreditation, see Sachar, 1976, pp. 34–38; Richlin, 1974, pp. 78–79; author interview with Sachar; "Materials Submitted to Pre-Medical Approving Authority," 1951. For emphasis on national role and recruitment of ex-Harvardians, see Sachar, 1976, pp. 26, 32–34, 39, 44ff.; "Materials Submitted to Pre-Medical Approving Authority," 1951, Schedule 3a, 3b; author interview with Sachar.

15. For interpretation of Sachar's ideas, see D. Richlin, 1974, pp. 31ff., 83; Richlin interviews with Goldstein, Berger; author interview with Sachar. For Goldstein criticisms, see I. Goldstein, 1951, pp. 119–21; Richlin interview with Goldstein. For Sachar inaugural, see Richlin, 1974, p. 89; author interview with Sachar.

16. For start-up, see A. Sachar, 1976, pp. 29, 38, 53–54; "Materials Submitted to Pre-Medical Approving Authority," 1951, Exh. 2. For student recruitment, see Richlin

interview with Berger. For faculty recruitment, see Sachar, 1976, pp. 39ff., 142; Richlin interview with Berger; author interview with Sachar.

17. For past difficulty obtaining money for Jewish university, see L. Newman, 1945; Richlin interview with Berger; author interview with Sachar. For Sachar on his constituency, see A. Sachar, 1976, Chapt. 6 and pp. 96–97, 113–14, 118, 168; D. Richlin, 1974; author interview with Sachar. For quote, see Sachar, 1976, pp. 25–26.

18. For description of early fund-raising efforts, see A. Sachar, 1976, Chapts. 5–8; also author interview with Sachar; "Materials Submitted to Pre-Medical Approving Authority," 1951, Schedule 6b. For expansion of trustees, see "Profile of Brandeis University," 1962, p. 148 and Appendix A. For statistics on annual giving, see Controller's Office, Sept. 30, 1980. For data on operating costs in early years, see "Materials Submitted to Pre-Medical Approving Authority," 1951, Exh. 6, Schedule 6b; also N. Madison Cartmell and Associates, Feb. 1956, Intro.-ii, I-11, I-13, II-5, 6, VI, VII-5, 6. For data on faculty salaries, see "Materials Submitted to Pre-Medical Approving Authority," 1951, Schedule 3a. For data on facilities in 1950, see "Materials Submitted to Pre-Medical Approving Authority," 1951, Schedule 4a.

19. For reliance on Jews for financial support, see A. Sachar, 1976, p. 60. For impact of past discrimination on admissions, see author interview with Eugene Black. For efforts to attract non-Jewish students, see Sachar, 1976, pp. 59, 282, 284; Richlin interview with Smith; author interview with Sachar. For Sachar attitude, see I. Goldstein, 1951, p. 111. For three chapels, see Sachar, 1976, Chapt. 7.

20. For Wessell appointment, see R. Miller, 1966, p. 712. For inaugural, see Nils Wessell, Dec. 9, 1953. For name change, see Public Relations Office, press release, March 23, 1955; TUAR (1955), 1; "Tufts: The Total University," 1973, Appendices, p. 119.

21. For faculty role, esp. Cohen, see author interviews with Sachar, Black, Cohen, Touster; Saul Cohen, Nov. 22, 1983; Saul Cohen, Dec. 1984. For view that BrU was initially conceived as collegiate institution, see I. Goldstein, 1951, p. 87; see also Richlin interview with Goldstein; D. Richlin, 1974, pp. 54, 87. For transition from college to university, see "Profile of Brandeis University," 1962, pp. 25ff.; "Re-Evaluation Report to the New England Association of Schools and Colleges," 1966, pp. 6–7. For quote, see ibid., 7. For Cohen appointment as dean, see A. Sachar, 1976, p. 40.

22. For Wessell inaugural and quote, see N. Wessell, Dec. 9, 1953. For Sachar on small-university idea, see A. Sachar, 1976, pp. 32ff.

23. For Sachar inaugural, see A. Sachar, 1976, p. 38; author interview with Sachar; D. Richlin, 1974, p. 89. For relationship of scholarship and teaching, see Sachar, 1976, p. 36. For negative views on professional programs and service activities, see ibid., Chapt. 17; "Profile of Brandeis University," 1962, p. 6. For general discussion of small-university idea, see Sachar, 1976, pp. 31–38. See also author interview with Cohen.

24. For symposium, see "The Role of the Small University in American Higher Education," Proceedings, Dec. 8, 1955. For Carnegie self-study, see "Tufts Self-Study," 1960; Tufts Self-Study, Executive Committee, Aug. 15, 1958; Tufts Self-Study, Study Committee on Faculty Personnel, Feb. 26, 1958; Tufts Self-Study, Leonard Mead, July 10, 1958; Tufts Self-Study, Kent Geiger, Sept. 1957; see also "Report of a Visiting Committee to Re-Evaluate Tufts University," Nov. 1, 1959. For Wessell views, see TUAR (1959), 1–4, 6; for quote, see ibid.; see also author interview with Wessell; Nils Wessell, Apr. 4, 1964.

25. For dentistry, see author interview with Wessell. For religion at TU, see "Tufts Self-Study," 1960, p. 13; author interview with Wessell; "The Role of the Small Uni-

versity in American Higher Education," Dec. 8, 1955, section on "Role of Religion in a Small University."

26. For Wessell on changes, see, for example, TUAR (1958) 1. For quotes, see TUAR (1960), 2–3.

27. For growth of graduate programs and faculty, see "Profile of Brandeis University," 1962; A. Sachar, 1976, Chapts. 9–13, 17; author interviews with Sachar, Cohen; S. Cohen, Dec. 1984. For general review of progress, see *Saturday Review*, March 17, 1962.

28. For admissions at TU, see "Tufts Self-Study," 1960, pp. 25, 31ff., 49; Tufts Self-Study, K. Geiger, Sept. 1957, pp. II-12, III-1; "Tufts: The Total University," 1973, Appendices, p. 123. Application data for 1950s from TUARs (1953–1960). For Wessell views, see TUAR (1953), 2, 3; TUAR (1955), 3. For admissions at Brandeis, see A. Sachar, 1976, p. 31; David A. Alexander, unpublished thesis, BrU, 1979, tables on size and SAT scores of entering classes. Admissions Office, "Statistics of the Class Enrolling in September 1959"; Cartmell et al., 1956, III-6, IV.

29. For accreditation, see "Report of a Visiting Committee to Re-evaluate Tufts University," Nov. 1959, Chapts. 5, 15; quote is on 49. For statistics on sponsored research, see TUR, Research Coordinator (1958). See also TUAR (1954), 6. For comments on problem of being both college and university, see author interview with John Dunn; Tuft's Self-Study, K. Geiger, Sept. 1957, p. 8.

30. For financial pressures, see TUAR (1953), 3; (1955), 4–5, 7; (1956), 3; (1957), 1–7; (1959). For additional material on financial needs, see Tufts Self-Study, Executive Committee, Aug. 15, 1958, "Financial Implications" and "Summary of Recommendations"; "Report of a Visiting Committee to Re-evaluate Tufts University," Nov. 1959, p. 12. For financial data, see TUTR (1952) compared with (1958); TUAR (1954), 6–7; TUR, Vice President for Development (1958). For Wessell on financial management in fifties, see TUAR (1956); see also author interview with Miller.

31. For faculty background, see "Profile of Brandeis University," 1962, pp. 27ff. For lighter teaching loads and specialized courses, see "Materials Submitted to Pre-Medical Approving Authority," 1951, Schedule 3q; "Profile," 1962, p. 9; Cartmell et al., 1956, III-3ff. For Cohen approach, see author interview with Cohen. For evolution of general education, see "Profile," 1962, pp. 77ff.; Committee on General Education, April 20, 1965; D. Alexander, 1979, pp. 4ff. For evolution of research program, see "Profile," 1962, pp. 48–55; author interview with Sachar. For "Brandeis has achieved," see "Profile," 1962, pp. 36–37.

32. TUAR (1960), 1–2.

33. For applications/admissions data, see TU, *Fact Book*, 1973, pp. 94–95; TUAR (1965); "Tufts: The Total University," 1973, pp. 60, 79; "A Re-evaluation Report to the Commission," April 1970, p. 13; quote is from TUR, Dean of Admissions (1967). For changing academic character of students, see TU, *Fact Book*, 1973, pp. 96–97; TUAR (1968), Chart 14; TUR, Dean of Admissions, (1958); (1963); (1968).

34. For changing social character of students, see "Tufts: The Total University," 1973, pp. 68, 78–80, 109; TU, *Fact Book*, 1973, pp. 96–97. For efforts to enroll blacks, see TUAR (1965); "Tufts: The Total University," 1973, pp. 74–75. For College of Special Studies, see TUAR (1962), 4–5; (1963), 3–4; (1964), 11; "Tufts: The Total University," 1973, Appendices, p. 121; "Report of a Visiting Committee to Re-evaluate Tufts University," Nov. 1959, p. 51.

35. For expansion of graduate programs, see TUR, Dean of Graduate School (1958); TUAR (1961), 4; TUAR (1964), 8; TUAR (1965), Charts 15, 16, 17; TUAR

(1967), 12; "Tufts: The Total University," 1973, p. 30, Appendices, pp. 109ff.; "Report of a Visiting Committee to Re-evaluate Tufts University," Nov. 1959, p. 18; Graduate Long-Range Planning Committee, May 1969, pp. 8–9. For faculty development, see "Tufts: The Total University," 1973, Appendices, pp. 123–24. For sponsored research, see TUTR, (1958); (1967).

36. My reviews of Crane, Fletcher, Medical, and Dental schools in 1960s are based on Wessell's TUARs and Wessell interview; see also Russell Miller, 1986, Chapts. 18, 19, 20. For growth of residential students, see TU, *Fact Book,* 1973, p. 125.

37. For fund-raising, see TUAR (1960); (1961); (1963), 1; "Tufts: The Total University," 1973, pp. 146–47; Howard Chase Associates, Inc., April 1961, pp. 1–2; "Tufts University, Original and Revised Goals and Trustees Development Committee Recommendations," Nov. 27, 1960. For assertion that Wessell's fund-raising brought in less usable support than he claimed, see John A. Dunn, Fall 1990, pp. 26–27; letter from Dunn to author. For financial pressures of 1960s, see TUAR (1959); (1960); (1961); (1962); author interview with Dunn; "Tufts: The Total University," 1973, p. 5. For sponsored research see TUAR (1967), 2–3; "Tufts: The Total University," 1973, p. 59. For financial data, see TUTR (1958); (1963); (1967). For policies on enrollment and tuition, see "Tufts: The Total University," 1973, pp. 5, 55–56, 63ff.; author interview with Dunn. For scholarship data, see TUAR (1967), Fig. F. For "no other factor," see TUAR (1964), 7. For "Since, during the 1960s," see "Tufts: The Total University," 1973, p. 56.

38. For "will make [those of] the last decade," see Nils Y. Wessell, April 15, 1965, pp. 9–10. For Mead appointment, see R. Miller, 1986, pp. 256ff. For data on rising faculty costs, see TUAR (1959); (1963); (1968); (1972); see also (1964), 10; "Tufts: The Total University," 1973, pp. 111, 124, Appendices, p. 125; Long-Range Planning Committee of the Faculty of Arts and Sciences, Aug. 5, 1968, pp. 1–6. For assessments of TU's financial position, see TUAR (1966), 5, 21, Figs. A, B; Graduate Long-Range Planning Committee, May 1969, pp. 13, 41ff.; data on per student expenditures derived from TUTRs and HUTRs. For graduate assessments, see TUAR (1966), 1; (1967), 16. For "deliberate long and hard," see TUAR (1966), 22.

39. For "you can't cross," see A. Sachar, 1976, p. 32. For impact of Ford grant, see author interviews with Sachar and Loomis. For data on financial growth during 1960s, see BrUFS (1958); (1963); (1968); Controller's Office, Sept. 30, 1980; "Re-evaluation Report to the New England Association of Schools and Colleges," 1966, pp. 102ff.; "Profile of Brandeis University," 1962, Chapts. 7, 8, 9; Sachar, 1976, Chapts. 7, 9.

40. For salaries, see "Re-evaluation Report to the New England Association of Schools and Colleges, 1966 p. 46; "Profile of Brandeis University," 1962, p. 33. DIR derived from BrUFS (1968). Sponsored Research from BrUFS (1968); see also "Re-evaluation Report," 1966, p. 178. For plant development, see A. Sachar, 1976, Chapt. 4; quote is on 289; Loomis interview. For endowment see Sachar, 1976, Chapt. 8; author interview with Sachar; BrUFS (1968).

41. Enrollment data from Mary Irvin, 1960; Todd Furniss, 1973. Expansion of graduate programs and reduction of teaching loads from "Re-evaluation Report to the New England Association of Schools and Colleges," 1966, pp. 2, 62. For faculty growth and quality, see ibid., pp. 44–45; M. Irvin, 1960; T. Furniss, 1973; A. Sachar, 1976, Chapts. 11–13.

42. For ACE rankings, see K. Roose and C. Anderson, 1970; see also L. Wilson, 1979, p. 223 and Appendix F.

43. For post-baccalaureate destinations of graduates, see "Profile of Brandeis Uni-

versity," 1962, pp. 22ff., Appendix B; "Re-evaluation Report to the New England Association of Schools and Colleges," 1966, pp. 69–70, 88, 160. For statistics on entering freshmen, see Admissions Office, "Statistics of the Class Enrolling in September 1961" and "Information on New Students Entering in 1967"; see also "Re-evaluation Report," 1966, pp. 72–73. For TYP, see author interview with Sachar; D. Alexander, 1979, VII-8, 11. For one of most selective, see Sachar, 1976, pp. 95–96.

44. For rising pressure on finances, see "Re-evaluation Report to the New England Association of Schools and Colleges," 1966, pp. 102–3; author interview with Loomis; Cartmell et al., 1956. For admissions, see Admissions Office, "Statistics of the Class Enrolling in September 1961" and "Information on New Students Entering in 1967"; D. Alexander, 1979, VIII-24–27; confidential source.

45. For Wessell's feelings for Tufts, see author interview with Wessell; letter from Ullman. For Maslow, see A. Sachar, 1976, p. 207.

46. For "New Plan," see R. Miller, 1966, pp. 360ff. For a critical view, see TUR, Dean of Liberal Arts (1935); (1938), 12–13. For Medical and Dental schools, see Miller, 1966, p. 689. For allocations of power, see "The Charter of the Trustees of Tufts College and Acts of the General Court of Massachusetts in Addition to and Amendment Thereof," May 1, 1951; "By-laws of the Trustees of Tufts College," May 21, 1923.

47. The best account of Cousens's approach to administration can be found in R. Miller, 1966, Chapt. 13.

48. For development of faculty and AAUP role, see R. Miller, 1966, pp. 624ff.; Office of the Vice President, April 28, 1961. For administrative/organizational change under Carmichael, see TUAR (1939), 12; (1950), 4–5; (1952), 8; Miller, 1966, pp. 658–59, and, generally, Chapt. 15. For limited role of faculty in planning under Carmichael, see TUAR (1952), 15.

49. For Wessell on importance of participation and salaries, see TUAR (1959), 5. For "Tufts College is rapidly becoming," see TUR, Vice President and Provost (1954), p. 11. For "had not held," see Tufts Self-Study, Executive Committee, Aug. 1958, "History of the Carnegie Study," 8. For evolution of personnel policy, see Tufts Self-Study, Study Committee on Faculty Personnel, 1958; Faculty Handbook, May 26, 1958, Sect. II; Handbook of Information, Faculty of Arts and Sciences, Sept. 1965, Sect. II; Faculty Handbook, 1970, Sect. III; author interview with Miller.

50. For administrative development under Wessell, see TUAR (1953), 4–5; (1954); (1955), 8; (1956), 2, 9; (1967), 2. For criticisms, see "Report of a Visiting Committee to Re-evaluate Tufts University," Nov. 1959, Chapts. 1, 7, 16. See also Graduate Long-Range Planning Committee, May 1969, p. 20ff.

51. For early organization of BrU, see A. Sachar, 1976, p. 99; "Materials Submitted to Pre-Medical Approving Authority," 1951; Cartmell et al., 1956; D. Alexander, 1979, "Academic Policy," 2; Committee on General Education, April 1965, pp. 4–5.

52. For consultants' review, see Cartmell et al., 1956; quote is on v. For changes of mid-1950s, see Faculty Handbook, 1958; 1962, p. 31; D. Alexander, 1979, "Academic Policy," 7–9; author interviews with Sachar, Cohen.

53. For Sachar attitude and continuing role, see author interviews with Sachar, Cohen, Kauffman. The organization charts, included in the 1966 accreditation report, display the lack of formal delegation from Sachar; see "Re-evaluation Report to the New England Association of Schools and Colleges," 1966. For AAUP talk, see A. Sachar, Dec. 6, 1963; for "aggressive public relations," see ibid., 1; for "fast buck," see ibid., 3; for "given every leeway," see ibid., 8. See also A. Sachar, 1976, pp. 202, 205; AAUP talked is discussed on p. 205.

54. Data for comparisons of faculty growth from M. Irvin, 1960; T. Furniss, 1973.

55. For Wessell approach, see letter from Ullman; Tufts Self-Study, Study Committee on Faculty Personnel, 1958; author interview with Wessell. For salary policy, see "Tufts: The Total University," 1973, p. 43. For "some individuals would interpret," see Tufts Self-Study, Study Committee on Faculty Personnel, 1958, pp. 23, 24.

56. For Sachar's willingness to oppose faculty, see A. Sachar, 1976, p. 205. See also author interview with Kauffman.

57. For administrative changes of 1960s, see "Re-evaluation Report to the New England Association of Schools and Colleges," 1966, pp. 25, 62, Exhs. A and B; Faculty Handbook, 1968. For Cuban missile crisis and graduate dean incidents, see A. Sachar, 1976, pp. 197ff., 204. For student protest activities, see D. Alexander, 1979, "Political Unrest," esp. 3, 5.

58. This account based on confidential sources. Sachar's own version of his decision to retire is found in A. Sachar, 1976, Chapt. 23.

59. For testimony by outsiders to Wessell's continuing popularity and Tufts' morale, see Howard Chase Associates, 1961, iii-1; "Report of a Visiting Committee to Re-evaluate Tufts University," Nov. 1959, p. 52. The authors of the Carnegie self-study, written in the late 1950s, could still use the term "family" to describe Tufts; see, for example, "Tufts Self-Study," 1960, p. 53. For Chancellor idea, see TUAR (1962), 6. For two committees, see Long-Range Planning Committee, Aug. 1968; Graduate Long-Range Planning Committee, May 1969.

60. For undergraduate group, see Long-Range Planning Committee, Aug. 1968, pp. 1–4, 6. For graduate group, see Graduate Long-Range Planning Committee, May 1969, Sect. II. Perceived needs to rekindle collegiate community and educational coherence were major themes of Wessell's successor, Burton Hallowell; see, for example, his proposal to create a university-wide advisory group—TUAR (1968), 6. For sense of inferiority, see Howard Chase Associates, 1961, 1-19.

61. For continuing emphasis on small-university idea at Brandeis, see "Profile of Brandeis University," 1962, pp. 69, 70, 74; author interview with Sachar. At Tufts, see Ad Hoc Committee, March 1969, Sect. II. For enrollments in 1968, see TU, *Fact Book*, 1973, p. 86; T. Furniss, 1973 (for Brandeis). For medical school decision, see A. Sachar, 1976, p. 208; author interview with Sachar.

62. For graduate enrollments, see TU, *Fact Book*, 1973, p. 86; T. Furniss, 1973 (for Brandeis); for comparisons with Harvard and MIT, see Chapt. 3, "Consolidating the New Focus." For a review of graduate education at Tufts in late 1960s, see Graduate Long-Range Planning Committee, May 1969.

63. For "less and less teacher oriented," see A. Sachar, Dec. 1963, p. 7. For Levy quote, see Memorandum from Levy to Sachar, March 16, 1964, p. 6. For workload controversy, see Memorandum from Sacks to Sachar and Levy, June 19, 1964; author interview with Black, who was associate dean during this period and involved with the issue; a different view of the workload controversy was obtained during author interview with Klein; see also D. Alexander, 1979, "Academic Policy," 9–10.

64. For evolution of general education in 1960s, see Committee on General Education, April 1965; see also "Re-evaluation Report to the New England Association of Schools and Colleges," 1966, pp. 30ff.; D. Alexander, 1979, "Academic Policy," 8ff.; author interview with Black. For "you may turn" and "moral decision-making," see Committee on General Education, April 1965, p. 6; for "abundant offerings," see ibid., 9. For final elimination of requirements, see Alexander, 1979, "Academic Policy," 9–11.

65. For Wessell views, see N. Wessell, April 1964; N. Wessell, April 1965. For Experimental College, see Wessell, April 1964, pp. 6–7; TUAR (1966), 28; (1967), 19; (1968), 15; Wessell letter to author. For seminar, see "The Tufts Seminar to Initiate New Experiments in Undergraduate Instruction," Aug.–Sept. 1965. For Plans of Study, see R. Miller, 1986, pp. 78–79.

66. For undergraduate committee, see Ad Hoc Committee, March 1969; for "is not a multiversity," see ibid., 1. For graduate committee, see Graduate Long-Range Planning Committee, May 1969; for "we see no evidence," see ibid., 2. For a more negative view of impact of graduate programs on undergraduate education, see "Tufts: The Total University," 1973, p. 62; the difference between this document and the 1969 report undoubtedly reflected the co-existence of different perceptions and values among the Tufts faculty and the biases of different presidents in selecting members of these committees.

67. For "shibboleth," see TUAR (1965), 5. For more critical account, see "Tufts: The Total University," 1973, p. 62.

68. For percent of Harvardians on faculty, see: "Report of a Visiting Committee to Re-evaluate Tufts University," Nov. 1959, p. 11; "Profile of Brandeis University," 1962, p. 27. For example, the decision of the Brandeis faculty to shift from a five- to a four-course load for students was strongly influenced by Harvard norms; see author interview with Black.

69. For Hallowell appointment, see R. Miller, 1986, pp. 257ff. For "has both lost and gained," see TUAR (1968) 12–13. For additional expressions of Hallowell views, see Burton Hallowell, Sept. 1967; Burton Hallowell, Aug. 1969; also TUAR (1969), 14–15.

70. For financial data, see TUAR (1968), 19–21; (1970), 41; (1972), Table 4; "Tufts: The Total University," 1973, pp. 43–44, 89, 104, 146–47; TU, *Fact Book*, 1973, Sect. 8; letter from Dunn to author. For Medical School see E. Cheit, 1971, p. 3. For "we need more faculty," see TUAR (1968), 6. For "the needs of students," see TUAR (1969), 16. For "the central economic question," see ibid., 5.

71. For debates and protests, see TUAR (1968), 8–9; (1969), 7–10; (1970), 7, 21ff., 27ff. For TU involvement in social problem solving, see TUAR (1966), 13; (1968), 29; (1970), 35ff.; (1975), 17–18, 22–24; see also B. Hallowell, Aug. 1969. For new emphasis on planning, see TUAR (1969), 24–25.

72. For Abram background and appointment, see Morris B. Abram, 1982; A. Sachar, 1976, pp. 291–92. For a discussion of Abram's ideas about BrU, see Abram, 1982, pp. 170ff. For "prune the luxuriant growth," see ibid., 192. For law school, see ibid., 192; D. Alexander, 1979, "Brandeis History," 16–17, 19.

73. For Abram's early exchanges with faculty, see M. Abram, 1982, pp. 179–80; for students, see ibid., 177–78, 180–82. For general discussion of student protest activity at BrU during these years, see D. Alexander, 1979, Chaps. 6–7; A. Sachar, 1976, 294–95.

74. For blacks, Ford Hall, and TYP, see M. Abram, 1982, pp. 171–72, 182–91; D. Alexander, 1979, "Political Unrest," 8ff. For Sachar, see Abram, 1982, pp. 168–70; author interview with Sachar. For "made up of layers of administrators," see Abram, 1982, p. 193. For "a cabal," see ibid., 176.

75. For Abram departure, see M. Abram, 1982, pp. 193–94; author interview with Sachar. For "I could cope with greed," and "keeper of the peace," see Abram, 1982, p. 194.

76. For Schottland appointment, see D. Alexander, 1979, "Brandeis History," 17. For student protest activity during Schottland, see ibid., "Political Unrest," 18ff.

CHAPTER 5. TRANSFORMATION OF THE URBAN UNIVERSITY: BOSTON UNIVERSITY, BOSTON COLLEGE, AND NORTHEASTERN, 1945–1972

1. For "we kept getting ready," see BUAR (1950), 24. For "when the war is over," see NUAR (1943), 7.

2. For postwar committee, see BUAR (1944); a copy of full report is in BUA, as is an "Analysis of Responses of the Deans of Boston University to the Proposals of the Committee on the University in the Postwar World." For religion, see BUAR (1942), 8; (1945), 25; (1946), 21–24; (1949), 5–9; (1950), 14, 16–17; also author interview with Perkins. For construction program, see BUAR (1945), 14, 20–21, 24. For BU's academic ambitions, see BUAR (1941), 3; (1946), 15–16; (1950), 7–9; see also BUAR (1944), 10ff., 19, and "Responses of Deans." For service, see BUAR (1941), 6–8; (1944), 7; (1946), 17; (1950), 32ff. For "an institution of Boston University's character," see BUAR (1944), 13. For "widening its geographical sphere," see ibid., 26.

3. For link between expansion and new development, see BUAR (1944), 40; (1948), 6. For Marsh's emphasis on construction, see BUAR (1950), 6; for skepticism of postwar committee about this emphasis, see Committee on the University in the Postwar World, 1944, p. 38; the deans also seemed doubtful, as indicated in ibid., "Responses of Deans," 3. For "Boston University cannot afford," see BUAR (1944), 13.

4. For Ell background and views, see above, Chapt. 1, "The Long Pause"; also NUAR (1948), 4–5. For Ell's emphasis on professional associations, see NUAR (1954), 19; (1958), 30ff.; (1959), 19–20. For his belief in close ties to industry, see NUAR (1950), 5; (1953), 9–10. For wartime planning at NU, see NUAR (1943), 17; (1944), 6, 11–12, 24; (1946), 8–9. For emphasis on day colleges, see NUAR (1945), 6; also R. Morris, 1977, p. 134. For "we believe that the long-established," see NUAR (1948). For "Northeastern has a definite mission," see NUAR (1946), 5.

5. For "dynamic . . . developing . . . flexible," see NUAR (1946), 7. For Ell's financial policies, see NUAR (1950), 7; (1956), 32; (1959), 18; also Carl Ell, May 1956. For NU's financial record under Ell, see NUAR (1948), 10; (1950), 12. For development of alumni organization, see NUAR (1948), 12; (1950), 11–12; (1951), 16; also E. Marston, 1961, p. 132–33. For NU's general orientation toward public relations, see R. Morris, 1977, p. 122.

6. For need to maintain Special Studies during war, see JEA, Executive Committee, Minutes, Oct. 5, 1942, p. 8 and April 27, 1943, p. 9; JEA, Executive Director, May 6, 1942, p. 6 and 1943, p. 13; JEA, Executive Committee, Digest of Meetings, 1939–44, p. 6. For "it would be fatal," see JEA, Executive Committee, Minutes, Oct. 5, 1942, p. 8. For "continue and . . . increase," see JEA, Executive Director, May 6, 1942, p. 6. For AAU and Pontifical Status, see JEA, Executive Committee, Digest of Meetings, 1939–44, p. 9. For postwar planning, see JEA, Executive Committee, Minutes, Nov. 5, 1943 and Oct. 17, 1944; JEA, Executive Committee, Digest of Meetings, 1939–44, p. 3; JEA, Executive Director, 1943, p. 3 and 1944, pp. 3, 5; JEA, Special *Bulletin* #33; Wilfred M. Mallon (ed.), Aug. 1948, pp. 8ff. For "to make a blueprint," see JEA, Special *Bulletin* #33, p. 2. For general's 1947 statement, see P. Fitzgerald, 1984, pp. 74–77; private communication from Fitzgerald.

7. For assignments to Special Studies, see JEA, Executive Director, 1943, p. 13. For determination to upgrade BC, see Charles F. Donovan, June 1979, p. 11; author interview with Walsh. For "the administration of the New England Province," see Donovan, June 1979, p. 11. For arrival of special studies graduates, see ibid., 11. For Keleher and McEleney, see: D. Dunigan, 1947, p. 306; author interview with Walsh.

8. For "the upheavals wrought," see BUAR (1946), 15. For growth of BU during

veterans period, see J. Perkins, 1977, Table 26; BUAR (1944), 9–10; (1945), 28; (1946), 14; (1947), 18ff.; (1948), 6; (1950), 8; W. Ault, 1973, p. 141. For NU, see NUAR (1945), 8; (1946), 9; (1950), 9; E. Marston, 1961, p. 143; R. Morris, 1977, p. 133. For BC, see D. Dunigan, 1947, pp. 305–10; Jack Frost, 1962, pp. 118, 129; author interview with Walsh; C. S. Marsh, 1940; A. J. Brumbaugh, 1948; JEA, *Directory,* 1947–48.

9. For tuition levels, see C. Marsh, 1940; A. Brumbaugh, 1948; but note: (1) prior to 1945 the different colleges of BU charged varying tuitions, so this comparison is based on average of the 1939 rates; (2) since NU ran a five-year program, the tuition rate has been recalculated to a four-year equivalent charge for purposes of comparison. For analysis of BU's finances, see BUTR (1948); also BUAR (1948), 13; W. Ault, 1973, p. 13. For construction at BU, see Harold Case, 1957; for chapel, see BUAR (1950), 34. For BC's finances, see BCFS (1948); see also D. Dunigan, 1947, p. 312. In the case of NU, accurate financial records are not available, but Ell made no secret of the basic strategy of using operating surpluses to generate working capital; see, for example, R. Morris, 1977, p. 133. For a more general discussion of the post-World War II building boom on American campuses, see "What the Colleges and Universities Plan to Spend," *School and Society,* Oct. 24, 1946.

10. F. Rudolph, 1977, observes that development of professional programs was widespread in the late 1940s. For "Boston University wants students," see BUAR (1950), 14; also (1945), 6–7. For NU as "community-service university," see NUAR (1950), 5ff. Note that BC's relationship to Zook's democratizing goals was more ambiguous. Though BC chiefly served low-income students in these years, the Jesuit tradition included a strong orientation toward elite academic values—as subsequent changes at BC would demonstrate. Father Gannon of Fordham, a leading Jesuit educator of the postwar years, vigorously attacked the admissions/enrollment recommendations of the President's Commission on Higher Education; see G. Kennedy (ed), 1952.

11. For changes at BU, see BUAR (1950), 8; (1951), 9; (1954), 22. For NU, see NUAR (1947), 9–10; (1949), 11; (1950), 7; (1950), 18; (1951), 5–6, 13; (1951), 5–6, 8–9; (1952), 6; (1957), 23; for law school, see A. Frederick, 1982, p. 213. For BC, see D. Dunigan, 1947, p. 309; J. Frost, 1962, pp. 119, 128; Walsh interview. For Education at BC, see author interview with Walsh; C. Donovan, June 1979, p. 12.

12. For fund-raising activities at NU, see NUAR (1950), 15; (1951); (1952), 30; (1953), 30. For BC, see J. Frost, 1962, pp. 119, 137; author interview with Walsh; Boston College Building-Fund Committee, 1946. For BU, see BUAR (1950), 26–7. For Loyola Fund, see Walsh interview. For NU special fund, see author interview with Ryder. For financial policies at BU, see BUAR (1950), 26–30; (1951), 5; (1952), 5, 14–16; Committee on the University in the Postwar World, 1944, pp. 38–43. For "quarter mile of solid Gothic," see BUAR (1950), 24.

13. For BU, see BUAR (1953), 10, 20; (1959). For BC, see Otis A. Singletary, 1968; BCFS (1958); J. Frost, 1962; Walsh interview. For NU, see NUAR (1953), 13–14; (1956), 7; (1959), 17, 53–54.

14. For Maxwell background and views, see Walsh interview. For changes in faculty, see ibid.; Task Force on Higher Education (TF-4), 1965. p. 10. For program change, see Faculty of Arts and Sciences, July 28, 1955; Boston College *Bulletin,* 1951; 1958; J. Frost, 1962, p. 136; Walsh, Fitzgerald interviews. For changes in students, see Faculty of Arts and Sciences, July 28, 1955, pp. 1, 8; for "ordinary B," see ibid., 9; for "little more than ten," see ibid., Subcommittee on Curriculum, Sect. VII; see also J. Frost 1962; Walsh interview.

15. For student change, see University Planning Committee, 1959–60, Attachment, 3; J. Frost, 1962, p. 139; Walsh interview. For faculty change, see University Planning

Committee, 1960–61, p. 17; Walsh interview. Discussion of JEA policies on admissions based on records in BCA.

16. Traditionally BC graduates entered local service occupations, especially in social welfare and education. P. Schrag, 1967, reports the high percentage of teachers and school administrators who were BC alumni/ae in the 1960s. The Citizen Seminars represented an effort to reach a more influential and wealthier support group. For material on seminars, see College of Business Administration, "10 Years of Public Service, Boston Citizen Seminars, 1954–64"; School of Management, "Boston Citizen Seminars, 1954–79"; W. Whitehill, 1966, p. 164; Walsh interview. For continuing significance of philosophy and theology, see Faculty of Arts and Sciences, July 28, 1955, Curriculum Subcommittee; University Planning Committee, 1959–60, p. 8; see also A. Greeley, 1967, p. 134ff.

17. For Case appointment and views, see BUAR (1951). For Case on religion, see ibid., 15–16; H. Case, 1957, p. 15. On public service, see BUAR (1951), 6; (1953), 5, 16–17; (1954), 5; (1959), 8–12, 17. On research and teaching, see BUAR (1951), 15; (1952), 21; (1953), 7–8; (1959), 11. For long-range planning, see BUAR (1951), 18; (1952), 7–8; (1953), 18; for "all things to all people," see ibid., 11. For Cohen, see Nora Ephron, Sept. 1977, p. 138. For construction program, see BUAR (1951), 18; (1952), 9.

18. For student change, see BUAR (1950), 29; (1952), 13; (1955); (1959), 7; (1967), 3; "Long-Range Planning: A Progress Report," 1966–67, vol. 2, p. 685. For School of Medicine, see Perkins interview; John S. Perkins, Nov. 1973, pp. 24–25. Summary of program change based on review of Boston University *Catalog*.

19. For vintage Ell statements on NU, see C. Ell, May 24, 1956, esp. 16–17; NUAR (1959), 7–11. For mission statement, see NUAR (1953), 8–9; E. Marston, 1961, Chapt. 6. For Ell's evolving views on research and graduate education, see NUAR (1952), 8, 12–13, 24; (1953), 17; (1954); (1955); (1956), 40; (1957), 9; (1959), 10, 23. See also Arthur A. Vernon, June 24, 1969; C. Ell, Aug. 1, 1958; A. Frederick, 1982, pp. 184–86; R. Morris, 1977, p. 133. For "best scholars," see NUAR (1953), 31. For admissions, see NUAR (1953), 29; (1957), 45; (1959), 47; C. Ell, Oct. 13, 1955. For "seldom, if ever," see NUAR (1957), 51.

20. For BU and demographic change, see BUAR (1952), 14; (1953), 10; (1959), 16. For NU and local economy, see NUAR (1955), 15; (1956); (1957), 51; C. Ell, Oct. 13, 1955. For concern about public sector growth, see BUAR (1954), 36–37.

21. For Walsh appointment, background, and views, see Walsh interview. For "my basic message," see JEA, "The Society of Jesus and Higher Education in America," Oct. 1964, pp. 28–29.

22. For Walsh's early priorities, see Walsh interview. For additional references, see J. Frost, 1962, pp. 143–45; "Toward Greater Heights," 1961. For reference to BC's longstanding academic ambitions, see C. Donovan, June 1979, p. 11. For "Spencer Tracy," see A. Greeley, 1967, p. 58. For "the bonanza years," see Walsh interview.

23. For focus on Arts and Sciences and initiatives in admissions, see Walsh interview. For "untapped" and "free," see ibid. For scholarships, see "Ten-Year Report: 1958–68," pp. 10, 20; University Planning Committee, 1959–60, p. 23; TUAR (1967), Tables; Walsh interview. For dormitories, see "Ten-Year Report: 1958–68," p. 19; C. Donovan, June 1979, p. 14; Admissions-Housing Committee, July 1977. For data on students, see *Boston College Fact Book*, 1972, p. 70; "Self-Study of the College of Arts and Sciences," 1963–64, Reports of Committees on Intellectual Climate and Guidance; University Planning Committee, 1959–60; "Re-evaluation Material," July 1966, p. 86;

"Ten-Year Report: 1958–68," p. 8; "Brief Facts," 1964, p. 2. For "noted with great pleasure," see University Planning Committee, 1960–61, pp. 7–8. Account of JEA discussions of admissions policy based on JEA records in BCA.

24. For Walsh on faculty recruitment and characteristics, see Walsh interview; JEA, "The Society of Jesus and Higher Education," Oct. 1964, p. 27; "Ten-Year Report: 1958–68," pp. 3–4. In recruiting lay faculty, Walsh followed the advice of the JEA Board of Governors and looked for individuals likely to conform to Jesuit goals; see Walsh interview and JEA, Executive Director, May 1958, pp. 8–10. For background of BC faculty, see *Boston College Fact Book*, 1972, p. 27; C. Donovan, June 1979, p. 11. For compensation and teaching loads, see "Self-Study," 1963–64, Research Subcommittee, Recommendation, 4; JEA, Executive Committee, Digest of Meetings, 1939–44, p. 5; University Planning Committee, 1959–60, p. 31; "Ten-Year Report: 1958–68," pp. 4, 20; BU, "Long-Range Planning," 1966–67, vol. 2, p. 615; Walsh interview. For changes in faculty, see SJ, *Catalogus Provinciae, Novae Angliae, Societatis Jesu*, 1958; 1968; M. Irvin, 1960; O. Singletary; "Re-evaluation Material," July 1966; University Planning Committee, 1959–60, p. 5; and 1960–61; "Ten-Year Report: 1958–68," p. 2; "Brief Facts," 1964, p. 3; Task Force on Higher Education (TF-4), 1965, p. 10; C. Donovan, June 1979, p. 16; Walsh interview.

25. For Walsh on importance of graduate programs, see Walsh interview; JEA, "The Society of Jesus and Higher Education," Oct. 1964, pp. 26–27; also A. Greeley, 1967, p. 56. For new programs during Walsh, see "Re-evaluation Material," July 1966; University Planning Committee, 1960–61, p. 12. For Walsh on graduates going to non-Catholic graduate schools, especially Harvard, see Walsh interview. For data on destinations of graduates, see JEA, "The Society of Jesus and Higher Education," Oct. 1964, p. 55ff.; "Ten-Year Report: 1958–68," p. 9; "Brief Facts," 1964, p. 2.

26. For professional programs, see Walsh interview; University Planning Committee, 1959–60, p. 19; "Re-evaluation Material," July 1966; see also D. Riesman and C. Jencks, 1962, p. 151. For "progress has not been uniform," see University Planning Committee, 1960–61, pp. 7–8. For applicant/enrollment data, see *Boston College Fact Book*, 1972, p. 67; "Re-evaluation Material," July 1966, University Planning Committee, 1959–60, p. 1.

27. For Walsh's approach to fund-raising, see Walsh interview. For examples of development materials and plans, see "Toward Greater Heights," 1961; "Planning Your Estate," 1965. For financial achievements, see "Ten-year Report: 1958–68," pp. 18, 20; Walsh interview; J. Frost, 1962, p. 137–38.

28. A comprehensive analysis of BC's rising costs in the 1960s can be found in Committee on University Priorities, Feb. 1, 1972. Analysis of direct instructional costs based on BCFS (1958); (1968); see also comparison of reported operating costs in "Brief Facts," July 1966, (for 1958) and "Ten-year Report: 1958–68," (for 1968). For more on endowment, see ibid., 20. On research, see: ibid., 4; University Planning Committee, 1959–60, p. 7. For tuition policy, see Walsh interview; also M. Irvin, 1960; O. Singletary, 1968; University Planning Committee, 1959–60, p. 22.

29. For end of Walsh's term, see Walsh interview. For a summary of changes in his years, see "Ten-year Report: 1958–68," "Re-evaluation Material," July 1966. For NORC study, see A. Greeley, 1967. For "the university has taken its place," see "Ten-year Report: 1958–68," p. 1. For ACE rankings, see K. Roose and C. Anderson, 1970. Comparisons of sponsored research based on treasurers' reports and financial statements for each campus. For undergraduate arts and sciences see Jack Gourman, 1967–68. SAT comparisons based on data in *Boston College Fact Book*, 1972; and TU, *Fact Book*,

1973. For an additional assessment, see D. Riesman and C. Jencks, 1962, p. 131, who claim that BC, even in the early years of the Walsh administration, belonged in the "top tenth" of American colleges nationally.

30. For Greeley, see A. Greeley, 1967, p. 31. For tradition of protecting the faith versus movement toward secular academic norms see ibid., Introduction, Chapt. 9; also JEA, "The Society of Jesus and Higher Education," Oct. 1964, pp. 39ff., 47; William F. Kelley, "Commission for the Study of American Jesuit Higher Education," 1966, pp. 10, 100. For Walsh role in debate, see Fitzgerald interview. For Walsh on curriculum reform, see Walsh interview. For 1962 conference, see R. J. Henle (ed.), Aug. 1962, pp. 108ff. For curriculum reform, see "Self-Study of the College," 1963–64, reports of Executive Committee and Total Curriculum Committee; impact of these changes also discussed in "Re-evaluation Material," July 1966. For additional discussion of curriculum change in 1960s, see "Report to the Commission on Institutions of Higher Education," Feb. 1976, p. 24.

31. For trend toward secularization under Walsh, see "The Jesuits at Boston College," Jan. 21, 1974; "Self-Study of the College," 1963–64, reports of Committee on Intellectual Climate and Committee on Research as well as Executive Committee; C. Donovan, June 1979, p. 11; University Planning Committee, 1960–61, pp. 8ff.; Walsh interview. Note also that the development materials produced by BC during the Walsh years are striking for their lack of reference to Catholic themes. For a scholarly comment on this pattern, see A. Greeley, 1967, pp. 67, 106ff. For Butterfield, see letter to Mahoney, Sept. 14, 1964, privately obtained. For "implicit derogation," see C. Donovan, June 1979, pp. 11, 14. For "had yet to devise," see Greeley, 1967, pp. 69–70. For Walsh's return to Catholic concerns, see Walsh interview; also his comments in JEA, "The Society of Jesus and Higher Education," Oct. 1964. For "religious functions of our colleges," see ibid., 22. For "it seems to me," see ibid., 28. For centennial colloquium, see Francis J. Sweeney, 1966.

32. For Knowles background/appointment, see A. Frederick, 1982, Chapt. 2. For Knowles view of NU, see E. Marston, 1961, p. 176; NUAR (1960), 6–7, 13–26. For Knowles on higher education generally, see Asa S. Knowles, Oct. 1957, pp. 329ff.; Asa S. Knowles, Jan. 1960, pp. 37ff.

33. For planning committees, see A. Frederick, 1982, p. 96; NUAR (1960), 13–14. For University College and Lincoln Institute, see Frederick, 1982, Chapts. 6, 8; NUAR (1960), 15. For outreach to business, see ibid., 24; NUAR (1963), 3. For adult and continuing education generally, see Frederick, 1982, Chapt. 11.

34. For Planning Office, see A. Frederick, 1982, p. 39; Thompson interview. For new colleges and programs, see Frederick, 1982, Chapts. 7, 12; NUAR (1960), 16; (1961); (1962); (1964), 17; a ten-year summary of new programs can be found in NUAR (1966). For graduate programs, see Frederick, 1982, Chapt. 9; NUAR (1960), 16; (1965), 35; (1969), 4. For statistics on enrollment growth, see NUARs. For claim to be largest, see NUAR (1967), 5. For a critical view of NU's growth, see R. Morris, 1977, pp. 55–56.

35. For Knowles interest in higher status, see NUAR (1965), 7–8; A. Frederick, 1982, pp. 22, 37. For "head table," see ibid., 45. For sense of NU in competitive context, see NUAR (1964), 3, 5; Frederick, 1982, p. 96; Frederick interview. For co-op, see Frederick, 1982, Chapt. 14; NUAR (1960), 30; (1964). For orientation toward business community, see Asa S. Knowles, July 1961, pp. 179ff.; for an illustrative example, see NUAR (1962), 12. For Knowles's attitude toward liberal arts, see communication from Frederick; Frederick, 1982, pp. 142–43; note also comments of accreditation team cited in "The Institutional Self-Study Report," Fall 1978, pp. 111, 116ff. For view that

NU was becoming too conventional under Knowles, see R. Morris, 1977, pp. 39–40, 55–56.

36. For Knowles on need to balance distinctive qualities with academic conventions, see NUAR (1965). For Knowles on graduate development, see NUAR (1964), 15; (1965), 11. On research, see NUAR (1960), 19–20; (1961), 16; (1962), 18, 36; (1964), 30; (1969), 3; also Frederick interview. Statistics on sponsored research from O. Singletary, 1968. For changes in student life, see A. Frederick, 1982, pp. 55–60; 351–52; NUAR (1969), 4. For Knowles on admissions, see NUAR (1960), 14, 19; (1961), 17; (1965), 29; (1966), 17; (1969), 4. For geographic distribution, see NUAR (1963); (1968). For dormitories, see Frederick, 1982, pp. 526–27. For SATs, see Singletary, 1968. For national evaluation, see J. Gourman, 1967–68.

37. For financial role of part-time programs, see NUAR (1968), 50. For fund-raising, including DADP, see NUAR (1960), 28; (1962), 32; (1963); NUAR (1971) contains a general summary of growth in alumni giving; A. Frederick, 1982, pp. 41, 60ff., 532; Planning Office, Nov. 15, 1976, IV-3–5. For growth of revenues from current operations, see Kenneth Ryder, March 18, 1969; "The Institutional Self-Study Report," Fall 1978, p. 70. For expansion of assets and facilities, see NUAR (1963), 32; (1969), 5; Planning Office, 1976. For statistics on financial growth in all categories, see M. Irvin, 1960; T. Furniss, 1973. For "rolling in money," see Knowles interview.

38. Calculations of student-faculty ratios from data in T. Furniss, 1973; see also R. Morris, 1977, pp. 71, 76; E. Marston, 1961, p. 159. For teaching loads, see A. Frederick, 1982, p. 219. For salaries, see AAUP *Bulletin* (Summer 1968); also Frederick, 1982, p. 387. For DAPD summary results, see NUAR (1974), 43; see also NUAR (1969), 5, for facilities; Frederick, 1982, p. 532 for endowment.

39. For "triple service role," see NUAR (1965), 6. For "the blooming," see R. Morris, 1977, p. 167ff. For legislative commission, see Knowles interview.

40. For physical development in 1960s, see BUAR (1967), 2–5, 12: Lawrence E. Steadman, unpublished DBA thesis, 1976, pp. 162–63. For financial analysis, see John S. Perkins, Sept. 10, 1970. Tuition and enrollment information from M. Irvin, 1960; O. Singletary, 1968; BUARs.

41. Case's own summary of change can be found in BUAR (1967). For announcement of planning exercise see BUAR (1966), 3–8. Actual report contained in, "Long-Range Planning," 1966–67; the consultants were Frederick Bolman and Miguel de Capriles—see "Consultant's Report on Institutional Planning and Development," 1966. For changes in students, see "Long-Range Planning," 1966–67, vol. 2, pp. 685–86; BUAR (1966); (1967), 2–3, 8; "Consultants' Report," 1966, p. 33; BU, *Fact Book,* 1962–63. For undergraduate curriculum change, see "Long-Range Planning," 1966–67, vol. 1, pp. 48, 52. For shift toward graduate, see BUAR (1966), 5; (1967), 10ff.

42. For data on size and distribution of BU faculty, see A. Brumbaugh, 1948; O. Singletary, 1968. For "growing prestige," see BUAR (1967), 7. For growth of research, see ibid., 5, 7; J. Perkins, Sept. 10, 1970, Sect. 10. For religion, see "Long-Range Planning," 1966–67, vol. 1, p. 120; "Consultants' Report," 1966, pp. 48ff. For "already done much" and "outstanding, modern, private," see ibid., 1, 6.

43. For salaries, see "Long-Range Planning," 1966–67, vol. 2, pp. 474ff., 587, 615–18; "Consultants' Report," 1966, pp. 14–15; L. Steadman, 1976, p. 164. For a review of other weaknesses, see ibid., pp. 164–65. For record on scholarships and research funds, see "Long-Range Planning," 1966–67, vol. 2, pp. 86, 100. Analysis of DIR, endowment based on data in J. Perkins, Sept. 10, 1970. For reputation, see "An Assessment of Boston University," 1967; for undergraduate evaluation, see J. Gourman, 1967–68; for ACE, see K. Roose and C. Anderson, 1970.

44. Comparisons of enrollment and faculty growth with BC and NU based on data in M. Irvin, 1960; O. Singletary, 1968; presidents' annual reports. For an analysis of BU's financial policies in 1960s, see John R. Silber, Dec. 1982. For "in a sense," see "Consultants' Report," 1966, p. 29.

45. For key recommendations, see "Long-Range Planning," 1966–67, vol. 1, pp. 115ff.; see also ibid., pp. ix, 5, 41. For consultants, see "Consultants' Report," 1966, pp. 1–2, 7–8, 16. For Massachusetts context, see ibid., pp. 2–4; "Long-Range Planning," 1966–67, vol. 1, pp. 4, 7, 25ff.

46. For a statement of BU's dilemma, see "Long-Range Planning," 1966–67, vol. 2, pp. 92ff.; see also ibid., vol. 1, p. iv; and "Consultants' Report," 1966, pp. 27ff. For costs rising faster than income, see "Long-Range Planning," 1966–67, vol 1, p. v; John S. Perkins, Dec. 1977, p. 61. For search for alternative sources of money, see "Long-Range Planning," 1966–67, vol. 2, pp. 471ff., 535ff.; "Consultants' Report," 1966, pp. 10, 27–28. For "the only way," see "Long-Range Planning," 1966–67, vol. 2, p. 478.

47. For projections of continued growth, see "Long-Range Planning," 1966–67, vol. 1, pp. 60, 113–15; ibid., vol. 2, pp. 249ff.; see also ibid., vol. 1, pp. 3–5. For general optimism about future, see L. Steadman, 1976, p. 157. On need for new leadership, see Perkins interview. For Christ-Janer appointment, see ibid.; interview with Farrago; N. Ephron, Sept. 1977, p. 138.

48. The traditional organization of BU is described in Faculty Manual, 1950, pts. I, II. Marsh also makes frequent references to organization in his annual reports; for example, see BUAR (1930). For evolution of NU organization, see E. Marston, 1961, pp. 60–62, 161–64; A. Frederick, 1982, pp. 466ff.; NUAR (1942), 13; (1956), 38.

49. On organizational traditions at BC, see P. Fitzgerald, 1984, Chaps. 1–4; A. Greeley, 1967, pp. 7–8, Chapt. 8; Walsh, Fitzgerald interviews; C. Donovan, June 1979, pp. 12, 15–16; JEA, Executive Director, May 1940. For "obedience, discipline, loyalty," see Greeley, 1967, p. 8. For Gannon, see Walsh interview.

50. For BU, see BUAR (1930); (1942), 15; (1944), 7; (1946), 25; (1950), 6, 18ff.; see also Faculty Manual, 1950. For NU, see NUAR (1941), 13; (1945), 3; (1950), 8; R. Morris, 1977, Chapts. 2, 3, 6; Thompson interview. For BC, see Walsh interview; Faculty of Arts and Sciences, July 1955, Report of Subcommittee on Faculty, 4.

51. On need for stronger coordination, see BUAR (1942), 15–17; (1944), 17ff.; (1945), 7ff.; (1950), 6, 17–19. For new Senate, see BUAR (1946), 20–21. Symptomatic of new activism were revised policies on salaries and personnel; see BUAR (1945), 16; (1947), 13ff.

52. Evolution of faculty role based on successive editions of BU Faculty Manual: 1950, 1952, 1957, 1962, 1967; see also BUAR (1966), 6; "Long-Range Planning," 1966–67, vol. 1, 67ff.; ibid., vol. 2, Chapt. 7.

53. For postwar committee, see BUAR (1944), 17; Committee on the University in the Postwar World, 1944, sect. on "Simplification of University's Organizational Structure." For evolution under Case, see BUAR (1953), 15–16; (1954), 6; (1959), 17; (1967), 5ff.; "Consultants' Report," 1966, pp. 8–11, 20ff.; "Long-Range Planning," 1966–67, vol. 1, pp. 36, 75, 94–97, 104–11; ibid., vol. 2, Chapt. 10, p. 511; L. Steadman, 1976, 163ff.; W. Ault, 1973, p. 153.

54. For postwar faculty pressures, see R. Morris, 1977, Chapt. 14. For Ell's efforts to accommodate new pressures, see NUAR (1946), 14; (1950), 7–10; (1956), 43; (1959), 24; C. Ell, May 24, 1956, p. 14; C. Ell, May 12, 1947. For administrative evolution under Ell, see NUAR (1950), 11–12, 14; (1953); (1956), 26; (1958); (1959), 26; C. Ell, Oct. 13, 1955; Morris, 1977, pp. 72–73; E. Marston, 1961, pp. 43–49. For con-

tinuity in top leadership, see ibid., 154, 165, Appendix B; NUAR (1959), 69. For "I doubt if any other," see ibid., 13.

55. For Knowles's early changes, see NUAR (1960), 6, 13, 17–18, 20; (1961), 20; E. Marston, 1961, pp. 59–60, 121, 178–79; A. Knowles, July 1959; see also Faculty Handbook, 1960–61. For organizational evolution under Knowles, see subsequent editions of Faculty Handbook: 1961–62, 1965–66, 1966–67, 1970–71, 1974; NUAR (1966), 19–20, 58–59; (1967), 17; A. Frederick, 1982, Chapts., 18, 19, 20; Frederick interview; "Data Prepared for the New England Association," Spring 1967, pt. I.

56. For growth of faculty, see data in NUAR (1959), 25; (1969), 4; T. Furniss, 1973; see also A. Frederick, 1982, p. 486. For growing assertiveness of faculty, see Frederick, 1982, Chapt. 18; Frederick interview. For role of faculty in selecting administrators, see Asa S. Knowles, Feb. 10, 1966.

57. For "dissatisfaction" and "greater participation," see Faculty of Arts and Sciences, July 28, 1955, Subcommittee on Faculty, 18, 20. For balance between clerical and lay, see Walsh interview. For emphasis on accreditation, see Faculty of Arts and Sciences, July 28, 1955, Subcommittee on Curriculum, 1; Fitzgerald interview.

58. For laicization and curriculum revision and governance changes, see Walsh interview. For Walsh control of Executive Committee of 1953 self-study, see "Self-Study of the College," 1963–64, "Introduction" to Executive Committee Report. For continuing control of chair appointments, see University Planning Committee, 1960–61, p. 11.

59. For demands for stronger faculty role, see "Self-Study of the College," 1963–64, Executive Committee, 10, 16, 23 and Intellectual Climate Committee, 2. For difficulty of balancing campus and order governance pressures, see Walsh interview; University Planning Committee, 1960–61. For need to escape order control, see Walsh interview; see also A. Greeley, 1967, pp. 6, 9 on the conflict between order control and academic development. For Woodstock discussions, see JEA, "The Society of Jesus and Higher Education," Oct. 1964, p. 35, Chapt. 6. For 31st General Congregation, see Walsh interview; William F. Kelley, "Commission," 1966, was a background piece for the General Congregation prepared under Reinert's presidency.

60. For movement to separate incorporation in New England, see Task Force on Higher Education (TF-4), 1965. For tensions fostered by this movement at BC, see Walsh, Powers interviews. For implementation of separate incorporation at BC, see Walsh interview; files of Father Seavey Joyce, including a Memo to Joyce (father rector) from the Committee on Trustees on stationery of the Financial VP and Treasurer, with handwritten annotations, undated; "Triennial Report for St. Mary's Community," 1971–73.

61. For Case on Metrocenter, see BUAR (1966), 8–9; (1967), 13. For "it should be emphasized," see BUAR (1966), 9. For Bolman-de Capriles, see "Consultants' Report," 1966, pp. 43–46. For self-study, see "Long-Range Planning," 1966–67, vol. 1, pp. 25ff., 107; quotes are on 25, 27.

62. For UPC, see University Planning Committee, 1958–59, pp. 19, 25. For shift in Walsh's priorities and Social Work and Human Sciences, see Walsh interview and letter to author; "Toward Greater Heights," 1961. For BC's withdrawal from Boston and Mellon visit, see Walsh interview; also Committee on University Priorities, Feb. 1972, pp. 17, 23.

63. For Carnegie study, see Dan Waldorf, 1973. Waldorf reviews a range of community service projects. For additional discussion of NU's responses to local urban conditions, see A. Frederick, 1982, Chapts. 15, 17. For minority enrollments, see ibid., 405.

64. For Knowles quote, see D. Waldorf, 1973, p. 94. For "a private university," see title to ibid.

65. For Joyce appointment and views, see Walsh interview; "The University and the City of Man," 1969. For "the outstanding Catholic university," see *Bridge,* "Father Joyce, Where Do You Go From Here?" Feb. 1972, pp. 3–4. For Joyce views on separate incorporation, see Walsh interview. For "a sense of class," see *Bridge,* "Father Joyce, Where?" Feb. 1972.

66. A sense of Joyce's early difficulties can be gleaned from his memos to the BC community on file in BCA; for commentary on this period, see *Boston Globe,* "Father Joyce Steps Down," editorial, Feb. 28, 1972; Walsh interview. For weakness of BC's administrative apparatus, see ibid.; Committee on University Priorities, Feb. 1972, p. 20; communication from Doyle; in letter to author, Father C. Donovan states that this paragraph gives too little credit to BC's Jesuit administrators. For evolution of governance under Joyce, see interviews with Walsh, Donovan; "University and City of Man," 1969, p. 3; André Daniere, undated response to 1972 report of Priorities Committee, p. 10.

67. For data on BC finances, see *Boston College Fact Book,* 1972; Committee on University Priorities, Feb. 1972, p. 12ff. For Walsh financial legacy, see Walsh interview; "Ten-Year Report: 1958–68," pp. 20, 22; Committee on University Priorities, Feb. 1972, pp. 12ff. For deficits see ibid., 12. For fund-raising under Joyce, see "University and City of Man," 1969; Committee on University Priorities, Feb. 1972, p. 20; Walsh interview. For enrollments, tuition, and housing crisis, see ibid.; "University and City of Man," 1969, p. 14; Committee on University Priorities, Feb. 1972, p. 8.

68. For 1970 strike, see Committee on University Priorities, Feb. 1972, p. 4, "Testament"; Walsh interview. For "genuine terror" and "mob," see *Bridge,* "Father Joyce, Where?" Feb. 1972, p. 4. For removal as rector, see *Boston Globe,* "Father Joyce Steps Down," editorial, Feb. 28, 1972; Committee on Trustees, undated. For committee, see Committee on University Priorities, Feb. 1972. For resignation, see *Bridge,* "The President Resigns" and "Father Joyce, Where?" Feb. 1972; see also *Boston Globe,* "Father Joyce Steps Down," Feb. 28, 1972; Walsh interview.

69. For Christ-Janer's early positions, see BUAR (1968). For long-range planning, see L. Steadman, 1976, p. 203. For perceptions of Christ-Janer's presidency and resignation, see N. Ephron, 1977, p. 138; Perkins interview.

70. For Perkins quote, see J. Perkins, Sept. 10, 1970, Sects. 1 and 9. For "had reached a crossroads" and "their task went well beyond," see Edward Kern, June 4, 1971, pp. 55, 57. For "appeared ready to take off," see ibid., 57.

71. For search process, Lee appointment, and Silber appearance, see E. Kern, June 4, 1971; N. Ephron, 1977, pp. 136, 138. Newspaper and magazine stories on Silber— his background, character, ideas—are endless. For an early appraisal, see Deckle McLean, March 5, 1972.

72. For "Dr. Lee will take us," see E. Kern, 1971. For Lee's priorities, see interview in *The Daily Free Press,* vol. 3, no. 7, Jan. 26, 1971. For *Life* quote, see Kern, 1971. For trustees' view of significance of Silber choice, see L. Steadman, 1976, p. 173.

73. For atmosphere and condition of NU in late 1960s and early 1970s, see Knowles, Frederick interviews; also A. Frederick, 1982. For enrollments, see NUAR (1972), 3–4; (1974); see also Frederick, 1982, p. 365. For redistribution of enrollments to new fields, see NUAR (1972), 4; see also NUAR (1971), 3; Frederick, 1982, p. 105.

74. My account of protest activity is based on A. Frederick, 1982, Chapt. 17; see also R. Morris, 1977, Chapt. 15; NUAR (1967), 7; (1968), 3; (1969), 6ff., 22; (1970), 3; D. Waldorf, 1973, p. 92. On Knowles's reactions to faculty and student claims for power,

see Frederick, 1982, Chapts. 17, 18, 20; see also Asa S. Knowles, "Higher Education Responds to Campus Unrest," undated address ca. 1970. For "when faculty and students," see NUAR (1973), 9.

75. For Knowles's revised assessment, see NUAR (1970), 14; see also NUAR (1971), 3. For tenure issue, see A. Frederick, 1982, pp. 451–52, 551; NUAR (1973), 8. For "by the Fall of 1972," see Frederick, 1982, p. 453. For resignation discussions, see ibid., 549.

CHAPTER 6. FROM STATE COLLEGE TO UNIVERSITY SYSTEM: THE UNIVERSITY OF MASSACHUSETTS, 1945–1973

1. For Baker's wartime advocacy, see MSCAR (1940); (1941); (1942); (1943); (1944), 17; (1945), 8, 19; (1946), 16–18. For "if there ever has been," see MSCAR (1943), 17. For wartime planning efforts, see MSCAR (1941), 15; (1943); (1944), 14–15, 22. For plans for future development, see MSCAR (1942), 6; (1944), 7, 15, 21–22; (1945), 8–10, 22–24; (1946), 22–23.

2. For Baker's anticipation of veterans, see MSCAR (1943), 17; (1944), 24–25; (1945), 2–3, 5. For "it will be tragic," see MSCAR (1943), 17. For 1944 report, see W. Cary, 1962, p. 168. For "unusually aggressive," see MSCAR (1945), 21. For "the college will be forced," see ibid., 7–8.

3. For Devens background and plan, see W. Cary, 1962, pp. 168ff.; MSCAR (1945); (1946); F. Troy, 1982, p. 3; Mather oral history interview, 7. For enrollments at Devens and Tobin's hopes, see Cary, 1962, p. 170. It should be noted that the creation of two-year feeder facilities was not unique to Massachusetts; a network of two-year facilities was created in Wisconsin.

4. For Baker's discouragement, see MSCAR (1946), 23ff. For "so little" and "fine promise," see ibid., 26. For his successor on Baker's decision to retire, see MSCAR (1947), 2.

5. For establishment of Mahar commission, see MGC, Staff of the Special Commission, 1962–65, p. 3; see also W. Cary, 1962, p. 173. For pro-UMass bills, see ibid., 172ff. For commission report, see MGC, Special Commission, April 1, 1948.

6. For increased postwar support, see: MSCAR (1946), 4. UMAR (1947), 4; (1948), 5ff.; (1952), 2; see also W. Cary, 1962, pp. 168–69, 190. For financial data, see MSCTR (1940); UMTR (1948); UMAR (1958), 4. For trustees' expansion plans, see UMAR (1947), 2. Comparison of Massachusetts to nation based on data from UMARs and American Council on Education, 1962. For comparison with New England, see UMAR (1949), 10–11; (1950), 11. For continuing enrollment pressures, see UMAR (1952), 2. For lobbying by veterans, see private communication from Troy.

7. For Van Meter appointment and background, see W. Cary, 1962, p. 175. For sense of new possibilities, see UMAR (1947), esp. 2, 5; (1948), 14. For inaugural, see Cary, 1962, p. 178.

8. For Van Meter's illness, see UMAR (1953), 3. For summary of program changes under Van Meter, see UMAR (1951), 6–15; see also (1947), 4, 12; (1948), 12; (1949), 10; W. Cary, 1962, pp. 178ff. For numerical growth, see UMARs for each year. For shift toward arts and sciences, see UMAR (1947), 7; also Cary, 1962, p. 177; F. Troy, 1982. For women, see UMAR (1950), 8. For treasurer and provost, see Cary, 1962, 176ff. Comparison of UMass with "typical" state university based on H. K. Allen, 1952, p. 10; see also UMAR (1949), 11; (1951), 10. For "starved to death," see Kenneth W. Johnson oral history interview, 3. For failure of state to support extracurricular programs or

research, see Kenneth W. Johnson, Dec. 31, 1973, p. 2. For failure to create Arts and Sciences, see Mather oral history interview, 3; see also UMAR (1947), 12; (1951), 2; (1953), 6. Note also that in 1950 the Schools of Liberal Arts, Science, and Engineering were all headed by full-time teachers since dean's positions were not yet available—see UMAR (1950), 6–7.

9. For campus conservatism on growth, see W. Cary, 1962, pp. 186–87; Mather oral history interview, 12; MSCR, Report of Dean (1944), 35. For Van Meter's approach to development, see Cary, 1962, 186–89; UMAR (1948), 13–14; (1949), 11–12. For "we are a small university," see UMAR (1948), 14. Comparison with BU and NU based on data in annual reports for all three.

10. For governor's attitude toward public higher education, see Mather oral history interview, 23. For private-sector opposition to Medical School, see Newman Commission on Political Intrusion in Higher Education, "University of Massachusetts Medical School at Worcester." For financial structure, see K. Johnson, 1973. For proposed Boston campus, see UMAR (1949), 12; (1950), 12; W. Cary, 1962, p. 173.

11. For Mather background, appointment, and perspective, see Mather oral history interview, 1–3, 23–24; Johnson oral history interview, 5–6, 10, 15; Marcus interview. For "small, comfy, cozy," see Mather oral history interview, 12. For "just rocked along," see ibid., 11. For "go for broke," see ibid., 19.

12. For Mather on "tidal wave" and planning for growth, see Mather oral history interview, 5ff., 7, 12, 39–40; W. Cary, 1962, pp. 189–91; UMAR (1953), 3–5; (1954), 5; (1955), 3; Johnson oral history, 11–13. For trustee support, see UMAR (1953), 19; Mather oral history interview, 11–12. For "I decided I will become," see ibid., 15. For approaches to press and governor, see ibid., 15ff. For "care for their own" and "the people of Massachusetts," see UMAR (1953), 4, 19.

13. A summary of administrative controls exercised by state agencies in the early 1950s can be found in MGC, Special Commission, Jan. 24, 1962, pp. 20–32. For more on personnel controls, see Mather oral history interview, 8–9; Johnson oral history interview, 5. For Baker, see MSCAR (1939), 9; (1941), 12–13. For Van Meter, see UMAR (1947), 6; (1948), 13; (1949). Link to Van Meter's illness in Johnson oral history interview, 8. For a general review of government control of public universities, see Committee on Government and Higher Education, 1959; Malcolm Moos and Francis E. Rourke, 1959; Lyman Glenny, 1959. For Massachusetts' standing within national pattern, see Moos and Rourke, 1959, pp. 8–9, Chapts. 4,5.

14. For "the idea was," see Johnson oral history interview, 8–9. For Mather on need for autonomy, see UMAR (1957), 11–15. For "anyone who read the name," see Mather oral history interview, 8.

15. For political, public changes that helped Mather, see Mather oral history interview, 42; private communication from Troy; Alec T. Barbrook, 1973, p. 92. For successes of early years, see UMAR (1954), 3; (1955), 2–3; (1956), 3–5; (1957), 3; Mather oral history interview, 24–26; Johnson oral history interview. For "the need for," see UMAR (1954), 3. For decision to halt dormitory construction, see Mather oral history interview, 3, 25–26.

16. For launching of "Freedom Bill" campaign, see Mather oral history interview, 27–36; Johnson oral history interview, 10; W. Cary, 1962, pp. 194ff; see also MGC, Special Commission, Jan. 24, 1962, pp. 21–23. For "the most significant single," see UMAR (1955), 3.

17. For political complexities of campaign, see Mather oral history interview, 20–21, 32–34; Johnson oral history interview, 10; Ian Menzies, in *Boston Globe*, "He Put UMass on the Map," Dec. 4, 1984. For "cufflink" episode and two versions of famous

quote, see Mather oral history interview 31; Richard Stafford and Larry Lustberg, Fall 1978, p. 15. For conclusion of "Freedom Bill" campaign, see Mather oral history interview, 27ff.; John W. Lederle oral history interview, 17; UMAR (1956), 4–5; W. Cary, 1962, p. 195; I. Menzies in *Boston Globe*, Dec. 4, 1984.

18. For UM growth 1953–58, see K. Johnson, 1973; UMAR (1958), 4–6; Long-Range Academic Planning Committee, June 5, 1962, pp. 24–25. Comparisons with other states based on data in American Council on Education, 1962; 1974 (enrollments and state expenditures); Roger Freeman, 1965, p. 127 (state appropriations); J. Corson, 1975, p. 5 (enrollments). For 1958 trustee decision, see UMAR (1958), 6–7. For apathy and private opposition, see UMAR (1957), 8–9, 11–15; (1958), 10–18. For impact of Mather personality on politics and "dead right" quote, see R. Stafford and L. Lustberg, Fall 1978, p. 15; also Walsh interview. For salary bill, and resignation, see Mather oral history interview, 37–39, 43; W. Cary, 1962, p. 196; Marcus, Walsh interviews. For political fallout from resignation, see Troy interview.

19. For Massachusetts politics and economy in mid-1950s, see A. Barbrook, 1973, pp. 65–66, 81, 98–100; Mather oral history interview, 14. For attitudes of privates, see ibid., 42; MGC, Special Commission, March 26, 1958, pp. 29–30.

20. For Furcolo's efforts to promote public higher education, see A. Barbrook, 1973, pp. 105–6; MGC, Special Commission, June 1965, p. 103. For audit of state needs, see MGC, Special Commission, March 26, 1958. For "crisis in higher education," see ibid., 7. For earlier commission reports, see, for example, MGC, Report on the Massachusetts State Teachers Colleges, Oct. 1954, summary attached to MGC, Staff of the Special Commission, 1962–1965. For Furcolo's political problems, see A. Barbrook, 1973, pp. 103–6, 131; Murray B. Levin and George Blackwood, 1962, pp. 58–68, 98, 200.

21. This account of Massachusetts politics in the 1950s is based on A. Barbrook, 1973; M. Levin and G. Blackwood, 1962; D. Lockard, 1959; Edgar Litt, 1965. For membership in General Court by party, see MGC, *Manual for the Use of the General Court* for 1950s. For D. Riesman and C. Jencks, see 1962, p. 135.

22. For program change under Mather, see UMAR (1953); (1954); (1955); (1956); (1957); W. Cary, 1962, pp. 179–88; Mather and Johnson oral history interviews. A good summary of change patterns can be found in Faculty Senate Long-Range Planning Committee, Sept. 1970, p. 5ff. For emphasis on research/graduate, see UMAR (1953), 16, 18; (1954), 6; (1957), 3, 16–17; (1958), 9; UMR, Dean of Arts and Sciences (1957), 1–3; Long-Range Academic Planning Committee, June 5, 1962, pp. 30, 34; Faculty Senate Long-Range Planning Committee, Sept. 1970, p. 8; Mather oral history interview, 38. For emphasis on academic culture, see ibid.; Percheron story is on 28. For Mather on academic standards, see UMAR (1957), 10; (1958), 10–11.

23. For rising selectivity, see UMAR (1956); (1957), 8–11, 15–16; UMR, Registrar (1957), 2–3; (1963), 2. For Mather's perspective, see private communication from Troy.

24. D. Riesman and C. Jencks, 1962. For "up to the present," see ibid., 146. One indication of tension among competing models was the statement of the dean of Arts and Sciences that "the movement toward the large lecture pattern is proceeding rapidly" but "there remain areas of resistance"; see UMR, Dean of Arts and Sciences (1959), 8.

25. For enrollment growth, see K. Johnson, 1973 (total university); Faculty Senate Long-Range Planning Committee, Sept. 1970, p. 8 (UM/A); UMAR (1970), 7 (UM/B). For financial growth, see ibid., 8; K. Johnson, 1973; R. Stafford and L. Lustberg, Fall 1978. For Medical School, see UMAR (1969), 7. For salaries, see UMAR (1970) (total

university); BU, Long-Range Planning, 1967, vol. 2, 615 (UM/B); Lederle oral history interview, 23.

26. For data on all public higher education, see MGC, Special Commission, June 1965, pp. 92–97; R. Stafford and L. Lustberg, Fall 1978, p. 7. For growth in financial support, see ibid., Table 8; CM, Executive Office of Educational Affairs, 1980; MGC, Special Commission, June 1965, p. 117. Comparisons with national trends based on data in American Council on Education, 1974, Table 74.107. For salaries, see Lederle oral history interview, 21; MGC, Special Commission, June 1965, p. 542.

27. For awareness of demographic pressures, see MGC, Special Commission, June 1965, pp. 112, 114, 379, 405–7, Appendix 5–10 on 467. For Catholic attitudes, see S. Thernstrom, 1973, pp. 174–75; "Tuition Policy for the University of Massachusetts," p. 3; Lederle oral history interview, 51; J. Whitaker, Dec. 1985. For Walsh attitude, see interview; R. Stafford and L. Lustberg, Fall 1978, note that the growth of public higher education did not reflect reduced numbers of state residents in private schools but rather increased numbers attending college. According to Lederle, even though some alumni politicians, like David Bartley, were major allies of UM in the 1960s, the alumni/ ae in general were not a major source of support for expansion as they tended to cling to the old state college ideal; see Lederle oral history interview, 103.

28. For a review of social and economic trends in relation to educational needs, see MGC, Special Commission, June 1965, Chapt 3; see also the commission's interim report, issued Dec. 1964 and attached as an appendix to the final report, 528–29. For general changes in political environment, see John K. White, 1983, esp. 43–44.

29. For Menzies/Forman, see Ian Menzies and Ian Forman, Sept. 1961. For changed legislative environment, see R. Stafford and L. Lustberg, Fall 1978, pp. 14– 18. For Willis-Harrington, see MGC, Special Commission, June 1965.

30. This account of Massachusetts politics in the 1960s is based on E. Litt, 1965; J. White, 1983; M. Levin and G. Blackwood, 1962; A. Barbrook, 1973; see also Lederle oral history interview, 12, 17, 80, 95, 132, 138; R. Stafford and L. Lustberg, Fall 1978, pp. 10–11; W. Cary, 1962, pp. 201–2. In a letter to Kevin Harrington dated Oct. 15, 1968, former UM/B Chancellor Ryan stated that the Boston campus had been starved by Volpe but saved by the legislature—copy privately obtained.

31. For Lederle appointment, background, and orientation, see W. Cary, 1962, pp. 196–97; Lederle oral history interview, 2–3; Lederle interview; UMAR (1960), 3; UMAR (1961), 1. For Lederle's emphasis on legislative and public relations, see interviews with Lederle, Marcus; private communication from Troy; Mather oral history interview, 39; UMAR (1964), 2; (1970). For examples of public-relations documents, see Office of the President, "Let's Face the Problem," 1960; UMAR (1961); (1968).

32. For Lederle's views on importance of fiscal autonomy, see Lederle oral history interview, 1–6, 9; F. Troy, 1982, p. 3; see also Lederle's paper on state relations with public universities included as Appendix A to M. Moos and F. Rourke, 1959. For campaign for fiscal autonomy, see Lederle oral history interview, 10ff.; W. Cary, 1962, pp. 201ff.; UMAR (1970), 2–3; Walsh interview. Note that Leo Redfern, Lederle's assistant and legislative liaison on this matter, had written his doctoral thesis at Harvard in 1957 on "State Budgets and State Universities in New England," which was cited by Moos and Rourke, 1959, p. 54. For commission report, see MGC, Special Commission, Jan. 24, 1962; see also MGC, Legislative Research Council, May 9, 1962. For significance of autonomy, see UMAR (1963), 6, 9; (1969), 19; (1970), 7. For "with the university's new birth," see UMAR (1963), 6.

33. For Lederle's commitment to public service/land grant ideal, see UMAR (1960); (1961); (1963), 10; (1970), 6; Marcus, Troy interviews. For desire to raise status/pro-

mote research and graduate education, see Lederle oral history interview, 29–30, 34, 61; Lederle interview; UMAR (1960), 7; (1961), 1; (1963), 5–6; W. Cary, 1962, pp. 197–98. For commitment to growth, see Lederle oral history interview, 76, 97.

34. For inaugural, see UMAR (1960). For "we have the demand," see ibid., 4–5; for additional statements of tension between size and quality, see UMAR (1961), 3–5. For understanding of legislature's primary interest in undergraduate education and growth, see Lederle oral history interview, 28–29, 40.

35. For a review of planning activities during 1960s, see Faculty Senate Long-Range Planning Committee, Sept. 1970, pp. 15ff. For successive iterations, see Long-Range Academic Planning Committee, June 5, 1962; Office of Dean of Administration, July 18, 1966; "Preliminary Master Plan," Feb. 1969, Chapts I–IV; Faculty Senate Long-Range Planning Committee, Sept. 1970. For continuing education, living/learning, black students, UMass Press, Phi Beta Kappa, five-college cooperation, and football, see UMAR (1964), 4; (1965), 7; (1969), 5; (1970), 3; Lederle oral history interview, 95, 100, 110ff.; Lederle interview.

36. For increasing selectivity/rising standards, see data on applications and acceptances, board scores, and high school rank of entering students in UMAR, Registrar (1963); (1968); see also "Accreditation Self-Study," 1978; UMAR (1967), 15. For "the quiet revolution," see UMAR (1963), 6–7.

37. For statistics on student income levels, see President's Committee on the Future, Dec. 1971, pp. 21–28; MBHE, 1969, pp. 10, 32–35. For declining yield rates, see UMAR, Registrar (1968), 3. For "cannot adopt," see Faculty Senate Long-Range Planning Committee, Sept. 1970, pp. 4–5; for recommendation that socio-economic status be taken into account in admissions, see committee's "Summary," ibid., 5–6. For Lederle on tuition, see Lederle interview.

38. For data on new programs and enrollment growth, see Faculty Senate Long-Range Planning Committee, Sept. 1970, pp. 8, 11–12, 14; UMAR (1970), 7. For rising emphasis on research, see UMAR (1964), 3; (1965), 10; UM/AR, Dean of Graduate School (1968); "Accreditation Self-Study," 1978, Table B-6. For ACE rankings, see K. Roose and C. Anderson, 1970; also UMAR (1971). For continuing interest in doctoral development, see MBHE, "A Study of Graduate Education in Massachusetts," 1969, pp. 27–29. For professional school, see UMAR (1968); Office of Dean of Administration, July 18, 1966; "Preliminary Master Plan," Feb. 1969, p. 23.

39. For "despite the trend," see Faculty Senate Long-Range Planning Committee, Sept. 1970, pp. 7–8. For "in keeping with our concern," see ibid., 9. For "a proper balance," see ibid., 11.

40. For "moved too far," see Lederle oral history interview, 91–92. For initiatives on undergraduate education, see ibid., 73, 92–94; UMAR (1966), 4, 11, 14; (1967), 5; Lederle interview.

41. For Lederle on his senior appointments, see Lederle oral history interview, 27–28, 34–35, 37; also UMAR (1961), 6. For "we had to shake this place," see Lederle oral history interview, 41. For Tippo, see ibid., 28–30; F. Troy, 1982, pp. 4–5; private communication from Troy. For "infusing the instructional staff," see Lederle oral history interview, 28.

42. For Van Meter and Mather, see: UMAR (1949); Mather oral history interview, 43. For 1962 report, see Long-Range Academic Planning Committee, June 5, 1962, p. 56. For Lederle view and "had to get into Boston," see Lederle oral history interview, 80; also Lederle interview. For Willis-Harrington, see MGC, Special Commission, June 1965, p. 101.

43. For key dates in founding of UM/B, see "University of Massachusetts-Boston

Date Sheet." For Lederle's account, see Lederle oral history interview, 80ff. For trustee discussions, see Board of Trustees, Minutes, May 11, 1964; May 22, 1964; June 2, 1964; June 6, 1964; Board of Trustees Executive Committee, Minutes, April 30, 1964. For Boston State, State Colleges, Case, and Knowles, see Gagnon interview; *Boston Herald,* "UMass Branch Here Wins First Test," June 14, 1964, Sect. 1, pp. 1, 11; F. Troy, 1982, p. 6; Knowles interview. For Donohue role, see R. Stafford and L. Lustberg, Fall 1978, p. 9.

44. For early planning for UM/B, see "University of Massachusetts-Boston Date Sheet"; Board of Trustees Executive Committee, Minutes, April 30, 1964; Board of Trustees, Minutes, July 2, 1964; July 30, 1964, and subsequent; see also "Budgeting Requests for FY 1965," p. 1, attached to Board of Trustees, Minutes, Dec. 1964. For "would be a complete activity," see Board of Trustees Executive Committee, Minutes, April 30, 1964. For "a quality institution," see Board of Trustees, Minutes, July 2, 1964; see also Board of Trustees Executive Committee, Minutes, April 30, 1964. For Ryan, see Lederle oral history interview, 30; Lederle interview; Board of Trustees Committee on Faculty and Educational Policy, Minutes, March 3, 1966. For "to the best of our knowledge," see Board of Trustees, Minutes, Dec. 1964, "Budgeting Requests for FY 1965," p. 2.

45. For limited financial support at outset, see Lederle oral history interview, 80ff.; also private communication from Lederle. Note that press reports quoted both Kevin Harrington and Robert Quinn to the effect that the leadership of the Amherst campus and the Board of Trustees was sabotaging Boston by not pushing for adequate financial support; see *Boston Herald Traveler,* "Sen. Harrington Hits UMass Double Talk," Jan. 8, 1968, p. 3; and Thomas C. Gallagher, "New University Set-up Eyed" in ibid., Feb. 2, 1968, p. 8; Lederle vigorously rebuts this view and insists he gave full support to Boston, citing John A. Ryan, Oct. 15, 1968. For Volpe and legislature, see Ryan, Oct. 15, 1968. For public attitudes toward UM/B and controversy over campus location, see Lederle oral history interview, 80ff.; BU, "An Assessment of BU," 1967.

46. For fiscal year 1969 budget, see "Response To the Governor's Budget Recommendations" March 1, 1969. For "among all of the new campuses," see ibid., 12.

47. For enrollment growth, see UMAR (1970), 7. For character of students, see MBHE, 1971, p. 35; Organization for Social and Technical Innovation, Appendix B, Oct. 1973, p. B-144; President's Committee on the Future, Dec. 1971, pp. 22–25.

48. For size and distribution of faculty, see UM/B, *Catalog* 1969–70. Statement about focus of Lederle and trustee interest based on review of Board of Trustees, Minutes; Lederle interview. For Gagnon views, see Paul Gagnon, May 10, 1979; see also "Statement of Purpose, University of Massachusetts, Boston," June 1965. Another example of a former MSC activist who came to UM/B was Alvin Ryan; see W. Cary, 1962, p. 155. For 1969 Master Plan, see "Master Plan to 1980," June 9, 1969; see also Board of Trustees, Minutes, June 30, 1969.

49. For tension between early plans for UM/B and the pressures of an urban constituency, see Richard M. Freeland, Oct. 7, 1970. For City College, see Nathan Glazer, "City College" in D. Riesman and V. Stadtman, 1973. For Lederle's view of UM/B, see Lederle interview. For Troy, see F. Troy, 1982, p. 8. For trustee resolution, see Board of Trustees, Minutes, Jan. 30, 1970, pp. 2–3. For public and community service, see Francis L. Broderick, Dec. 1970.

50. For slowness of organizational change at Amherst, see Faculty Senate Long-Range Planning Committee, Sept. 1970, pp. 12ff. For Van Meter on organization, see UMAR (1947), 5; Johnson oral history interview, 4–5. For Mather, see Mather oral his-

tory interview, 11–12, 18–19. For traditional organizational arrangements at Amherst, see "Standard Practice Instruction" (1939); (1950); (1954). For "there was a practical," see Mather oral history interview, 18–19.

51. For Senate, see "Constitution of the University of Massachusetts Faculty Senate," Feb. 28, 1957. For evolution of personnel policy at Amherst following fiscal autonomy, see "Statement on Professional Personnel Policies," T63–050; Trustee Document T64–061; "Statement of Professional Personnel Policies," 1968 revision; Moyer Hunsberger, Jan. 2, 1969. On continuing domination by administrative hierarchy in 1960s, see Subcommittee on the Role of Faculty in Decision-Making at the University, 1969. On Senate role in 1960s, see Faculty Senate Long-Range Planning Committee, Sept. 1970. For 1969 committee, see Subcommittee on the Role of Faculty in Decision-making, 1969; for background of this committee, see Faculty Senate Long-Range Planning Committee, Sept. 1970, p. 17.

52. For history of Medical School issue, see "The Massachusetts Medical School," Appendix A, 6ff.; MGC, Special Commission, June 1965, p. 20; MGC, Staff of the Special Commission, 1962–1965, UMAR (1963), 10; Long-Range Academic Planning Committee, June 5, 1962, pp. 41, 45: Mather oral history interview 44. TU, R. Miller, 1966, p. 688; NU, Knowles interview. For trustee discussions of location, see Lederle oral history interview, 48ff., 61; F. Troy, 1982, pp. 5–6; R. Stafford and L. Lustberg, Fall 1978, Newman Commission on Political Intrusion, "University of Massachusetts Medical School at Worcester."

53. For initial organization of UM/B, see "Academic Organization," Oct. 2, 1967; "University of Massachusetts-Boston," May 15, 1967; R. Freeland, Oct. 7, 1970. For defeat of proposed programs, see Freeland, Oct. 7, 1970.

54. For new constitution, see "The Proposal for University Governance," Nov. 11, 1969; Donald C. Babcock, Nov. 19, 1969.

55. For efforts to solidify UM/A position as graduate/research center, see Office of Dean of Administration, July 18, 1966; Faculty Senate Long-Range Planning Committee, Sept. 1970, p. 19. For early thinking about intercampus relations, see UMAR (1966), 6; Office of Dean of Administration, July 18, 1966, p. 13; Faculty Senate Long-Range Planning Committee, Sept. 1970, "Summary." For intercampus tension in 1960s, see ibid., 37.

56. For relations between UMass and other public campuses, see Lederle oral history interview, 11–13; private communication from Lederle; Long-Range Academic Planning Committee, June 5, 1962, p. 56ff.; Faculty Senate Long-Range Planning Committee, Sept. 1970, p. 28. For Lederle's advocacy of statewide authority, see UMAR (1964), 3–5; Lederle oral history interview, 118; Board of Trustees, Minutes, July 2, 1964. For "the problem is," see Lederle oral history interview, 118. For earlier expressions of need for statewide coordination, see MGC, Special Commission, Jan. 24, 1962; MGC, Special Commission, Mar. 26, 1958, pp. 43–45.

57. For work and recommendations of Willis-Harrington, see MGC, Special Commission, June 1965, 168ff., 535–36; see also preliminary report, Dec. 1964, attached as appendix to June 1965 report; Lederle oral history interview, 117–22; Robert D. Gaudet, Summer/Fall 1987, p. 66ff. For "sole public university," see MSC, Special Commission, June 1965, p. 539–40. For legislative action on Willis-Harrington, see Lederle oral history interview, 120; David Wilson in *Boston Herald* April 4, 1965; "Preliminary Master Plan," Feb. 13, 1969, p. 5.

58. For early years of BHE, see Lederle oral history interview 117–23; F. Troy, 1982, pp. 6–7; Faculty Senate Long-Range Planning Committee, Sept. 1970, p. 24. For

creation of additional universities, see Lederle oral history interview, 118–19, 124; R. ford and L. Lustberg, 1978, p. 10; Board of Trustees, Minutes, Feb. 23, 1970; Thomas Gallagher in *Boston Herald*, Feb. 2, 1968.

59. For Willis-Harrington on aid to privates, see MGC, Special Commission, June 1965, pp. 405–6, 428. For discussion of scholarships for attendance at privates as an alternative to public expansion, see MGC, Legislative Research Council, April 13, 1964, pp. 36–37; "The Massachusetts Medical School," Appendix A, p. 38ff. Discussion of organization of AICUM based on minutes of Association of Independent Colleges and Universities, Executive Committee for March 6, 1967; May 16, 1967; and June 14, 1967; also Walsh, Tredinnick interviews.

60. Early history of AICUM based on Executive Committee minutes. For discussions of institutional aid, see ibid. for following dates: May 10, 1968; Sept. 25, 1968; Oct. 14, 1968; Dec. 12, 1968; Feb. 5, 1969; March 7, 1969; May 8, 1969; July 14, 1969; Sept. 16, 1969; Dec. 10, 1969; Jan. 22, 1970. For select committee, see Select Committee for the Study of Financial Problems, Jan. 1970. For AICUM review of goals in wake of initial experience see Executive Committee minutes for following dates: May 8, 1969; Sept. 16, 1969; Nov. 19, 1969; Dec. 10, 1970.

61. For Lederle and Boyden resignations, see UMAR (1970); Lederle oral history interview, 126ff. For Marcus report, see Board of Trustees, "Attachment to T70–032"; see also Ad Hoc Committee on Campus-Central Office Relations, Feb. 12, 1976, pp. 7–8; Healey to Morris, Dec. 29, 1971, and Healey to Booth, Sept. 17, 1975 (with attached minutes of trustee discussion); UMAR (1970), 7; (1975), 6. For trustee decision on system-wide organization, see Board of Trustees, T70–032.

62. For Tippo elevation, see Lederle oral history interview. For Wood background and appointment, see Richard M. Weintraub, May 27, 1973.

63. For organization of system office, see UMAR (1971). Comments on this period also reflect author's personal observations as assistant to Wood. See also Hay Associates, March 1975, p. 4. For a subsequent reconsideration of implications of bringing secretary's office into system president's office, see Ad Hoc Committee on Board Operations and Organization, June 1978, UMSO.

64. For new policy on governance, see Faculty Senate Long-Range Planning Committee, Sept. 1970, pp. 2, 17–18. For rising tension as Wood increased presidential role, see "Report to the University Assembly by the Boston Representatives to the Pan-University Study Group for Review of Governance Procedures," Feb. 8, 1973; Healey to Morris, Dec. 29, 1971; Francis L. Broderick, Nov. 30, 1971. For Tippo resignation and campus reaction, see Healey to Morris, Dec. 29, 1971. For AAUP guidelines, see Healey to Wellman, Dec. 29, 1971. Discussion of Broderick resignation based on author's observations.

65. Discussion of new governance policy (T73–098) based on review of file on "Governance (University-wide) 1969–73" in UMSO, which contains a full set of materials on the work of the faculty, student, administration committee; see particularly Pan-University Study Group for Review of University Governance, March 1, 1973. For unionization, see UMAR (1973), 14; F. Troy, 1982, p. 9; Ad Hoc Committee on Campus-Central Office Relations, 1976, p. 9.

66. For Wood's inaugural, including quotes, see R. Weintraub, May 27, 1973, p. 18. For additional statements of Wood's emphasis on innovation over traditionalism or continuity, see UMAR (1971), 1; (1973), 12.

67. For policy review, see "Trustees Policy Review," Dec. 28–29, 1970; for similar estimates from other university sources, see "Preliminary Master Plan," Feb. 13, 1969,

p. 3; Board of Trustees, Minutes, March 30, 1969. For Future Committee, see President's Committee on the Future, 1971, p. 16ff.

68. For Law School, see Committee to Determine the Feasibility of Establishing a Law School, May 12, 1972. For UM/W, see "Trustees Policy Review," Dec. 1970, pp. 3–4; President's Committee on the Future, 1971, p. 84. For UM/B see "Trustees Policy Review," Dec. 1970, 2–3. For Future Committee, see President's Committee on the Future, 1971.

69. For fiscal year 1973 budget, see David Nyhan in *Boston Globe,* Jan. 25, 1972, p. 7 and Jan. 27, 1972, p. 1; Kenneth D. Campbell in ibid., Jan. 26, 1972, p. 1; Jonathan Fuerbringer in ibid., Jan. 27, 1972, p. 4; see also K. Johnson, Dec. 1973. For Wood reaction, see UMAR (1973), 5.

70. For Lederle's financial concerns, see UMAR (1968); (1969), 2. For "is unlikely to come," see Francis L. Broderick, Feb. 16, 1971. For additional statements of new financial situation, see Faculty Senate Long-Range Planning Committee, Sept. 1970, pp. 2–3, 38; K. Johnson, 1973, pp. 5–6.

71. For Massachusetts economy and pressures on state revenues, see Academy for Educational Development, June 1973, pp. 141–42; "Tuition Policy for the University of Massachusetts," 3; K. Johnson, 1973, p. 5. For proposals for new taxes, see Academy for Educational Development, June 1973, p. 142. For "the State House will be" see F. Broderick, Feb. 16, 1971.

72. For altered political environment, see Lederle oral history interview, 137ff. For student protests see ibid., 140ff; UMAR (1967); (1969), 4–5; Faculty Senate Long-Range Planning Committee, Sept. 1970, p. 2. For growing public/private tension, see AICUM, minutes of Feb. 11, 1971; March 11, 1971; May 13, 1971; June 7, 1971; Sept. 9, 1971; Oct. 14, 1971; Nov. 11, 1971; K. Johnson, 1973; R. Weintraub, May 27, 1973, pp. 10, 18; TUAR (1972), 11. For opposition to Law School, see *Boston Globe*, Dec. 16, 1972, p. 3; Feb. 4, 1973, p. A-3; Peter Edelman, Nov. 13, 1972. For a general review of problems of this period, see Robert C. Wood, Summer/Fall 1987, pp. 8–9.

73. For impact of PhD glut and cutbacks in other states, see Lederle oral history interview, 137, 151; Faculty Senate Long-Range Planning Committee, Sept. 1970, "Summary," 1, 3. For new projections, see Organization for Social and Technical Innovation, 1973, Appendix A, esp. p. A-26.

74. For Organization for Social and Technical Innovation, see their 1973 report; for Academy for Educational Development, see their 1973 report. For background on the three reports, see R. Wood, Summer/Fall 1987 p. 10.

75. For Law School, see Lederle oral history interview, 122–23; *Boston Globe*, Feb. 4, 1973, p. A-3. For changes in UM enrollment policy, see Robert C. Wood, June 1974; UMAR (1977), 8–9. For "the strategy of growth," see UMAR (1973), 4.

CHAPTER 7. THE INSTITUTIONAL COMPLEX AND ACADEMIC ADAPTATION, 1945–1980

1. For a general discussion of change in admission policies at public and private institutions in the postwar years, see C. Jencks and D. Riesman, 1968, pp. 279ff.

2. On the limited ability of even top universities to be selective in admissions before World War II, see R. Geiger, 1986, pp. 129ff. Jencks and Riesman stress the potency of changes in admissions policy—if conditions permit it—as a means of bringing about broadbased change in the character of a college; see C. Jencks and D. Riesman, 1968, p. 254.

3. Clark has observed that when student demand is strong, institutional decisions about program change tend to be determined by the interests of internal groups, but that when demand is weak, institutions are pressed to make choices based on student interests; see B. Clark, 1983, p. 211. Abbott makes a related point in noting that an institution's readiness to adapt to its environment varies inversely with its prestige; see Walter Abbott, 1974, pp. 401–7.

4. As early as 1947, the Zook commission criticized institutions for "megalomania" in pursuing "sheer bigness"; see U.S. President, Commission on Higher Education, vol. 3, 1947, pp. 22–23. The tendency of all organizations to grow as a path to prestige has been widely noted by students of organizational behavior; see, for example, J. Haas and T. Drabek, 1973, p. 195. See also B. Clark, 1983, p. 198.

5. For additional discussion of stages through which institutions pass as they develop, see D. Riesman and C. Jencks, 1962, pp. 118ff.; Frank Pinner, in Nevitt Sanford, 1962, p. 941; J. Ben-David, 1972, p. 43. Ben-David notes the tendency to generate resources for high-prestige functions by cultivating constituency support for technical programs.

6. Ashby put it this way: "In theory universities could have turned down opportunities for luxuriant growth of their scientific research; in practice it would have been impossible: any university which turned aside from such opportunities would have lost its place in the hierarchy." See E. Ashby, 1971, p. 82.

7. For the evolution of higher education's role as the channel of upward mobility for the middle class, see C. Jencks and D. Riesman, 1968, pp. 20–27; also, generally, B. Bledstein, 1976.

8. Blau asserts another dimension of the relationship between academic prestige and social class—the tendency of top-ranked institutions to recruit faculty from upper-class backgrounds. See P. Blau, 1973, p. 251.

9. A. Touraine, 1974, p. 170.

10. For Walsh quote, see above, Chapt. 5, "The Bonanza Years at Boston College."

11. For durability of prestige rankings, see B. Clark, 1983, p. 195.

12. On the self-reinforcing qualities of the prestige hierarchy, see J. Ben-David, 1972, p. 39; Neil Smelser and Robin Content, 1980, p. 7. For the tendency of federal funding to perpetuate the established hierarchy, see E. Ashby, 1971, p. 84.

13. For a general discussion of campus cultures and their role in institutional development, see Ellen E. Chaffee and William G. Tierney, 1988.

14. For role of intellectual values in universities, see discussion of the "cognitive complex" in T. Parsons and G. Platt, 1973, esp. Chapt. 2. For Morison quote, see J. Killian, 1985, p. 400. For Morison's account of biology at MIT, see ibid., 206ff.

15. Frey discusses the pressure on universities to maintain "legitimacy" with their supporters by engaging in activities that express conformity with the dominant social values of those external groups in J. Frey, 1977, p. 7.

16. For students as carriers of social and political concerns in 1960s, see Carnegie Commission on Higher Education, *Digest*, 1974, p. 126; W. Quine, in *Daedalus*, Fall 1974, p. 39.

17. For Clark on durability of values, see B. Clark, 1956.

18. For Jencks and Riesman on the inherent conflict between institutional interests and service to disadvantaged students, see C. Jencks and D. Riesman, 1968, p. 130.

19. A typical discussion of the devolution of universities into warring interest groups can be found in Special Committee on Campus Tensions, 1970, pp. 22–23, 26, 30, 34; see also J. Frey, 1977, pp. 110–11. P. Blau, 1973, p. 216, is one of many to argue that

academic specialization generates little interdependence among discipline-based subunits and therefore tends to divide institutions into unrelated components.

20. Blau's research supports the argument that presidents who lead their institutions upward in prestige by hiring more professionally oriented faculty are likely in the end to experience conflict with that faculty by pointing out that the balance of power between faculty and administration tends to shift toward the faculty as campus prestige rises; see P. Blau, 1973, pp. 164–66, 186.

21. The classic statement of diminished presidential authority can be found in C. Kerr, 1963, pp. 29ff.; see also F. Rourke and G. Brooks, 1966, pp. 109ff.; J. Millett, 1952, p. 213; President's Task Force on Higher Education, 1970, p. 17; Assembly on University Goals and Governance, 1971, p. 10.

22. M. Cohen and J. March, 1974, pp. 1, 2, 203. B. Clark, 1983, pp. 234–35, contains an interesting discussion of unplanned, uncoordinated change within institutions of higher education.

23. Derek Bok, who succeeded Pusey as president of Harvard in 1970, takes on the Cohen/March view and attempts to characterize the possibilities of the modern university presidency in D. Bok, 1986, pp. 191ff.

24. For discussions of the importance of coherence among different aspects and functions of universities, see E. Chaffee and W. Tierney, 1988, Chapt. 10; Carnegie Commission on Higher Education, *Digest,* 1974, pp. 185–86. For pattern of building research/graduate activities on technical/service bases, see J. Ben-David, 1972, pp. 43–44.

25. Though Harvard and other Ivy League universities are often cited as being better able to combine undergraduate teaching with graduate education and research than giant public institutions, Riesman has expressed doubts about Harvard's ability to be both a good college and a good research university; see S. Lipset and D. Riesman, 1975, p. 378.

26. M. Trow has argued that there is a fundamental incompatibility between elite higher education at the undergraduate level and the dynamics of public systems; he notes that there are virtually no examples of limited-size, high-quality, undergraduate institutions in the public sector; see M. Trow, 1976, p. 374. See also J. Ben-David, 1972, p. 42.

27. Wessell disputes the view taken here in a letter to the author, arguing that his approach was the only one possible for him, given Tuft's entrenched faculty and the prosperity of the period. He argues that Sachar's style would not have worked at Tufts.

28. For the importance of institutional "personality," see J. Killian, 1985, p. 147. For a scholarly discussion of the value to institutions of establishing a "protective niche" in a competitive system, see B. Clark, 1983, pp. 220, 223.

29. For 1971 national projections, see Carnegie Commission on Higher Education, *Digest,* 1974, p. 77. For 1975 state projections see MBHE, ca. 1975; see also L. Lustford and R. Stafford, Fall 1978, p. 20. For actual enrollment trends nationally and in Massachusetts, see U.S. Department of Education, 1990, Table 174; see also Verne A. Stadtman, 1980, pp. 7, 17, 92; Carnegie Council on Policy Studies, 1982, pp. 55ff., 72; Executive Office of Educational Affairs, 1979.

30. For nontraditional students, see V. Stadtman, 1980, pp. 17–19, 41–43; Carnegie Council on Policy Studies, 1982, Supplement B; Reginald Wilson and Sarah E. Melendez, Fall 1985, p. 46; James Blackwell, July 1985. For intensified recruitment and marketing, see Stadtman, 1980, pp. 43, 122, 167; "Colleges Learn the Hard Sell," *Business Week,* Feb. 14, 1977, pp. 92–93; Liz Murphy, May 13, 1985, pp. 50–53. For growth

at most institutions, see Stadtman, 1980, p. 120; Carnegie Council on Policy Studies, 1982, p. 10. For Carnegie Council survey, see Stadtman, 1980, pp. 88, 92.

31. For Cheit and Bowen, see C. Finn, 1978, pp. 26–27. For total income and per student expenditures, see V. Stadtman, 1980, p. 119; Carnegie Council on Policy Studies, 1982, pp. 10, 140. For federal funding in 1970s, see C. Finn, 1978, p. 12; Stadtman, 1980, pp. 13, 133; Carnegie Council on Policy Studies, 1982, pp. 12, 25, 112, Supplement J. For state funding, see Stadtman, 1980, p. 133; Carnegie Council on Policy Studies, 1982, p. 12; "Analysis of State Funds for Higher Education," *Chronicle of Higher Education,* Oct. 10, 1978, p. 14; Carnegie Foundation, 1976. For contributions to revenue, see Carnegie Council on Policy Studies, 1982, pp. 14–18, 140. For "the 1970s was," see Carnegie Council on Policy Studies, 1982, p. 13. For economic conditions of 1970s, see Stadtman, 1980, pp. 6, 12, 120.

32. For changes in academic labor market, see N. Smelser and R. Content, 1980, Chapt. 8; L. Wilson, 1979, pp. 51ff.; W. Metzger, 1987, pp. 156–57; V. Stadtman, 1980, pp. 49, 53–54; Carnegie Council on Policy Studies, 1982, p. 81. For impact of "PhD glut," see Stadtman, 1980, pp. 48, 55–56, 58, 62–63; Carnegie Council on Policy Studies, 1982, pp. 80–82.

33. For power shifts, see V. Stadtman, 1980, pp. 79–80, 86–87. For unionization, see W. Metzger, 1987, pp. 170–78; Stadtman, 1980, pp. 69ff.; Carnegie Council on Policy Studies, 1982, p. 82.

34. For growth of statewide boards, see T. R. McConnell, in Philip G. Altbach and Robert O. Berdahl, 1981, esp. 46; E. D. Duryea, in ibid.; Robert O. Berdahl, 1975; Carnegie Council on Policy Studies, 1982, p. 23. For increase in federal controls, see McConnell and Duryea in Altbach and Berdahl, 1981; V. Stadtman, 1980, pp. 9–10; Brewster interview in *Boston Globe,* March 20, 1977. For general discussions of increases in external controls, see L. Wilson, 1979, pp. 97, 115; Carnegie Commission on Higher Education, *Governance,* 1973; George Keller, 1983, pp. 24–26. For "regulated industry," see Carnegie Council on Policy Studies, 1982, p. 14. For "the market conditions," see Burton R. Clark, in Van de Graaf et al., 1978, p. 120. For impact of rise of external controls in Massachusetts, see HUAR (1973); (1975); TUAR (1973); (1975); MIT, D. Garvin, 1977. For movement toward stronger statewide control of public system in Massachusetts, see James Collins, 1982.

35. For Harvard search, see R. Smith, 1986, pp. 270ff.; S. Lipset and D. Riesman, 1975, pp. 235–36; HUAR (1971), 6; University Committee on Governance, April 1970. For Bok background, see Smith, 1986, pp. 273–74, 279ff., 333; C. Vigeland, 1986, pp. 19–24, 131–32; N. Aldrich, 1977.

36. For MIT search, see J. Killian, 1985, p. 274. For Weisner background, see *Technology Review* vol. 73, April 1971, pp. 89–90; For Gray background, see ibid., 91–92.

37. For president/chancellor system at MIT, see MITAR (1972), 12–13; (1980), 7. For Press committee see MITAR (1976). For Bok's reorganization of HU, see HUAR (1971), 22ff.; (1972) 24ff.; (1973), 5, 28; University Committee on Governance, March 1971 and February 1972; R. Smith, 1986, pp. 285–89; C. Vigeland, 1986, pp. 8, 20; J. Bethell, March–Apr. 1979; N. Aldrich, March 1977, p. 47; Shenton, O'Brien interviews.

38. For HU finances and budget controls in early 1970s, see R. Smith, 1986, p. 288; HUAR (1971); (1972), 25; (1973), 7ff.; N. Aldrich, March 1977, pp. 39, 47. For Harvard Management Corporation, see C. Vigeland, 1986, pp. 118–19, 143, 151ff. For decline in federal support, see Vigeland, 1986, p. 28; HUTR (1968); (1978), 9. For energy plant, see Vigeland, 1986, pp. 132, 210. For mix of revenue sources, see HUAR

(1976), 39ff. For salaries and staff cuts, see Vigeland, 1986, p. 111; HUTR (1978); HUAR (1974), 4. For 350th, see Vigeland, 1986, pp. 52, 73, 111.

39. For general discussion of MIT finances, see MITAR (1972), 1; (1974), 10, 18; (1976), A38; (1980), 1. For federal cutbacks, see D. Garvin 1977, pp. 43, 49, 59, 62, 74–75, 79, 82; MITAR (1976), A40. In a letter to the author, former President Paul Gray notes that the impact of the overall decline in federal support in the early 1970s was lessened by the fact that dollar support for sponsored projects among MIT's core faculty (as opposed to the Draper and Lincoln labs) actually increased. For cost controls, see ibid., A38; Committee on MIT Research Structure, June 21, 1976, p. 111. For enrollment and tuition, see MITAR (1972), 14; (1977), 2; (1980), 16; MITB (1972); (1980). For MIT-industry ties, see MITAR (1972), 7 (1974), 19; (1976), A40-1. For "share in its guidance," see MITAR (1976), A40. For capital campaign, see MITAR (1977), 1; J. Killian, 1985, pp. 261, 276–77. For changed mix of revenue sources, see MITTR (1971); (1980). For "have managed to adjust," see Garvin, 1977, p. 82.

40. For general statement of Bok's priorities, see D. Bok, 1986, p. 158. For "to be blunt," see HUAR (1971), 16. For undergraduate reform, see HUAR (1971), 18; (1972); P. Keller, 1982, p. 34; C. Vigeland, 1986, p. 20. For ethics and public service, see HUAR (1974); (1976), 36–37; Bok, 1986, pp. 112–13, 127ff., 141; R. Smith, 1986, pp. 322, 324, 334. For Bok's view of presidency, see Smith, 1986, pp. 283, 289–90, 295–96, 301–2, 304, 330, 338.

41. For emphasis on continuity, see Weisner in *Technology Review*, vol. 73, April 1971, p. 91. For social implications of science and sociotechnical systems, see ibid., 93; MITAR (1976), A46; (1977) 1. For educational priorities, see Gray in *Technology Review*, vol. 73, April 1971, pp. 89–94; MITAR (1972), 9ff.; (1973); (1976), A38, A47-48; (1977), 7–8; (1980), 11–12. For "trying to solve," see MITAR (1976), A41.

42. For Hallowell on professionalism, see TUAR (1973), 14–15; (1974), 15–16. For "man, not knowledge," see Burton C. Hallowell, Sept. 24, 1967. For undergraduate education, see TUAR (1970), 3–5; (1971), 3–4; (1972); (1974); (1975), 1; (1976), 1. For "live and act," see TUAR (1971), 3–4. For "vision" and "new environment," see B. Hallowell, Sept. 24, 1967. For program innovation, see TUAR (1970), 3–5; (1971), 4–5; (1974), 5–10. For reaffirmation of Tufts as "college-centered university," see TUAR (1974).

43. For enrollments, faculty numbers, and tuition rates, see TU, *Fact Book*, 1977–78. For salaries, see "Tufts: The Total University," 1973, pp. 44–45. For "may prove to be," see TUAR (1971), 3–4. For USC and CUE, see TUAR (1971), "Recommendations"; "Tufts: The Total University," 1973, p. 34.

44. For CUE, see Committee on Undergraduate Education, Jan. 1973. For USC, see "Tufts: The Total University," 1973. For Hallowell reaction to reports, see TUAR (1973), 13–14. For statistics on private giving, enrollments, faculty numbers, and student preparation and selectivity, see TU, *Fact Book*, 1977–78. For rising standards for promotion, see "Tufts: The Total University," 1973, pp. 46, 52; TUAR (1973), 4–5, 15.

45. For Bernstein appointment and views, see *Justice*, Sept. 14, 1971; Oct. 21, 1971; Nov. 2, 1971; Nov. 16, 1971; Dec. 7, 1971; Dec. 14, 1971; Marver H. Bernstein, Oct. 5, 1972; letter from Black. For financial difficulties of early 1970, see Bernstein interview; *Justice*, Jan. 11, 1972; Feb. 15, 1972; Feb. 22, 1972; May 2, 1972; May 9, 1972; Oct. 31, 1972; Dec. 12, 1972; Sept. 18, 1973; Nov. 7, 1973; Dec. 4, 1973; Dec. 11, 1973; Feb. 5, 1974; Feb. 12, 1974; Dec. 10, 1974; Dec. 16, 1974; Feb. 18, 1975; Mar. 18, 1975. D. Alexander, 1979, "Political Unrest," p. 22; "Report of Brandeis University for the Commission," Oct. 1976, "Report to the Faculty," p. 2.

46. For sources of financial problems, see Bernstein, Sachar, Klein interviews. For annual giving, see Controller's Office, "Gifts Received," 1980; D. Alexander, 1979, "History," 17. For financial data, see BrUFS, (1970); (1973); (1978). For student protest activity, see Alexander, 1979, "Political Unrest," 21ff. For sizes of entering classes see ibid., Table on "Enrollment"; Office of Admissions and financial Aid, "Seven-Year Trend Study, 1974–80"; Sachar, Bernstein interviews.

47. For declining graduate enrollments and higher teaching loads, see "Report of Brandeis University for the Commission," Oct. 1976, Goldstein letter to Bernstein. For declining selectivity and board scores, see Gould interview; Office of Admissions and Financial Aid, Statistics on Entering Classes, (1972) and "Seven-Year Trend Study, 1974–80"; "Report of Brandeis University for the Commission" Oct. 1976, Sect. Va; D. Alexander, 1979, Tables on class size, SATs. For faculty shrinkage and lower personnel standards, see "Report of Brandeis University for the Commission," Oct. 1976, Academic Planning Committee, 5–6, 13; *Justice,* Dec. 7, 1971. For "we have many," see *Newsweek,* May 30, 1977, p. 83. For Goldstein letter, see "Report of Brandeis University for the Commission," Oct. 1976.

48. For finances during Bernstein's final years, see *Justice,* Feb. 16, 1982; Feb. 26, 1982; March 9, 1982; April 29, 1982; Sept. 14, 1982; Oct. 13, 1982; March 8, 1983. For student data, see *Justice,* April 29, 1982; Oct. 5, 1982; March 15, 1983; March 22, 1983; Office of Admissions and Financial Aid, Statistics on Entering Classes, "Seven-Year Trend Study, 1974–80." For rating, see Lewis C. Salmon and Alexander W. Astin, Sept. 1981, pp. 23–28. For 30th anniversary, see *Newsweek,* May 30, 1977; *Boston Globe,* Oct. 2, 1977; Oct. 5, 1978; Oct. 31, 1978. For Sachar continuing role, see Bernstein interview; M. Abram, 1982, p. 196.

49. For enrollments, see NUARs. For DAPD, see NUAR (1971); (1974). For Ryder, see A. Frederick, 1982, pp. 552ff.

50. For collective bargaining, see A. Frederick, 1982, pp. 558ff.; *Boston Herald American,* Feb. 20, 1977, p. A16.

51. For collective bargaining, see N. Ephron, 1977, p. 144; John S. Perkins, "Is the Silber Storm Coming to an End?" 3ff. For "upside potential" vs. "downside risk," see Ephron, Sept. 1977, p. 140. For "compete on price" vs. "compete on quality," see J. Silber, Dec. 8, 1982, p. 11. For "terribly understaffed," see *Currents,* vol. 3, no. 16, Jan. 21, 1971, p. 1. For faculty appointments, see Ephron, Sept. 1977, p. 140; Charles Radin, Feb. 15, 1976; D. McLean, March 5, 1972, p. 14; "An Interview with Dr. Silber" in *Bostonia,* March 1971, pp. 10–11. On program initiatives, see Board of Trustees, BU, "Boston University, 1971–1981," p. 10; Charles Radin, Nov. 11, 1976. For new deans, see Ephron, Sept. 1977, p. 141.

52. For BU finances, see J. Perkins, 1977, pp. 68ff.; Charles W. Smith, Sept. 1, 1975; J. Silber, Dec. 8, 1982; Charles Radin, Nov. 8, 1976; Board of Trustees, BU, "Boston University, 1971–1981"; L. Steadman, 1976, pp. 177ff. For "going to go broke," see ibid., p. 177. For enrollments, see ibid., pp. 187ff.; J. Silber, Dec. 8, 1982; Charles Radin, Nov. 7, 1976, p. 4; Board of Trustees, BU, "Boston University, 1971–1981." For need to cut 150 faculty, see *The News,* Oct. 1974, p. 8.

53. For political crisis of mid-1970s, see C. Radin, Nov. 7, 1976; "Executive Sweep" in *Commonwealth Monthly,* Sept. 76; N. Ephron, Sept. 1977, pp. 144–45. For Silber's strong support from board, see interview with Estin in *Boston Globe,* March 5, 1972.

54. Silber tells the story of the admissions/enrollment turnaround in Board of Trustees, BU "Boston University, 1971–1981," pp. 48–52, 63–69; see also J. Silber, Dec. 8, 1982; D. C. Denison, April 10, 1983. For glossy, see Board of Trustees, BU,

"Boston University, 1971–1981." For a critical perspective on Silber's managerial effectiveness, see Peter Gabriel comments quoted in N. Ephron, Sept. 1977, p. 144.

55. For Monan appointment and background, see *Bridge,* "The President Resigns," Feb. 1972, and "Author, Scholar, Administrator, Athlete," Sept. 1972. For BC needs, see Walsh interview.

56. For BC finances, see "Boston College, 1972–1977"; Frank B. Campanella, April 1976; Jim Delay, Oct. 1971; John Tessitore, Nov. 1972; "Report to the Commission," Feb. 1976; Walsh, Donovan interviews. For enrollments, see *Boston College Fact Book,* 1978; "Boston College, 1972–1977"; communication from Doyle. For Newton College and "may rank in importance," see Charles Donovan et al., 1990, pp. 426–430. For faculty size and salaries, see *Boston College Fact Book,* 1972; 1978; Walsh interview; "Boston College, 1972–1977." For fund-raising, see "Boston College, New Heights Advancement Campaign," 1976; "Boston College, 1972–1977."

57. For planning committee, see University Academic Planning Council, Feb. 1975. For goals, see ibid., 1–11. For Monan reaction, see "Boston College, 1972–1977." For additional comment on Monan's BC, see C. Donovan, 1979; "Report to the Commission," Feb. 1976; Walsh interview.

58. For enrollments, see: UMAR (1977), 8, 30–32; "Accreditation Self-Study," 1978, pp. 14, 17; Robert Wood, May 5, 1977, Appendix I, II; "UMass Medical Center," ca. 1985. For state economy and impact on higher education, see Lynn E. Browne and John S. Hekman, 1988; R. Stafford and L. Lustberg, Fall 1978, pp. 25ff.; Executive Office of Educational Affairs, 1979; "Analysis of State Funds" in *Chronicle of Higher Education,* Oct. 10, 1978, p. 14; UMAR (1975). For UM budget data, see UMAR (1977), 30–32; Stafford and Lustberg, Fall 1978, p. 10; "Accreditation Self-Study," 1978, pp. 15, 16, 18; Long-Range Planning Committee, July 27, 1977, p. 10. For "boom-bust" pattern, see Stafford and Lustberg, Fall 1978, p. 26.

59. For graduate dean report, see UMAR (1973), 6. For commission, see Commission on Missions and Goals, April 1976. For Puryear, see *Chronicle of Higher Education,* May 9, 1977, p. 4. For reaccreditation report, see Evaluation Team Representing, March 1979. For "unable or unwilling," see ibid., 7.

60. For Golino years, see New Directions Committee, June 1974; Long-Range Planning Committee, ca. 1977; Evaluation Team of the Commission, ca 1978; John Hubner, March 9, 1979.

61. For evolution of system office, see UMAR (1973), 13–14; (1977), 4, 11ff.; "Central Administration Self-Study," Sept. 8, 1978. For Wood's general perspective on university administration, see R. Wood, in *Daedalus,* Winter 1975. For heightened emphasis on management in mid-1970s, see Hay Associates, March 1975; R. Wood, Jan. 11, 1977; see also, generally, filed labeled "Organization Design Review Committee" in UMSO; UMAR (1975), 5, 7. For steps reflecting heightened system office/campus tensions, see R. Wood, "Chancellor's Council," June 15, 1976; R. Wood, "Campus Visits," June 15, 1976.

62. For Wood's involvement in academic planning for campuses, see UMAR (1977), 12–13; R. Wood, April 26, 1977; see also materials in Secretary's Files, Trustee Committee on Long-Range Planning, 1974–78 in UMSO. For rejection of two PhDs see Ian Menzies, "UMass after Wood: A better university," *Boston Globe,* Feb. 21, 1978. For conflicts with UM/A faculty, see *Chronicle of Higher Education,* "4 Presidents Under Fire," May 9, 1977, p. 4; Rules Committee of Faculty Senate, Aug. 1975; Healey to Booth, Sept. 17, 1975; Ad Hoc Committee on Campus-Central Office Relations, Feb. 12, 1976. For background to votes on unionization at UM/B, see J. Hubner, 1979, p. 20; *Mass Media,* "Faculty, Wood, Dead End Confrontation," March 22, 1977.

63. For Wood's account of struggle with Dukakis, see UMAR (1975), 1–3; (1977), 1–2, 21, 24–26; R. Wood, 1987, pp. 14–15; Wood oral history interview, 33–38. For an example of media coverage, see "Dukakis vs. Wood—Two Gladiators Get Ready for the Battle," in *Boston Globe*, Dec. 22, 1974, p. 1. For Dukakis effort to control trustees, see UMAR (1977), 25; F. Troy, 1982, p. 10; "UMass Trustee Quits, Blasts Dukakis," in *Boston Globe*, Oct. 27, 1977, p. 14; Frank Thompson, "High-Level Exodus at UMass Laid to Dukakis Trustee Appointments," in *Boston Herald American*, Sept. 24, 1978, p. A3; J. Hubner, 1979, p. 20. For reorganization struggle, see UMAR (1977), 9; R. Wood, 1987, p. 19; Muriel Cohen, "Pride, problems for Wood in a final UMass report," in *Boston Globe*, Jan. 8, 1978; R. Stafford and L. Lustberg, Fall 1978, pp. 24, 37, 39–42, 44, 46–49; J. Collins, 1982.

64. For tensions within public sector, see R. Stafford and L. Lustberg, Fall 1978, pp. 46–47. For public-private relations generally, see: UMAR (1973), 10, 16; (1977), 26–29; R. Wood, June 1974; TUAR (1973), 12, 21–22; "Tufts: The Total University," 1973, pp. 119ff. Asa S. Knowles, June 1974; AICUM Executive Committee, minutes, 1970s; Stafford and Lustberg, Fall 1978, pp. 66ff. For tuition policy, see UMAR (1975), 7; "Staff Paper on Tuition," Jan. 18, 1974; R. Wood, Sept. 25, 1975; R. Wood, Nov. 20, 1975; "Tufts: The Total University," 1973, p. 120; Academy for Educational Development, June 1973; "Tuition Policy for the University of Massachusetts." For public-private forum, see R. Wood, 1987.

65. For Wood final report, see UMAR (1977); quote is on 10. For Wood's own assessment of his presidency, see his oral history interview, 55ff. For accreditation team quote, see "Evaluation Team Representing," March 1979, p. 12. For dates of campus chancellorships, "Dates of Campus Chancellors."

66. While, in the aggregate, tuition provided an increased proportion of campus budgets in the 1970s, the shift was much more evident at institutions that had large streams of revenue from nontuition sources—like endowment or federal grants—than at those that had continued to rely mostly on student charges. Thus Harvard's dependence on student payments rose measurably while BU and BC registered little change in this respect. For data on student aid expenditures, see BU, C. Smith, Sept. 1, 1975, Appendix 4; BCFS (1972); (1977); "Tufts: The Total University," 1973, Appendix G; TUTR (1975); BrUFS (1972); (1978); HUTR (1978). For BU admission strategy, see Board of Trustees, BU, "Boston University, 1971–1986," p. 130. For Tufts's shift toward private school graduates, see TU, *Fact Book*, 1977–1978.

67. For problems of middle-income students in 1970s, see C. Finn, 1978, pp. 69n, 92; R. Stafford and L. Lustberg, Fall 1978, pp. 103ff. For Silber, see Board of Trustees, BU, "Boston University, 1971–1981," p. 52. For Sloan report, see Stafford and Lustberg, Fall 1978, pp. 103ff., 117. For Harvard, see HUTR (1978), 13; HUAR (1981), 20–22.

68. For national data on minority enrollments, see V. Stadtman, 1980, pp. 36, 127, 131; Academic Collective Bargaining Information Service, June 1985; R. Wilson and S. Melendez, 1985, p. 46; George Keller, 1988–89, pp. 43ff. For institutional patterns, see TU, *Fact Book*, 1977–78; TUAR (1977); "Tufts: The Total University," 1973, pp. 74–77; Board of Trustees, BU, "Boston University, 1971–1981," contains no reference to minority enrollments, but the subsequent update, Board of Trustees, BU "Boston University, 1971–1986," reports a decline in minorities in 1970s and subsequent efforts to reverse this trend (see pp. 52, 126ff.); *Boston College Fact Book*, 1978; HUAR (1971), 7–8; Derek Bok, Feb. 27, 1981; R. Smith, 1986, p. 310; MITAR (1974); (1980), 16; MIT, D. Garvin, 1977, p. 31; MITR, Director of Admissions (1974), 312; UM/B, Long-Range Planning Committee, 1977, p. 43; UM/B, Evaluation Team of the Com-

mission, 1978, p. 15; *Northeastern University Fact Book,* 1983. For general review of minority enrollments in Massachusetts institutions in early 1980s, see Richard G. King, 1987. For TYP, see M. Abram, 1982, pp. 171–72, 182–88; Bernstein interview; D. Alexander, 1979, "Academic Policy," 11; *Justice,* Mar. 3, 1975; Apr. 15, 1975; Apr. 22, 1975; May 6, 1975; Sept. 9, 1975; Apr. 11, 1978; Apr. 18, 1978; Sept. 6, 1978; Oct. 17, 1978; Oct. 31, 1978; Feb. 13, 1979; May 1, 1979.

69. V. Stadtman, 1980, pp. 20–21, reports a national pattern of declining academic standards among nonselective campuses in the 1970s, combined with higher standards at selective schools. For Bok, see D. Bok, Feb. 27, 1981. For Silber, see Board of Trustees, BU, "Boston University, 1971–1986," pp. 52, 126ff.

70. Jencks and Riesman, argue that a major reason why higher education in the U.S. did not become totally class dominated was the permissiveness of this country, in contrast to European states, in allowing new institutions to be created by those excluded from established campuses; see C. Jencks and D. Riesman, 1968, p. 105. See also A. Touraine, 1974, p. 142.

71. For Bok, see HUAR (1972); (1973), 6; (1974), 1ff. For Silber, see D. McLean, 1972. For Hallowell, see above, Chapt. 7, n42. For Wood, see Committee on the Future, 1971, p. 72. For Bernstein, see M. Bernstein, Oct. 5, 1972, p. 4. For Gray, see above, Chapt. 7, n36. For Monan, see "Boston College, 1972–1977," p. 14, also University Academic Planning Council, Feb. 1975, p. 18. For Knowles, see NUAR (1971), 4.

72. For Hallowell, see above, Chapt. 7, n42. For Bernstein, see M. Bernstein, Oct. 5, 1972, p. 5; Bernstein interview; "Report of Brandeis University for the Commission," Nov. 1976, Questions 4a, 4b, 4c. For MIT, see MITAR (1973), 5–6; (1974), 7–10; (1977), 2; (1979). For UM/B, see work of Daisy Tagliacozzo as dean of College I, Tagliacozzo interview. For Silber, see Board of Trustees, BU, "Boston University, 1971–1981," pp. 8–12. For Bok, see D. Bok, 1986, Chapt. 2. For review of national trends in curriculum reform, see Zelda F. Gamsen, 1987.

73. For concern about enrollments, see HU, Edward B. Fiske, Dec. 5, 1977; "Report of Brandeis University for the Commission," Nov. 1976, "Report of Academic Planning Committee"; BC, Committee on University Priorities, 1972; V. Stadtman, 1980, pp. 166, 170. For impact of new clienteles, see UMAR (1977), 16–17; P. Keller, 1982, p. 42; R. Smith, 1986, p. 283; Stadtman, 1980, pp. 136ff., 151; Z. Gamsen, 1987. On shift toward career interests, see BrU, *Justice,* March 16, 1982; MITAR (1980), 1; UM/B, New Directions Committee, 1974, p. 3; Stadtman, 1980, pp. 7–8, 22–26; Jan Krukowski, "What Do Students Want? Status," in *Change,* vol. 17 (May/June 1985).

74. For link to financial pressures, see P. Keller, 1982, pp. 37, 134–35; Office of the Dean, Oct. 1974, pp. 2, 6. For "can we assume," see ibid., 9. For "an educated person," see Change Magazine Press, 1979, p. 7. For HU, see also Keller, 1982, pp. 35ff. For TU, see TUAR (1974), 5–10. For BrU, see "Report of Brandeis University for the Commission," Nov. 1976, "Report of Academic Planning Committee," 11–12; D. Alexander, 1979, "Academic Policy," pp. 11–12; *Justice,* Sept. 12, 1978, Sept. 26, 1978; Oct. 24, 1978; Feb. 13, 1979; Mar. 20, 1979; May 1, 1979. For MIT, see Committee on the HASS Requirements, Aug. 25, 1986. See also Z. Gamsen, 1987, pp. 12ff.

75. For a critical perspective on HU's core, see Barry O'Connell, in Change Magazine Press, 1979; R. Smith, 1986, p. 320; see also D. Bok, 1986, p. 45. For Hallowell on limits of reform, see TUAR (1974); (1976), 12. For lack of national consensus on undergraduate requirements, see P. Keller, 1982, pp. 143–45. For an assessment of organizational problems in educational reform, see Arthur Levine, 1980.

76. For scholarly standing as key to institutional reputation, see: L. Wilson, 1979,

p. 219; James Thompson, 1967, p. 93. For survey, see L. Salmon and A. Astin, 1981, pp. 23–28. For beginnings of assessment movement, see Z. Gamsen, 1987, p. 436. For limits of student pressure on curriculum reform, see D. Bok, 1986, p. 179; D. Riesman and V. Stadtman, 1973, pp. 453ff.; a contrary example, however, appears to be Brown University, where student activists played a major role in curriculum reform during the 1970s—see Friedman interview.

77. For early Bok statements and initiatives relative to strengthening teaching, see HUAR (1971), 18–19; (1976), 10; R. Smith, 1986, p. 290; Change Magazine Press, 1979, p. 6. For Bok's acceptance of established, research-oriented criteria for appointments/promotions, see HUAR (1976), 10. For Bok's rejection of popular teachers, see Smith, 1986, p. 288. Note that, as his presidency wound down in the 1980s, Bok continued to lament inadequate attention to teaching, while also claiming some gains during his years; see D. Bok, 1986, pp. 6, 45, 174; Colin Campbell, July 20, 1986, p. 17. For Silber statements and initiatives to improve teaching, see Board of Trustees, BU, "Boston University, 1971–1981," p. 12; "An Interview," *Bostonia*, 1971, p. 20. For Vendler, see *New York Times Magazine*, April 23, 1989, p. 74. V. Stadtman, 1980, p. 56, reports a slight decline nationally in faculty interest in teaching in the 1970s, which he attributes to the increased proportion of professors with PhDs.

78. For Brandeis, see Bernstein, Oct. 5, 1972 p. 7; Bernstein interview; "Report of Brandeis University for the Commission," Nov. 1976, sect. III. For BC, see University Academic Planning Council, 1975, p. 54. For need to reduce size of GSAS at HU, see Committee on the Future of the Graduate School, 1969, pp. 13–15. For enrollment patterns, see institutional sources—*Fact Books,* registrars' reports, accreditation reports. For national patterns parallel to Massachusetts, see N. Smelser and R. Content, 1980, p. 46.

79. For Bernstein, see author interview. Early in his presidency, Bok called for more attention to preparation for teaching in doctoral programs (see HUAR (1973)), but his review of steps that should be taken to improve teaching produced toward the end of his presidency was silent on this possibility (see D. Bok, 1986). For similar sentiments from Hallowell, see TUAR (1973), 15. For DA, see Paul L. Dressell and Magdala Thompson, 1978. For relationship of research and teaching, see D. Webster, 1985, p. 60.

80. For MIT, see MITAR (1973), 3–4; (1976), A38–39; Committee on MIT Research Structure, 1976. For other examples, see UMAR (1977), 18–20; Board of Trustees, BU, "Boston University, 1971–1981," p. 27; *Northeastern University Fact Book,* 1983, p. 33. For a general discussion of impact of market pressures on professional education, see J. Ben-David, 1977, p. 64–67.

81. J. Ben-David, 1972, p. 35.

82. For similarity of institutional responses to proposals for core curricula, see B. O'Connell, in Change Magazine Press, 1979, p. 27. For standardization/professionalization of academic administration, see: R. Birnbaum, 1983, pp. 72ff.; E. Duryea, and T. McConnell, in P. Altbach and R. Berdahl, 1981.

83. For Carnegie council, see Carnegie Council on Policy Studies, 1982; V. Stadtman, 1980, pp. 97ff. For scholarly literature, see B. Clark, 1983, esp. Chapt. 7; R. Birnbaum, 1983; E. Gross and P. Grambsch, 1974, Chapt. 3; J. Corson, 1975. For a different slant on impact of competition, see J. Frey, 1977, who argues that conditions of scarcity promote interinstitutional collaboration. For "the road to survival," see Carnegie Council on Policy Studies, 1982, p. 30. For Riesman, see D. C. Denison, 1983. See also J. Ben-David, 1972, p. 35. R. Birnbaum, 1983 (esp. pp. 22ff., 183ff.), argues that long-term change in the academic system does not derive from institutional change

but from processes of "natural selection" and institutional "mortality"; this macro-level assessment is useful and provocative but understates, in the author's view, the importance of the evolutionary changes that flow from the kinds of institutional adaptations chronicled in this book.

84. For "leagues," see E. Gross, and P. Grambsch, 1974, p. 3. For diversity within institutions, see Carnegie Council on Policy Studies, 1982, p. 22; J. Ben-David, 1977; A. K. Rice, 1970, p 85.

85. For reports, see Martin Trow, 1987; Z. Gamson, 1987.

86. For state action, see Z. Gamson, 1987, p. 437. For argument that greater external control of higher education is needed to promote institutional change, see B. Richman and R. Farmer, 1974; J. Hefferlin, 1969.

87. For a similar view of benefits of competitive systems in meeting social needs, see B. Clark, 1983, pp. 212–13, 270. For a critical view of statewide governing boards, see Hugh D. Graham, in *Chronicle of Higher Education,* Nov. 4, 1987, p. A60; for an extended statement, see Hugh Graham, 1989.

Bibliography

The bibliography is divided into two sections. The first part focuses on specific institutions and lists all sources, published and unpublished, used in my studies of individual universities. The second part is a general bibliography of sources consulted for those portions of the book that discuss broad academic patterns at the state and national levels. Sources used for both aspects of the book are listed only in the section of the bibliography associated with their primary contribution to my research.

INSTITUTIONAL SOURCES

Boston College

Books and Periodicals

Boston Globe. Selected dates.

Bridge (magazine of the BC Jesuit community). "Author, Scholar, Administrator, Athlete." Sept. 1972.

———. "Father Joyce, Where Do You Go From Here?" Feb. 1972.

———. "The President Resigns." Feb. 1972.

Brosnahan, Timothy. "President Eliot and the Jesuit Colleges." *Sacred Heart Review,* Jan. 13, 1900.

Delay, Jim. "One Hundred Cents—Under the Money Tree with Things Looking Up." *Bridge,* Oct. 1971.

Donovan, Charles F. "A Cheerful Reminiscence." *Boston College Magazine,* June 1979.

Donovan, Charles F., David R. Dunigan, and Paul M. Fitzgerald. *History of Boston College.* Chestnut Hill: The University Press of Boston College, 1990.

Dunigan, David R. *A History of Boston College.* Milwaukee: The Burke Publishing Co., 1947.

Fitzgerald, Paul A. and Charles F. Donovan. *Boston College, A Pictorial History.* Chestnut Hill: University Archives, Boston College, 1981.

Fitzgerald, Paul A. *The Governance of Jesuit Colleges in the United States, 1920–1970.* Notre Dame: University of Notre Dame Press, 1984.

Foley, Ernest B. "St. Ignatius Lives." *Bridge,* March 1973.

Frost, Jack. *The Crowned Hilltop.* Redding: Hawthorne Press, 1962.

Greeley, Andrew M. *The Changing Catholic College.* Chicago: Aldine Publishing Co., 1967.

Meisenzahl, Stuart B, ed. *Centennial History of Boston College.* Boston: Sub Turry, Boston College Yearbook, 1963.

Riesman, David and Christopher Jencks. "Boston College," in "The Viability of the American College." In Nevitt Sanford, ed. *The American College*. New York: John Wiley & Sons, 1962.

Stylus (campus periodical). Selected dates.

Sweeney, Francis J., ed. *The Centennial Colloquium at Boston College*. New York: Farrar, Strauss, 1966.

Tessitore, John. "B.C. Finances—Getting Better All the Time." *Bridge*. Nov. 1972.

Published Reports and Documents, Boston College

Boston College Building Fund Committee. "Boston College Builds." 1946.

Boston College *Bulletin*. 1950s and 1960s.

"Boston College, Chestnut Hill, Massachusetts" (fund-raising letter, development program). 1966.

Boston College Fact Book. 1972, 1978.

"Boston College, New Heights Advancement Campaign" (development brochure). 1976.

"Boston College, 1972–1977, A Report" (report of the president).

"Brief Facts About Boston College." 100th Anniversary Development Program. 1964.

College of Business Administration. "10 Years of Public Service, Boston Citizen Seminars, 1954–64."

"Planning Your Estate" (development brochure). 1965.

School of Management. "Boston Citizen Seminars, 1954–79."

"The Story of Boston College" (fund-raising pamphlet). 1926.

"Ten-Year Report: 1958–1968 at the University called Boston College" (report of the president).

"Toward Greater Heights." The Boston College Program for Strength in Excellence. 1961.

"The University and the City of Man." The Boston College Program for Strength in Excellence. 1969.

University Faculty Manual. 1953, 1957.

"University Statutes." 1960, 1968, 1970, 1973, 1980.

Published Reports and Documents, Society of Jesus

Farrell, Allan P. and Matthew J. Fitzsimons. "A Study of Jesuit Education." Jesuit Educational Association, 1958.

Jesuit Educational Association. *Bulletin*. Selected dates.

Jesuit Educational Association. *Directory*. Selected dates.

Jesuit Educational Quarterly. Selected dates.

Kelley, William F. "Commission for the Study of American Jesuit Higher Education, Report to the 31st General Congregation." Milwaukee: Wisconsin Jesuit Province, 1966.

———. "The Jesuit Order and Higher Education in the U.S., 1789–1966." Milwaukee: Wisconsin Jesuit Province, 1966.

Society of Jesus. *Catalogus Provinciae, Novae Angliae, Societatis Jesu*. Rome: RP. Bibliothecatio, 1958, 1968.

Unpublished Documents, Boston College

Admissions-Housing Committee. "Report on the Demand for and Supply of Resident Spaces at Boston College." July 1977. BCA.

Annual Financial Statements for years ended 1948, 1953, 1958, 1963, 1968, 1973, 1977. BCA.

Butterfield, Victor. Letter to John L. Mahoney, Sept. 14, 1964.

Campanella, Frank B. "The Boston College Long-Range Financial Plan." April 1976. BCA.

Committee on Trustees. "Memo to Father Rector." Undated, ca. 1970. BCA.

Committee on University Priorities. "Report to the President." Feb. 1, 1972. BCA.

Daniere, André. "A Faculty View on University Priorities." Undated, ca. 1971. BCA.

Faculty of Arts and Sciences. "A Study of the College of Arts and Sciences, Final Report of the Subcommittees." July 28, 1955. BCA.

"The Jesuits at Boston College." Jan. 21, 1974. Privately obtained.

Joyce, W. Seavey. President's file. BCA.

"Re-evaluation Material Prepared for the New England Association of Colleges and Secondary Schools." July 1966. BCA.

"Report to the Commission on Institutions of Higher Education of the NEACSS." Feb. 1976. BCA.

"Self-Study of the College of Arts and Sciences." 1963–64. BCA.

"Triennial Report for St. Mary's Community, 1971–1973." BCA.

University Academic Planning Council. "Report to the President." Feb. 1975. BCA.

University Planning Committee. "Report." 1959–60 and 1960–61. BCA.

Unpublished Documents, Society of Jesus

Henle, R. J., ed. "Final Report of the Workshop on the Role of Philosophy and Theology as Academic Disciplines." Aug. 6–14, 1962. BCA.

Jesuit Educational Association. "The Society of Jesus and Higher Education in America." Proceedings of the Woodstock Institute, Oct. 9–11, 1964. BCA.

Jesuit Educational Association, Executive Committee. Digests of Meetings. Selected dates. BCA.

Jesuit Educational Association, Executive Committee. Minutes. Selected dates. BCA.

Jesuit Educational Association, Executive Director. Reports to the Board of Governors and Responses by Governors. Selected dates. BCA.

Mallon, Wilfred M., ed. "Proceedings of the Institute for Jesuit Deans." JEA, Aug 3–13, 1948. BCA.

Task Force on Higher Education (TF-4). "Report." Society of Jesus, New England Province, ca. 1965. CHA.

Interviews and Correspondence

Father Charles F. Donovan, S.J.; Arthur Doyle; Father Paul A. Fitzgerald, S.J.; John Neuhauser; Father J. Powers, S.J.; Father Michael P. Walsh, S.J.

Boston University

Books and Periodicals

Ault, Warren O. *Boston University, The College of Liberal Arts, 1873–1973*. Boston: Trustees of Boston University, 1973.

Bostonia (campus periodical). Selected dates.

Case, Harold. "Harvest from the Seed" (speech to Newcomen Society). Boston University, 1957.

Commonwealth Monthly (campus periodical). Selected dates.
Currents (campus periodical). Selected dates.
Daily Free Press (campus periodical). Selected dates.
Ephron, Nora. "Academic Gore." *Esquire.* Sept. 1977.
Kern, Edward. "Quest for the Silver Unicorn." *Life,* June 4, 1971.
McLean, Deckle. "Vision of Greatness." *Boston Globe Magazine,* March 5, 1972.
The News (campus periodical). Selected dates.
Radin, Charles. *Boston Globe* (two-part series), Feb. 15–16, 1976.
————. *Boston Globe* (five-part series), Nov. 7–12, 1976.

Published Reports and Documents

Annual Report of the Treasurer for years ended 1940, 1948, 1958.
Board of Trustees, Boston University. "Boston University, 1971–1981."
————. "Boston University, 1971–1986."
Boston University *Catalog.* selected dates.
Boston University Fact Book. 1962–63, 1977–78.
"Boston University Financial Report." 1977.
Boston University News Bureau. "In New Administrative Organization Board of Trustees Vote for Continuation of Silber Administration." May 1976.
Faculty Manual. 1950, 1952, 1957, 1962, 1967, 1970.
President's Annual Report. 1930, 1938–1967.
Smith, Charles W. "Five-Year Report of the Vice President for Finance, 1971–75."

Unpublished Reports and Documents

"An Assessment of Boston University by the Influence Leaders of Boston." Office of University Affairs, 1967. BUA.
Committee on the University in the Postwar World. "Analysis of Responses of the Deans of Boston University to the Proposals of the Committee on the University in the Postwar World." Undated, ca. 1944. BUA.
————. "Report." 1944. BUA.
"Consultants' Report on Institutional Planning and Development." 1966. BUA.
"Long-Range Planning, A Progress Report." 4 vols. 1966–67. BUA.
Perkins, John S. "Boston University Medical Center: FACT Review." Nov. 1973. Privately obtained.
————. "Financial History of Boston University in the 1960s." Sept. 10, 1970. BUA.
————. "How Did We Get Here From There?" Dec. 1977. Privately obtained.
————. "Is the Silber Storm Coming to an End?" Undated. Privately obtained.
President's Commission. "Preliminary Report." June 1976. BUA.
Provost's Task Force on Faculty and Student Life. "Students and Faculty in a Learning Environment." Dec. 1978. BUA.
Silber, John R. "Letter to the Faculty of Boston University." Dec. 8, 1982. BUA.
Steadman, Lawrence E. *College and University Management.* Unpublished DBA thesis, Graduate School of Business Administration, Harvard University, 1976.
Task Force 'B'. "University/City Relations." Dec. 1978. BUA.

Interviews and Correspondence

Charles Beye, Peter Farrago, Kurt Hertzfeld, John S. Perkins.

Brandeis

Books and Periodicals

Abram, Morris. *The Day is Short: An Autobiography.* New York: Harcourt Brace Jovanovich, 1982.
Boston Globe. Selected dates.
Brandeis Review (campus periodical). Winter 1983.
Goldstein, Israel. *Brandeis University: Chapter of its Founding.* New York: Bloch Publishing Co., 1951.
Justice (campus periodical). Selected dates.
Newman, Louis I. *Biting on Granite.* New York: Bloch Publishing Co., 1946.
Sachar, Abram. *A Host at Last.* Boston: Atlantic Monthly Press, 1976.
Saturday Review. "Brandeis: A Young University in A Hurry." March 17, 1962.

Published Reports and Documents

Bernstein, Marver. "Inaugural Address." Oct. 5, 1972.
Brandeis *Catalogue.* Selected dates.
Centennial Fund Committee. "The Brandeis Centennial Year." 1956.
Faculty Handbook. 1958, 1962, 1968, 1972, 1976.
Ford Foundation. "Toward Greatness in Higher Education." Dec. 1964.
"This is Brandeis." Undated admissions brochure.
Werner, Alfred. "A Jewish University." National Community Relations Advisory Council, 1948.

Unpublished Reports and Documents

Admissions Office (later Office of Admissions and Financial Aid). Data on entering classes (various titles). 1957, 1959, 1961, 1967, 1972. Privately obtained.
———. "Seven-Year Trend Study, 1974–80." Privately obtained.
Alexander, David A. *The Brandeis Challenge.* Unpublished thesis, Brandeis University, 1979.
Financial Statements for years ended 1949, 1953, 1958, 1963, 1968, 1973, 1978. Privately obtained.
Cohen, Saul. "Art, Science, Neuroscience and Brandeis." Dec. 1984. Privately obtained.
———. (speech). "Prepared for the Boston Latin School Association." Nov. 22, 1983. Privately obtained.
Committee on General Education. "Report." April 20, 1965. Privately obtained.
Controller's Office. "Gifts Received During Fiscal Years Ended June 30, 1948 to 1980." Sept. 30, 1980. Privately obtained.
"Faculty Student Relations." Unsigned memo to Leonard Levy. March 5, 1965. Privately obtained.
Levy, Leonard. Memo to Deans Morrissey and Black et al. "Faculty-Student Relations." March 29, 1965. Privately obtained.
———. Memo to President Sachar. "Faculty Work Load." March 16, 1964. Privately obtained.
———. Memo to the Educational Policy Committee. "Faculty Work Load." April 20, 1964. Privately obtained.

"Materials Submitted to Massachusetts Pre-Medical Approving Authority." 1951. BrUA.

N. Madison Cartmell and Associates. "Administrative Survey/Brandeis University." Feb. 15, 1956. Privately obtained.

"Profile of Brandeis University, 1948–1972." Undated, ca. 1962. Privately obtained.

"Re-evaluation Report to the New England Association of Schools and Colleges, Inc." 1966. Privately obtained.

"Report of Brandeis University for the Commission on Institutions of Higher Education of the New England Association of Schools and Colleges, Inc." Nov. 1976. Privately obtained.

Richlin, Dean. *The Founding of Brandeis University: American Jewry's Search for Security.* Unpublished thesis, Wesleyan University, 1974.

Sachar, Abram. "A President's View of University Governance." Address to AAUP, Dec. 6, 1963. Privately obtained.

Sacks, I. Milton. Memo to President Sachar and Dean Levy. "Faculty Work Load." June 19, 1964. Privately obtained.

Interviews and Correspondence

Author: Marver Bernstein, Eugene Black, Saul Cohen, David Gould, Joseph Kauffman, Morton Keller, Attila Klein, Harold Levine, Lester Loomis, Saul Touster, Abram Sachar. Taped interviews from Dean Richlin: George Alpert, Clarence Berger, Israel Goldstein, Otto Nathan, Abram Sachar, C. Ruggles Smith and Dudley Kimball.

Harvard

Books and Periodicals

Aldrich, Nelson W., Jr. "Harvard on the Way Down." *Harper's,* March 1976, pp. 39–52.

Baltzell, E. Digby. "Puritan Harvard and Quaker Penn." The *Pennsylvania Gazette,* Nov. 1979.

Bethell, John T. "The University on Trial." *Harvard Magazine,* March–April, 1979.

Bok, Derek, *Beyond the Ivory Tower.* Cambridge: Harvard University Press, 1982.

———. *Higher Learning.* Cambridge: Harvard University Press, 1986.

Bundy, McGeorge. "Were Those the Days?" *Daedalus,* vol. 99 (Summer 1970).

Cabot, Paul C. "Chasing the Budget, My Twelve Years as Treasurer." *Harvard Alumni Bulletin,* May 1963, pp. 634–37.

Campbell, Colin. "The Harvard Factor." *New York Times Magazine,* July 20, 1986.

Conant, James B. "America Remembers the University." *Atlantic Monthly,* vol. 177, May 1946.

———. *Education in a Divided World.* Cambridge: Harvard University Press, 1948.

———. *My Several Lives.* New York: Harper and Row, 1970.

Fiske, Edward B. "After Criticism, Harvard Acts to Improve Quality Teaching," *New York Times,* Dec. 5, 1977, pp. 1, 26.

French, Peter. *The Long Reach.* New York: Ives Washburn, 1962.

Harris, Seymour. *The Economics of Harvard.* New York: McGraw-Hill, 1970.

Harvard Committee. *General Education in a Free Society.* Cambridge: Harvard University Press, 1945.

Hawkins, Hugh. *Between Harvard and America.* New York: Oxford University Press, 1972.

Kahn, E. J., Jr. *Harvard, Through Change and Through Storm.* New York: W. W. Norton, 1969.

Keller, Phyllis. *Getting At The Core.* Cambridge: Harvard University Press, 1982.

Kern, Edward. "Close-up: Derek Bok, Harvard Picks a Young Face for the '70s." *Life,* Jan. 22, 1971, pp. 34–36.

Kistiakowsky, George B. "James Bryant Conant, 1893–1978." *Biographical Memoirs of Fellows of the Royal Society,* vol. 25, Nov. 1979.

Kuklick, Bruce. *Rise of American Philosophy.* New Haven: Yale University Press, 1977.

Larkin, Al. "The Cautious Presidency of Derek Bok." *Boston Globe Magazine,* June 4, 1978, pp. 6ff.

Lipset, Seymour Martin and David Riesman. *Education and Politics at Harvard.* New York: McGraw-Hill, 1975.

Lowell, A. Lawrence. *At War With Academic Traditions in America.* Cambridge: Harvard University Press, 1934.

————. *What a University President Has Learned.* New York: The Macmillan Co., 1938.

Meyer, Marshall. "After the Bust: Student Politics at Harvard, 1969–1972." In David Riesman and Verne Stadtman. *Academic Transformation.* New York: McGraw-Hill, 1973.

Morison, Samuel E. *Three Centuries of Harvard, 1636–1936.* Cambridge: Harvard University Press, 1942.

The New York Times. Selected dates.

O'Connell, Barry. "Where Does Harvard Lead Us?" In Change Magazine Press. *The Great Core Curriculum Debate.* New Rochelle: Change Magazine Press, 1979.

Powell, Arthur G. *The Uncertain Profession.* Cambridge: Harvard University Press, 1980.

Pusey, Nathan M. *Age of the Scholar.* Cambridge: Harvard University Press, 1964.

————. *American Higher Education.* Cambridge: Harvard University Press, 1978.

Rosovsky, Henry. *The University, An Owner's Manual.* New York: W. W. Norton, 1990.

Sacks, David Harris. "Bok's Harvard: Ethics 350." *Boston Review,* Oct. 1986.

Sinnott, Marcia G. *The Half-Opened Door.* Westport: Greenwood Press, 1979.

Smith, Richard N. *The Harvard Century.* New York: Simon and Schuster, 1986.

Special Committee. *The Harvard Report on Some Problems of Personnel in the Faculty of Arts and Sciences.* Cambridge: Harvard University Press, 1939.

"Still Smiling After Fifteen Years." *Harvard Magazine,* Sept.–Oct. 1986.

Story, Ronald. *The Forging of an Aristocracy: Harvard and the Boston Upper Class, 1800–1870.* Middletown: Wesleyan University Press, 1980.

————. "Harvard and the Boston Brahmins: A Study in Institutional and Class Development, 1800–1865." *Journal of Social History,* vol. 8, Spring 1975, pp. 94–121.

Ulam, Adam. *The Fall of the American University.* New York: The Library Press, 1972.

Vigeland, Carl A. *Great Good Fortune.* Boston: Houghton Mifflin, 1986.

Yeomans, H. A. *Abbott Lawrence Lowell, 1856–1943.* Cambridge: Harvard University Press, 1948.

Published Reports and Documents

Bok, Derek, "Issues of Race at Harvard: An Open Letter to the Harvard Community." Feb. 27, 1981.

————. "Reflections on the Ethical Responsibilities of the University in Society: Open Letter to the Harvard Community." March 9, 1979.

Committee on Admission (later Admission and Scholarship Committee). Annual Reports. 1930, 1940, 1947, 1948, 1952, 1953, 1954, 1960, 1967, 1968, 1969.

Committee on the University and the City. "Report on the University and the City." Dec. 1968.

Dean of Arts and Sciences Report. 1955, 1956.

"Growth and Changes at Harvard: Ten Years in Statistical Summary." 1964.

Harvard University *Catalogue.* Selected dates.

Office of the Dean, Faculty of Arts and Sciences. "A Letter to the Faculty on Undergraduate Education." Oct. 1974.

———. "Report to the Faculty and Students on the Core Curriculum." May 1979.

President's Report. 1908, 1942–1980.

Pusey, Nathan M. "Harvard and the Federal Government: A Report to the Faculties and the Governing Boards of the University." Sept. 1961.

Treasurer's Report for years ended 1930, 1940, 1948, 1953, 1958, 1963, 1968, 1978.

"The University and Its Resources." 1968.

University Committee on Governance. "Discussion Memorandum Concerning the Choice of a New President." April 1970.

———. "Harvard and Money, A Memorandum on Issues and Choices." Nov. 1970.

———. "The Nature and Purposes of the University, A Discussion Memorandum." Jan. 1971.

———. "The Organization and Functions of the Governing Boards and the President's Office, A Discussion Memorandum." March 1971.

———. "Tentative Recommendations Concerning a University Senate and the Council of Deans." Feb. 1972.

Unpublished Reports and Documents

Committee of Fifteen, Faculty of Arts and Sciences. "Interim Report on the Causes of the Recent Crisis." June 9, 1969. HUA.

Committee on Appointments, Promotions and Retirements, Faculty of Arts and Sciences. "Report." March 14, 1956. HUA.

Committee on the Future of the Graduate School, Faculty of Arts and Sciences. "Report." 1969. HUA.

Committee on the Organization of the Faculty of Arts and Sciences, Faculty of Arts and Sciences. "Report." Oct. 17, 1969. HUA.

Committee on the Recruitment and Retention of Faculty, Faculty of Arts and Sciences. "Report." May 1968. HUA.

Committee to Consider Aspects of the Harvard-Radcliffe Relationship that Affect Administrative Arrangements, Admissions, Financial Aid and Educational Policy. "Report." Feb. 1975. HUA.

Conant, James B. "Diversity in Higher Education." Speech at Northeastern's 50th anniversary. NUA.

Feldman, Penny H. *Recruiting an Elite: Admission to Harvard College.* Unpublished thesis, Harvard College, 1975.

Galeota, William R. *Resource Allocation in Harvard University.* Unpublished thesis, Harvard College, 1970.

Special Committee of the Board of Overseers on the Financial Requirements of the University and the Deficit Incurred During Recent Years. "Report." 1904. HUA.

Special Committee on College Admission Policy, Faculty of Arts and Sciences. "Admission to Harvard College." 1960. HUA.

Special Committee to Review the Present Status and Problems of the General Education Program. "Report." May 1964. HUA.
Task Force on the Core Curriculum. Faculty of Arts and Sciences. "Report." Sept. 1976. HUA.

Interviews and Correspondence

William Bentinck-Smith, McGeorge Bundy, Alfred D. Chandler, Thurston Child, Franklin Ford, Hugh Hawkins, Phyllis Keller, George Kistiakowsky, Henry Murray, Thomas O'Brien, Nathan Pusey, David Riesman, David Z. Robinson, Robert Shenton, Robert C. Wood.

Massachusetts Institute of Technology

Books and Periodicals

Blackwood, James R. *The House on College Avenue: The Comptons at Wooster, 1891–1913.* Cambridge: MIT Press, 1968.
Burchard, John E. *Mid-Century: The Social Implications of Scientific Progress.* Cambridge: The Technology Press, 1950.
———. *Q.E.D.: MIT in World War II.* New York: The Technology Press, 1948.
Compton, Karl T. "Cultural Aspects of Engineering Education." *Journal of Engineering Education,* vol. 23, Oct. 1932, pp. 69–76.
———. "Educational Objectives at M.I.T." *The Technology Review,* March 1932, pp. 242ff.
———. "The Future of Engineering." *The Technology Review,* Feb. 1932, pp. 163ff.
———. "The Government's Responsibilities in Science." *Science.* April 12, 1935, pp. 347–55.
———. "Universities and the Public Welfare." Reprint of address at Abbott Laboratories, undated. MITA.
Geiger, Roger L. "Institutional Patterns: MIT." Draft section of *To Utilize Knowledge: The Growth of American Research Universities. 1940 to the Present.* Dec. 1986.
Killian, James R., Jr. *The Education of a College President.* Cambridge: The MIT Press, 1985.
Noble, David. *America By Design.* New York: Oxford University Press, 1977.
Pearson, Henry G. *Richard Cockburn Maclaurin.* New York: Macmillan Co., 1937.
Prescott, Samuel C. *When MIT Was "Boston Tech."* Cambridge: The Technology Press, 1954.
Snyder, Benson. "Change Despite Turmoil at MIT." In David Riesman and Verne Stadtman. *Academic Transformation.* New York: McGraw-Hill, 1973.
Technology Review (campus publication). Selected dates.
Weeks, Edward. *The Lowells and Their Institute.* Boston: Little, Brown and Co., 1966.

Published Reports and Documents

"By-Laws of the Corporation" (later "Corporation By-Laws"). 1934, 1962, 1971.
Commission on MIT Education. *Report: Creative Renewal in a Time of Crisis.* Nov. 1970.
Committee on Educational Survey. *Report.* 1949.
Committee on Financing Development. "Funding MIT's Independence." 1948.
———. "MIT—A New Era." 1948.
———. "Statement of the MIT Fund-Raising Plans." 1948.
Director of Admissions Report (later Admissions Office, Office of Admissions). 1935, 1940, 1948, 1953, 1968, 1974, 1978.

"Liberal Education at the Massachusetts Institute of Technology" (brochure). 1952.

MIT *Bulletin*. Selected dates.

"Policies and Procedures." 1939, 1940, 1945, 1947, 1952, 1957, 1961, 1966, 1979.

President's Report. 1931–1980.

Registrar's Report, 1930, 1935, 1940, 1944, 1945, 1947, 1948, 1953, 1958, 1963, 1968, 1973, 1978.

"Rules and Regulations of the Faculty." 1930, 1975.

Second-Century Program. "From Strength to Greater Strength" (undated fund-raising material). Ca. 1961.

―――. "In Common Cause: to representatives of Massachusetts business and industry." 1961.

Treasurer's Report for years ended 1930, 1940, 1947, 1948, 1953, 1958, 1963, 1968, 1973, 1978.

Unpublished Reports and Documents

Ad Hoc Committee on Enrollment. "Report." Feb. 23, 1956. MITA.

Ad Hoc Committee on Outside Commitments. "Report." Feb. 15, 1970. MITA.

Committee on Curriculum Content Planning. "Report." May 1964. MITA.

Committee on Educational Policy. "Changing the Undergraduate Curriculum at MIT." 1964. MITA.

―――. "Report on MIT Faculty Survey." 1964. MITA.

Committee on Faculty Responsibility. "Report." Feb. 1963. MITA.

Committee on MIT Research Structure. "Report." June 21, 1976. MITA.

Committee on Staff Environment. "Report." 1949. MITA.

Committee on Student Environment. "Undergraduate Housing in the 1970s." 1973. MITA.

Committee on the Future of the Graduate School. "Report." Feb. 7, 1958. MITA.

Committee on the HASS Requirements. "Report." Aug. 5, 1986. Privately obtained.

Committee on Undergraduate Admissions and Student Aid. "Report, March 1967 to June 1969." Oct. 10, 1969. MITA.

Committee on Undergraduate Policy. "Final Draft, Recommendation to be presented to the Faculty at the April Meeting." April 3, 1956. MITA.

Division of Industrial Cooperation. Files contained in MITA collection "Office of the President, 1897–1932" and "Office of the President, 1930–1958."

Faculty Records. March 21, 1956. "Circulated with the call for the meeting of April 18, 1956." MITA.

Garvin, David. "MIT and the Federal Government." Unpublished report for the Sloan Commission on Government and Higher Education. 1977. Privately obtained.

Graduate School Study Committee. "Report." 1968. MITA.

Gutierrez, Manuel G. *Description and Analysis of the MIT Budgeting Process*. Unpublished thesis, Sloan School of Management, 1977.

Ladd, P. J. "The Massachusetts Institute of Technology: 1865–1947." Sept. 1947. Paper prepared for Committee on Educational Survey. MITA.

Marquis, Kathleen and Helen Samuels. "Technology Moves to Cambridge." Undated draft essay. MITA.

Norton, C. L. "Five Years on the Technology Plan." In President's file, AC-4 under "Industrial Cooperation and Research, New Dean, 1924–29." MITA.

Planning Committee for the work of the Commission on Nature and Purposes of MIT Education. "Preliminary Report." Aug. 4, 1969. MITA.

"Proposal to Establish a Graduate School, reported by the Faculty Council to the Faculty for discussion at its meeting on Wednesday, February 17th, 1932." MITA.

Romanowski, Roslyn. "Notes on Chairman of the Corporation Papers, 1939–54." MITA.

Tatlow, Thomas. "November Actions." Unpublished paper. Nov. 1969. MITA.

Thresher, B. A. Letter to Frederick R. Keppel, Carnegie Corporation, on enrollment stabilization, with attachments. Jan. 3, 1939. President's file. MITA.

Interviews and Correspondence

Gordon Brown, Alfred D. Chandler, David Garvin, Paul E. Gray, Howard W. Johnson, James R. Killian, Jr., Loretta Mannix, Leo Marx, Sandra Morgan, Elting Morison, Ray Pariser, Walter Rosenblith, Helen W. Samuels, Martin Sirbu, Julius Stratton, Robert C. Wood, Jerrold Zacharias.

Northeastern

Books and Periodicals

Boston Herald American. Selected dates.

Frederick, Antoinette. *Northeastern University, An Emerging Giant: 1959–1975.* Boston: Northeastern University Custom Book Program, 1982.

Knowles, Asa S. "Emerging Features of Tomorrow's Higher Education." *The Educational Record,* Oct. 1957.

———. "The Influence of Industries on Local Academic Programs." *The Educational Record,* July 1961.

———. "Orientation of a College President." *The Educational Record,* Jan. 1960.

Marston, Everett C. *Origin and Development of Northeastern University.* Boston: Northeastern University, 1961.

Morris, Rudolph M. *Where? On Huntington Avenue.* North Quincy: The Christopher Publishing House, 1977.

Northeastern News (campus periodical). Selected dates.

"Northeastern to Establish 'University College,' Trustees Approve Plan to Provide Appropriate Status for Adult Education" (periodical article). Undated, ca. 1960. Knowles papers, NUA.

The Northeastern Edition (campus periodical). Selected dates.

Waldorf, Dan. "Northeastern University: A Private University Serving the Urban Proletariat." In George Nash et al. *The University and the City.* New York: McGraw-Hill, 1973.

Published Reports and Documents

"An Opportunity for Investment" (fund-raising brochure). Jan. 20, 1931.

"Blazing a New Trail in Higher Education" (fund-raising brochure). 1935.

"Condensed Financial Statements, Year Ending June 30, 1979."

Ell, Carl. "Northeastern at Boston, Adventure in Education to Develop Latent Talents." Speech to Newcomen Society, May 24, 1956.

Faculty Handbooks. 1938, 1941, 1944, 1949, 1954, 1957, 1961, 1962, 1966, 1967, 1971, 1974.

Northeastern University *Catalog.* Selected dates.

"The Northeastern University Corporation: The University and Its Governing Body." Jan. 1955.

Northeastern University Fact Book. 1983.
President's Annual Report. 1941–1974.

Unpublished Reports and Documents

"Accreditation Information." Undated, ca. 1941. NUA.
"Data Prepared for the New England Association of Colleges and Secondary Schools by Northeastern University." Spring 1967. NVA.
Ell, Carl. Letter to Speare. Feb. 8, 1932. NVA.
———. Memo to Churchill et al. "Committee on University Policies Affecting the Faculty." May 12, 1947. NUA.
———. "Remarks to Executive Committee of Trustees." Oct. 13, 1955. NUA.
———. "Statement in Regard to Northeastern University." Jan. 23, 1937. NUA.
———. "Statement in Regard to the University and its Faculty." Aug. 1, 1958. NUA.
Financial Statement and Auditor's Report for year ended June 30, 1977.
"The Institutional Self-study Report Prepared for the New England Association of Schools and Colleges." 2 vols. Fall 1978. NUA.
Knowles, Asa S. "Higher Education Responds to Campus Unrest." Undated speech, ca. 1970. NUA.
———. Letter to Troupe. Nov. 15, 1966. NUA.
———. Letter to White. Feb. 10, 1966. NUA.
———. Memo to Members of the Faculty and Staff. "The University and Urban Renewal Planning in Boston." Sept. 13, 1961.
———. "University Advisory Committee on Faculty Policy." July 1959. NUA.
Lovely, William A. Memo to Professor Bateson. "Center for Continuing Education, Cost-Revenue Examination." Oct. 27, 1970. Privately obtained.
"New England Association of Colleges and Secondary Schools, Information Blank, Senior Colleges." Sept. 30, 1940. NUA.
"Northeastern University Accreditation, Historical Notes." Jan. 15, 1960. NUA.
Office of University Planning. "Obsolescent Projections." March 22, 1971. Privately obtained.
Planning Office. "Boston Campus Master Plan." Nov. 15, 1976. Privately obtained.
Ryder, Kenneth. Memo to all concerned. "Information Concerning the University Budget." March 18, 1969. NUA.
Vernon, Arthur A. "History of Graduate Work at Northeastern University." June 24, 1969. NUA

Interviews and Correspondence

Antoinette Frederick, Asa S. Knowles. Rudolph Morris, Kenneth Ryder, Loring Thompson.

Tufts

Books and Periodicals

Cousens, John A. "Tufts College—Its Future." Tufts College *Graduate*, Dec. 1925–Feb. 1926, pp. 69ff.
———. "The Two-Year College." Tufts College *Graduate*, Sept.–Nov. 1925, pp. 28ff.
Dunn, John A., Jr. "Entrepreneurial Planning: Tufts University." *New Directions for Institutional Research*, no. 67, Fall 1990.

Miller, Russell E. *Light on the Hill, A History of Tufts College 1852–1952*. Boston: Beacon Press, 1966.

––––––. *Light on the Hill*, volume 2, *A History of Tufts University Since 1952*. Cambridge: MassMarket Books, 1986.

Tufts College *Graduate* (campus periodical). Selected dates.

Tufts *Weekly* (campus periodical). Selected dates.

Published Reports and Documents

"Actions by the Trustees of Tufts College." Dec. 1969.

"By-Laws of the Trustees of Tufts College." 1923, 1955, 1962, 1970.

Carmichael, Leonard. "Tufts College: Its Science and Technology; A Centennial View." Speech to Newcomen Society, 1952.

"The Charter of the Trustees of Tufts College and Actions of the General Court of Massachusetts in Addition to and Antecedent Thereof." May 1, 1951.

Faculty Handbook. 1958, 1965, 1970, 1979.

Public Relations Office. "For Release Wednesday A.M. March 23," (1955) (announcement of name change). TUA.

"The Role of the Small University in American Higher Education." Proceedings of symposium. Dec. 8, 1955.

Treasurer's Report for years ended 1920, 1930, 1940, 1948, 1967, 1975.

"Tufts Self-Study." 1960.

"The Tufts Seminar to Initiate New Experiments in Undergraduate Education." Proceedings, Aug. 30–Sept. 11, 1965.

"Tufts: The Total University in Changing Times, A Report to the President by the University Steering Committee." 1973.

Tufts University *Fact Book*. 1973, 1977–78.

Unpublished Reports and Documents

Ad Hoc Committee to make a searching investigation into the present educational arrangements of the College of Liberal Arts, Jackson College, and the College of Engineering. "Tufts in Medford." March 1969. TUA.

Advisory Committee on Faculty Personnel. Memo proposing amendments to the Arts and Sciences By-laws. March 10, 1969. TUA.

––––––. "Recommendations . . . for changes in the Faculty Manual." Feb. 1961. TUA.

Barton-Gillet Company. "Communications Planning for Tufts University." Nov. 1979. TUA.

Committee on Undergraduate Education. "Report." Jan. 1973. TUA.

Cousens, John A. Correspondence with General Education Board. 1920–21. TUA.

––––––. "Memorandum concerning an organization for college education." June 1921. TUA.

––––––. Speech to Boston Tufts Club. Jan. 20, 1926. TUA.

––––––. Speech to Faculty of Arts and Sciences. June 1924. TUA.

––––––. Speech to Tufts Teachers' Association. Nov. 10, 1923. TUA.

––––––. Speech to Tufts Teachers' Association. Oct. 31, 1925. TUA.

Deans' Annual Reports (Admissions, Liberal Arts, Jackson, Engineering, Medical School, Dental School, Graduate School). Selected dates. TUA.

Graduate Long-Range Planning Committee. "Report to the Faculty of Arts and Sciences." May 1969. TUA.

Hallowell, Burton C. Installation speech. Sept. 24, 1967. TUA.

————. "The University: Neutral or Engaged?" Speech at Boston University. Aug. 16, 1969. TUA.

"Handbook of Information, Faculty of Arts and Sciences." Sept. 1, 1965. TUA.

Howard Chase Associates, Inc. "Report on Analysis of Tufts University." April 1961. TUA.

Long-Range Planning Committee of the Faculty of Arts and Sciences. "An Interim Report." Aug. 5, 1968. TUA.

Memo to Members of the Board of Trustees, untitled, listing by-law amendments since 1972. Jan. 31, 1973. TUA.

Office of the Vice President. "Memo to Members of the Faculty of Arts and Sciences." April 28, 1961.

President's Annual Report. 1920–1980, TUA.

"A Re-evaluation Report to the Commission on Institutions of Higher Education, NEASCC, Inc." April 5–7, 1970. TUA.

"Report of Ad Hoc Committee: comparison of the 1940 AAUP Statement of Policy Regarding Academic Tenure and the Statement of the Trustees of Tufts College." June 1963. TUA.

"Report of a Visiting Committee to Re-evaluate Tufts University to the Standing Committee on Institutions of Higher Education of the New England Association of Colleges and Secondary Schools." Nov. 1, 1959. TUA.

Research Coordinator. Annual report. Selected dates. TUA.

Tufts Self-Study. Executive Committee. "Final Report." Aug. 15, 1958. TUA.

————. Geiger, Kent. "A Report to the Study Committee on Admissions." Sept. 1957. TUA.

————. Mead, Leonard. "Andover Commentary on the Final Report of the Study Committee on Faculty Personnel." July 10, 1958. TUA.

————. Study Committee on Faculty Personnel. "Final Report to the Executive Committee." Feb. 26, 1958. TUA.

"Tufts University, Original and Revised Goals and Trustees Development Committee Recommendations: A Capital Funds Program for Tufts University." Oct. 27, 1960. TUA.

Vice President and Provost. Annual report. Selected dates. TUA.

Vice President for Development. Annual report. Selected dates. TUA.

Wessell, Nils Y. "Are We Using the Wrong Yardsticks in College Admissions?" Undated speech. TUA.

————. "Education and Renewal." President's Day address. April 4, 1964. TUA.

————. "President's Address." Inaugural. Tufts *Weekly,* Dec. 9, 1953, p. 1. TUA.

————. "Report to Trustees." April 15, 1965. TUA.

"Women at Tufts." Dec. 1972. TUA.

Interviews and Correspondence

Burton C. Hallowell, John A. Dunn, Robert Johnson-Lally, Leonard C. Mead, Russell E. Miller, Franklin K. Patterson, Albert D. Ullman, Nils Y. Wessell.

University of Massachusetts

Books and Periodicals

Barbrook, Alec T. *God Save the Commonwealth: An Electoral History of Massachusetts.* Amherst: University of Massachusetts Press, 1973.

Boston Globe, selected dates.

Boston Herald, Boston Herald American, Boston Herald Traveler. Selected dates.

Cary, Harold Whiting. *The University of Massachusetts: A History of One Hundred Years.* Amherst: University of Massachusetts, 1962.

Gaudet, Robert D. "The Willis-Harrington Commission: The Politics of Education Reform." *New England Journal of Public Policy,* vol. 3, Summer/Fall 1987, pp. 66–87.

Hubner, John. "Last Chance for UMass/Boston." *Real Paper,* March 9, 1979.

Litt, Edgar. *Political Cultures of Massachusetts.* Cambridge: MIT Press, 1965.

Lockhard, Duane. *New England State Politics.* Princeton: Princeton University Press, 1959.

Mass Media (campus publication, Boston). Selected dates.

Menzies, Ian and Ian Forman. "The Mess in Education." *Boston Globe.* Sept. 17–22, 1961; Sept. 24, 1961.

Meyerson, Martin and Edward Banfield. *Boston: The Job Ahead.* Cambridge: Harvard University Press, 1966.

Rand, Christopher. *Cambridge, U.S.A.* New York: Oxford University Press, 1964.

Rand, Frank P. *Yesterdays at Massachusetts State College.* Massachusetts State College, 1933.

Riesman, David and Christopher Jencks. "The University of Massachusetts." In Nevitt Sanford, ed. *The American College.* New York: John Wiley & Sons, Inc., 1962.

Schrag, Peter. *Village School Downtown.* Boston: Beacon Press, 1967.

Thernstrom, Stephan. *The Other Bostonians: Poverty and Progress in the American Metropolis, 1880–1970.* Cambridge: Harvard University Press, 1973.

Weintraub, Richard M. "Robert Wood and the University of Massachusetts." *Boston Globe Magazine,* May 27, 1973.

White, John K. *The Fractured Electorate.* Hanover: University Press of New England, 1983.

White, William. *Streetcorner Society.* Chicago: University of Chicago Press, 1943.

Wood, Robert C. "Academe Sings the Blues." *Daedalus,* vol. 104, Winter 1975, pp. 45–55.

———. "The Public-Private Forum: Good Intentions Randomize Behavior." *New England Journal of Public Policy,* vol. 3, Summer/Fall 1987, pp. 6–20.

Published Reports and Documents: University of Massachusetts

"Academic Personnel Policy of the University of Massachusetts at Amherst, Boston, Worcester." Approved by trustees as T75–125, T76–081.

Deans' Annual Reports (includes MSC). Selected dates.

"The Massachusetts Medical School." Case Study C14-75-001. Kennedy School of Government, Harvard University.

"The Massachusetts Medical School: Sequel." Case Study C94-75-0015. Kennedy School of Government, Harvard University.

President's Annual Report (includes MSC). 1930–1977.

President's Committee on the Future University of Massachusetts. "Report." Dec. 1971. Privately obtained.

Registrar's Annual Report (includes MSC). Selected dates.

Treasurer's Annual Report for years ended 1930, 1948, 1958, 1968.

"UMass Medical Center: a local, regional and statewide resource" (undated brochure). Ca. 1985.

"Tuition Policy for the University of Massachusetts." Case Study 9-179-044. Harvard Business School, Harvard University.

University of Massachusetts at Boston *Catalog*. Selected dates.

Published Reports and Documents: Commonwealth of Massachusetts

Academy for Educational Development. *Higher Education in Massachusetts: A New Look At Some Major Policy Issues*. A study for the Massachusetts Advisory Council on Education. June 1973.

Mass. Board of Higher Education. *Higher Education in the Boston Metropolitan Area*. 1969.

———. *Higher Education in the Boston Metropolitan Area. Follow-up Study*. 1971.

Mass. General Court. *Manual for the Use of the General Court*. Selected dates from 1945–1946 to 1985–1986.

SDL, Systems Research Group. "The Economic Impact of Colleges and Universities on the Boston Area." Feb. 1974.

Select Committee for the Study of Financial Problems of Private Institutions of Higher Education in the Commonwealth of Massachusetts. "Report." Jan. 1970.

Unpublished Reports and Documents: UMass Trustees and (post-1970) System Office

Ad Hoc Committee on Board Operations and Organization. "Memo." June 1970. UMSO.

"Attachment to T70-072" (Marcus Report). UMSO.

Board of Trustees. Minutes of Meetings. Selected dates. UMSO.

Board of Trustees. T-70-032 (policy creating system office). UMSO.

Board of Trustees Executive Committee. Minutes of Meetings. Selected dates. UMSO.

Board of Trustees Faculty and Educational Policy Committee. Minutes of Meetings. Selected dates. UMSO.

"Central Administration Self-Study." Sept. 8, 1978. UMSO.

Committee to Determine the Feasibility of Establishing a Law School at the University of Massachusetts. "Report." May 12, 1972. UMSO.

"Dates of Campus Chancellors." File designation. UMSO.

Edelman, Peter. Letter to Manoil. Nov. 3, 1972. UMSO.

"Governance (University-wide), 1969–73" (file designation). UMSO.

Hay Associates. "A Study of the Administrative Resources within the University of Mass." March 19, 1975. SHL.

Healey, Joseph. Letter to Booth. Sept. 17, 1975. UMSO.

———. Letter to Morris. Dec. 29, 1971. UMSO.

———. Letter to Wellman. Dec. 29, 1971. UMSO.

Johnson, Kenneth W. "The Financial Structure of the University of Massachusetts." Dec. 31, 1973. UMSO.

Newman Commission on Political Intrusion in Higher Education. Files and notes of Dorothy Marshall. Privately obtained.

———. "University of Massachusetts Medical School at Worcester." Case study prepared by S. Young, 1985. Privately obtained.

"Organization Design Review Committee" (file designation). UMSO.

Pan-University Study Group for Review of University Governance. "Memo to Board of Trustees." March 1, 1973. UMSO.

"Staff Paper on Tuition." Jan. 18, 1974. UMSO.

Troy, Frederick. "Some Observations on the Development of the University of Massachusetts." 1982. Privately obtained.

"Trustee Committee on Long-Range Planning" (file designation). 1974–1978. UMSO.

"Trustees Policy Review." Dec. 28–29, 1970. UMSO.

Wood, Robert C. "Campus Visits." Memorandum to senior staff. June 15, 1976. UMSO.

———. "Chancellors' Council and Other Consultative Arrangements." Memorandum to Chancellors. June 15, 1976. UMSO.

———. "The Planning Process." Memorandum to Board of Trustees. April 26, 1977. UMSO.

———. "Special Meeting on May 10, 1977." Memorandum to Faculty and Educational Policy Committee," with appendices. May 5, 1977. UMSO.

———. "Status of University Organization and Executive Staffing." Memorandum to Organization Design Review Committee. Jan. 11, 1977. UMSO.

———. "Tuition." Memorandum to Board of Trustees. Sept. 25, 1975. UMSO.

———. "Tuition." Nov. 20, 1975. UMSO.

Unpublished Reports and Documents: UMass/ Amherst (formerly Mass. Agricultural College, Mass. State College)

"Accreditation Self-Study." 1978. UMSO.

Ad Hoc Committee on Campus-Central Office Relations. "Final Report." Feb. 12, 1976. UMSO.

Board of Admissions and Records. "Annual Report." 1968. Attached to president's Annual Report.

Commission on Mission and Goals. "Public Service Through Academic Excellence." April 1976. UMSO.

"Constitution of the University of Massachusetts Faculty Senate." Approved by trustees Feb. 28, 1957; revised Oct. 1962. UMSO.

Dean of the Graduate School. Annual Report. 1968.

Evaluation Team Representing the Commission on Institutions of Higher Education of the NEASC. "Report." March 15, 1979. UMSO.

Faculty Senate Long-Range Planning Committee. "Directions for the Seventies." Sept. 1970. SHL.

Hunsberger, Moyer I. "Statement on Faculty Personnel Policy in the College of Arts and Sciences." Jan. 2, 1969. UMSO.

Long-Range Academic Planning Committee. "Report." June 5, 1962. SHL.

Office of Dean of Administration. "The University of Massachusetts: Toward 1975." Revised draft. July 18, 1966. UMSO.

Office of the President. "Major Higher Educational Problems in Massachusetts, 1960–75." 1960. SHL.

———. Staff Study. "Let's Face the Problem." 1960. SHL.

"Preliminary Master Plan." Unsigned. Feb. 13, 1969. USMO.

Rules Committee of Faculty Senate. "Statement of Concerns." Aug. 1975. UMSO.

"Standard Practice Instruction." 1939, 1950, 1954. UMSO.

"Statement of Professional Personnel Policies at the University of Massachusetts," with revisions of Jan. 1968. Approved by trustees as T63-050. UMSO.

Subcommittee on the Role of the Faculty in Decision-making at the University. "Report." 1969. UMSO.

Trustee Document T64-061 (regarding personnel policy). Approved May 11, 1964. UMSO.

Unpublished Reports and Documents: UMass/Boston

"Academic Organization, University of Massachusetts at Boston." Oct. 2, 1967. Attached to minutes of Trustee Committee on Faculty and Educational Policy, Oct. 16, 1967. UMSO.

Babcock, Donald C. "Principal Features of the Proposed Constitution." Nov. 19, 1969. UMSO.

Broderick, Francis L. "Memorandum to Members of the Faculty at UMass/Boston." Feb. 16, 1971. UMSO.

———. "Next Steps at UMass/Boston." Dec. 1970. UMSO.

———. "University Organization." Memorandum to President Wood. Nov. 30, 1971. UMSO.

Evaluation Team of the Commission on Institutions of Higher Education of the NEASC. "Report to the Faculty, Administration, Trustees, Students of the University of Massachusetts at Boston." Ca. 1978. Privately obtained.

Freeland, Richard M. "Report on UMass/Boston and Models of Urban Universities." Memo to Wood. Oct. 7, 1970. Privately obtained.

Gagnon, Paul. "The Real Paper Story and the University." Memorandum to "my students and other interested parties." May 10, 1979. Privately obtained.

Long-Range Planning Committee. "Commentary on Document T77-094." July 27, 1977. UMSO.

Long-Range Planning Committee. "Interim Long-Range Plan." Ca. 1977. Privately obtained.

"Master Plan to 1980." June 9, 1969. UMSO.

New Directions Committee. "New Directions." June 1974. Privately obtained.

"The Proposal for University Governance." Nov. 11, 1969. Approved by trustees as T70-061. UMSO.

"Report to the University Assembly by the Boston Representatives to the Pan-University Study Group for Review of Governance Procedures." Feb. 8, 1973. UMSO.

"Response to the Governor's Budget Recommendations for Fiscal 1969 for the University of Massachusetts, Boston." March 1, 1969. UMSO.

Ryan, John A. Letter to Harrington. Oct. 15, 1968. Privately obtained.

"Statement of Purpose, University of Massachusetts, Boston." June 1965. Privately obtained.

"University of Massachusetts-Boston Date Sheet." UMSO.

"University of Massachusetts-Boston General Administrative Structure." May 15, 1967. Approved by trustees as T67-63. UMSO.

"University of Massachusetts-Boston, General Statement of Objectives and Purposes." April 14, 1969. SHL.

Unpublished Reports and Documents: Commonwealth of Massachusetts

Association of Independent Colleges and Universities in Massachusetts. Minutes of Executive Committee meetings and annual meetings. Selected dates. Privately obtained.

———. "Proposed Association of Independent Colleges and Universities in Massachusetts," with 1967 constitution attached. Privately obtained.

Collins, James. "The Reorganization of Massachusetts Public Higher Education." Thesis proposal, UMass/Amherst, 1982. Privately obtained.

Executive Office of Educational Affairs. "Higher Education in Massachusetts." 1979. Privately obtained.

———. "Profile of Higher Education in Massachusetts." 1980. Privately obtained.

Harvard University Task Force on Higher Education. "Higher Education in Massachusetts: Policies for the Near Future." 1974. HUA.

Knowles, Asa S. "Issues in Massachusetts Higher Education, A Private View." June 1974. Privately obtained.

Massachusetts Board of Higher Education. "Enrollment Projections for the Commonwealth of Massachusetts through 1990." Undated, ca. 1975. Privately obtained.

———. "A Study of Graduate Education in Massachusetts." Staff paper by C.E. Hay. 1969. Privately obtained.

Massachusetts General Court, Legislative Research Council. "Higher Education for Greater Boston." Senate #864. April 13, 1964. SHL.

———. "Report Relative to Proposed 'Fiscal Independence' for the University of Massachusetts and Lowell Technical Institute." May 9, 1962. SHL.

Massachusetts General Court. Commission for an Investigation Relative to Opportunities and Methods for Technical and Higher Education in the Commonwealth. "Report." House 1700. Dec. 1923. SHL.

———. Special Commission Established to Investigate and Study Certain Problems of Education in the Commonwealth. "Final Report." House #2050. April 1, 1948. SHL.

———. Special Commission Established to Make an Investigation and Study Relative to Improving and Extending Educational Facilities in the Commonwealth. "Report." House #4300. June 1965. SHL.

———. Special Commission on Audit of State Needs. "Needs in Massachusetts Higher Education." House #3035. March 26, 1958. SHL.

———. Special Commission on Budgetary Powers of the University of Massachusetts and Certain Related Matters. "Report." House #3350. Jan. 24, 1962. SHL.

———. Staff of the Special Commission Established to Make an Investigation . . . 1962–1965. "A Study of Massachusetts Education Studies, 1900–63." SHL.

Organization for Social and Technical Innovation, Inc. "A Master Planning Process for Higher Education in Massachusetts." Oct. 1973. Privately obtained.

———. Appendix A: "Demand and Supply of Higher Education in Massachusetts." Oct. 1973.

———. Appendix B. "A Summary of Responses to the OSTI Questionnaire." Oct. 1973.

Sargent, Francis W. Letter to Suddath (establishing select committee). April 17, 1969. Privately obtained.

Smith, Elden T. "A Summary of Studies of the Financing of Independent Institutions of Higher Education Conducted in Five States." June 2, 1969. Privately obtained.

Stafford, Richard and Larry Lustberg. "Higher Education in Massachusetts: Issues in Their Context." Staff report for the Sloan Commission on Government and Higher Education. Fall 1978. Privately obtained.

Whitaker, John. "The Influence of the American Catholic Population on the Development of Public Higher Education in Massachusetts." Graduate student paper, UMass/Amherst, Dec. 1985. Privately obtained.

Wood, Robert C. "Issues in Massachusetts Higher Education, A Public View." June 1974. Privately obtained.

Interviews and Correspondence

Author: Francis L. Broderick, Paul Gagnon, William Kornegay, John Lederle, Ernest Lynton, Joseph Marcus, Oswald Tippo, Frank A. Tredinnick, Daisy M. Tagliacozzo, Frederick Troy. UMass Oral History Project Interviews in UMAA: Kenneth Johnson, John Lederle, Jean Paul Mather, Robert C. Wood.

GENERAL BIBLIOGRAPHY

Federal Government Reports and Documents

Advisory Committee on Education. *Report of Committee.* 75th Cong., 3d sess., 1938. H. Doc. 529.

Advisory Committee on Higher Education to the Secretary of Health, Education and Welfare. *The Federal Government and Higher Education.* Washington, D.C.: GPO, 1968.

Chase, John L. *Graduate Assistants in American Universities.* Washington, D.C.: GPO, 1970.

National Science Board. National Science Foundation. *Graduate Education: Parameters for Public Policy.* Washington, D.C.: GPO, 1969.

————. *Toward a Public Policy for Graduate Education in the Sciences.* Washington, D.C.: GPO, 1969.

President's Commission on Campus Unrest. *Campus Unrest.* Washington, D.C.: GPO, 1970.

President's Committee on Education Beyond the High School. *First Interim Report to the President.* Washington, D.C.: GPO, 1956.

————. *Second Interim Report to the President.* Washington, D.C.: GPO, 1957.

President's Scientific Research Board. *Science and Public Policy: A Program for the Nation.* Vol. 1. Washington, D.C.: GPO, 1947.

President's Task Force on Higher Education. *Priorities in Higher Education.* Washington, D.C.: GPO, August 1970.

U.S. Bureau of the Census. *Historical Statistics of the United States, from Colonial Times to 1970.* Bicentennial Edition. Part 1. Washington, D.C.: GPO, 1975.

————. *Special Demographic Analysis, CAS 85-1, Education in the United States, 1940–83.* Washington, D.C.: GPO, 1985.

U.S. Congress. House. *Postwar Education Opportunities for Service Personnel.* 78th Cong., 1st sess., 1943.

————. House. *Report 214.* 79th Cong., 1st sess., 1945.

————. Senate. Committee on Education and Labor. *Hearings on S1295 and S1509.* 78th Cong., 1st sess. 1943.

U.S. Department of Education. Office of Educational Research and Improvement. National Center for Educational Statistics. *Digest of Educational Statistics.* Washington, D.C.: GPO, 1988, 1990.

U.S. Department of Health, Education and Welfare. *Report on Higher Education.* Washington, D.C.: GPO, 1971.

U.S. Office of Education. *Biennial Survey of Education.* Washington, D.C.: GPO, selected dates.

————. *Opening Fall Enrollments, 1955.* Washington, D.C.: GPO, 1956.

U.S. President, Commission on Higher Education. *Higher Education for American Democracy.* 6 Vols. Washington, D.C.: GPO, 1947–48.

Other Reports and Documents

Academic Collective Bargaining Information Service. "Fact Sheet, #131, Fair Employment Practices." Washington, D.C.: Labor Studies Center, University of the District of Columbia, June 1985.

American Council on Education. *The Federal Investment in Higher Education: Needed Next Steps*. Washington, D.C.: American Council on Education, 1969.

The Assembly on University Goals and Governance. *A First Report*. Cambridge, Mass. American Academy of Arts and Sciences, 1971.

Association of American Universities. *The Federal Financing of Higher Education*. Washington, D.C.: Association of American Universities, April 1968.

Engineer's Council for Professional Development. *Annual Reports, 1933–39*. MITA

The Exploratory Committee on Financing Higher Education and Research. *Report*. Rockefeller Foundation, Aug. 1948. Rockefeller Foundation Archives.

"The Family Remembers." *Hebrew College Bulletin*, 5, June 1975.

Kauffman, Polly. "Boston Women and City School Politics, 1892–1905." Unpublished thesis, Boston University, 1978.

Medalia, Leon S. "The Hebrew Teacher's College: Beginnings." *Hebrew Teacher's College Bulletin*, Feb. 1957.

National Board on Graduate Education. *Federal Policy Alternatives Toward Graduate Education*. Washington, D.C.: National Academy of Sciences, Jan. 1974.

Special Committee on Campus Tensions. *Campus Tensions: Analysis and Recommendations*. Washington, D.C.: American Council on Education, 1970.

Books and Periodicals

Abbot, Walter F. "Prestige Goals in American Universities." *Social Forces*, vol. 52(3), 1974, pp. 401–7.

Aldrich, Howard E. *Organizations and Environments*. Englewood Cliffs: Prentice Hall, 1979.

Allen, H. K. *State Public Finance and State Institutions of Higher Education in the US*. New York: Columbia Univ. Press, 1952.

Altbach, Philip G. and Robert O. Berdahl. *Higher Education in American Society*. Buffalo: Prometheus Books, 1981.

American Association of University Professors. *Bulletin*. Selected dates.

————. *Depression, Recovery, and Higher Education*. New York: Methuen, 1937.

American Council on Education, comp. and ed. *Fact Book on Higher Education*. Washington: American Council on Education, 1962, 1974.

Ashby, Eric. *Adapting Universities to a Technological Society*. San Francisco: Jossey-Bass, 1974.

————. *Any Person, Any Study: An Essay on Higher Education in the United States*. New York: McGraw-Hill, 1971.

Babbidge, Homer D. and Robert M. Rosenzweig. *The Federal Interest in Higher Education*. New York: McGraw-Hill, 1962.

Baldridge, J. Victor. *Power and Conflict in the University: Research in the Sociology of Complex Organizations*. New York: John Wiley, 1971.

Baldridge, J. Victor, et al. *Policy-Making and Effective Leadership*. San Francisco: Jossey-Bass, 1978.

Baltzell, E. Digby. *Puritan Boston and Quaker Philadelphia: Two Protestant Ethics and the Spirit of Class Authority and Leadership*. New York: Free Press, 1979.

Barzun, Jacques. *The American University: How It Runs, Where It Is Going.* New York: Harper & Row, 1968.

Baumol, William J. and Peggy Heim. "The Economic Status of the Academic Profession; Taking Stock, 1964–65." AAUP Bulletin, Summer 1965, pp. 246–301.

Bell, Daniel. *The Reforming of General Education: The Columbia College Experience in Its National Setting.* New York: Columbia Univ. Press, 1966.

Ben-David, Joseph. *American Higher Education: Directions Old and New.* New York: McGraw-Hill, 1972.

———. *Centers of Learning: Britain, France, Germany, United States: An Essay.* New York: McGraw-Hill, 1977.

Berdahl, Robert O. "Evaluating Statewide Boards." In *Evaluating Statewide Boards.* San Francisco: Jossey-Bass, 1975.

Berelson, Bernard. *Graduate Education in the United States.* New York: McGraw-Hill, 1960.

Berg, Ivar. *Education and Jobs: The Great Training Robbery.* New York: Praeger, 1970.

Birnbaum, Robert. *Maintaining Diversity in Higher Education.* San Francisco: Jossey-Bass, 1983.

Blackwell, James. "Increasing Access and Retention for Minority Students in Graduate and Professional Schools." Education Testing Service, July 1985.

Blau, Peter M. *The Organization of Academic Work.* New York: John Wiley, 1973.

Blau, Peter M. and Ellen L. Slaughter. "Institutional Conditions and Student Demonstrations." *Social Problems,* Spring 1971, pp. 475ff.

Bledstein, Burton J. *Culture of Professionalism: The Middle Class and the Development of Higher Education in America.* New York: W. W. Norton, 1976.

Bloland, Harlan G. and Sue M. Bloland. *American Learned Societies in Transition: The Impact of Dissent and Recession.* New York: McGraw-Hill, 1974.

Browne, Lynn E. and John S. Hekman. "New England's Economy in the 1980's." In David R. Lampe, ed. *The Massachusetts Miracle.* Cambridge: MIT Press, 1988.

Brubacher, John S. and Willis Rudy. *Higher Education in Transition: A History of American Colleges and Universities, 1630–1968.* New York: Harper & Row, 1976.

Brumbaugh, A. J., ed. *American Universities and Colleges.* 5th edition. Washington, D.C.: American Council on Education, 1948.

Burke, Colin G. *American Collegiate Populations: A Test of the Traditional View.* New York: New York Univ. Press, 1982.

Bush, George G. *History of Higher Education in Massachusetts.* Washington, D.C.: U.S. Bureau of Education, 1891.

Bush, Vannevar. *Pieces of the Action.* New York: William Morrow & Company, 1970.

———. *Science, the Endless Frontier.* Washington, D.C.: GPO, 1945.

Caplow, Theodore and Reece J. McGee. *The Academic Marketplace.* New York: Basic Books, 1958.

Carnegie Commission on Higher Education. *The Campus and the City, Maximizing Assets and Reducing Liabilities.* New York: McGraw-Hill, 1972.

———. *A Chance to Learn.* New York: McGraw-Hill, 1970.

———. *A Digest of Reports of the Carnegie Commission on Higher Education.* New York: McGraw-Hill, 1974.

———. *Higher Education: Who Pays? Who Benefits? Who Should Pay?* New York: McGraw-Hill, 1973.

———. *Governance of Higher Education: Six Priority Problems.* New York: McGraw-Hill, 1973.

————. *A Learning Society.* New York: McGraw-Hill, 1977.

————. *Less Time, More Options: Education Beyond the High School.* New York: McGraw-Hill, 1971.

————. *New Students and New Places: Policies for Future Growth and Development of Higher Education.* New York: McGraw-Hill, 1971.

————. *Priorities for Action: Final Report of the Carnegie Commission on Higher Education.* New York: McGraw-Hill, 1973.

————. *Reform on Campus: Changing Students, Changing Academic Programs.* New York: McGraw-Hill, 1972.

————. *Sponsored Research of the Carnegie Commission on Higher Education.* New York: McGraw-Hill, 1975.

Carnegie Council on Policy Studies in Higher Education. *The States and Private Higher Education: Problems and Policies in a New Era.* San Francisco: Jossey-Bass, 1977.

————. *Three Thousand Futures: The Next Twenty Years for Higher Education.* San Francisco: Jossey-Bass, 1982.

Carnegie Foundation. *States and Higher Education: A Proud Past and Vital Future.* San Francisco: Jossey-Bass, 1976.

Cartter, Allan M. *Ph.D.'s and the Academic Labor Market.* New York: McGraw-Hill, 1976.

————. ed. *American Universities and Colleges.* 9th ed. Washington, D.C.: American Council on Education, 1964.

Chaffee, Ellen E. "The Concept of Strategy: From Business to Higher Education." In John C. Smart, ed. *Higher Education: Handbook of Theory and Research.* Vol. I. New York: Agathon Press, 1985.

Chaffee, Ellen E. and William G. Tierney. *Collegiate Culture and Leadership Strategies.* New York: Macmillan, 1988.

Change. Selected dates.

Change Magazine Press. *The Great Core-Curriculum Debate.* New Rochelle: Change Magazine Press, 1979.

Cheit, Earl F. *The New Depression in Higher Education: A Study of Financial Conditions at 41 Colleges and Universities.* New York: McGraw-Hill, 1971.

Chronicle of Higher Education. Selected dates.

Clark, Burton R. *The Higher Education System: Academic Organization in Cross-National Perspective.* Berkeley: Univ. of California Press, 1983.

————. "Organizational Adaptation and Precarious Values: A Case Study." *American Sociological Review,* June 1956, pp. 327–33.

————. "The United States." In Van de Graaf, John H., Burton R. Clark, Dorothea Furth, Dietrich Goldschmidt, and Donald Wheeler. *Academic Power: Patterns of Authority in Seven National Systems of Higher Education.* New York: Praeger, 1978.

Cohen, Michael D. and James G. March. *Leadership and Ambiguity: The American College President.* New York: McGraw-Hill, 1974.

Commission on Financing Higher Education. *Nature and Needs of Higher Education.* New York: Columbia Univ. Press, 1952.

Committee on Government and Higher Education. *The Efficiency of Freedom.* Baltimore: Johns Hopkins University Press, 1959.

Corson, John J. *The Governance of Colleges and Universities: Modernizing Structure and Processes.* New York: McGraw-Hill, 1975.

Corwin, Ronald G. *A Sociology of Education: Emerging Patterns of Class, Status, and Power in the Public Schools.* New York: Appleton-Century-Crofts, 1965.

Cremin, Lawrence. *The Transformation of the School: Progressivism in American Education, 1876–1957.* New York: Knopf, 1961.

Daedalus. American Higher Education: Toward An Uncertain Future. vol. 103, Fall 1974; and vol. 104, Winter 1975.

———. *The Embattled University.* vol. 99, Winter 1970.

———. *Rights and Responsibilities: The University's Dilemma.* vol. 99, Summer 1970.

Denison, D. C. "Selling College in a Buyer's Market." *New York Times Magazine,* April 10, 1983.

Dresch, Stephen P. *The College, The University and the State: A Critical Examination of Institutional Support in the Context of Historical Development.* New Haven: Yale University Press, 1974.

———. *An Economic Perspective on the Evolution of Graduate Education: A Technical Report Presented to the National Board on Graduate Education.* Washington, D.C.: National Board on Graduate Education, March 1974.

Dresch, Stephen and Adair L. Waldenberg. *Labor Market Indicators, Intellectual Competence and College Attendance.* New Haven: Institute for Demographic and Economic Studies, 1978.

Dressel, Paul L. *The Confidence Crisis.* San Francisco: Jossey-Bass, 1970.

Dressel, Paul L. and Magdala Thompson. *A Degree for College Teachers: The Doctorate of Arts.* Carnegie Council on Policy Studies in Higher Education. San Francisco: Jossey-Bass, 1978.

Dunham, E. Alden. *Colleges of the Forgotten Americans: A Profile of State Colleges and Regional Universities.* New York: McGraw-Hill, 1969.

Edwards, Newton and Herman G. Richey. *The School in the American Social Order.* Boston: Houghton Mifflin, 1963.

Emmerson, George S. *Engineering Education: A Social History.* New York: Crane, Russak and Company, 1973.

Fernandez, Luis. *U.S. Faculty after the Boom: Demographic Projections to 2000.* Berkeley: Carnegie Council on Policy Studies in Higher Education, 1978.

Fine, Benjamin. *Democratic Education.* New York: Thomas Y. Crowell, 1945.

Finn, Chester E. *Scholars, Dollars and Bureaucrats.* Washington, D.C.: Brookings Institution, 1978.

Flexner, Abraham. *Universities, American, English, German.* New York: Oxford, 1930.

Freeman, Roger A. *Crisis in College Finance? Time for New Solutions.* Washington D.C.: Institute for Social Science Research, 1965.

Frey, James H. *An Organizational Analysis of University Environmental Relations.* Washington: University Press of America, 1977.

Furniss, Todd, ed. *American Universities and Colleges.* 11th edition. Washington, D.C.: American Council on Education, 1973.

Gamson, Zelda, F. "An Academic Counter-Revolution." *Education Policy,* 1987, pp. 429–444.

Gans, Herbert. *Urban Villagers: Group and Class in the Life of Italian-Americans.* New York: Free Press, 1982.

Geiger, Roger. *To Advance Knowledge: The Growth of American Research Universities, 1900–1940.* New York: Oxford Univ. Press, 1986.

Gerald, Grant and David Riesman. *The Perpetual Dream: Reform and Experiment in the American College.* Chicago: Univ. of Chicago Press, 1978.

Glenny, Lyman A. *Autonomy of Public Colleges: The Challenge of Coordination.* New York: McGraw-Hill, 1959.

Gourman, Jack. *The Gourman Report: Ratings of American Colleges,* 1967–68 edition. Phoenix: Continuing Education Institute.

Graham, Hugh D. "Structure and Governance in American Higher Education: Historical and Comparative Analysis in State Policy." *Journal of Policy History,* vol. 1, no. 1, 1989.

Green, Martin. *The Problem of Boston: Some Readings in Cultural History.* New York: W.W. Norton, 1966.

Gross, Edward and Paul V. Grambsch. *Changes in University Organization, 1964–71.* Carnegie Commission on Higher Education. New York: McGraw-Hill, 1974.

Haas, J. Eugene and Thomas E. Drabek. *Complex Organizations: A Sociological Perspective.* New York: The Macmillan Co., 1973.

Handlin, Oscar and Mary F. Handlin. *The American College and American Culture: Socialization as a Function of Higher Education.* New York: McGraw-Hill, 1970.

Harris, Seymour E. *Statistical Portrait of Higher Education.* New York: McGraw-Hill, 1972.

Hart, Albert Bushnell, ed. *Commonwealth History of Massachusetts: Colony, Province and State.* 5 vols. New York: States History Company, 1927–30.

Hefferlin, J. B. Lon. *Dynamics of Academic Reform.* San Francisco: Jossey-Bass, 1969.

Henry, David D. *Challenges Past, Challenges Present: An Analysis of American Higher Education Since 1930.* San Francisco: Jossey-Bass, 1975.

Hillway, Tyrus. *The American Two-Year College.* New York: Harper & Row, 1958.

Hodgkinson, Harold. *Institutions in Transition: A Profile of Change in Higher Education.* New York: McGraw-Hill, 1971.

Hofstadter, Richard and C. De Witt Hardy. *The Development and Scope of Higher Education in the United States.* New York: Columbia Univ. Press, 1952.

Hutchins, Robert M. *The Higher Learning in America.* New Haven: Yale Univ. Press, 1936.

Irvin, Mary, ed. *American Universities and Colleges.* 6th, 7th and 8th editions. Washington, D.C.: American Council on Education, 1952, 1956, 1960.

Jencks, Christopher and David Riesman. *The Academic Revolution.* Garden City: Doubleday, 1968.

Joughlin, Louis, ed. *Academic Freedom and Tenure: A Handbook of the American Association of University Professors.* Madison: Univ. of Wisconsin Press, 1967.

Katz, Daniel and Robert L. Kahn. *The Social Psychology of Organizations.* New York: John Wiley & Sons, 1966.

Kaysen, Carl. *The Higher Learning, the Universities, and the Public.* Princeton: Princeton Univ. Press, 1969.

Keller, George. *Academic Strategy: The Management Revolution in American Higher Education.* Baltimore: Johns Hopkins University Press, 1983.

———. "Black Students in Higher Education: Why So Few?" *Planning for Higher Education,* 17:3, 1988–89.

Kennedy, Gail, ed. *Education for Democracy: The Debate over the Report of the President's Commission on Higher Education.* Boston: Heath, 1952.

Kerr, Clark. *Uses of the University.* Cambridge: Harvard Univ. Press, 1963.

King, Richard G. "Minorities in Higher Education: A New England Perspective." In Joseph M. Cronin and Sylvia Q. Simmons, *Student Loans: Risks and Realities.* Dover: Auburn House, 1987.

Leavitt, Harold J., William R. Dill, and Henry B. Eyring. *The Organizational World.* New York: Harcourt Brace Jovanovich, 1973.

Levin, Murray B. and George B. Blackwood. *The Compleat Politician: Political Strategy in Massachusetts*. Indianapolis: Bobbs-Merrill, 1962.

Levine, Arthur. *Why Innovation Fails*. Albany: SUNY Press, 1986.

Levine, David O. *The American College and the Culture of Aspiration, 1915–1940*. Ithaca: Cornell Univ. Press, 1986.

Loring, Augustus P. "A Short Account of the Massachusetts Constitutional Convention, 1917–1919." Supplement to the *New England Quarterly*, vol. 6, no. 1. 1933, pp. 25–36.

Margulies, Rebecca Zames and Peter M. Blau. "America's Leading Professional Schools." *Change*, Nov. 1973, pp. 21–27.

Marsh, C. S. *American Universities and Colleges*. 3rd and 4th editions. Washington, D.C.: American Council on Education, 1936 and 1940.

Mayhew, Lewis. *Higher Education in the Revolutionary Decades*. Berkeley: McCutchan Publishing Corporation, 1967.

Metzger, Walter P. "The Academic Profession in the United States." In Burton R. Clark, ed. *The Academic Profession: National, Disciplinary and Institutional Settings*, Berkeley: Univ. of California Press, 1987.

Miles, Robert H. *Macro Organizational Behavior*. Santa Monica: Goodyear, 1980.

Millett, John David. *The Academic Community: An Essay on Organization*. New York: McGraw-Hill, 1962.

———. *Financing Higher Education in the United States: The Staff Report of the Commission on Financing Higher Education*. New York: Columbia Univ. Press, 1952.

Moos, Malcolm and Francis E. Rourke. *The Campus and the State*. Baltimore: Johns Hopkins University Press, 1959.

Morrison, A. and D. McIntyre. *Schools and Socialization*. Manchester: Penguin Books, 1971.

Moynihan, Daniel P. and Frederick Mosteller, eds. *On Equality of Educational Opportunity*. New York: Random House, 1972.

Murphy, Liz. "Market or Perish." *Sales & Marketing Management*, May 1985, pp. 50–53.

Newman, Frank, et al. *The Second Newman Report: National Policy and Higher Education; Report of a Special Task Force to the Secretary of Health, Education, and Welfare*. Cambridge: MIT Press, 1973.

Nisbet, Robert. *The Degradation of the Academic Dogma: The University in America, 1945–1970*. New York: Basic Books, 1971.

Olson, Keith W. *The GI Bill, the Veterans, and the Colleges*. Lexington: Univ. of Kentucky Press, 1974.

O'Neill, June A. *Resource Use in Higher Education: Trends in Output and Input, 1930–1970*. Berkeley: Carnegie Commission on Higher Education, 1971.

———. *Sources of Funds to Colleges and Universities*. Berkeley: Carnegie Commission on Higher Education, 1973.

Orlans, Harold, ed. *Science Policy and the University*. Washington, D.C.: Brookings Institution, 1968.

Pace, C. Robert. *Education and Evangelism: A Profile of Protestant Colleges*. New York: McGraw-Hill, 1972.

Parsons, Talcott and Gerald M. Platt. *The American University*. Cambridge: Harvard Univ. Press, 1973.

Perrow, Charles. "Organizational Prestige." *American Journal of Sociology*. vol. 66, Jan. 1961, pp. 335–41.

Peterson, Marvin and Lisa Mets. *Key Resources on Higher Education Governance, Management and Leadership: A Guide to the Literature.* San Francisco: Jossey-Bass, 1987.

Pifer, Alan, John Shea, David Henry, and Lyman Glenny. *Systems of Higher Education: The United States.* New York: International Council for Educational Development, 1978.

The Public Interest, no. 13, Fall 1968. "Special Issue, The Universities."

Pusey, Nathan M. *American Higher Education.* Cambridge: Harvard Univ. Press, 1978.

Ravitch, Diane. *The Troubled Crusade: American Education 1945–1980.* New York: Basic Books, 1983.

Rice, A. K. *The Modern University: A Model Organization.* London: Tavistock, 1970.

Richman, Barry M. and Richard N. Farmer. *Leadership, Goals and Power in Higher Education.* San Francisco: Jossey-Bass, 1974.

Riesman, David. *Constraint and Variety in American Higher Education.* Garden City: Doubleday Anchor Books, 1958.

Riesman, David and Verne A. Stadtman. *Academic Transformation, Seventeen Institutions under Pressure.* New York: McGraw-Hill, 1973.

Rivlin, Alice M. *The Role of the Federal Government in Financing Higher Education.* Washington, D.C.: Brookings Institution, 1961.

Roose, Kenneth D. and Charles J. Anderson. *A Rating of Graduate Programs.* Washington, D.C.: American Council on Education, 1970.

Ross, Davis R. B. *Preparing for Ulysses: Politics and Veterans During World War I.* New York: Columbia Univ. Press, 1969.

Rourke, Francis E. and Glenn E. Brooks. *The Managerial Revolution in Higher Education.* Baltimore: Johns Hopkins University Press, 1966.

Rudolph, Frederick. *The American College and University: A History.* New York: Knopf, 1962.

———. *Curriculum: A History of the American Undergraduate Course of Study Since 1636.* San Francisco: Jossey-Bass, 1977.

Russell, J. D., ed. "Emergent Responsibilities of Higher Education." vol. 17. In *Proceedings of the Institute for Administrative Officers of Higher Institutions.* Chicago: Univ. of Chicago Press, 1945.

———. "Higher Education in the Postwar Period." vol. 16. *Proceedings of the Institute for Administrative Officers of Higher Institutions.* Chicago: Univ. of Chicago Press, 1944.

———. "The Outlook for Higher Education." vol. 2. *Proceedings of the Institute for Administrative Officers of Higher Institutions.* Chicago: Univ. of Chicago Press, 1939.

Salmon, Lewis C. and Alexander W. Astin. "A New Study of Excellence in Undergraduate Education." Part One. *Change.* Sept. 1981, pp. 23–28.

Sanford, Nevitt, ed. *The American College: A Psychological and Social Interpretation of the Higher Learning.* New York: John Wiley, 1962.

School and Society. Selected dates.

Scott, J. W. and Mohammed El-Assai. "Multiversity, University Size, University Quality and Student Protest." *American Sociological Review,* Oct. 1969.

Selden, William, K. *Accreditation.* New York: Harper & Row, 1960.

Shepard's Acts and Cases By Popular Names, Third Edition, pt. I. Colorado Springs: 1986.

Singletary, Otis A., ed. *American Universities and Colleges.* 10th edition. Washington, D.C.: American Council on Education, 1968.

Smelser, Neil and Robin Content. *The Changing Academic Market.* Berkeley: Univ. of California Press, 1980.

Smith Bruce L. R. and Joseph J. Karlesky. *The State of Academic Science.* vols. 1 and 2. New York: Change Magazine Press, 1977, 1978.

Stadtman, Verne A. *Academic Adaptations: Higher Education Prepares for the 1980s and 1990s.* San Francisco: Jossey-Bass, 1980.

Taubman, Paul and Terence Wales. *Mental Ability and Higher Educational Attainment in the 20th Century.* New York: National Bureau of Economic Research, 1972.

Tewksbury, Donald G. *The Founding of American Colleges Before the Civil War, with Particular Reference to the Religious Influences Bearing upon the College Movement.* Hamden: Archon Books, 1965.

Thernstrom, Stephan. *Poverty, Planning, and Politics in the New Boston.* New York: Basic Books, 1969.

Thompson, James D. *Organizations in Action: Social Science Bases of Administrative Theory.* New York: McGraw-Hill, 1967.

Touraine, Alain. *The Academic System in American Society.* New York: McGraw-Hill, 1974.

Trow, Martin. "Elite and Mass Higher Education: American Models and European Realities." In *Research Into Higher Education: Processes and Structures.* Report from a Conference in June 1978. Stockholm: National Board of Universities and Colleges, 1979.

———. "Elite Higher Education: An Endangered Species?" *Minerva,* Autumn 1976, 355–76.

———. "The National Reports on Higher Education: A Skeptical View." *Educational Policy,* 1987, 411–427.

———. "Problems in the Transition from Elite to Mass Higher Education." In *Policies for Higher Education.* General Report of the Conference on Future Structure of Post-Secondary Education. Paris: O.E.C.D., 1974.

Valentine, P. F., ed. *The American College.* New York: Philosophical Library, Inc., 1949.

Veblen, Thorstein. *The Higher Learning in America: A Memorandum on the Conduct of Universities by Business Men.* Stanford: Academic Reprints, 1954.

Veysey, Laurence. *The Emergence of the American University.* Chicago: Univ. of Chicago Press, 1965.

Wallerstein, Immanuel and Paul Starr. *The University Crisis Reader.* New York: Random House, 1971.

Webster, David S. "Does Research Productivity Enhance Teaching?" *Educational Record,* Fall 1985, pp. 60–62.

Weick, Karl E. "Educational Organizations as Loosely Coupled Systems." *Administrative Science Quarterly,* March 1976, pp. 1–19.

Whitaker, John P. "The Impact of the State Constitutional Convention of 1917 on State Aid to Higher Education in Massachusetts." *New England Journal of Public Policy,* vol. 7, no. 1, Spring/Summer 1991, pp. 39–54.

Whitehill, Walter M. *Boston in the Age of John Fitzgerald Kennedy.* Norman: University of Oklahoma Press, 1966.

Who's Who. London: Adam and Charles Black, 1946–47.

Wiebe, Robert H. *The Search for Order, 1877–1920.* New York: Hill and Wang, 1967.

Wilson, Logan. *The Academic Man: A Study in the Sociology of a Profession.* New York: Oxford Univ. Press, 1942.

———. *American Academics: Then and Now.* New York: Oxford Univ. Press, 1979.

Wilson, Reginald and Sarah E. Melendez. "Down the Up Staircase." *Educational Record,* Fall 1985, 46–50.

Wolfe, Dael. *America's Resources of Specialized Talent: A Current Appraisal and a Look Ahead; Report.* New York: Harper & Bros., 1954.

Index

Abram, Morris, 230–32, 372
Academic ideas and values, as factor in institutional change, 8, 10, 11, 45–48, 117, 364–68, 375
Academic Planning Committee. *See* Brandeis University.
Academy for Educational Development, 350
Accreditation, 25, 62, 189–90, 194; accrediting agencies, development of, 50–51; influence on campus policies, 9, 63, 65, 95. *See also individual campus references.*
Admission practices: discrimination in, 3–4, 41–42, 100, 118–19, 154, 160–61, 181–82, 251, 324, 341, 356–57, 402, 404–5; Massachusetts patterns, 6, 77, 102–3, 356–57, 366–67, 402–5; national debates about and patterns, 73, 76–77, 86–89, 100–103, 119, 380, 402–5, 473n2; toward minorities, 3–4, 7, 10, 76–77, 100–101, 115, 160, 203, 210–11, 231, 288, 296, 302, 324, 357, 366–68, 402, 404–5; toward women, 7, 46, 101, 128, 160, 199, 255, 395, 402; World War II, impact of on, 7. *See also individual campus references.*
African-American students. *See* Black students.
Albert Einstein Educational Foundation. *See* Brandeis University.
Allison, Graham, 172–73
Alpert, George, 186–88, 190–91
Alumni/ae: role in traditional colleges, 5, 48, 275; as source of financial support for institutions in golden age, 89–90, 93, 99. *See also individual campus references.*
American Academy of Arts and Sciences, 100. *See also* Assembly on University Goals and Governance.

American Association for the Advancement of Science, 48
American Association of Collegiate Registrars and Admissions Officers, 87–88
American Association of Junior Colleges, 97
American Association of University Professors, 50, 59, 95, 97, 214–15, 253, 267, 271–72, 276–78, 280, 382, 388; Statement of Principles on Academic Freedom and Tenure, 95; Statement on Government of Colleges and Universities, 97; Statement on Procedural Standards in Faculty Dismissal Proceedings, 95; Statement on Recruitment and Resignation of Faculty Members, 95–96; Statement on Standards for Notice of Nonreappointment, 96
American Chemical Society, 48
American Council of Learned Societies, 95
American Council on Education, 61–62, 73–74, 87, 100, 105, 209, 254, 257, 265, 325
American Federation of Labor, 29, 66
American Legion, 74
American Mathematical Association, 48
American Medical Association, 50, 180
Amherst College, 31, 41, 79
Andrews, Kenneth, 165
Arrupe, Pedro, S.J., 284
Assembly on University Goals and Governance, 100, 105, 108, 199
Association of American Universities, 54, 62, 76, 87, 100, 104, 125, 238; "Federal Financing of Universities," 104
Association of Governing Boards of Colleges and Universities, 97

funded research, 201; finances and
fund-raising, 188, 190–92, 201, 207–
8, 210–12, 216–17, 219, 356, 387,
389, 390–91; founding, 5, 186–88,
449n11; Friends of Brandeis Music,
191; general education, 189, 200–201,
225, 407; graduate education, 118,
195, 197, 200, 208–9, 216–19, 224,
228, 263, 357–58, 366, 368, 389–90,
411–12; Graduate School of Arts and
Sciences, 194; Heller School of Social
Welfare, 197, 209, 220; and Jewish
community, 10, 179, 185, 197, 211–
12, 357, 389, 416–17; Lemburg
Center for the Study of Violence, 220;
and Middlesex University, 186–88;
mission and purposes, 5, 188–90, 246;
organization, 212, 216–22; public
service activities, 112, 195, 286;
research, 106–7, 118, 194, 201, 208–
9, 224, 263, 357, 360, 366, 390;
Sachar presidency (*see* Sachar, Abram);
Schottland presidency (*see* Schottland,
Charles); science at, 201, 209; student
characteristics, 189–90, 199, 232, 332,
357; student protests of 1960s, 98,
221, 231; Transitional Year Program,
210, 231, 404; tuition policy, 191,
221, 356, 390; undergraduate
education, 108, 118, 179, 188–89,
190, 194–95, 200–201, 208–10, 225–
26, 228, 263, 272, 358, 376, 389–91,
407, 414; Wein Scholarships, 220;
Yom Kippur War, 389
Broderick, Francis L., 332–33, 337,
344–45, 348–49
Bromery, Randolph, 397
Brooks, Glenn, 113
Buck, Paul, 76, 79, 127
Bundy, McGeorge, 140, 254, 341
Burr, Hooks, 383
Bush, Vannevar, 71–73, 82, 90–91, 131
Butterfield, Kenyon, 29, 67, 308

California Institute of Technology, 150
Cambridge Electron Accelerator, 170
Capen, Elmer, 22, 23, 36, 37
Capriles, Miguel de, 271, 273, 287
Carmichael, Leonard: and academic
appointments, 183–84; and academic
research, 60, 64, 181, 184, 193;
administrative/leadership style, 214;
appointed president of Tufts, 60; end
of term, 182, 184–85; and federal
funding, 71, 179–80; financial policies

and fund-raising, 90, 180; and general
education, 79; and graduate
education, 60, 183–84; institutional
changes during presidency of, 181–85;
institutional goals of, 60, 179–81; pre-
presidential career, 60, 180;
presidency evaluated, 184–85; and
undergraduate admissions, 181, 184–
85, 448n5; and undergraduate
education, 60, 79, 181
Carnegie Commission on Higher
Education, 100, 106–10, 113–14,
288–89, 379, 412
Carnegie Corporation, 88–89
Carnegie Council on Policy Studies in
Higher Education, 100, 380–81, 415–
16
Carnegie Foundation, 50, 75, 100
Carnegie Institution, 71–72
Cartter, Alan, 207
Case, Harold: and academic
appointments, 273; administrative/
leadership style, 247, 372; appointed
president of B.U., 242; and Charles
River campus, 268–69, 373; end of
term, 270; financial policies and fund-
raising, 272; and graduate admissions,
248, 356; institutional changes during
presidency of, 269–70, 272;
institutional goals of, 247–48, 357;
presidency evaluated, 356–57, 372;
and undergraduate admissions, 244,
248, 250, 269, 272, 356
Catholic University of America, 62
Catholics and higher education, 4, 10,
21, 23–24, 37, 41–42, 44, 68, 78, 192,
246–47, 252, 257, 316–17, 320, 336,
344, 359, 360–61, 365, 402, 416–17;
conflict between religious and
academic values, 10, 22, 43, 251;
impact of immigration, 22, 33, 43, 251
Change among universities: competition
as cause of, 8, 11, 35–39, 40–45, 117–
18, 355–60, 374–79, 415–18; external
conditions as cause of, 11, 116, 117,
357, 380, 415, 424n8, 473n3; ideas
and values as cause of, 8, 10, 45–48,
117, 364–68, 374–79; internal power
distribution as cause of, 8, 9, 45–48,
116, 369–74, 374–79, 414–15, 424n8,
473n3; literature concerning, 8–9,
116, 424n8; in Massachusetts, 6, 9–10;
national patterns, 3–4, 5–6;
organizational characteristics as factor
in, 116, 117, 369–74. *See also*